Cases on Historical Thinking and Gamification in Social Studies and Humanities Education

María Martínez-Hita
University of Murcia, Spain

Cosme Jesús Gómez Carrasco
University of Murcia, Spain

Pedro Miralles-Martínez
University of Murcia, Spain

IGI Global
PUBLISHER of TIMELY KNOWLEDGE

A volume in the Advances in Game-Based Learning (AGBL) Book Series

Published in the United States of America by
IGI Global
Information Science Reference (an imprint of IGI Global)
701 E. Chocolate Avenue
Hershey PA, USA 17033
Tel: 717-533-8845
Fax: 717-533-8661
E-mail: cust@igi-global.com
Web site: http://www.igi-global.com

Library of Congress Cataloging-in-Publication Data

Names: Martínez-Hita, María, DATE- editor. | Gómez Carrasco, Cosme Jesús, editor. | Miralles Martínez, Pedro, editor.
Title: Cases on historical thinking and gamification in social studies and humanities education / Maria Martínez-Hita, Cosme Gómez Carrasco, and Pedro Miralles-Martínez, editors.
Description: Hershey, PA : Information Science Reference, [2023] | Includes bibliographical references and index. | Summary: "The objective of this book is to respond to the needs of the teachers of social sciences and studies in humanities and shortcomings generated by COVID-19, proposing new epistemological and methodological approaches for the teaching of history in a multidisciplinary context"-- Provided by publisher.
Identifiers: LCCN 2022023416 (print) | LCCN 2022023417 (ebook) | ISBN 9781668452400 (Hardcover) | ISBN 9781668452448 (Paperback) | ISBN 9781668452417 (eBook)
Subjects: LCSH: Active learning--Research. | Gamification--Research. | Social sciences--Study and teaching--Computer network resources. | Humanities--Study and teaching--Computer network resources. | History--Study and teaching--Computer network resources.
Classification: LCC LB1027.23 .C23 2023 (print) | LCC LB1027.23 (ebook) | DDC 371.3--dc23/eng/20220810
LC record available at https://lccn.loc.gov/2022023416
LC ebook record available at https://lccn.loc.gov/2022023417

This book is published in the IGI Global book series Advances in Game-Based Learning (AGBL) (ISSN: 2327-1825; eISSN: 2327-1833)

British Cataloguing in Publication Data
A Cataloguing in Publication record for this book is available from the British Library.

Advances in Game-Based Learning (AGBL) Book Series

Robert D. Tennyson
University of Minnesota, USA

ISSN:2327-1825
EISSN:2327-1833

Mission

The **Advances in Game-Based Learning (AGBL) Book Series** aims to cover all aspects of serious games applied to any area of education. The definition and concept of education has begun to morph significantly in the past decades and game-based learning has become a popular way to encourage more active learning in a creative and alternative manner for students in K-12 classrooms, higher education, and adult education. **AGBL** presents titles that address many applications, theories, and principles surrounding this growing area of educational theory and practice.

Coverage

- Curriculum Development Using Educational Games
- Digital Game-Based Learning
- Edutainment
- Electronic Educational Games
- Game Design and Development of Educational Games
- MMOs in Education
- Pedagogical Theory of Game-Based Learning
- Psychological Study of Students Involved in Game-Based Learning
- Role of instructors
- Virtual worlds and game-based learning

The Advances in Game-Based Learning (AGBL) Book Series (ISSN 2327-1825) is published by IGI Global, 701 E. Chocolate Avenue, Hershey, PA 17033-1240, USA, www.igi-global.com. This series is composed of titles available for purchase individually; each title is edited to be contextually exclusive from any other title within the series. For pricing and ordering information please visit http://www.igi-global.com/book-series/advances-game-based-learning/73680. Postmaster: Send all address changes to above address.

Titles in this Series

For a list of additional titles in this series, please visit: www.igi-global.com/book-series/advances-game-based-learning/73680

Handbook of Research on the Influence and Effectiveness of Gamification in Education
Oscar Bernardes (ISCAP, ISEP, Polytechnic Institute of Porto, Portugal & University of Aveiro, Portugal) Vanessa Amorim (ISCAP, Polytechnic Institute of Porto, Portugal) and Antonio Carrizo Moreira (University of Aveiro, Porugal)
Information Science Reference • © 2022 • 835pp • H/C (ISBN: 9781668442876) • US $295.00

Handbook of Research on International Approaches and Practices for Gamifying Mathematics
Cristina A. Huertas-Abril (University of Córdoba, Spain) Elvira Fernández-Ahumada (University of Córdoba, Spain) and Natividad Adamuz-Povedano (University of Córdoba, pain)
Information Science Reference • © 2022 • 422pp • H/C (ISBN: 9781799896609) • US $270.00

Handbook of Research on Using Disruptive Methodologies and Game-Based Learning to Foster Transversal Skills
Irene Rivera-Trigueros (University of Granada, Spain) Abigail López-Alcarria (University of Granada, Spain) Diego-Pablo Ruiz-Padillo (University of Granada, Spain) María Dolores Olvera-Lobo (University of Granada, Spain) and José Gutiérrez-Pérez (University of Granada, Spain)
Information Science Reference • © 2022 • 507pp • H/C (ISBN: 9781799886457) • US $285.00

Handbook of Research on Acquiring 21st Century Literacy Skills Through Game-Based Learning
Carol-Ann Lane (University of Toronto, Canada)
Information Science Reference • © 2022 • 958pp • H/C (ISBN: 9781799872719) • US $525.00

Esports Research and Its Integration in Education
Miles M. Harvey (University of New Mexico, USA) and Rick Marlatt (New Mexico State University, USA)
Information Science Reference • © 2021 • 313pp • H/C (ISBN: 9781799870692) • US $215.00

Exploring the Cognitive, Social, Cultural, and Psychological Aspects of Gaming and Simulations
Brock R. Dubbels (McMaster University, Canada)
Information Science Reference • © 2019 • 333pp • H/C (ISBN: 9781522574613) • US $190.00

Design, Motivation, and Frameworks in Game-Based Learning
Wee Hoe Tan (Sultan Idris Education University, Malaysia)
Information Science Reference • © 2019 • 306pp • H/C (ISBN: 9781522560265) • US $175.00

IGI Global
PUBLISHER of TIMELY KNOWLEDGE

701 East Chocolate Avenue, Hershey, PA 17033, USA
Tel: 717-533-8845 x100 • Fax: 717-533-8661
E-Mail: cust@igi-global.com • www.igi-global.com

Table of Contents

Detailed Table of Contents

of sources and the identification of causes and consequences of historical events. The study concludes that Spanish publishers need to increase the presence of activities that promote history learning through thinking competencies.

It is evident that the integration of key competences in the educational panorama and in the curriculum is not perceptible in the practical development of the classroom. Given the lack of clear and practical proposals in the legislation that facilitate this implementation, this chapter aims to analyse—through an updated bibliography—the role of the school and the teacher in making key competences effective in the teaching of social sciences. In the same way, it sets out what is considered to be the most effective way of working on key competences in social sciences: through the development of historical thinking and the concepts that define it, as well as the critical spirit, providing students with skills for their personal development, the ability to transfer concepts to everyday situations, as well as empathy and commitment to their social environment.

The need for a transformation of the teaching and learning process of history has long been called for from the field of history education research. A change is advocated which affects both the methodology and the epistemology of the field and promotes the development of historical thinking. This chapter presents an intervention programme aimed at primary education students in Spain and validated via expert judgement with the aim of contributing to the aforementioned change in the teaching of history by including work on the historical thinking skills along with the use of active methodologies such as gamification. The objective of this chapter is to present this gamified project for the development of historical thinking in such a way that it can serve as a point of reference and to propose a series of steps to facilitate the design of gamified learning experiments.

The use of active methodologies in the teaching-learning process is increasing in popularity. However, with regard to History, this is not the case. Nevertheless, History teaching trends emphasise the importance of their integration to achieve a practical and student-centred learning process to encourage students to develop skills such as reflection and critical thinking. The acquisition of these competences along with knowledge about History is known as historical thinking. In this quantitative study, a gamification methodology was compared to a lecture-based one. To this aim, over the period of a unit of work, two groups from two different schools participated in the study. Results show that, although both groups had the same knowledge before the intervention, the gamification group performed at a significantly higher academic level after it. In addition, a reduced version of the instructional material motivational survey, which was given to the gamification class before and after the intervention, verified that students prefer the gamification dynamic compared to their usual lessons.

In recent years, the literature has identified the need to influence teacher training so that teachers promote historical thinking metaconcepts and innovative methodological strategies that actually encourage learning of these history skills in the classroom. To that end, n=36 students of the Master's Degree in Teaching in Secondary Education at the University of Zaragoza (Geography and History specialty) were presented with two gamified experiences for secondary education, developed during the pandemic, so they could reflect on their usefulness, benefits, and possible challenges or limitations. Based on the preservice teachers' evaluation, their prior conceptions of the usefulness of gamification in encouraging historical thinking skills and the educational scope of introducing good practices in teacher training were analyzed using mixed methods research.

The reality is that students show a lack of interest in certain school subjects. In Social Sciences, teaching has predominantly been based on transmission, which has only amplified the problem. It has also prevented new work and intervention techniques that boost students' interest in historical and geographical concepts

The development of historical thinking in students using active methodologies is an unavoidable opportunity to approach key events in the history of humanity, such as the Nuremberg trials. This chapter presents a proposal for gamification in the classroom through role-playing using a card game designed ad hoc in order to develop historical empathy in students. The objectives of this proposal are to determine the responsibilities of individuals and organisations for the execution of the German extermination programme, decide the seriousness of the facts proven through documentation and sources provided, value respect for life and tolerance as the foundations of democracy and human rights, investigate and become aware of the crimes committed by those involved, and value respect for life and tolerance as the foundations of democracy and human rights. This activity introduces students to a controversial topic such as the Nuremberg trials through activities such as the creation of a preliminary commission, the performance of the trial, and a debate.

Chapter 13
The Use of WebQuests to Promote Democratic Education in a Higher Education Context 228
José María Campillo-Ferrer, University of Murcia, Spain

During the last decades, literature has demonstrated the benefits of WebQuests as a potential resource for promoting critical thinking skills and knowledge. However, in higher education contexts, research on the use of WebQuests as a tool to promote democratic education is extremely scarce. Although there are some studies involving student teachers on the appropriateness and effectiveness of the WebQuest approach to learning, few studies have focused on the development of democratic education by students with the support of other ICT resources. The present study investigated the impact of WebQuests in higher education classrooms and on democratic education in the Region of Murcia, Spain. The design and planning of WebQuests was encouraged along with other electronic resources to help foster learning and networking among future teachers.

Chapter 14
The Perceptions of Pre-Service Teachers Regarding the Teaching Methodology of Primary Education Social Science Teachers 246
Catalina Guerrero-Romera, University of Murcia, Spain

This chapter has been proposed with the aim of discovering and analysing how Social Sciences teachers represent and develop knowledge in their teaching practice through the perspective of pre-service teachers. To achieve this, the methodological model of primary education teachers will be analysed via observations carried out by students of an undergraduate degree in Primary Education during their period of teaching practice, paying particular attention to the development of the historical thinking skills and the use of ICT resources and of learning strategies, resources, and assessment. These observations by trainees reflect how pre-service teachers are more aware of the importance of encouraging a wider variety of learning and assessment strategies and activities for the achievement of historical thinking competences and more complex thinking skills.

Preface

Cases on Historical Thinking and Gamification in Social Studies and Humanities Education focuses on the necessary renewal of the teaching-learning process of history and social sciences through active learning methods, digital resources, gamification and the historical thinking approach, as well as the combination of them.

The reason that has led to this book arises from the doctoral thesis entitled "El pensamiento histórico en Educación Primaria. Diseño y evaluación de un programa de intervención gamificado" [Historical thinking in Primary Education. Design and evaluation of a gamified intervention programme] authored by María Martínez-Hita and supervised by Cosme J. Gómez Carrasco and Pedro Miralles-Martínez at the University of Murcia (Spain) (Martínez-Hita, 2022). Likewise, from the research projects "The geographical and historical thinking of the Primary Education student in the Region of Murcia: innovative methodological proposals for quality education" (20874/PI/18), funded by the Fundación Séneca-Agencia de Ciencia y Tecnología de la Región de Murcia; "The teaching and learning of historical competences in baccalaureate education: a challenge for the achievement of a critical and democratic citizenship" (PID2020-113453RB-I00), funded by MCIN/AEI/10.13039/501100011033; and "HistoryLab for European Civic Engagement: open e-Toolkit to train History Teachers on Digital Teaching and Learning", funded by SEPIE under the ERASMUS+ KA226 call (2020-1-ES01-KA226-HE-095430).

In addition, as this is a casebook, research and projects from other universities and research groups have been added, such as the University of Castilla-La Mancha, the University of Zaragoza, the University of Granada, the University of Huelva, Çukurova University, Gazi University, Aksaray University, Kastamonu University, Ahi Evran University or Giresun University, among others.

This book contributes to the configuration of an incipient line of research that analyzes the joint work of historical thinking with active learning methods such as gamification.

Research on history education and historical thinking is becoming increasingly relevant internationally (Metzger & Harris, 2018; Thorp & Persson, 2020). This research highlights the need for a history education renewal that pursues the development of historical thinking as opposed to a repetitive and conceptual learning of history. History education research advocates a teaching model based on the development of historical thinking among learners so that students can understand history as a form of knowledge that is the result of an investigation. This approach allows the development of more complex cognitive skills from a constructivist perspective.

Historical thinking makes reference to the use of historical sources and to the skills employed by the historian and requires understanding rather than the mere memorisation of closed narratives.

In order to develop historical thinking, two complementary aspects are required: a substantive knowledge of first-order concepts about the past; and a knowledge of second-order historical concepts. The former are the concepts which history addresses (i.e., the contents), whereas the second type of historical knowledge provides the necessary tools for the study of the past and the construction of historical explanations (Lee, 2005; Lee & Ashby, 2000).

According to Seixas and Morton (2013), six big concepts of historical thinking can be identified: historical relevance, source and evidence, causes and consquences, historical perspective or empathy, change and continuity, and the ethical dimension. These concepts are those which make it possible to organise and give meaning to substantive first-order contents (factual, chronological knowledge) and, therefore, provide students with an understanding of the subject of History.

The need for a renewal of history education is not only justified by the epistemology of history itself, but also by the demand for a methodological change in education in general, making students active protagonists in the construction of their own learning and based on the development of competencies.

The new educational paradigm promotes student learning in an active and motivating way, since the simple transmission of theoretical knowledge no longer makes sense. Among these new pedagogical approaches, gamification is one of the most popular alternatives, due to its playful and motivating nature.

In this book, gamification is proposed and analyzed as a pedagogical innovation that can enable the renewal of the teaching and learning process of history, facilitating the active learning of historical thinking concepts.

Gamification consists of applying elements which normally form part of games to a non-game context. It has become very popular in the educational field in recent years, since it can provide a solution to the current problems of education, such as the lack of motivation and interest of students in the teaching-learning process (Deterding et al., 2011; Kapp, 2012).

Gamification in education can be defined as the application of the elements of which games are made up to the teaching process in order to improve students' motivation, learning and engagement, among others. Some of these elements are the narrative, challenges, missions, badges, levels, points, rewards, avatars, collaboration, competition or progression.

However, gamification is often confused with other concepts such as the use of games and serious games in the classroom or with other pedagogical approaches, for example, those based exclusively on the use of points, badges and leaderboards (*pointsification*). Gamification does not consist of the use of serious games or complete games in class, but makes use of the elements of which the former consist in order to modify the teaching process and to create a learning experience which is similar to a game.

Since it is necessary to clarify the conceptual issue related to gamification, this book aims to contribute to this, providing different definitions and educational proposals to help clear up this term and consequently facilitate its correct application in the classroom.

Although there are numerous studies that analyze the effects of the use of gamification in the teaching-learning process, there is a lack of research on its use in the teaching of social sciences and history in particular. Because of that, further study on the potential use of gamification within social studies and humanities education is required to understand its benefits and challenges

Moreover, gamification and active learning methodologies combined with Information and Communication Technology (ICT) are an inexhaustible and powerful resource for acquiring new knowledge and improving the teaching-learning process.

There are many ICT applications and tools that can be implemented in the classroom combined with these methodologies to create more motivating learning experiences for students. Different digital resources such as video games, WebQuests or numerous applications can be used to complement the teacher's explanations, to create new materials or for formative and final evaluation of students, among other uses.

Despite the introduction of digital resources in the educational field, teachers do not have sufficient level of digital competence for the correct use of technology as a teaching tool, as pointed out in the scientific literature. The same happens with the implementation of the historical thinking approach and gamification in the classroom. Therefore, a transfer of research results is also necessary to promote the inclusion of historical thinking and gamified and digital methods in initial and continuing teacher training.

Hence, *Cases on Historical Thinking and Gamification in Social Studies and Humanities Education* is an ideal book for teachers, researchers, academicians, practitioners, instructors, and prospective teachers interested in history education and gamification as well as who wish to improve the quality of the teaching and learning process of history, social studies and humanities education.

The book is organized into fifteen chapters. A brief description of each of the chapters follows:

Chapter 1, "Changes in Primary School Students' Ideas About History After Implementing a Gamified Intervention Programme," is a quasi-experimental research that analyses the evolution of the conceptions on history as a discipline of students in the fourth year of primary education in Spain. For this purpose, an experimental group, which worked with an active learning methodology based on gamification and historical thinking, was compared with a control group, which followed a traditional methodology. Significant differences were identified between the two groups regarding their conceptions of history and, therefore, their understanding of the subject and their development of historical thinking skills.

Chapter 2, "Historical Thinking Skills and Cognitive Levels in Spanish High School History Textbooks," checks how history textbooks in Spain contribute to the teaching of historical thinking competencies. To reach this goal there are two specific objectives. The first one is to investigate the existence of historical thinking skills in History textbooks in Spanish Baccalaureate. The second is to establish what level of cognitive difficulty there is in the textbook activities when developing historical thinking competencies.

Chapter 3, "Historical Thinking as a Dynamic Vehicle for Teaching Through Key Competences: The Roles of the Teacher and the School," aims to analyse—through an updated bibliography—the role of the school and the teacher in making key competences effective in the teaching of social sciences. In the same way, it sets out what is considered to be the most effective way of working on key competences in social sciences: through the development of historical thinking and the concepts that define it, as well as the critical spirit, providing students with skills for their personal development, the ability to transfer concepts to everyday situations, as well as empathy and commitment to their social environment.

Chapter 4, "A Proposal for the Design of a Gamified Experience for the Teaching of Historical Thinking in Primary Education," presents an intervention programme aimed at primary education students in Spain and validated via expert judgement with the aim of contributing to the aforementioned change in the teaching of history by including work on the historical thinking skills along with the use of active methodologies such as gamification. The objective of this chapter is to present this gamified project for the development of historical thinking in such a way that it can serve as a point of reference and to propose a series of steps to facilitate the design of gamified learning experiments.

Chapter 5, "Impact of a Gamified Experience on the Promotion of Historical Thinking in Primary Education," aims to contribute to expanding knowledge about the possibilities of uniting historical thinking and gamification through a technology-based gamified environment in a didactic intervention with sixth-year Primary Education students (11-12 years old) and measure their results based on academic performance and motivation.

Chapter 6, "Historical Thinking Development Through Gamification: Secondary Education and Teacher Training Applications," analyses, based on the preservice teachers' evaluation, their prior conceptions of the usefulness of gamification in encouraging historical thinking skills and the educational scope of introducing good practices in teacher training. For this purpose, two gamified activities for fostering historical reasoning during the secondary education stage were presented to students of the Master's Degree in Teaching in Secondary Education at the University of Zaragoza (Geography and History specialty), so they could reflect on their usefulness, benefits, and possible challenges or limitations.

Chapter 7, "Gamified Teaching Strategies to Work on Historical Thinking: Methodological Applications," presents a potential application of gamification, based on existing models such as the BIG 6 developed by Eisenberg and Berkowitz in 1990, which will be linked to the skills to be developed, the way in which information is presented and the characteristics of the game or activity to be gamified. This model will help to promote didactic proposals that apply this work methodology in the future.

Chapter 8, "Gamification: A Learning Technique for the Dynamization of the Teaching of Social Sciences," carries out an analysis of the particularities that make up gamification as a learning technique for educational revitalization and updating. From a holistic perspective, a tour of the terminological particularities of gamification, constituent elements, benefits and limitations are made. Likewise, this chapter takes a tour of the main techno-pedagogical resources for the gamification of the Social Sciences classroom, focusing on the subject of History and the development of historical thinking skills, presenting different gamification experiences from a transversal perspective and proposes a compendium of gamified activities based on active learning.

Chapter 9, "Gamification Through Mobile Learning in University Students: A Teaching Innovation Proposal," presents an experience of teaching innovation carried out with gamification, mobile learning and flipped classroom resources and tools for trainee teachers at a Spanish university. Specifically, the experience was aimed at making classrooms more dynamic with mobile applications for self-assessment and reinforcement of learning using mobile devices.

Chapter 10, "Use of Digital Historical Material and Alternative Teaching Tools in History Lessons Project TEBIT," introduces the turkish project TEBIT whose aim is to provide history teachers with digital historical resources and alternative teaching tools that they can use in history education in order to help students gain high-level thinking skills in addition to knowledge in history courses. To achieve this, a needs analysis for Turkish history teachers was performed to determine which subjects should be focused on in history courses, and what kind of digital historical resources and alternative teaching tools are required.

Chapter 11, "What Do Secondary Students Know About Video Games? Previous Ideas and Predisposition to Learning Social Sciences With Video Games," sets out the results of a questionnaire given to secondary school students (12-13 years) about the use of video games for the teaching and learning of Social Sciences, and more specifically for History, as well as their opinions on the introduction of this resource in the classroom.

Chapter 12, "Learning to Understand Historical Context: Role-Playing Game 'The Nuremberg Prosecutors'," presents a proposal for gamification in the classroom through role-playing using a card game designed ad hoc in order to develop historical empathy in students. This activity introduces students to a controversial topic such as the Nuremberg trials through activities such as the creation of a preliminary commission, the performance of the trial and a debate.

Chapter 13, "The Use of WebQuests to Promote Democratic Education in a Higher Education Context," investigates the impact of WebQuests in higher education classrooms and on democratic education in the Region of Murcia, Spain. The design and planning of WebQuests was encouraged along with other electronic resources to help foster learning and networking among future teachers.

Chapter 14, "The Perceptions of Pre-Service Teachers Regarding the Teaching Methodology of Primary Education Social Science Teachers," analyses how Social Sciences teachers represent and develop knowledge in their teaching practice through the perspective of pre-service teachers. To achieve this, the methodological model of primary education teachers will be analysed via observations carried out by students of an undergraduate degree in Primary Education during their period of teaching practice, paying particular attention to the development of the historical thinking skills and the use of ICT resources and of learning strategies, resources and assessment.

Chapter 15, "Evaluation of a Training Program for Trainee Teachers in Active Methodologies for Teaching Social Sciences," investigates the opinions and conceptions of Primary education teachers undergoing initial training on active methodologies and evaluates a training program that uses these methodologies with a particular focus on the teaching of Social Sciences.

The results and conclusions of this book can serve as motivation and a reference point for promoting the implementation of gamification in history, social studies, and humanities education in order to develop historical thinking among students and improve the teaching and learning process, as well as for orienting teacher training programmes towards a necessary epistemological and methodological change.

In conclusion, this book contributes to an emerging line of research concerning the combination of historical thinking with active learning methods such as gamification. In addition, it allows us to move towards the necessary renewal of the teaching-learning process in the social sciences and history in particular.

María Martínez-Hita
University de Murcia, Spain

Cosme Jesús Gómez Carrasco
University of Murcia, Spain

Pedro Miralles-Martínez
University of Murcia, Spain

REFERENCES

Deterding, S., Dixon, D., Khaled, R., & Nacke, L. (2011). From game design elements to gamefulness: Defining "gamification". In A. Lugmayr (Ed.), *Proceedings of the 15th international academic MindTrek Conference: Envisioning future media environments* (pp. 9-15). ACM. 10.1145/2181037.2181040

Kapp, K. M. (2012). *The Gamification of Learning and Instruction. Game-Based Methods and Strategies for Training and Education.* John Wiley & Sons.

Lee, P. (2005). Putting Principles into Practice: Understanding History. In M. S. Donovan & J. D. Bransford (Eds.), *How students learn: History in the classroom* (pp. 29–78). National Academies Press.

Lee, P., & Ashby, R. (2000). Progression in Historical Understanding among Students Ages 7-14. In P. N. Stearns, P. Seixas, & S. Wineburg (Eds.), *Knowing, Teaching, and Learning History: National and International Perspectives* (pp. 199–222). New York University Press.

Martínez-Hita, M. (2022). *El pensamiento histórico en Educación Primaria. Diseño y evaluación de un programa de intervención gamificado* [Historical thinking in Primary Education. Design and evaluation of a gamified intervention programme] [Doctoral thesis, University of Murcia]. Digitum: Repositorio Institucional de la Universidad de Murcia. http://hdl.handle.net/10201/116267

Metzger, S. A., & Harris, L. M. (Eds.). (2018). *The Wiley International Handbook of history teaching and learning*. Wiley. doi:10.1002/9781119100812

Seixas, P., & Morton, T. (2013). *The Big Six Historical Thinking Concepts*. Nelson Education Ltd.

Thorp, R., & Persson, A. (2020). On historical thinking and the history educational challenge. *Educational Philosophy and Theory*, *52*(8), 891–901. doi:10.1080/00131857.2020.1712550

Acknowledgment

This book is the result of the research projects "The geographical and historical thinking of primary education students in the Region of Murcia: an innovative methodological proposal for quality education" (20874/PI/18), funded by the Fundación Séneca-Agencia de Ciencia y Tecnología de la Región de Murcia; "The teaching and learning of historical competences in baccalaureate education: a challenge for the achievement of a critical and democratic citizenship" (PID2020-113453RB-I00), funded by MCIN/AEI/10.13039/501100011033; and "HistoryLab for European Civic Engagement: open e-Toolkit to train History Teachers on Digital Teaching and Learning", funded by SEPIE under the ERASMUS+ KA226 call (2020-1-ES01-KA226-HE-095430).

MINISTERIO DE CIENCIA E INNOVACIÓN

AGENCIA ESTATAL DE INVESTIGACIÓN

Región de Murcia

f SéNeCa(+)

Agencia de Ciencia y Tecnología Región de Murcia

Chapter 1
Changes in Primary School Students' Ideas About History After Implementing a Gamified Intervention Programme

María Martínez-Hita
University of Murcia, Spain

Cosme Gómez Carrasco
University of Murcia, Spain

Pedro Miralles-Martínez
https://orcid.org/0000-0002-9143-2145
University of Murcia, Spain

EXECUTIVE SUMMARY

The teaching of history requires a process of change to encourage the active learning of historical research methods rather than the mere memorisation and the learning of concepts. The use of gamification can facilitate the development of the historical thinking skills. This quasi-experimental research had the aim of analysing the evolution of the conceptions on history as a subject of students in the fourth year of primary education in Spain. An experimental group, which worked with an active learning methodology based on gamification and historical thinking, was compared with a control group, which followed a traditional methodology. To achieve the aims of the research, a mixed performance test was applied to the students before and after the classroom intervention. The results demonstrated a higher degree of evolution in the students' conceptions in the experimental group. Therefore, the use of gamified active learning methodologies based on historical thinking is recommended in order to contribute towards the improvement of history education.

DOI: 10.4018/978-1-6684-5240-0.ch001

INTRODUCTION

Historical thinking is becoming increasingly popular in international research on history education (Metzger & Harris, 2018; Thorp & Persson, 2020). This phenomenon is having an impact on the teaching of history, in which the learning of historical contents based on memorisation is slowly losing ground in favour of the active learning of historical research methods, i.e., the development of historical thinking (Lévesque & Clark, 2018). In addition, this approach to history teaching is in line with current trends in education, which advocate the inclusion of active learning methods in the classroom (Gómez et al., 2018).

Teaching based on historical thinking requires an awareness of how historical knowledge is constructed and of how historians work. The view that students have of history as a subject and the construction of knowledge can either favour or hinder their understanding of history (Miguel-Revilla et al., 2020; VanSledright & Maggioni, 2016).

However, students tend to have incomplete or erroneous conceptions of history and a lack of knowledge of the work of the historian and the usefulness of historical sources (Brophy & VanSledright, 1992; Brophy et al., 1992; Fraile-Delgado, 2020; Fuentes, 2002, 2006; Miguel-Revilla et al., 2020; Shemilt, 1987a, 1987b).

The methodology employed in the classroom has an influence on students' conceptions of history and can be modified positively via an active methodology which is based on the historical thinking skills (Brophy et al., 1992; Fraile-Delgado, 2020; Fuentes, 2002, 2006; Miguel-Revilla et al., 2020; Shemilt, 1987a, 1987b).

However, prior research has tended to study learners from higher levels of education (VanSledright & Maggioni, 2016), largely ignoring primary schoolchildren.

The present study aims to contribute towards correcting this imbalance in research by analysing the conceptions held by children in the fourth year of primary education on history as a subject, comparing a control group and an experimental group both before and after a differentiated teaching intervention in each of the groups.

HISTORICAL THINKING

The teaching and learning process of history takes place in two main ways in the classroom: On the one hand, education based on the use of the textbook and the learning by heart of information, dates and concepts; on the other hand, history may be taught based on constructivism and active methodologies which seek the comprehension of history as a narrative or interpretation of the past, placing emphasis on the historical method (Santisteban, 2010). The first method of teaching implies the transition of the idea of history as closed and neutral knowledge, whereas the second shows history as knowledge which can be questioned and is open to democratic debate (Miralles & Gómez, 2021; Shemilt, 1987b).

The latter approach is that which is related to historical thinking and, therefore, favours its development. It implies that students do not merely memorise past events, information and dates, which are known as first-order concepts, but that they should also develop the capacity to analyse, interpret and explain the past based on the critical analysis of sources. In other words, they learn the methods and techniques of historical research which make reference to strategic second-order concepts (Domínguez, 2015; Seixas & Morton, 2013; Thorp & Persson, 2020; VanSledright, 2004, 2011).

According to Seixas & Morton (2013), these second-order concepts are as follows: historical relevance, evidence or sources, change and continuity, causes and consequences, historical perspective and the ethical dimension of history. These concepts, which are also known as methodological concepts or historical thinking skills, are those which make it possible to organise and give meaning to substantive first-order contents and, therefore, provide students with an understanding of the subject of history (Lee, 2005; Lee & Ashby, 2000).

Wineburg (1999, 2001) states that explicit teaching of historical thinking is necessary as it is not developed in a natural way. Therefore, when history is taught, it is necessary to explain and give evidence of how history is written and how historians work.

Thus, in order to teach and learn history in an appropriate way, a methodological and epistemological change is required (Gómez et al., 2021; Martínez-Hita et al., 2021) in which students learn and understand the methods of which the subject consists (in other words, how historical knowledge is constructed). This learning requires an epistemological basis for the understanding of history (Santacana, 2005; Shemilt, 1987b).

It can be said, then, that to improve history education, a change in teaching approach is needed which makes it possible to understand what history is and the way in which it is constructed, i.e., the work of the historian, which forms the basis of historical thinking. Furthermore, the views students have of these aspects should be taken into consideration (Valls & López-Facal, 2011).

However, it has been stated that one of the main problems of history education is that it tends to focus on the transmission of first-order concepts rather than on the understanding of history as a subject and the development of the historical thinking skills (Lévesque, 2008; Seixas & Morton, 2013; Thorp & Persson, 2020).

In the case of Spain, educational practice is determined by two main elements: the curriculum and textbooks. Prior studies have shown that the presence of historical thinking in these two elements is negligible (Gómez, 2014; Martínez-Hita, 2019; Martínez-Hita & Gómez, 2018; Sáiz, 2011, 2013; Sáiz & Colomer, 2014). This implies that students' knowledge of what history is and of the work of the historian (and, therefore, their education in relation to historical thinking) is clearly lacking.

STUDENTS' CONCEPTIONS OF HISTORY

Students' ideas and perceptions concerning history and the work of historians have been the object of study for decades. One of the first studies on this issue was that carried out by Shemilt in the 1980s (Shemilt, 1987b).

This author evaluated the results of a pioneering history teaching project based on the approach of historical thinking which began in 1972 in Great Britain under the name of History Project 13-16, later becoming known as the School History Project (SHP). Shemilt (1987b) observed that students of the SHP (aged between 13 and 16 years of age) understood the nature of history better than those studying conventional courses. For example, students who did not form part of the SHP defined history as a compendium of pre-existing and unalienable facts and a memory-based subject, whereas those who had participated in the project to renovate the history curriculum expressed the idea that Historians create knowledge based on evidence, these creations are debatable and history is a problem-solving subject (Shemilt, 1987b). Shemilt (1987b) defended, therefore, that in order to understand history, it is necessary to address methodological aspects and historical explanation in such a way as to also understand the methods, the logic and the perspectives of the discipline.

Later, Fuentes (2002) carried out a review of the vision of history held by teenagers in the United States and the United Kingdom. As far as the United Kingdom is concerned, Fuentes makes reference to the prior study by Shemilt (1987a) in which four stages of evolution in student perceptions of historical sources and the work of the historian were established. These ideas evolved from a conception of history as an absolute truth engraved into textbooks to the consideration that history is a reconstruction of past events via the analysis of sources. As has previously been stated, it was the students of the experimental group (i.e., those who participated in the history teaching innovation project) who developed an idea of history associated with the analysis and interpretation of sources, rather than those of the control group, who considered that history was a description of past events.

With regard to research on this issue in the United States, the studies carried out in the 1990s by Brophy & VanSledright (1992) and Brophy et al. (1992) are particularly worthy of note. The former study (Brophy & VanSledright, 1992) demonstrated that the majority of students considered history to be the study of significant events of the past and that they had difficulty distinguishing the work carried out by historians. The latter study (Brophy et al., 1992) complemented the former by analysing student perceptions before and after a teaching intervention in order to observe how they evolved. An active methodology was employed, bringing about an improvement in the understanding of history as a discipline and of the work of the historian. For example, before the intervention, the students were unaware of the role of the historian and confused it with that of an archaeologist, whereas following the teaching intervention, they understood the role of the historian and how to analyse sources.

In summary, following the review of prior research, Fuentes (2002) stated that the majority thereof concluded that learners considered history to be unchangeable and closed knowledge based on the description of the most significant events of the past. However, these student perceptions on history are related with the way in which history is taught in the classroom and can, therefore, be modified via the use of new methodologies. In the same way, as regards the work of the historian, most students considered that these professionals are responsible for describing the past, which is already written down in sources or books, although they did not allude to the critical analysis, interpretation or research of history. However, the explanations of the work of the historian by those students who had worked with sources in class were more complete. Finally, she stated the importance and necessity of increasing the amount of research which would make it possible to understand students' perspectives of history.

Years later, the same author (Fuentes, 2006) carried out an analysis of the perceptions of secondary education students on history as a field of knowledge and a school subject. Focusing on history as a field of knowledge, students were asked about the definition of history, its object of study and the role of the historian. The results show that the majority of the students related history with knowledge of the past and had difficulties in explaining the work of historians. However, students who had worked with historical sources in the classroom had a more complete vision of both the role of the historian and of history as a discipline.

More recently, VanSledright & Maggioni (2016) have carried out a review of the main studies published on epistemological cognition in history. These authors highlight the importance of understanding the epistemology of each subject in order to improve learning thereof as, in the case of history, epistemological beliefs on what history is and how its knowledge is created are associated with historical thinking and historical comprehension. Furthermore, they conclude by stating the need to make progress in terms of research in this area with more empirical and systematic studies.

Another recent study by Fraile-Delgado (2020) analyses the evolution of the historiographic conceptions of first-year secondary education students by using a methodology based on working with the competencies associated to historical thinking.

Before the classroom intervention, as far as their vision of history is concerned, most of the students considered it as the study of past events, followed by a confusion between history and the past. With regard to the work of the historian, a high percentage of the students were unaware of what this consisted of and confused it with the work of the archaeologist, scientist or teacher. Finally, in relation to how the past is studied, the majority did not know or associated it with the search for information, although a quarter of the students made reference to the analysis of sources.

Following the classroom intervention, the students' conceptions evolved in a favourable way, particularly as far as the work of the historian is concerned, as a large proportion of the students identified the historian or archaeologist as somebody who investigates the past via the analysis and interpretation of sources. Thus, Fraile-Delgado (2020) concludes that a methodology based on historical thinking facilitates the positive evolution of students' historiographic conceptions (and, therefore, the development of historical thinking) as these are essential for historical literacy.

Miguel-Revilla et al. (2020) examined the epistemological beliefs concerning history of pre-service teachers (i.e., university students), both in primary and secondary education via the Beliefs About History Questionnaire (BHQ), with a qualitative analysis employing a questionnaire which focused on four categories: the nature of history, the interpretation of history, objectivity and subjectivity and the role of sources. Differences were detected between pre-service primary and secondary teachers. With regard to primary teachers, second-year undergraduates confused the past with history and did not take historical sources into consideration, whereas third-year students demonstrated conceptions which were a little more complete having previously studied subjects dealing with these contents. The pre-service secondary teachers, on the other hand, had the view of history as a science and emphasised the critical analysis of sources. The authors concluded by stressing the importance of teaching to modify epistemological beliefs.

Therefore, these studies reflect an erroneous or insufficient initial knowledge of history among students, which can hinder its comprehension and the development of historical thinking (Miguel-Revilla et al., 2020; VanSledright & Maggioni, 2016). Furthermore, it is highlighted that the use of an active methodology based on historical thinking brings about modifications in students' conceptions towards a better understanding of the work of the historian and of history as a discipline.

However, these prior studies have focused on the analysis of students of secondary or higher education (VanSledright & Maggioni, 2016) and, thus, there is a lack of research in the level of primary education. This fact can probably be attributed to the influence of Piagetian theory, which considers that it is difficult for students of these ages to understand history and to develop historical thinking (Éthier et al., 2010; Fuentes, 2002).

Nonetheless, other studies have demonstrated that primary schoolchildren are capable of understanding history and thinking historically and also point out the importance of the use of active methodologies in order to improve historical comprehension (Booth, 1983, 1987; Éthier et al., 2010; Fuentes, 2002).

The present study is based on such ideas and on the lack of research in the primary stage. In addition, it aims to complement prior research by including a quantitative analysis of students' conceptions on history, making it possible to carry out a statistical study of the differences in their evolution. Thus, its objective was to analyse students' conceptions of history as a subject following a classroom intervention, comparing an experimental group which worked with an active methodology based on gamification and historical thinking (Martínez-Hita & Miralles, 2020) with a control group which followed a traditional methodology based on the use of the textbook.

METHOD

Objectives

The main objective of this research was to discover how conceptions on history as a subject evolved among fourth-year primary schoolchildren following a classroom intervention, comparing an experimental group, which followed an active methodology based on gamification and historical thinking (Martínez-Hita & Miralles, 2020), with a control group, which worked on the same contents but applying a traditional methodology.

This general objective can be broken down into the following research questions:

1. Are there significant differences in the students' conceptions of history as a subject in the experimental group following the classroom intervention (pretest-posttest)?
2. Are there significant differences in the students' conceptions of history as a subject in the control group following the classroom intervention (pretest-posttest)?
3. Are there significant differences in the students' conceptions of history as a subject between the control group and the experimental group?

Research Design

The present study employed a quasi-experimental design with an experimental group and a control group, along with a pretest and a posttest.

Participants

A total of 44 children from the fourth year of primary education (aged between 9 and 10 years of age) attending a publicly-funded school in the Region of Murcia (Spain) participated in this research.

The selection of the sample for this research, which was carried out during the 2017/2018 academic year, was non-probabilistic and incidental in nature as it was based on the criteria of accessibility to the subjects and their fit with the aims of the study (Bisquerra, 2014).

The participants were divided into two groups which corresponded to their natural class groups. One of the groups, consisting of 21 students, was the control group, which worked with a traditional methodology, while the experimental group was made up of 23 children and followed an approach based on historical thinking. More specifically, the experimental group followed a gamified intervention programme based on historical thinking which included active and inclusive learning methods such as cooperative work (Martínez-Hita & Miralles, 2020).

Table 1. Items of the data collection tool and their respective concepts

Item	Concept
1. What is history for you?	Definition of history
2. How is history written?	Construction of historical knowledge
3. Who writes history?	Work of the historian
4. What is a historical source? What is its purpose?	Role of historical sources

Source: Own

Data Collection Tool

For the data collection, a performance test was employed which was created ad hoc with the aim of obtaining information on the students' views of history and historical research. Specifically, the following four short open-response items, which formed part of the aforementioned test, were analysed (see Table 1).

The performance test was validated via the expert judge technique. The analyses carried out of the psychometric characteristics demonstrated both content validity (Escobar-Pérez & Cuervo Martínez, 2008) and a high degree of internal consistency, with a Cronbach's alpha value of .850 for these four items (Bisquerra, 1992).

Data Analysis

The responses given by the students were coded and analysed using the SPSS v.24 statistical program. A 5-point (0-4) scale was employed to carry out the process of coding and evaluation of the data collected in the posttest, assigning a specific achievement indicator to each value for each of the items (see Table 2).

In the statistical analysis, the descriptive statistics, frequencies and intergroup and intragroup differences were calculated.

The intragroup comparison was carried out via the non-parametric Wilcoxon signed-rank test, whereas the comparison between the control group and the experimental group was made employing the Mann-Whitney U test. Statistical significance was established with a p-value £ .05.

The effect size was also calculated using Rosenthal's r (Rosenthal, 1991) with the aim of measuring the magnitude of the differences in the intergroup and intragroup comparisons.

RESULTS

The results are presented in accordance with the research questions.

1. **Are there significant differences in the students' conceptions of history as a subject in the experimental group following the classroom intervention (pretest-posttest)?**

Table 3 shows the descriptive statistics of the experimental group in the pretest. Extremely low scores were observed in the four items, with a mode of zero in three of them, i.e., the most repeated response which was equivalent to a lack of knowledge on the aspects asked.

Table 2. Achievement indicators for the evaluation of each of the items

Item	Scale and achievement indicators		Example
1. What is history for you?	0	Lack of knowledge. Blank or completely incorrect.	"It is a book". "It is a world which has a story."
	1	Name a past event.	"When fire/writing was invented."
	2	Confusion between history and the past.	"It's something that happened a long time ago, like Egypt, Prehistory"
	3	Identification of history as a science, albeit without specifying the object of study.	"It's science which investigates." "History is what historians investigate."
	4	A science which studies the past.	"It's the science of investigating the past of people and human societies."
2. How is history written?	0	Lack of knowledge. Blank or completely incorrect.	"With ancient letters." "In drawings and in letters."
	1	No reference is made to research. It is already written.	"They search for it on the internet." "I think they imagine it." "In books."
	2	Short answer: researching.	"It is written by researching." "They write what they research."
	3	Researching and analysing, without mentioning sources. Or mentioning sources but not research.	"History is written by analysing information. Then it is summarised and written." "Historians have to analyse, research and, with this information, they write history."
	4	Reference is made to research and the analysis of sources.	"Analysing historical sources and researching them." "They searched for historical sources, analysed them and wrote history."
3. Who writes history	0	Lack of knowledge. Blank or completely incorrect.	"God."
	1	People.	"People who have studied it."
	2	Writer, author of a book.	"A writer and illustrator." "The author of the book."
	3	Scientist, archaeologist, researcher.	"Archaeologists." "Researchers."
	4	Historians.	"Historians."
4. What is a historical source? What is its purpose?	0	Lack of knowledge. Blank or completely incorrect.	"Its purpose is to say if it is written/oral."
	1	Only states that information is given, without specifying that it is from the past.	"A source is what gives you information and serves to accumulate information."
	2	An example of a source without explaining what its purpose is. States what its purpose is but not what it is.	"It is a text which talks about history." "It is a place where there are many things, such as ruins, painted caves."
	3	A correct explanation without stating that history is written via its analysis.	"It is an object from the past which serves to see how people lived in the past."
	4	A correct and detailed explanation.	"The marks of the past. It serves to analyse them and, then, to write history."

Source: Own

The descriptive statistics of the posttest for the experimental group can be observed in Table 4. There was an increase in the scores of all the items which reflected an improvement in the knowledge of history among the students following the classroom intervention. Both the median and the mean of the four items was equal to or higher than 2 (the mean value of the evaluation scale of the responses).

Table 3. Descriptive statistics of the experimental group in the pretest

	N	Mean	Median	Mode	Standard deviation	Minimum	Maximum
Item_1	23	1.13	2.00	2	.968	0	2
Item_2	23	.96	1.00	0	.928	0	3
Item_3	23	.83	1.00	0	.887	0	3
Item_4	23	.39	.00	0	.891	0	3

Source: Own

Table 4. Descriptive statistics of the experimental group in the posttest

	N	Mean	Median	Mode	Standard deviation	Minimum	Maximum
Item_1	23	2.83	3.00	4	1.370	0	4
Item_2	23	2.87	3.00	3	1.180	0	4
Item_3	23	3.91	4.00	4	.288	3	4
Item_4	23	2.00	2.00	0	1.567	0	4

Source: Own

In order to determine whether this increase in the scores in the posttest compared with the pretest is significant, and to provide an answer to the first research question, the Wilcoxon's W non-parametric contrast test for two dependent or related samples was performed (see Table 5). The results showed that there were statistically significant differences in all of the items in the experimental group between the pretest and the posttest ($p < .05$).

In addition, the effect size (i.e., how big these differences were) was calculated, indicating moderate modifications in the students' conceptions of history as a subject among the experimental group, in accordance with Cohen's (1988) criteria.

Table 5. Wilcoxon's W testa for the posttest/pretest of the experimental group with their respective effect size

Item	Mean	Z (Sig.)	ES
Item_1_pre	1.13	-3.859[b] (.000)	0.569
Item_1_pos	2.83		
Item_2_pre	.96	-3.966[b] (.000)	0.585
Item_2_pos	2.87		
Item_3_pre	.83	-4.255[b] (.000)	0.627
Item_3_pos	3.91		
Item_4_pre	.39	-3.548[b] (.000)	0.523
Item_4_pos	2.00		

a. Wilcoxon's signed-rank test
b. Based on negative ranges
Source: Own

Table 6. Descriptive statistics of the control group in the pretest

	N	Mean	Median	Mode	Standard deviation	Minimum	Maximum
Item_1	21	1.19	2.00	2	.928	0	2
Item_2	21	.90	.00	0	1.044	0	3
Item_3	21	1.14	.00	0	1.352	0	3
Item_4	21	.24	.00	0	.889	0	4

Source: Own

From a more qualitative point of view, as regards the first item on what history is, in the pretest, the majority of the students confused history with the past (52.2%) or did not know what it was (39.1%). In the posttest, a high percentage of the students (43.5%) defined history as a science which studies the past, although 21.7% of the participants still confused history with the past. An example of the evolution in the responses was noted in that one of the students defined history as "Things which happened a long time ago" in the pretest, whereas, in the posttest, he stated that "For me, history is the science which investigates the past" (student 8).

With regard to the second item relating to how historical knowledge is constructed, in the pretest, the majority of the students (39.1%) did not know, followed by 30.4% who stated that history appears in books and on the Internet, without making reference to research. The remaining students mentioned research, albeit briefly and without mention of historical sources, e.g., "It is written by researching" (student 2). In the posttest, an evolution could be observed in the responses. 30.4% of the students made reference to research and the analysis of sources (e.g., "They searched for historical sources and analysed them and write history" (student 15)) and 47.8% mentioned the process of research and analysis, albeit without mention of sources, or made reference to sources but not research ("It is necessary to research, analyse and, when they have finished, write it down" (student 7)).

As far as the third item (Who writes history?) is concerned, in the pretest, the majority of the students (43.5%) did not know, responding that it was people (34.8%) or authors and the writers of books (17.4%). In the posttest, these responses underwent a modification, with 91.3% stating that it was historians. This is in line with the quantitative results obtained with regard to the effect size as it was this item which obtained the greatest effect size (0.627) (see Table 5).

Finally, as far as historical sources are concerned, in the pretest, the vast majority of the students (82.6%) did not know what they were or what purpose they served. However, in the posttest, their responses were more varied. 21.7% offered correct and detailed responses, as was the case of student 13 who stated that "it is something which is preserved from the past and serves to write history". However, there were still 30.4% of the students who were not capable of explaining their meaning or use. An example of evolution can be observed in student 2 who was unaware of historical sources in the pretest, leaving the question unanswered, but, in the posttest, defined them as "the marks left by the past which serve to write history".

2. **Are there significant differences in the students' conceptions of history as a subject in the control group following the classroom intervention (pretest-posttest)?**

Table 7. Descriptive statistics of the control group in the posttest

	N	Mean	Median	Mode	Standard deviation	Minimum	Maximum
Item_1	21	1.29	2.00	2	1.007	0	3
Item_2	21	1.33	2.00	0	1.197	0	3
Item_3	21	2.48	3.00	4	1.750	0	4
Item_4	21	.86	.00	0	1.315	0	4

Source: Own

The descriptive statistics of the control group in the pretest can be observed in Table 6. All of the items obtained extremely low scores, which demonstrates insufficient knowledge of history and historical research.

The descriptive statistics of the posttest for the control group show an increase in the scores of the items (see Table 7). However, with the exception of item 3, these scores are still low, particularly in the case of item 4.

In order to respond to the second research question (Are there significant differences in the students' conceptions of history as a subject in the control group following the classroom intervention (pretest-posttest)?), Wilcoxon's signed-rank test was performed. As shown in Table 8, there were no significant differences between the pretest and the posttest for items 1 and 2, although there were in the case of items 3 and 4 ($p < .05$). The effect size (ES) was small, i.e., the differences were small as they were below the value of .50 (Cohen, 1988).

In a more qualitative approach to the students' responses to the first item regarding what history is, in the pretest, more than half of the children (52.4%) confused history with the past and 33.3% did not know what history was. In the posttest, almost the same percentages were maintained as in the pretest, which is reflected in the lack of statistically significant differences in the quantitative analysis. For example, the response of one student to this item in the pretest was "For me, it is what happened in the past"; and in the posttest "For me, it is the events which occurred in the past" (student 35).

Table 8. Wilcoxon's W test a of the posttest/pretest for the control group with their respective effect sizes

Item	Mean	Z (Sig.)	ES
Item_1_pre	1.19	-.649[b] (.516)	.100
Item_1_pos	1.29		
Item_2_pre	.90	-1.852[b] (.064)	.286
Item_2_pos	1.33		
Item_3_pre	1.14	-2.954[b] (.003)	.456
Item_3_pos	2.48		
Item_4_pre	.24	-1.994[b] (.046)	.308
Item_4_pos	.86		

a. Wilcoxon's signed-rank test
b. Based on negative ranges.
Source: Own

Table 9. Results of the Mann-Whitney U test for the pretest between the control group and the experimental group

	Group	Average range	Sum of ranges	*U* (Sig.)	Z
Item_1	Experimental	22.20	510.50	234.500 (.855)	-.183
	Control	22.83	479.50		
Item_2	Experimental	23.00	529.00	230.000 (.772)	-.289
	Control	21.95	461.00		
Item_3	Experimental	21.78	501.00	225.000 (.678)	-.415
	Control	23.29	489.00		
Item_4	Experimental	23.33	536.50	222.500 (.454)	-.749
	Control	21.60	453.50		

Source: Own

As far as the second item regarding how history is written is concerned, in the pretest, 52.4% of the students were unable to answer, followed by 33.3% who merely mentioned research. In the posttest, the number of students who did not know how historical knowledge was built reduced (38.1%), 33.3% still made only a brief reference to research, but there was an increase to 19% of those students who provided a better, albeit still incomplete, explanation of research. For example, in the posttest, responses were given such as "Researching things from the past (student 34), "Researching everywhere" (student 35) and "With the historical sources found" (student 41).

In relation to the third item, concerning who writes history, approximately half of the students (52.4%) did not know, although 28.6% made mention of archaeologists or researchers. In the posttest, the percentage of students who did not know who wrote history reduced to 28.6%, with 23.8% mentioning archaeologists or researchers and 42.9% referring to historians.

Finally, as far as historical sources are concerned, as was the case in the experimental group, in the pretest, the majority did not know what they were or what purpose they served (90.5%). In the posttest, although this percentage went down, it remained high at 66.7% of those who were unable to answer this question, followed by 19% who provided some kind of example of historical source or explained their use, but not their significance. For example, "Maps" (student 26) or "They are objects from the past" (student 41).

3. **Are there significant differences in the students' conceptions of history as a subject between the control group and the experimental group?**

Before responding to the third research question, it was verified that there were no prior differences between the two groups before the classroom intervention.

Table 9 shows the comparison of the results obtained in the pretest for the control group and the experimental group. The non-parametric Mann-Whitney U test for two independent samples showed that there were no statistically significant differences between the control group and the experimental group in any of the items ($p > .05$).

Table 10. Results of the Mann-Whitney U test for the posttest between the control group and the experimental group with their respective effect sizes

	Group	Average range	Sum of ranges	*U* (Sig.)	Z	TE
Item_1	Experimental	29.20	671.50	87.500 (.000)	-3.760	.567
	Control	15.17	318.50			
Item_2	Experimental	29.39	676.00	83.000 (.000)	-3.849	.580
	Control	14.95	314.00			
Item_3	Experimental	27.89	641.50	117.500 (.000)	-3.542	.534
	Control	16.60	348.50			
Item_4	Experimental	26.80	616.50	142.500 (.013)	-2.485	.375
	Control	17.79	373.50			

Source: Own

Having verified the absence of prior differences between the groups, a comparison of the posttest results was carried out in order to answer the third research question (Are there significant differences in the students' conceptions of history as a subject between the control group and the experimental group?)

The Mann-Whitney U test demonstrated that there were differences in all of the items between the control group and the experimental group, with the results obtained by the experimental group being higher than those of the control group (see Table 10). Furthermore, these differences, with the exception of item 4, were moderate as reflected in the values of the effect size (ES), which were higher than .50 (Cohen, 1988).

DISCUSSION AND CONCLUSION

In spite of the increasing presence of historical thinking and the defence of teaching innovation in research on history education (Domínguez, 2015; Lévesque & Clark, 2018; Seixas & Morton, 2013; Thorp & Persson, 2020), the results obtained, which showed a deficient initial perspective of history before the classroom intervention in both groups, coincide with those of different studies carried out decades ago (Brophy & VanSledright, 1992; Brophy et al., 1992; Fuentes, 2002, 2006).

However, following the classroom intervention, it became clear that there had been an evolution in the conceptions of both groups. This phenomenon was greater in the experimental group, with statistical significance in all of the items and a moderate effect size. In addition, all of the items exceeded (both in their mean and their median) the mean value of the evaluation scale of the responses, which would imply knowledge that is more than sufficient. On the other hand, although the students in the control group also improved their conceptions, these modifications were lower, with significant differences only being found in two of the four items and a small effect size. To this must be added the fact that the mean of only one of the items obtained a higher score than the mean value of the scale.

Likewise, the intergroup comparison reflected the existence of statistically significant differences between the experimental group and the control group in the posttest which did not exist in the pretest. Therefore, the results indicate that the type of methodology employed did, indeed, have an influence on the modifications of the students' conceptions of history as a subject. The students of the experimental group, who followed a teaching approach based on historical thinking and active learning methods, had a more complete vision of history than those of the control group, who worked with a traditional methodology based on the use of the textbook.

These results are in line with prior research (Brophy et al., 1992; Fraile-Delgado, 2020; Fuentes, 2002, 2006; Shemilt, 1987a, 1987b), which has highlighted the greater understanding of history as a subject and of the work of historians among students who have worked with active methodologies based on historical thinking in the classroom. Consequently, there is agreement on the importance and significance of methodology as a relevant factor in the modification of students' conceptions regarding historical research.

Furthermore, as highlighted by VanSledright & Maggioni (2016), if what is sought is an improvement in the learning of history, an understanding of the specific epistemology of the subject is required as the vision of what history is and how its knowledge is created is related with historical thinking and, therefore, with the comprehension of history.

The use of an active methodology based on historical thinking makes it possible to work in the classroom on the methodological aspects of the subject and, in this way, to know how historical knowledge is constructed. This epistemological basis is necessary for a good level of teaching and understanding of history as it makes it possible to progress from a conception of history as neutral and closed knowledge towards the view of history as a construction, a narrative or an interpretation of the past based on evidence (Santisteban, 2010; Shemilt, 1987b).

Consequently, it is possible to provide a solution to one of the main problems of history education, which has been highlighted in research in this field; namely, the prominence of substantive first-order concepts rather than the understanding of history (Lévesque, 2008; Martínez-Hita & Gómez, 2018). Thus, it is possible to improve history education by bringing about both a methodological and an epistemological change (Gómez et al., 2021; Martínez-Hita et al, 2021).

It has also been noted that it would be feasible to develop knowledge of history among primary education students, as has been stated in other prior research (Booth, 1983, 1987; Éthier et al., 2010; Fuentes, 2002), rather than diffuse ideas due to the influence of Piaget's theory on the impossibility of students of these ages learning history (Éthier et al., 2010; Fuentes, 2002).

This research has demonstrated the capacity of fourth-year primary education students to evolve from erroneous or deficient conceptions of history as a subject towards a more complete vision thereof, particularly if an active methodology based on historical thinking is employed. For this reason, it is proposed that students learn from an early age about how to construct historical knowledge and the work of the historian, as has already been put forward in research on history education (VanSledright, 2011). This learning should be carried out via methodologies which make it possible to overcome reliance on textbooks and master classes in order to progress towards an approach based on historical thinking combined with active methods, such as gamification, in line with current trends in education (Gómez et al., 2018; Martínez-Hita et al., 2021).

To conclude, it is necessary to state that the limitations of this study, such as the sample size and the fact that only one researcher took part in the evaluation of the students' responses, should be taken into consideration. Therefore, it is recommended that future research on this issue should increase the number of participants and levels of education analysed and include more researchers, thus enabling a triangulation of the data and eliminating the possible bias of a single researcher.

ACKNOWLEDGMENT

This study is the result of the research projects "The geographical and historical thinking of primary education students in the Region of Murcia: an innovative methodological proposal for quality education" [20874/PI/18], funded by the Fundación Séneca-Agencia de Ciencia y Tecnología de la Región de Murcia; "HistoryLab for European Civic Engagement: open e-Toolkit to train History Teachers on Digital Teaching and Learning", funded by SEPIE under the ERASMUS + KA226 call [2020-1-ES01-KA226-HE-095430]; and the research project PID2020-113453RB-I00, funded by the Spanish State Research Agency [AEI/10.13039/501100011033].

REFERENCES

Bisquerra, R. (1992). *Introducción a la estadística aplicada a la investigación educativa.* PPU.

Bisquerra, R. (Coord.). (2014). Metodología de la investigación educativa (4ª ed.). La Muralla.

Booth, M. B. (1983). Skills, concepts and attitudes: The development of adolescent children's historical thinking. *History and Theory*, *22*(4), 101–107. doi:10.2307/2505218

Booth, M. B. (1987). Ages and concepts: a critique of the Piagetian approach to history teaching. In C. Portal (Ed.), *The history curriculum for teachers* (pp. 22–38). The Falmer Press.

Brophy, J., & VanSledright, B. (1992). Storytelling, imagination and fanciful elaboration in children's historical reconstructions. *American Educational Research Journal*, *20*(4), 837–859.

Brophy, J., VanSledright, B., & Brendin, S. (1992). Fifth graders' ideas about history expressed before and after their introduction to the subject. *Theory and Research in Social Education*, *XX*(4), 440–489. doi:10.1080/00933104.1992.10505682

Cohen, J. (1988). *Statistical Power Analysis for the Behavioral Sciences* (2nd ed.). Lawrence Erlbaum Associates.

Domínguez, J. (2015). *Pensamiento histórico y evaluación de competencias*. Graó.

Escobar-Pérez, J., & Cuervo-Martínez, Á. (2008). Validez de contenido y juicio de expertos: Una aproximación a su utilización. *Avances en Medición*, *6*, 27–36.

Éthier, M. A., Demers, S. & Lefrançois, D. (2010). Las investigaciones en didáctica sobre el desarrollo del pensamiento histórico en la enseñanza primaria. Una panorámica de la literatura publicada en francés e inglés desde el año 1990. *Enseñanza de las ciencias sociales, 9*, 61-74.

Fraile-Delgado, F. J. (2020). Pensar en Clío: la evolución de las concepciones historiográficas del alumnado de 1º de Educación Secundaria Obligatoria. *Didáctica de las ciencias experimentales y sociales*, *39*, 3-16. doi:10.7203/dces.39.15512

Fuentes, C. (2002). La visión de la historia por los adolescentes: revisión del estado de la cuestión en Estados Unidos y el Reino Unido. *Enseñanza de las ciencias sociales, 1*, 55-68.

Fuentes, C. (2006). Concepciones de los alumnos sobre la Historia. *Educar em Revista, 22*(spe), 219–239. doi:10.1590/0104-4060.407

Gómez, C. J. (2014). Pensamiento histórico y contenidos disciplinares en los libros de texto. Un análisis exploratorio de la Edad Moderna en 2.° de la ESO. *Ensayos. Revista de la Facultad de Educación de Albacete, 29*(1), 131–158.

Gómez, C. J., Ortuño, J., & Miralles, P. (2018). *Enseñar ciencias sociales con métodos activos de aprendizaje. Reflexiones y propuestas a través de la indagación*. Octaedro.

Gómez, C. J., Rodríguez-Medina, J., Miralles, P., & Arias, V. B. (2021). Efectos de un programa de formación del profesorado en la motivación y satisfacción de los estudiantes de historia en enseñanza secundaria. *Revista de Psicodidáctica, 26*(1), 45–52. doi:10.1016/j.psicod.2020.07.002

Lee, P. (2005). Putting Principles into Practice: Understanding History. In M. S. Donovan & J. D. Bransford (Eds.), *How students learn: History in the classroom* (pp. 29–78). National Academies Press.

Lee, P., & Ashby, R. (2000). Progression in Historical Understanding among Students Ages 7-14. In P. N. Stearns, P. Seixas, & S. Wineburg (Eds.), *Knowing, Teaching, and Learning History: National and International Perspectives* (pp. 199–222). New York University Press.

Lévesque, S. (2008). Thinking historically: Educating students for the twenty-first century. Toronto University Press.

Lévesque, S., & Clark, P. (2018). Historical Thinking: Definitions and Educational Applications. In S. Metzger & L. M. Harris (Eds.), *The Wiley International Handbook of History Teaching and Learning* (pp. 119–148). John Wiley & Sons, Inc. doi:10.1002/9781119100812.ch5

Martínez-Hita, M. (2019). Análisis comparativo del modelo cognitivo y conceptos históricos en el currículum español e inglés. In *IV Jornadas Doctorales Escuela Internacional de Doctorado de la Universidad de Murcia (EIDUM)* (pp. 560–563). Editum.

Martínez-Hita, M., & Gómez, C. J. (2018). Nivel cognitivo y competencias de pensamiento histórico en los libros de texto de Historia de España e Inglaterra. Un estudio comparativo. *Review of Education, 379*, 145–169. doi:10.4438/1988-592X-RE-2017-379-364

Martínez-Hita, M., Gómez-Carrasco, C. J., & Miralles-Martínez, P. (2021). The effects of a gamified project based on historical thinking on the academic performance of primary school children. *Humanit Soc Sci Commun, 8*(1), 122. doi:10.105741599-021-00796-9

Martínez-Hita, M., & Miralles, P. (2020). Evaluación del diseño de un programa de intervención gamificado para el desarrollo del pensamiento histórico en Educación Primaria. *RIFOP, 34*(2), 187–204. doi:10.47553/rifop.v34i2.78420

Metzger, S. A., & Harris, L. M. (Eds.). (2018). *The Wiley International Handbook of history teaching and learning*. Wiley. doi:10.1002/9781119100812

Miguel-Revilla, D., Carril-Merino, T., & Sánchez-Agustí, M. (2020). An examination of epistemic beliefs about history in initial teacher training: A comparative analysis between primary and secondary education prospective teachers. *Journal of Experimental Education*, *89*(1), 54–73. doi:10.1080/00220973.2020.1718059

Miralles, P., & Gómez, C. J. (2021). El pensamiento histórico del alumnado y su relación con las competencias. In *Educación histórica para el siglo XXI. Principios epistemológicos y metodológico.* (pp. 83-114). Universidad del Valle y Universidad Icesi.

Rosenthal, R. (1991). *Meta-analytic procedures for social research* (2nd ed.). Sage. doi:10.4135/9781412984997

Sáiz, J. (2011). Actividades de libros de texto de Historia, competencias básicas y destrezas cognitivas, una difícil relación: análisis de manuales de 1° y 2° de ESO. *Didáctica de las ciencias experimentales y sociales, 25*, 37-64.

Sáiz, J. (2013). Alfabetización histórica y competencias básicas en libros de texto de historia y en aprendizajes de estudiantes. *Didáctica de las ciencias experimentales y sociales, 27*, 43-66. doi:10.7203/dces.27.2648

Sáiz, J. & Colomer, J. C. (2014). ¿Se enseña pensamiento histórico en libros de texto de Educación Primaria? Análisis de actividades de historia para alumnos de 10-12 años de edad. *CLIO. History and History teaching, 40*.

Santacana, J. (2005). Reflexiones en torno al laboratorio escolar de ciencias sociales, *Íber: Didáctica de las Ciencias Sociales. Geografía e Historia*, *43*, 7–14.

Santisteban, A. (2010). La formación de competencias de pensamiento histórico. *Clío & Asociados, 14*, 34-56.

Seixas, P., & Morton, T. (2013). *The Big Six Historical Thinking Concepts*. Nelson Education Ltd.

Shemilt, D. (1987a). Adolescent ideas about evidence and methodology in History. In C. Portal (Ed.), *The history curriculum for teachers* (pp. 39–61). The Falmer Press.

Shemilt, D. J. (1987b). El proyecto «Historia 13-16» del Schools Council: pasado, presente y futuro. In *La geografía y la Historia dentro de las Ciencias Sociales: hacia un currículum integrado* (pp. 173–208). Centro de Publicaciones del M.E.C.

Thorp, R., & Persson, A. (2020). On historical thinking and the history educational challenge. *Educational Philosophy and Theory*, *52*(8), 891–901. doi:10.1080/00131857.2020.1712550

Valls, R., & López-Facal, R. (2011). ¿Un nuevo paradigma para la enseñanza de la historia? Los problemas reales y las polémicas interesadas al respecto en España y en el contexto del mundo occidental. *Enseñanza de las ciencias sociales, 10*, 75-86.

VanSledright, B. A. (2004). What Does It Mean to Think Historically... and How Do You Teach It? *Social Education*, *68*(3), 230–233.

VanSledright, B. A. (2011). *The Challenge of Rethinking History Education. On Practice, Theories, and Policy*. Routledge.

VanSledright, B. A., & Maggioni, L. (2016). Epistemic cognition in history. In J. A. Greene, W. A. Sandoval, & I. Bråten (Eds.), *Handbook of epistemic cognition* (pp. 128–146). Routledge.

Wineburg, S. (1999). Historical Thinking and Other Unnatural Acts. *Phi Delta Kappan*, *80*(7), 488–499.

Wineburg, S. (2001). *Historical Thinking and other Unnatural Acts. Charting the Future of Teaching the Past*. Temple University Press.

KEY TERMS AND DEFINITIONS

Conceptions of History: Ideas and perceptions concerning history and the work of historians.

First-Order Concepts: Substantive knowledge of the content about the past, that is, past events, concepts, and dates.

Historians: Person who studies, researches, and writes about the past.

Historical Source: Source of information about the past whose analysis and interpretation allows the generation of historical narratives.

Historical Thinking: Creative process based on the analysis and interpretation of different historical sources in order to generate historical narratives.

History: Science of investigating the past of people and human societies by analyzing different historical sources.

Second-Order Concepts: Procedural ideas about history that provide the necessary tools for the study of the past and the construction of historical explanations.

Chapter 2
Historical Thinking Skills and Cognitive Levels in Spanish High School History Textbooks

Juan Ramón Moreno-Vera
University of Murcia, Spain

Raquel Sánchez-Ibáñez
University of Murcia, Spain

EXECUTIVE SUMMARY

The main purpose of this study is to check how history textbooks in Spain contribute to the teaching of historical thinking competencies. To reach this goal, there are two specific objectives. The first one is to investigate the existence of historical thinking skills in History textbooks in Spanish Baccalaureate. The second is to establish what level of cognitive difficulty there is in the textbook activities when developing historical thinking competencies. For this purpose, a sample of almost 4000 activities from five Spanish textbooks publishers has been selected. The methodology is quantitative and based on descriptive analysis. The results show that the textbooks include few activities working on historical thinking competencies and with a low-medium cognitive skill level. The most frequent historical competencies are the analysis of sources and the identification of causes and consequences of historical events. The study concludes that Spanish publishers need to increase the presence of activities that promote history learning through thinking competencies.

INTRODUCTION

History has traditionally been present since the first attempts to create national curriculums in all "Western" countries at the beginning of the 19th century. Obviously, the reasons for studying history have evolved as societies have developed. First of all, history was of great importance in the construction of modern nations (19th century) and in the justification of the new model of state-centered power. In the present day, history education must fill an extremely significant gap due to the fact that the new objectives of

DOI: 10.4018/978-1-6684-5240-0.ch002

contemporary society have evolved towards an understanding of current social problems, democratic values, civic engagement, racism and the environment. As Prats and Santacana (2001) have pointed out, history is useful for students to understand the society they live in and how to behave and solve social problems to become good citizens in the future (Lévesque, 2008).

In recent decades, in the field of social sciences education, there has been a growing insistence on promoting competency-based history teaching. This involves teaching students not only historical contents (dates, facts, relevant figures), but also a series of skills related to epistemology and the historical method of investigation (Alvén, 2017; Bertram, 2016; Carretero, 2019; Eliasson et al., 2015; Ercikan & Seixas, 2015; Gómez et al., 2018).

For this reason, the main objective of this study is to reveal how history textbooks in Spain contribute towards developing these historical thinking skills. According to authors such as Lee (2011) and Seixas and Morton (2013), the historical thinking skills enable students to become more critical and to base their arguments more on scientific evidence, with up to six historical thinking concepts having been distinguished: the analysis of sources and evidence, the identification of causes and consequences, the identification of changes and continuities over time, historical perspective, historical relevance and the ethical dimension of history.

THEORICAL FRAMEWORK

Learning History Must be More than a Conglomeration of Facts and Dates

Current debates in both Italy and Spain, and, indeed, in all "Western" countries, concerning democratic values such as national identity and the interests of market forces influence new political discussions on the development of curriculums (Whitty, 1989). In this sense, it is of particular relevance to turn the discussion towards new teaching and learning topics, such as the development of concepts for historical thinking, the use of practical and active methodologies such as field work and investigation and the use of sources and evidence in the classroom.

As Wineburg (2002) stated in his book *Historical thinking and other unnatural acts*, it may be the case that we are asking the wrong questions. From ancient times, all societies have lamented young people's lack of historical knowledge, warning themselves that they were being condemned to repeat the same mistakes. In this regard, authors such as Dewey (1900) at the beginning of the 20th century were already advocating the teaching of history in accordance with the scientific method, using evidence and transforming the classroom into a historical laboratory in order to enable students to work like professional historians by carrying out research and investigation via the use of primary sources.

According to García (2021) historical positivism is still the hegemonic narrative in history education today. This kind of approach is closely linked to the "official history" of countries and the concept of nation. For this reason, Wineburg (2002) considers that we, as educators, should not ask "what history do we teach in the classroom?", but rather "why is it important to learn history today". The same author (Wineburg, 2002) also states that learning history is more than learning one fact after another. Our aim as history teachers is to enable students to work like professional historians, following a method, analyzing evidence, interpreting documents and pictures and understanding the complex relationships that lie behind people and events in the past. Furthermore, it should be debated and argued how these facts are related to the present and how we must act in the future in order to solve the current problems of society.

Indeed, other historians, such as Fontana (2006), have asked a very similar question when reflecting upon history education in Spain: What kind of history should we teach for the 21st century? In his opinion, a model of history education based on wars and battles (which he named "State biographies") is not what is required. Rather, there is a need for a change of approach towards a more social history, in the sense that it must be focused more on people's lives and new actors should be made visible, who, until now, have been invisible in historical narratives (women, African and Asian cultures, pre-Hispanic civilizations, children, old people or racial and sexual minorities) (Ortega, 2018).

In order to develop these new approaches to history education, Seixas and Morton (2013) summarized *the big six concepts for historical thinking*. They distinguished two kinds of concepts: first-order concepts, such as dates, facts, eras and the minimum chronological foundation to build historical knowledge; and second-order concepts, which are more related to developing historical thinking skills in a similar way to that exercised by professional historians (historical perspective, the use of evidence, the explanation of causes and consequences, pointing out changes and continuities, historical relevance and debating the ethical approach of important historical topics.

Seixas (2006) noted that it is important to understand that these six historical thinking concepts are not "skills but rather a set of underlying concepts that guide and shape the practice of history" (Seixas, 2006, p. 2).

According to Peck and Seixas (2004) and Seixas and Peck (2008), the six historical thinking concepts could be defined as:

- Historical significance: establishing why we care today about specific facts, dates and characters of the past. This requires our students to reflect upon why we choose to study certain characters and events and not others. What makes an event important in history?

The two main aspects to be taken into account in terms of historical significance are: "resulting in change" (if the event or person had profound consequences for many people over a long period of time) and "revealing" (if the event or person sheds light on enduring issues in history or was important at some point in history within the collective memory of a social group).

- Historical evidence: this aspect implies the use of primary sources in the classroom in order to build strong and scientific historical narratives. It is important that students understand that history is not a tale. Historical knowledge is built through evidence and sources (documents, pictures, films, archeological sites, architecture, letters, oral sources, objects, images, books, etc.). As Prats and Santacana (2001) pointed out, the best way to learn history is to allow our students to build history themselves. The implementation of this competency is crucial in contemplating the history classroom as Dewey did with his "laboratory school" at the beginning of the 20th century (Fallace & Fantozzi, 2017). Active learning methodologies, in which students work in collaborative teams and carry out research by themselves (always with the teacher guiding the experience and facilitating sources), are the best way to acquire this competency.

Seixas (2006) highlighted the fact that employing historical evidence in the classroom increases students' capacities to find, compare, select, contextualize and interpret different sources for a historical argument. At the same time, this implies increasing their critical thinking skills and teaching them to confront fake news in their daily lives.

- Change and continuity: identifying what has changed in history as well as what has remained over time. Students should be required to understand that not only are there events or facts that produce changes in history, but also that there are always facts that remain the same. Some visible changes are present in our cities, heritage and laws but less visible changes can also be found in mentalities, ideas, technology, industry or the Arts.

It is also important to encourage students to reflect upon the speed and depth of changes. Do these changes remove social and historical structures? Are the changes important for a large number of people or do they just affect a small portion of the population? Fernand Braudel has defined a structure of long duration as "an organization, a coherence of fixed relationships between social masses" (Casali, 2007, p. 5).

Seixas (2006) stated that continuity and change in terms of opinion are interrelated and usually continuous, rather than being isolated into specific events. In this sense, learning chronology is fundamental in historical thinking. Chronology may help to order and understand historical processes if they are clearly linked to the corresponding historical period and context.

- Cause and consequence: analyzing causes and consequences is essential for students to form their own understanding of historical complexity. In this regard, Seixas (2006) remarks that students have to know the role that people play in promoting, shaping and resisting change in history. Causes are different to motivations (or intentions) and may be related to long-term ideologies and conditions or short-term events that develop facts and new events.

As far as causes are concerned, there are two aspects which are of particular importance when developing this historical thinking competence. On the one hand, it should be understood that people provoke changes in history, although they are always limited by the context in which they live (natural environment, geography, historical legacies, laws, other countries, etc.). On the other hand, during the course of history it is not unusual for events to bring about unintended consequences.

- Historical perspective: this can be considered to be one of the most difficult competencies to acquire. As Seixas (2006) stated, "the past is a foreign country" and, therefore, it is sometimes difficult to understand people's languages, intentions, beliefs, laws or motivations due to their past contexts. It is necessary to think historically regarding their behavior, their social organization and the knowledge that they had when they experienced a historical event.

In the words of Powell (2003), presentism often appears in young students' historical narratives. For this author, presentism includes the imposition of modern values, beliefs or awareness onto a past era. A teacher may use students' "presentist" perspective to compare historical events with relevant problems in their daily lives. This may be of interest for students in order to understand that historical knowledge is important when interpreting the world in which they live. However, at the same time, it can be dangerous to have a merely "presentist" vision of the past as this is an open door for legitimizing a selective tradition over others. Teachers must pay attention to this mechanism of historical knowledge in such a way as to avoid populism, nationalist and supremacist narratives and hatred against other cultures or countries.

For Seixas (2006), certain aspects to be taken into account when developing historical perspective are as follows: the perspective of historical actors, always based on evidence of what life was like in past contexts (avoiding presentism); a specific historical fact could have many different interpretations depending on the people involved and their diverse perspectives thereof; and, although it may seem obvious, taking the perspective of a historical actor into consideration does not mean that the students identify themselves with that actor.

- Moral dimension in history: As Heller (1990) noted, history (among many other social sciences) is a scientific field based on evidence which requires interpretation by historians. In this regard, the interpretation of historical events could allow for multiple points of view, leading to historical knowledge always being open and critical.

This competency implies the argumentation and justification of moral judgments in history in terms of actors and events which were harmful for people in the past. It is not related to making presentist reinterpretations regarding controversial actors or events. However, teachers must allow their students to define whether past deeds were positive or negative depending on who suffered (or not) the event. As Seixas (2006) remarked, "we should expect to learn something from the past that helps us in facing the moral issues of today" (p. 11).

There are three important aspects to be taken into account when developing the competency of the moral dimension of history: all meaningful events of the past involve an implicit or explicit judgment; there is always the risk of interpreting that moral judgment with our present standards; and the facts must be evaluated taking into account the historical context and all the different points of view.

The use of this competency-based model grounded in historical thinking in the classroom will obviously have further consequences. As Körber (2011) explained, this model calls for an integration of the field of commemoration and memory into formal history education. Such an approach would enable teachers to include the topic of recent history in their lessons, an issue which is frequently controversial for society. The historical thinking skills make it possible to study specific controversial subjects through the filter of scientific knowledge, transferring the methods of the historian to the classroom: research, use of evidence, argumentation, comparison and critical reflection.

In the 1960s (Lukacs, 1968) and the mid-1970s, authors such as Weintraub (1975) and Gadamer and Fantel (1975) defined historical consciousness as "the privilege of modern man to have a full awareness of the historicity of everything present and the relativity of all opinions" (p. 8). This approach continued during the 1980s with authors such as Ross (1984) and Funkenstein (1989), who reflected on problems such as academic history, the construction of the modern concept of nation and the changes and variations of collective memories and historical consciousness.

In this sense, Seixas (2004) identified five principles to gain an understanding of historical consciousness: 1) The relationship between academic history and popular history, i.e., to recognize the complex relationship between historical scientific knowledge and the popular practice of history, in which there are a wide variety of purposes. 2) The relationship between theoretical history and practice. History has to be continuously tested and applied, as well as systematically reworked in the light of new findings. 3) It is necessary to compare the diverse points of views of historical events. Historical consciousness implies understanding the different implications of a fact depending on people, countries, cultures or values without applying a Western lens. 4) It is important to develop historical consciousness in order to promote an open and democratic society and to contribute to curriculum and other public-policy applications. 5) Historicizing the study of historical consciousness.

In the words of Gergen (2005), the study of historical narratives is still seen as concatenation of historical conceptions (realistic, phenomenological, psychodynamic, cognitive, textual, rhetorical, etc.).

Each of these conceptions contributes different implications for the understanding of history. For this reason, it is important in history education to develop the historical thinking skills among students. In this way, they will become more critical, use evidence to build the knowledge themselves, develop their own historical consciousness and, last but not least, achieve a more civic and democratic identity.

Along similar lines, Sáiz and López-Facal (2015) commented that the majority of students and pre-service teachers based their historical narratives on substantive contents which were not closely related to the historical thinking skills. Their research highlights the importance of history education in improving thinking skills among students.

The Historical Thinking Skills: A Comparison of European Countries

Domínguez (2016) claimed that the Spanish education system had failed when assessing the historical thinking skills, pointing out that most of the evaluations that the students completed were based on developing facts, dates and key actors. However, it is of interest to take into consideration the situation in other European countries.

A similar situation can be found in other European countries, although differences can be identified between countries. For example, Gómez and Chapman (2016) carried out a comparative study between Spain and England, looking for the historical thinking skills in their national curriculums. A similar study was carried out by Martínez-Hita and Gómez (2018) comparing in this case the textbooks of the two countries. The conclusions of both studies were similar: they appreciated that in the case of Spain there were less cognitive complex activities and a significant lack of historical thinking skills. In the case of England, on the other hand, the data showed a better situation in terms of cognitive skills, although there was still the need for improvement in the development of the historical thinking concepts.

Moreno-Vera and Alvén (2020) compared the Spanish and Swedish primary education curriculums with the aim of identifying the presence of the historical thinking concepts. These authors sought to analyze whether these key concepts can enable new active learning methodologies in the Social Sciences classroom. They compared five dimensions of each curriculum: structure, educational methodologies, objectives and evaluation criteria and, last of all, contents. The presence of the historical thinking skills in these dimensions was extremely low in both countries. In fact, these competencies were not the main aim for primary education. Above all, Moreno-Vera and Alvén (2020) suggested that "the low presence of historical thinking competencies is linked to traditional teaching models still based on positivism and memorization" (p.1).

Another comparative study was carried out by Gómez et al. (2020) analyzing the cognitive skills found in Spanish, Portuguese and English history textbooks. In this case, the authors analyzed the transition stage between primary and secondary education (11 to 13 years old), examining 6561 activities in 27 school textbooks. The results revealed that books in Spain and Portugal mainly include activities situated between a basic and intermediate cognitive level while in the case of England the cognitive level of their activities is medium or high. It is important to note, according to Gómez et al. (2020) that the activities with a higher cognitive level correspond to those of creation and essays or exercises that work on empathy and historical relevance (Gago, 2018; Magalhães, 2013).

Last of all, Sánchez-Ibáñez et al. (2020) compared the cognitive skills of activities in Italian history textbooks. The results were similar to those of countries such as Spain, Portugal and France. In the case of Italy, the activities analyzed in history textbooks also presented a low cognitive level. Indeed, according to Sánchez Ibáñez et al. (2020) they required students to reproduce the conceptual contents of the books textually, thereby making it difficult for them to learn critical and reflective historical thinking (Cajani, 2006).

Activities and Cognitive Skills in History Education

In recent years, researchers such as Ansari et al. (2011) have highlighted the importance of creating greater connections between education and cognitive neuroscience. In their opinion, the education system must build an infrastructure, mainly through interdisciplinary training, to assess the obstacles and difficulties of learning processes for students.

Goldman (2004) had previously stated that the development of practical skills would be important in the field of education in the 21st century. In fact, for this author, such skills would be crucial in all subjects related to human development in order to face the challenges of the new century. To her mind, these skills must be encouraged to understand all the information resources that were "becoming ubiquitous in society through various new multimedia technologies" (p. 317).

Goldman's (2004) reflection is of particular importance if we transfer her hypothesis to the field of history education, in which recent studies (Gómez et al., 2014) show the significance of learning history through thinking skills (Seixas & Morton, 2013). In this sense, one of the most important competencies for Seixas and Morton (2013) is to construct historical narratives using evidence and primary sources. Thus, if students are able to research, select and construct information from historical sources, they will learn the scientific method of history, the importance of inquiring, comparing and being critical with sources and, even, to make their own interpretation of historical events (Prats & Santacana, 2001).

In terms of history education, paying attention to the management of information and sources is especially encouraged for teachers:

These resources appear in a variety of media and forms. For example, information continues to come in traditional forms such as print-based text, but it is now also appearing in forms we do not typically think of as text, such as the oral "text" of a video, branched and linked text in hypertext environments, and the "text" of a visual image or picture. (Goldman, 2004, p. 317)

According to Tarman and Kuran (2015), Turkish Social Sciences textbooks have made significant changes and have been rearranged in accordance with the theories of constructivism (Vygotsky, 1988). For these authors, the main goal of these changes is to enable students to acquire higher-order cognitive skills. As is the case in other studies, such as that of Assaly and Smady (2015), the authors employed Bloom's Taxonomy (Shabatura, 2014) to analyze the activities contained in Turkish Social Sciences textbooks. In their results, they focused on types of activities and the cognitive skills required to carry them out. They found that multiple-choice questions required an extremely low cognitive level (85% of the total). Also prep questions (all those questions related to the reproduction of something that is contained in the textbook, such as "observe the text and highlight…" or "what is the meaning of…?") demonstrated a low level of cognitive skills (84.2% of the total). On the other hand, a high level was noted for open-ended questions (71.3% of the total), in which students were encouraged to create their own historical or geographical narratives, explaining contents in their own words, examining causes and consequences or changes and continuities and arguing concepts creatively.

When analyzing cognitive skills, it is crucial to note the division made by Bloom in his Taxonomy. This framework emerged in 1956 under the title "Taxonomy of educational objectives: the classification of educational goals. Handbook 1: cognitive domain" (Bloom et al., 1956) as a way of measuring annual examinations. The original framework of Bloom's Taxonomy was divided into six categories: knowledge (involving the recall of specifics and universals), comprehension (the individual knows what is being communicated and can use it but without necessarily relating it to other knowledge), application (using abstractions in particular and concrete situations), analysis (understanding elements or parts between classifying them into a hierarchical order), synthesis (putting together different elements so as to form a coherent whole) and evaluation (being capable of making judgements about the value of the contents).

Later revisions, such as that made by Anderson et al. (2001), reduce the Taxonomy to just four categories (the types of knowledge used in cognition) to make them less confusing (Krathwohl, 2010; Adams, 2015). These authors proposed verbs and gerunds to label and specify their categories of cognitive skills (and a large number of subcategories). With the following "action words" the cognitive processes could be described and easily recognized: remember (recognizing, recalling); understand (summarizing, explaining), apply (executing, implementing), analyze (differentiating, attributing), evaluate (checking, critiquing) and create (generating, producing).

While it is true that the original Taxonomy was conceived to evaluate educational objectives, Bloom et al. (1956) saw the categories as something more than a measurement tool, considering them to be:

- A tool in common language regarding learning targets, facilitating communication across teachers, subject contents and grade levels.
- The basis for clearly determining the curriculum and standards.
- A way to specify the coherence between objectives, activities and their evaluation.
- A complete panorama of the educational possibilities valid for any particular educational content.

In this sense, Bloom's Taxonomy proved to be a useful tool for analyzing not only didactic objectives, but also activities, evaluation criteria and specific educational standards. Through this framework, authors such as Athanassiou et al. (2003) have remarked that the Taxonomy makes it possible to analyze the level of critical thinking in learning activities in the classroom. Along similar lines, Riazi and Mosalanejad (2010) highlighted that it is also useful when analyzing the activities contained in textbooks. Halawi at al. (2009) also use the framework to evaluate e-learning educational programs on the basis of Bloom's Taxonomy.

METHODOLOGICAL FRAMEWORK

Objectives

As has been stated above, the main target of this research is to analyze the presence of the historical thinking skills and the cognitive skills developed in Spanish baccalaureate textbooks.

This objective is based on two specific objectives:

- S.O. 1: To ascertain the presence of historical thinking skills in History textbooks in pre-university Baccalaureate education (16 to 18 years of age). Six skills are analyzed (Peck & Seixas, 2008; Seixas, 2017): the analysis of sources and evidence, the identification of causes and consequences, the identification of changes and continuities over time, historical perspective, historical relevance and the ethical dimension of history.

- S.O. 2: To consider the level of cognitive difficulty contained in the activities proposed in the textbooks analyzed in order to verify the degree of reflection, analysis and application of the contents required of students. For this purpose, a classification has been applied which proposes a division into three levels of cognitive ability: high, intermediate and low (Sáiz, 2013, 2015).

A low cognitive level is represented by tasks consisting of content reproduction and imitation. The intermediate level includes tasks which require students to understand the contents (explanation of facts, summaries, diagrams, concept maps or timelines). The high cognitive level is present when students are asked to demonstrate understanding and knowledge of the scientific method (the formulation of hypotheses, analysis of sources, contrasting of information and drawing conclusions) and to apply their knowledge or create their own contents (elaboration of historical narratives from sources).

Context and Textbooks

Textbooks were chosen as a source of analysis due to the fact that, at present, in Spain they are still the most widely used didactic resource for the teaching of history (Martínez, 2014). For this reason, a sample of five publishers of Spanish textbooks (Anaya, Oxford, Santillana, SM and Vicens Vives) was selected. These publishers were chosen due to the fact that they are the most widely sold in Spain and, therefore, have the greatest presence in schools at the baccalaureate stage (16 to 18 years of age).

Specifically, the first year of this stage, which corresponds to the 16-17 age range, was selected for the analysis, as the contents of the syllabus, corresponding to the History of the Contemporary World, are universal. These contents are mandatory for the curriculum established by the Organic Law for the Improvement of Educational Quality, which has been in force in Spain since 2013. This universal history syllabus makes it possible to compare the results of this study on an international level, based on other similar studies carried out in other European countries (Portugal, France, Italy, the Netherlands).

Research Procedure and Tool

A quantitative research method was employed in order to analyze both the presence of the historical thinking skills and the level of cognitive skills contained in the activities of the textbooks. This procedure has been used in several previous studies in the field of social sciences education, such as Gómez et al. (2019, 2020) and Moreno-Vera et al. (2020, 2021).

The present study is an example of diagnostic research in the field of education and is based on descriptive analyses. These analyses focused on the activities present in the textbooks. In total, almost 4000 activities were analyzed, taking into account the objectives of the research. The descriptive analysis shows the frequency of the six historical thinking skills in the activities of the textbooks and their cognitive levels.

Figure 1. Level of cognitive skills found in textbooks
Source: Own elaboration

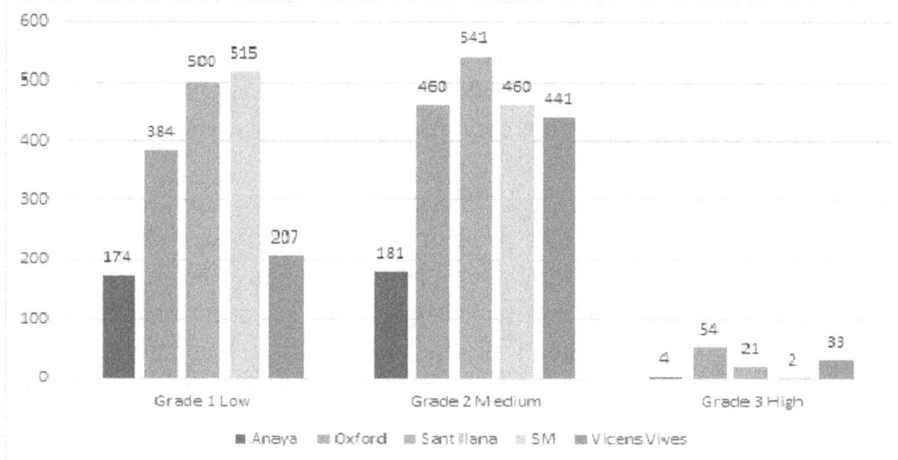

RESULTS

As far as specific objective 1 (S.O. 1), regarding the level of cognitive skills, is concerned, the results show that in Spanish baccalaureate History textbooks (16 to 18 years of age), in general, the activities proposed correspond to a low to medium cognitive level.

In fact, as can be seen in Figure 1, of the 3977 activities analyzed among the five textbooks, 1780 activities were found to be linked to Grade 1 (low cognitive skill required), representing 44.75% of the total. Regarding Grade 2 (medium cognitive skill), it can be observed that there were 2083 exercises, representing 52.37% of the activities. Finally, as far as the higher level of cognitive skills is concerned (Grade 3), only 114 activities were observed, representing 3.62% of the total, demonstrating a very poor result and the need to improve the number of such activities.

Analyzing the results of the cognitive skills grade by grade, it was found that, in relation to Grade 1 (low), the publisher SM presents more than 53% of activities at this level. The other textbooks were situated between 43% and 47%, with the exception of Vicens Vives, which shows the best results with just 30% of such activities. As far as Grade 2 (medium) is concerned, the best result is, again, for the Vicens Vives textbook as more than 65% of its activities were found to encourage historical analysis skills. Santillana, Oxford and Anaya also show good results as more than 50% of their activities correspond to Grade 2. Finally, although the presence of activities related to Grade 3 (high) promoting critical thinking skills is, in general, very poor, the highest number of such activities were observed in the books by Oxford (6% of its activities) and Vicens Vives (5%).

Consequently, it can be stated that it is common to find activities whose sole purpose is the reproduction and comprehension of theoretical contents which are already included in the textbook (Grades 1 and 2). Furthermore, activities which encourage analysis, reflection or critical thinking among students (Grade 3) are not frequent.

Taking specific objective 2 (S.O.2) into consideration, as far as the level of historical competencies is concerned, activities involving the analysis of sources and the identification of causes and consequences

Figure 2. Historical thinking skills in Spanish textbooks
Source: Own elaboration

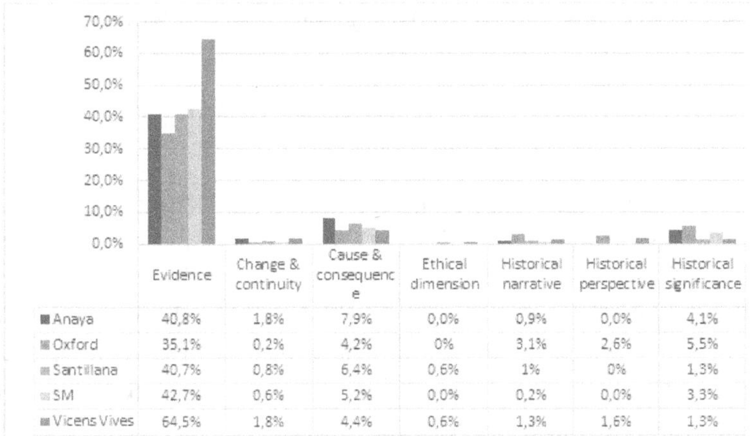

of historical events and processes were the most frequent. However, a significant difference could be observed between these competencies, as can be observed in Figure 2.

If the results are analyzed publisher by publisher, it can be observed that, in the case of the Vicens Vives textbook, the activities relating to the use of sources and evidence make up more than 64% of the activities, which is a very good result taking into account that these kinds of exercises encourage investigation and cooperative work among students and their own construction of historical knowledge. The remaining publishers analyzed obtained a more modest result when using evidence.

However, as stated above, there is a big gap between the competencies. Activities based on "cause and consequence" and "historical significance" are those which obtain better results. Activities regarding cause and consequence are more notable in the Anaya textbook (7.9% of its activities) while in the other publishers analyzed they represent between 4% and 6% of the total. As regards historical significance, the best result is for the Oxford textbook with 5.5% of the activities, with the other textbooks containing between 1% and 4% of such exercises.

Activities which appear at a lower level are those related to change and continuity, historical perspective and the ethical dimension of history. The analysis highlights the very low number of activities related to these competencies. The best results in terms of change and continuity were found in the Anaya and Vicens Vives textbooks, with a mere 1.8% of the activities. As far as the ethical dimension of history is concerned, the best results were for Santillana and Vicens Vives with an extremely low 0.6% of the total. Finally, as far as historical perspective is concerned, the best result was for the Oxford textbook, with 2.6% of the activities.

In Figure 2, it can be observed that the study included one more category related to activities focused on asking students to create their own "Historical narratives". This kind of activity is extremely interesting from the point of view of critical thinking and the students' construction of their own historical knowledge. These activities also obtain very low results (a mere 3.1% in the case of the Oxford textbook and around 1% in the other publishers). These kinds of creative exercises must be encouraged by publishers as they enable students to research by themselves, to use evidence to construct their narrative and to argue the topic using causes and consequences, reflecting on changes and continuities and, even, forming their own thoughts about ethical issues in past events.

The comparative study reveals that Oxford and Vicens Vives offer activities in which the learning of historical competencies is encouraged more than is the case with the other publishers. Furthermore, they offer activities in which students are required to have a greater capacity for analysis and critical reflection.

CONCLUSION

The study concludes that it is necessary for publishers in Spain to increase the presence of activities that encourage the learning of historical thinking skills among students, in line with the research carried out by Sáiz and López-Facal (2015), who evaluated the historical narratives of secondary students and pre-service history teachers. It would be of interest for publishers and textbooks to count on the assistance of specialists in the area of Social Sciences Education. In fact, the two publishers that do have professionals with this profile among their editorial teams are those which have offered the best results.

An important limitation of this study is to contrast the results with teaching practice in history classrooms, through research based on observation of teacher methodology. The use of textbooks by teachers could also have been explored in more depth by means of interviews or questionnaires. Finally, one way of extending this study would be to carry out a longitudinal study to ascertain the evolution of the treatment of historical thinking skills in textbooks at the Baccalaureate stage in Spain.

At the same time, it is necessary for history curriculums to incorporate the historical thinking skills (Moreno-Vera & Alvén, 2020) as a fundamental aspect of this discipline in all educational stages (from primary to baccalaureate). Students need to learn not only historical knowledge (memorization) but also skills related to historical thinking, which will help them to understand today's society in a critical way (Funkenstein, 1989; Lévesque, 2008; Seixas, 2017). In a digitalized and global society such as that of the 21st century, knowledge can easily be found but it is not easily learnt by students. In order to help them to learn history and to be critical, it is of great importance to incorporate the historical thinking skills into the school environment (Cajani, 2006; Gago, 2018; Magalhães, 2013; Schmidt & Fronza, 2018; Solé & Barca, 2018; Wineburg, 2018). For this reason, teacher training is also an essential aspect to be taken into consideration.

There is an urgent need to change the traditional teaching approach to a competency-based approach to history teaching, in line with the needs of today's society (Zanazanian, 2015). Indeed, this aspect is fundamental: the reflective capacity of society is a guarantee of a critical spirit and provides citizens with the necessary tools to distance themselves from totalitarianism, stereotypes, fake news, etc. For all of the above reasons, the promotion of critical thinking based on the development of historical competencies (Seixas, 2017; Seixas & Morton, 2013; Lee, 2011) in the stage of baccalaureate education (16-18 years of age) is key for this research (Prats & Santacana, 2001).

There are, nowadays, many different studies which establish the use of resources other than the textbook (which is over-used in the teaching of history), which diversify the strategies employed based on educational innovation, mainly concerning research and the use of other resources such as videogames and historical, artistic and cultural heritage (Gómez et al., 2018; Orts, 2019). Therefore, a new methodological focus is essential in teaching, one which promotes greater interaction and the development of skills which enable students to argue, debate and construct historical contents dealt with in the classroom, promoting the use of more active methodologies, such as problem-based learning, service-learning, challenge-based learning and gamification and the use of videogames and virtual reality (Sáez et al., 2016; Olmos, 2017; Palacios, 2020). Such strategies and methods are more related with a critical approach to the teaching of the social sciences (Giménez, 2019; Gómez et al., 2018) and encourage the development of the historical thinking skills (Seixas & Morton, 2013). This has important educational repercussions for the initial training of teachers as it involves analyzing the university training programs that are being carried out and introducing new training models for teachers in which importance is given not only to disciplinary knowledge but also to didactic training and to a historical education based on competences (Parra & Fuertes, 2019; Sánchez et al., 2021). It is also essential to strengthen the actions for the continuous training of teachers so that teachers can update and innovate their teaching practices through the results of research carried out in the field of social science teaching and in the construction of historical knowledge.

ACKNOWLEDGMENT

This research was supported by the MICIN [PID2020-113453RB-I00 / AEI / 10.13039/501100011033] "The teaching and learning of historical competences at baccalaureate level: a challenge for critical and democratic citizenship".

REFERENCES

Adams, N. E. (2015). Bloom's taxonomy of cognitive learning objectives. *Journal of the Medical Library Association: JMLA*, *103*(3), 152–153. doi:10.3163/1536-5050.103.3.010 PMID:26213509

Alvén, F. (2017). *Tänka rätt och tycka lämplig: historieämnet I skärningspunkten mellan att fostra kulturbärare och förbereda kulturbyggare*. Malmö Högskola.

Anderson, L. W., Krathwohl, D. R., Airasian, P., Cruikshank, K., Mayer, R., Pintrich, P., Raths, J., & Wittrock, M. (2001). *Taxonomy for Learning, Teaching, and Assessing, A: A Revision of Bloo''s Taxonomy of Educational Objectives*. Longman.

Ansari, D., Coch, D., & De Smedt, B. (2011). Connecting education and cognitive neuroscience: Where will the journey take us? *Educational Philosophy and Theory*, *43*(1), 37–42. doi:10.1111/j.1469-5812.2010.00705.x

Assaly, I., & Smadi, O. M. (2015). Using Bloom's Taxonomy to evaluate the cognitive levels of Master class textebook's questions. *English Language Teaching*, *8*(5), 100–110. doi:10.5539/elt.v8n5p100

Athanassiou, N., McNett, J., & Harvey, C. (2003). Critical thinking in the management classroom: Bloom's taxonomy as a learning tool. *Journal of Management Education*, *27*(5), 533–555. doi:10.1177/1052562903252515

Bertram, C. (2016). Recontextualising principles for the selection, sequencing and progression of history knowledge in four school curricula. *Journal of Education*, *64*(64), 27–54. doi:10.17159/i64a02

Bloom, B., Englehart, M. D., Furst, E. J., Hill, W. H., & Krathwohl, D. (1956). *Taxonomy of educational objectives: The classification of educational goals. In Handbook 1: Cognitive domain*. Longsman.

Cajani, L. (2006). Italian history textbooks on the brink of the twenty-first century. In J. Nicholls (Ed.), *School history textbooks across cultures: International debates and perspectives* (pp. 27-41). Symposium Books.

Carretero, M. (2019). Pensamiento histórico e historia global como nuevos desafíos para la enseñanza. *Cuadernos de Pedagogía, 495*, 59–63.

Casali Fuentes, A. (2007). Una adaptación del estructuralismo a la historia. La larga duración histórica: clave metodológica de las diferentes temporalidades. *Analecta: revista de humanidades, 2,* 1-17.

Dewey, J. (1900). The aim of history in elementary education. *Elementary School Record, 1*(4), 203.

Domínguez, J. (2016). Enseñar y evaluar el pensamiento histórico: competencias, conceptos y destrezas cognitivas. *Íber, didáctica de las ciencias sociales, geografía e historia, 82,* 43-49.

Eliasson, P., Alvén, F., Yngveus, C. A., & Rosenlund, D. (2015). Historical consciousness and historical thinking reflected in large-scale assessment in Sweden. In K. Ercikan & P. Seixas (Eds.), *New directions in assessing historical thinking* (pp. 171–182). Routledge.

Ercikan, K., & Seixas, P. (2015). Issues in designing assessment of historical thinking. *Theory into Practice, 54*(3), 255–262. doi:10.1080/00405841.2015.1044375

Fallace, T., & Fantozzi, V. (2017). The Dewey School as Triumph, Tragedy, and Misunderstood: Exploring the Myths and Historiography of the University of Chicago Laboratory School. *Teachers College Record: The Voice of Scholarship in Education, 119*(2). doi:10.1177/016146811711900205

Fontana, J. (2006). ¿Qué Historia para el siglo XXI? *Analecta: Revista de Humanidades, 1*, 1-12.

Funkenstein, A. (1989). Collective memory and historical consciousness. *History & Memory, 1*(1), 5–26. https://www.jstor.org/stable/25618571

Gadamer, H. G., & Fantel, H. (1975). The problema of historical consciousness. *Graduate Faculty Philosophy Journal, 5*(1), 8–52. doi:10.5840/gfpj1975512

Gago, M. (2018). *Consciência histórica e narrativa na aula de História- concepções de professores.* Edições Afrontamento.

García Fernández, G. A. (2021). Enseñar historia en las escuelas públicas del siglo XXI. ¿Qué historia enseñar y para qué? *Revista Didáctica de las Ciencias Experimentales y Sociales, 40*(40), 35–50. doi:10.7203/dces.40.16835

Gerge, K. J. (2005). Narrative, moral identity and historical consciousness. In J. Straub (Ed.), *Narration, identity and historical consciousness* (pp. 99–119). Berghahn Books.

Giménez, J. E. (2019). Investigar para innovar: El caso del Ámbito de Investigación de las sociedades actuales e históricas. *Revista de Investigación en Didáctica de las Ciencias Sociales, 1*, 4. doi:10.17398/2531-0968.04.4

Goldman, S. R. (2004). Cognitive aspects of constructing meaning through and across multiple texts. In N. Shuart Faris, & D. Bloome (Eds.), Uses of intertextuality in classroom and educational research (pp. 317-351). Information Age Publishing.

Gómez, C. J., Ortuño, J., & Miralles, P. (2018). *Enseñar ciencias sociales con métodos activos de aprendizaje. Reflexiones y propuestas a través de la indagación*. Octaedro.

Gómez-Carrasco, C. J., & Chapman, A. (2016). Pensamiento histórico y evaluación de competencias en el currículo de Inglaterra y España. Un estudio comparativo. In R. López-Facal (Ed.), *Ciencias Sociales, educación y futuro. Investigaciones en didáctica de las ciencias sociales* (pp. 432–445). Universidad de Santiago de Compostela.

Gómez Carrasco, C. J., Molina, S., & Ortuño, J (2014). Aprender a pensar históricamente. Retos para la historia en el siglo XXI. *Tempo e argumento, 6*(11), 5-27. doi:10.5965/2175180306112014005

Gómez Carrasco, C. J., Monteagudo, J., Moreno-Vera, J. R., & Sáinz, M. (2019). Effects of a gamification and flipped-classroom program for teachers in training on motivation and learning perception. *Education Sciences*, *9*(4), 299. doi:10.3390/educsci9040299

Gómez Carrasco, C. J., Monteagudo, J., Moreno-Vera, J. R., & Sáinz, M. (2020). Evaluation of a gamification and flipped-classroom program used in teacher training: Perception of learning and outcome. *PLoS One*, *15*(10), e0241892. doi:10.1371/journal.pone.0241892 PMID:33119687

Gómez Carrasco, C. J., Solé, G., Miralles, P., & Sánchez-Ibáñez, R. (2020). Analysis of cognitive skills in history textbook (Spain-England-Portugal). *Frontiers in Psychology*, *11*, 521115. doi:10.3389/fpsyg.2020.521115 PMID:33329167

Halawi, L., McCarthy, R., & Pires, S. (2009). An evaluation of E-Learning on the basis of Bloom's taxonomy: An exploration study. *Journal of Education for Business*, *84*(6), 374–380. doi:10.3200/JOEB.84.6.374-380

Heller, A. (1990). *Can modernity survive?* University of California Press.

Körber, A. (2005). German history didactics: from historical consciousness to historical competencies and beyond? In H. Bjerg, C. Lenz, & E. Thorstensen (Eds.), *Historicizing the uses of the past. Scandinavian perspective on history culture, historical consciousness and didactics of history related to World War II* (pp. 145–164). Transcript Verlag.

Krathwohl, D. R. (2010). A revision of Bloom's taxonomy: An overview. *Theory into Practice*, *41*(4), 212–218. doi:10.120715430421tip4104_2

Lee, P. (2011). History education and historical literacy. In I. Davies (Ed.), *Debates in History Teaching* (pp. 63–72). Routledge.

Lévesque, S. (2008). *Thinking Historically. Educating Students for the 21th Century*. University of Toronto Press.

Lukacs, J. (1968). *Historical consciousness: the remembered past*. Transaction publishers.

Magalhães, O. (2013). Em torno da escolha do manual escolar: opções de professors. In T. García, M. A. Schmidt, & R. Valls (Eds.), Didática, História e manuais escolares: contextos ibero-americanos (pp. 231-246). Ijuí: Editora Unijuí.

Martínez-Hita, M., & Gómez, C. J. (2018). Cognitive level and thinking historically competencies in history textbooks from Spain and England: A comparative study. *Review of Education, 379*, 136–159.

Martínez Valcárcel, N. (2014). *La historia de España en los recuerdos escolares*. Nau Llibres.

Moreno-Vera, J. R., & Alvén, F. (2020). Concepts for historical and geographical thinking in Sweden's and Spain's Primary Education curricula. *Humanities & Social Sciences Communications, 7*(1), 107. doi:10.105741599-020-00601-z

Moreno-Vera, J. R., Ponsoda-López de Atalaya, S., & Blanes-Mora, R. (2021). By Toutatis! Trainee Teachers' Motivation When Using Comics to Learn History. *Frontiers in Psychology, 27*, 778792. Advance online publication. doi:10.3389/fpsyg.2021.778792 PMID:34777186

Moreno-Vera, J. R., Ponsoda-López de Atalaya, S., López-Fernández, J. A., & Blanes-Mora, R. (2020). Holistic or Traditional Conceptions of Heritage among Early-Childhood and Primary Trainee Teachers. *Sustainability, 12*(21), 8921. doi:10.3390u12218921

Olmos, R. (2017). Kahoot: ¡Un, dos, tres! Análisis de una aplicación de cuestionarios. *Íber. Didáctica de las Ciencias Sociales, Geografía e Historia, 86*, 51-56. Available at: https://dialnet.unirioja.es/ejemplar/456181

Ortega Sánchez, D. (2018). Las mujeres en la historia enseñada: Resultados de un programa docente en formación inicial del profesorado. *Enseñanza de las Ciencias Sociales, 17*(2018.17), 13–21. doi:10.1344/ECCSS2018.17.2

Orts, M. (2019). El uso de móviles en el instituto. Reflexiones en el instituto Jaume Vicens Vives (Girona). *Aula de Secundaria, 32*, 35-39.

Palacios, R. J. (2020). *Experimentación y análisis del uso de los videojuegos para la Educación Patrimonial. Estudio de caso en 1.º de ESO*. Universidad de Huelva.

Parra, D., & Fuertes, C. (Coords.). (2019). *Reinterpretar la tradición, transformar las prácticas. Ciencias Sociales para una educación crítica*. Tirant humanidades.

Peck, C., & Seixas, P. (2008). Benchmarks of Historical Thinking: First Steps. *Canadian Journal of Education, 31*(4), 1015–1038.

Powell, Ch. (2003). Challenging the pluralism of our past: Presentism and the selective tradition in historical fiction written for young people. *Research in the Teaching of English, 37*, 425–466.

Prats, J., & Santacana, J. (2001). *Enseñar historia: notas para una didáctica renovadora*. Junta de Extremadura.

Riazi, A. M., & Mosalanejad, N. (2010). Evaluation of Learning Objectives in Iranian High-School and Pre-University English Textbooks Using Bloom's Taxonomy. *The Electronic Journal for English as a Second Language, 13*(4), 1-16.

Ross, D. (1984). Historical consciousness in nineteenth-century America. *The American Historical Review, 89*(4), 909–928. doi:10.2307/1866398

Sáez, J. M., Cózar, R., & Domínguez, J. (2016). Realidad aumentada en Educación Primaria: Comprensión de elementos artísticos y aplicación didáctica en ciencias sociales. *Digital Education Review*, *34*, 59–75.

Sáiz, J. (2013). Alfabetización histórica y competencias básicas en libros de texto de historia y en aprendizaje de los estudiantes. *Didáctica de las Ciencias Experimentales y Sociales*, *27*, 43–66.

Sáiz, J., & López-Facal, R. (2015). Competencias y narrativas históricas: El pensamiento histórico de estudiantes y futuros profesores españoles de educación secundaria. *Revista de Estudios Sociales*, *52*, 87–101.

Sánchez-Ibáñez, R., Famà, K., & Escribano Miralles, A. (2020). I livelli cognitivi nei manuali di storia dell'Istruzione Secondaria Superiore in Italia. *Didattica Della Storia, Journal of Research and Didactics of History, 2*(1), 180-195. doi:10.6092/issn.2704-8217/11020

Sánchez-Ibáñez, R., Guerrero-Romera, C., & Miralles-Martínez, P. (2021). Primary and secondary school teachers' perceptions of their social science training needs. *Humanities and Social Sciences Communications*, *8*(1), 26. doi:10.105741599-021-00705-0

Schmidt, M. A. & Fronza, M. (2018). Jovens, consciência histórica e avaliação da aprendizagem: o caso do Exame Nacional do Ensino Médio no Brasil entre 2009/2015. *Educatio Siglo XXI, 36*, 149-171. doi:10.6018/j/324211

Seixas, P. (2004). *Theorizing historical consciousness*. University of Toronto Press. doi:10.3138/9781442682610

Seixas, P. (2006). *Benchmarks of historical thinking: a framework for assessment in Canada*. Centre for the Study of Historical Consciousness.

Seixas, P. (2017). Historical Counsciousness and Historical Thinking. In M. Carretero, M. Grever, & S. Berger (Eds.), *Palgrave Handbook of Research in Historical Culture and Education* (pp. 59–72). Palgrave McMillan. doi:10.1057/978-1-137-52908-4_3

Seixas, P., & Morton, T. (2013). *The big six: historical thinking concepts*. Nelson College Indigenous.

Seixas, P., & Peck, C. (2004). Teaching historical thinking. In A. Sears & I. Wright (Eds.), *Challenges and Prospects for Canadian Social Studies* (pp. 109–117). Pacific Educational Press.

Shabatura, J. (2014). *Bloom's Taxonomy verb chart*. University of Arkansas. Retrieved May 10, 2022, from https://tips.uark.edu/blooms-taxonomy-verb-chart/

Solé, G., & Barca, I. (2018). *O Manual Escolar no Ensino da História: Visões Historiográficas e Didática*. Associação de Professores de História. Available at: https://aph.pt/o-manual-escolar-no-ensino-da-historia-visoes-historiograficas-e-didaticas/

Tarman, B., & Kuran, B. (2015). Examination of the cognitive level of questions in social studies textbooks and the views of teachers based on Bloom Taxonomy. *Educational Sciences: Theory and Practice*, *15*(1), 213–222. doi:10.12738/estp.2015.1.2625

Vygotsky, L. S. (1988). *El desarrollo de los procesos psicológicos superiores*. Editorial Crítica.

Weintraub, K. J. (1975). Autobiography and historical consciousness. *Critical Inquiry*, *1*(4), 821–848. doi:10.1086/447818

Whitty, G. (1989). The new right and the national curriculum: State control or market forces? *Journal of Education Policy*, *4*(4), 329–341. doi:10.1080/0268093890040402

Wineburg, S. (2002). *Historical thinking and Another unnatural acts. Charting the future of teaching the past*. Temple University Press.

Wineburg, S. (2018). *Why Learn History (When It's Already on Your Phone)*. Chicago University Press. doi:10.7208/chicago/9780226357355.001.0001

Zanazanian, P. (2015). Historical consciousness and metaphor: Charting new directions for grasping human historical sense-making patterns for knowing and acting in time. *Historical Encounters*, *2*, 16–33.

KEY TERMS AND DEFINITIONS

Cause and Consequence: The understanding of the reasons (deep or direct) that develop a historical process and the repercussion that the event has for the society.

Change and Continuity: Permanence and transformations in historical events and processes over time.

Cognitive Skill: Ability associated with thinking processes and the application of theoretical knowledge through procedural activities.

Ethical Dimension: Thinking skill associated with the explanation of historical facts taking into account the ethical codes and mentality of the context to allow the student to make their own moral judgements.

Historical Evidence: Building historical narratives through the use of primary and secondary sources asking and interpreting the resources found.

Historical Perspective: Thinking skill associated with the understanding of facts in their historical context taking in account the mentality of the people that lived that event.

Historical Relevance: The explanation of the historical importance of facts and personalities based on the repercussions that events or characters have overtime.

Chapter 3
Historical Thinking as a Dynamic Vehicle for Teaching Through Key Competences:
The Roles of the Teacher and the School

Maria Glória Parra Santos Solé
University of Minho, Portugal

Francisco Javier Trigueros Cano
University of Murcia, Spain

Ana María Rubio Leiva
University of Murcia, Spain

Jesús Molina Saorín
https://orcid.org/0000-0002-9919-0910
University of Murcia, Spain

EXECUTIVE SUMMARY

It is evident that the integration of key competences in the educational panorama and in the curriculum is not perceptible in the practical development of the classroom. Given the lack of clear and practical proposals in the legislation that facilitate this implementation, this chapter aims to analyse—through an updated bibliography—the role of the school and the teacher in making key competences effective in the teaching of social sciences. In the same way, it sets out what is considered to be the most effective way of working on key competences in social sciences: through the development of historical thinking and the concepts that define it, as well as the critical spirit, providing students with skills for their personal development, the ability to transfer concepts to everyday situations, as well as empathy and commitment to their social environment.

DOI: 10.4018/978-1-6684-5240-0.ch003

INTRODUCTION

In recent decades, education in Spain has been evolving — at a dizzying pace — at the same time as its society has been changing, in order to generate the necessary and most suitable educational scenarios for each context. This constant adaptation seeks — at all times — that the student, in addition to achieving a predominantly conceptual learning, is also capable of applying it -subsequently- in his or her development at different levels. In other words, the aim is to teach in a way that enables the transfer of the learning acquired. This is why we speak of teaching through key competences, since they are those that enable the transfer of both knowledge and skills to situations of a varied nature (Miralles and Gómez, 2021).

However, the integration of competences in curriculum development is not carried out in a way that is visible and practical for teachers and transferable to the reality of the classroom and the school (mired in a disarray between theory and practice) is failing. In this sense, the administration must make the necessary resources and tools available to teachers and educational centres for the performance of their daily tasks, and must be responsible for ensuring -therefore- that this curricular integration of competences is effective, not a mere addition, but that it is perfectly threaded into the planning of the teacher in the teaching-learning process (Álvarez, Díaz and Molina, 2021). Of course, the main way is through a transition in competency training, in which the theoretical and generic scope of the concept is transferred to the way in which this competency approach can be transferred to daily tasks (López, Velasco, Santidrián and Armas, 2011). In other words, teachers must be able to relate key competences to other curricular elements, so that they understand this competence approach from a practical and transferable perspective.

HISTORICAL THINKING AS A FACILITATING VEHICLE FOR THE COMPETENCY-BASED APPROACH IN SOCIAL SCIENCES

Currently, the concept of competences -despite being included in educational legislation for more than a decade- is still new (and not always understood) by the educational community, which assimilates the competence approach as something diffuse, since it is not clear how it should be worked on by students both in the classroom and outside it.

However, as a result of this generalised lack of knowledge, there is currently a mistaken belief that less content is taught through competences, when the reality is that, in addition to acquiring the same content established in the curriculum of the Spanish education system, pupils work on a series of skills that will enable them to understand, reason and apply this knowledge later on. With the inclusion of these key competences in teaching practice, there is a clear need to assess both the acquisition of the content established in the curriculum and, on the other hand, the acquisition of skills or aptitudes that allow them to apply this knowledge in their development as individuals and in the transfer to real situations in their day-to-day lives (Molina, Ortuño and Miralles, 2011). It is therefore a tool at the service of teachers through which the teacher enjoys a greater margin of autonomy, while the student obtains a more significant and transferable learning to their everyday context, it is essential for teaching practice to know the episteme that surrounds competences in order to be able to introduce, use and assess them (Campos, 2008).

In the Social Sciences, Geography and History class, students' learning should not be based solely and exclusively on the memorisation of dates and events in the past, but rather on the students' ability to interpret these concepts and content, which should help them to decipher and understand the socio-economic, political and cultural context in which they find themselves (Gómez, Ortuño and Molina, 2014; Gómez and Miralles, 2015; Minte and Ibagón, 2017). To this end, it is recommended that the way of working on key competences should be accompanied by a methodology that has historical thinking as its main axis, which Peck and Seixas (2008 p. 1024) identify through the following concepts:

- Historical relevance, understood as the importance that past events have in the present day, being remembered, remembered, or considered as conditioning factors for the construction of the current reality, in terms of society.
- Historical sources, in relation to the analysis and understanding of these sources, being able to reflect, interpret them and apply knowledge to construct conclusions in this respect. In the same way, it is important to know how to value these sources, and to have the critical capacity to discern in the case of contradictory sources in the same period.
- Change and continuity, concepts that allude to the process of evolution of a society through historical events, knowing how to differentiate key points or events and their repercussions in this sense.
- Causes and consequences is a concept of great importance in the development of historical thinking, as it puts into value the knowledge acquired in reference to a certain event, in order to know how to find the origin of the event, the triggering factors and, subsequently, the effects that this event may have had on society. In this way, they gain an understanding of the importance of certain historical events and their repercussions. It also equips them with the ability to understand current events, such as armed conflicts, analysing their causes and hypothesising about the possible effects they may have had, on a social, cultural, political or economic level, among others.
- Historical perspective, understood as the ability to understand a given period seen as a context which is, in turn, understood on a social, artistic, cultural, political and intellectual level, in order to be able to interpret events from a period point of view, developing empathy to some extent.
- The moral or ethical dimension of history enables pupils to judge historical events through the previously described historical perspective, i.e. by considering these events within a context, rather than looking at them through contemporary eyes (Seixas and Morton, 2013).

These dimensions, which require relational skills and the application of knowledge on the part of students, represent a considerable cognitive difficulty due to the old way in which students have been taught and which neglects the processual and transferable sphere of History. Even so - in no case - can this difficulty (however unjustified it may seem) be ignored by teachers, since otherwise the methodologies used - however appropriate they may appear to be - would have no impact either on the students or on the results they obtain. The question then arises as to the role of the teacher, since, if the teacher's role is only to transmit conceptual content (dates, facts or data in textbooks), perhaps the teacher is not indispensable in this purely content-based teaching-learning system.

In this sense, the role of the teacher in the teaching of Social Sciences is crucial, who, according to Vansledright (2013) must know how to transmit first-order knowledge or knowledge related to specific events (dates, places, characters, etc.) as well as second-order knowledge (strategies, historical perspective or selection of sources, among others). It is this first-order knowledge that has always received the most attention in the teaching of Social Sciences (and in general in the Spanish education system), being the main object or aim of teachers, who seek to memorise content in order to subsequently evaluate it by means of simple theoretical written tests, without actually relating facts. As Gómez, Ortuño and Molina

(2014, p. 142) state, recent studies developed over the last two decades show the few benefits of the assessment of historical knowledge through the exams and textbooks used, as the predominant model in these materials is of a conceptual and descriptive nature, forcing memorisation (Álvarez, Molina, Trigueros and Miralles 2021; Ibagón and Miralles, 2019). However, nowadays - and with increasing urgency - there is a need to transmit second-order knowledge to students, more specifically the ability to analyse historical sources, investigate and produce logical conclusions about a given historical event. However, when it comes to teaching History from this perspective, the shortcomings in the training of teachers in our educational system are most glaring, and far from venturing to use active methodologies in the classroom, they prefer to continue to stick to the exclusive use of the textbook, as well as to traditional teaching and assessment methods. In the same way, it should be noted that the curriculum includes the objectives, content and assessment criteria considered basic to be developed or achieved in each subject; these can be subsequently expanded by teachers in their teaching programmes, although the reality is that in most cases it is only these curricular contents present in the regulations that are applied in the classroom; So much so that authors such as Miralles, Gómez and Sánchez (2014), state the suitability of focusing the subject of Social Sciences on more specific and reduced content, so that it can be dealt with in greater depth in the classroom. In this way, through a curricular specification of the contents, students could focus on them and develop them through research, analysis of sources, written productions or classroom discussions. For their part, Miralles and Molina (2011) highlight the excessive use of superficial learning -based solely on memorisation- and which presents a low degree of empathy and commitment to the social environment as it includes an excessive number of subjects in the curriculum for each educational stage.

For this reason, Domínguez (2016), in his analysis of how to teach and assess historical thinking, stresses the importance of an assessment proposal in line with a methodology that promotes historical thinking in order to develop competences. To this end, he affirms the consideration of the figure of the historian and the work he or she carries out, as well as the importance he or she plays in learning about past events. The author defines history as empirical knowledge whose nature is based on documentary evidence or testimonies based on theoretical concepts, and which therefore cannot be compared to sciences such as physics, which apply scientific laws and are based on experimentation. It also highlights the great value for the development of students' historical thinking, so that they are aware of the importance of not only knowing "what happened", but also of having a broader impact on "why we know today what happened". With all this, the role of the historian, his or her work and historical research as a source of information is greatly enhanced, thus - according to the author - leading to a comprehensive historical education, which combines knowledge and methodologies. It is this type of teaching that is considered optimal for the acquisition of competences by the student, working on historical thinking in its concepts as stated by Seixas and Morton (2013).

One of the key elements when working on historical thinking is the importance that the teacher attaches to the analysis and interpretation of historical sources for the development of this thinking in students (Álvarez, Miralles, Molina and Trigueros 2021; Ibagón, 2021), making it immediate to think about the different types of sources that can be analysed and used in the classroom, and also to ask which are those that provoke the most significant learning. Domínguez (2015), in his writings on historical thinking and the assessment of competences, establishes the association with iconic and material sources (images, videos, clothing, materials or objects from the past, etc.) as those considered most attractive by pupils. This type of source provides more implicit than explicit information, which makes it very convenient for use in the beginnings of this type of analysis, but which should be combined with written sources in order to develop a more complete work. On the other hand, the author makes a distinction between primary and secondary sources, both of which are valid and extremely useful in the development of teaching practice. Primary sources are those that belong to the period or place to which they refer, while secondary sources refer to documents or materials produced after the historical event, the result of research (articles, books, etc.).

In reference to the above, the author Jesús Domínguez (2015, p. 73) details certain guidelines when using primary and secondary sources in the teaching and learning process of Social Sciences. He states that the ideal way to put this into practice would be to combine both types: a secondary source can provide basic theoretical knowledge about the historical context, in order to be able to situate and better understand a primary source. On the other hand, secondary sources can present different versions of the same event, which can be particularly didactic insofar as pupils can compare and analyse these elements on the basis of information previously acquired from primary sources. It should be added that, through the use of these historical sources, students' historical thinking would be developed and, therefore, the competences in the subject would be included.

THE DEVELOPMENT OF HISTORICAL THINKING AT SCHOOL AND IN THE CLASSROOM

In relation to the development of historical thinking in the classroom and its assessment, Jesús Domínguez (2016) establishes a link between these cognitive skills on which the competences are based and the specific case of causal explanation. The author sets out what he considers to be the cognitive skills to which special attention should be paid when developing this causal explanation in Social Sciences, Geography and History classes, presenting them in five blocks (Domínguez 2016, p. 48), which include a series of skills that can easily be developed and assessed in the classroom using current methodologies, i.e. through activities or questions that start from the concrete and move on to the more abstract. The first of these blocks corresponds to the identification of causes and consequences in history, being able to differentiate both terms and relate the effect that the former has on the latter, as well as the effects it may have today. Block two focuses on the cognitive skill of classifying causes according to a series of criteria, such as their duration in time, the importance they acquire in relation to the effect they produce, or the content and functions of these causes. The third block details the analysis of the existing nexus between causes and consequences, through a study of these possible connections, as well as the relations that some causes may have between them to derive in a specific event, with their respective effects. With regard to block number four, it is of great importance to judge those possible scenarios that finally did not occur due to different circumstances, analysing the factors that could have led to this type of possible events and those that triggered others. Finally, the fifth and last block of these cognitive skills focuses on synthesis and communication, through the formulation of hypotheses and the explanation of causes, as well as the assessment and analysis of sources of historical information. In short, through these five groups of skills, it is possible to work on the aforementioned causal explanation of history, developing in turn historical thinking, and with all this, the key competences in the subject of Social Sciences, Geography and History.

However, working on historical thinking is no easy task, since, as Sáiz and López (2015) state, in order to educate historically, it is necessary to develop students' historical thinking from early stages, given that this characteristic is neither innate nor intuitive, and of course it is not knowledge that is acquired immediately; rather it requires a training process in which the teacher must integrate gradually and continuously, combining first and second order concepts in a balanced way in the teaching-learning process. In this sense, in Spain, such methodologies are hardly used, causing certain deficiencies at various levels but which, according to Molina, Rodríguez and Sánchez (2013), can be corrected through the transmission of historical research to students from a very early age; which would be a clear enrichment, going beyond the minimum content of the educational stage to which it is attached. It is therefore a question of bringing scientific research into the classroom, thus developing different concepts of historical thought, fundamentally the use of historical sources, the moral or ethical dimension of history or historical relevance. From this, in practice, aspects such as the ability to establish causes and consequences through the analysis of events in their context would also be developed.

With regard to the historical perspective, it is important to point out the importance of teaching history within a context, studied from various angles. The key to meaningful and transferable learning is to come to understand history through concepts, characteristics of the society of the time, art, clothing, the scientific and technological situation at the time, among others. In this way, and being closely related to the concept of causes and consequences, a given event is understood in its context, facilitating the understanding of its origin, working on empathy, and also valuing the consequences it had, both at the time and today, estimating the repercussions that this event may have had on our current society (López and Valls 2012). On the other hand, history is considered to have been learnt well when the pupil, faced with current events, is capable of taking a position, having a logical and reasoned opinion, understanding the origin of the event, and critically analysing what is happening, applying the knowledge acquired in Social Sciences and making a real transfer of this knowledge to everyday situations, so that education becomes complete, to develop people with critical, thinking, analysing and reasoning skills. All of this means that, through historical thinking, the competences in Social Sciences are worked on.

THE ROLE OF THE TEACHER IN THE DEVELOPMENT OF HISTORICAL THINKING

It seems indisputable that it is difficult for teachers to carry out competence-based assessment without departing from what is established in the curriculum. In this sense, legislation sometimes poses a barrier when teachers aim to develop assessment based on active methodologies in which the student is the focus and assessment is understood as a process and not as an end, transcending beyond the memorisation of concepts in order to develop -thus- historical thinking and a critical spirit in the student, being able to transfer concepts to real life. As Polo (2010) states, there is a disconnection or lack of normative concreteness insofar as the competences are described but at no point is the way to develop and assess them specified, nor the measures to be adopted in the event of noticing cases in which pupils present problems in the acquisition of these key competences. According to Molina, Ortuño and Miralles (2011), assessment - or rather, good assessment - does not neglect the motivating and guiding function that it should have, forming part of this process on an ongoing basis, avoiding focusing its consideration as a merely qualifying element. Likewise, this test or examination, which will be graded, must be important when planning teaching activity and choosing the most appropriate methodologies for its successful achievement. Furthermore, the authors also refer to a balance in the assessment of knowledge in its three modalities (conceptual, procedural and attitudinal), avoiding giving top priority to one of them, as is currently the case with concept tests.

In this sense, Calatayud (2000) states in his analysis of the current abuse and hegemony of the exam in primary education assessment, the preponderance of the use of exams or objective written tests in student assessment systems is still in force, resulting in an erroneous understanding of the exam as an end and not as an instrument. This translates into an erroneous view of assessment within the teaching and learning process, understood as a merely qualifying element, which marks the pupil and classifies and differentiates them according to a mark; instead of being conceived in its orienting, motivating and accompanying function, going parallel to the construction of knowledge, instead of being placed only at the end, as a judgement. For their part, Miralles, Gómez and Sánchez (2014), in their study on the content and skills assessed in examinations in the third cycle of Primary Education, reflect on the need to adapt assessment today if we want to achieve the proposed goal: "in fact, if the main objective of the teaching of social sciences is to prepare students for democratic citizenship, beyond the mere acquisition of information, the assessment of this knowledge must be adjusted to this purpose". However, this desired change implies for the teacher an adaptation and a change in the conception of teaching methods, to introduce others that include a series of modifications, especially focused on this evaluation; such as the introduction of new indicators of the students' progress or difficulties, such as interviews, conceptual schemes, written productions, direct observation, participation in debates, round tables, analysis of sources, etc.). In this way, by fostering competences in the subject through these assessment tools, students' historical thinking is also developed, increasing their critical and reflective capacity, as well as their ability to solve problems and be able to express this knowledge. In order to achieve this, the didactic means and resources available to the teacher for transmitting knowledge in the subject of Social Sciences are decisive. Thus, as a preliminary step, it is imperative to distinguish between traditional materials, present and used even today, and those that have emerged in recent years, which are closely linked to digital competence: Information and Communication Technologies (ICT). Currently, the former are as important as the latter, being complementary and in no case substituting each other, as Sáiz and López (2015, p. 89) state, "in the teaching-learning of historical thinking competences, the use of narratives is fundamental". 89), "in the teaching-learning of historical thinking skills, the use of narratives is fundamental", which, according to the authors, are valid and necessary instruments in the process, to be used both to teach and to evaluate meta-concepts of a historical nature, since by developing these narratives, the student structures and organises his or her thinking logically and gives meaning to the expression of a specific historical event. For his part, Carretero (2009), in addition to defending narratives as key tools for the understanding of history, as they capture events and their causes in a logical order, on the other hand assures that there is an underlying danger in the use of this type of material, which is to forget that they are incomplete chronicles. Students should be aware of the simplification involved in capturing what happened years ago in textual form; inevitably, many details, stories and characters are forgotten because they are not included in these materials.

Another of the risks posed by the author is the students' conception of history as a series of events that follow one another in a logical narrative thread that leads to a specific end, almost always, and optimistically, towards progress. The third risk that arises in reference to these historical narratives is the belief that they are history in themselves, forgetting that they are tools created by specific figures with the capacity to decide who or what is told in them. On the other hand, reference is made to the individual narrative, understood as a tool that focuses its description on a specific figure or character, as an element that presents a certain duality in its use: on the one hand, they humanise historical events, calling on students' empathy and their ability to put themselves in the place of the characters in the context in which they are included; but on the other, the causal nature of the narrative is lost, focusing on the specific case instead of generalising factors such as social, economic or political factors.

Regarding the use of more up-to-date tools in the teaching-learning process, it is inevitable to adapt the school to the reality of the society in which we live (Carretero, 2019). The changes that occur day after day in terms of technology must be included in the school, making demands at a material and human level; since on the one hand it requires the acquisition or updating of devices, and on the other, it requires teachers to have up-to-date training in technological matters, as well as new approaches in the classroom, all with a single purpose: to favour student learning. ICT are nowadays a key element in the classroom, as they facilitate and provoke the incorporation of students into the digital reality we live in (Seva, Vera and Soriano, 2017). In this sense, Soriano (2011) directly relates the use of ICT to greater motivation and attention in the teaching-learning process, thus favouring the acquisition of knowledge of a different nature and the development of digital competence, which is present in the curriculum. For their part, Olmos (2018) and Zou (2020) reinforce this idea of increased motivation by introducing methodologies that encourage the use of these technologies through the gamification of content in a timely manner, increasing motivation, the desire to excel and therefore interest in the subject.

We therefore find a series of limitations or conditioning factors that hinder the incorporation of this competence-based approach in the classroom by the teacher, who, in a suitable context, can favour the development of historical thinking in the students. In the first place, this lack of training in competences is a key element in this question; and in order to address it consequently, it is necessary to address the concept of assessment, understanding it as a training and learning tool within the process and not only as an element of assessment or verification of the acquisition of certain knowledge. In this sense, Gómez, C., Rodríguez, R. and Monteagudo, J., (2017, p. 159) affirm the need for "a methodological renewal that favours work through active strategies, such as projects, case studies or PBL that encourage the autonomous action of students through cooperative work structures. This is done by placing students in practical situations that require knowledge, skills and attitudes to be able to respond positively to these situations, but not before having gone through a process of meditation and reasoning to arrive at possible solutions, which helps students to think critically". They also claim that this type of more active methodology, in which students are confronted with practical questions, can serve as an evaluation in itself, as it allows them to assess their understanding of the historical events dealt with and their contextualisation.

This change in the way of assessing involves a major approach to a more meaningful teaching-learning methodology. Dispensing with written tests in which -after having finished watching some content in class- a series of questions are posed in which the only questions to be answered are those that encourage memorisation or the retention of dates and data with no kind of association of what has been learned; and on the other hand, bringing assessment closer to the process, understanding it as part of it, in the subject of social sciences it involves a contextualised understanding of society, generating relationships between events, times, facts or places; being able, in the same way, to connect this knowledge with the present day (Martins, 2019; Santisteban, 2017).

However, the reality is that teachers, for various reasons (lack of knowledge, fear, etc.) do not implement these teaching-learning methods in the classroom. It is true that the curriculum cites the competences, their importance and the benefits of methodologies with a student-oriented approach; however, there is a clear lack of real and practical guidelines to be applied in the classroom, which, if included in Spanish educational laws, would bring teachers closer to the reality of their application.

FUTURE RESEARCH DIRECTIONS

Through this chapter, new lines of research emerge through which more light could be shed on historical thinking as a way of working on key competences in the social sciences. A future analysis of pupils' historical thinking through the concepts of historical relevance, historical sources, change and continuity, causes and consequences, historical perspective and the moral or ethical dimension of history is extremely interesting. In other words, a study of the current situation in this sense, in order to be able, on the basis of this reality, to develop new lines of research and work to be taken to the classroom and put into practice, which is in all cases the most complex part and the part which is least carried out.

On the other hand, following the analysis of current assessment methods and the affirmation of the large gap between these and active methodologies (rarely applied), another future line of research emerges concerning the most appropriate assessment procedures for the implementation of competences in general, and historical thinking in particular.

The inclusion of a new line of research is also proposed, the development of which is very interesting, relating to the study of the current perception of primary school pupils in the last stage (prior to secondary and baccalaureate studies) of competences, the role of the teacher and the assessment system applied in the classroom.

CONCLUSION

Following the development of the previous chapters, the need for transformation that both the school and the Spanish education system require becomes clear. However, despite the existence of a pedagogical approach such as teaching by competences, which is already supported by educational regulations, the lack of a practical basis for its implementation in the classroom makes it extremely complicated for teachers. This is why teachers - in their day-to-day work - must be able to count on theoretical and practical support and also on a support that allows them to face the various problems that may arise in the exercise of their profession when implementing learning by competences (Domínguez, 2015).

It should be noted that this recent focus on competences in the field of education has aroused great interest in terms of their incorporation into Spanish school curricula. This is due, to a large extent, to its pragmatic nature, whereby teachings are proposed that arise from society's own needs and whose contents are, for the most part, procedural in nature (rather than conceptual -Gómez et al, 2017-). All this has triggered a renewal of education legislation, involving education policies at both national and international level, thus questioning the univocal thinking on quality education.

Despite the latest changes, in the current context, the concept of competences - for teachers - is a noble purpose but ineffective in its incorporation, perhaps because clear examples have not yet been defined that allow these new approaches to be put into practice (Álvarez, Trigueros, Miralles and Molina, 2020). Despite its incorporation into educational regulations, the lack of clear and practical proposals regarding this transfer among teachers trained in traditional models and without pragmatic references experienced first-hand, it is difficult to venture which is the best proposal for teaching by competences to be extended. Likewise, given the limited training in terms of competences that today's teachers have, they are reluctant to implement this new teaching perspective (Gómez and Miralles, 2016). Therefore, it is immediate to look at the perception that they have in relation to the teaching of social sciences. In this sense, the research by Sánchez, Campillo and Guerrero (2020) on the perceptions of primary and secondary school students regarding the teaching of history stands out, in order to discern which methodologies focused on the development of historical thinking they value most positively. Through this study, there is evidence of progress in the use of strategies that encourage greater student involvement and participation, although it is still necessary to strengthen didactic and methodological training in university teacher training studies in order to update the teaching and learning process and teaching practices in the classroom; Although the weight of these didactics, and specifically in the didactics of Social Sciences, has been increasing in undergraduate and postgraduate courses since the last decades of the 20th century (Pagès 2002), there is still a long way to go in these aspects.

In order to understand these perceptions of teachers, who are different in many ways and also diverse in terms of the context in which they are inserted, it is worth considering the different approaches that the teaching-learning process can adopt; both the more traditional ones in which the teacher takes on the leading role, and those charged with innovation in terms of methodology, in which the student becomes the centre of the process and acquires greater attention (Martín, Pozo, Mateos, Martín and Del Puy, 2014; Schmidt, 2019).

It is undoubtedly interesting to know the teachers' perception of the training they once received from teachers in this subject, as it can somehow influence the way in which they perceive the teaching of the subject, both in negative and positive aspects. With the analysis of Gómez, Rodríguez and Mirete (2018), referring to this perception or memories of social studies students, a study carried out two decades ago by Cuesta (1998) is updated. However, the results obtained after this study denounce the lack of reform in the teaching of history, with an absolute predominance of traditional methods such as lectures, which are not at all participative, with the book as the main resource and the absence of debates, analysis of sources or problem solving. Once again, this shows that the change for the better in the field of active methodologies in the classroom is taking place but is still insufficient, making good teacher training in didactics essential in order to evolve and improve this perception of the teacher and with it the figure of the teacher.

In the same way, returning to the case of assessment, and, specifically, to the Assessable Learning Standards, understood according to Royal Decree 126/2014, of 28 February, which establishes the basic curriculum for Primary Education, as "specifications of the assessment criteria that define the learning outcomes, and which specify what the student should know, understand and know how to do in each subject". The preponderance of the conceptual nature of these standards is evident, as opposed to the procedural and attitudinal ones, which are more intrinsically related to the methodologies described above, and which are therefore more favourable to the acquisition and assessment of these competences. It is clear, therefore, that the regulations need to adapt the assessment elements for teachers, who are currently subject to very marked guidelines that are far removed from the meaningful learning that is so much sought after.

In accordance with recent regulations in Spain, specifically Royal Decree 984/2021, of 16 November, which regulates assessment and promotion in Primary Education, as well as assessment, promotion and qualifications in Compulsory Secondary Education, Baccalaureate and Vocational Training; and Royal Decree 157/2022, of 1 March, which establishes the orientation and minimum teaching standards for Primary Education, these standards are now used as a guideline for assessment.

Annex I of Order ECD/65/2015, of 21 January, which describes the relationships between the competences, contents and assessment criteria for primary education, compulsory secondary education and baccalaureate, establishes and details the key competences established in the Spanish education system; as well as the importance of the use of active methodologies as opposed to traditional methodologies for the acquisition of these competences, given that they allow students to develop social, management, analysis, organisation and decision-making practices, among others.

In addition, Annex II of the Order describes methodological strategies considered favourable for the practice of teaching through competences. These are guidelines to facilitate implementation, based on good planning on the part of the teacher (objectives, resources, etc.) and the importance of understanding and adapting this practice to the context in which it is to be carried out. In the same way, the aforementioned Annex II highlights the importance of boosting student motivation, generating curiosity and dynamising the sessions through student participation, which is essential in the subject of Social Sciences for the development of historical thinking and student involvement.

In this sense, if teachers have to be able to develop all these functions in order to become competent in their profession, it is also important to point out that there is no clear interpretation of what specific performances educational professionals should have. This validity or teaching competence is therefore demonstrated through the analysis and critical reflection of the teacher's practice in the classroom, and at various levels (Seixas, 2006). This concludes that there is no single valid professional model, but that the very variety of profiles shows that, despite being different, many of them could be considered valid. Furthermore, with the aim of educating by competences and the express will to do so under the dictates of educational regulations, it can be affirmed that educational centres, perhaps due to a misinterpretation of the legislation (perhaps because of excessive influence from publishers), far from approaching the proposed model, continue to apply outdated and canned methodologies, completely ignoring the reality of society and of the students themselves (Álvarez et al, 2021).

ACKNOWLEDGMENT

This study is the result of the research projects "The geographical and historical thinking of primary education students in the Region of Murcia: an innovative methodological proposal for quality education" (20874/PI/18), funded by the Fundación Séneca-Agencia de Ciencia y Tecnología de la Región de Murcia; and "The teaching and learning of historical competences in baccalaureate education: a challenge for the achievement of a critical and democratic citizenship" (PID2020-113453RB-I00), funded by MCIN/AEI/10.13039/501100011033.

REFERENCES

Álvarez, J. M., Díaz, Y., & Molina, J. (2021). *El Código Cuomo. Las fábulas de María: una niña a la que no le gustaba la escuela* [The Cuomo Code. Mary's fables: a girl who didn't like school]. Dykinson.

Álvarez, J. M., Miralles, P., Molina, J., & Trigueros, F. J. (2021). Secondary School Students' Perception of the Acquisition of Social Science Skill. *Social Sciences*, *10*(4), 126. Advance online publication. doi:10.3390ocsci10040126

Álvarez, J. M., Molina, J., Miralles, P., & Trigueros, F. J. (2021). Key Competences and the Transfer of Social Knowledge: Perceptions of Secondary School Pupils. *Sustainability*, *13*(4).

Álvarez, J. M., Molina, J., Trigueros, F. J., & Miralles, P. (2021). The Development of Historical Competencies in Secondary Education: A Study Based on the Analysis of Sources in Spanish and Italian History Textbooks. *International Journal of Learning, Teaching and Educational Research, 20*(4), 137–151. doi:10.26803/ijlter.20.4.8

Álvarez, J. M., Trigueros, F. J., Miralles, P., & Molina, J. (2020). Assessment by Competences in Social Sciences: Secondary Students Perception Based on the EPECOCISO Scale. *Sustainability, 12*(23), 1–15. doi:10.3390u122310056

Calatayud, M. A. (2000). La supremacía del examen, la evaluación como examen: Su uso y abuso, aún, en la educación primaria [The supremacy of the test, assessment as test: its use and abuse, even in primary education]. *Bordón, 52*(2), 165–178.

Campos, M. (2008). La evaluación por competencias, mitos, peligros, desafíos [Competency-based assessment, myths, dangers, challenges]. *Educere. Foro Universitario, 43*, 805–814.

Carretero, M. (2019). Pensamiento histórico e historia global como nuevos desafíos para la enseñanza [Historical thinking and global history as new teaching challenges]. *Cuadernos de Pedagogía, 495*, 59–63.

Carretero, M., & López, C. (2009). Estudios cognitivos sobre el conocimiento histórico: Aportaciones para la enseñanza y alfabetización histórica [Cognitive Studies on Historical Knowledge: Contributions to Historical Literacy and Education]. *Enseñanza de las Ciencias Sociales, 8*, 79–93.

Cuesta, R. (1998). *Clío en las aulas. La enseñanza de la Historia en España entre reformas, ilusiones y rutinas* [Clio in the classroom. History teaching in Spain between reforms, illusions and routines]. Akal.

Domínguez, J. (2015). *Pensamiento histórico y evaluación de competencias* [Historical thinking and competence assessment]. Graó.

Domínguez, J. (2016). Enseñar y evaluar el pensamiento histórico. Competencias, conceptos y destrezas cognitivas [Teaching and assessing historical thinking. Cognitive skills, concepts and competences]. *Íber: Didáctica de las ciencias sociales, geografía e historia, 82*, 43-49.

Gómez, C., Rodríguez, R., & Monteagudo, J. (2017). Las competencias históricas en los procesos de evaluación: libros de texto y exámenes [Historical competences in assessment processes: textbooks and exams]. In Enseñanza de la historia y competencias educativas [History teaching and educational competences] (pp. 141-165). Graó.

Gómez, C. J., & Miralles, P. (2015). ¿Pensar históricamente o memorizar el pasado? La evaluación de los contenidos históricos en la educación obligatoria en España [Thinking historically or memorising the past? The evaluation of historical content in compulsory education in Spain]. *Revista de Estudios Sociales, 52*(52), 52–68. doi:10.7440/res52.2015.04

Gómez, C. J. & Miralles, P. (2016). Las competencias históricas en educación obligatoria: evaluación, estrategias basadas en la indagación, y argumentación de los estudiantes [Historical competencies in compulsory education: assessment, inquiry-based strategies, and student argumentation]. *New approaches in educational research, 5*(2), 139-146. doi:10.7821/naer.2016.7.172

Gómez, C. J., Ortuño, J., & Molina, S. (2014). Aprender a pensar históricamente. Retos para la historia en el siglo XXI [Learning to think historically. Challenges for history in the 21st century]. *Revista Tempo e Argumento*, *6*(11), 5–27. doi:10.5965/2175180306112014005

Gómez, C. J., Rodríguez, R. A., & Mirete, A. B. (2018). Percepción de la enseñanza de la historia y concepciones epistemológicas. Una investigación para futuros maestros [Perceptions of history teaching and epistemological conceptions. An investigation for future teachers]. *Revista Complutense de Educación*, *29*(1), 237–250. doi:10.5209/RCED.52233

Ibagón, N. J. (2021). El uso de fuentes históricas en la escuela y el desarrollo del pensamiento histórico del estudiantado [The use of historical sources in schools and the development of students' historical thinking]. In Educación histórica para el siglo XXI, principios epistemológicos y metodológicos [History Education for the 21st century, epistemological and methodological principles] (pp. 155-183). Universidad Icesi y Universidad del Valle.

Ibagón, N. J., & Miralles, P. (2019). Historia a enseñar, historia enseñada e historia aprendida. Posibilidades investigativas en el campo de la educación Histórica en Iberoamérica [History to be taught, taught history and learned history. Research possibilities in the field of history education in Ibero-America]. *Historia y Espacio*, *15*(53), 9–18.

López Facal, R., & Valls, R. (2012). La necesidad cívica de saber historia y geografía [The civic need to know history and geography]. In N. de Alba, F. F. García, & A. S. Fernández (Eds.), *Educar para la participación ciudadana en la enseñanza de las Ciencias Sociales* [Educating for civic participation in social science education] (pp. 185–192). Díada Editora. https://cutt.ly/2u5HA2R

López Facal, R., Velasco, L., Santidrián, V. M., & Armas Castro, X. A. (Coords.). (2011). *Pensar históricamente en tiempos de globalización: actas del I Congreso Internacional sobre enseñanza de la historia* [Thinking Historically in Times of Globalisation: Proceedings of the 1st International Conference on History Education]. Universidade de Santiago de Compostela.

Martín, E., Pozo, J. I., Mateos, M., Martín, A., & Del Puy, M. (2014). Infant, primary and secondary teacher's conceptions of learning and teaching and their relation to educational variables. *Revista Latinoamericana de Psicología*, *46*(3), 211–221. doi:10.1016/S0120-0534(14)70024-X

Martins, E. (2019). História, historiografia e pesquisa em educação histórica [History, historiography and research in history education]. *Educar em Revista*, *35*(74), 17–33. doi:10.1590/0104-4060.63035

Minte, A., & Ibagón, N. (2017). Pensamiento crítico ¿competencia olvidada en la enseñanza de la historia? [Critical thinking, a neglected skill in history teaching?]. *Revista Entramado*, *13*(2), 186–198. doi:10.18041/entramado.2017v13n2.26228

Miralles, P., & Gómez, C. J. (2021). El pensamiento histórico del alumnado y su relación con las competencias [Students' historical thinking and its relationship to competences]. In Educación histórica para el siglo XXI, principios epistemológicos y metodológicos [History Education for the 21st century, epistemological and methodological principles] (pp. 83-114). Universidad Icesi y Universidad del Valle.

Miralles, P., Gómez, C. J., & Sánchez, R. (2014). Dime qué preguntas y te diré qué evalúas y enseñas. Análisis de los exámenes de Ciencias Sociales en tercer ciclo de Educación Primaria [Tell me what questions you ask and I will tell you what you assess and teach. Analysis of the Social Sciences examinations in the third cycle of Primary Education]. *Aula Abierta*, *42*(2), 83–89. doi:10.1016/j.aula.2014.05.002

Miralles, P., Molina, S., & Ortuño, J. (2011). La Investigación en Didáctica de las Ciencias Sociales [Research in Social Sciences Didactics]. *Educatio Siglo XXI, 29*(1), 149-174. https://revistas.um.es/educatio/article/view/119921/112891

Molina, S., Ortuño, J., & Miralles, P. (2011). El comentario de fuentes primarias como herramienta para la evaluación de competencias básicas en Historia [The commentary of primary sources as a tool for the assessment of basic skills in History]. In P. Miralles, S. Molina, & A. Santisteban (Eds.), *La evaluación en el proceso de enseñanza y aprendizaje de las ciencias sociales* [Assessment in the teaching and learning process in the social sciences] (Vol. 1, pp. 295–306). AUPDCS.

Molina, S., Rodríguez, R., & Sánchez, R. (2013). Investigar, enseñar y divulgar la historia social: La experiencia del Seminario y grupo de investigación Familia y Élite de Poder de la Universidad de Murcia [Researching, teaching and disseminating social history: the experience of the Seminar and research group Family and Power Elite at the University of Murcia]. *Clio*, 39.

Olmos, R. (2018). Kahoot! Una aplicación para la gamificación en el aula [Kahoot! An application for classroom gamification]. In *EDUNOVATIC 2017. Conference Proceedings. 2nd Virtual International Conference on Education, Innovation and ICT* (pp. 862-869). Adaya Press.

Order ECD/65/2015, of 21 January, which describes the relationships between the competences, contents and assessment criteria of primary education, compulsory secondary education and baccalaureate. (2015, January). *Boletín Oficial del Estado*, *25*(29), 6986–7003.

Organic Law 3/2020 of 29 December 2020, which amends Organic Law 2/2006 of 3 May on Education. (2020, December). *Boletín Oficial del Estado*, *340*(30), 122868–122953.

Pagès, J. (2002). Aprender a enseñar historia y ciencias sociales: El currículo y la didáctica de las ciencias sociales [Learning to teach history and social sciences: the curriculum and the didactic of social sciences]. *Pensamiento Educativo: Revista de Investigacion Educacional Latinoamericana*, *30*(1), 255–269.

Peck, C., & Seixas, P. (2008). Benchmarks of Historical Thinking: First Steps. *Canadian Journal of Education*, *31*(4), 1015–1038.

Polo, I. (2010). La evaluación de las competencias básicas [The assessment of basic skills]. *Avances en supervisión educativa, 12*.

Royal Decree 126/2014, of 28 February, establishing the basic curriculum for Primary Education. (2014, March). *Boletín Oficial del Estado*, *1*(52).

Royal Decree 157/2022, of 1 March, which establishes the orientation and minimum teachings of Primary Education. (2022, March). *Boletín Oficial del Estado*, *2*(52).

Royal Decree 984/2021, of 16 November, which regulates assessment and promotion in Primary Education, as well as assessment, promotion and qualifications in Compulsory Secondary Education, Baccalaureate and Vocational Training. (2021, November). *Official State Gazette*, *17*(275), 141583–141595.

Sáiz, J., & López, R. (2015). Competencias y narrativas históricas: El pensamiento histórico de estudiantes y futuros profesores de educación secundaria [Historical skills and narratives: the historical thinking of students and prospective secondary school teachers]. *Revista de Estudios Sociales*, *52*(52), 87–101. doi:10.7440/res52.2015.06

Sánchez, R., Campillo, J. M., & Guerrero, C. (2020). Percepciones del profesorado de primaria y secundaria sobre la enseñanza de la historia [Primary and secondary school teachers' perceptions of history teaching]. *Revista Interuniversitaria de Formación del Profesorado, 34*(3), 57-76. https://www.redalyc.org/journal/274/27468063003/html/

Santisteban, A. (2017). Del tiempo histórico a la conciencia histórica: Cambios en la enseñanza y el aprendizaje de la historia en los últimos 25 años [From historical time to historical consciousness: changes in the teaching and learning of history in the last 25 years]. *Diálogo Andino*, *53*, 87–99.

Schmidt, M. (2019). El turno de la didáctica de la historia: contribuciones para un debate [The turn of history didactics: contributions to a debate]. *Historia y espacio, 15*(53), 21-42.

Seixas, P. (2006). *Teacher Notes: Benchmarks of Historical Thinking, a framework for Assessment in Canada.* UBC: Centre for the Study of Historical Consciousness. https://www.edu.gov.mb.ca/k12/cur/socstud/foundation_gr8/tns/tn1.pdf

Seixas, P., & Morton, T. (2013). The big six historical thinking concepts. Academic Press.

Seva, F., Vera, M. I., & Soriano, M. C. (2017). La percepción del alumnado de Ciencias Sociales ante la utilización de las tecnologías de la información y la comunicación en clase. Las TIC favorecen el aprendizaje de las Ciencias Sociales, según el alumnado [Social Studies pupils' perception of the use of information and communication technologies in class. According to pupils, ICT favour the learning of Social Sciences.]. In *Investigación en Didáctica de las Ciencias Sociales. Retos, preguntas y líneas de investigación* [Research in Didactics of Social Sciences. Challenges, questions and lines of research] (pp. 782-799). Asociación Universitaria de Profesorado de Didáctica de las Ciencias Sociales. http://rua.ua.es/dspace/handle/10045/71843

Vansledright, B. (2013). *Assessing historical thinking and understanding. Innovate designs for new standards*. Routledge. doi:10.4324/9780203464632

Zou, D. (2020). Gamified flipped EFL classroom for primary education: Student and teacher perceptions. *Journal of Computers in Education,* 1-16. doi:10.1007/s40692-020-00153-w

Chapter 4
A Proposal for the Design of a Gamified Experience for the Teaching of Historical Thinking in Primary Education

María Martínez-Hita
University of Murcia, Spain

Cosme Gómez Carrasco
University of Murcia, Spain

Pedro Miralles-Martínez
https://orcid.org/0000-0002-9143-2145
University of Murcia, Spain

EXECUTIVE SUMMARY

The need for a transformation of the teaching and learning process of history has long been called for from the field of history education research. A change is advocated which affects both the methodology and the epistemology of the field and promotes the development of historical thinking. This chapter presents an intervention programme aimed at primary education students in Spain and validated via expert judgement with the aim of contributing to the aforementioned change in the teaching of history by including work on the historical thinking skills along with the use of active methodologies such as gamification. The objective of this chapter is to present this gamified project for the development of historical thinking in such a way that it can serve as a point of reference and to propose a series of steps to facilitate the design of gamified learning experiments.

DOI: 10.4018/978-1-6684-5240-0.ch004

INTRODUCTION

Research on the teaching of history advocates the need for a change in the teaching and learning process and the redefinition of the current model of history education by introducing historical thinking into the classroom (Carretero et al., 2017; Metzger & Harris, 2018; Thorp & Persson, 2020; VanSledright, 2011, 2014).

In order to achieve an education in historical thinking, it is necessary to move beyond the mere memorisation of dates and information and to work on second-order concepts which provide the necessary tools for the study of the past and the construction of historical explanations (Domínguez, 2015; Lee, 2005; Lee & Ashby, 2000; Seixas & Morton, 2013).

Furthermore, it is argued that the traditional teaching practices employed in the majority of schools for the teaching of history should be substituted by active methodologies which attribute a leading role to students in the construction of their own learning (Gómez et al., 2018; Martínez-Hita et al., 2021).

Gamification is a teaching innovation which is gradually gaining in popularity in schools due to its positive effects on aspects such as learning and motivation (Huang et al., 2020; Kocakoyun & Ozdamli, 2018; Landers, 2014; Sailer & Homner, 2020; Swacha, 2021). Therefore, this chapter proposes the use of gamification as a tool which can facilitate the active learning of historical thinking concepts.

HISTORICAL THINKING

Research into historical thinking is increasingly gaining relevance (Epstein & Salinas, 2018; Lévesque & Clark, 2018; Thorp & Persson, 2020) as can be observed in the recent monographs on this issue (Carretero et al., 2017; Counsell et al., 2016; Metzger & Harris, 2018). Within this field, two main trends can be identified (Seixas, 2017); one based on historical consciousness and controversial issues (Barton & Levstik, 2004; Domínguez-Almansa & López-Facal, 2017; Rüsen, 2012), which complements another focused on historical thinking (De Groot-Reuvekamp et al., 2018; Lévesque & Clark, 2018; Thorp & Persson, 2020; VanSledright, 2014).

In spite of the proliferation of research on history education, and historical thinking in particular, Lévesque & Clark (2018) have stated that history teachers have not fully integrated proposals made as a result of this research into their teaching practice, although it is true that the education curriculums of some countries have incorporated historical thinking (Brant et al., 2016; Clark, 2018; Domínguez, 2015; Parkes & Donnelly, 2014).

The lack of relationship between the research on historical thinking and classroom teaching experience (Lévesque & Clark, 2018) explains the fact that researchers continue to defend the need to carry out a renovation of history education towards the development of historical thinking. This necessity is also justified by the very epistemology of history and its aims, as well as by the guidelines set out in education curriculums (Gómez et al., 2018).

In order to develop historical thinking, two complementary aspects are required: a substantive knowledge of first-order concepts about the past (*substantive history*); and a knowledge of second-order historical concepts (*second-order or procedural ideas about history*). The former are the concepts which history addresses (i.e., the contents), whereas the second type of historical knowledge provides the necessary tools for the study of the past and the construction of historical explanations. Without these second-order concepts, it would be impossible to give meaning to the substantive (first-order) contents as they determine the way towards "making history" (i.e., the work of the historian), and make it possible to organise our knowledge, providing understanding of this subject (Lee, 2005; Lee & Ashby, 2000).

The changes required in history education in order to teach and think historically are based on modifying the approach to teaching and learning. This should not consist merely of the acquisition and memorisation of first-order concepts (dates, information, etc.), which is what occurs in most classes (Gómez-Carrasco et al., 2018; Monteagudo-Fernández et al., 2020). Rather, in the teaching of history, students must, not only learn these first-order concepts, but it is also of great importance for them to acquire the skills of the historian (i.e., the historical thinking skills, methodological concepts and second-order concepts).

According to Seixas & Morton (2013), six historical thinking concepts can be identified which correspond with second-order concepts:

- Historical relevance: this refers to why certain past events or characters are selected today as worthy of being remembered.
- Evidence or sources: taken to be the critical analysis and interpretation thereof in order to build a particular historical argument.
- Change and continuity: the capacity to identify what changes and what remains the same as time goes by.
- Causes and consequences: this refers to the need to analyse which factors led to a specific past event and what their repercussions were.
- Historical perspective: this consists of understanding the past as a foreign country in which the social, cultural, intellectual and even emotional context is different and has an influence on the way of life and the actions of the people of that age.
- The ethical dimension of history: making ethical judgements on past actions and evaluating the sacrifices and injustices of the past and their consequences in the present from a historical perspective (i.e., taking into account their historical context).

In order to achieve an education in historical thinking, these second-order concepts must be complemented by first-order concepts, among which the following two types can be identified (Gómez & Miralles, 2015):

- Chronology: this refers to knowledge of the dates in which certain events occurred or certain people lived in the past.
- Conceptual/factual: relating to the knowledge of a past concept or event.

In addition, in order to improve history education and to put an end to the erroneous conception of history as closed knowledge which must be memorised, it is necessary to pay attention not only to epistemology, but also to the methodology employed for the teaching of history.

Thus, to carry out a renewal of history education fostering the development of historical thinking among students, a methodological change must take place to encourage students to actively participate in the construction of their own historical knowledge. Although there are different teaching methods and strategies which can contribute towards this methodological change (Gómez et al., 2018), this study proposes gamification as a tool which is capable of bringing about this constructivist learning based on historical thinking. Furthermore, it can also contribute towards putting an end to students' negative conceptions of history as a boring and unstimulating subject (Liceras, 2016; Llopis & Balaguer, 2016; Sanz et al., 2017; Van Straaten et al., 2018).

Prior research has shown that the use of gamification in the classroom contributes to the improvement of students' perceptions of the subject in question, increasing interest therein and the perception that the classes are enjoyable and entertaining (Álvaro-Tordesillas et al., 2020; Cózar-Gutiérrez & Sáez-López, 2016; Ortiz-Colón et al., 2018; Prieto, 2020).

GAMIFICATION

Gamification has increased in popularity over recent years and has become a relevant field of study in education research (Huang et al., 2020; Kocakoyun & Ozdamli, 2018; Landers, 2014; Manzano-León et al., 2021; Sailer & Homner, 2020; Swacha, 2021).

However, it is frequently confused with other terms such as the use of games and serious games in the classroom. Gamification does not consist of the use of serious games or complete games in class, but makes use of the elements of which the former consist in order to modify the teaching process and to create a learning experience which is similar to a game (Deterding et al., 2011; Marczewski, 2015; Sailer & Homner, 2020).

According to Kapp (2012, p.10), "Gamification is using game-based mechanics, aesthetics and game thinking to engage people, motivate action, promote learning, and solve problems".

Therefore, gamification consists of applying the elements of which games are made up to the teaching process. Although there are different classifications for these elements, two of the most commonly used taxonomies are outlined below.

Hunicke et al. (2004) proposed the MDA (*Mechanics, Dynamics and Aesthetics*) framework in which the following three types of elements are differentiated:

- The mechanics are the basic rules of the game which establish how to play it. Points, badges and leaderboards (the so-called PBL system) are examples of mechanics.
- The dynamics refer to the behaviours and actions of the participants during the situations created by applying the mechanics. Collaboration, competition and progression are examples of dynamics.
- Aesthetics are related with the sensorial and emotional responses of the participants. They refer to their perceptions of the experience and, thus, it must be attractive in order to catch their attention and get them involved. Therefore, it is important to take into account the characteristics of those participating. The narrative (i.e., the story in which the experience is framed) is a key element in order to generate stimulating aesthetics.

The second classification is that put forward by Werbach & Hunter (2012) which differentiates three categories of the elements of gamification: the dynamics, the mechanics and the components.

- The dynamics are the highest level of abstraction of gamification and include the most general aspects, such as limitations, emotions, relationships, narrative and progression.
- The mechanics are the basic processes which stimulate the development of the activity, such as competition, cooperation, missions, rewards and feedback.

- The components are the specific elements of a game, such as points, badges, leaderboards, avatars and levels, among others.

The incorporation of these elements into practical teaching makes it possible to transform the teaching and learning process into an immersive experience similar to a game. In this way, gamification contributes to the improvement of different aspects such as learning, motivation, interest and student involvement (Area & González, 2015; Bai et al., 2020; Chapman & Rich, 2018; Da Rocha-Seixas et al., 2016; Hamari et al., 2014; Huang et al., 2020; Martínez-Hita et al., 2021; Ortiz-Colón et al., 2018; Prieto, 2020; Sailer & Homner, 2020).

These benefits of gamification are explained by different theories, such as Csikszentmihalyi's (1990) Flow Theory or Lander's (2014) Theory of Gamified Learning.

Flow Theory (Csikszentmihalyi, 1990) makes reference to the concept of flow understood as the mental state of total concentration, involvement and enjoyment of the activity being carried out. This can be encouraged by setting clear targets, providing immediate feedback and establishing a balance between the level of the challenge and the participant's skill.

On the other hand, Lander's (2014) Theory of Gamified Learning explains the relationship between gamification and learning via four components: instructional content, behaviours and attitudes, game characteristics and learning outcomes. Gamification has an effect on learning outcomes by modifying the behaviours and attitudes which are relevant for learning.

Prior studies on the application of gamification have shown contradictory results, reporting both positive (Chapman & Rich, 2018; Da Rocha-Seixas et al., 2016; Hamari et al., 2014; Martínez-Hita et al., 2021; Ortiz-Colón et al., 2018; Prieto, 2020) and negative effects or even the absence of effects (Domínguez et al., 2013; Hanus & Fox, 2015; Mekler et al., 2017). However, most research, as has been shown by recent systematic reviews, reflects that gamification is an effective teaching strategy which brings about improvements in learning, behaviour, interest, participation, involvement and motivation among students (Bai et al., 2020; Huang et al., 2020; Manzano-León et al., 2021; Sailer & Homner, 2020).

Prior studies have also stated that the majority of studies on gamification are limited to the use of points, badges and leaderboards (so-called *pointsification* (Hamari et al., 2014; Huang et al., 2020; Majuri et al., 2018; Manzano-León et al., 2021; Seaborn & Fels, 2015). However, gamification cannot be based purely on *pointsification*, but should also include other elements, such as narrative, which helps to increase the potential of this pedagogical innovation, facilitating learning and obtaining better results (Huang et al., 2020; Kapp, 2012; Landers, 2014; Manzano-León et al., 2021).

Furthermore, most studies which analyse the use of gamification in education focus on the area of Computer Science and higher levels of education (Prieto, 2020; Swacha, 2021; Sailer & Homner, 2020), with there being an almost total lack of learning experiments linking historical thinking and gamification in primary education (Martínez-Hita, 2022; Martínez-Hita et al., 2021).

Thus, it is possible to identify a series of deficiencies in research, such as knowledge areas and levels of education in which gamification is applied, and a lack of clarity regarding the term, which makes it difficult to create gamified experiences due to its confusion with the use of games or serious games or with the exclusive use of points, badges and leaderboards.

Thus, it is necessary, on the one hand, to structure the elements of gamification and the steps to be followed for the design of gamified learning experiences and, on the other, to present examples which can serve as a point of reference in the field of education.

OBJECTIVE

The objective of this chapter is to present a gamified intervention programme for the development of historical thinking in primary education with the aim of it serving as a point of reference for the design of gamified learning experiences.

In addition, it proposes a series of steps which can facilitate the gamification of the teaching and learning process, exemplified in the aforementioned gamified project, the design of which was validated via the expert judgement technique (Martínez-Hita, 2022; Martínez-Hita & Miralles-Martínez, 2020).

CASE DESCRIPTION

For the creation of a gamified intervention programme, the following five steps are proposed:

1. Know the characteristics of the context and the students.
2. Determine the objectives and curricular aspects.
3. Create a narrative.
4. Design the missions and challenges.
5. Integrate the elements of gamification.

1) Know the Characteristics of the Context and the Students

The first step in the design of a gamified learning experience is to analyse the context and the students in order to discover their characteristics and needs.

The gamified intervention presented here is set in the context of the fourth year of primary education in Spain, i.e., with children aged between 9 and 10 years of age.

Following the CIPP evaluation model, an evaluation of the context was carried out, which showed deficiencies in the teaching of historical thinking among students in Spain (Martínez-Hita & Gómez, 2018) and their negative perception of the learning of history (Liceras, 2016; Llopis & Balaguer, 2016; Sanz et al., 2017; Van Straaten et al., 2018). This justified the need for the intervention programme to be focused on historical thinking and gamification.

Furthermore, when designing a gamified experience, the level of education and the ages and preferences of the students should be taken into consideration in order to respond to their characteristics, attract their attention and motivate them to learn.

2) Determine the Objectives and Curricular Aspects

The second step in the design of a gamified learning experience implies the clear establishment of the objectives sought and the delimitation of all of the aspects of the curriculum which will form part of the gamified intervention programme.

As far as the proposal presented here is concerned, the main learning objectives which were established based on the Spanish education curriculum (CARM, 2014) can be observed in Table 1, along with their relationship with the concepts of historical thinking.

Table 1. Objectives of the gamified intervention programme designed and their relationship with the concepts of historical thinking

Objectives	Concepts of historical thinking
To recognise the events which mark the beginnings and ends of different historical periods.	Chronology Conceptual/Factual
To identify the characteristics of Prehistory.	Historical sources and evidence
To explain the importance of writing, agriculture and pastoral farming as discoveries which profoundly changed human societies.	Historical relevance Change and continuity
To use different techniques (timelines, maps) in order to locate past events in time and space.	Chronology Historical sources and evidence
To explain the differences in the periods into which Prehistory is divided and the basic characteristics of ways of life in these periods.	Historical perspective
To explain aspects related with the way of life and social organisation of Spain in Ancient History.	Historical perspective
To deepen students' knowledge of Prehistory and Ancient History via different media: comics, magazines, videos, books.	Historical sources and evidence

Source: Own, based on the Spanish education curriculum (CARM, 2014).

3) Create a Narrative

The narrative refers to the history or context which serves as the central theme of the whole learning experience. Therefore, it is of great importance to select a topic which attracts the students' attention and permits them to work on the necessary contents in a coherent way in order to achieve the proposed aims.

The narrative becomes an essential element of the gamification process and is extremely effective in attracting the students' attention and guiding them through the whole experience (Kapp, 2012; Landers, 2014; Manzano-León et al., 2021; Sailer & Homner, 2020).

In this case, the narrative created for the work on historical thinking was as follows (Martínez-Hita, 2022):

We are a mission of aliens who have been on the Earth throughout the year investigating humans and completing the missions our boss has given us. We are divided into five work groups with each group coming from a different planet. Now the time has come for us all to return to our own planets. However, there is one problem: our boss wants to check if we really deserve to go back home. Our spaceships are blocked and we do not know the passwords to make them work again. In order to get the numbers which will enable us to go home, we must complete a series of missions. Depending on how we perform in these missions, we will achieve points which will determine how we will be remembered or considered on our planets when we return home. It all depends on us.

First of all, we know that on Earth, humans are living in a historical age called the Contemporary Age. However, on our planets, not everything is the same as here. For example, in the continent where we live, we are experiencing an age which is more advanced than here on Earth, which is what enabled us to come here. However, not all of the continents are like this and the rest of the planet is living in a completely different historical age.

Our boss has challenged us to investigate what age it is according to human eras and to report back to her. To do this, we have to work as a team and be extremely precise so as not to forget any small details or to be tricked.

To introduce this narrative to the class, a video-trailer of the gamification process was shown in class with the aim of catching the students' attention and immersing them in the story created.

Table 2. Missions and challenges of the gamified intervention programme for the development of historical thinking

Phase	Session	Development	Historical concept
Introduction Motivation Previously held ideas	1. Introduction to the project	Introduction of the narrative via a video. Identification of previously held ideas.	
Development	2. History and historical sources	An explanation of what history, historical research and sources are. An analysis of different types of historical sources and their classification.	Sources and evidence
Development	3. Historical time	Jigsaw classroom technique to obtain information about historical periods. The construction of a timeline in small groups.	Chronology Conceptual/Factual
Development	4. Mission 1: Construction of a chronological axis	The construction of a chronological axis using the scale in accordance with the duration of each period.	Chronology Conceptual/Factual
Development	5. Mission 2: Sources	The analysis of sources to verify and reason the historical period in which each planet is situated.	Sources
Development	6. Mission 3: Historical perspective	Individual narration in which it is explained how the natives live on their planet (housing, clothing, food, government, society, economy, etc.).	Historical perspective
Development	7. Mission 4: Changes and continuities	The creation of a comic in which the historical period being experienced on their planet is compared with that on Earth.	Changes and continuities
Development	8. Mission 5: Historical relevance	An essay responding to the question: What is the main invention or discovery made on your planet in the current historical age? What changes has it caused in your life?	Historical relevance
Development	9. Mission 6: Sources and heritage	Identification of a work of art which corresponds with the period. Justification and drawing of the work of art in order to be able to make a replica on their own planet.	Sources
Synthesis Evaluation	10. Mission 7: Escape room-breakout	An escape room is made in small groups with tests relating to everything worked on throughout the project.	Chronology Conceptual/Factual Sources Historical relevance Historical perspective
Evaluation	11. Demonstration of knowledge	An individual written test to evaluate student learning.	Chronology Conceptual/Factual Sources Historical relevance Historical perspective
Synthesis Evaluation	12. End of the missions	Discussion on the gamified experience and awarding of medals to each learner according to the level achieved.	

Source: Own, based on the gamified intervention programme (Martínez-Hita, 2022)

4) Design the Missions and Challenges

The missions and challenges make reference to the activities and tasks which the students must carry out. These can be individual, in small groups or as the whole class. In addition, it is important for these missions to be coherent with the narrative created due to the fact that if they are absorbed by an attractive narrative, they will be more motivated to complete the tasks (Manzano-León et al., 2021).

The missions designed in the gamified intervention programme for the development of historical thinking can be observed in Table 2.

In addition to the missions presented here, the project also included voluntary missions, among which videos were watched with questions via Edpuzzle and stories were read and analysed relating to the historical issues in question. The students also had a mission diary in which they wrote down the work corresponding to each of the missions and challenges, as well as an outline of the missions of which the project consisted. This was given to them in the first session to serve as a guide throughout the learning experience.

As pointed out by Landers (2014) in his Theory of Gamified Learning, it is essential for the missions (i.e., the tasks) to be well designed in order to facilitate the learning of the contents. If the contents to be taught are not of sufficient quality and if they do not help the students to learn, the gamification of these contents alone cannot bring about learning.

Likewise, Csikszentmihalyi's (1990) Flow Theory should also be taken into account. For students to achieve a state of flow, taken to be the moment in which a person is totally immersed in and concentrating on the enjoyment of the task being carried out, it is necessary for there to be a balance between the level of challenge required of the students and their skills. Therefore, the missions designed should be achievable, whilst also implying a challenge.

5) Integrate the Elements of Gamification

Different gamification elements were integrated into the proposal designed for the development of historical thinking, some of which, such as narrative and missions have already been presented. Others include collaboration, competition, progression, feedback, rewards, avatars, levels, badges and points, among others.

In the gamified project, cooperation and collaboration among the participants were encouraged rather than competition in order to avoid the negative effects of competitivity, as has been shown in prior research (Area & González, 2015; Hamari et al., 2014; Hanus & Fox, 2015; Huang et al., 2020). Thus, a competitive spirit was not encouraged among the students with each student competing against him/herself, whilst cooperating with his/her peers in order to achieve common aims.

Bearing this in mind, different active methodologies were used in this gamified intervention programme, including cooperative learning. The students worked in heterogeneous teams which allowed for peer tutoring and mutual assistance, without neglecting individual work to respond to different types of learning. Specifically, the students were divided into five groups, with a different historical period corresponding to each of them: Palaeolithic, Neolithic, Metal Age, Ancient History (pre-Roman peoples, Iberians), Ancient History (Rome). In turn, each student had a different role within their cooperative group (captain or spokesperson, time controller, noise controller, secretary and materials manager).

In addition to these cooperative roles, cooperative learning techniques were also used, such as puzzles, Aronson's jigsaw classroom and Spencer Kagan cooperative structures, such as *Numbered Heads Together*.

Avatars are a personal representation of each student within the gamified experience, which fosters a greater degree of emotional attachment (Teixes, 2014). As with the missions and any other gamification element, avatars should be coherent with the narrative created. For the gamified intervention programme designed, the *ClassDojo* platform was employed, which includes avatars with similar aesthetics to aliens, in line with the story created.

The same platform (*ClassDojo*) was also used to award points to the students. These points represent numeric values which indicate progress made within the gamification process and can be obtained by completing the missions or via certain behaviours and actions. Table 3 presents some of the items which lead to points being awarded.

Table 3. Items for the obtention of points in the gamified project

Items	Score
Mission completed	5 points
Helping others	1 point
Teamwork	1 point
Working hard	1 point
Challenge overcome	2 points

Source: Own, based on the gamified intervention programme (Martínez-Hita, 2022)

The points, in turn, made it possible to acquire rewards. These consisted of various prizes of different values which the students were free to choose in exchange for their points.

In addition, the students were able to achieve badges for completing certain missions or for certain behaviours and attitudes. These badges are collectable visual icons which reflect the students' achievements. It is recommended that a transparent system be used in which the badges achieved by each student are visible. In this way, the students can challenge themselves and their motivation is increased in order to achieve the medals which they have not yet attained (Sailer & Homner, 2020).

Badges are also useful as progress markers, as a form of recognition and as a way of providing immediate feedback to students regarding their performance (Bai et al., 2020).

Last of all, the levels make reference to the degree of progress made within the gamified experience. Passing from one level to another can be established according to different criteria (number of points obtained, badges achieved, missions completed, etc.). In the gamified proposal presented here for the development of historical thinking, five levels were established according to the number of points accumulated and badges obtained. The levels, related to the narrative, were as follows (from lowest to highest): Legend; Superhero; Hero; Hero's assistant; Mission companion.

CONCLUSION

Gamification is a strategy which is increasingly gaining prominence in the field of education due to its positive effects on aspects such as motivation, interest, participation, behaviour and student learning

(Bai et al., 2020; Chapman & Rich, 2018; Da Rocha-Seixas et al., 2016; Hamari et al., 2014; Huang et al., 2020; Manzano-León et al., 2021; Ortiz-Colón et al., 2018; Prieto, 2020; Sailer & Homner, 2020).

Indeed, as Bai et al. (2020) have pointed out in their systematic review, the results of student learning with the use of gamification are significantly better than those cases in which this innovative technique is not used. Furthermore, the effect size in learning is greater in gamified groups than in control groups (Huang et al., 2020).

This coincides with the results obtained in the application of the gamified intervention programme for the development of historical thinking presented in this chapter. The academic performance of students who worked with this programme was significantly higher than that of students in the control group, who followed a traditional methodology based on the use of the textbook as the main teaching resource (Martínez-Hita, 2022; Martínez-Hita et al, 2021).

The design of the gamified intervention programme for the development of historical thinking included different elements of gamification which extended beyond mere *pointsification*. In this regard, attention was paid to the recommendations of research regarding the need to move beyond the mere use of points, badges and leaderboards and progress towards learning experiences with a greater potential to facilitate learning by including other elements such as a narrative, missions and collaboration between participants (Huang et al., 2020; Kapp, 2012; Landers, 2014; Manzano-León et al., 2021).

The inclusion of a narrative makes it possible to situate learning in a specific context and to guide students throughout the whole process. This narrative is an element of immersion which encompasses the tasks in an attractive story for the students, thus fostering motivation towards these tasks and, as a consequence, student learning (Kapp, 2012; Landers, 2014; Manzano-León et al., 2021; Sailer & Homner, 2020). These benefits of gamification on learning are in line with Lander's (2014) Theory of Gamified Learning.

This immersion is also fostered by the use of avatars and missions which are coherent with the narrative created. Therefore, the use of a narrative and of missions is becoming increasingly more relevant in the design of gamified projects in the field of education (Manzano-León et al., 2021).

The feedback provided to students is also of great importance as far as learning is concerned. A gamified process which includes elements such as badges, points and levels provides students with direct and immediate feedback on their progress and performance, thus favouring the state of flow proposed by Csikszentmihalyi (1990).

Therefore, the gamified project presented in this chapter can serve as an example and as a point of reference for the creation of other learning experiences which are, in effect, deep gamification processes and are not based merely on *pointsification*, thus avoiding confusion with learning based on games.

In addition, the steps proposed for the creation of a gamified intervention programme can facilitate and promote the design of gamified experiences by organising and structuring the stages which are to be followed in a more guided way.

It has also been corroborated that the use of gamification is compatible with the historical thinking approach which is advocated from the field of history education research (Carretero et al., 2017; Metzger & Harris, 2018; Thorp & Persson, 2020; VanSledright, 2011, 2014). Thus, it can be a tool which contributes towards the transformation of the teaching and learning process of history catering to both epistemology and methodology (Martínez-Hita, 2022; Martínez-Hita et al., 2021).

For the above reasons, it is recommended that this line of research be continued, examining the possibilities of the use of gamification for the teaching of history and historical thinking. It would be of interest to analyse teaching and learning experiences in which gamification is employed in combination with historical thinking in different levels of education and in different contexts.

ACKNOWLEDGMENT

This study is the result of the research projects "The geographical and historical thinking of primary education students in the Region of Murcia: an innovative methodological proposal for quality education" [20874/PI/18], funded by the Fundación Séneca-Agencia de Ciencia y Tecnología de la Región de Murcia; "HistoryLab for European Civic Engagement: open e-Toolkit to train History Teachers on Digital Teaching and Learning", funded by SEPIE under the ERASMUS + KA226 call [2020-1-ES01-KA226-HE-095430]; and the research project PID2020-113453RB-I00, funded by the Spanish State Research Agency [AEI/10.13039/501100011033].

REFERENCES

Álvaro-Tordesillas, A., Alonso-Rodríguez, M., Poza-Casado, I., & Galván-Desvaux, N. (2020). Gamification experience in the subject of Descriptive Geometry for Architecture. *Educación XX1, 23*(1), 373-408. doi:10.5944/educxx1.23591

Area, M., & González, C. S. (2015). De la enseñanza con libros de texto al aprendizaje en espacios online gamificados. *Educatio Siglo XXI, 33*(3), 15–38. doi:10.6018/j/240791

Bai, S., Hew, K. F., & Huang, B. (2020). Does gamification improve student learning outcome? Evidence from a meta-analysis and synthesis of qualitative data in educational contexts. *Educational Research Review, 30*, 100322. doi:10.1016/j.edurev.2020.100322

Barton, K., & Levstik, L. (2004). *Teaching History for the Common Good.* Lawrence Erlbau. doi:10.4324/9781410610508

Brant, J., Chapman, A., & Isaacs, T. (2016). International instructional systems: Social studies. *Curriculum Journal, 27*(1), 62–79. doi:10.1080/09585176.2015.1134340

CARM (Comunidad Autónoma de la Región de Murcia) (2014). Decreto 198/2014, de 5 de septiembre, por el que se establece el currículo de la Educación Primaria en la Comunidad Autónoma de la Región de Murcia. *BORM (Boletín Oficial de la Región de Murcia), 206*, 6 de septiembre de 2014.

Carretero, M., Berger, S., & Grever, M. (Eds.). (2017). *Palgrave Handbook of Research in Historical Culture and Education.* Palgrave Macmillan. doi:10.1057/978-1-137-52908-4

Chapman, J. R., & Rich, P. J. (2018). Does educational gamification improve students' motivation? If so, which game elements work best? *Journal of Education for Business, 93*(7), 315–322. doi:10.1080/08832323.2018.1490687

Clark, P. (2018). History Education Debates: Canadian Identity, Historical Thinking and Historical Consciousness. *Arbor. Ciencia. Pensamiento y Cultura, 194*(788), 1–13. doi:10.3989/arbor.2018.788n2001

Counsell, C., Burn, K., & Chapman, A. (2016). *MasterClass in history education. Transforming teaching and learning*. Bloomsbury. doi:10.5040/9781474285476

Cózar-Gutiérrez, R., & Sáez-López, J. M. (2016). Game-based learning and gamification in initial teacher training in the social sciences: An experiment with MinecraftEdu. *International Journal of Educational Technology in Higher Education*, *13*(2), 2. Advance online publication. doi:10.118641239-016-0003-4

Csikszentmihalyi, M. (1990). *Flow. The Psychology of Optimal Experience*. Harper & Row.

Da Rocha-Seixas, L., Gomes, A. S., & De Melo-Filho, I. J. (2016). Effectiveness of gamification in the engagement of students. *Computers in Human Behavior*, *58*, 48–63. doi:10.1016/j.chb.2015.11.021

De Groot-Reuvekamp, M., Ros, A., & Van Boxtel, C. (2018). A successful professional development program in history: What matters? *Teaching and Teacher Education*, *75*, 290–301. doi:10.1016/j.tate.2018.07.005

Deterding, S., Dixon, D., Khaled, R., & Nacke, L. (2011). From game design elements to gamefulness: Defining "gamification". In A. Lugmayr (Ed.), *Proceedings of the 15th international academic MindTrek Conference: Envisioning future media environments* (pp. 9-15). ACM. 10.1145/2181037.2181040

Domínguez, A., Saenz-de-Navarrete, J., de-Marcos, L., Fernández-Sanz, L., Pagés, C., & Martínez, J. J. (2013). Gamifying learning experiences: Practical implications and outcomes. *Computers & Education*, *63*, 380–392. doi:10.1016/j.compedu.2012.12.020

Domínguez, J. (2015). *Pensamiento histórico y evaluación de competencias*. Graó.

Domínguez-Almansa, A., & López Facal, R. (2017). Patrimonios en conflictos. Competencias cívicas y formación profesional en educación primaria. *Review of Education*, *375*, 86–109. doi:10.4438/1988-592X-RE-2016-375-336

Epstein, T., & Salinas, C. S. (2018). Research methodologies in history education. In S. A. Metzger & L. M. Harris (Eds.), *The Wiley International Handbook of history teaching and learning* (pp. 61–92). Wiley. doi:10.1002/9781119100812.ch3

Gómez, C. J., & Miralles, P. (2015). ¿Pensar históricamente o memorizar el pasado? La evaluación de los contenidos históricos en la educación obligatoria en España. *Revista de Estudios Sociales*, (52), 52–68. doi:10.7440/res52.2015.04

Gómez, C. J., Ortuño, J., & Miralles, P. (2018). *Enseñar ciencias sociales con métodos activos de aprendizaje. Reflexiones y propuestas a través de la indagación*. Octaedro.

Gómez-Carrasco, C. J., Rodríguez-Pérez, R. A., & Mirete, A. B. (2018). Metodología didáctica y concepciones epistemológicas sobre la enseñanza de la historia. Una investigación con futuros maestros. *Revista Complutense de Educación*, *24*(1), 237–250. doi:10.5209/RCED.52233

Hamari, J., Koivisto, J., & Sarsa, H. (2014). Does Gamification Work?– A Literature Review of Empirical Studies on Gamification. In R. H. Sprague (Ed.), *47th Hawaii International Conference on System Science (HICSS)* (pp. 3025-3034). IEEE Computer Society. /HICSS.2014.37710.1109/HICSS.2014.377

Hanus, M. D., & Fox, J. (2015). Assessing the effects of gamification in the classroom: A longitudinal study on intrinsic motivation, social comparison, satisfaction, effort, and academic performance. *Computers & Education, 80*, 152–161. doi:10.1016/j.compedu.2014.08.019

Huang, R., Ritzhaupt, A. D., Sommer, M., Zhu, J., Stephen, A., Valle, N., Hampton, J., & Li, J. (2020). The impact of gamification in educational settings on student learning outcomes: A meta-analysis. *Educational Technology Research and Development, 68*(4), 1875–1901. doi:10.100711423-020-09807-z

Hunicke, R., Leblanc, M., & Zubek, R. (2004). MDA: A formal approach to game design and game research. In D. Fu, S. Henke, & J. Orkin (Eds.), *Proceedings of the AAAI-04 Workshop on Challenges in Game AI* (pp. 1-5). AAAI Press.

Kapp, K. M. (2012). *The Gamification of Learning and Instruction. Game-Based Methods and Strategies for Training and Education*. John Wiley & Sons.

Kocakoyun, S., & Ozdamli, F. (2018). A Review of Research on Gamification Approach in Education. In R. Morese, S. Palermo & J. Nervo (Eds.), Socialization - A Multidimensional Perspective (pp. 51-72). IntechOpen. doi:10.5772/intechopen.74131

Landers, R. N. (2014). Developing a Theory of Gamified Learning: Linking Serious Games and Gamification of Learning. *Simulation & Gaming, 45*(6), 752–768. doi:10.1177/1046878114563660

Lee, P. (2005). Putting Principles into Practice: Understanding History. In M. S. Donovan & J. D. Bransford (Eds.), *How students learn: History in the classroom* (pp. 29–78). National Academies Press.

Lee, P., & Ashby, R. (2000). Progression in Historical Understanding among Students Ages 7-14. In P. N. Stearns, P. Seixas, & S. Wineburg (Eds.), *Knowing, Teaching, and Learning History: National and International Perspectives* (pp. 199–222). New York University Press.

Lévesque, S., & Clark, P. (2018). Historical Thinking: Definitions and Educational Applications. In S. A. Metzger & L. M. Harris (Eds.), *The Wiley International Handbook of history teaching and learning* (pp. 119–148). Wiley. doi:10.1002/9781119100812.ch5

Liceras, A. (2016). Las dificultades en la enseñanza y el aprendizaje de las ciencias sociales. In A. Liceras & G. Romero (Coords.), Didáctica de las Ciencias Sociales. Fundamentos, contextos y propuestas (pp. 95-118). Pirámide.

Llopis, M. A., & Balaguer, P. (2016). El uso del juego en educación. Gamificación. In O. Chiva & M. Martí (Coords.), Métodos pedagógicos activos y globalizadores (pp. 85-101). Graó.

Majuri, J., Koivisto, J., & Hamari, J. (2018). Gamification of education and learning: A review of empirical literature. In J. Koivisto & J. Hamari (Eds.), *Proceedings of the 2nd International GamiFIN Conference* (pp. 11–19). CEUR Workshop Proceedings.

Manzano-León, A., Camacho-Lazarraga, P., Guerrero, M. A., Guerrero-Puerta, L., Aguilar-Parra, J. M., Trigueros, R., & Alias, A. (2021). Between Level Up and Game Over: A Systematic Literature Review of Gamification in Education. *Sustainability, 13*(4), 2247. doi:10.3390u13042247

Marczewski, A. (2015). *Even Ninja Monkeys Like to Play: Gamification, Game Thinking and Motivational Design*. CreateSpace Independent Publishing Platform.

Martínez-Hita, M. (2022). *El pensamiento histórico en Educación Primaria. Diseño y evaluación de un programa de intervención gamificado* [Historical thinking in Primary Education. Design and evaluation of a gamified intervention programme] [Doctoral thesis, University of Murcia]. Digitum: Repositorio Institucional de la Universidad de Murcia. http://hdl.handle.net/10201/116267

Martínez-Hita, M., & Gómez, C. J. (2018). Nivel cognitivo y competencias de pensamiento histórico en los libros de texto de Historia de España e Inglaterra. Un estudio comparativo. *Review of Education, 379*, 145–169. doi:10.4438/1988-592X-RE-2017-379-364

Martínez-Hita, M., Gómez-Carrasco, C. J., & Miralles-Martínez, P. (2021). The effects of a gamified project based on historical thinking on the academic performance of primary school children. *Humanit Soc Sci Commun, 8*(1), 122. doi:10.105741599-021-00796-9

Martínez-Hita, M., & Miralles-Martínez, P. (2020). Evaluación del diseño de un programa de intervención gamificado para el desarrollo del pensamiento histórico en Educación Primaria. *RIFOP, 34*(2), 187–204. doi:10.47553/rifop.v34i2.78420

Mekler, E. D., Brühlmann, F., Tuch, A. N., & Opwis, K. (2017). Towards understanding the effects of individual gamification elements on intrinsic motivation and performance. *Computers in Human Behavior, 71*, 525-534. https://doi.org/10.1016/j.chb.2015.08.048

Metzger, S. A., & Harris, L. M. (Eds.). (2018). *The Wiley International Handbook of history teaching and learning*. Wiley. doi:10.1002/9781119100812

Monteagudo-Fernández, J., Rodríguez Pérez, R. A., Escribano-Miralles, A., & Rodríguez García, A. M. (2020). Percepciones de los estudiantes de Educación Secundaria sobre la enseñanza de la historia, a través del uso de las TIC y recursos digitales. *Revista Electrónica Interuniversitaria de Formación del Profesorado, 23*(2). Advance online publication. doi:10.6018/reifop.417611

Ortiz-Colón, A. M., Jordán, J., & Agredal, M. (2018). Gamificación en educación: Una panorámica sobre el estado de la cuestión. *Educação e Pesquisa, 44*(0), 1–17. doi:10.15901678-4634201844173773

Parkes, R. J., & Donnelly, D. (2014). Changing conceptions of historical thinking in History education: An Australian case study. *Revista Tempo e Argumento, 6*(11), 113–136. doi:10.5965/2175180306112014113

Prieto, J. M. (2020). Una revisión sistemática sobre gamificación, motivación y aprendizaje en universitarios. *Teoría de la Educación. Revista Interuniversitaria, 32*(1), 73–99. doi:10.14201/teri.20625

Rüsen, J. (2012). Tradition: A principle of historical sense-generation and its logic and effect in historical culture. *History and Theory, 51*(4), 45–59. doi:10.1111/j.1468-2303.2012.00646.x

Sailer, M., & Homner, L. (2020). The Gamification of Learning: A Meta-analysis. *Educational Psychology Review, 32*(1), 77–112. doi:10.100710648-019-09498-w

Sanz, P., Molero, J. M., & Rodríguez, D. (Eds.). (2017). *La historia en el aula. Innovación docente y enseñanza de la historia en la educación secundaria*. Milenio.

Seaborn, K., & Fels, D. I. (2015). Gamification in theory and action: A survey. *International Journal of Human-Computer Studies, 74*, 14–31. doi:10.1016/j.ijhcs.2014.09.006

Seixas, P. (2017). Historical Consciousness and Historical Thinking. In M. Carretero, S. Berger, & M. Grever (Eds.), *Palgrave Handbook of Research in Historical Culture and Education*. Palgrave Macmillan. doi:10.1057/978-1-137-52908-4_3

Seixas, P., & Morton, T. (2013). *The Big Six Historical Thinking Concepts*. Nelson Education Ltd.

Swacha, J. (2021). State of Research on Gamification in Education: A Bibliometric Survey. *Education in Science*, *11*(2), 69. doi:10.3390/educsci11020069

Teixes, F. (2014). *Gamificación: fundamentos y aplicaciones*. Editorial UOC.

Thorp, R., & Persson, A. (2020). On historical thinking and the history educational challenge. *Educational Philosophy and Theory*, *52*(8), 891–901. doi:10.1080/00131857.2020.1712550

Van Straaten, D., Wilschut, A., & Oostdam, R. (2018). Measuring students' appraisals of the relevance of history: The construction and validation of the Relevance of History Measurement Scale (RHMS). *Studies in Educational Evaluation*, *56*, 102–111. doi:10.1016/j.stueduc.2017.12.002

VanSledright, B. A. (2011). *The Challenge of Rethinking History Education. On Practice, Theories, and Policy*. Routledge.

VanSledright, B. A. (2014). *Assessing historical thinking and understanding. Innovate designs for new standards*. Routledge.

Werbach, K., & Hunter, D. (2012). *For the Win: How Game Thinking Can Revolutionize Your Business*. Wharton Digital Press.

KEY TERMS AND DEFINITIONS

Avatar: A personal representation of each student within the gamified experience.

Badges: Collectable visual icons which reflect the students' achievements in a gamified learning experience.

First-Order Concepts: Substantive knowledge of the content about the past, that is, past events, concepts, and dates.

Gamification: The application of the elements of which games are made up to the teaching process in order to improve students' motivation, learning and engagement, among others.

Historical Thinking: Creative process based on the analysis and interpretation of different historical sources in order to generate historical narratives.

Missions: Activities and tasks which the students must carry out in a gamified learning experience.

Narrative: The history or context which serves as the central theme of the whole gamified learning experience.

Second-Order Concepts: Procedural ideas about history that provide the necessary tools for the study of the past and the construction of historical explanations.

Chapter 5
Impact of a Gamified Experience on the Promotion of Historical Thinking in Primary Education

Carlota López-Fernández
Lab of Technology Integration in Classrooms, Faculty of Education of Albacete, Spain

Sergio Tirado-Olivares
https://orcid.org/0000-0002-8557-5115
Lab of Technology Integration in Classrooms, Faculty of Education of Albacete, Spain

Rafael Villena-Taranilla
https://orcid.org/0000-0002-7665-775X
Lab of Technology Integration in Classrooms, Faculty of Education of Albacete, Spain

Ramón Cózar-Gutiérrez
https://orcid.org/0000-0001-8255-6376
Lab of Technology Integration in Classrooms, Faculty of Education of Albacete, Spain

EXECUTIVE SUMMARY

The use of active methodologies in the teaching-learning process is increasing in popularity. However, with regard to History, this is not the case. Nevertheless, History teaching trends emphasise the importance of their integration to achieve a practical and student-centred learning process to encourage students to develop skills such as reflection and critical thinking. The acquisition of these competences along with knowledge about History is known as historical thinking. In this quantitative study, a gamification methodology was compared to a lecture-based one. To this aim, over the period of a unit of work, two groups from two different schools participated in the study. Results show that, although both groups had the same knowledge before the intervention, the gamification group performed at a significantly higher academic level after it. In addition, a reduced version of the instructional material motivational survey, which was given to the gamification class before and after the intervention, verified that students prefer the gamification dynamic compared to their usual lessons.

DOI: 10.4018/978-1-6684-5240-0.ch005

INTRODUCTION

In recent years, research into the didactics of History has found the need for a renewal and redefinition of the teaching of History to students (Gómez Carrasco & Miralles Martínez, 2018). A pedagogical model focused on the need to promote critical thinking in students is proposed. This model, in contrast to the traditional one, avoids the mere memorization and repetition of past events presented as closed knowledge. In addition, this renewal of the model is justified according to the new History curriculum. This curriculum demands a greater commitment to the acquisition of new skills beyond theoretical knowledge (López-Facal, 2014). Among these competences, we can highlight the importance of being able to identify reliable sources of information, critical reflection, or the ability to express oneself autonomously based on the information analysed (Gómez-Carrasco et al., 2018). From this perspective, an alternative approach, or methodological change, in History teaching is proposed. This alternative aims to develop skills, abilities, and attitudes similar to those used by historians in their professional lives. This way of educating about History content is called historical thinking.

In short, it consists of preparing students, for society in the 21st century. The mere transmission of theoretical knowledge no longer makes sense as, thanks to emerging technologies, information is at hand. Thus, historical thinking aims to put the students in the shoes of historians; learning to reflect as historians do. The new educational paradigm promotes student learning in an active and motivating way; something which makes much more sense nowadays. Among these new pedagogical approaches, gamification is presented as one of the alternatives which is becoming more popular, due to its marked playful nature (Kapp, 2012). Therefore, in the present study, an intervention is presented with the use of gamification in which historical thinking is encouraged. The results obtained, both academic and motivational, were compared with a control group using traditional classroom methodology.

BACKGROUND

Historical Thinking: Changing What our Students Need to Remember

Often, the teaching-learning process of History is based on the mere transmission of theoretical knowledge (concepts, data, dates, etc.) which students must memorize (Martínez-Hita & Gómez-Carrasco, 2018). However, as Miralles Martínez, Gómez-Carrasco and Sánchez-Ibáñez (2014) point out in their study, the methodology most commonly used by teachers continues to be lecture-based, supported by the use of a textbook. Likewise, these authors affirm that this teaching, in addition to not providing lasting learning over time to students, has become obsolete, since due to emerging technologies we have instant access to this purely theoretical knowledge. Therefore, not only does theoretical History learning make no sense, but it also means that students perceive History as closed, immutable and useless (Burenheide, 2007; Liceras, 2016). Martínez-Hita and Gómez-Carrasco (2018) point out that the students' conception of History can be altered by changing the way History is taught in class. Therefore, a renewal of History teaching towards a reflexive, critical and open-to-debate approach is necessary, through which students are able to question information and understand its usefulness. This is what we know as historical thinking (Domínguez, 2015; Lee & Ashby, 2000; Seixas & Morton, 2013; VanSledright, 2011; Wineburg, 2001).

In the seventies, we find the roots of this alternative teaching approach, seeking to learn historical methods at the same time as accumulating knowledge about purely theoretical content. Since then, different definitions of what historical thinking is have been proposed. One of the most common is the proposal by Seixas and Morton (2013) who defined historical thinking as the creative process that historians develop in order to interpret the evidence of the past and generate the historical narrative. If we focus on its integration in the educational field, Van Drie and van Boxtel (2008) point out that historical reasoning focuses on the activity of students, helping them to interpret the past and the present while providing them with knowledge about History.

This approach allows students not only to develop more complex cognitive skills from a constructivist perspective, but it also enables them to acquire learning skills such as research, evidence-based argumentation, or reflection. These critical thinking skills are essential in today's society. If we analyse the current educational law, we can appreciate that it emphasizes the importance of making the students more critical, responsible, active and autonomous citizens (Gómez-Carrasco & Miralles-Martínez, 2017; VanSledrigh, 2004).

In this paradigm, research on historical thinking is becoming more and more relevant, especially in recent years. However, there is a certain disconnection between research and educational experiences in the classroom (Levesque & Clark, 2018). This lack of a relationship is demonstrated in different educational aspects such as the curriculum or teaching resources (e.g., textbooks) and the classroom (Martínez-Hita & Gómez-Carrasco, 2016, 2018). This disconnection explains why it is necessary to continue emphasising the need to carry out a renewal of historical education that pursues the development of historical thinking (Gómez-Carrasco et al., 2018).

Moreover, the gap between historical research and classroom reality is greater in Spain than in other countries (Martínez-Hita, 2022). In England, the development of the History curriculum and textbooks have taken into account the contributions of research, focusing the teaching-learning process of History on historical research (Cooper, 2014; Zarmati, 2019). Consequently, students must use sources to infer information and understand that History is not closed knowledge, but that the past can be interpreted in different ways, while at the same time they must develop critical thinking (Cooper, 2014).

However, Seixas and Morton (2013) devised a way to eliminate this gap and bring the development of historical thinking closer to the classroom by creating activities that work on the "big six" concepts that they believe are the core concepts: cause and consequence, relevance, change and continuity, ethical dimension, historical perspective and sources. Furthermore, they claim that these concepts are the first step towards reflecting on the way History is taught, and that they will enable students to construct History. In other words, they serve as a basis on which to build a new way of teaching History, while encouraging students to make their own interpretations of History. These are the guidelines followed by the curriculum of the province of British Columbia (Canada), which seeks to develop these six historical concepts that students can apply to almost any information and use to solve problems, make choices and convey their ideas in an effective way (Zarmati, 2019).

Making the Classroom an Active Learning Space: The Case of Gamification

Currently, there is a consensus about the possibility of using active and participatory methodologies to carry out this renewal of History teaching. Moreover, introducing emerging technologies, due to their possibilities in the teaching-learning process, is important too. In this regard, authors such as Kori et al. (2014) claim that the use of technology in the classroom promotes inquiry learning and the acquisition of knowledge and skills by students; these can also be developed with the help and assistance of their teachers and technological tools designed to help teachers during the teaching-learning process. Related to this, Miralles-Martínez et al. (2019) have proven that the use of ICT can provide different advantages, such as the promotion of self-regulation, the individualization of the learning process, and a higher level of communication among students, and between students and their teachers. However, although the use of ICT in active methodologies is extensive in many areas, this is not the case in Social Sciences in schools. This statement is justified to some extent by the premise that the didactics of History is at a disadvantage in contrast to other areas of knowledge, such as the experimental sciences, due to the unfeasibility of reproducing historical events (Acosta Barros, 2010). Due to this fact, in order to demystify teaching historical knowledge from a fully traditional perspective, an idea which is very popular in our society, it is necessary to carry out more studies using methodologies that encourage active participation via ICT (Gómez-Carrasco et al., 2020). Thus, in recent years, the design of a theoretical framework that responds to the needs of teachers to enable them to feel qualified to use these methodologies in the teaching of History, and thus improve this didactic, has been strongly encouraged (Miralles-Martínez et al., 2019).

Thus, continuing this line of research in this area in particular is important. Implementing active methodologies and ICT in History classrooms at school could lead to promising results. One of the methodologies or approaches that can combine both options is gamification, due to its active and ludic character. In recent years, gamification has increased in popularity. This can be demonstrated by the numerous experiments and the amount of research carried out that have been published in this field over recent years (Nacke & Deterding, 2017). But what is gamification?

Although it is true that there are many definitions of what we mean by gamification, one of the best known and most widespread is the one proposed by Kapp (2012). This author defines gamification as the integration of characteristics, mechanics and aesthetics of games in non-playful contexts with the main objective of engaging the receivers of this gamification. Related to this, Deterding et al. (2011) summarize this definition in a single sentence: "Gamification is the use of game design elements in non-game contexts" (p. 10). In the educational context, this methodology offers an attractive learning space to students, through motivating experiences, with challenges, rewards, and the use of a token economy. These elements seek to stimulate participation, motivating students to take action; this is essential to achieve the main objective which is to create a meaningful experience, promoting learning by solving problems (Kapp, 2012). So, as we can see, there are precedents in the literature concerning this methodology in which different studies have proven that games can be considered effective pedagogical resources, promoting the acquisition of theoretical content, interest and critical thinking (Talan et al., 2020; Martínez Navarro, 2017). At this point, since its interest and potential have already been stated in the literature, we must consider how to correctly implement gamification within the area of History. For this reason, investigating the elements that make up gamification is necessary.

If we review the current literature on how gamification is integrated into the classroom, related to its development, we can see that gamification is based on the use of different elements, which may vary depending on the framework used (Hunicke et al., 2004; Werback & Hunters, 2012; 2015; Landers et al., 2014; Marczewsky, 2014). These game elements are the ones that act as essential ingredients for the design and planning of a gamified activity (Pujolá & Herrera, 2019). It is the interrelation between these elements that can create an engaging and immersive learning environment (Kapp, 2012). The framework developed by Werbach and Hunter (2012) is one of the most commonly used.

These authors propose a classification of the elements of gamification based around a pyramid with three segments (Figure 1), with the components at the base, the mechanics in the central part and the dynamics at the apex. From the bottom to top, these concepts become more abstract. Components refer to specific implementations of dynamics and mechanics. Some examples of components are achievements,

Figure 1. The Game Element Hierarchy
Source: Werbach and Hunter (2012)

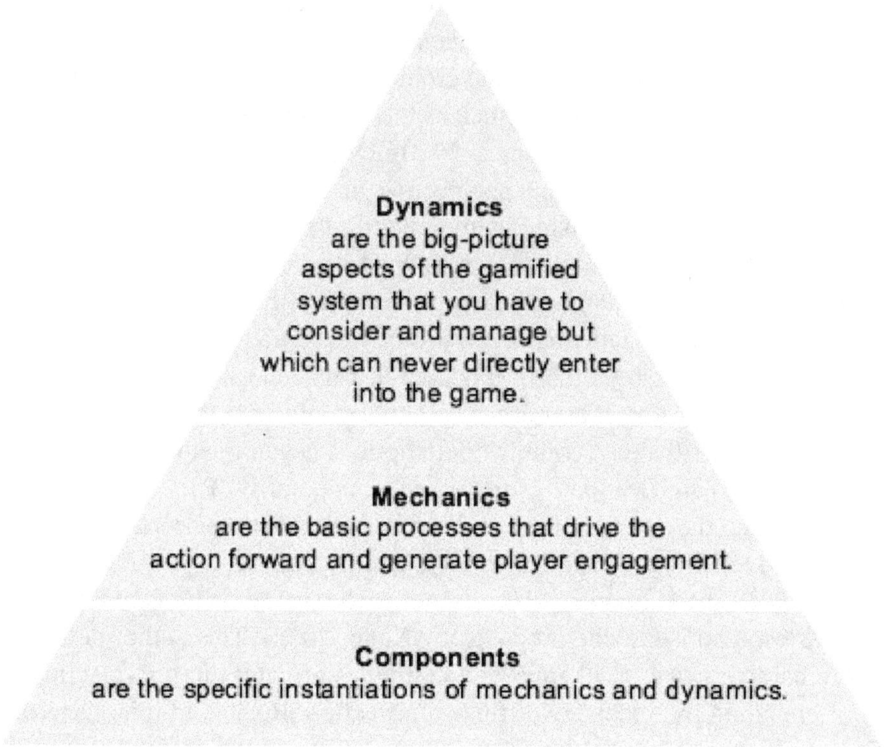

avatars, badges, points, or leaderboards. Mechanics are the processes that produce the development of the game. When we talk about feedback, competition, cooperation, rewards or challenges, the authors are referring to the mechanics of the game. Finally, dynamics are the most abstract group and define the main structure of the game. Examples of dynamics are the proposed restrictions, the relationships with the environment or the narrative of the activity.

It is not necessary to use all the elements to gamify an educational activity. It is enough to adapt the dynamics, the mechanics and the components to the educational context (Prados Sánchez et al., 2021). However, the number of elements used will determine how the activity is gamified and the effects it produces on student motivation (Pujolà & Herrera, 2019). Marczewski (2014) introduces a distinction between thin gamification and deep gamification according to the level of motivation. The former, called thin-layer gamification, is based on the introduction of components into the game, such as points, badges and leaderboards. This type of gamification usually only affects the extrinsic motivation of the students. On the contrary, deep level gamification usually integrates all the elements of gamification (dynamics, mechanics and components). Layer gamification enables the immersion of the student in a relevant and long-lasting activity which tries to stimulate intrinsic motivation.

Although the theoretical foundations set out above concerning gamification are independent of whether the gamified context is digital or non-digital, the vast majority of current examples of gamification in educational contexts are carried out through the use of technology. This conclusion was reached by the systematic review carried out by Zainuddin et al. (2020), in which the current state of the literature on gamification in educational domains is analysed.

Focusing on the History teaching field, we can find interesting proposals and research that revolve around the gamification of learning through immersive, adventure or educational games (serious games) (Cózar-Gutiérrez & Sáez-López, 2016; Rivero, 2017). However, most of the innovative experiences of the application of gamification have focused on Secondary Education and Higher Education, with few examples in Primary Education (Martínez Hita et al., 2021).

Considering this previously described framework, this work aims to contribute to expanding knowledge about the possibilities of uniting historical thinking and gamification through a technology-based gamified environment in a didactic intervention with sixth-year Primary Education students (11-12 years old) and measure their results based on academic performance and motivation. Thus, the present study is focused on the following questions:

- What effect does the use of gamification have on a student's performance compared to a traditional methodology such as teacher-based lessons?
- Is there an improvement in motivation through the use of gamification in History classes compared to the use of a teacher-based methodology?

MATERIALS AND METHODS

Participants

A total of 41 students from two Spanish schools participated in the study. In particular, this study was carried out in the sixth grade of primary education (11-12 years old). All the participants used the same Social Science textbook. However, during the study, while the students from the first school continued with their class dynamic (using the textbook and teacher-based learning), in the second school the gamification dynamic was employed. The students from the first school were the control group (hereinafter, CG), and the students from the second school were the intervention group (hereinafter, IG). Regarding the ethical aspects of data collection and processing, this piece of research was part of a larger project approved by the corresponding committee of the community to which the schools participating in this study belonged.

Design

To analyse the established objectives, we carried out a quasi-experimental study using a quantitative methodology. Measurements were taken before and after the intervention. Then, a pre-post design was developed. Through this design, we intended to discover how the implementation of an active methodology, such as gamification, affects both the academic achievement and motivation of primary school students.

Procedure

At the beginning of the project, both schools were going to study the same curricular contents in Social Sciences: Spanish History in the XIX century. The experimental phase consisted of 5 sessions of

45 minutes each. During these sessions, the procedure followed was the same in each lesson. In each CG session, the traditional teacher-based methodology was used. Firstly, students started the lesson collectively reading the information given in their Social Science textbook. The teacher explained the information and answered any questions that students had. Finally, at the end of the session, the students answered the questions and completed the task given in the textbook. Their answers were checked at the end of the class.

In the IG sessions, the gamification methodology was presented to students as a journalism project. In particular, different historical sources (documents, images, maps, etc.) were distributed among the students. Then, taking into account this information, the students worked in groups to develop their own newspaper. In this newspaper, the students had to depict historical events and life during the XIX century in Spain. In addition, while the students prepared their newspapers autonomously, the teacher in charge of the group distributed points to each student through the digital *ClassDojo* platform. These points were based on different aspects of the teaching-learning process: behaviour, team cooperation, the use of the historical sources and how the students deliberated about them, etc. Finally, although the students could perceive the project as a single task, the teacher had previously divided the theoretical contents, for each session, that the students had to learn by the end of the project. At the end of each session, the students demonstrated what they had learned in each session through a *Kahoot!* quiz. The points attained in this Kahoot! were also integrated in the ClassDojo platform individually for each student.

Instruments and Statistical Analysis

To analyze the effect of gamification on academic performance, an ad hoc test was designed based on the exam models proposed by the publishers of the textbooks normally used in both schools. This test was used with both groups, before and after the implementation of the unit on "Spanish History in the XIX century".

To measure motivation, a reduced instrument of the Instructional Material Motivational Survey (IMMS) by Keller (2010), developed and validated by Loorbach et al. (2015), was used. In this questionnaire, the 36 items of the original version are reduced to the 12 most representative ones, on which the four dimensions motivation is made up of, according to Keller's ARCS model (1987) are based: attention, relevance, confidence and satisfaction. The first arises if the learner notices a gap between his/her current knowledge and the knowledge being acquired; the second depends on the perceived usefulness of that learning; the third one varies according to confidence and it is closely linked to past experiences; and the last one is the dimension on which the previous ones converge, resulting in the prediction of good results during task performance. The motivation is composed of the interaction of these four dimensions. Attention leads to relevance, relevance to confidence and all of them to satisfaction (Cabero et al., 2017). Measurements are made on a five-level Likert-type scale (ranging from 1, strongly disagree, to 5, strongly agree).

All the data collected were exported to a database for analysis using the SPSS version 24 software. After, different descriptive and inferential analyses were carried out; all of them with an alpha level of .05. So, regarding the first objective, a U Mann Whitney test was used to find out significant differences before the intervention between groups, and also to find out if the experimental condition influences the participant's learning score. In relation to the second objective, a Wilcoxon test was used to check the items of the motivational test both before and after the intervention. In addition, an analysis by dimensions was also carried out. Finally, as a measure of the effect size, r is reported for all the comparisons.

According to Cohen (1988), values of 0.1, 0.3 and 0.5 can be interpreted as small, medium and large, respectively.

RESULTS

The results obtained have been divided into sections corresponding to each objective. In the first section, the analysis carried out was to contrast the two methodologies implemented according to the academic achievement of the students. Then, in the second section, the analysis shown was done to contrast the motivation levels of the students by groups.

Differences in Academic Achievement depending on the Methodology

The descriptive statistical data can be seen in Table 1. As can be seen, there is an improvement in academic achievement in both groups. While in the pre-test students from both groups show a low level of knowledge about this topic, there is a greater improvement in knowledge attained in the case of the intervention group which used gamification. To evaluate the statistical effect of this difference, an inferential analysis was analysed.

Table 1. Descriptive statistical data obtained in the pre-test and in the post-test in IG and CG groups

	Group	n	M	SD
Pre-test	CG	19	1.00	.72
	IG	22	.81	.43
Post-test	CG	19	6.31	2.52
	IG	22	8.45	.96

IG: intervention group; gamification methodology; CG: control group; lecture-based methodology.

After checking that the normal assumption was not attained, the Mann Whitney U test was used to compare the results obtained. Regarding the pre-test results, the Mann Whitney U test reported that there was no statistically significant difference between the groups before the intervention (U=178.5; p=.424). However, according to the post-test results, there is a significant difference between the CG and the IG in favour of the latter (U=84.5; p=.001; *r*= 0.5085). Thus, according to these results, it can be seen that before the intervention both groups have a similar level of knowledge about this topic. However, after the intervention phase, the students from the IG achieved a significantly greater academic level. So, the gamification methodology implemented has a positive effect on the students' academic achievement.

Table 2. Results of the motivation questionnaire for each item in the pre-test and post-test

	Pre-M (SD)	Post-M (SD)	Z	*p*
1. The quality of the activities helped to hold my attention.	2.36 (.79)	4.73 (.55)	-4.17	0.000
2. The way the information is arranged helped hold my attention.	2.64 (1.14)	4.73 (.55)	-4.04	0.000
3. The variety of activities helped hold my attention in the class.	2.23 (1.27)	4.82 (.4)	-3.97	0.000
4. It is clear to me how the activities are related to things I already know.	3.45 (1.06)	2.86 (.35)	-2.44	0.015
5. The contents and activities convey the impression that the contents of the lesson are worth knowing.	3.41 (1.3)	4.59 (.5)	-3.13	0.002
6. The contents of the activities will be useful for me.	4.23 (1.07)	4.77 (.43)	-2.23	0.026
7. As I worked with these activities, I was confident that I was going to learn the contents.	3.64 (1.18)	4.46 (.67)	-2.92	0.003
8. After working with these activities for a while, I was confident that I would be able to complete an exam on the subject.	3.36 (1.65)	4.59 (.59)	-2.95	0.003
9. The good organization of the activities helped me be confident that I would learn the contents.	2.91 (1.02)	4.68 (.48)	-3.84	0.000
10. I enjoyed working with these activities so much that I would like to know more about the topics.	1.73 (1.03)	4.55 (.74)	-4.02	0.000
11. I really enjoyed working with these activities.	2.05 (1.05)	4.68 (.57)	-4.15	0.000
12. It was a pleasure to work with such well-designed activities.	2.27 (.99)	4.68 (.48)	-4.14	0.000

Motivational Results within the IG

To check what the students thought about the gamification methodology used, the motivational test was given to them before and after the intervention. Table 2 shows the results obtained by the participants in the IG for each of the items of the Reduced Instructional Material Motivational Survey both in the pre-test and post-test. Also, the values obtained in the test for the comparison of related samples are shown. The Wilcoxon test shows significant differences in all the items presented in the questionnaire.

Based on the analysis by dimensions following Keller's ARCS model (1987, 2010), Table 3 shows the results obtained in each of the four dimensions. These results have also been compared between the pre-test and the post-test. The Wilcoxon test shows significant differences in the four dimensions of the ARCS model. Additionally, the effect sizes can be considered as large-sized. For this reason, we can state that the use of methodologies such as Gamification seems to have a positive impact on the motivation of pupils regarding the teaching of the contents.

DISCUSSION

Emerging technologies have enabled new resources and ways of teaching which are very different from those we had not too many years ago. Renowned reports such as the 2021 Horizon report emphasize the importance of integrating these technologies within the teaching-learning processes precisely for this reason: for the new and diverse pedagogical possibilities that would be unattainable without them (Pelletier et al. 2021). Despite this need for a pedagogical renewal in this area of knowledge, the didactics of History continues to have a marked rote learning and expository character. The teacher, contrary to

Table 3. Total score and partial scores for each dimension in the motivation test for the pre-test and post-test in the intervention group

	Pre-M (SD)	Post-M (SD)	Z	*p*	*r*
Attention	2.41 (.78)	4.76 (.34)	-4.120	0.000	0.6211
Relevance	3.7 (.78)	4.08 (.25)	-2.217	0.027	0.3342
Confidence	3.3 (.98)	4.58 (.37)	-3.852	0.000	0.5807
Satisfaction	2.02 (.73)	4.64 (.33)	-4.123	0.000	0.6216
Total Motivation	2.86 (.65)	4.51 (.25)	-4.109	0.000	0.6195

current pedagogical principles, continues to be the main element of the teaching-learning process, while the students attend these classes passively listen to theoretical contents that they need to memorize to later demonstrate in a final summative assessment (e. g. exam) (Miralles-Martínez et al., 2014; Tirado-Olivares et al., 2021). This way of teaching not only fails to provide students with a solid knowledge base (Miralles-Martínez et al., 2014), but it also contributes to History being seen as closed, boring and useless knowledge (Burenheide, 2007; Liceras, 2016). Against this view, other authors emphasize the need to promote other thinking skills such as reflection, synthesis or argumentation. Something that is synthesized in developing among the students the work that historians carry out during their professional lives. This is understood as the promotion of historical thinking (Domínguez, 2015; Lee & Ashby, 2000; Seixas & Morton, 2013; VanSledright, 2011). For this reason, adopting new active educational methodologies is required (Gómez-Carrasco et al., 2018; Tirado-Olivares et al., 2021).

In this search for innovative pedagogical approaches, the use of methodologies with a markedly practical and playful character are increasingly being used (Pelletier et al., 2021; Gómez-Carrasco et al., 2021). An example of one of the best known of these methodologies is gamification. In relation to this methodology, although there are numerous studies that address the potential benefits of its use during the teaching-learning process (Bai et al., 2020; Huang et al., 2020), there is an evident lack of studies that use it within the didactics of History. For this reason, the main purpose of this study was to contribute to the educational community based on evidence about its use in this area of knowledge. In particular, this study wanted to verify the usefulness of implementing gamification in primary education in relation to the improvement in two of the most important variables to analyse during the teaching-learning process: academic achievement and motivation.

Based on the first objective of this investigation, we can appreciate how the integration of this active methodology has a significantly positive effect on the academic performance of primary school students. Through the pre-test and post-test comparison, we can see that students from both schools had the same knowledge base before the intervention. After the intervention, it can be seen that both the IG and the CG improved their test scores; however, those students who received the gamification lessons improved significantly more compared to those who followed the traditional or lecturer-based classes. According to the current literature, the positive impact appreciated here was also obtained in previous studies (Bai et al., 2020; Sailer & Hommer,2020). However, as mentioned before, few studies have been developed in the area of History (Martinez-Hita et al., 2021). For this reason, the results obtained in this area of knowledge seem to validate more studies similar to the one presented here.

In addition, it is important that the integration of these innovative approaches is carried out considering that at the same time it promotes a better playful context that favours a higher level of student motivation towards the contents of History (Tirado-Olivares et al., 2021). In this regard, in this study the potential of this active and ludic methodology is compared to a traditional or lecturer-based methodology. Based on the motivational results obtained in a reduced version of the Instructional Materials Motivation Survey, there clearly seem to be higher students' motivational levels after the intervention. After the gamification, students show significantly greater levels of motivation based on the all items and dimensions analysed: attention, relevance, confidence and satisfaction. This has also been reported in previous studies (Bai et al., 2020; Huang et al., 2020; Sailer & Homner, 2020). However, this is even more important in our area of knowledge. Different authors have pointed out the alarming motivational situation that students show with regard to knowledge about History (Burenheide, 2007; Martínez-Hita et al., 2021). Something that is justified by the many statements made by students regarding how difficult History is, and that the contents are not very interesting (Liceras, 2016). For this reason, obtaining this significant improvement in motivation towards History classes could mark a line of action worth following in the future.

Limitations and Proposals for Future Research

During the research, new hypotheses arose that could be interesting to examine with the aim of obtaining additional interesting results. Some of them arise from aspects of the study itself that could be improved in future research in order to verify the relevance of the results obtained.

Firstly, one of the most important limitations of the study presented here is the sample size. Despite having two different schools for this study, we were able to access only one class in each centre. Therefore, extending this sample size in future studies would allow for greater external validity of the conclusions drawn here. In addition, although the control group followed their usual lecturer-based class dynamic, the instructor in the sessions was different to their regular schoolteacher. This variable must be taken into account when understanding the data both in performance - reported here - and in motivation - not collected for this group in the present study.

Finally, it would be interesting to carry out further studies using alternative instruments that help researchers to assess not only the academic performance of students, but also the students' acquisition of skills related to historical thinking; following the recommendations of different authors such as Gómez-Carrasco and Miralles-Martínez (2017). The instrument used in the present study was developed to assess the factual contents, but it was not designed to analyse these more complex skills.

All in all, due to the lack of studies in our field similar to the one presented here, the methodology presented here could be a starting point for new ways of approaching History classes at the primary school level.

CONCLUSIONS

Despite the tradition of educational research on the use of gamification and its effects (e.g., Bai et al., 2020; Sailer & Hommer, 2020), there is still a smaller number of studies in the area of social sciences (Martínez-Hita, 2022). In the present study, we have corroborated the statistically significant positive effect of integrating gamification in terms of academic performance in Social Sciences in Primary Education. By integrating elements of the games proposed by Werbach and Hunter (2012) in the teaching-learning process itself, students are not only more motivated to learn, as has also been analysed and verified in this study and corroborated in the literature (e.g. Martínez-Hita et al., 2021), but the learning process has been more effective compared to an expository class based on the use of the textbook too. Thus, after the conclusions obtained in the present study, continuing in this line of research in this area of knowledge is interesting.

ACKNOWLEDGMENT

This work was supported by the MCIN/AEI/10.13039/501100011033 under grant PID2020-113453RB-I00; by the University of Castilla-La Mancha and European Regional Development Funds under grant 2021-grin-31060, and by The Ministry of Universities of Spain under grant FPU20-02375.

REFERENCES

Acosta Barros, L. (2010). La enseñanza-aprendizaje de la historia en bachillerato y las TIC: La introducción de la estrategia Webquest. *Clío: History and History Teaching, 36*(8), 1–10. http://clio.rediris.es/n36/didactica/lmacosta_iehcan.pdf

Bai, S., Hew, K. F., & Huang, B. (2020). Does gamification improve student learning outcome? Evidence from a meta-analysis and synthesis of qualitative data in educational contexts. *Educational Research Review*, *30*, 100322. doi:10.1016/j.edurev.2020.100322

Burenheide, B. (2007). I Can Do This: Revelations on Teaching with Historical Thinking. *The History Teacher*, *41*(1), 55–61.

Cabero, J., Fernández, B., & Marín, V. (2017). Dispositivos móviles y realidad aumentada en el aprendizaje del alumnado universitario. *RIED-Revista Iberoamericana De Educación a Distancia*, *20*(2), 167–185. doi:10.5944/ried.20.2.17245

Cohen, J. (1988). *Statistical power analysis for the behavioral sciences*. Erlbaum.

Cooper, H. (2014). Why Are There No History Text Books in English Primary Schools? *Ensayos. Revista de la Facultad de Educación de Albacete*, *29*(1), 27–42.

Cózar-Gutiérrez, R., & Sáez-López, J. M. (2016). Game-based learning and gamification in initial teacher training in the social sciences: An experiment with MinecraftEdu. *International Journal of Educational Technology in Higher Education*, *13*(2), 2. Advance online publication. doi:10.118641239-016-0003-4

Deterding, S., Dixon, D., Khaled, R., & Nacke, L. (2011) From game design elements to gamefulness: defining "gamification". In *Proceedings of the 15th international academic MindTrek conference: envisioning future media environments*. ACM. 10.1145/2181037.2181040

Domínguez, J. (2015). *Pensamiento histórico y evaluación de competencias*. Graó.

Gómez-Carrasco, C. J., Chaparro Sainz, Á., Felices de la Fuente, M., & Cózar Gutiérrez, R. (2020). Estrategias metodológicas y uso de recursos digitales para la enseñanza de la historia. Análisis de recuerdos y opiniones del profesorado en formación inicial. *Aula Abierta*, *49*(1), 65–74. doi:10.17811/rifie.49.1.2020.65-74

Gómez-Carrasco, C. J., Martínez-Miralles, P., & López-Facal, R. (2021). *Handbook of Research on Teacher Education in History and Geography*. Peter Lang Publishing. doi:10.3726/b18091

Gómez-Carrasco, C. J., & Miralles Martínez, P. (2017). *Los espejos de Clío. Usos y abusos de la Historia en el ámbito escolar*. Sílex.

Gómez-Carrasco, C. J., & Miralles Martínez, P. (2018). Las competencias históricas en perspectiva comparada. Enfoques internacionales sobre su desarrollo y evaluación. *Educatio Siglo XXI*, *36*(1), 11–20.

Gómez-Carrasco, C. J., Ortuño Molina, J., & Miralles Martínez, P. (2018). *Enseñar ciencias sociales con métodos activos de aprendizaje. Reflexiones y propuestas a través de la indagación*. Octaedro.

Huang, R., Ritzhaupt, A. D., Sommer, M., Zhu, J., Stephen, A., Valle, N., Hampton, J., & Li, J. (2020). The impact of gamification in educational settings on student learning outcomes: A meta-analysis. *Educational Technology Research and Development*, *68*(4), 1875–1901. doi:10.100711423-020-09807-z

Hunicke, R., Leblanc, M., & Zubek, R. (2004). MDA: A Formal Approach to Game Design and Game Research. In *Proceedings of the AAAI Workshop on Challenges in Game AI*. AAAI Press.

Kapp, K. (2012). *The gamification of learning and instruction: Game-based methods and strategies for training and education*. John Wiley & Sons.

Keller, J. M. (1987). Development and use of the ARCS model of instructional design. *Journal of Instructional Development*, *10*(3), 2–10. doi:10.1007/BF02905780

Keller, J. M. (2010). *Motivational design for learning and performance: The ARCS model approach*. Springer US. doi:10.1007/978-1-4419-1250-3

Kori, K., Mäeots, M., & Pedaste, M. (2014). Guided reflection to support quality of reflection and inquiry in web-based learning. *Procedia: Social and Behavioral Sciences*, *112*, 242–251. doi:10.1016/j.sbspro.2014.01.1161

Landers, R. N. (2014). Developing a Theory of Gamified Learning. *Simulation & Gaming*, *45*(6), 752–768. doi:10.1177/1046878114563660

Lee, P., & Ashby, R. (2000). Progression in Historical Understanding among Students Ages 7-14. In Knowing, Teaching, and Leaming History: National and Intemational Perspectives (pp. 199-222). University Press.

Lévesque, S., & Clark, P. (2018). Historical Thinking: Definitions and Educational Applications. In S. A. Metzger & L. M. Harris (Eds.), *The Wiley International Handbook of History teaching and Learning* (pp. 119–148). Wiley. doi:10.1002/9781119100812.ch5

Liceras, A. (2016). Las dificultades en la enseñanza y el aprendizaje de las ciencias sociales. In Didáctica de las Ciencias Sociales. Fundamentos, contextos y propuestas (pp. 95-118). Pirámide.

Loorbach, N., Peters, O., Karreman, J., & Steehouder, M. (2015). Validation of the Instructional Materials Motivation Survey (IMMS) in a self-directed instructional setting aimed at working with technology. *British Journal of Educational Technology*, *46*(1), 204–218. doi:10.1111/bjet.12138

López-Facal, R. (2014). La LOMCE y la competencia histórica. *Ayer*, *94*, 273–285.

Marczewski, A. (2014). *Thin Layer vs Deep Level Gamification*. Gamasutra. The Art and Business of Making Games. https://www.gamasutra.com/blogs/AndrzejMarczewski/ 20140120/208924/ Thin_Layer_vs_Deep_Level_Gamification.php

Martínez Hita, M. (2022). *El pensamiento histórico en Educación Primaria. Diseño y evaluación de un programa de intervención gamificado* [Tesis de Doctorado, Universidad de Murcia]. Repositorio Institucional de la Universidad de Murcia.

Martínez-Hita, M., & Gómez, C. J. (2016). Diferentes enfoques sobre la enseñanza de la historia y del pensamiento histórico en el currículo español y canadiense. In J. Maquilón, C. J. Gómez, & M. B. Alfageme (Eds.), De la investigación a la mejora educativa en las aulas (pp. 19–32). Academic Press.

Martínez-Hita, M., & Gómez, C. J. (2018). Nivel cognitivo y competencias de pensamiento histórico en los libros de texto de Historia de España e Inglaterra. Un estudio comparativo. *Review of Education*, *379*, 145–169. doi:10.4438/1988-592X-RE-2017-379-364

Martínez-Hita, M., Gómez-Carrasco, C. J., & Miralles-Martínez, P. (2021). The effects of a gamified project based on historical thinking on the academic performance of primary school children. *Humanities and Social Sciences Communications*, *8*(1), 122. doi:10.105741599-021-00796-9

Martínez Navarro, G. (2017). Tecnologías y nuevas tendencias en educación: aprender jugando. El caso de Kahoot. *Opción: Revista de Ciencias Humanas y Sociales, 33*(83), 252–277. https://produccioncientificaluz.org/index.php/opcion/article/view/23116

Miralles Martínez, P., Gómez Carrasco, C. J., & Monteagudo Fernández, J. (2019). Percepciones sobre el uso de recursos TIC y «MASS-MEDIA» Para la enseñanza de la historia. Un estudio comparativo en futuros docentes de España-Inglaterra. *Educación XX1, 22*(2). doi:10.5944/educxx1.21377

Miralles Martínez, P., Gómez Carrasco, C. J., & Sánchez Ibañez, R. (2014). Dime qué preguntas y te diré qué evalúas y enseñas. Análisis de los exámenes de ciencias sociales en tercer ciclo de Educación Primaria. *Aula Abierta*, *42*(02), 83–89. doi:10.1016/j.aula.2014.05.002

Nacke, L. E., & Deterding, S. (2017). The maturing of gamification research. *Computers in Human Behavior*, *71*, 450–454. doi:10.1016/j.chb.2016.11.062

Pelletier, K., Brown, M., Brooks, D. C., McCormack, M., Reeves, J., Arbino, N., Bozkurt, A., Crawford, S., Czerniewicz, L., Gibson, R., Linder, K., Mason, J., & Mondelli, V. (2021). *2021 EDUCAUSE Horizon Report Teaching and Learning Edition*. EDU. https://www.learntechlib.org/p/219489/

Prados Sánchez, G., Cózar-Gutiérrez, R., del Olmo-Muñoz, J., & González-Calero, J. A. (2021). Impact of a gamified platform in the promotion of reading comprehension and attitudes towards reading in primary education. *Computer Assisted Language Learning*, 1–25. Advance online publication. doi: 10.1080/09588221.2021.1939388

Pujolà, J. T., & Herrera, F. J. (2019). Gamificación. In J. M. Basols, E. Gironzetti, & M. Lacorte (Eds.), *The Routledge Handbook of Spanish Language Teaching. Metodologías, contextos y recursos para la enseñanza del español L2* (pp. 583–595). Routledge.

Rivero, P. (Coord.). (2017). Gamificación para aprender ciencias sociales. *Íber: Didáctica de las ciencias sociales, geografía e historia*, 86.

Rüsen, J. (2012). Tradition: A principle of historical sense-generation and its logic and effect in historical culture. *History and Theory*, *51*(4), 45–59. doi:10.1111/j.1468-2303.2012.00646.x

Sailer, M., & Homner, L. (2020). The Gamification of Learning: A Meta-analysis. *Educational Psychology Review*, *32*(1), 77–112. doi:10.100710648-019-09498-w

Seixas, P., & Morton, T. (2013). The big six historical thinking concepts. Academic Press.

Talan, T., Doğan, Y., & Batdı, V. (2020). Efficiency of digital and non-digital educational games: A comparative meta-analysis and a meta-thematic analysis. *Journal of Research on Technology in Education*, *52*(4), 474–514. doi:10.1080/15391523.2020.1743798

Tirado-Olivares, S., Cózar-Gutiérrez, R., García-Olivares, R., & González-Calero, J. A. (2021). Active learning in History teaching in higher education: The effect of inquiry-based learning and a student response system-based formative assessment in teacher training. *Australasian Journal of Educational Technology*, *37*(5), 61–76. doi:10.14742/ajet.7087

Van Drie, J., & van Boxtel, C. (2008). Historical reasoning: Towards a framework for analyzing students' reasoning about the past. *Educational Psychology Review*, *20*(2), 87–110. doi:10.100710648-007-9056-1

VanSledright, B. A. (2004). What Does It Mean to Think Historically ... and How Do You Teach It? *Social Education*, *68*(3), 230–233.

VanSledright, B. A. (2011). *The Challenge of Rethinking History Education. On Practice, Theories, and Policy*. Routledge.

Werbach, K., & Hunter, D. (2012). *For the Win: How Game Thinking Can Revolutionize Your Business*. Wharton School Press.

Werbach, K., & Hunter, D. (2015). *The Gamification Toolkit: Dynamics, Mechanics, and Components for the Win*. Wharton School Press.

Wineburg, S. (2001). *Historical Thinking and other Unnatural Acts. Charting the Future of Teaching the Past*. Temple University Press.

Zainuddin, Z., Chu, S. K. W., Shujahat, M., & Perera, C. J. (2020). The impact of gamification on learning and instruction: A systematic review of empirical evidence. *Educational Research Review*, *30*, 100326. doi:10.1016/j.edurev.2020.100326

Zarmati, L. (2019). Future of Education and Skills 2030: Curriculum analysis. Learning progression in History. OECD.

Chapter 6
Historical Thinking Development Through Gamification:
Secondary Education and Teacher Training Applications

Borja Aso
University of Zaragoza, Spain

Alodia Rubio-Navarro
University of Zaragoza, Spain

Silvia García-Ceballos
University of Zaragoza, Spain

EXECUTIVE SUMMARY

In recent years, the literature has identified the need to influence teacher training so that teachers promote historical thinking metaconcepts and innovative methodological strategies that actually encourage learning of these history skills in the classroom. To that end, n=36 students of the Master's Degree in Teaching in Secondary Education at the University of Zaragoza (Geography and History specialty) were presented with two gamified experiences for secondary education, developed during the pandemic, so they could reflect on their usefulness, benefits, and possible challenges or limitations. Based on the preservice teachers' evaluation, their prior conceptions of the usefulness of gamification in encouraging historical thinking skills and the educational scope of introducing good practices in teacher training were analyzed using mixed methods research.

INTRODUCTION

As a result of the COVID-19 pandemic, lockdown measures were imposed in Spain from March 2020,

DOI: 10.4018/978-1-6684-5240-0.ch006

forcing students to continue their education online until the end of the academic year in June. As in many other countries, the following academic years at Spanish education centers have involved restrictions such as the use of masks, limits on sharing materials, and social distancing. The academic consequences of all these measures still persist, since a drop in student performance and motivation has been detected worldwide (Hoofman & Secord, 2021; Moliner & Alegre, 2021).

In this context of the "new normal," many social sciences teachers have continued to bring ideas to their classrooms to foster historical thinking skills while addressing their students' new educational needs. Consequently, the alternative of designing gamified activities fulfills both aspirations, since research has shown the ability of this method to impact students' historical reasoning and encourage their engagement (Colomo-Magaña et al., 2020; Martínez-Hita et al., 2021; Martínez-Hita & Miralles-Martínez, 2020).

Two gamified activities for fostering historical reasoning during the secondary education stage are presented below; one has been designed specifically to deal with the "new normal" circumstances, and the other dates from before the pandemic but has been adapted. Although both incorporate gamification elements, the new activity could be defined as non-tech and the adapted one as low-tech, since they aim to limit excessive exposure to the digital resources students experienced during lockdown.

Despite garnering positive results in the teachers' evaluation of these proposals in terms of student learning and rating, it was decided that both would be assessed by experts, namely n=48 students of the Master's Degree in Teaching in Secondary Education at the University of Zaragoza (Geography and History specialty). Taking advantage of the inclusion of both activities in the master's degree program, the preservice teachers' level of training in this method was also analyzed, as well as their prior conceptions about the potential of gamification to develop historical thinking metaconcepts. The main objective of presenting these activities to preservice teachers is, therefore, to subject the gamified proposals to external evaluation to identify their strengths, limitations, and aspects that can be improved. There are three other secondary objectives: 1) analyzing preservice teachers' conception of the usefulness of gamification in developing historical thinking; 2) checking whether experimenting with and evaluating good practices contribute to improving this prior conception; and 3) evaluating whether presenting good practices and experiencing them give teachers more tools to design gamified activities than the theoretical explanation of this method type.

BACKGROUND

Gamification. Definition and Educational Applications

The term "gamification," used for the first time in relation to the field of digital communication (Werbach & Hunter, 2012), has been around for just two decades. After these dynamics became popular and spread to other environments, such as business, health and education, Deterding et al. (2011) coined a definition of gamification common to the fields where it is applied: "the use of game design elements in non-game contexts" (p. 10). Although this broad characterization of gamification can be extrapolated to many fields, several authors have tried to provide a more precise definition of the elements needed to design and evaluate gamified learning activities. Educational gamification has been defined as a "a set of activities and processes to solve problems related to learning and education by using or applying the games mechanics" (Kim et al., 2018, p. 29) as well as "the introduction of game mechanics and dynamics in the classroom" (Rivero, 2017, p. 5). These definitions refer to a series of elements or categories—"mechanics" and "dynamics"—that must also be specified. Although several authors have suggested varying classifications (Deterding et al., 2011; Robson et al., 2015; Werbach & Hunter, 2012), the characteristics identified by Kapp (2012) have been taken as a reference here, since they specifically refer to education.

- **Mechanics:** These are dynamics that structure most of the games, such as the use of levels, scoring systems, or time limits.
- **Aesthetics:** These refer to game appearance, such as the attractive design of activities or graphics (if using a virtual platform).
- **Game thinking:** For Kapp this is the distinctive feature of gamification compared with another type of activity, which requires the integration of "competition, cooperation, exploration, and story-telling" (Kapp, 2012, p. 11). This category would include the "dynamics" other authors refer to.

When we refer to gamification for educational purposes, there is also some disagreement, or confusion, between the terms "gamification," "serious games," "serious gaming," and "game-based learning." Some contemporary definitions of these terms have been constructed on the association of "game" with "video game," or digital platform (Belova & Zowada, 2020; Boyle et al., 2011; Deterding et al., 2011). Marczewski (2015) establishes a categorization that differentiates between gamified strategies aspiring to immersion in the virtual world and those that do not. Consequently, he maintains that gamification would be those proposals incorporating game aesthetics and game elements, while "serious games" are those including the virtual world and game play. For all this, the definition of gamification cannot be limited to just digital formats or the use of video games, although it is true that most proposals use this type of technology (Buckley & Doyle, 2016).

The real scope of games and gamification as strategies to encourage motivation and learning is still uncertain. Some studies have highlighted a positive effect on students as they acquire skills and content and also become more interested and engaged in learning (Bai et al., 2020; Buckley & Boyle, 2016; Kapp, 2012; Putz et al., 2020; Sailer & Homner, 2019; Yildiz et al., 2021). However, some researchers have diagnosed a negative long-term impact on students' satisfaction, motivation, and performance (Hanus & Fox, 2015; Hernández-Fernández et al., 2020; Sanchez et al., 2020), while others have simply emphasized how difficult it is to determine the type of learning outcomes games provide (Connolly et al., 2012).

Historical Thinking and How It Is Developed Through Gamification

In the specific case of history instruction, gamification has been singled out because it has the potential to bring about a necessary updating of methodologies linked to fostering historical thinking skills (Martínez-Hita et al., 2021). These skills—also known as second-order concepts or metaconcepts—could be defined as the typical abilities of a professional historian and the aim of introducing them in history instruction is for students to be capable of reasoning with past data and of giving meaning to historical narratives. Consequently, rather than dispensing with knowledge of past events, processes and figures (first-order contents), these skills imply students understand and use this knowledge critically beyond simple rote memorization (Lévesque, 2008; Seixas & Morton, 2013; Seixas & Peck, 2004; VanSledright, 2011; Wineburg, 2001). This curricular focus therefore requires new methodological approaches and new evaluation systems in which students play a leading role and are given opportunities to reason historically rather than only memorize information (Metzer & Harris, 2018). Nevertheless, even though international efforts to incorporate methodological approaches fostering historical thinking can be seen in many curricula, textbooks, and teachers, Spain seems to have been more reticent in incorporating this curricular focus (Gómez-Carrasco et al., 2018; Martínez-Hita & Gómez-Carrasco, 2017; Moreno-Vera & Alvén, 2020).

As mentioned, gamification has proved to be a methodological strategy capable of sparking students' interest in educational content. Furthermore, several studies have stressed that gamification can improve learning outcomes in the subject of history in both primary (Li et al., 2019) and secondary education (Alshikhabobakr et al., 2020). Besides this motivational and learning improvement of first-order contents the question remains as to how far gamification actually manages to develop historical thinking skills: Can it help students establish causality relationships between several events? Can it give them tools to determine the current relevance of a past event?

Hardly any studies explore this line of educational research. Nonetheless, the research on primary education by Martínez-Hita & Miralles-Martínez (2020) and by Martínez-Hita et al. (2021) has recently produced some favorable results concerning the gamification–historical thinking symbiosis. Despite these pioneering attempts, there are still huge gaps in the study of inter-relationships between both fields. We believe it is essential to explore, first, the specific way in which this methodology fosters each of the skills forming this type of reasoning, as well as the cognitive processes these skills require, and, second, the reasons why barely any research has focused on applying case studies combining gamification and historical thinking in secondary education, or on their actual effectiveness, despite both gaining in popularity in recent decades.

Teachers' View of Gamification and Historical Thinking

To learn the possible reasons for the scarcity of research proposals on gamification applications to develop historical thinking in secondary education, at least two possible causes of this lack of case studies must be examined.

On the one hand, it would be reasonable to assume that some history teachers have never thought about combining gamification and historical thinking in their classes as their previous educational experiences are a determining factor in their later teaching performance (Monteagudo-Fernández et al., 2020). Since history instruction in Spanish education is still marked by the influence of the expository-reproductive method and overuse of textbooks (Gómez-Carrasco et al., 2018), many teachers of this subject likely reproduce the curricular methods and approaches they experienced in their early phases of education. Consequently, appropriate training of preservice teachers, which also includes experiencing methods and approaches that some have not previously been exposed to, could be crucial to break the continuity of these dynamics.

On the other hand, inservice and preservice teachers' conceptions of gamification or historical thinking could be negative. However, research has shown that teachers generally take a favorable stance toward the use of gamification in the classroom (Mee et al., 2020; Sajinčič et al., 2022; Sánchez-Mena & Martí-Parreño, 2017). In the particular case of history and social sciences instruction, this positive view is maintained and focuses on this methodological strategy's ability to increase students' motivation and active participation, encourage creativity and skill development, and foster the integration of learning as its main strength (Colomo-Magaña et al., 2020; Cózar-Gutiérrez & Sáez-López, 2016). Yet, one factor that dissuades teachers from applying gamified strategies in the classroom is their perception of how hard it is to design these activities as they do not believe they are skilled enough for this process (Cózar-Gutiérrez & Sáez-López, 2016; Sánchez-Mena & Martí-Parreño, 2017). It is difficult to evaluate the possible conception teachers in Spain may have of strategies to foster historical thinking, since most preservice teachers demonstrate no or scant familiarization with this type of reasoning and, therefore, a lack of knowledge of it (Sáiz-Serrano & López-Facal, 2015; Sáiz-Serrano et al., 2018).

To mitigate these factors, teacher training must provide opportunities to discover methodological approaches that differ from traditional ones, and to be educated in areas where teachers have or recognize shortcomings. Consequently, one possibility is presenting good practices that have successfully managed to combine gamification and historical thinking; by experiencing them, preservice teachers will not only have the option to reflect theoretically on the contributions and potential of these activities, but they can also train practically in strategies and tools that they can then use in their history classrooms. Several gamified experiences have been implemented in the classrooms of both the primary education degree and the master's degree in teacher training to check their instructional effectiveness in higher education. However, few studies have analyzed what preservice teachers think about their usefulness after experimenting with these practices (Figg & Jaipal-Jamani, 2018), and those focused on social sciences teachers are even more limited (Colomo-Magaña et al., 2020).

TWO CASES FOR HISTORY INSTRUCTION IN SECONDARY EDUCATION

Two learning experiences were selected to work on gamification possibilities as a method to develop historical thinking in the master's degree in teacher training at the University of Zaragoza (Table 1). These had been designed by members of the ARGOS research group in social sciences didactics, which is part of the same university. There were three reasons for selecting them:

1. They are for use in secondary education—the stage which the master's degree concerns—but with completely different levels: first year of compulsory secondary education (12–13 years old) and first year of post-compulsory secondary education (16–17 years old). As a result, preservice teachers can observe various educational strategies depending on the students' level of cognitive development.
2. Neither requires a digital platform for implementation, which attempts to refute the generalized association among the preservice teachers in the sample that gamification consists of adapting or developing video games for education.
3. They have been rated positively or they have led to good learning outcomes among the secondary school students they were designed for.

Case 1. Escape Room on the Cold War

The main objective of this educational project is to create attractive learning environments and proposals to work on the metaconcepts of historical thinking, specifically those linked to primary source work, understanding historical multicausality (cause and consequence), and continuity and change. The activity

Table 1. Main elements of the cases presented in the Teachers Master's Degree

	"Archaeology to Discover Hellas"	"Escape Room on the Cold War"
Subject and level	Geography and history, first year of compulsory secondary education	Contemporary world history, first year of post-compulsory secondary education
School and academic year	Secondary Education School "Ramón y Cajal", 2020–2021	School "La Salle Santo Ángel", 2017–2018 / 2019–2020 / 2020–2021
Educational objectives	• To extract information from several textual sources and be able to use it to generate or corroborate explanations for several events and historical-cultural processes. • To acquire specific vocabulary on the main economic, social, cultural, and artistic aspects of the Greek civilization. • To list the main periods of Greek civilization and to identify their timeframe and geographical location.	• To develop cooperative working strategies and to spark interest in the subject and the content studied. • To use information and communication technologies (ICTs) critically. • To understand the causes and consequences of the Cold War, as well as its various stages and the most important events that enable students to recognize the main characteristics of the two opposing socioeconomic models (capitalist and communist).
Content	• Geographical framework of the Greek civilization. Chronological framework and the series of periods from the Cretan civilization to Hellenism. • Timelines and other resources for understanding synchronic and diachronic processes in the past. Techniques for interpreting maps and other cartographic tools. • Dialogue and cooperative work for learning. Value of Greek heritage and cultural legacy.	• Formation of the communist block versus the capitalist block: the Cold War. • Social and cultural characteristics of two different political models: communism and capitalism. • United States and the USSR as models. The two superpowers. • Conflicts: from the Cold War to peaceful coexistence and détente. • The USSR and popular democracies. • The emergence of Gorbachev: *perestroika* and *glasnost*. The disintegration of the USSR: CIS, Russian Federation and the new former Soviet republics. • The fall of the Berlin Wall and the development of central and eastern European countries.
Timing	• 3rd term. • 3 sessions (50 minutes).	• 3rd term. • 4 sessions (55 minutes).
Metaconcept worked on	• Use of sources.	• Cause and consequence. • Historical evidence (use of sources). • Continuity and change.
Method	• Non-tech gamification. • Cooperative learning.	• Low-tech gamification. • Cooperative learning.
Resources	• Cards printed with clues. • PowerPoint presentation. • Reward cards. • Textbook.	• Several clues (newspaper cuttings, images, printed texts, QR code, video, web pages). • Textbook. • Students' digital devices.

Source: Own (2022)

aims to create a work context related to the world of espionage, as this was a vital tool during the Cold War. A series of "enticing" enigmas has been designed based on this context; students have to solve them in an orderly fashion and then write about them in a final research report. This learning experience adopts the characteristics of escape room activities, whose effectiveness for academic improvement has already been reported by authors such as Eukel & Morrell (2021) and Li et al. (2019).

This educational project on the Cold War has been designed for implementation in the contemporary world history subject in the first year of post-compulsory secondary education with a mean class size of thirty divided into teams. It is estimated to last around four class sessions (55 minutes per session).

Table 2. Textual and photographic historical sources worked on in the Cold War project depending on the students' teams

	Textual historical source	Photographic historical source
Team 1	Zhdanov: Cominform inaugural speech	Vietnam War
Team 2	On the missile crisis	Missiles to Cuba
Team 3	Warsaw Pact	Mathias Rust in Red Square
Team 4	NATO	Assassination of JFK
Team 5	Winston Churchill on the Iron Curtain	Checkpoint Charlie
Team 6	Yuri Gagarin and the space race	Yuri Gagarin
Team 7	Truman Doctrine	Fall of the Berlin Wall

Source: Own (2022)

The students need electronic devices and text manuals to perform the activity, since many of the clues have to be solved using technology.

In the first session, each group receives a sealed envelope differing in size, shape, and content. The enigmas included in the envelope have a letter of the Greek alphabet on the right side, which tells the students the order in which to solve the enigmas. The envelope also includes some clues to solve the enigmas. From an educational viewpoint, the enigmas can be grouped into two levels: general or specific. The general part focuses on knowledge of the Cold War in a broad sense—definition, causes and consequences, stages, and so on—while the specific part seeks to delve more deeply into more concrete aspects of the period. In this part, each group has to solve different enigmas depending on the envelope they have been given, since each contains different photographic and textural primary historical sources (Table 2).

Given that uncertainty and the enigma dominate the classroom, several analog and digital resources and materials are used. Every team starts with a sealed envelope with a series of papers inside: a photograph (with a link to the Padlet platform at the bottom); a press cutting with notes; a card with a graphic explanation of Greek orders; a napkin with a series of numbers written on it that the students have to decipher; a library catalog card that reads "Summary-Truman Doctrine (Marshall Plan) vs. Zhdanov Doctrine (COMECON)"; a primary historical source; and a small piece of paper saying "WrIT eA CoMmMEntarYonTheeE hIStorrRical soUrce dentro." In addition, hidden underneath one of each group's tables is a QR code linking to a video on the digital platform YouTube; watching it extends the series of numbers written on the napkin and enables the students to solve the enigma with the help of the text manual: the numbers correspond to the page, line and word numbers.

Our challenge as history teachers lies in creating attractive learning contexts and proposals that make it possible to engage students' interest and emotions, thereby activating a series of cognitive processes whose aim is to work on historical thinking metaconcepts, the ultimate goal of our teaching (Figure 1).

In this project we propose, on the one hand, to combine curricular content (the Cold War) with gamification (the escape room) and the use of technologies, and, on the other, to work on three of the six historical thinking metaconcepts: cause and consequence, historical evidence (source work), and continuity and change.

The results obtained from both the students' evaluation and the project itself—the teacher's journal and the ad hoc rubric are used as assessment tools to evaluate the students' research report—invite us

Figure 1. Students working on their respective projects and solving the proposed enigmas
Source: Photographs taken by the authors (2017/2018)

to continue along the path of educational innovation and research with actual possibilities of changing the paradigm in history instruction in third millennium classrooms.

Case 2. Archaeology to Discover Hellas

VanSledright (2014) defines evidence work as a staple supporting a historian's method and, as a consequence, as the starting point of historical reasoning. Familiarization with this second-order concept—consisting of identifying, contextualizing, interpreting, corroborating, and evaluating past testimonies on which historical discourse is based—is therefore revealed as a prior requisite in the first stages of historical thinking, which are the foundations on which other metaconcepts can be developed, such as perspective (VanSledright, 2014) or historical empathy (Lee, 1983). Consequently, after diagnosing that students in the first year of compulsory secondary education, in which the geography and history subject was taught in the academic year 2020–2021, had not worked on historical thinking skills in primary education, it was decided to introduce them to this type of reasoning through source work.

Taking the specifications of the Spanish curriculum as a starting point, which state that first-year students of compulsory secondary education must be capable of classifying and identifying historical sources, the aim is to go one step further by requiring students to work critically with these sources. To that end, an experience was designed aiming to initiate n=78 students in evidence work while adhering to the content in the Classical Greece block of the educational curriculum. Students are asked to reconstruct the series of civilizations and periods of ancient Greece as a terminological, chronological, and geographical framework for working on the rest of the educational unit. Nevertheless, the task is tackled from a constructivist focus: based on an analysis of a series of primary and secondary sources, the students work out the changes that took place in antiquity around the Aegean Sea. The design adapts to the limitations imposed by the context: restricted use of digital devices at the school and health measures due to COVID-19.

Considering the cognitive demand of the activity, since the students have not previously worked with historical thinking metaconcepts, a gamified method is used to introduce it in the classroom and encourage the students' interest and engagement in the proposed task. The scant availability of textual sources on the Cretan and Mycenaean civilizations is the reason why this proposal is inspired by a simulation of

Figure 2. Back and front of the first clue (α)
Source: Own (2021)

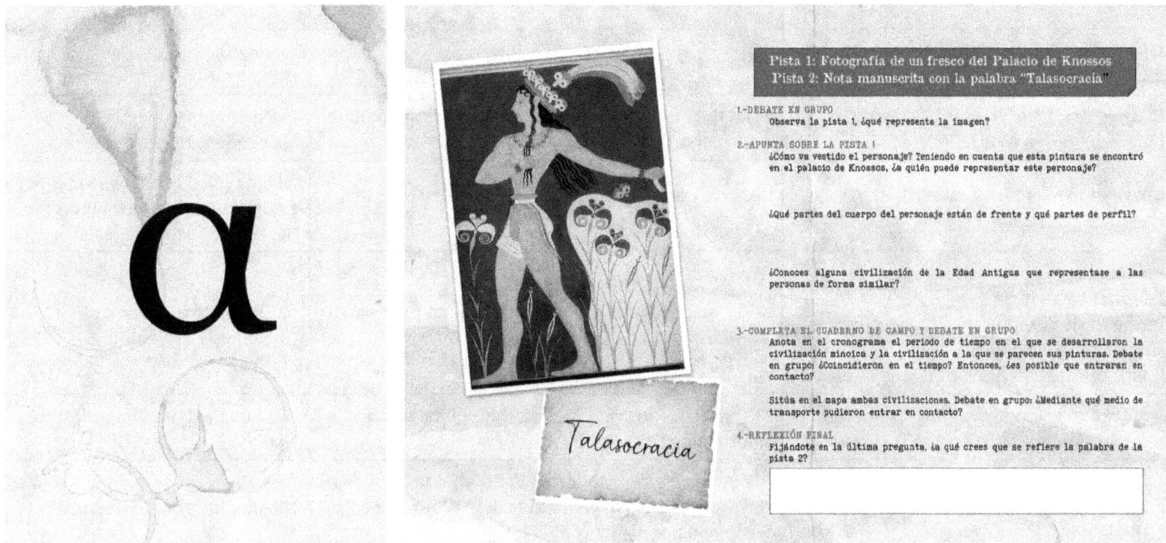

the archaeological method, resulting in the students analyzing archaeological sites and pieces of art. This decision is backed by the educational and motivational benefits stemming from introducing archaeology in formal education, as well as by their proven ability to encourage historical reasoning (Egea-Vivancos & Arias-Ferrer, 2018; Mendioroz-Lacambra & Erce-Domínguez, 2020).

Consequently, the activity is introduced into the classroom based on the following premise, which, in turn, defines the aesthetics component of gamification.

For some months, you have been training to be archaeologists at the prestigious Huesca Institute of Pyrenean Archaeology, led by the archaeologist Honor Frost. After spending several weeks excavating with her in Greece, on returning to Huesca she has realized that her field journal has gone missing on the flight back from Athens to Huesca. In teams, you archaeologists must go back to visit the most important sites and monuments of ancient Greece to try to fill in her field journal again. This will lead you to face several challenges, although you will also be rewarded for your efforts. The team with the most complete and rigorous journals will have the honor of disseminating them to the scientific community (they will be published in Google Classroom) and will receive the title of Young Promise of Pyrenean Archaeology.

Alongside the activity presentation, a series of cards identified with letters of the Greek alphabet are distributed among the group tables (Figure 2).

The first challenge is, therefore, to order the clues correctly following an alphabetical criterion. All the student groups will uncover the clues as the teacher guides them on a "tour" through ancient Greece using a presentation of images. At the same time, they must note down the information they deem relevant in an individual "field journal" that the teacher will use as an assessment tool. A challenge associated with a particular source is proposed in every stage resulting in a total of six activities focused on the evidence work aspects proposed by Seixas & Morton (2013) (Table 3).

Table 3. Sources, challenges and evidence work aspects that the clues lead to

Source	Challenge	Evidence work aspects (Seixas & Morton, 2013)
Image of *The Prince of the Lilies* fresco (Palace of Knossos)	"What was the thalassocracy?"	Taking the context into consideration
• Image of the Lion Gate (Mycenae) • Fragment of *The Oresteia*	"Did the mask that Schliemann found really belong to a man called Agamemnon?"	Corroborating inferences: checking against other sources
• Image of the Dipylon krater • Fragment of *The Odyssey*	"Are two sources enough to tell us everything that happened over a period of 400 years?"	Asking good questions to propel a study (inductive reasoning, from the source to the context)
• Map of Greek colonization around the Mediterranean Sea • Image of the sculptures of Riace Warriors (Calabria) and the god Asclepius (Empuries) • Image of the sculpture of Perseus (Athens)	"Can we prove that culture in the colonies was the same as culture in the metropolis?"	Corroborating inferences (hypothesis validation)
• Image of the painting *Pericles' Funeral Oration* (Philipp von Foltz, 1852)	"Which questions can we ask this source to get information?"	Asking good questions to propel a study
• Fragment of *Parallel Lives*	"Is Plutarch's description of the Battle of Granicus the same as a Persian would make? Which aspects would change and why?"	Making insightful inferences

Source: Own (2022)

The aim of the rewards each group can obtain on correctly solving every challenge is to facilitate solving the next ones (Figure 3), while the final reward consists of showing the field journal on the Google Classroom platform, which fosters cooperative learning as these materials help other students prepare for the final assessment test. As in the previous case, pointification is avoided, and badge systems or leaderboards are not used as they have been proved to promote social comparison and decrease intrinsic motivation (Hamari et al., 2014; Hanus & Fox, 2015).

EXPERIMENTATION AND EVALUATION OF CASES BY PRESERVICE TEACHERS

Method

The above-described cases are presented to n=48 students of the Master's Degree in Teaching in Secondary Education at the University of Zaragoza (Geography and History specialty) during the academic year 2021–2022. Given that the objectives pursued by introducing the activities into the master's degree are obtaining ratings on both and analyzing preservice teachers' perceptions of the gamification and historical thinking binomial, our work is based on mixed-method research combining qualitative and quantitative approaches—backed in studies into social sciences didactics by authors such as Barton (2005) and Grant (2001). Two ad hoc questionnaires were designed for data collection. They include open-ended questions and rating scales (five-point Likert scale). The open-ended questions were chosen so as not to determine the students' responses, thus allowing possible implicit beliefs or conceptualizations to emerge. It also prevents the perspective of the authors of both cases from conditioning the results, since they are also the authors of the questionnaire. A pre-post testing methodology was adopted for the rating scales. This

Figure 3. Rewards for the various challenges
Source: Own (2021)

method attempts to determine the impact of experiencing activities on teachers' conceptions of potential uses of gamification. As 12 students did not fully complete the post-test, the final sample was n=36 participants; the corresponding 12 questionnaires were excluded from the initial test.

The questions included in both questionnaires (pre-test and post-test) are in line with the following research objectives (Table 4):

1. Evaluating positive aspects, aspects that can be improved, and the limitations of both cases;
2. Describing the students' level of familiarization with gamified proposals in social sciences and their general perception of these proposals;
3. Analyzing the level of usefulness that the students allocate to gamification to encourage historical thinking;
4. Discovering the students' self-perception of their knowledge of gamification and valuing the usefulness of practical examples in their training.

Results

Below are the results categorized on the basis of their research objective.

Table 4. Categorization and type of questions in the questionnaires (pre- and post-test)

	Question
RO1	1_post: What are the strong points of the Cold War game of clues for working on the causality metaconcept in the first year of post-compulsory secondary education? Which weaknesses or limitations can it have? 2_post: For the Cold War proposal, to what extent do you think historical thinking metaconcepts are worked on? 3_post: What are the strong points of "Archaeology to Discover Hellas" for working on the source work metaconcept in the first year of compulsory secondary education? Which weaknesses or limitations can it have? 4_post: For the Hellas proposal, to what extent do you think historical thinking metaconcepts are worked on? 5_post: In general terms, which difficulties did you come across in the gamified proposals when developing historical thinking metaconcepts?
RO2	1_pre: Do you know of any gamified proposal related to social sciences instruction? 2_pre: What do you think are the main benefits of introducing gamified proposals in the classroom? 3_pre: Do you think it could have any negative impacts? Which one(s)? 4_pre: What do you think are the difficulties a teacher faces in introducing gamification in the classroom?
RO3	5_pre and 7_post: Gamification is a strategy that only motivates students. 6_pre and 7_post: Gamification can help develop historical thinking metaconcepts. 7 pre and 8_post: Gamification should be introduced in the secondary classroom to foster historical thinking metaconcepts. 10_pre: To which extent would you include gamified proposals in the classroom to teach social sciences? 6_post: In which stage do you think it is more appropriate to develop historical thinking metaconcepts?
RO4	8_pre and 10_post: I feel sufficiently trained to be capable of designing a gamified proposal based on historical thinking metaconcepts. 9_pre: The master's degree in teacher training should allocate more time to training in active methods such as gamification. 11_post: The presentation of practical examples has given me ideas and strategies to design gamified proposals based on historical thinking metaconcepts.

Source: Own (2022)

RO1: Evaluating Positive Aspects, Aspects That Can Be Improved and the Limitations of Both Cases

An emerging categorization is made of the participants' ratings of the activities (Table 5). The highest rated aspects in both are their ability to spark students' interest. Case 1 is highlighted specifically for its constructivist approach, while most participants attribute case 2 with a high ability to reason historically with students using evidence. Concerning aspects that can be improved or difficulties that may be involved in implementing the activity, they say that case 1 can take up too much teacher planning time and make it complex to control the various groups, compared with case 2, in which the participants mostly emphasize its excessive cognitive complexity.

Concerning the ability both proposals to encourage historical reasoning, both activities are rated with 3.78 points out of a scale of 5. When asked for a qualitative analysis of the possible limitations of these cases in conveying historical thinking approaches to secondary education (Q5_post), there is a wide range of responses that are hard to classify. Responses unrelated to the category asked about were given by 33.3%. Several participants pointed out the difficulty of first-order contents as a hindrance to working on metaconcepts in detail (19.4%), as well as the large number of time resources both activities require from the teacher (8.3%). In general, 27.8% of preservice teachers provide responses revealing a low level of understanding of historical thinking; they insist on the idea that all metaconcepts must be worked on simultaneously—therefore conceiving them as an indivisible whole—or justify it as an approach that students must assimilate subconsciously.

They can't all be covered at once; some have to be combined. [P3]

Table 5. Emerging categorization of responses to Q1_post and Q3_post

Positive aspects	Case 1	Case 2	Aspects that can be improved and limitations	Case 1	Case 2
Fosters motivation and engagement	61.1%	52.1%	Possible lack of motivation and engagement	8.3%	
Fosters student autonomy	22.2%		Excessive student autonomy		16.7%
Fosters cooperative learning and suitable active method approach	33.3%		Possible timing or development problems	41.7%	8.3%
Quantity and appropriate detail of first-order concepts	16.7%	25%	Scant development of first-order concepts	13.9%	
Fosters the specific metaconcept guiding the proposal	13.9%	58.3%	Scant development of the specific metaconcept guiding the proposal	11.1%	
Appropriate introduction for students to typical historical thinking methods	11.1%	13.9%	Excessive difficulty of the activity	30.6%	47.2%

Source: Own (2022)

The main difficulties I find are that they get more involved in the research task than in the task of assimilating them subconsciously. [P8]

Only one participant (2.8% of the sample) shows appropriate understanding of historical thinking and rates the drawbacks that gamification may involve for developing it, although their reflection is general and not focused on the presented cases.

The game dynamics may limit our possibilities for developing some concepts. Historical empathy, for example, could be supplanted by the fun dynamics of gamification. Nonetheless, other metaconcepts, such as change and continuity, could be worked on using it, in their own way. Game dynamics could help us highlight these factors, depending on the approach. Ultimately, it would depend on the type of concept to be worked on and on the dynamics applied. [P17]

RO2: Describing the Students' Level of Familiarization with Gamified Proposals in Social Sciences and Their General Perception of These Proposals

In Q1_pre, 77.8% of the participants say they know about gamified proposals for social sciences, and they provide examples such as MinecraftEdu, ClassCraft, or others worked on in subjects in the master's degree in teacher training. Concerning the benefits of gamification (Q2_pre), they cite their ability to motivate students and make content more interesting (66.7%), to facilitate understanding (25%), and, to a lesser extent, to foster significant learning, interdisciplinarity, digital skills, and historical reasoning (13.9%). The main negative aspects highlighted in Q3_pre are that students only focus on the fun aspects (83.3%), that it furthers competitiveness (27.8%), the content is not worked on in depth (11.1%), and that it is hard to apply in the educational context (8.3%). Out of the preservice teachers, 19.4% do not see any drawbacks to gamification. The difficulties that teachers can have in introducing gamification into their classroom (Q4_pre) are: not managing to produce proposals that attract their students' interest (66.7%), training shortcomings in designing games and digital platforms (58.3%), the lack of material and time resources (44.4%), and meeting with possible disapproval from the school or legal guardians (11.1%).

Table 6. Mean scores of RO3 items in a Likert scale

Item	Pre-test	Post-test
Gamification is a strategy that only motivates students	2.56	2.67
Gamification can help develop historical thinking metaconcepts	3.89	4
Gamification should be introduced in the secondary classroom to foster historical thinking metaconcepts	3.56	4.11
Extent to which participants would include gamified proposals in the classroom to teach social sciences	2.22	-

Source: Own (2022)

RO3: Analyzing the Level of Usefulness That the Students Allocate to Gamification to Encourage Historical Thinking

The results obtained on the students' perception of the use of gamification as a strategy to foster historical thinking are presented in Table 6.

Concerning Q6_post, 77.8% of the recorded responses point out that historical thinking skills must be improved in any educational stage by adjusting the activities to the students' cognitive development level. The remaining 21.2% of the participants consider that metaconcepts should only be introduced in the last academic years of secondary education.

For the post-compulsory secondary education stage because I believe their cognitive level has developed sufficiently to arrive at the conclusions we want them to reach. If done for a lower stage, besides them not being able to understand anything because they don't know it in depth, they are just going to play and try to solve the "Clue" game, thus missing out on the objective, which is knowledge of the Cold War; this all stems from not knowing the subject and the lack of context. [P26]

RO4: Discovering the Students' Self-Perception of Their Knowledge of Gamification and Valuing the Usefulness of Presenting Practical Examples

Preservice teachers exhibit a desire for the master's degree to give more prominence to training in active methodologies and a low rating of their current ability to design gamified proposals. Experimenting with the presented cases partially improves the latter aspect (0.45 points), although the experience is rated very positively (Table 7).

Discussion of the Results

The evaluation performed by the preservice teachers after experiencing the two gamified proposals comprises ratings that mostly focus on positive aspects; it allocates both a relatively high ability to foster historical thinking in secondary education (3.78 points out of a scale of 5). More than half of the participants rate positively their ability to stimulate students' motivation and engagement (61.1% in case 1 and 52.1% in case 2). Furthermore, preservice teachers refer to the adequacy of both first- and second-order contents addressed with these gamified activities, so it can be deduced that both cases are able to properly stimulate historical thinking skills. It is nevertheless noteworthy that, while 13.9%

Table 7. Mean scores of RO4 items in a Likert scale

Item	Pre-test	Post-test
I feel sufficiently trained to be capable of designing a gamified proposal based on historical thinking metaconcepts	2.22	2.67
The master's degree should allocate more time to training in active methods such as gamification	4.56	-
The presentation of practical examples has given me ideas and strategies to design gamified proposals based on historical thinking metaconcepts	-	4.22

Source: Own (2022)

of participants comment on the usefulness of the "Escape Room on the Cold War" to promote certain metaconcepts, this percentage rises to 58.3% in the case of "Archaeology to Discover Hellas". This is attributed less to a greater capacity of the activity to foster historical thinking than to the fact that in this case the instructions for developing metaconcepts are more explicit—since it is an activity intended to introduce students to this type of reasoning and requires more precise instructions.

On the other hand, the main shortcomings that preservice teachers identify in these gamified proposals are their high cognitive demand (30.6% in case 1 and 47.2% in case 2), and the potential difficulties regarding their development or timing (particularly in case 1, where 41.7% of the participants refer to this possible challenge). When asked about the general challenges of developing gamified activities to foster historical thinking, their evaluations point again to these two drawbacks: the students' possible limitations in understanding certain metaconcepts due to their complexity, and the large amount of time needed both to design gamified activities and to implement them in the classroom. It is also relevant to highlight the remarks made by some participants, who insist on the impossibility of developing several metaconcepts in a single gamified activity, or on how the competitive dynamics that gamification can generate might be detrimental to promoting metaconcepts with an ethical dimension, such as historical empathy. Unfortunately, the preservice teachers' responses tend to be superficial and do not explicitly state the possible factors that have led them to these arguments, thus in many cases they do not specify exactly what these difficulties consist of or which their causes are—an issue that must be solved by refining the instrument of analysis in the future.

Nevertheless, these results obtained in relation to RO1 cannot be considered conclusive, since two determining conceptual gaps can be inferred from the preservice teachers' responses: an apparent lack of knowledge of gamification elements and game design, and an imprecise conceptualization of historical thinking.

The first conceptual shortcoming is related to the complete lack of mention of the mechanics, aesthetics, and game thinking of both gamified activities. There are considerable design differences between both proposals, such as the use of pointification, narrative, or the students' freedom to explore, which were expected to appeal to participants and invite comparison. However, most positive evaluations focus mainly on the motivational aspects of both practices, thus coinciding with the results of other research on gamification among preservice teachers of social sciences or other subjects (Alajaji et al., 2021; Cózar-Gutiérrez & Sáez-López, 2016; Sánchez-Mena & Martí-Parreño, 2017). Although this result could be due to an appropriate design of both proposals, it is partly attributed to the fact that this methodology could have been presented previously in the master's degree, emphasizing its benefits to spark students' interest, but without working on strategies on how to design it or its ability to aid significant learning. Consequently, the preservice teachers may have been resorting to "platitudes," since the main benefits, drawbacks, and difficulties they mention when evaluating both cases in relation to working on historical skills often coincide with the generic ratings they give to gamification in the questions associated with RO2.

The second supposition has arisen from the emerging categorization of the preservice teachers' positive evaluations (Q1_post and Q3_post). Comments on the appropriate incorporation and handling of first-order concepts specified by the Spanish curriculum double the percentage of those referring to the way in which the cases address historical thinking or influence working on a specific metaconcept. As a result, the high percentage (58.3%) of participants underscoring the evidence work in case 2 as a valuable aspect is exceptional, which could be associated with the fact that this experience provides specific instructions for fostering this historical skill. Even though the proposal's design may have been perfectly suitable for introducing secondary students to this type of skill, over a quarter (27.8%) of the preservice teachers' ratings explicitly show an imprecise conception of historical thinking. This figure casts doubts on the starting assumptions on which preservice teachers rate the application of metaconcepts. Given that almost all participants already have a university degree in history, we should not necessarily assume they do not subconsciously apply reasoning based on causality or the historical perspective in their discipline (Sáiz-Serrano & López-Facal, 2015). Nonetheless, this is no guarantee they have worked on their theoretical conceptualization and have transferred them to their educational practice (Bohan & David, 1998).

This second hypothesis seems to be confirmed by observing the RO3 results. They show that preservice teachers attribute considerable potential to the combination of gamification and historical thinking in secondary education. They also demonstrate that practical experimentation with activities and their later evaluation improves this rating, thus confirming the educational benefits for preservice teachers of evaluating programs and activities focused on this curricular approach, a line furthered by other research such as that by Guerrero-Romera et al. (2019). However, again a significant percentage of the participants puts forward that metaconcept work must be introduced in later academic years, since they conceive historical thinking as conceptual content and not, therefore, as a procedural focus, apparently suffering from an imprecise conception of historical skills.

The results obtained in relation to RO4 are consistent with other studies focused on learning the level of training teachers believe they have to produce gamification activities (Cózar-Gutiérrez & Sáez-López, 2016; Sajinčič et al., 2020; Sánchez-Mena & Martí-Parreño, 2017). The preservice teachers in the sample mostly consider that the master's degree should place more of an emphasis on training in methodologies such as gamification, and they seem to agree that the current level of instruction does not suffice to develop these activities. Therefore, presenting and discussing both cases in the classroom have proven to be educationally effective, and the students, who allocate a score of 4.22 out of 5 points to the usefulness of this practice, rate them very highly and increase their feeling of being skilled in gamification by 0.45 points.

CONCLUSION

This study explores a field that has received scant attention from researchers into social sciences didactics, namely preservice teachers' conceptions of the potential of certain constructivist methodologies, such as gamification, to foster historical thinking in the history classroom. Our research reveals that the participants' perception of the didactic usefulness of gamification is generally positive, although they point out as hindrances its limitations to promote ethical metaconcepts, the difficulty to combine several metaconcepts in just one activity, and the long time required for its design and implementation. Considering the shortcomings preservice teachers attribute to gamification, we propose some recommendations to improve their perception of gamification. Firstly, it is necessary to design and present cases related to the ethical dimension or historical perspectives, demonstrating that a methodology such as gamification does not have to be necessarily a limitation when it comes to teaching certain contents or metaconcepts. Secondly, this experience reveals that a further step is needed, not only to enable preservice teachers to experiment with gamified activities, but also to invite them to design their own activities in order to test the possibility of grounding these on various metaconcepts. If possible, it would also be beneficial if preservice teachers could put them into practice during their internship in secondary schools—compulsory in Spain during the master's degree in teacher training—, so they could personally observe how this type of methodologies grounded in constructivist assumptions do not necessarily imply a lack of control of the classroom's dynamics; instead, with the teacher's proper guidance, gamification can be developed in an appropriate way and with an appropriate timing. The implementation of gamified activities by the preservice teachers themselves could also contribute to improving their perception of the time invested in designing them, since, although this type of activities requires more preparation time than traditional expository lessons, it provides better results both in terms of learning and satisfaction among students.

Furthermore, the results of this research show that, when analyzing the ratings preservice teachers give to methodologies or programs to work on approaches such as historical thinking, the level of knowledge they have of historical skills needs to be established first. Therefore, the research tool the participants use to rate practices for fostering historical thinking must be refined to further this line of research. This would enable preservice teachers' ratings to become more defined and turn into specific improvements of the two presented cases. Nevertheless, by making it possible for students to provide open-ended responses, extremely interesting implicit conceptions were identified, such as the absence of in-depth focus on game design during the master's degree and certain limitations in conceptualizing historical thinking metaconcepts. In short, presenting, experiencing, and evaluating good practices in teachers master's degrees is considered to be doubly beneficial as it offers students tools to reflect on and design their own educational proposals, and it provides inservice teachers with educational and discipline feedback on their approaches. Consequently, it is a future line of research requiring more study.

Conflict of Interest

The authors of this publication declare there is no conflict of interest.

Funding Agency

This research was supported by the research project "Desarrollo de competencias de pensamiento histórico en el aula. El nuevo desafío curricular de Ciencias Sociales" (JIUZ-2021-SOC-09); and ARGOS research group (S50_20R).

REFERENCES

Alajaji, D., & Alshwiah, A. (2021). Effect of Combining Gamification and a Scavenger Hunt on Pre-Service Teachers' Perceptions and Achievement. *Journal of Information Technology Education, 20*, 283–308. doi:10.28945/4809

Alshikhabobakr, H., Khan, S., Gedawy, H., Hussein, N., & Razak, S. (2020). Gamified Stories in History Classrooms. In *ICETC'20: 2020 12th International Conference on Education Technology and Computers* (pp. 76-81). Association for Computing Machinery. 10.1145/3436756.3437024

Bai, S., Hew, K. F., & Huang, B. (2020). Does gamification improve student learning outcome? Evidence from a meta-analysis and synthesis of qualitative data in educational contexts. *Educational Research Review, 30*, 100322. doi:10.1016/j.edurev.2020.100322

Barton, K. C. (2005). "Best Not to Forget Them": Adolescents' Judgments of Historical Significance in Northern Ireland. *Theory and Research in Social Education, 33*(1), 9–44. doi:10.1080/00933104.2005.10473270

Belova, N., & Zowada, C. (2020). Innovating Higher Education via Game-Based Learning on Misconceptions. *Education Sciences, 10*(9), 221. doi:10.3390/educsci10090221

Bohan, C. H., & Davis, O. L. Jr. (1998). Historical Constructions: How Social Studies Student Teachers' Historical Thinking is Reflected in Their Writing of History. *Theory and Research in Social Education, 26*(2), 173–197. doi:10.1080/00933104.1998.10505843

Boyle, E., Connolly, T., & Hainey, T. (2011). The role of psychology in understanding the impact of computer games. *Entertainment Computing, 2*(2), 69–74. doi:10.1016/j.entcom.2010.12.002

Buckley, P., & Doyle, E. (2016). Gamification and student motivation. *Interactive Learning Environments, 24*(6), 1162–1175. doi:10.1080/10494820.2014.964263

Colomo-Magaña, E., Sánchez-Rivas, E., Ruiz-Palmero, J., & Sánchez-Rodríguez, J. (2020). Percepción docente sobre la gamificación de la evaluación en la asignatura de Historia en educación secundaria [Teaching perception about gamification of the evaluation in the subject of History in secondary education]. *Información Tecnológica, 31*(4), 233–242. doi:10.4067/S0718-07642020000400233

Connolly, T. M., Boyle, E. A., MacArthur, E., Hainey, T., & Boyle, J. M. (2012). A systematic literature review of empirical evidence on computer games and serious games. *Computers & Education, 59*(2), 661–686. doi:10.1016/j.compedu.2012.03.004

Cózar-Gutiérrez, R., & Sáez-López, J. M. (2016). Game-based learning and gamification in initial teacher training in the social sciences: An experiment with MinecraftEdu. *International Journal of Educational Technology in Higher Education, 13*(1), 1–11. doi:10.118641239-016-0003-4

Deterding, S., Dixon, D., Khaled, R., & Nacke, L. (2011). From game design elements to gamefulness: defining "gamification". In *MindTrek '11: Proceedings of the 15th International Academic MindTrek Conference: Envisioning Future Media Environments* (pp. 9-15). Association for Computing Machinery. 10.1145/2181037.2181040

Egea-Vivancos, A., & Arias-Ferrer, L. (2018). El desafío de enseñar a pensar históricamente a través de la arqueología [The challenge of teaching historical thinking through archaeology]. In A. Egea-Vivancos, L. Arias-Ferrer, & J. Santacana-i-Mestre (Coords.), Y la arqueología llegó al aula: La cultura material y el método arqueológico para la enseñanza de la historia y el patrimonio (pp.329-343). Ediciones Trea.

Eukel, H., & Morrell, B. (2021). Ensuring Educational Escape-Room Success: The Process of Designing, Piloting, Evaluating, Redesigning, and Re-Evaluating Educational Escape Rooms. *Simulation & Gaming*, *52*(1), 18–23. doi:10.1177/1046878120953453

Figg, C., & Jaipal-Jamani, K. (2018). Developing Teacher Knowledge About Gamification as an Instructional Strategy. In M. Niess & H. Gillow-Wiles (Eds.), *Handbook of Research on Teacher Education in the Digital Age* (pp. 663–690). IGI Global.

Gómez-Carrasco, C. J., Rodríguez-Pérez, R. A., & Mirete-Ruiz, A. B. (2018). Percepción de la enseñanza de la historia y concepciones epistemológicas. Una investigación con futuros maestros [Perception of teaching history and epistemological conceptions. Research with future teachers]. *Revista Complutense de Educación*, *29*(1), 237–250. doi:10.5209/RCED.52233

Grant, S. G. (2001). It's Just the Facts, or Is It? The Relationship between Teachers' Practices and Students' Understandings of History. *Theory and Research in Social Education*, *29*(1), 65–108. doi:10.1080/00933104.2001.10505930

Guerrero-Romera, C., López-García, A., & Monteagudo-Fernández, J. (2019). Development of historical thinking in the classroom through a training programme for Secondary Education. *Revista Electrónica Interuniversitaria de Formación del Profesorado*, *22*(2). Advance online publication. doi:10.6018/reifop.22.2.363911

Hamari, J., Koivisto, J., & Sarsa, H. (2014). Does Gamification Work? – A Literature Review of Empirical Studies on Gamification. In *2014 47th Hawaii International Conference on System Sciences* (pp.3025-3034). IEEE. 10.1109/HICSS.2014.377

Hanus, M. D., & Fox, J. (2015). Assessing the effects of gamification in the classroom: A longitudinal study on intrinsic motivation, social comparison, satisfaction, effort, and academic performance. *Computers & Education*, *80*, 152–161. doi:10.1016/j.compedu.2014.08.019

Hernández-Fernández, A., Olmedo-Torre, N., & Peña, M. (2020). Is Classroom Gamification Opposed to Performance? *Sustainability*, *12*(23), 9958. doi:10.3390u12239958

Hoofman, J., & Secord, E. (2021). The Effect of COVID-19 on Education. *Pediatric Clinics of North America*, *68*(5), 1071–1079. doi:10.1016/j.pcl.2021.05.009 PMID:34538299

Kapp, K. (2012). *The Gamification of Learning and Instruction: Game-Based Methods and Strategies for Training and Education*. John Wiley & Sons.

Kim, S., Song, K., Lockee, B., & Burton, J. (2018). What is Gamification in Learning and Education? In S. Kim, K. Song, B. Lockee, & J. Burton (Eds.), *Gamification in Learning and Education* (pp. 25–38). Springer International Publishing. doi:10.1007/978-3-319-47283-6_4

Lee, P. J. (1983). History Teaching and Philosophy of History. *History and Theory*, *22*(4), 19–49. doi:10.2307/2505214

Lévesque, S. (2008). *Thinking historically. Educating students for the twenty-first century*. University of Toronto Press.

Li, C., Lee, M., Lien, Y., Huang, Y., Wang, C., & Hou, H. (2019). A Real Escape Gamification Teaching Activity Integrated with Situated Learning and Multi-dimensional Scaffolding for Elementary School Social Studies Course. In *2019 8th International Congress on Advanced Applied Informatics (IIAI-AAI)* (pp. 1051-1052). IEEE. 10.1109/IIAI-AAI.2019.00222

Marczewski, A. (2015). *Even Ninja Monkeys Like to Play: Gamification, Game Thinking and Motivational Design*. Independently Published.

Martínez-Hita, M., & Gómez-Carrasco, C. J. (2017). Nivel cognitivo y competencias de pensamiento histórico en los libros de texto de Historia de España e Inglaterra. Un estudio comparativo [Cognitive level and historical thinking competencies in history textbooks from Spain and England. A comparative study]. *Review of Education*, *379*, 145–169. doi:10.4438/1988-592X-RE-2017-379-364

Martínez-Hita, M., Gómez-Carrasco, C. J., & Miralles-Martínez, P. (2021). The effects of a gamified project based on historical thinking on the academic performance of primary school children. *Humanities and Social Sciences Communications*, *8*(1), 122. doi:10.105741599-021-00796-9

Martínez-Hita, M., & Miralles-Martínez, P. (2020). Evaluación del diseño de un programa de intervención gamificado para el desarrollo del pensamiento histórico en el alumnado de Educación Primaria [Evaluation of the design of a gamified intervention program to develop historical thinking competencies in primary school students]. *Revista Interuniversitaria De Formación Del Profesorado*, *34*(2). Advance online publication. doi:10.47553/rifop.v34i2.78420

Mee, R. W., Shahdan, T. S., Ismail, R., Ghani, K. A., Pek, L. S., Von, W. Y., Woo, A., & Rao, Y. S. (2020). Role of gamification in classroom teaching: Pre-service teachers' view. *International Journal of Evaluation and Research in Education*, *9*(3), 684–690. doi:10.11591/ijere.v9i3.20622

Mendioroz-Lacambra, A., & Erce-Domínguez, A. (2020). El método arqueológico simulado para desarrollar competencias históricas en educación infantil [Working with archeology in early childhood education to develop historical skills]. *Arte. Individuo y Sociedad*, *32*(3), 767–781. doi:10.5209/aris.65825

Metzer, S. A., & Harris, L. M. (Eds.). (2018). *The Wiley International Handbook of History Teaching and Learning*. John Wiley & Sons. doi:10.1002/9781119100812

Moliner, L., & Alegre, F. (2021). COVID-19 Restrictions and Its Influence on Students' Mathematics Achievement in Spain. *Education Sciences*, *12*(2), 105. doi:10.3390/educsci12020105

Monteagudo-Fernández, J., Rodríguez Pérez, R. A., Escribano-Miralles, A., & Rodríguez García, A. M. (2020). Percepciones de los estudiantes de Educación Secundaria sobre la enseñanza de la historia, a través del uso de las TIC y recursos digitales [Perceptions of Secondary Education students onthe teaching of history, through the use of ICT and digital resources]. *Revista Electrónica Interuniversitaria de Formación del Profesorado*, *23*(2), 67–79. doi:10.6018/reifop.417611

Moreno-Vera, J. R., & Alvén, F. (2020). Concepts for historical and geographical thinking in Sweden's and Spain's Primary Education curricula. *Humanities and Social Sciences Communications*, *7*(1), 107. doi:10.105741599-020-00601-z

Putz, L. M., Hofbauer, F., & Treiblmaier, H. (2020). Can gamification help to improve education? Findings from a longitudinal study. *Computers in Human Behavior*, *110*, 106392. doi:10.1016/j.chb.2020.106392

Rivero, P. (2017). Proceso de gamificación en el aula de ciencias sociales [Gamification process in the social sciences classroom]. *Íber. Didáctica de las Ciencias Sociales. Geografía e Historia*, *86*, 4–6.

Robson, K., Plangger, K., Kietzmann, J. H., McCarthy, I., & Pitt, L. (2015). Is it all a game? Understanding the principles of gamification. *Business Horizons*, *58*(4), 411–420. doi:10.1016/j.bushor.2015.03.006

Sailer, M., & Homner, L. (2020). The Gamification of Learning: A Meta-analysis. *Educational Psychology Review*, *32*(1), 77–112. doi:10.100710648-019-09498-w

Sáiz-Serrano, J., Gómez-Carrasco, C. J., & López-Facal, R. (2018). Historical thinking, causal explanation and narrative discourse in trainee teachers in Spain. *Historical Encounters: A Journal of Historical Consciousness, Historical Cultures, and History Education*, *5*(1), 16-30. http://hdl.handle.net/10347/17000

Sáiz-Serrano, J., & López-Facal, R. (2015). Competencias y narrativas históricas: El pensamiento histórico de estudiantes y futuros profesores españoles de educación secundaria [Historical Competencies and Narratives: The Historical Thinking of Students and Pre-Service Teachers]. *Revista de Estudios Sociales*, *52*(52), 87–101. doi:10.7440/res52.2015.06

Sajinčič, N., Sandak, A., & Istenič, A. (2022). Pre-Service and In-Service Teachers' Views on Gamification. *International Journal of Emerging Technologies in Learning*, *17*(3), 83–103. doi:10.3991/ijet.v17i03.26761

Sanchez, D. R., Langer, M., & Kaur, R. (2020). Gamification in the classroom: Examining the impact of gamified quizzes on student learning. *Computers & Education*, *144*, 103666. doi:10.1016/j.compedu.2019.103666

Sánchez-Mena, A., & Martí-Parreño, J. (2017). Drivers and Barriers to Adopting Gamification: Teachers' Perspectives. *The Electronic Journal of e-Learning, 15*(5), 434-443.

Seixas, P., & Morton, T. (2013). *The big six historical thinking concepts*. Nelson Education.

Seixas, P., & Peck, C. (2004). Teaching historical thinking. In A. Sears & I. Wright (Eds.), *Challenges and Prospects for Canadian Social Studies* (pp. 109–117). Pacific Educational Press.

VanSledright, B. (2011). *The challenge of rethinking history education: on practices, theories, and policy*. Routledge.

VanSledright, B. (2014). What Does It Mean To Think Historically… and How To Teach It? *Social Education*, *68*(3), 230–233.

Werbach, K., & Hunter, D. (2012). *For the Win: How Game Thinking Can Revolutionize Your Business*. Wharton Digital Press.

Wineburg, S. (2001). *Historical thinking and other unnatural acts: charting the future of teaching the past*. Temple University Press.

Yildiz, İ., Topçu, E., & Kaymakci, S. (2021). The effect of gamification on motivation in the education of pre-service social studies teachers. *Thinking Skills and Creativity*, *42*, 100907. doi:10.1016/j.tsc.2021.100907

Chapter 7
Gamified Teaching Strategies to Work on Historical Thinking:
Methodological Applications

Juan Carlos Colomer Rubio
Universitat de València, Spain

EXECUTIVE SUMMARY

The reality is that students show a lack of interest in certain school subjects. In Social Sciences, teaching has predominantly been based on transmission, which has only amplified the problem. It has also prevented new work and intervention techniques that boost students' interest in historical and geographical concepts from being developed. Including gamified didactic sequences to develop competences associated with historical thinking is one way in which this could change. In this chapter, the authors present a potential application of gamification, based on existing models such as the BIG 6 developed by Eisenberg and Berkowitz in 1990, which the authors link to the skills to be developed, the way in which information is presented, and the characteristics of the game or activity to be gamified. This model will help to promote didactic proposals that apply this work methodology in the future.

INTRODUCTION

In recent years, general educational research and specific didactics have noted a problem that is a common occurrence in the classroom: a lack of motivation. This leads students to approach school activities with apathy and disinterest, thus negatively affecting learning and resulting in school failure (Solbes, 2007). Widespread opinions that define the "usefulness" of a student in society as the knowledge he/she can acquire and the numerical value of the grades he/she is able to obtain pose an additional obstacle (Gajardo, 1993). Combining these two aspects, we have a school context with certain dissonances, inconsistencies and problems with regard to fundamental questions: What should we teach? What do students want to learn? How can we tackle the fact that they do not want to learn? What strategies can we use to improve student learning?

DOI: 10.4018/978-1-6684-5240-0.ch007

These questions have formed the basis of reflection on school and learning since the beginnings of modern pedagogy. In fact, Ivan Illich already stated the following (cited in Carbonell, 2015):

"School is an institution built on the axiom that learning is the result of teaching. And institutional wisdom continues to accept this axiom, despite overwhelming evidence to the contrary. We have all learned most of what we know outside of school. Students do most of their learning without their teachers, and often despite their teachers." (Illich cited by Carbonell, 2015, p. 25).

There may be many reasons, apart from those inherent to the school institution itself, that lead to apathy, disinterest and finally school failure. These include socioeconomic difficulties, pedagogical reasons, psychological causes and family situations. These circumstances, although often not in the teacher's hands to change, represent an opportunity for us to transform teaching methods in order to obtain a different result than the one obtained at school (Bécares, Busto & de Hoyos, 2016). These new methodologies may involve implementing dynamic activities associated with play in educational practice or with widespread social matters such as the use of technological media, especially video games, for the teaching and learning of Geography and History. Using these new methodological resources, we can try to contribute to the learning of content, without forgetting the importance of subjecting this content to questioning or criticism, and while remembering where these resources or strategies can help.

In the current context, teachers are progressively moving away from their traditional role of "transmitter" of knowledge to instead become the driver of sessions, almost an "entertainer", in a world submerged with new teaching methodologies that perpetuate technical and moralizing models, rather than being based on critical paradigms (Colomer, Fuertes & Parra, 2022). Thus, the appearance of presumably new methodologies can help to improve teaching practice as long as they are associated with new educational practices. Within these methodologies, the concept of "gamification" has taken a prominent role. It is understood as the introduction of game-related characteristics (such as challenges, obstacles and tests to be solved) as an element in the development of a social or educational activity (Dicheva et al., 2015; McGonigal, 2013; Rodríguez & Santiago, 2015). The introduction of these dynamic activities is not new in the history of education, but their inclusion in specific subjects in an extensive way is. This includes, for example, the use of video games in the classroom to complete certain tasks, work on certain content or achieve certain competencies (Cuenca-López & Martín, 2010; Delgado-Algarra, 2022; Gros & Garrido-Miranda, 2008; Guevara & Colomer, 2017; Jiménez-Palacios & Cuenca-López, 2021; Mugueta, 2019; Rivero, 2017; Van der Schilden & Heijltjes, 2017).

Despite the emergence of these new gamified practices, few can be linked to the development of competencies in students related to the construction of historical thinking in the case of Social Sciences. This is understood as the way in which we represent the past thanks to our knowledge of it, which is understood as substantive or first-order content (dates, data, figures, concepts, etc.), but also use skills to give it meaning, in other words second-order content or historical meta-concepts. These skills, which give meaning to and help us understand the past as done in historical research, have been a fundamental reference framework in the field of Didactics of Social Sciences until very recently (Colomer, Sáiz, Morales, 2021; Éthier, Demers, & Lefrançois, 2010; Sáiz & Colomer, 2014).

Therefore, in this chapter we will present the concept of gamification and the relevant link with the construction of historical thinking. This will be based on different categories associated with this type of thinking, according to a model of information literacy (BIG 6). This will allow us to outline the methodological basis for the creation of possible didactic interventions - one of which is presented in this article - that develop second-order concepts by means of gamified activities.

BACKGROUND

Gamification is a tool which can be used in the classroom to promote change in the teaching and learning processes within the Social Sciences. This technique is characterized by introducing game mechanics in sectors that are not related to them. There are many advantages to this type of methodological strategy, including a progressive increase in the motivation acquired by participants and the use of experiential learning (Guevara and Colomer, 2017; McGonigal, 2013). However, despite the attractiveness of this practice, it is essential for teachers to use it well in order to have the right impact on students and to be effective in the long-term (Huang & Soman, 2013; Lee & Hammer, 2011).

With the concept of gamification, we refer to the methodological practice used by transferring different game mechanics to the educational-professional environment to increase motivation, better absorb certain knowledge, improve skills or to add a compensatory purpose for some main actions (Gaitán, 2013). Given its playful nature and introduction in environments generally unrelated to the game, there are many authors who claim that it comes out ahead of methodologies of a more traditional nature, since it increases motivation towards a specific aspect of the subject and helps to facilitate understanding (Rivero, 2017). In fact, Fernandez-Enguita pointed out the following in the case of simulation games:

"While the school institution and the teaching profession abhorred video games, other institutions and groups, more concerned with efficiency and results than with tradition and dogma, rushed to incorporate them with notable success. Simulations and games in the strict sense are now a common component in the training of soldiers, pilots, heavy machinery operators, business managers, sportsmen, stockbrokers and surgeons." (Fernández-Enguita, p. 168).

There are several reasons which show the great value of using games as an educational resource (Chamoso et al., 2004). The first is the natural position of the game for the student, where he/she adopts and develops a collaborative spirit and enjoys its dynamics, which he/she considers natural. On the other hand, it also favors, to a great extent, the development of social skills and self-control and increases the generation of ideas. Finally, this type of activities, depending on how they are planned, can expand critical thinking and develop it more deeply, given that it makes greater use of the students' imagination and individual creativity and forces them to make autonomous decisions. In fact, games involve many elements that, when combined, can favor learning: from the ability to understand and retain information of both simple and complex elements in memory to other aspects such as creativity and innovation (UNESCO, 1980).

As Quintero (2018) explains, the use of video games may also entail negative consequences such as social isolation or addiction (Gros, 2008). In the case of Social Sciences, Arancibia and Badia (2013) pointed out that some use of ICT is widely related to backward pedagogical practices that already came from models developed prior to the emergence of digital technology. On the one hand, these authors note theories of information processing that approach a transmissive conception of disciplinary content using computers or portable devices in a behaviorist manner. This methodology is based on a teaching method that is dedicated to delivering information and to showing reality as external elements to the subject, pursuing learning that must be a faithful reproduction (a copy) of that external reality. This model is the one that clearly prevails in the use of certain technologies in the Social Sciences classroom, as can be seen in the abuse of digital presentations or videos without the ensuing didactic or epistemological reflection.

On the other hand, Arancibia and Badia propose another approach, which is the use of technology derived from cognitive tools associated with individual constructivism. In this type of strategy, the student decides on itineraries, activities, and goals. This implies the use of technology to support individual cognitive development, associated with a conception of learning and teaching that focuses on the individual interests of the student through specific platforms or applications. This way of working, which is less conditioned than the previous one, points to practices that place the act of teaching at the heart.

In this vein, Jiménez-Palacios and Cuenca-López (2021) have pointed out that digital resources associated with gamification, such as video games, allow the development of substantive knowledge about our true heritage if teachers use them correctly. In this way, gamification as a teaching practice, in this case using video games, would allow students to work on abstract content, increase their social knowledge and make learning an attractive, meaningful process that is close to their interests (del Pozo, 2015; Kapell & Elliott, 2013; Martínez-Hita, Gómez-Carrasco & Miralles-Martínez, 2021; McCall, 2012; Moseikina, Toktamysov, & Danshina, 2022; Parra-González et al., 2021)

In short, this intervention technique associated with active pedagogies can, therefore, be linked to other strategies, which also actively engage cognitive construction that can be included within the term of historical thinking in the case of Social Sciences. On this point, it is difficult to clarify which competencies are covered by historical thinking. To do so, we must try to answer the following question: What does it mean to be competent in this type of thinking (Santisteban, 2010)?

In the classroom, the Social Sciences teacher must, based on the principles of historical thinking, build a series of conceptual structures that will progressively become more complex for the understanding of this type of thinking. This is necessary since historical time also interferes with the conception of other times such as social, philosophical, biological and/or physical times (Pagès and Santisteban, 2010). In addition, as well as including methodology and learning, it can be observed that the construction of historical thinking fundamentally leads to the development of critical citizens (Soria, 2014).

As mentioned in the previous point, to be competent in historical thinking it is necessary to use different categories as a basis so that these conceptual structures are gradually perfected. In this way, the development of these categories in a gamified structure, even if it involves complexity, will always allow the student to have some second-order elements when working with historical content.

Thus, following the model explained by Santisteban (Santisteban, 2010) and which is best suited to the gamified activities that we would like to develop, we have aspects related to historical-temporal awareness, based on the concept of past, present and future. It is important to note that these are not independent elements; they are strictly related since the intention of the construction of this concept claims the past as learning for the conception of the future (Pagès & Santisteban, 2010).

Regarding the representation of history, it is necessary to understand that a gamified narrative stirs awareness in individuals. There is a very important related element for any student, which is when the historical narration of a past fact is contrary to the historical representation of the general culture. That is why we seek to create a completely rational representation of the temporal facts and include, above all, the cause and consequence of the historical facts (with documentation that can be explored parallel to the gamified process). In this way, students have an initial vision and are able to develop critical thinking.

In this same model, we use gamification to demonstrate the importance of historical imagination, since it can help develop aspects implicit in the historical thinking model itself, such as historical empathy or a basis for contextualizing the facts (Bel, 2021). It has always been useful to develop empathy by putting oneself in the place of the other. Thus, knowing the context of a certain historical period thanks to a gamified activity can lead us to understand the reasons behind certain events or different forms of human thought over the years. To focus on the development of critical thinking in students, gamification also serves a purpose by enabling students to discover themselves through gamified research or reconstructions; they may look at why a certain person or group carried out certain actions and judge for themselves using their opinion and reasoning. In fact, historical empathy is a skill that goes beyond putting oneself in the shoes of historical characters. It is about setting in motion controlled and contextualized imagination that helps recreate historical contexts and projects feelings or beliefs that are present in the student to the past (Sáiz, 2013).

Finally, we find historical interpretation, which is closely related to all the above. This is the result of a learning process that endows different human actions with historical content in a context.

Thus, as we can see, we are faced with two types of History learning (Santisteban, 2010). On the one hand, we have a type of learning that is based on the accumulation of information, facts, data, figures, and so on. This type focuses on chronology as the central axis of the discourse and instills a closed and untouchable vision of History, like the textbook model. The second relies mainly on the construction of a historical narrative and the contextualization of events. This mode accentuates the learning of social changes, examines the provenance of sources and above all explores the arguments to be questioned and debated.

These capabilities can be related to the elements implicit in any gamified activity, which we will develop in the following part. This will serve as a basis for the possible construction of didactic sequences based on this model, such as the one we will present in this paper.

HISTORICAL THINKING AND GAMIFICATION

Introducing the student to a historian's own working method by evaluating facts and sources is, as we have seen, of the utmost importance. Thus, based on the interpretation of manuals for teaching history and theoretical approaches, we can begin to link elements of the types of games for teaching together with the competencies of historical thinking that we wish to develop (Santisteban, 2010).

This should awaken the student's involvement in the imaginative reconstruction of the life of people from a given period through play, since it is not only a matter of studying political phenomena, but of being able to link them to everyday life. This contains another very important diachronic element, which is the comparison between the relevant period in the past and the contemporary period (Carretero, Pozo & Asensio, 1989). We also suggest the study of local history as a point of interest, since it is what really surrounds the students and is directly connected to them. It would be a matter of applying the elements known by the students and relating them to a broader and more personal context.

On this basis, a gamified activity with an information literacy model such as the one we will present will allow the following points to be achieved:

1. Understanding that causal factors occur together, never in isolation.
2. Understanding that explaining something in a causal way does not mean that it is inevitable.
3. Historical evidence and sources should not be understood in the same way as secondary narratives.

Table 1. Linking gamification features to historical thinking skills

Characteristics of gamification	Historical thinking competencies developed
It helps bypass the organizational structure of textbooks.	Historical interpretation
It allows us to learn about history more deeply, but also link it to other realities.	Historical-temporal awareness Historical interpretation Historical imagination
It generates historical knowledge conceived as debatable knowledge.	Historical interpretation Historical imagination Representation of history
It presents aspects of people's lives beyond war or political events.	Historical interpretation Historical imagination Representation of history
It boosts students' motivation, allowing them to progress to the core content of the discipline more quickly.	Historical-temporal awareness Historical interpretation Historical imagination Representation of history
It helps students tackle the problematic content of the discipline.	Historical-temporal awareness Historical interpretation Historical imagination Representation of history
It questions the very concept of the interpretation of history by comparing sources with the manual or textbook.	Historical interpretation Representation of history
It allows us to contemplate what happened in a sort of "natural state" and puts students in direct contact with the past.	Historical-temporal awareness Historical interpretation Historical imagination Representation of history
It facilitates students' autonomy, allowing them to take control of their own reconstruction of history.	Historical interpretation Representation of history
It enables the development of historical competencies since it emphasizes the progressive acquisition of skills and concepts rather than a series of events.	Historical-temporal awareness Historical interpretation Historical imagination Representation of history

Source: own work

4. Understanding that historical explanations often provide a "reduction of uncertainty", but almost never a complete solution.

According to these principles, the first stage should be dedicated to teaching a set of methodical skills accompanied by a series of analytical tools specific to history. Basically, this enables the student to reason about problems that are normally simplified in textbooks. A second stage, based on the previous one, would consist of studying the great conceptual nuclei of History. This would give the student general and overall ideas about the most important concepts for understanding life and social organization.

In order to apply these stages, it is necessary to combine the characteristics of any gamified product with the conceptual cores of History. A didactic activity or sequence that uses gamification with the above characteristics and links them to the elements present in the historical thinking scheme described above will undoubtedly make progress in the construction thereof (Table 1).

In this vein, in order to design a gamified activity that incorporates historical thinking, it is important to consider how information is organized, referring to models such as the BIG 6. This model was designed

Table 2. Outline of use of the BIG 6 method

Step	Activity	Summary question
1 - Defining the task to be performed: in this step, the aim will be to determine what the objective of the information we are looking for is and to define the needs related to it. In the case of history, for example, we need to know what specific data we want to obtain from the information we find.	Focus	What is the problem?
2 - Strategies for searching for information: when the problem is defined, the range of possible sources of information opens up. Here a filter will be necessary to find out which sources are reliable and which are more relevant.	Planning the search	How should I research?
3 - Identification and access: this is the point that is most related to research. After selecting the appropriate form of information research, it is put into practice.	Classify	What did I find?
4 - Use of information: after identifying and accessing the source, interact with the information to obtain what is relevant to the need.	Select	What is important?
5 - Synthesis: restructure the useful information obtained to meet the requirements of the work.	Synthesize and produce	How does it fit into the task?
6 - Evaluation: the task is processed in its entirety to analyze how effective it has been with respect to the need it sought to solve.	Evaluate, reflect	What has been learned?

Source: own work

by Mike Eisenberg and Bob Berkowitz for the purpose of searching for and organizing information and allows the information that must be used to tackle a problem to be managed. As a result, it can be defined as a systematic process of problem solving with a critical thinking basis and, in addition, a method of information management (Eisenberg & Berkowitz, 1990) (Table 2).

In the case of a gamified activity that pursues the desired competencies of historical thinking, the BIG 6 structure or model can help to organize the different phases of the game from the initial question to the result or synthesis of the gamified product or challenge posed to the students.

To conclude this section, does all this mean that the BIG 6 model is the best option when applying gamification in our field? This option presents us with a tool that should be subject to significant consideration given that its method – dividing the task into small objectives – is very complete. If the intention is to gamify an activity due to the work structure involved (achieving small objectives/rewards, among other reasons) this model can be very useful (Sánchez & Colomer, 2017).

METHODOLOGICAL PROPOSAL WITH MINECRAFT.EDU

Based on the BIG 6 model proposed and the importance of applying gamified methodological approaches for the development of historical thinking in our field of knowledge, we provide a proposal for the learning of Social Sciences aimed at Primary Education, although it would be perfectly possible to use in the early stages of Secondary Education. For the development of this gamified activity, we will use the educational version of the video game Minecraft developed by Microsoft, Minecraft.Edu, which has been appropriately applied in other didactic interventions of interest (Guevara & Colomer, 2017; Bourdeau, Coulon & Petit, 2021).

Minecraft is a video game developed by the company, Mojang, which was acquired in 2014 by Microsoft. It is what we call a sandbox: an open-world video game in which the player has the freedom to move around the map without any limitations. There are two versions of Minecraft available, a portable version which includes the educational part and which is better optimized, and another traditional version for PC. One of the main features of the program in its latest versions is that it has been fully optimized, since the goal is that it can be used by anyone without the need to have a high-performing computer or tablet (https://education.minecraft.net/getstarted/). Microsoft conceived Minecraft.Edu with a local perspective, i.e. the idea is that students play together in a classroom under the teacher's control, which subsequently implies a larger role for the teacher in the learning experience.

It is worth noting that a recent study has confirmed the effectiveness of the implementation of the program at this educational stage. In this study, 98% of those consulted noted a significant increase in students' problem-solving skills. In addition, significant improvements were observed in creativity, reading, collaboration, problem solving and computational thinking. All of this confirms that the educational use of gamification has substantial learning outcomes. (Karsenti, Bugmann & Gros, 2017).

We will now suggest a gamified activity following the BIG 6 structure proposed above and whose learning objectives are to provide students with sufficient tools to collect primary sources, perform a critical analysis and contrast the sources to extract traces of the historical process. The aim is to introduce historical thinking in a playful and collaborative way. To this end, a transmedia narrative is used, inventing a story about a medieval merchant who has been trapped in time in a city and asks the students for help. Some of the most significant urban elements of the Middle Ages (city hall, cathedral, etc.) are recreated, with a script that follows the narrative of the selected contents. Students will play cooperatively and with total freedom. This world has a life of its own as it is complemented by the presence of computer-controlled characters – that Minecraft allows – characterized with elements of the period. The characters have their own lines of text and information that provide the support necessary to solve the different challenges (Figure 1).

The activities are introduced into the game by means of quests – missions – which involve solving questions, searching for and obtaining elements, and completing an "adventurer's diary" (Phase 5 of the BIG 6 model). The purpose of the quests is to analyze the social structure in the Middle Ages, as well as its main cultural and economic features, which are understood as a set of interrelated elements. These quests, in turn, are complemented with activities outside the video game, through the "fourth wall". This is a phenomenon whereby characters in the virtual environment directly address the player to claim some element outside the game, as a primary source to be analyzed as an external element. Finally, as the sessions progress, the students will go from one level to another – several screens of Minecraft – that will allow them to observe the historical evolution of the city and the construction of chronological axes in other network applications. Finally, there is an evaluation session (Phase 6 of the BIG 6 model) where the students present the "adventurer's diary", that collects the resolution of the main quests of the gamified intervention, to the rest of their classmates.

All of these activities form an introduction to historical research in a playful way. Primary sources are used with a simple character, allowing them to observe that history goes beyond the textbook. It is an adventure that transcends the video game and links them with their environment, generating a complete and meaningful experience, where both content and values are promoted.

Thinking of the competencies involved, we integrate historical thinking skills and link them with other competencies such as digital skills, since technological skills are tested in the handling of the video game, as well as information processing and the creation of documentation through the "adventurer's

Figure 1. Screenshot of Minecraft.Edu
Source: Wikimedia commons

diary". We also develop the competence of learning to learn, encouraging autonomy and collaboration among peers as cornerstones in the design and integration of new content, seeking analysis and reasoning to achieve knowledge. Finally, we deal with social and civic competence, promoting the development of values such as empathy, tolerance, collaboration, or effort, which are all fundamental for social and citizen development. In order to evaluate this experience, we created a framework that links the activities proposed, including the "adventurer's diary", with the competencies that have been developed during the activity (Table 3).

CONCLUSION

Modifying methodologies is, therefore, a key part of educational practice. Playful learning environments can help us here. Gamification, for example, consists of the use of game mechanics in environments that are traditionally far from playful to enhance motivation, effort and all the values that are developed in a game in the teaching process. Gamification has been highly criticized in educational circles for its lack of rigor, but the reality is that this type of methodology involves greater planning and gives students more agency, awakening intrinsic motivations aimed at developing knowledge.

We should not make the mistake of thinking that an activity of a more playful, fun nature implies less learning. McGonigal (2013) already pointed out the importance of starting to imitate some of the actions that happen when we play, since they guarantee a much faster learning process. In addition, they help us overcome the fear of failure, since, if we lose, we can simply try again. In addition, a game involves rules that every player has to comply with. The rules are the methodology and the evaluation

Table 3. Synthesis of the phases of the gamified intervention with Minecraft.Edu and its link with the BIG 6 model

Step according to BIG 6 model	Activity	Summary question
1 - Defining the task to be performed	Listen to the teacher's explanation of the activity instructions and familiarize self with the Minecraft.Edu game environment.	What is the problem?
2 - Strategies for searching for information	Carry out different quests and develop various strategies used to search for information.	How should I research?
3 - Identification and access	Within the game itself and with the use of documentation and external sources, locate the answer to the different quests posed by different characters.	What did I find?
4 - Use of information	Select the information needed to solve the different problems found during the game.	What is important?
5 - Synthesis	Create an "adventurer's diary" containing the resolution of all the quests presented in the game.	How does it fit into the task?
6 - Evaluation	Share the "adventurer's diary" with the rest of the class.	What has been learned?

Source: own work

system. They are not conceived as an imposition but as factors to be met to overcome the game, which ultimately involves learning and fun not just as a means to reach an end, but for the social interaction with classmates and the teacher.

In the case at hand – the implementation of methodological gamified strategies for the development of historical thinking skills – we have seen that existing models, such as BIG 6, combined with gamified environments, such as Minecraft.Edu, allow logical sequencing of activities. This sequencing helps students to work on the major conceptual cores of history, in a collaborative way and without sacrificing the rigor and analytical nature of the historian's own analysis of sources. The recourse to gamification, linked to pre-existing schemes of historical thinking, can from the basis of didactic sequences that help students learn how to organize information - based on the BIG 6 model proposed or others - and develop the acquisition of competencies. However, it remains to be seen whether this type of intervention is successful in the long term and, more importantly, whether this type of strategy leads to more well-founded and critical knowledge or, on the contrary, remains a mere gimmick associated with this type of audiovisual tools.

As limitations to the study presented, although it is evident, as confirmed by scientific articles, that the use of gamified methodologies increases student motivation and improves educational processes, we must have empirical data on the proposal we have put forward. Therefore, after successfully implementing proposals such as the one with Minecraft, an in-depth study combining qualitative and quantitative studies would be necessary. These studies would make it possible to answer the questions: Which dimensions are worked on more? Which dimensions are developed less by means of gamified proposals? Having empirical data that demonstrate the didactic suitability of the proposal presented is fundamental to approach evidence-based educational practices.

In any case, within gamification, the use of technological resources such as video games or collaborative online applications can help us to improve our students' learning. That is why we are presenting this proposal, where teamwork and the development of values is a key element for students developing these kinds of skills. The aim is to develop a critical view of history, one that questions and that does not understand it in an uncritical way but as the basis on which we build ourselves socially and personally.

REFERENCES

Arancibia, M., & Badia, A. (2013). Caracterización y valoración de los usos educativos de las TIC en 10 secuencias didácticas de historia en enseñanza secundaria. *Estudios Pedagógicos (Valdivia)*, *39*(Especial), 7–24. doi:10.4067/S0718-07052013000300002

Bécares, L., Busto, M., & de Hoyos, C. (2016). Sentarse, escuchar y repetir. ¿Existe otra forma de enseñar historia? *Ikastorratza.e-Revista de Didáctica*, (16), 15-38.

Bel, J. C. (2021). *La imaginación histórica en la didáctica de la historia: génesis del concepto, percepciones del profesorado y estudio de caso en Educación Primaria*. Universitat de València.

Carbonell, J. (2015). *Pedagogías del siglo XXI: Alternativas para la innovación educativa*. Octaedro.

Carretero, M., Pozo, J. I., & Asensio, M. (Eds.). (1989). *La enseñanza de las Ciencias Sociales*. Visor.

Chamoso, J. M., Durán, J., García, F., Martín, J., & Rodríguez, M. (2004). Análisis y experimentación de juegos como instrumentos para enseñar matemáticas. *Suma*, (47), 47–58.

Colomer, J. C., Fuertes, C., & Parra, D. (2022). Tecnología educativa y enfoque sociocrítico en enseñanza de la Historia. ¿Dónde estamos?¿ Hacia dónde vamos? *Con-ciencia social. Segunda Época*, (5), 143–160.

Colomer, J. C., Sáiz, J., & Morales, A. (2021). History and geographical thinking skills: between disciplinary knowledge and knowledge for teaching in Teacher Education. In Handbook of Research on Teacher Education in History and Geography (pp. 159-176). Peter Lang Publishing Group.

Cuenca-López, J.-M., & Martín, M. (2010). La resolución de problemas en la enseñanza de las ciencias sociales a través de videojuegos. *Íber. Didáctica de las Ciencias Sociales. Geografía e Historia*, (63), 32–42.

del Pozo, M. M. (2015). Videojuegos y aprendizaje colaborativo. Experiencias en torno a la etapa de Educación Primaria. *Teoría de la Educación*, *16*(2), 69–89.

Delgado-Algarra, E. J. (2022). Gamification and Game-Based Learning: Motivating Social Sciences Education. In Information Resources Management Association (Ed.), Research Anthology on Developments in Gamification and Game-Based Learning (pp. 932-956). IGI Global.

Dicheva, D., Dichev, C., Agre, G., & Angelova, G. (2015). Gamification in education: A systematic mapping study. *Journal of Educational Technology & Society*, *18*(3), 75–88.

Eisenberg, M., & Berkowitz, R. E. (1990). *Information Problem Solving: The Big Six Skills*. Linworth.

Éthier, M. A., Demers, S., & Lefrançois, D. (2010). El desarrollo del pensamiento histórico de la literatura publicada en francés e inglés. *Enseñanza de las ciencias sociales: revista de investigación*, (9), 61-74.

Fernández-Enguita, M. (2016). *La educación en la encrucijada*. Santillana.

Gaitán, V. (2013). *Gamificación: el aprendizaje divertido*. Accessed on May 25, 2022, at https://www.educativa.com/blog-articulos/gamificacion-el-aprendizaje-divertido/

Gajardo, M. (1993). Ivan Illich. *Prospects*, *23*(3-4), 711–720. doi:10.1007/BF02195145

Gros, B. (Coord.). (2008). Videojuegos y aprendizaje. Barcelona, Spain: Graó.

Gros, B., & Garrido-Miranda, J. M. (2008). "Con el dedo en la pantalla": El uso de un videojuego de estrategia en la mediación de aprendizajes curriculares. *Teoría de la Educación. Educación y Cultura en la Sociedad de la Información*, *9*(3), 108–129.

Guevara, J. M., & Colomer, J. C. (2017). Minecraft y Eduloc, en historia y geografía. *Íber. Didáctica de las Ciencias Sociales. Geografía e Historia*, (86), 16–23.

Huang, W. H., & Soman, D. (2013). *Gamification Of Education*. Accessed on May 25, 2022, at https://mybrainware.com/wp-content/uploads/2017/11/Gamification-in-Education-Huang.pdf

Jiménez-Palacios, R., & Cuenca-López, J. M. (2021). La enseñanza y aprendizaje de las Ciencias Sociales a través del patrimonio, videojuegos y emociones. Estudio de caso en un IES de Huelva (España). *Panta Rei. Revista digital de Historia y Didáctica de la Historia*, (15), 103-133.

Kapell, M. W., & Elliott, A. B. R. (2013). *Playing with the Past: Digital Games and the Simulation of History*. Bloomsbury.

Karsenti, T., Bugmann, J., & Gros, P. P. (2017). *Transforming Education with Minecraft? Results of an exploratory study conducted with 118 elementary-school students*. CRIFPE.

Lee, J. J., & Hammer, J. (2011). Gamification in Education: What, How, Why Bother? *Academic Exchange Quarterly*, *15*(2), 1–5.

Martínez-Hita, M., Gómez-Carrasco, C. J., & Miralles-Martínez, P. (2021). The effects of a gamified project based on historical thinking on the academic performance of primary school children. *Humanities and Social Sciences Communications*, *8*(1), 1–10. doi:10.105741599-021-00796-9

McCall, J. (2012). Gaming the past: Using video games to teach secondary history. In *Gaming the Past: Using Video Games to Teach Secondary History*. Routledge.

McGonigal, J. (2013). *Por qué los videojuegos pueden mejorar tu vida y cambiar el mundo?: un encuentro entre el mundo virtual y el real en el que las personas salen favorecidas*. Siglo XXI.

Moseikina, M., Toktamysov, S., & Danshina, S. (2022). Modern Technologies and Gamification in Historical Education. *Simulation & Gaming*, *53*(2), 135–156. doi:10.1177/10468781221075965

Mugueta, Í. (2019). El campus escolar «Historia y videojuegos»: Diseño, resultados y conclusiones. *Clío: History and History Teaching*, (44), 9–25.

Pagès, J., & Santisteban, A. (2010). La enseñanza y el aprendizaje del tiempo histórico en Educación Primaria. *Cad. Cedes, Campinas*, *30*(82), 281–309. doi:10.1590/S0101-32622010000300002

Parra-González, M. E., López-Belmonte, J., Segura-Robles, A., & Moreno-Guerrero, A. J. (2021). Gamification and flipped learning and their influence on aspects related to the teaching-learning process. *Heliyon*, *7*(2), e06254. doi:10.1016/j.heliyon.2021.e06254 PMID:33659757

Quintero, D. (2018). Didáctica de las Ciencias Sociales a través de los videojuegos: Investigación y experimentación del juego Assassin's Creed Origins, para posible propuesta didáctica sobre la enseñanza del patrimonio y la cultura del Antiguo Egipto. *Clío: History and History Teaching*, (44), 1–28.

Rivero, P. (2017). Procesos de gamificación en el aula de Ciencias Sociales. *Íber. Didáctica de las Ciencias Sociales. Geografía e Historia*, *86*, 5–6.

Rodríguez, F., & Santiago, R. (2015). *Gamificación: Cómo motivar a tu alumnado y mejorar el clima en el aula*. Digital Text.

Sáiz, J. (2013). Alfabetización histórica y competencias básicas en libros de texto de historia y en aprendizajes de estudiantes. *Didáctica de las ciencias experimentales y sociales*, (27), 43-66.

Sáiz, J., & Colomer, J. C. (2014). ¿Se enseña pensamiento histórico en libros de texto de Educación Primaria? Análisis de actividades de historia para alumnos de 10-12 años de edad. *Clío: History and History Teaching*, (40), 1–19.

Sánchez, A., & Colomer, J. C. (2017). Gamificación y construcción del pensamiento histórico: Desarrollo de competencias en actividades gamificadas. *Clío: History and History Teaching*, (43), 1–12.

Santisteban, A. (2010). La formación de competencias de pensamiento histórico. *Clio y Asociados*, (14), 34–56. doi:10.14409/cya.v1i14.1674

Solbes, J. (2007). El desinterés del alumnado hacia el aprendizaje de la ciencia: implicaciones en su enseñanza. *Didáctica de las ciencias experimentales y sociales*, (21), 91-117.

Soria, G. M. (2014). El pensamiento histórico en la educación primaria: Estudio de casos a partir de narraciones históricas. *Enseñanza de las Ciencias Sociales*, (14), 83–95.

UNESCO. (1980). *El niño y el juego Planteamientos teóricos y aplicaciones pedagógicas. Estudios y documentos de educación*. UNESCO.

Van der Schilden, R., & Heijltjes, B. (2017). Herald. How Wispfire used history to create fiction. In A. A. A. Mol, C. E. Ariese-Vandemeulebroucke, & K. H. J. Boom y Aris Politopoulos (Eds.), *The interactive past: Archaeology, heritage & video games* (pp. 73–82). Sidestone Press.

KEY TERMS AND DEFINITIONS

Gamification: The introduction of game-related features (such as challenges, obstacles and problems to be solved) as an element in the development of a social or educational activity.

Historical Empathy: Reconstruction of the points of view of relevant figures through knowledge and understanding of the historical contexts in which these people have taken part.

Historical Thinking: The creative process carried out by historians to interpret past sources and generate historical narratives.

History Education: Aimed at providing students with an understanding of the way in which historians "make history."

Minecraft.Edu: The educational version of the Minecraft video game. This tool allows the creation of Game-Based Learning experiences with which skills can be developed and creativity can be fostered.

Video Games: An interactive entertainment-oriented application that, through certain commands or controls, simulates experiences on the screen of a TV, computer, or other electronic device.

Chapter 8
Gamification:
A Learning Technique for the Dynamization of the Teaching of Social Sciences

Juan-Carlos de la Cruz-Campos
https://orcid.org/0000-0002-9263-6799
Universidad de Granada, Spain

Santiago Pozo-Sánchez
https://orcid.org/0000-0001-8125-4990
University of Granada, Spain

Blanca Berral-Ortiz
University of Granada, Spain

Santiago Alonso-García
University of Granada, Spain

EXECUTIVE SUMMARY

The search for the optimization of educational processes has led to gamification becoming one of the teaching strategies that has received the most attention in recent years. This chapter carries out an analysis of the particularities that make up gamification as a learning technique for educational revitalization and updating. From a holistic perspective, a tour of the terminological particularities of gamification, constituent elements, benefits, and limitations is made. Likewise, this chapter reviews the main techno-pedagogical resources for the gamification of the Social Sciences classroom, focusing on the subject of History and the development of historical thinking skills, presenting different gamification experiences from a transversal perspective and proposes a compendium of gamified activities based on active learning. This work serves as a starting point for those teachers who intend to carry out gamified activities in their classroom within the field of Social Sciences.

DOI: 10.4018/978-1-6684-5240-0.ch008

INTRODUCTION

During the last decades, education has experienced an authentic stage of revolution in terms of its way of being conceived. There has been a true restructuring of the way of conceiving teaching, as well as the teaching and learning process. This revolution has been especially enhanced by the inclusion of digital technologies and spaces in educational contexts (Greenhow et al., 2021). In this way, the new socio-educational reality has made a methodological commitment characterized by the prominence of active learning and the development of student skills (Hinojo-Lucena et al., 2019).

Education is the main tool for social and economic progress worldwide and educational institutions are constantly working to update education to the needs of today's students (Howell, 2021). Despite this, it is necessary to continue working, betting on research, teaching, innovation and knowledge transfer to solve current problems and continue progress towards educational updating (Ramlo, 2021). In this search for the optimization of educational processes, gamification has become one of the teaching strategies that has received the most attention in recent years (Behl et al., 2022). This impulse of gamification has been based mainly on its numerous benefits within the teaching and learning process, as well as on the proliferation of techno-pedagogy, which has allowed the implementation of pedagogical proposals updated to the current reality (Fernández, 2021).

This work is configured as an analysis of the particularities that make up gamification as a learning technique for educational revitalization and updating. It is intended to carry out a tour of its terminological particularities, its constituent elements, as well as its benefits and limitations, from a holistic perspective. Likewise, it is intended to carry out a tour of the main techno-pedagogical resources for the gamification of the Social Sciences classroom, expose different gamification experiences from a transversal perspective and propose a compendium of gamified activities based on active learning. In this way, the present work aims to establish itself as a starting point for those teachers who intend to carry out gamified activities in their classroom, within the field of Social Sciences.

ACTIVE LEARNING METHODOLOGIES AND THE IMPLEMENTATION OF TECHNO-PEDAGOGY: TWO KEY ISSUES FOR EDUCATIONAL UPDATE

The global health crisis generated by covid-19 has caused a new socio-educational reality in which specific methodologies for virtual learning have had to be carried out (Crawford et al., 2020). This health crisis has led to a real revolution in the educational field, since teachers have been forced to address the teaching and learning process with the support of digital devices, virtual platforms and online learning management systems (Mhlanga and Moloi, 2020). For this reason, the constant search for updating and educational innovation becomes essential in a constantly evolving social landscape in which techno-pedagogy is the way forward (Cabero, 2021).

Importance of Technopedagogy and Digital Competence

In order to achieve pedagogical updating and innovation, teachers must have appropriate knowledge of innovative pedagogical models and the correct use and implementation of technology as a teaching tool (Moreno et al., 2018). Consequently, teachers must have an adequate level of digital competence to be able to put into practice these innovative methodologies complemented by ICT (Information and

Communication Technology), since a poor level of competence in digital material can become a limiting factor. for its use and its combination with pedagogical innovation (Elche and Yubero, 2019).

Based on this teaching update and his search for training in digital competence, technopedagogy was born. Technopedagogy is defined as a group of concepts, ideas and practices associated with innovation and development in the area of education in the digital age (Fernández et al., 2018). Technopedagogy is based on phygital competence, a competence that brings together all those skills and abilities related to ICT and that enable its management and use effectively, being one of the fundamental competences for professionals. of the digital age (Castañeda et al., 2019). Following what was stated by the National Institute of Educational Technologies and Teacher Training (2017), digital skills are grouped into the following areas: Information and Information Literacy; Communication and Collaboration; Creation of Digital Contents; Security; Problem resolution.

Despite the integration of technology and digital resources in the educational field, the scientific literature has drawn attention to the insufficient level of digital competence of teachers (Fuentes et al., 2019). This fact can suppose an important limitation for the comprehensive and up-to-date training of students and a great obstacle for the optimal inclusion of ICTs in daily pedagogical life (Huda et al., 2017).

Active Methodologies in Current Education: Definitions and Types

Bonwell and Eison (1991) defined active learning as that derived from an instructional method that connects students with the learning process and causes them to think reflectively about what processes they are carrying out. In a similar vein, Meyer and Jones (1993) define active methods as those that provide the student with the opportunity to listen, write, read and reflect on academic content for themselves. Johnson et al., (1999) affirm that the action of learning is not carried out by the student in a contemplative way, but rather occurs thanks to his active participation and his complete immersion in the processes that constitute him. Sáez-Pérez (2011) approaches his definition of active learning by focusing on the context that surrounds the teaching process itself, alluding to the paramount importance that the immersion of the student in scenarios that present real problems of the professional world has within active methods. or of social reality itself.

Benito and Cruz (2007) establish five key objectives pursued by active methods, from the student's perspective: interact with the peer group to exchange significant experiences; assume a leading role and build their own knowledge; formulate achievable goals for himself, plan the steps to achieve them and self-assess them in a critical-reflective way; relate to the social environment to be able to adapt quickly to changes; develop metacognition to reflect on the processes carried out.

Luelmo (2018) summarizes the main typologies of existing methodologies that have emerged since the first proposals: the participatory lecture, learning by simulation, learning through case studies, cooperative learning, the flipped classroom and flipped learning, project-based learning, problem-based learning, competency-based learning, and portfolio learning. Other authors incorporate –in addition to those mentioned here– other recently expanded methodologies such as didactic contract learning, thought-based learning and Design Thinking (Hussein and Fast, 2020).

In short, despite the multiple typologies of existing active methods, in general terms they are based on the same pedagogical principles that make them plural and common resources at the same time. The basis on which these methods are based is the student's own assumption of responsibility to build their own learning (Coll, 2018). This responsibility is managed by the teacher, who stands as a counselor and guide who offers students various opportunities to successfully complete their teaching and learning process (Friesen, 2013). Likewise, the evaluation will be constituted as an integrating and continuous action that will analyze the teaching and learning process developed by the student, more than the results themselves (Morales and Landa, 2004).

Benefits and Limitations of the Implementation of Gamified Proposals

There is a multitude of research that supports the benefits of implementing active methodologies in the teaching and learning process. Following Colomer et al., (2020), active methodologies promote commitment and responsibility to achieve the didactic function and aim to train the student in a transversal, comprehensive and self-critical way. Pedocentrism favors the construction of knowledge autonomously and promotes learning by discovery in the search for certainties.

Active methodologies improve memorization by promoting the use of all mental faculties and generate a high level of participation and motivation in students. In short, these methodologies transform the teaching and learning process into an effective procedure.

On the other hand, some studies warn that the implementation of active methodologies has some limitations to consider. Following Zuhir et al., (2021), the ineffective design of some activities can lead to poor time management. These methodologies require the effort and perseverance of both teachers and students. A bad design or a bad implementation of the programming times of the classroom can generate difficulties in the teaching of all the proposed curricular contents.

Likewise, these methodologies can generate moments of disorganization and indiscipline when the instructions are not explained clearly and concisely, even some tasks can generate an unequal distribution of work. Learning may be affected by pre-existing poor relationships between students at the time of methodological implementation and there may be some resistance to alternative assessment methods.

GAMIFICATION: A HOLISTIC APPROACH TO ITS PEDAGOGICAL IMPLEMENTATION

Gamification places the student as the main protagonist of his or her learning. This change of perspective is plausible thanks to the restructuring of the roles that both teachers and students have undergone in recent years and which have made the latter the fundamental axis in the production of knowledge, with students being active agents who take an interest in their learning and develop a series of skills that allow them to act autonomously in the learning process.

In Spain, numerous experiences on gamification have been published, involving teachers and students of social, humanities, health and technical degrees, although its implementation is less than in culturally related countries (Alonso-García et al., 2021a). Gamification has been studied alone or associated with other flipped classroom methodologies, studying the effects on motivation through surveys and questionnaires, demonstrating positive effects on learning and academic performance.

Terminology Issue: Gamification, Serious Game, Game-Based Learning

Gamification is defined as a didactic strategy whose objective is to transfer the mechanics of games to the educational environment and, therefore, to the teaching-learning process (Aznar-Díaz et al., 2017). Its main purpose is to achieve better results (knowledge retention, acquisition of new skills or greater reinforcement of existing ones or rewarding actions, among others) through playful and especially motivating learning. The use of games and gamification in learning contexts, although not yet common, has become widely accepted as teachers are convinced that gamification is a more than stimulating tool for students, improves enthusiasm in the classroom work of students and influences the acquisition of key competences (Aznar-Díaz et al., 2017).

Despite this, its terminology has generated some problems when it comes to its implementation, with points in common but also differences between other pedagogical proposals such as game-based learning or serious play.

A search for "digital games in education" on Google Scholar yielded almost 46700 article records published in 2021 alone, of which most were in the social sciences (42700), but many are still confused about the distinction between serious games, educational games, game-based learning and gamification.

This section aims to clarify the conceptual issue by providing different definitions from among those proposed by the existing scientific corpus to help reach a consensus on what we mean if we want to make progress.

For Becker (2021) Game has the following criteria, although it is not necessary to fulfil them strictly but the general feeling (Table 1):

It is interactive, has rules, has one or more goals, has a quantifiable measure of progress (or success) and has a recognisable end.

Serious games are specifically designed for learning for purposes other than or in addition to pure entertainment including health games (from surgical trainers to pain management games), games focused on social justice issues, advergames (games for advertising), political games, etc. In the educational environment, serious games can be used in formal face-to-face educational settings and virtual learning platforms, although game-based learning can also include professional development and informal learning. Michael and Chen (2006) state that serious games are games that exclude fun, entertainment and enjoyment from their important objectives. However, serious games still provide entertainment, joy and happiness to their users, with a hidden purpose.

Gamification is not necessarily about learning as it can be used in multiple contexts such as in companies seeking to incentivize their employees as well as, association and brand loyalty. In education, it often involves attempts to wrap a game narrative around a course, topic, project or assessments (Becker, 2021).

In parallel, game-based learning helps individuals and teams to improve performance, engage and take responsibility for learning, gain knowledge, achieve and sustain engagement, promote transformative mindsets and open minds to creative thinking and innovation, as Ahmed and Sutton (2017) indicate.

In game-based pedagogy, it is necessary to identify the skills required for teachers to effectively use the tools necessary to enhance learning acquisition. In this context, teaching competence comprises cognitive, skill-based and affective elements: knowledge, skills, attitudes, values and ethics (Nousiainen et al., 2018). In addition to these capacities, teachers must have a deep theoretical knowledge of each educational subject, the practical skills to apply this knowledge effectively and a certain attitude and stance (characteristics such as openness, responsiveness, persistence and the ability to see failures and mistakes as learning opportunities) (Binkley et al., 2012).

Table 1. Differences between different types of teaching and learning using games

	PROCESS	GAMES			GUIDELINES	
	Gamification	**Serious game**	**Game to learn**	**Game**	**Game based learning**	**Game-based Pedagogy**
Basic definition	Use of game elements in a non-game context.	Game designed for purposes other than, or including, pure entertainment.	Game designed specifically towards some learning goals.	Includes both serious games and games to learn.	Process and practice of learning using games (from the students' point of view).	Process and practice of teaching using games (from the point of view of teachers).
Purpose	Improve motivation and have fun.	Change behavior, attitude, health, and understanding of knowledge.	Connect with some educational goals.	Can be used for any purpose.	It is not a game but an approach to knowledge.	It is not a game but an approach to knowledge.
Primary conductor (why is it used)	Take advantage of extrinsic or intrinsic rewards (or both) depending on how you target.	Receive game message.	Learn something.	It can be both the game and the reward (or both).	Improve learning and increase its effectiveness.	Improving teaching practice and its effectiveness.
Key issues	Does it improve profits in business? Is it beneficial in education?	Is the message being received?	It is effective?	It's fun?	Am I learning what I am supposed/need to learn?	Am I teaching what I should teach?
Center focus	User experiences (How to)	Content/message (What?)	Content/message (What?)	Player experience (How to)	Learning objectives (What and how?)	Pedagogical objectives (What and how?)
Cost	From next to nothing to tens of thousands.	From next to nothing to hundreds of thousands.	From next to nothing to hundreds of thousands.	From next to nothing to hundreds of millions.	Usually part of an institutional budget. Largely irrelevant to the user.	Usually part of an institutional budget. Largely irrelevant to the user.
Business model	Producers pay.	Producers pay.	It varies.	User pays.	Pay the institution.	Pay the institution.
Catalytic concept	What is used in learning generally affects how things are taught and managed rather than what is taught.	Message.	Effectiveness or knowledge gap.	The main thing is to have fun.	The game is the lesson or a part of it.	The game is the lesson or a part of it.
Loyalty	Not applicable. If there is a narrative, it doesn't have to have anything to do with what is being gamified.	Fidelity to the message is essential.	Fidelity to the message is essential.	Self consistent, otherwise irrelevant.	Fidelity to the message is essential.	Fidelity to the message is essential.

Source: Modified from Becker (2021)

Constituent Elements of Gamification

When facing the challenge of designing competence-based learning strategies, teachers need to adapt the general characteristics of this approach to the given teaching context in order to integrate the elements of game design into learning activities.

According to Bartel et al., (2015) the five most important dynamics of competence-based gamification are (Table 2):

- Constraints

In the game design, quantitative variables such as time required, objectives achieved or quality of the results have to be defined. In gamification, learners/players must respect time limits (finish a mission in a given time) and be aware that they will be able to receive grades on their performance based on the competences defined in the teaching guides. The initial definition will include what units are measured in a given activity, when they are collected, how values are reflected and how these rules (from the learner/player's point of view) are transparent.

- Emotions

In gamified learning processes it is necessary to induce, stimulate, enhance, intrinsic motivation (Buckley and Doyle, 2016) through a set of dynamic emotions such as wonder, joy or curiosity (Mullins and Sabherwal, 2020) to integrate them in the acquisition of competences. Environmental conditions can often be connected to gamification scenarios to create certain types of emotions. Emotions, by their nature, once unlocked, cannot be confined to a specific game, but can easily be extrapolated, both to gamification activities and outside the classroom as they induce very personal, concrete meanings in learners. Therefore, the elicitation of learning competences through emotions must be well defined and responsibly weighed as they are aimed at learners with different sensitivities.

- Narrative Dynamics

The script, key points, characters, plot, etc., must be considered as a whole in order to provide overall academic learning for the learners, considering the learning objectives that drive this training action. It is not a question of designing a flat, rigid map, but rather the dynamic narrative can be used in a flexible, multidimensional way, to enable different, but specific, individual learning paths, considering the students' previous training (course, stage, training line, academic path, etc.) and their previously acquired competences. Teachers and learners can use the narrative map to insert the state of learning progression, grades, badges and limits to learning so that the former can evaluate the acquisition of competences and the latter to know the possible options for improvement.

- Progression

Progression in learning is identified through the acquisition of competences by progressing through levels of play or different levels of complexity. It requires objective indicators that can be measured with

Table 2. Elements of gamification dynamics

Dynamics of the game	Emotions	Narrative	Progression	Relations
• Constraints. • Balancing Constraints. • Player Freedom. • Rewards. • Solutions.	• Appear in the game. • Remain outside the game. • Long-term commitment of the player.	• Explicit or implicit history. • Consistent. • Own internal logic. • Placed in a context.	• Player growth and development. • During the game. • Various possibilities.	• Social interactions of players. • Promotion of social links.

Source: Modified from Werbach and Hunter (2015)

various techniques through cognitive ranking models or through the achievement of complex competences (Jagušt et al., 2018).

- Relationships

One of the main objectives of learning through gamification is to interact with environment and peers, to socialise by playing in order to learn to relate to each other by creating bonds of camaraderie, fellowship, altruism, social status, etc. Both situations foster motivation to create social bonds in the classroom and to succeed, both in learning and socialising (de Sousa Borges et al., 2014) and the ability to obtain information, select it and transmit it efficiently (Stott and Neustaedter, 2013).

The combination of good game design and good instructional design is a demanding task. To reach the learner at that level, the basic requirements (which have their roots in instructional design) are (Martens and Mueller, 2016):

Clear definition of the intended learning objectives; reduction of the learning material to a level appropriate for the target group; and redesigning the learning content in a way that is interesting for the target group. This includes: closeness to the everyday experiences of the target group; allowing for the construction of one's own mental knowledge; and allowing for increasing levels of complexity (i.e. finding the right level of challenge).

The main elements of the game are (Martens and Mueller, 2016):

- Interaction elements: Elements of the game with which a user can interact (implements, non-player stage characters, the dream world, etc.
- Qualification elements: Elements that provide feedback to the student body (awards, levels, badges, scoring systems, grades, dossiers, etc.).
- Game interface elements: These are the objects that the student can perceive (see, touch or feel in the real world) and with which he/she interacts in the game with the rest of his/her peers (such as scenarios, dialogues, information screens, implements, furniture, panels, boards, costumes, tokens, etc.) and that define each game.
- Operational elements: These are the elements that describe the rules of the game and the conditions to which all players must submit and which are usually known as game mechanics. For the gamification process to be effective, it is important to highlight the game mechanics and elements, which refer to the fundamental rules that must be respected during the gamification processes, fundamental to obtain the maximum benefits of this methodology and to ensure the true involve-

ment and active participation of students in the teaching-learning processes (Alonso-García et al., 2021b).

The operational elements can be separated into subcategories:

- Rules. They require a thorough reading and understanding by the students so that they understand the ways to interact with their peers, how to communicate and behave with them, as well as the opportunities they can develop to progress in the game. These can be defined as the objectives to be achieved in order to progress or obtain a badge and it is essential that learners are able to define more or less risky game strategies to reach the objectives in a bold way.
- Roles representing the typical environments in which students operate (captain, player, starter, substitute, etc.) in order to understand the multiple interactions that can take place.
- Plot that defines the interaction of the elements of the game with the participants.

The Reward System

Meaningful gamification is the use of play and recreational activities to help a user find personal connections that motivate engagement with a specific context for long-term change.

Gamification-based learning attaches particular importance to the belief and values that learners attach to rewards, as well as to the positive effects that rewards have on players' motivation. Rapp (2017) gives importance to the two factors mentioned above (student belief and positive effects on motivation) for two reasons.

- Subjective approach to the value that players attach to rewards: The attributed values reveal how players realize the incentives offered by the game. Players attach meaning to rewards in order to adhere to the game. This effect may transcend the intended goals of the educators/game designers as learners attach different value to the reward depending on the effort to achieve it.
- Possibility of transferring the elements of the game to other circumstances. Indeed, studying the perceived effects of rewards on players is a prerequisite for transferring such design elements to other environments. Of course, not all experiences induce this positive effect. It is up to the designers of the activities to induce or understand what kind of experience they are able to produce in learners and under what conditions they can suggest how and when it is appropriate to reproduce such an experience in non-game contexts.

Both reasons can be linked. Often in the classroom, players do not seek the tangible rewards defined in the game but rely on the game for social gratifications, opportunities to expose their skills, possibilities to acquire reputation, i.e. for all those 'social' rewards that give value to their experience in the game. The robustness of the most successful games (such as World of Warcraft) lies in the fact that the reward structure combines tangible or concrete and visible rewards (such as badges, ratings, positions, etc.) with immaterial incentives (Rapp, 2017) (Table 2).

However, while reward-based gamification can be useful for short-term goals and situations where participants do not have personal connections or intrinsic motivation to participate in a context, rewards can reduce intrinsic motivation and long-term desire to participate in the real-world context (Nicholson, 2015). If long-term change is the goal, rewards should be avoided and other game-based elements

Table 3. Reward classification

Category	Attributed values	Experimental effects	Examples	Gambling situations that make prizes visible
Enabling rewards	• Procedures. • Progression. • Perceived effort.	• Improved performance and motivation. • Possible addiction.	• Experience and/or reputation points. • Badges, skills, social rewards. • Rewards for players who favor the group.	• Discharges at the end of missions. • Instances and raids. • Access to guilds and group games. • Social recognition of players' skills.
Reward exchange	• Instrumental.	• Increased retention. • Possible automation of actions.	• Gold badges . • Professions. • Duplicate ítems.	• Agriculture. • Crafting. • Social engagement with guild roles.
Flexible rewards	• Appearance. • Sociability. • Empowerment.	• Behavioural change. • Possible abandonment.	• Team level. • Legendary team. • Rare pets. • Extremely difficult achievements.	• Completion of quests. • Global battles. • Quest completion.

Source: Modified from Rapp (2017).

should be used to create a system based on meaningful gamification concepts. Nicholson (2015) defines six concepts (Reflection, Exposure, Choice, Information, Play, and Engagement) to guide designers of gamification systems that rely on non-reward-based game elements to help people find personal connections and meaning in a real-world context.

Benefits and Limitations of the Implementation of Gamified Proposals

This section will address the main advantages and limitations of implementing gamification in the classroom. Some of the benefits pointed out by the literature on gamification are the promotion of unconscious involvement in the learning objectives, it allows the adaptation of new realities configured under the parameters that the teacher considers most positive for their students, it improves physical and mental activities, cooperation, collaboration, problem-solving skills and poses challenges that allow increasing the autonomy of students by achieving in a playful way an objective that would otherwise have been more difficult to achieve.

Gamification has had a large number of studies in the field of education since the emergence of the term. However, there is a lack of primary and secondary studies that explore the negative effects that gamification, and gamified learning design, can have on learners, and there is also a lack of studies that analyse gamification design that may be linked to these negative effects. Toda et al., (2017) have conducted a systematic mapping study to identify these negative effects, identifying the decrease or loss of performance, undesired behaviours, indifference and diminishing effects of the application of gamification.

Loss of performance was the most frequent effect and, in the league table, the most cited game design element, among 11 other elements. In addition, they were able to link elements and effects to identify how these elements may have influenced these outcomes. According to their results, game design can have a negative impact, especially in relation to leaderboards which are strongly associated with many negative effects.

The decrease in performance arises when in the gamification process there are tasks and situations that impair or hinder the learning process of students, especially when they have to spend too much time to complete the gamification objectives. However, most studies indicate mixed results, with both positive and negative outcomes after applying gamification in their learning contexts (Toda et al., 2017).

The occurrence of undesirable behaviours may be due to the fact that gamification may have a different effect (positive or negative) on the learning context in which it is applied, either due to poor planning or lack of planning. These behaviours include learners complaining that the bonus system was not satisfactory and they did not receive most gamified notifications due to system problems (Singer and Schneider, 2012), that the system was not enjoyable and a waste of time (Domínguez et al., 2013), the appearance of demotivation due to excessive competition (Codish and Ravid, 2012; Campos, et al., 2015), focus more on dynamics than on learning (Snow et al., 2015), as well as excessive difficulty or dissatisfaction with not achieving badges (McDaniels et al., 2012).

In some studies, students showed indifference, which is typical of undesirable behaviour. De Marcos et al., (2014) indicated that, in general, gamification did not improve learners' knowledge acquisition compared to the traditional learning method, as well as in cognition and performance. Domínguez et al., (2013), Papadopoulos et al., (2016), and Haaranen et al., (2014) have agreed that learners felt indifferent towards the gamified application and that for them it was neither fun nor boring. Buisman and van Eekelen (2014) reported that gamification did not affect students' motivation and engagement. Finally, Berkling and Thomas (2013) also reported that some students were not interested in the gamification used, preferring traditional methods over gamified ones.

Gradual loss of motivation and engagement in gamification processes is common because learners are initially motivated by the novelty of the proposal, but motivation, interest, novelty, is lost over time, which can also lead to loss of performance (Berkling and Thomas, 2013; Hanus and Fox, 2014). On other occasions, a lack of understanding of the rules or reluctance to use gamified assessment (for fear that it would affect their grades) can also be negative effects (Campos et al., 2015).

In the future, further analysis of primary studies would be necessary in order to identify their objectives and to statistically analyze how these negative effects influence each other, as well as to conduct individual analyses of each game element in the respective gamification designs in order to understand their influence, positive or negative, on the determinants of student learning.

RELATIONSHIP OF GAMIFICATION TO HISTORY TEACHING AND HISTORICAL THINKING SKILLS

In the review by Shavab et al., (2021) it is shown that gamification in history learning affects students in several ways, including motivation, interests, learning process, learning interactions and understanding of the material. Gamification also elicits good perceptions from teachers and students after being implemented in history learning activities. Equipment is also a component of gamification that should be considered in history learning. These results can be used as a reference in history learning research using gamification.

Moseikina et al., (2021) conclude that gamification in history teaching has a positive effect on the evolutionary development of a personality adaptive to the socio-economic conditions of the 21st century for a complete vertical and horizontal evolutionary development of the personality, thus fostering historical thinking skills in learners.

TECHNO-PEDAGOGICAL RESOURCES FOR THE GAMIFICATION OF THE SOCIAL SCIENCES CLASSROOM

In the digital era in which we find ourselves, it is considered crucial to have a rigorous and critical point of view on the way in which technologies are managed and thus the different technological resources within a pedagogical design. In this sense, it is interesting to note how, since the year 2000, technopedagogical tools have been introduced into the educational system, and the accompaniment of these tools has been considered as pedagogical strategies. In line with the above, educational institutions try to incorporate technological tools because they improve and facilitate the way of producing, disseminating, organizing, accessing knowledge and controlling knowledge (Santos-Rego, 2017). As Bernate and Vargas (2020) state, one of the challenges in today's society is to make effective use of technology in all areas of the individual and, in particular, in educational contexts. For this, it is appropriate and necessary to have adequate digital competence (Concha-Maquisaca and Álvarez-Lozano, 2021), in addition to a critical, creative and safe use of ICTs in order to achieve the objectives related to learning, use of leisure time, work, inclusion and participation in society.

Among the advantages found in the use of techno-pedagogical tools are: motivation, trying to teach in an attractive and fun way; interest, since the use of graphic resources, audios, videos and interactive activities reinforces multimedia comprehension; creativity and initiative, which give students an active role, where they are given autonomy to select the information they consider appropriate; and cooperation, which allows students and collaborators to carry out joint projects or work together.

From the perspective of Karatas et al., (2017), the inclusion of technologies as essential resources to develop teaching-learning processes facilitates and encourages innovation of traditional strategies with new horizons of understanding education by teachers.

Authors such as Alarcón-San Lucas and Millán-Ibarra (2021) argue that a literate subject trained in technological media will make it easier to be reflective, critical, autonomous and participatory in the digitalized society in which we currently live. On the other hand, it is understood that media and visual literacy is necessary in digital and advanced knowledge societies due to the fact that most of the information received is received through visual media, so the use of photography, comics and press in the classroom is necessary.

All of the above takes on a more inescapable character in the field of knowledge of the social sciences, where the main function is the formation of citizenship. As has been done in recent decades, the need to I ntegrate ICT in the teaching of social sciences, as in other applied sciences, has been emphasized. Technologies represent an opportunity for the teacher as the main generator of virtual images in time and space, since the purpose of social science didactics is to design, analyze and investigate techniques of dissemination, didactics and communication of the contents of history, art history and geography. Therefore, the use of resources increases the options for experimentation in the social sciences (Miralles-Martínez et al., 2019).

It is a generalized opinion that the use of ICT in the classroom and the path towards a virtual classroom is a valuable tool in the learning of social sciences at all educational levels (Acosta, 2010). The main advantages of using technology to teach history, geography and other social sciences revolve around the fact that ICTs promote and allow for self-regulated and meaningful learning, and, as shown in the resources in Table 4, they enable collaboration among the students themselves and between students and teachers.

As Rodríguez and Gutiérrez (2016) point out, the interaction with technopedagogical tools allows to effectively enhance historical education.

On the other hand, gamification is considered as one of the methodological strategies that are being used successfully and have acquired significant progress to work social sciences in the classroom. In this sense, Ayén (2017) sheds works where they explain the methodological dynamics and the procedures they follow to establish points and rakings; Guevara and Colomer (2017) carry out experiences to evaluate the use of Minecraft and Maté (2017) establishing guidelines to work with role-playing games favoring attitudinal changes and facilitating learning through experiences. In all the works, positive results have been provided in two aspects: the motivation shown by the students, which predisposes them for learning and makes such learning more meaningful. The following is a list of some useful teaching technology resources for social sciences teaching and their functionalities, in which gamification plays an important role (Table 4) (Trejo, 2019; Rojas-Viteri et al., 2020).

Each and every one of the tools mentioned above are ideal for implementing gamification in the classroom, i.e., to encourage students to learn in a fun way through play. The creation of games where they compete with each other to see who gets the highest score can stimulate them to acquire and fix their knowledge in all subjects. Research such as that conducted by González-Acosta et al., (2020), shows that gamification keeps students interested in the tasks set for much longer than in traditional homework and, frequently, individuals' grades tend to improve.

PROPOSAL OF GAMIFIED ACTIVITIES BASED ON ACTIVE LEARNING

If we conclude that the objective of gamification is to influence the motivation of students to achieve a certain behavior, this subject must be at the center of the thinking of those who design a gamified activity and at the center of the definition. Gamification consists of making game experiences live within a non-game context, and this is measured by the player's enjoyment during the process (Zambrano-Álava et al., 2020).

In line with the above, the idea of gamification is that the learner has the feeling of living a game experience. Therefore, all activities that aim to be configured with the learning technique "gamification" should consist of placing the participants in real protagonists, in addition, the activities should propose challenges using certain elements of the game and progress through the levels proposed. In educational environments there are many gamification proposals, mainly in Primary and Secondary Education, however, in Higher Education there is still little incidence (Cornella et al., 2020).

Below are two educational activities that have recently become fashionable: Escape Room and Breakout (Sierra and Fernández-Sánchez, 2019; Moreno, 2019). Both games are applicable to any educational stage, from Kindergarten to Higher Education. They require the resolution of enigmas and puzzles to achieve the ultimate goal: in the case of Breakout it is to open a box guarded by various padlocks and the Escape Room the goal is to escape from a locked room. Likewise, both require the team of players to make decisions that will lead them to failure or success. So, they have to make interesting and risky decisions. Both types of games have an extra element to achieve the objective: a maximum time limit. This type of learning, motivates students and are experiences that are fun for everyone, in addition, can be adapted to any curricular content and likewise, curricular adaptations can be made, if necessary. On the other hand, they promote teamwork and collaboration, improve group and individual communication skills, develop problem solving skills and critical thinking, students learn to work under pressure, it is a learning based on research, develops deductive thinking, this type of educational games challenges players to persevere and learning revolves around the student.

Table 4. Examples of technopedagogical resources

Technopedagogical resources	Operation of the resources
Arcademics	• They are educational video games whose objective is to produce a high learning rate through exciting and focused repetition that allows to achieve automaticity and fluency quickly. • It includes a number of interactive games to learn English or exercise mental arithmetic.
Brainscape	• It is a flashcard mode application, so you do not have to type the answers, just think what the solution is and turn the cards over by pressing "Reveal answer", thus, it will check if you have guessed it or not. • It allows you to learn languages and so on, in a simple way thanks to its repetition system.
Cerebriti	• The application helps Primary and Secondary students to fix the knowledge through the development of games and their active participation in a fun and entertaining way. • All subjects can be worked on, the games are classified in 16 areas, among which are located material from the school curriculum.
ChemCaper	• It is a video game that teaches the principles of chemistry, experiment techniques, instruments, among others. • You get immediate feedback.
Classcraft	• Each student is part of a team (healers, mages or warriors), through various combats, players can level up and gain life, action or money points. • Students have to create team strategies to prevent teammates from falling in combat or to ensure that they level up.
ClassDojo	• It is an educational communication platform that students, teachers and families use to build united communities by sharing what they experience at home through videos, messages and photos. • It is about listening to teachers, students and families, with the goal of working as a community.
CodeCombat	• It is a management platform whose objective is to manage an educational classroom by scoring student behavior. The interface is simple, allows customization and the participation of parents, students and teachers. Although the teacher is the one who grades. • If the student does a brilliant job, he/she will earn points; on the contrary, if he/she disturbs his/her classmates, he/she will receive a negative score.
Edmodo	• It is an application whose main objective is to allow communication between teachers and students. It was created for specific use in education, providing the teacher with a private and closed virtual environment where messages, files, links and a classroom calendar can be shared.
Genially	• It is an online tool whose objective is to help create interactive content, by creating quizzes, graphs, presentations, infographics, timelines, among others, for any purpose and subject, but of quality without costing you too much effort. • In addition, it allows the student to interact with the content instead of being merely observed passively.
Kahoot!	• It is considered a useful tool for students and teachers to review and learn concepts in entertaining ways, as if it were a quiz. The most common way is through quiz questions, although there are also spaces for debate and discussion. • Anyone can create a game board for any subject.
Knowre	• The objective of this platform is to personalize the mathematical learning process. It consists of question and answer sessions to evaluate the individual strengths and weaknesses of each student in order to build personalized curricula adapted to the progress of each student in real time. • Once the data is collected, the platform automatically builds an individual evaluation sheet with the contents that the student is not assimilating properly.
Minecraft (Education Edition)	• It is an educational version of the video game Minecraft. This resource enables the creation of game-based learning experiences that develop creativity, collaborative experiences, STEM skills and problem solving among students. It is used to teach curricular content and inspire Project Based Learning (PBL). • Also, this educational version enables the inclusion of evaluation tools and multiplayer, to work in teams.
Monster Kit	• This game enables students to develop creative skills by working on drawing, reading and writing, calculating and developing their imagination. It also makes it possible to create monsters and work alone or with others. • The objective is to develop creation in fun ways.
Pear Deck	• It enables an active role for students by providing a context of questions and exercises. This tool provides the teacher with real time information, therefore, the feedback on student learning is immediate. • It is coupled to Google Slides.
Play Brighter	• Once the teacher is registered on the platform, he/she begins to configure his/her classes. The resource enables children to learn by playing, improving problem solving and activating their role in their own learning. • Once the students are registered, the teacher assigns games, missions, challenges and problems to each of them according to their needs. The tool also offers teachers the possibility of monitoring their work.
Quizizz	• It is a website that enables the creation of fun and playful online quizzes, through which students can respond in three different ways: as homework, playing live or individually. • Teachers make use of this application to evaluate student learning as it allows immediate feedback on the answers given by the students and, of course, to gamify the Teaching-Learning (T-L) processes.
Quizlet	• The purpose of this application is to learn vocabulary. It consists mainly of creating classes and lists of words that can then be used to study. • The application includes games, statistics on what they have studied and vocabulary (flashcards). Students have to join the classes through a. link or by searching in the search engine.
The World Peace Game	• It is a game that takes place in specific workshops and camps. It introduces students to a simulation, offering them the opportunity to explore and make new contacts in a community suffering from economic, social and environmental crises with the possibility and danger of entering a major war. •The objective is to save humanity by alleviating all the problems.
Toovari	• It is a technological program of support, reinforcement and academic improvement aimed at parents, teachers and students with the objective of improving motivation in the T-L processes, through the incorporation of techniques, games and dynamics. • They are self-evaluating activities for students to exercise in an autonomous way, enabling self-learning, discipline and study habits, in addition to promoting communication, collaboration and the development of social skills. • The activities are adaptive because they cater to the student's profile, encourage deepening in those that have gone wrong, incorporate game techniques and elements to capture the attention and interest of students and learning is marked by achievements that the student will collect as he/she progresses through the program.
Trivinet	• This collaborative educational resource is an online trivia game in which you can demonstrate your knowledge of various subjects or topics through questions, as well as compete against other players or against your group of friends. • The tool has a multitude of questions prepared by subjects, educational levels and thematic areas. It gives you the possibility for the teacher to manage and create collaborative trivia. The teacher receives if the students have assimilated the contents or not, statistics are generated where the successes and failures of each group or each of them are located.

Source: Own elaboration.

FUTURE RESEARCH DIRECTIONS

Next, the following lines of research on gamification in the area of Social Sciences are proposed:

- Analyze the effects of the combination of gamification as a learning technique together with other pedagogical proposals: Flipped Learning, Project-Based Learning, Cooperative Learning, Problem-Based Learning, Design Thinking, Thinking Based Learning and Competency-Based Learning, among other proposals.
- It carries out a comparative analysis in which the different results of the application of gamification in the teaching and learning process in the different subjects of Social Sciences are analyzed. For example, its effect could be comparatively analyzed in the classroom of: History, Geography, Economics, Anthropology, Psychology, Sociology, et.
- Related to the previous proposal, it is proposed to analyze the effectiveness of gamification by comparing the different educational stages, to verify the relevance of its implementation: early childhood education, primary education, secondary education, higher education and professional training.
- Carry out a longitudinal study that analyzes the effectiveness of gamification over a given period of time. In this way it will be possible to verify if part of the positive effects of gamification are conditioned by its novel component.
- Analyze the effects of the application of gamification in Social Sciences in comparison with other areas of knowledge. In this way, it will be possible to know the specific degree of effectiveness for each area of knowledge.
- Carry out a bibliometric analysis that allows knowing the research trends of gamification research in the area of Social Sciences. This analysis is especially important in the knowledge of the thematic centers of interest during the last years.
- Extend the limits of face-to-face gamification and establish a comparative analysis between gamification applied in physical learning contexts and gamification implemented in virtual spaces, through digital tools.

CONCLUSION

This work has carried out an analysis of the particularities that make up gamification as a learning technique for educational revitalization and updating. A tour has been made of its terminological particularities, its constitutive elements, as well as its benefits and limitations. The main techno-pedagogical resources for the gamification of the Social Sciences classroom, different gamification experiences from a transversal perspective and proposals for gamified activities based on active learning have been proposed.

In short, gamification has become a very effective pedagogical technique for training and learning acquisition in the area of Social Sciences. The ambivalent motivational power of game elements in technology-supported learning environments has been costly. Gamification creates learning experiences through fun, thus making learning more meaningful and functional. For this, it is essential that the teacher creates affective ties between the student and the game (bond or loyalty) so that they commit to what they are working on. Teachers need to constantly motivate them to continue to achieve goals and improve their learning and reward them for a job well done. In this way, a correctly implemented gamification can cause highly positive benefits in the teaching and learning process. For this reason, this chapter aims to serve as a starting point for those teachers who intend to carry out gamified activities in their classroom effectively to dynamize their Social Sciences classrooms.

As it has been stated throughout this paper, gamification is not only useful for learning, but also for changing behaviors in the classroom and for the student to improve. This educational technique ensures learning based on healthy competition, helps to socialize, equality, equity and non-discrimination of students, also contributes to personal and emotional well-being. In short, gamification is here to stay because it prepares students better, but it requires teachers to adapt and train themselves.

In the same way, we must adapt to the demands of today's society and, thus, integrate technologies in the teaching-learning process and make adequate use of the technopedagogical resources that have been proposed, such as ClassDojo, Edmodo, Kahoot!, among others.

ACKNOWLEDGMENT

This research received no specific grant from any funding agency in the public, commercial, or not-for-profit sectors.

REFERENCES

Acosta, L.M. (2010). La enseñanza-aprendizaje de la historia en bachillerato y las TIC: la introducción de la estrategia Webquest. *Clío. History and History Teaching, 36.*

Ahmed, A., & Sutton, M. J. (2017). Gamification, serious games, simulations, and immersive learning environments in knowledge management initiatives. *World Journal of Science, Technology and Sustainable Development, 14*(2/3), 78–83. doi:10.1108/WJSTSD-02-2017-0005

Alarcón-San Lucas, M., & Millán-Ibarra, A. (2021). La relación entre el uso responsable de la tecnología y el aprendizaje en los estudiantes del Subnivel Básica Media de la Escuela Leónidas Plaza. *593 Digital Publisher CEIT, 6*(1), 120-138. doi:10.33386/593dp.2021.2-1.528

Alonso-García, S., Martínez-Domingo, J. A., Berral-Ortiz, B., & De la Cruz-Campos, J. C. (2021a). Gamificación en Educación Superior. Revisión de experiencias realizadas en España en los últimos años. *Hachetetepé. Revista científica de Educación y Comunicación, 23*, 1-21. . doi:10.25267/Hachetetepe.2021.i23.2205

Alonso-García, S., Rodríguez-Jiménez, C., De la Cruz-Campos, J. C., & Santos-Villalba, M. J. (2021b). Applications of Gamification in the Context of Higher Education. A Theoretical Approach. In *International Conference in Methodologies and intelligent Systems for Techhnology Enhanced Learning* (pp. 147-155). Springer. 10.1007/978-3-030-86618-1_15

Ayén, F. (2017). ¿Qué es la gamificación y el ABJ? *Íber. Didáctica de las Ciencias Sociales. Geografía e Historia, 86*, 7–15.

Aznar-Díaz, I., Raso-Sánchez, F., Hinojo-Lucena, M. A., & Romero-Díaz de la Guardia, J. J. (2017). Percepciones de los futuros docentes respecto al potencial de la ludificación y la inclusión de los videojuegos en los procesos de enseñanza-aprendizaje. *Educar*, *53*(1), 11–28. doi:10.5565/rev/educar.840

Bartel, A., Figas, P., & Hagel, G. (2015). Towards a competency-based education with gamification design elements. In *Proceedings of the 2015 Annual Symposium on Computer-Human Interaction in Play* (pp. 457-462). 10.1145/2793107.2810325

Becker, K. (2021). What's the difference between gamification, serious games, educational games, and game-based learning? *Academia Letters*. Advance online publication. doi:10.20935/AL209

Behl, A., Jayawardena, N., Pereira, V., Islam, N., Del Giudice, M., & Choudrie, J. (2022). Gamification and e-learning for young learners: A systematic literature review, bibliometric analysis, and future research agenda. *Technological Forecasting and Social Change*, *176*, 121–145. doi:10.1016/j.techfore.2021.121445

Benito, A., & Cruz, A. (2007). *Nuevas claves para la Docencia Universitaria*. Narcea.

Berkling, K., & Thomas, C. (2013). Gamification of a software engineering course and a detailed analysis of the factors that lead to it's failure. *2013 International Conference on Interactive Collaborative Learning (ICL)*, 525–530. 10.1109/ICL.2013.6644642

Bernate, J. A., & Vargas, J. A. (2020). Desafíos y tendencias del siglo XXI en la educación superior. *Revista de Ciencias Sociales*, *26*(2), 141–154.

Binkley, M., Erstad, O., Herman, J., Raizen, S., Ripley, M., Miller-Ricci, M., & Rumble, M. (2012). Defining twenty-first century skills. In *Assessment and teaching of 21st century skills* (pp. 17–66). Springer. doi:10.1007/978-94-007-2324-5_2

Bonwell, C., & Eison, J. (1991). *Active learning:creating excitement in the classroom*. The George Washington University.

Buckley, P., & Doyle, E. (2016). Gamification and student motivation. *Interactive Learning Environments*, *24*(6), 1162–1175. doi:10.1080/10494820.2014.964263

Buisman, A. L. D., & van Eekelen, M. C. J. D. (2014) Gamification in educational software development. *Proceedings of the Computer Science Education Research Conference*, 55, 9–20. 10.1145/2691352.2691353

Cabero, J. (2021). And COVID-19 transformed the educational system: Reflections and experiences to learn. *International Journal of Educational Research and Innovation*, (15), 218–228. doi:10.46661/ijeri.5246

Campos, A., Batista, E., Signoretti, A., Gardiman, R., & Madeira, C. (2015). Gamifying activities in a higher education course. In*: Proceedings of the European Conference on Games-Based Learning* (pp. 117–124). Academic Conferences International Limited. Retrieved from https://www.proquest.com/conference-papers-proceedings/gamifying-activities-higher-education-course/docview/1728409632/se-2?accountid=14542

Castañeda, L., Esteve, F., & Adell, J. (2018). ¿Por qué es necesario repensar la competencia docente para el mundo digital? *Revista de Educación a Distancia*, *56*(56), 1–20. doi:10.6018/red/56/6

Codish, D., & Ravid, G. (2012) Personality based gamification: how differente personalities perceive gamification. *Proceedings of the 22nd European Conference on Information Systems*, 11. https://cutt.ly/gGnfmdE

Coll, C. (2018). La personalización del aprendizaje escolar, una exigencia de la nueva ecología del aprendizaje. *Personalización del aprendizaje*, 5-11.

Colomer, J., Serra, T., Cañabate, D., & Bubnys, R. (2020). Reflective Learning in Higher Education: Active Methodologies for Transformative Practices. *Sustainability*, *12*(9), 3827. doi:10.3390u12093827

Concha-Maquisaca, J. A., & Álvarez-Lozano, M. I. (2021). Aplicación del sistema del conocimiento a través de herramientas tecnopedagógicas en Cañar durante el COVID-19. *Espisteme Koinonia*, *4*(8), 204–288. doi:10.35381/e.k.v4i8.1353

Cornella, P., Estebanell, M., & Brusi, D. (2020). Gamificación y aprendizaje basado en juegos: Consideraciones generales y algunos ejemplos para la Enseñanza de la Geología. *Enseñanza de las ciencias de la tierra. Revista de la Asociación Española para la Enseñanza de las Ciencias de la Tierra*, *28*(1), 5–19.

Crawford, J., Butler-Henderson, K., Rudolph, J., Malkawi, B., Glowatz, M., Burton, R., & Lam, S. (2020). COVID-19: 20 countries' higher education intra-period digital pedagogy responses. *Journal of Applied Learning & Teaching*, *3*(1), 1–20. doi:10.37074/jalt.2020.3.1.7

De-Marcos, L., Domínguez, A., Saenz-de-Navarrete, J., & Pagés, C. (2014). An empirical study comparing gamification and social networking on e-learning. *Computers & Education*, *75*, 82–91. doi:10.1016/j.compedu.2014.01.012

De Sousa Borges, S., Durelli, V. H., Reis, H. M., & Isotani, S. (2014). A systematic mapping on gamification applied to education. In *Proceedings of the 29th annual ACM symposium on applied computing* (pp. 216-222). 10.1145/2554850.2554956

Domínguez, A., Saenz-de-Navarrete, J., De-Marcos, L., Fernández-Sanz, L., Pagés, C., & Martínez-Herráiz, J. (2013). Gamifying learning experiences: Practical implications and outcomes. *Computers & Education*, *63*, 380–392. doi:10.1016/j.compedu.2012.12.020

Elche, M., & Yubero, S. (2019). The influence of reading habits on the use of internet: A study with university students. *Investigación Bibliotecológica*, *33*(79), 51–66. doi:10.22201/iibi.24488321xe.2019.79.57985

Fernández, F. J., Fernández, M. J., & Rodríguez, J. M. (2018). El proceso de integración y uso pedagógico de las TIC en los centros educativos madrileños. *Educación XX1, 21*(2), 395-416. doi:10.5944/educxx1.17907

Fernandez, S. (2021). Making space in higher education: Disability, digital technology, and the inclusive prospect of digital collaborative making. *International Journal of Inclusive Education*, *25*(12), 1375–1390. doi:10.1080/13603116.2019.1610806

Friesen, N. (2013). Learning analytics: Readiness and rewards. *Canadian Journal of Learning and Technology*, *39*(4), 1–12. doi:10.21432/T2J01B

Fuentes, A., López, J., & Pozo, S. (2019). Análisis de la competencia digital docente: Factor clave en el desempeño de pedagogías activas con Realidad Aumentada. *Revista Electrónica Iberoamericana sobre Calidad, Eficacia y Cambio en Educación*, *17*(2), 27–42. doi:10.15366/reice2019.17.2.002

González-Acosta, E., Almeida-González, M., Torres-Chils, A., & Traba-Montejo, Y. M. (2020). La gamificación como herramienta educativa: El estudiante de contabilidad en el rol del gerente, del contador y del auditor. *Formación Universitaria*, *13*(5), 155–164. doi:10.4067/S0718-50062020000500155

Greenhow, C., Lewin, C., & Staudt Willet, K. B. (2021). The educational response to Covid-19 across two countries: A critical examination of initial digital pedagogy adoption. *Technology, Pedagogy and Education*, *30*(1), 7–25. doi:10.1080/1475939X.2020.1866654

Guevara, J. M., & Colomer, J. C. (2017). Minecraft y Eduloc en historia y geografía. *Íber. Didáctica de las Ciencias Sociales. Geografía e Historia*, *86*, 16–23.

Haaranen, L., Ihantola, P., Hakulinen, L., & Korhonen, A. (2014) How (not) to introduce badges to online exercises. *Proceedings of the 45th ACM Technical Symposium on Computer Science Education*, 33–38. 10.1145/2538862.2538921

Hanus, M. D., & Fox, J. (2014). Assessing the effects of gamification in the classroom: A longitudinal study on intrinsic motivation, social comparison, satisfaction, effort, and academic performance. *Computers & Education*, *80*, 152–161. doi:10.1016/j.compedu.2014.08.019

Hinojo-Lucena, F. J., Aznar-Díaz, I., Cáceres-Reche, M. P., & Romero-Rodríguez, J. M. (2019). Flipped Classroom Method for the Teacher Training for Secondary Education: A Case Study in the University of Granada, Spain. *International Journal of Emerging Technologies in Learning*, *14*(11), 202–208. doi:10.3991/ijet.v14i11.9853

Howell, R. A. (2021). Engaging students in education for sustainable development: The benefits of active learning, reflective practices and flipped classroom pedagogies. *Journal of Cleaner Production*, *325*, 129–168. doi:10.1016/j.jclepro.2021.129318

Huda, M., Maseleno, A., Shahrill, M., Jasmi, K. A., Mustari, I., & Basiron, B. (2017). Exploring adaptive teaching competencies in big data era. *International Journal of Emerging Technologies in Learning*, *12*(3), 68–83. doi:10.3991/ijet.v12i03.6434

Hussein, M. T., & Fast, O. (2020). Gut feeling: A grounded theory study to identify clinical educators' reasoning processes in putting students on a learning contract. *Journal of Clinical Nursing*, *29*(1-2), 75–84. doi:10.1111/jocn.15058 PMID:31512306

Jagušt, T., Boticki, I., & So, H. J. (2018). Examining competitive, collaborative and adaptive gamification in young learners' math learning. *Computers & Education*, *125*, 444–457. doi:10.1016/j.compedu.2018.06.022

Johnson, R. T., Johnson, D. W., & Holubec, E. J. (1999). *El aprendizaje cooperativo en el aula*. Paidós.

Karatas, I., Tunc, M., Yilmaz, N., & Karaci, G. (2017). An Investigation of Technological Pedagogical Content Knowledge, Self-Confidence, and Perception of Pre-Service Middle School Mathematics Teachers towards Instructional *Technologies. Journal of Educational Technology & Society*, *20*(3), 122–132. https://jstor.org/stable/26196124

Luelmo, M. J. (2018). Origen y desarrollo de las Metodologías Activas dentro del sistema educativo español. *Encuentro Journal*, (27), 4-21. http://www3.uah.es/encuentrojournal/index.php/encuentro/article/view/2

Martens, A., & Mueller, W. (2016). Gamification - A Structured Analysis. *2016 IEEE 16th International Conference on Advanced Learning Technologies (ICALT),* 138-142. 10.1109/ICALT.2016.72

Maté, I. (2017). Juegos de rol. Pautas para su uso en clase. *Íber. Didáctica de las Ciencias Sociales. Geografía e Historia*, *86*, 24–29.

McDaniel, R., Lindgren, R., & Friskics, J. (2012) Using badges for shaping interactions in online learning environments. *IEEE International Professional Communication Conference*, 12–15. 10.1109/IPCC.2012.6408619

Meyer, C., & Jones, T. (1993). *Promoting active learning: Strategies for the college classroom.* Jossey-Bass.

Mhlanga, D., & Moloi, T. (2020). COVID-19 and the Digital Transformation of Education: What Are We Learning on 4IR in South Africa? *Education Sciences*, *10*(7), 1–11. doi:10.3390/educsci10070180

Michael, D. R., & Chen, S. L. (2005). Serious Games: Games That Educate, Train, and Inform. *Education*, 1–95. https://dl.acm.org/doi/abs/10.5555/1051239

Miralles-Martínez, P., Gómez-Carrasco, C.J., & Monteagudo-Fernández, J. (2019). Perceptions on the use of ICT resources and mass-media for the teaching of History. A comparative study among future teachers of Spain-England. *Educación XX1, 22*(2), 187-211. https://doi.org. doi:10.5944/educxx1.21377

Morales, P., & Landa, V. (2004). Aprendizaje Basado en Problemas. *Theoria*, 145–157. https://cmapspublic.ihmc.us/rid=1152868048651_1396346847_11204/pbl1.pdf

Moreno, E. (2019). El "Breakout EDU" como herramienta clave para la gamificación en la formación inicial de maestros/as. EDUTEC. Revista electrónica de tecnología educativa, (67), 66-79. doi:10.21556/edutec.2019.67.1247

Moreno, N., López, E., & Leiva, J. (2018). El uso de tecnologías emergentes como recursos didácticos en ámbitos educativos. *International Studies on Law and Education*, *29*(30), 131–146. http://www.hottopos.com/isle29_30/131-146Moreno.pdf

Moseikina, M., Toktamysov, S., & Danshina, S. (2022). Modern Technologies and Gamification in Historical Education. *Simulation & Gaming*, *53*(2), 135–156. doi:10.1177/10468781221075965

Mullins, J. K., & Sabherwal, R. (2020). Gamification: A cognitive-emotional view. *Journal of Business Research*, *106*, 304–314. doi:10.1016/j.jbusres.2018.09.023

National Institute of Educational Technologies and Teacher Training. (2017). *Marco de Competencia Digital.* Ministerio de Educación, Ciencia y Deportes.

Nicholson, S. (2015). A recipe for meaningful gamification. In *Gamification in education and business* (pp. 1–20). Springer. https://scottnicholson.com/pubs/recipepreprint.pdf

Nousiainen, T., Kangas, M., Rikala, J., & Vesisenaho, M. (2018). Teacher competencies in game-based pedagogy. *Teaching and Teacher Education*, *74*, 85–97. doi:10.1016/j.tate.2018.04.012

Papadopoulos, P. M., Lagkas, T., & Demetriadis, S. N. (2016). How revealing rankings affects student attitude and performance in a peer review learning environment. In S. Zvacek, M. T. Restivo, J. Uhomoibhi, & M. Helfert (Eds.), *CSEDU 2015. CCIS* (Vol. 583, pp. 225–240). Springer. doi:10.1007/978-3-319-29585-5_13

Ramlo, S. E. (2021). Universities and the COVID-19 Pandemic: Comparing Views about How to Address the Financial Impact. *Innovative Higher Education*, *46*(6), 777–793. doi:10.100710755-021-09561-x PMID:34177079

Rapp, A. (2017). From games to gamification: A classification of rewards in World of Warcraft for the design of gamified systems. *Simulation & Gaming*, *48*(3), 381–401. doi:10.1177/1046878117697147

Rodríguez, M. A., & Gutiérrez, D. (2016). Innovación en el aula de ciencias sociales a través de los videojuegos. *Revista Iberoamericana de Educación*, *72*(2), 181–200.

Rojas-Viteri, J., Álvarez-Zurita, A., & Bracero-Huertas, D. (2021). Uso de Kahoot como elemento motivador en el proceso enseñanza-aprendizaje. *Revista Cátedra*, *4*(1), 98–114. doi:10.29166/catedra.v4i1.2815

Sáez-Pérez, M. P. (2011). *Metodologías Activas y Aprendizaje. Propuesta de innovación en el grado de ingeniería de edificación*. Universidad de Granada.

Santos-Rego, M. (2017). La educación intercultural y el pluralismo religioso: Propuestas pedagógicas para el diálogo [Intercultural education and religious pluralism: pedagogical proposals for dialogue]. *Educación (Lima)*, *21*(1), 1–4. doi:10.5944/educxx1.17489

Shavab, O. A. K., Yulifar, L., Supriatna, N., & Mulyana, A. (2021). Gamification in History Learning: A Literature Review. In *6th International Conference on Education & Social Sciences (ICESS 2021)* (pp. 254-258). Atlantis Press. 10.2991/assehr.k.210918.047

Sierra, M. C., & Fernández-Sánchez, M. R. (2019). Gamificando el aula universitaria. Análisis de una experiencia de Escape Room en educación superior. *REXE-Revista de Estudios y Experiencias en Educación*, *18*(36), 105–115. doi:10.21703/rexe.20191836sierra15

Singer, L., & Schneider, K. (2012) It was a bit of a race: gamification of version control. *2012 2nd International Workshop on Games Software Engineering (GAS*), 5–8. 10.1109/GAS.2012.6225927

Snow, E.L., Allen, L.K., Jackson, G.T., & McNamara, D.S. (2015) Spendency: students' propensity to use system currency. *Int. J. Artif. Intell. Educ.*, *25*(3), 407–427. doi:10.1007/s40593-015-0044-1

Stott, A., & Neustaedter, C. (2013). *Analysis of gamification in education*. http://clab.iat.sfu.ca/pubs/Stott-Gamification.pdf

Toda, A. M., Valle, P. H., & Isotani, S. (2017). The dark side of gamification: An overview of negative effects of gamification in education. In *Researcher links workshop: higher education for all* (pp. 143–156). Springer. doi:10.1007/978-3-319-97934-2

Trejo, H. (2019). Recursos tecnológicos para la integración de la gamificación en el aula. *Tecnología. Ciência & Educação (Bauru)*, *13*, 75–117.

Werbach, K., & Hunter, D. (2015). *The Gamification Toolkit: Dynamics, Mechanics, and Components for the Win*. Wharton Digital Press. https://www.coursera.org/learn/gamification

Zambrano-Álava, A. P., Lucas-Zambrano, M. D. L. Á., Luque-Alcívar, K. E., & Lucas-Zambrano, A. T. (2020). La Gamificación: Herramientas innovadoras para promover el aprendizaje autorregulado. *Dominio de las Ciencias*, *6*(3), 349–369. doi:10.23857/dc.v6i3.1402

Zuhir, A., Mohammed, E. Y., Al Arab, A. R., Alara, M., & Al-Rawashdeh, B. (2021). Advantages and Disadvantages of Using e-Learning in University Education: Analyzing Students' Perspectives. *Electronic Journal of e-Learning, 19*(3), 107-117. doi:10.34190/ejel.19.3.2168

ADDITIONAL READING

Cózar-Gutiérrez, R., & Sáez-López, J. M. (2016). Game-based learning and gamification in initial teacher training in the social sciences: An experiment with MinecraftEdu. *International Journal of Educational Technology in Higher Education*, *13*(1), 1–11. doi:10.118641239-016-0003-4

Fayzullayevna, N. (2021). History of Gamification and Its Role in the Educational Process. *International Journal of Multicultural and Multireligious Understanding*, *8*(5), 212–216. doi:10.18415/ijmmu.v8i5.2640

Gómez-Trigueros, I. (2019). Methodologies Gamified as Didactic Resources for Social Sciences. *International Journal of Emerging Technologies in Learning*, *14*(23), 193–207. doi:10.3991/ijet.v14i23.10794

Kalogiannakis, M., Papadakis, S., & Zourmpakis, A. I. (2021). Gamification in science education. A systematic review of the literature. *Education Sciences*, *11*(1), 22–37. doi:10.3390/educsci11010022

Mahfuzah-Mohamad, S. N., Safwana-Sazali, N. S., & Mohd-Salleh, M. A. (2018). Gamification approach in education to increase learning engagement. *International Journal of Humanities. Arts and Social Sciences*, *4*(1), 22–32. doi:10.20469/ijhss.4.10003-1

Putz, L. M., Hofbauer, F., & Treiblmaier, H. (2020). Can gamification help to improve education? Findings from a longitudinal study. *Computers in Human Behavior*, *110*, 106392. doi:10.1016/j.chb.2020.106392

Raitskaya, L., & Tikhonova, E. (2019). Gamification as a field landmark in educational research. *Journal of Language and Education*, *5*(3), 4–10. doi:10.17323/jle.2019.10688

Van Gaalen, A. E. J., Brouwer, J., Schönrock-Adema, J., Bouwkamp-Timmer, T., Jaarsma, A. D. C., & Georgiadis, J. R. (2021). Gamification of health professions education: A systematic review. *Advances in Health Sciences Education: Theory and Practice*, *26*(2), 683–711. doi:10.100710459-020-10000-3 PMID:33128662

Yildiz, İ., Topçu, E., & Kaymakci, S. (2021). The effect of gamification on motivation in the education of pre-service social studies teachers. *Thinking Skills and Creativity*, *42*, 109–147. doi:10.1016/j.tsc.2021.100907

KEY TERMS AND DEFINITIONS

Active Methodologies: Methodologies that encourage the interaction of the student with the constituent elements of the training process and enhance the participation and satisfaction of the agents involved in the teaching and learning process.

Feedback: Key element of the teaching and learning process, which provides the student with information about what he has done well or not, what he can improve and how to do it.

Game-Based Learning: Introduction of games, both analog and digital, in the classroom as a learning tool.

Gamification: Use of some elements and mechanisms typical of a game, such as scoring or setting levels to be overcome, in a non-game environment.

Learning Role: Position and importance that each agent of the educational process occupies within the teaching and learning process.

Serious Game: Games specifically designed with a training purpose, with the intention of creating a message, encouraging reflection, or promoting learning on any subject.

Technopedagogy: Group of concepts, ideas and practices associated with innovation and development in the area of education in the digital age.

Chapter 9
Gamification Through Mobile Learning in University Students:
A Teaching Innovation Proposal

Inmaculada Aznar-Díaz
University of Granada, Spain

María Pilar Cáceres Reche
University of Granada, Spain

Juan-Manuel Trujillo-Torres
https://orcid.org/0000-0002-2761-3523
University of Granada, Spain

José-María Romero-Rodríguez
University of Granada, Spain

EXECUTIVE SUMMARY

Gamification is being implemented in university teaching as an innovative method in the teaching-learning process in line with 20th century society and the current type of student. The purpose of this chapter was to develop the experience of teaching innovation carried out with gamification, mobile learning, and flipped classroom resources and tools for trainee teachers at a Spanish university. Specifically, the experience was aimed at making classrooms more dynamic with mobile applications for self-assessment and reinforcement of learning using mobile devices. The results showed that students increased their autonomy, the acquisition of new knowledge, improved academic performance and content retention thanks to gamification. Finally, the use of mobile devices and applications brings students closer to the social and everyday reality outside the classroom.

DOI: 10.4018/978-1-6684-5240-0.ch009

INTRODUCTION

Methodologies combined with Information and Communication Technologies (ICT) are an inexhaustible source of resources for acquiring knowledge in a deeper and more lasting way, such as the flipped classroom. This methodology could be defined as the inversion of roles in the classroom, where the student acquires theoretical knowledge outside the classroom and the classroom becomes a space conducive to the resolution of doubts and cooperative work (Strayer, 2012). Thus, students work previously on theoretical concepts in non-formal contexts, using digital devices with which they can expand the information through their search and documentation on the web, to later present them in the classroom through small working groups (O'Flaherty & Phillips, 2015). Along the same lines, gamification is acquiring a relevant role in current teaching models where it was previously unthinkable to introduce this type of resource. Gamification is the use of a playful resource that has no didactic intention in formal educational contexts (Kapp, 2012).

In the university environment, gamification seeks to achieve greater student involvement in the subject (Huang et al., 2019), being able to develop certain skills associated with digital games such as those indicated by Contreras (2016): motivation towards learning; improved attention; social skills; and decision-making. Depending in the first instance on the game dynamics that the teacher intends to implement (competitive and/or cooperative). Competitive games are also fuelled by the intrinsic motivation to outperform one's peers and to achieve the reward individually or as a group, if competing in groups. While introducing the cooperative nuance encourages the development of social skills and group resolution, since the relationship and communication between teammates is fundamental to achieve success in the game.

In relation to the possibility of gamification from the introduction of mobile devices, mobile applications (apps) greatly facilitate compatibility and introduction because they are resources already created, tested and available to the public. Following Sánchez (2012), we could classify apps that promote learning through mobile devices into three types: self-assessment, sequential and support. With regard to the first, the central theme of the innovation project, we find as an example the MobiEval application developed by Méndez et al. (2013) for student self-assessment so that each student can detect their weak points and reinforce them before the assessment.

In this scenario, several experiences of gamification of apps with mobile devices have emerged in the university environment. Among them, we find Rodríguez-Fernández (2017), who used the *Kahoot!* app, which allows creating a game of questions and answers with an optionality between 2-4 items, which must be answered in a given time. The student who answers in the shortest possible time and correctly receives the highest score. The implementation dynamics applied with 43 university students consisted of accessing the contents from home beforehand, and then attending a classroom class where, at the end of the class, a *Kahoot!,* was held on the topics worked on. At the end of the experience, a survey was given to the students to get their opinion, highlighting two main benefits: improvement of learning and reduction of study time.

It should be noted that the potential of this type of self-assessment resource is further intensified in education degrees, as it has a double effect on both the development of students' skills and the possibility of transferring them to those who will teach them in the future.

Specifically, the experience was carried out in different subjects of the Bachelor's Degrees in Primary Education, Early Childhood Education, Social Education and Pedagogy. And also in postgraduate courses in the official university Master's Degree in Secondary Education, Baccalaureate, Vocational Training and Languages.

Finally, the aim of the teaching innovation project was to dynamise classrooms with self-assessment and learning reinforcement apps using mobile devices. To this end, the planning was based on the principles and methodology of the flipped classroom, and with the learning achievement established according to Bloom's taxonomy and linked to the three phases of the flipped classroom (before class, during and after). In this sense, the starting point was work by the students at home (before class) with the viewing of videos searched for and produced for each subject by the teaching staff, and on the other hand, reading and working on documents also created specifically for the contents of the subjects.

BACKGROUND

The origin of the flipped classroom methodology lies in the concern of two teachers who, in order to deal with absenteeism in the classroom, began to record their presentations with audio to offer it as support material to students (Bergmann & Sams, 2012). From this experience they realised that this teaching method favoured the development of certain benefits, among them: development of a collaborative learning environment; dynamisation of the student's role; updating of the teaching role; favours autonomous learning; fosters student skills; facilitates participatory and interactive activities. These benefits have been confirmed in various research studies carried out on the flipped classroom method (Akçayır & Akçayır, 2018; Altakhayneh, 2022; Chick et al., 2020; Chuang et al., 2019; Förster et al., 2022; Mingorance et al., 2017).

Specifically, the characteristics of the flipped classroom are as follows (González et al., 2017; Miragall & García-Soriano, 2016):

- The content is worked on in advance and in greater depth.
- The student acquires an active and meaningful role in his or her learning, basing this methodology on constructivism and the social theory of learning.
- The teacher acts as a guide to learning.

Therefore, taking these considerations into account, there is a change of roles with respect to the traditional model of the master class, in which the student was a mere receiver of content and the teacher was limited to transmitting information. In contrast, the flipped classroom turns this situation on its head and the student takes a leading role in their learning, while the teacher acts as a guide facilitating the learning content. Thus, in its implementation, the teacher selects a series of videos that can be accompanied by questions that the student can consult outside the classroom, with the possibility of noting down individual doubts to bring them back to class. Similarly, by working on the subject beforehand, the formation of cooperative groups in the classroom is encouraged in order to reinforce the content among equals.

In terms of classroom experiences, we can highlight, among many, those carried out by: Ros and Rodríguez (2021) in the Primary Education Teaching Degree, a control group was formed whose learning development was through the master class and another experimental group that followed a flipped classroom dynamic. The authors' findings were linked to a significant improvement in academic performance, a favourable change in expectations and the development of positive attitudes towards learning; Espada et al. (2020), who implemented a flipped classroom at university level, found that students achieved better academic results with the flipped classroom than with the traditional method. In addition, students also highlighted that the flipped classroom allowed them to make better use of their time and achieve better learning; Rivero-Guerra (2019), who found that the flipped classroom methodology had a significant impact on the development of academic outcomes, which satisfied students throughout the semester; Canales-Ronda and Hernández-Fernández (2019), observed positive effects that have had an impact on the improvement of the perception of learning, teamwork and satisfaction of students in the subjects where it has been applied; Sánchez-Cruzado et al. (2019), concluded that the flipped classroom adapted to different learning paces and needs, students felt that they had an efficient use of their time in class, effective learning and recognised that their learning had improved.

Considering the empirical research data, it can be concluded that the flipped classroom methodology brings with it a real change of roles that is specified in its positive results, due to its way of proceeding in which the student deepens the content with the help of ICT. Moreover, it can be implemented using mobile devices (Artal et al., 2017).

For their part, games that require the use of technology have been branded as distracting and harmful to users, when their content has not really been analysed and, consequently, certain benefits associated with them such as the development of problem-solving skills, logical thinking, decision-making, among others, have been overlooked (Aznar-Díaz et al., 2017). Some authors go further and state that future teachers should experience gamification first-hand in order to be able to make a value judgement on its possible application and add it to their teaching background so that in the future they can implement it in their school (Pérez-López & Rivera, 2017).

Apps facilitate gamification, since any app can be gamified with a dynamic that structures the game, mechanics that guide the player and components that motivate them to continue playing (Carceller, 2016). Thus, the app must follow a systematic thread that allows the learner to follow a logical development and progress that guides the actions to be taken, while rewards (e.g. through badges) are a key component to maintain attention and enthusiasm. Consequently, we can call mobile gamification the fact of using a specific gamified app and/or gamifying any resource for use with a smartphone or tablet.

All of this is made possible through mobile learning, defined as a method that uses mobile devices for learning to take place (Romero-Rodríguez et al., 2020). Along these lines, several experiences of gamification based on mobile learning in the university environment have been collected:

Ortiz-Martínez et al. (2022) compared the grades of 232 students of Financial Accounting of the Business and Management Degree at the University of Murcia (Spain). The sample consisted of two groups of students, depending on whether or not they used games in the classroom, and the grades of the continuous assessment exercises, the exam and the final grade of the course were compared to see if there were significant differences between the groups. Finally, the results indicated that students who played games obtained better academic results than those who did not use the *Kahoot!* app.

Alawadhi and Abu-Ayyash (2021), applied the *Kahoot!* app in an English language course in a federal school in the United Arab Emirates. They found that there was an overall positive response to *Kahoot!*, increased motivation, greater classroom participation and a better learning experience.

Morais et al. (2021), applied the tools *Kahoot!, Socrative, Quizizz* and *Nearpods* to the third year of the management course at the Polytechnic Institute of Bragança, the results were satisfactory, implying a greater dynamic and interest during the class on the part of the students.

Martínez-Jiménez et al. (2021), analysed the relationship between the use of *Kahoot!* and students' learning outcomes, measured through their academic grades. The results showed a positive relationship between students' *Kahoot!* test scores and final grade. Also, students' academic results improved when *Kahoot!* was used as an assessment tool.

In short, mobile gamification enables new scenarios for learning, taking into account various motivational and educational components. It is the task of teachers to plan resources that can be gamified within a systematic learning process, where pedagogical objectives and didactic programming are established. The motivational components depend on the characteristics of the students themselves and the rewards associated with the game as feedback to maintain interest. However, the benefits are not only limited to motivation and positive results, but also the development of certain skills such as problem solving, teamwork, decision making, among others, due to the type of content that the implemented game may entail.

In this context, the role of the teacher in selecting the appropriate content for the development of the subject syllabus and specifically their level of digital competence, which is key to the development of the subject, is once again highlighted: To clarify a good search for information on the web about the app or resource to be implemented; to create audiovisual content if needed or complementary to the gamified resource; to establish communication mechanisms through social networks among the students participating in the activity; to solve problems associated with the implementation of the digital resource; and finally, to transmit values related to responsible and appropriate use of the web to the students.

In this line, the development of digital competence in university education is an essential element (Farías-Gaytán et al., 2022). Its relevance is accentuated if we take into account that the labour market demands professionals with digital skills who know how to function effectively in the 21st century society, so it is a key competence that favours labour market insertion. However, its acquisition is of particular interest in the training of future teachers, as it equips them with technological resources for their subsequent professional practice (Cabero-Almenara et al., 2022; Fernández-Batanero et al., 2022).

Given the advantages and benefits associated with mobile gamification, it is only a matter of time before more experiences and research emerge at university and other educational levels. Therefore, in a few years there will be a wide range of successful experiences that will serve as a reference model for teachers who want to join the introduction of this type of innovative resources in the classroom.

EDUCATIONAL EXPERIENCE

The educational experience had three phases and involved a total of 373 students from the Bachelor's Degrees in Primary Education, Early Childhood Education, Social Education and Pedagogy at the University of Granada.

The first phase consisted of autonomous work on the part of the student, carried out before class, and which involved the tasks of watching videos searched for and created for each subject by the teaching staff, and on the other hand, reading and working on documents also created specifically for the contents of the subjects. In the second phase, during the class sessions, students highlighted the most relevant aspects of the videos and/or documents, doubts were resolved and tasks related to the subjects of the university degree were carried out using gamification, self-assessment and the use of apps with mobile learning. Finally, in the third phase, a formative assessment was carried out to verify the acquisition and understanding of the contents.

For its part, the project also focused on developing a cooperative methodology centred on the active participation of the student in which there was interaction not only between the teacher and the students but also among the students themselves, through the use of virtual resources such as the Moodle platform

"Leader group", the virtual learning environment of the University of Granada and the social network Twitter, which provided students with the facility to develop autonomous and cooperative learning within the university training process established by the EHEA (European Higher Education Area), as well as enriching the teacher's training work, improving in both cases basic competences and specifically digital competence.

In terms of time distribution, the undergraduate subjects consisted of 6 ECTS credits divided into: two hours of theory per week and two/three hours for seminars. This time was used to develop the content of the subject at a theoretical and practical level and to propose an integrated project between the weekly hours of theory and the hours of seminars, based on the following approaches:

- Cooperation in terms of flipped classroom methodology to improve teaching in Higher Education, by the teaching staff participating in the project and to generate the development of new academic competences, by the students.
- Dynamic and interactive, linking theoretical and practical content worked on in class and structuring it through the flipped classroom methodology and using the established apps, with special emphasis on self-assessment and reinforcement of learning with a system of points and badges in situ.

With regard to the educational apps used, although there are numerous tools that students can use online to learn and carry out tasks in a different way, the following were used specifically based on the planning of the activities and the objectives of the project:

- Evernote or Pages, for taking notes.
- MyHomework, TimeTable or Google Calendar, to manage the agenda.
- Google Drive, SkyDrive, or Dropbox to share documents.
- Google classroom, to manage a class.
- WordPress or Blogger, to create blogs.
- SlideShare or Prezi to make interactive presentations.
- Canva to create infographics, stickers.
- Idoceo to keep the teacher's diary with notes and students.
- Powtton, to create audiovisual videos.
- Quiver and CHROM ville to work with augmented reality.
- Kahoot! for self-assessment of learning via mobile phones.
- ClassDojo, for assigning badges.

Likewise, the methodology used consisted of a series of specific actions: (i) presentation of the project at the beginning of each degree subject; (ii) presentation of the platform, structure, use and discharges; (iii) preparation of the specific teaching guide for the project, which guided the student's learning process and highlighted the methodology to be used and the virtual resources available; (iv) application of an initial diagnostic questionnaire, created ad hoc, on knowledge of the use of innovative methodologies and the use of ICT in other university subjects (examples of items: Did mobile learning for gamification activities directly influence your academic performance? Was content retention an important point to consider the positive effect of self-assessment apps?); (v) specific training seminars for teaching staff and monitoring-achievement of the established objectives; (vi) face-to-face classes with the use of apps

Figure 1. Students using an augmented reality app for the development of content and gamified activities and challenges

for the development of content and gamified activities and challenges (Figure 1); (vii) registration in the social network, use and management of the same, purpose of its use. Use as feedback in question-answer activities in class; (viii) monitoring of work, participation and involvement in the subject through the use of social networks and the use of our learning platforms: Moodle and Leader group; (ix) monitoring of student learning with the use of various *Kahoot!* throughout the development of the subjects; (x) rewards with badges, points under *ClassDojo* and the group's own; (xi) creation of group-specific and student-specific badges on stickers, cards (snapshots) and in 3D with own creations-drawings, resulting in on-site badges; (xii) Flipchart-cork-mural displaying the badges in snapshots and 3D drawings to encourage students' motivation and generate more effort; (xiii) visual compilation in scrapbooks of the work done with the resources and products generated; (xiv) snapshots with direct convergence to social networks (SocialMatic); (xv) creation of ICT materials that were based on the use of Scratch programming, augmented reality, 3D material and were exhibited in groups at the end of the project; (xvi) self-evaluation of the project after one year: follow-up report; (xvii) final evaluation of the project: application of questionnaires and elaboration of a report.

Table 1. Key aspects of expert judgement

Validation objectives	Validate the different items collected in the questionnaire
Experts	Three experts from the field of Higher Education, specialising in educational technology
Validation mode	Individual method by which information was obtained from each expert without them being in contact with each other

With regard to the data collection instrument, the initial diagnostic questionnaire on knowledge of the use of innovative methodologies and the use of ICT in other university subjects was drawn up ad hoc for this educational experience. However, a content validation by expert judgement was carried out (Cabero & Llorente, 2013). Table 1 shows the main aspects followed for the expert judgement.

The experts were contacted through a personal invitation and by email, in which they were provided with a set of documents (formal letter with information about the research and the respective validation instructions and questionnaire).

In relation to the suggestions for improvement made by the different experts, all the proposals were taken into account, and the scale was finally composed of 19 items on a Likert scale of 1 to 4 (1 = Strongly disagree, 2 = Disagree, 3 = Agree, 4 = Strongly agree). The reliability obtained for this study was good (Cronbach's alpha = .91).

RESULTS

The degree of acquisition of the different objectives set out in the project was satisfactory, working with ICT methodologies complementary to the flipped classroom based on mobile learning and gamification.

A higher percentage of students have managed to achieve a higher level of autonomous work and cooperative learning has been promoted through the use of social networks, which has also helped to dynamically monitor their learning process and involvement in the subjects. In this sense, most of the

Figure 2. Percentage of time devoted to self-study

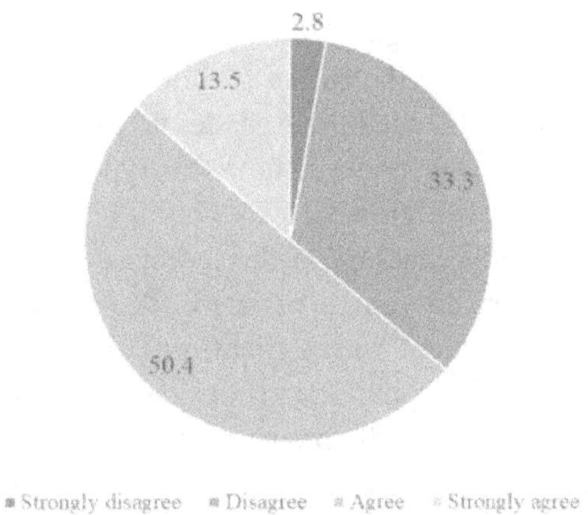

Figure 3. Influence of mobile learning on academic performance

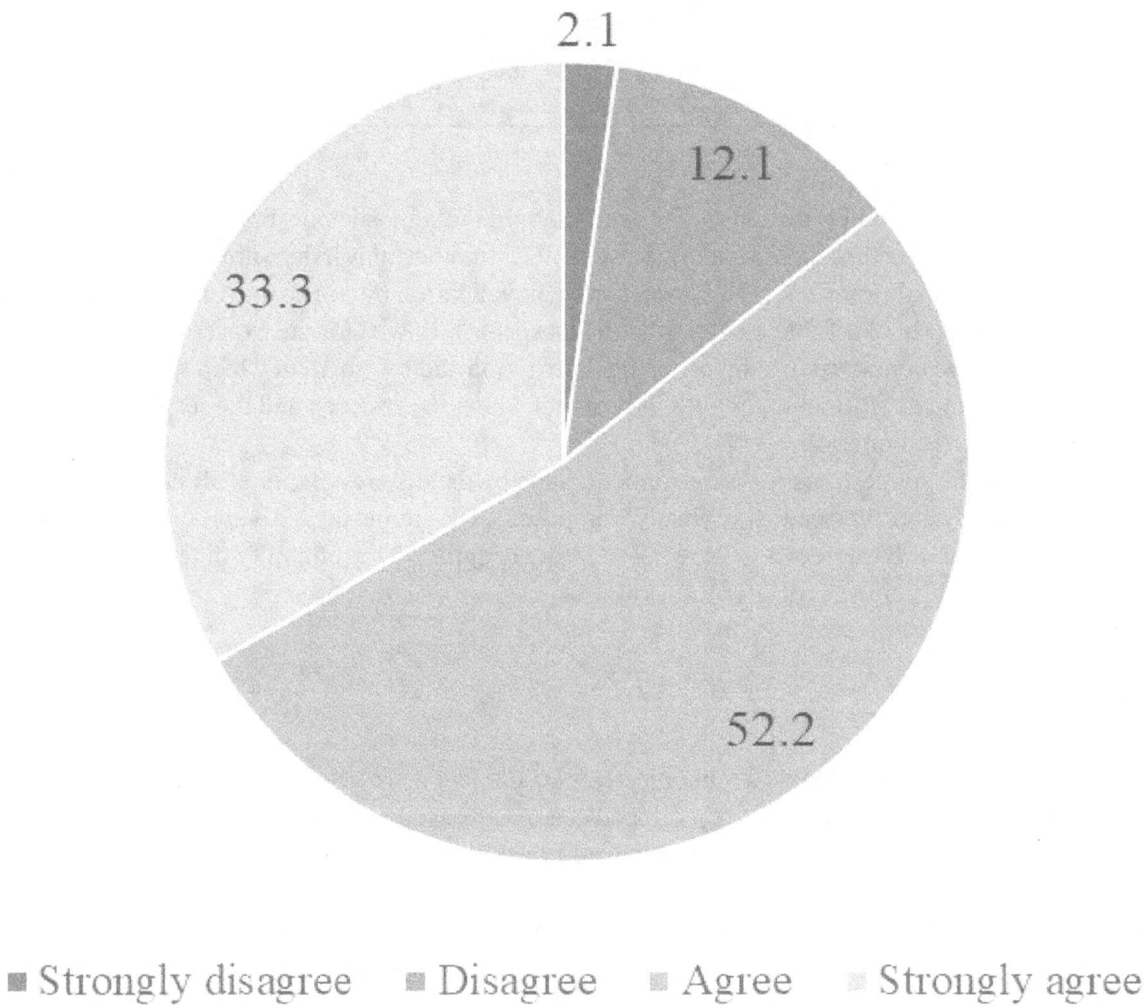

students (63.9%), considered that the use of these methodologies in the classroom meant devoting more time to autonomous work in the subject (Figure 2).

On the other hand, students stated that the use of mobile devices through mobile learning to carry out gamification activities directly influenced their academic performance. In such a way that 85.8% stated an improvement in their grades when performing this type of self-assessment activities through apps to learn the content of the subject (Figure 3).

In terms of learning new knowledge, the use of the mobile device and gamification have provided students with tools for its acquisition. In sum, a majority (96.5%) stated that these types of didactic resources were key to acquiring the content for the first time (Figure 4).

Finally, content retention was an important point to consider the effect of self-assessment apps, where 92.2% stated that their use positively influenced content retention, being better and longer lasting (Figure 5).

Figure 4. Acquisition of new content

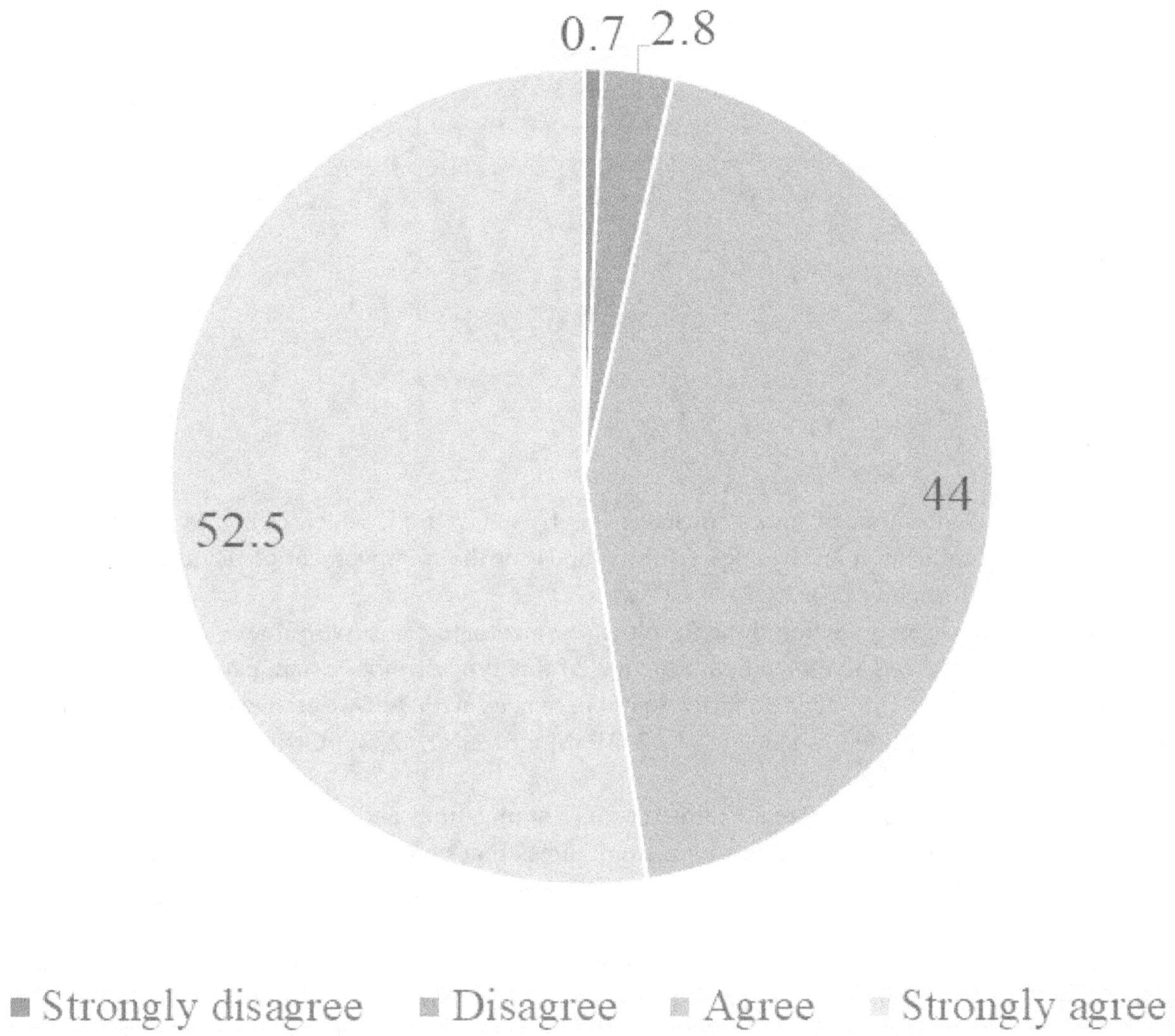

DISCUSION AND CONCLUSIONS

Gamification as a teaching and learning methodology has been understood from a playful perspective that makes students learn the content in a more attractive way, and in turn, the characteristics of the game make students motivated to continue advancing.

Among the results obtained, autonomous and cooperative work increased with the implementation of these teaching methodologies, which is in line with previous studies (Altakhayneh, 2022; Chick et al., 2020; Chuang et al., 2019; Förster et al., 2022).

For its part, gamification has had an impact on students' perception of improved academic performance, as specified by Huang et al. (2019), gamification achieves greater student involvement. In this sense, the experience carried out confirms this premise.

Figure 5. Influence on content retention

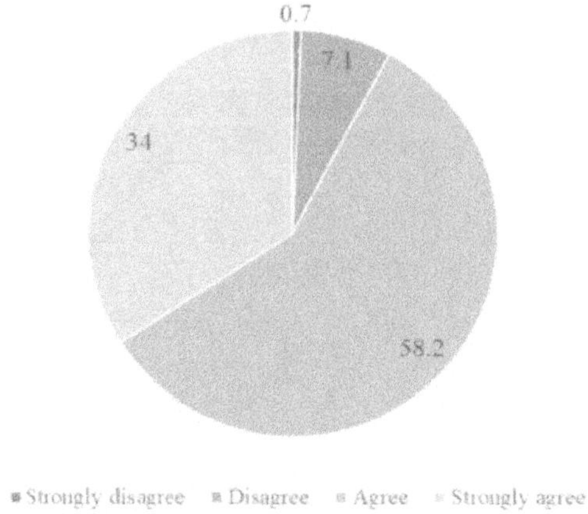

Likewise, the acquisition of new knowledge has been favoured, which indicates that the use of m-learning and gamification are two powerful methods for the improvement of the teaching-learning process (Cabero-Almenara et al., 2022).

In terms of knowledge retention through self-assessment apps, positive values were collected indicating that the content was reinforced with the use of this type of mobile applications. This is in line with the results obtained in other gamification experiences with self-assessment apps (Alawadhi & Abu-Ayyash, 2021; Martínez-Jiménez et al., 2021; Morais et al., 2021; Ortiz-Martínez et al., 2022; Rodríguez-Fernández, 2017).

As this chapter has shown, there are numerous ICT applications and tools that allow this methodology to be put into practice in the classroom, from games that complement the teacher's explanations and serve to check how the contents learned have been consolidated, to tools for creating material and evaluating the student.

On the other hand, it is important that teachers have acquired a certain digital competence that allows them to develop gamification correctly in their classes. To do so, not only do they need to know the tools that allow them to implement this methodology, but they also need to know how to handle ICT, and which tool is best for each moment and teaching process.

This results in the fact that by using video games for learning, group work and coexistence can also be implied by having to achieve an objective with the help of other classmates, learning to make decisions in the face of numerous questions, increasing motivation by trying to overcome the set of challenges presented to them, and it must always be a game close to the interests of the student.

Specifically, the experience carried out shows that gamification through self-assessment apps allows students to increase autonomy in tasks, retain new knowledge and improve academic performance and content retention. Therefore, we have a useful tool for implementation in higher education. In addition, there is the potential of using apps through complementary methods such as flipped classroom and mobile learning.

Finally, this project has aimed to go a step further in terms of digital competences by working with web applications and platforms using mobile devices, with a special emphasis on: (i) motivation towards learning; (ii) improved academic performance; and (iii) greater involvement of students in the classroom.

FUTURE RESEARCH DIRECTIONS

The teaching experience developed gathers data of interest for the scientific community and especially for academics interested in gamification and mobile learning. From the data obtained, a series of future lines of research can be derived:

- Further investigate the use of mobile learning and reverse the trend in research, which is mostly based on research on perceptions and adoption of mobile learning in a theoretical way. In order to initiate a more practical line of research related to the actual application in the classroom.
- Validate a training plan on the use of self-assessment apps to improve the teaching-learning process.
- Establish mechanisms to improve the application of methodologies such as flipped classroom and mobile learning in order to have reference examples that can be used by other teachers in their implementation.
- To compile good teaching practices in teaching with mobile devices in order to generate a repository of successful practices, useful for the teaching community when starting or improving their teaching.

Thus, as practical implications of this project, new opportunities are established at the academic level when initiating projects related to the use of ICT in the teaching-learning process. In this sense, the opportunities for establishing new and diverse virtual teaching-learning environments are expanded. Other resources generated by the project are the specific presentations of the project, the evaluation *Kahoot!*, the videos and texts used under the flipped classroom methodology, the diagnostic questionnaires and the final assessment questionnaires of the project, the badges in the different formats generated in labels/stickers, snapshots and in 3D through the drawings with 3D pencils that will be collected continuously on a wall, flipchart and at the end in a scrapbook to visualise all the products generated.

ACKNOWLEDGMENT

This research was supported with public funds and in competitive concurrence by the Unit of Quality, Innovation and Prospective of the University of Granada, in its call for Projects of Teaching Innovation and Good Practices Advanced and Coordinated of the Plan FIDO UGR 2018-2020 with title "Dynamization of the classroom with apps and web platforms for self-assessment and reinforcement of learning by gamification in undergraduate and postgraduate students under the use of mobile devices and flipped classroom methodology"[grant number 443].

REFERENCES

Akçayır, G., & Akçayır, M. (2018). The flipped classroom: A review of its advantages and challenges. *Computers & Education*, *126*, 334–345. doi:10.1016/j.compedu.2018.07.021

Alawadhi, A., & Abu-Ayyash, E. A. S. (2021). Students' perceptions of Kahoot!: An exploratory mixed-method study in EFL undergraduate classrooms in the UAE. *Education and Information Technologies, 26*(4), 3629–3658. doi:10.100710639-020-10425-8

Altakhayneh, B. (2022). Impact of Using Flipped Classroom Strategy in Developing the Mathematical Thinking of Pre-Service Teachers in Open Education Systems in Jordan. *International Journal of Emerging Technologies in Learning, 17*(3), 228–244. doi:10.3991/ijet.v17i03.24973

Artal, J. S., Casanova, O., Serrano, R. M., & Romero, E. (2017). Mobile devices and flipped classroom. A multidisciplinary experience of university teachers. *Edutec. Revista Electrónica de Tecnología Educativa, 59*, 1–13. doi:10.21556/edutec.2017.59.817

Aznar-Díaz, I., Raso, F., Hinojo, M. A., & Romero, J. J. (2017). Perceptions of future teachers regarding the potential of gamification and the inclusion of video games in the teaching-learning process. *Educar, 53*(1), 11–28. doi:10.5565/rev/educar.840

Bergmann, J., & Sams, A. (2012). *Flip your classroom: Reach every student in every class every day.* International Society for Technology in Education.

Cabero, J., & Llorente, M. C. (2013). The application of expert judgement as a technique for evaluating information technology (ICT). *Eduweb. Revista de Tecnología de Información y Comunicación en Educación, 7*(2), 11–22.

Cabero-Almenara, J., Guillen-Gámez, F. D., Ruiz-Palmero, J., & Palacios-Rodríguez, A. (2022). Teachers' digital competence to assist students with functional diversity: Identification of factors through logistic regression methods. *British Journal of Educational Technology, 53*(1), 41–57. doi:10.1111/bjet.13151

Canales-Ronda, P., & Hernández-Fernández, A. (2019). Flipped classroom methodology in university teaching. *Revista Iberoamericana de Educación Superior, 10*(28), 116–130. doi:10.22201/iisue.20072872e.2019.28.432

Carceller, C. J. (2016). Gamification in green mobile applications: Analysis of game components and game elements. *Sphera Publica, 1*(16), 95–113.

Chick, R. C., Clifton, G. T., Peace, K. M., Propper, B. W., Hale, D. F., Alseidi, A. A., & Vreeland, T. J. (2020). Using Technology to Maintain the Education of Residents During the COVID-19 Pandemic. *Journal of Surgical Education, 77*(4), 729–732. doi:10.1016/j.jsurg.2020.03.018 PMID:32253133

Chuang, H. H., Weng, C. Y., & Chen, C. H. (2018). Which students benefit most from a flipped classroom approach to language learning? *British Journal of Educational Technology, 49*(1), 56–68. doi:10.1111/bjet.12530

Contreras, R. S. (2016). Digital games and gamification applied in the field of education. *RIED. Revista Iberoamericana de Educación a Distancia, 19*(2), 27–33. doi:10.5944/ried.19.2.16143

Espada, M., Rocu, P., Navia, J. A., & Gómez-López, M. (2020). Academic performance and university student satisfaction with the flipped classroom method. *Profesorado, 24*(1), 116–135. doi:10.30827/profesorado.v24i1.8710

Farías-Gaytán, S., Aguaded, I., & Ramírez-Montoya, M. S. (2022). Transformation and digital literacy: Systematic literature mapping. *Education and Information Technologies*, *27*(4), 1417–1437. doi:10.100710639-021-10624-x

Fernández-Batanero, J. M., Cabero-Almenara, J., Román-Graván, P., & Palacios-Rodríguez, A. (2022). Knowledge of university teachers on the use of digital resources to assist people with disabilities. The case of Spain. *Education and Information Technologies*, 1–15. doi:10.100710639-022-10965-1 PMID:35340536

Förster, M., Maur, A., Weiser, C., & Winkel, K. (2022). Pre-class video watching fosters achievement and knowledge retention in a flipped classroom. *Computers & Education*, *179*, 104399. doi:10.1016/j.compedu.2021.104399

González, D., Jeong, J. S., Cañada, F., & Gallego, A. (2017). The teaching of science content through a "Flipped" model: An instructional proposal for students in Primary Education. *Enseñanza de las Ciencias*, *35*(2), 71–87. doi:10.5565/rev/ensciencias.2233

Huang, B., Hew, K. F., & Lo, C. K. (2019). Investigating the effects of gamification-enhanced flipped learning on undergraduate students' behavioral and cognitive engagement. *Interactive Learning Environments*, *27*(8), 1106–1126. doi:10.1080/10494820.2018.1495653

Kapp, K. M. (2012). *The Gamification of Learning and Instruction: Game-based Methods and Strategies for Training and Education*. John Wiley & Sons.

Martínez-Jiménez, R., Pedrosa-Ortega, C., Licerán-Gutiérrez, A., Ruiz-Jiménez, M. C., & García-Martí, E. (2021). Kahoot! as a tool to improve student academic performance in business management subjects. *Sustainability*, *13*(5), 2969. doi:10.3390u13052969

Méndez, P., Lage, F., & Cataldi, Z. (2013). M-learning in higher education: Application for mobile devices focusing on self-assessment. In 1er Congreso Nacional de Ingeniería Informática/Sistemas de Informaci6n. Proceedings (pp. 1–10). National Technological University.

Mingorance, A. C., Trujillo, J. M., Cáceres, P., & Torres, C. (2017). Improving academic performance through the inverted classroom methodology focused on active learning for university students of educational sciences. *Journal of Sport and Health Research*, *9*(1), 129–136. doi:10.36097/rsan.v0i31.601.s244

Miragall, M., & García-Soriano, G. (2016). Transforming an undergraduate psychology class into a flipped classroom. *@tic. Revista d'innovació educativa, 17,* 21–29. doi:10.7203/attic.17.9097

Morais, L., Goncalves, V., & De Assis, L. B. (2021). A Case Study on the use of Gamification in the Flipped Classroom. *16th Iberian Conference on Information Systems and Technologies, CISTI. Code 170402*. 10.23919/CISTI52073.2021.9476257

O'Flaherty, J., & Phillips, C. (2015). The use of flipped classrooms in higher education: A scoping review. *Internet and Higher Education*, *25*, 85–95. doi:10.1016/j.iheduc.2015.02.002

Ortiz-Martínez, E., Santos-Jaén, J. M., & Palacios-Manzano, M. (2022). Games in the classroom? Analysis of their effects on financial accounting marks in higher education. *International Journal of Management Education*, *20*(1), 100584. doi:10.1016/j.ijme.2021.100584

Pérez-López, I., & Rivera, E. (2017). Training teachers, training people: Analysis of the learning achieved by university students from a gamification experience. *Signo y Pensamiento*, *36*(70), 112–129. doi:10.11144/Javeriana.syp36-70.fdfp

Rivero-Guerra, A. O. (2019). Impact of three teaching models in university general botany courses on the academic results of students. *Formación Universitaria*, *12*(3), 67–80. doi:10.4067/S0718-50062019000300067

Rodríguez-Fernández, L. (2017). Smartphones and learning: The use of Kahoot in the university classroom. *Revista Mediterránea de Comunicación*, *8*(1), 181–190. doi:10.14198/MEDCOM2017.8.1.13

Romero-Rodríguez, J. M., Aznar-Díaz, I., Hinojo-Lucena, F. J., & Gómez-García, G. (2020). Mobile Learning in Higher Education: Structural Equation Model for Good Teaching Practices. *IEEE Access: Practical Innovations, Open Solutions*, *8*(1), 91761–91769. doi:10.1109/ACCESS.2020.2994967 PMID:34192098

Ros, G., & Rodríguez, M. T. (2021). Influence of the flipped classroom in the scientific training of pre-service teachers: Benefits in the teaching-learning process, attitudes and expectations towards science. *Revista de Investigación Educacional*, *39*(2), 463–482. doi:10.6018/rie.434131

Sánchez, M. M. (2012). Designing digital resources for e-learning environments in university education. *RIED. Revista Iberoamericana de Educación a Distancia*, *15*(2), 53–74.

Sánchez-Cruzado, C., Sánchez-Compaña, M. T., & Ruiz-Palmero, J. (2019). Experiences of flipped classroom as a methodological strategy in university education. *Publicaciones*, *49*(2), 39–58. doi:10.30827/publicaciones.v49i2.8270

Strayer, J. F. (2012). How learning in an inverted classroom influences cooperation, innovation and task orientation. *Learning Environments Research*, *15*(2), 171–193. doi:10.100710984-012-9108-4

ADDITIONAL READING

Aznar-Díaz, I., Cáceres-Reche, M. P., & Romero-Rodríguez, J. M. (2018). Effect of the mobile learning methodology in university education: Meta-analysis of the research published in WOS and Scopus. *RISTI. Revista Ibérica de Sistemas y Tecnologías de la Información*, *30*, 1–16. doi:10.17013/risti.30.1-16

Aznar-Díaz, I., Cáceres-Reche, M. P., & Romero-Rodríguez, J. M. (2018). Quality indicators to evaluate good teaching practices of mobile learning in Higher Education. *Education in the Knowledge Society*, *19*(3), 53–68. doi:10.14201/eks20181935368

Aznar-Díaz, I., Hinojo-Lucena, F. J., Cáceres-Reche, M. P., & Romero-Rodríguez, J. M. (2020). Analysis of the determining factors of good teaching practices of mobile learning at the Spanish University. An explanatory model. *Computers & Education*, *159*, 104007. doi:10.1016/j.compedu.2020.104007

Aznar-Díaz, I., Hinojo-Lucena, F. J., Cáceres-Reche, M. P., & Romero-Rodríguez, J. M. (2020). Pedagogical approaches in the knowledge society: The Flipped Classroom method for the development of creativity and dialogical learning. *International Journal of Emerging Technologies in Learning*, *15*(3), 4–14. doi:10.3991/ijet.v15i03.11664

Romero-Rodríguez, J. M., Aznar-Díaz, I., Hinojo-Lucena, F. J., & Cáceres-Reche, M. P. (2020). Models of good teaching practices for mobile learning in higher education. *Palgrave Communications*, *6*(80), 1–7. doi:10.105741599-020-0468-6

Romero-Rodríguez, J. M., Aznar-Díaz, I., Hinojo-Lucena, F. J., & Gómez-García, G. (2020). Mobile Learning in Higher Education: Structural Equation Model for Good Teaching Practices. *IEEE Access: Practical Innovations, Open Solutions*, *8*(1), 91761–91769. doi:10.1109/ACCESS.2020.2994967 PMID:34192098

Romero-Rodríguez, J. M., Aznar-Díaz, I., Trujillo-Torres, J. M., & Moreno-Guerrero, A. J. (2021). Best practices in the use of mobile learning by university teachers of Didactics Language-Literature. *Revista Conhecimento Online*, *3*(13), 6–25. doi:10.25112/rco.v3.2772

Sola-Martínez, T., Aznar-Díaz, I., Romero-Rodríguez, J. M., & Rodríguez-García, A. M. (2019). Eficacia del Método Flipped Classroom en la Universidad: Meta-Análisis de la Producción Científica de Impacto. *REICE. Revista Electrónica Iberoamericana sobre Calidad, Eficacia y Cambio en Educación*, *17*(1), 25–38. doi:10.15366/reice2019.17.1.002

Chapter 10
Use of Digital Historical Material and Alternative Teaching Tools in History Lessons Project TEBIT

Neval Akça Berk
Çukurova University, Turkey

Fatma Gültekin
Aksaray University, Turkey

Fatih Berk
Gazi University, Turkey

Mutlu Üstündağ
https://orcid.org/0000-0001-6198-2819
Gazi University, Turkey

Erhan Güneş
https://orcid.org/0000-0002-4268-4645
Ahi Evran University, Turkey

Gülin Karabağ
Gazi University, Turkey

Mustafa Tanrıverdi
Gazi University, Turkey

Mevlüt Uysal
Gazi University, Turkey

Selahattin Kaymakcı
Kastamonu UNiversity, Turkey

Ahmet Tokdemir
Giresun University, Turkey

EXECUTIVE SUMMARY

The aim of this chapter is to provide history teachers with digital historical resources and alternative teaching tools that they can use in history education in order to help students gain high-level thinking skills in addition to knowledge in history courses. To achieve this, a needs analysis for Turkish history teachers was performed to determine which subjects should be focused on in history courses, and what kind of digital historical resources and alternative teaching tools are required. The findings have shown that history teachers face difficulties in teaching ancient civilizations. Teachers have expressed that they remain abstract and incomprehensible to the students due to the inefficacy of materials and teaching tools. It has been determined that they need proper digital historical sources and alternatives most fitting for the subject at hand.

DOI: 10.4018/978-1-6684-5240-0.ch010

INTRODUCTION

The developments and problems -such as the development of computer technology, unlimited access via the internet, combined with students who are bored with the classical teacher role and classroom atmosphere- that have arisen with the 21st century have raised the need to train students who can deliberate on and question information they are given. This emphasizes the importance of teaching history, which is a pool of human experience with the potential to bring solutions to the problems of the present by taking advantage of the past. For this reason, it is important to provide students with high-level cognitive skills such as analysis, interpretation, critical thinking, historical empathy, reasoning, problem solving and questioning in addition to knowledge in history courses.

Developing these skills in history lessons is related to the epistemological beliefs of history teachers, the training they receive, and their tendency to integrate different practices into the classroom. Researches support this situation. Gómez-Carrasco, et al. (2021) in their study to analyze the teaching approaches of trainee history teachers and future secondary school teachers, they revealed that there are important gender differences. In the Approaches to Teaching Inventory (ATI) questionnaire, which was used as a data collection tool in this study, men gave a more positive opinion on the items related to the subject-based approach, while women presented statistically significant data in favor of the items related to the student-based approach. There are also studies showing that women are more prone to student-based teaching approaches, as well as have a more positive view of innovative methods for teaching history, especially the use of ICT resources and mass media (Gómez Carrasco et al., 2021)

In a study examining the difficulties faced by prospective history teachers in understanding and applying the history curriculum focused on historical reasoning (Paricio, et al. 2022), it has been revealed that the prospective history teachers who have advanced epistemic beliefs do not think of the curriculum in terms of an inquiry-based approach to historical problems and exhibit a transmissive-productive understanding of history teaching. Based on the results of the research, it is suggested that history teachers should adopt a learning approach that considers knowledge as questioning and reasoning.

There are studies showing that the prominence of skills as well as knowledge in history lessons is related to the epistemological beliefs of history teachers. For example, Wansink (2017) focused on teachers' beliefs in his study and revealed that pre-service and experienced teachers mentioned interpretive history as an important goal, but teachers had contradictory beliefs in this sense. History teachers combine historical knowledge with the objectives of history education, representing factual and interpretive; revealed that pre-service teachers had difficulty in balancing between teaching and interpreting the facts.

The question then becomes how can history educators integrate skills into history lessons? How can these skills be developed through courses? How does a historian work in the 21st century, and how can this work process be included in the history class? Finding the answers to these questions may lead history teachers to make methodological, pedagogical and technological changes to their approach. The COVID-19 pandemic quickly increased the need for technological changes in education, and led to the use of online applications and ongoing hybrid applications . The pandemic has raised the need in the field of history education for a methodological change that integrates active learning methods, digital resources and emerging technologies so that students can participate in non-current courses. The work carried out within the scope of this project is partially meant to address these needs.

Before the pandemic, the first steps towards helping with the needs of history teachers in Turkey, the development of historical thinking skills and historical awareness in students and the creation of an innovative understanding of history teaching were taken in 2010 by Euroclio activities and teaching materials designed within the framework of the project "A Key to Europe, Innovative Methodology in Turkish School History" (Safran, 2006; Köksal et al., 2012 Aktekin et al., 2009, Ata, 2013). But recently, the intensive use of web-based educational tools in teaching, the availability of historical evidence from multiple environments, as well as the integration of technological improvements such as VR and AR into educational environments have revealed new needs and the necessity for transformations in the field. Based on these needs, a national project called "The Project TEBAG; Development of Alternative Teaching Tools to Improve the Contextualization Skill in History Education" has recently been designed. It is also supported within the scope of the "Call for the Improvement of History Education" announced by TÜBITAK. Another name for the project shared with the target audience is **TEBİT** (**T**arih **E**ğitiminde **B**ağlamsallaştrma **İ**çin **T**eknoloji), as it can be explained more easily and gain traction. The project team includes six education specialists working in Aksaray, Çukurova, Gazi, Kastamonu and Kırşehir Ahi Evran Universities and the Directorate of State Archives, four educational technologists, two Management Information Specialists, three scholarship students and four master and PhD students participating as volunteers. This project also brought on 72 history teachers working in different provinces and types of high schools in Turkey. The needs of these teachers were identified, and then digital historical resources and alternative teaching tools were designed to meet these needs.

In this section, the results of the needs analysis regarding history teachers (the studies conducted in accordance with the needs of history teachers and the activities they produced at the end of these studies) will be presented. This will be followed-up with explanations regarding digital history contents and alternative teaching tools produced as materials based on the finding that history teachers have difficulty teaching ancient civilizations.

BACKGROUND

The main problem this project focuses on is helping students gain historical thinking skills and the process of teaching students these skills in history courses. The starting point of the project is upon the contextualization skills that provide an opportunity to conjointly evaluate the factors of time, space, and humanity that make up the focus of history.

By studying the thinking processes of historians, Wineburg (1991) has identified three heuristics in his approach to documents: corroboration, sourcing, and contextualization. He defined corroboration as 'the act of comparing documents with each other', sourcing, or questioning their source, as 'the act of looking first to the source of the document before reading the body of the text', and contextualization as 'the act of situating a document in its temporal and spatial context'. These three heuristics have helped readers decipher the contradictions contained in documents, make distinctions between different types of evidence, and reach an understanding of the subject. The temporal dimension of contextualization is defined as 'the act of placing events in chronological order', and the spatial dimension as 'placing events in tangible spaces and determining the conditions under which they occur -geography, weather, climate and landscape'.

Havekes, Luttenberg and van Boxtel (2012) determined the elements involved in contextualization teaching based on Wineburg's definition of contextualization in their study based on the literature on historical thinking. They emphasize that when teaching historical contextualization it is important not only to know who and what happened, but also to know when and where. Haveke, et al. (2012) find common concepts important in establishing historical context as they enable relationships between facts and unique and general concepts.

Wineburg's conceptualization has been used within the same framework in other studies in the field (for example, Nokes, Dole&Hacker, 2007; Wooden, 2008; Reisman, 2012; Baron, 2016). For example, Nokes, Dole and Hacker (2007, 493) defined contextualization as 'an effort to imagine the particular geographical, political, historical and cultural context of an event and to comprehend documents within that context'. Although definitions are similar, the contextualization skill has been discussed within various other frameworks as well. Van Drie and Van Boxtel (2008) regarded questioning, resource use, use of concepts and contextual reasoning as components of historical reasoning.

The definition of contextualization in literature coincides with the goal of imparting knowledge to history students through high-level cognitive skills. Although they seem sufficient for the acquisition of knowledge, textbooks, which are the main teaching tools in the classroom, are limited in terms of information acquisition and content. Therefore, it is necessary to support skill-teaching in history courses with other tools. This support is often imagined as integrating first and second-hand resources into the history lesson. However, teachers often experience problems accessing and adapting these resources to the lesson.

In this sense, Andrews and Burke (2007) states that they have developed an approach that they describe as the "five C's of historical thinking" in the Teachers for a New Era project. He states that these concepts, which they express as change over time, causality, context, complexity and contingency, define the common foundations of the discipline of history. In practice, this approach provides a means for history teachers to learn how to formulate and support arguments based on primary and secondary sources, and to understand and question historical interpretations of historical thinking. However, in addition to providing such tools to history teachers, their epistemological beliefs also affect how they formulate and support arguments based on primary and secondary sources. As a matter of fact, VanSledright and Reddy (2014) focused on the epistemic beliefs of prospective history teachers in their study and evaluated how the epistemological positioning of prospective history teachers differed. This study revealed the epistemological wobble in the perspectives of prospective history teachers towards the sources they use and their approaches to the sources.

Of course, integrating ICT into history classes is another problematic that history teachers face. Chapman (2003) used two features of the Office Word application to develop historical thinking through ICT in his study to find a way to digitize history. He designed an activity that facilitates understanding through contextualization and provides an opportunity to encourage historical thinking. As a practitioner, Chapman highlights that while helping students categorize events on a timeline and consider their possible significance, some students take a long time to analyze the details, but eventually they all begin to ask questions about the importance of the topic covered in the exercise.

In addition, recent studies have shown the contrast of advantages and disadvantages of a wide variety of factors caused by the pandemic. Resources (Alam, 2020; Bozkurt, 2020; Sarı&Nayır, 2020; Bogdandy, Tamas &Toth, 2020) supplied by the Ministry of National Education due to schools being shut down and education being carried to online platforms, the need for secure education software that is available in Turkish, the problematic need for evaluation and inequality of technical infrastructure and opportunity between students are some examples of these complications. On the other hand, students think history books are off-putting and force students to mere recitation, are not valid sources for questioning, competitive critical thinkers, contain the same information at all levels of education and contain no content with practical applications, just triviality and raw information (Safran, 1993, Ulusoy, 2009: 20).

Havekes, Luttenberg and van Boxtel (2012) revealed in their study based on the work of Maggioni et al. that teachers' epistemic beliefs determine the relationship between knowing and doing history. For this reason, although it is considered important to integrate knowing and doing history in history teaching, it is emphasized that it is difficult for teachers and students.

Within the scope of this project, answers to the following questions were sought:

1. What are the subjects that history teachers have difficulty in teaching in the 9th grade history curriculum?
2. What are the reasons for their difficulties in teaching these subjects?
3. What kind of a solution proposal is presented for the problems faced by history teachers in the teaching of these subjects?

The aim of this project is to create a digital historical resource that supplements existing 9th grade history books. The hope is that it can be used by teachers to produce activities for the classroom and design, develop and evaluate alternative teaching tools that will improve students' contextualization skills utilized in history courses. In light of this, interest, need and expectations of teachers regarding course materials were analyzed, and teaching tools that advance contextualization skills of students and encapsulate their topics of interest, daily concerns and contemporary technology in history courses were designed for use. In addition, in order for history teachers to develop skills-based activities using these alternative teaching tools, digital historical content has been developed and sample events have been created in accordance with their interests, needs and expectations.

The reasons this project is based on 9th grade history courses are that students get acquainted with history and the principals of this science for the first time at this grade and that advanced courses are based on this grade. Therefore, it is important for history teachers to begin developing alternative teaching tools and skill-based activities for this level. It is also important for students to have access to context-appropriate historical information and get involved in the process through generating logical elaboration in accordance with historical reasoning.

Method

Exploratory case studies based on the theoretical framework of Datta (1990) were used (Cited by Davey, 1991). Since the project is a comprehensive study (such as history teachers-students-in-class practices…), it was first focused on history teachers; the functioning of the 9th grade history curriculum has been determined as a situation based on discovery of uncertainty about its problems.

The aim of the research is to determine the problems that history teachers encounter in 9th grade history teaching and the reasons behind these problems. It has been tried to put forward solutions for the described problems. In this sense, focus group interviews were conducted online with teachers in order to determine the problems they face teaching history in 9th grade classrooms and their needs related to these problems. A total of 72 history teachers who responded positively to the call for cooperation were reached through snowball sampling, and focus group interviews were subsequently conducted with them. After the preliminary interviews, they were asked to choose from a list of dates on a Google form, and focus group interviews were conducted with teachers who chose the same dates. There were four history teachers in each focus group, and the focus group interviews were completed by two history education experts and scholarship students within 18 days. The goal was to examine the problems faced by history teachers regarding the content of 9th grade history course programs, subjects on which they need material/alternative teaching tools and types of material/alternative teaching tools they were most inclined to implement.

The findings were analyzed descriptively and carried out in four stages. 1) Based on the research questions, the conceptual framework of the research, the dimensions in the interviews and observations, it was determined under which themes the data would be organized. 2) In this direction, the data was read and arranged. 3) The edited data is defined. It was determined which direct quotations would be. 4) The identified findings were explained, correlated and tried to make sense of it. The data obtained from the focus group interview were coded into the determined themes and expressed as percentages and frequencies. Since each teacher's answer cannot be expressed individually, examples were presented by citing teacher responses coded into themes.

Participant

Within the scope of the project, collaboration was called for research through social media groups and educational communities used by history teachers. 72 history teachers responded positively to the call for cooperation. Information on the characteristics of project working groups is shown in the tables below.

Table 1. Distribution of the working group of history teachers by gender

Gender	f	%
Female	40	56
Male	32	44
Total	72	100

72 teachers, 40 of them female and 32 male, participated in the focus group interview. The distribution of these teachers by years of professional experience.

Table 2. Distribution of the working group of history teachers by years of professional experience

Professional seniority	f	%
11-20 years	27	37,5
21-30 years	24	33,3
6-10 years	12	16,7
31 years and over	5	6,9
1-5 years	4	5,6
Total	72	100

Table 3. Distribution of the working group of history teachers on their educational status

Education Status	f	%
Post-graduate	36	50
Undergraduate	34	47,2
Doctorate	2	2,8
Total	72	100

As can be seen from the table above, professional experience was widely varied. The history teacher on the working group with the most seniority had 33 years of experience while the most junior member had 1.5 years of experience.

As can be seen from the table above, most of the history teachers completed their post-graduate studies and only two completed their doctoral degrees.

Results

Subjects That History Teachers have Difficulty in Teaching

In accordance with answers received from those who joined the focus group interview, the analysis of subjects that teachers have difficulty teaching is presented below.

Table 4. Distribution of subjects that 9th grade history teachers have difficulty teaching in the classroom

Units	Difficult	Partly Difficult	Not Difficult
	f	f	f
Unit 1-History and Time	34	29	9
Unit 2- The Early Stages of Humanity	37	26	9
Unit 3- The World in the Middle Ages	31	24	17
Unit 4- The Turkic World in the Early and Middle Ages	13	21	38
Unit 5- The Birth of Islamic Civilization	11	21	40
Unit 6- The Adoption of Islam by the Turks and the First Turkish Islamic States	10	19	43

"The Early Stages of Humanity" is the subject 9th grade teachers have the most difficulty teaching in the classroom. Ancient civilizations comes from this unit. They stated that subjects they had the least trouble teaching were the last three units. A reason for this is that students were able to more easily grasp the subjects they learned in the classroom through a multitude of films and series that serve as visualize examples of these time periods. They stated that the only subject they only had a hard time teaching in the last unit was the "Divans" in the Great Seljuk State, as it contains very detailed information, is expressed only through rote-based elements, and even the teachers themselves memorize the information before class and forget it behind after.

Table 5. The distribution of why history teachers have difficulty teaching

Reason	f
Lack of Materials	125
Intangibility of the Subjects	112
Problems Arising from the Presentation of Subjects in the Textbook	92
Unappealing Subject	84

When asked why they have difficulty teaching the unit "The Early Stages of Humanity", history teachers have given several reasons, which are presented in the table below.

Reasons Why History Teachers Have Difficulty

History teachers in the project working group identify the first reason they have difficulty with subjects included in "The Early Stages of Humanity" unit as lack of accessible materials on these subjects. For example, Teacher 52 stated that *"....these subjects are quite abstract and it's quite a waste of time to look for material to make it tangible. I don't even want to get into the way these subjects are described in the textbook..."* This statement highlights three issues "lack of materials, intangibility of the subjects and problems arising from the presentation of subjects in the textbook" at once. Teacher 23 states that *"...it is said that the textbook is thematic, but it is impossible to understand how this is a thematic approach. You focus on a specific subject and explain it chronologically, and you go back to the same place on another subject; this situation makes it difficult for us to even teach the student, let alone the student understanding what we teach..."* This statement draws attention to the problems arising from the manner in which information on the subject is presented in the textbook. Teacher 11 states *"...the students are very different from those we encountered three to five years ago. They don't want to read, they don't have information, but they have a lot of ideas. I try to teach them through dramatizing, otherwise subjects at hand don't interest them at all..."*

In their focus group interviews, history teachers stated that they primarily had difficulty during the online education process, as they did not know how to use most web-based teaching tools, and therefore could not teach effectively when implementing them. Obtained information has shown that history teachers need digital sources on prehistoric ages and prehistoric civilizations, and need training and application examples on web-based teaching tools and VR/AR applications.

Solution For Difficulties

Stage One: Web-Based Teaching Tools Training and Creating Activities

In the first stage of the project, since the participating history teachers did not know how to use web-based teaching tools, trainings were provided online in order to contribute to their professional development. As an end product of these trainings, they designed activities where they used web-based teaching tools.

At this stage, it was determined which web-based teaching tools could be used by history teachers to improve students' contextualization skills in their courses with the help of educational technologists and history education experts included in the project team. Methods for teaching the tools were decided

Figure 1. September 10-13 2021 1st Meeting

based on how capable each teacher was when it comes to educational technology. An online training program was prepared which included information on how to use selected web-based teaching tools, how to teach students contextualization skills in history courses, and what points to take into consideration while preparing activities (in order to establish subject-time-space relationships according to historical context by questioning, delivering evidence and using contextually proper terminology). Training on selected web-based teaching tools (Camtasia, Nearpod, Captivate, Edmodo, Padlet, Gitmind, Canva, WordClouds, Edpuzzle, Flipsnack, Crello, Storyjumper, Thinglink, Learningapps, LiveWorkSheet, Thinkercat) was provided during the spring of 2021.

After this program, teachers were requested to prepare an activity compatible to 9th grade history curriculum using a web-based teaching tool of their choice. Samples of activities are included in Appendix-1. History teachers who designed these activities shared them with their colleagues in an online environment. Through the sharing process, feedback was given on the activities produced, on development of contextualization skills, and the use of web-based teaching tools. Afterwards they were asked to finish designs of their activities and provide a finalized activity. From the delivered activities, activities with the highest potential to help develop students' contextualization skills were selected and added to the projects' website. A grand total of fifteen of the activities produced by the 72 history teachers were included in the project. The mentioned team of history teachers (fifteen history teachers) are as still working a core team on this project.

The history teachers who originally produced these fifteen activities were invited to Çukurova University, the institution which conducted the project, where they shared their activities and results. Between September 10-13 and November 5-7, 2021, they discussed their experiences about the practical advantages and disadvantages of these activities. While some caught the attention of students and motivated them to be involved in the teaching process, other web-based teaching tools seem to have come

Figure 2. November 5-7, 2021 2nd Meeting

up short regarding the goal to improve students' contextualization skills and teaching the principles of historical science.

During these meetings, teachers also expressed why they used which web-based teaching tool and what kind of experience they had when designing their courses with these tools. For example, teachers using the Gitmind web tool stated that students were unable to comprehend the relationships between concepts hierarchically or contextually when creating or examining a concept map. It has been found that the history teachers often use tools that they find more suitable for the working principles of historical science, that can help establish subject-time-space relationships when planning skill-based history lessons, and that provide a complete control scheme, such as Thinglink and Nearpod.

The Second Stage: Creating Digital Historical Material

In the needs analysis conducted at the first stage of the project, many teachers stated that they use visual materials (especially photos, images, and YouTube videos) to attract students' attention and to teach in a meaningful and tangible way in their courses. However, they also mentioned that they could only find a few usable visual materials, so they often failed to take into account the copyright of the images. Related to this, one of the important original aspects of the project was the creation of a visual history dictionary containing digital materials (3D modeling, videos, historical illustrations, photos and images). The ma-

Figure 3. Hunter-Gatherer Period

terials in the visual history dictionary on the project page were selected taking into account pedagogical concerns in accordance with the goals of the history course. The reason the visual history dictionary is included in the project is that history teachers and researchers would be able to design activities using these digital historical materials, and the combination of visuals are appropriate for the program achievements of history education. This source contributes to the productivity of history teachers.

The results of the needs analysis of history teachers revealed that teachers could not materialize the subjects they were teaching because they could not find visual materials, and therefore had difficulty while explaining the subjects. Consequently, the history education specialists in conjunction with the core teacher team included in the project team (history teachers involved in the process of producing activities) have determined which content should be produced as digital historical material related to "The Early Periods of Humanity" unit, which is the subject specifically mentioned as difficult in the needs analysis. A roadmap has been made with the help of history education specialists, educational technologist and graphic artists for the drawing, modeling and provision of the specified materials. In principle, drawings and modeling should be as close to historical reality as possible, so history education experts prepared storyboards for graphic artists to help draw images more realistically. In the storyboards, all details such as the historical background of the visuals and the point of view from which they should be drawn, (for example, a bird's-eye view of an ancient city, an eye-level view, a view of the spaces from the inside and outside) were included. The main goal was to make sure the digital historical materials reflect historical background knowledge, context, and help students establish a subject-time-space relationship in a way that can improve their contextualization skills. For this purpose, nine storyboards were prepared, and historical background information about an ancient city has been provided on each storyboard (of Mohenjo Daro, Nineveh, Ur, Assyria, Alacahöyük, Phrygia, Hunter-gatherer period and two of Phoenicia). In accordance with the aforementioned storyboards, 80 images were drawn by visual graphic artists. Sample images are included below.

The mentioned images were first drawn as sketches by the graphic designers and were delivered in their final forms after the necessary retouches were given by the field experts. These images can be found on the project's web page (http://tebit.cu.edu.tr/Authentication/Login?redirectAction=Index) which has also been included in the visual history dictionary.

Figure 4. Market in the City of Ur

This website was designed with technical ease of use in mind, as a main purpose was to include digital material that might be uploaded by the core group of history teachers and researchers. An educator who may want to prepare an activity using digital historical materials, plan a lesson, or upload materials are first verified as members of the page, and are then given access to related digital historical resources. A preliminary evaluation and declaration form has been prepared for those wanting to upload material. The form contains information such as the relevant type of material, its characteristics, for which grades it can be used and which learning outcome they are related to, whether it has copyright, whether it requires permission to use, and if permission is required whether the necessary permission has been obtained. Through this process, the teacher or researcher is able to upload their material, which is then forwarded to the reviewers of the visual project team. If the relevant reviewer deems it appropriate, the material can be added to the visual history dictionary.

The Third Stage: Creating Alternative Teaching Tools

Various alternative teaching tools have been developed and made available to history teachers and students via the web. These alternative teaching tools have been designed to improve the contextualization skills of students. Pedagogy of history education was taken into account while designing these alternative teaching tools developed with Web 2.0 technologies. In addition, pilot studies and trials were conducted for each of them during the project. The alternative teaching tools developed have received positive feedback from history teachers, students and subject area experts. Four were developed in the project: "Evidence Scale", "Seeing the Whole", "Concept Map" and "Lens-Image Cropping".

The Evidence Scale

In this alternative teaching tool, a dilemma situation is created for students. The aim is for the student to reach a decision based on evidence given within the activity. For this activity to be successful, it is necessary for the student to evaluate the evidence that was designed to establish a subject-time-space relationship, taking into account the relation of the evidence and the dilemma situation, in order to reach a direct conclusion, or to hesitate about the given evidence and find evidence that supports their interpretation using the dictionary of visual history. The "Proof Scale" tool offers an interactive scale with shrouds to the right and left of the screen. On the right and left, the student can see sentences regarding the dilemmas that were previously prepared by the teacher and saved in the system. According to which evidence supports which view in this dilemma and the effect of the evidence, the student places the evidence in the shroud that they find appropriate on the scale by the drag-and-drop method. The student can examine all the evidence in detail by clicking on it. They can change the distribution of evidence they have chosen until they make a final decision and finish. If they remain undecided about which opinion the evidence corresponds to, they can place it in the middle of the scale. The evidence may be in a wide variety of forms such as text, images, videos, etc. The quantity of evidence can also be determined by the teacher. As the student places the evidence on the scale, it reacts instantly. The student placing all the evidence is actually determining which opinion in the dilemma is more acceptable to them, that is, which opinion they agree with more. In addition, students who complete the activity using this tool are expected to create a historical background of 100-150 words and write their own assessment of the dilemma situation. This should reflect the conclusions they have drawn through their analysis of the activity. For this purpose, the system provides empty fields for questions set by the teacher and those for the students to fill out their answers. In these fields, the student can write their answers and add images or links using the rich text editor. At the end, they finalize their answers for evaluation. Through this alternative teaching tool, the student thinks, makes decisions, updates and interacts with the scale continuously, justifies their thoughts and comes to a conclusion. The elements of these activities, questions, evidence, etc. prepared specifically with the purpose of developing students' contextualization skills will contribute to the overall goals thanks to this tool. The activity completed by each student and the final status of the scale can be seen by the teacher, and feedback can be provided in this way.

Seeing The Whole

The "Seeing the Whole" alternative teaching tool is divided into visual parts designed with learning outcomes in mind. The student is expected to make the big picture visible by answering questions correctly. There are two factors to keep in mind for effective usage of this tool. The first of these is the preparation of a question bank including as many questions as the number of parts in the image, and the other is variation of questions. The logic behind "Seeing the Whole" is to enable students to access whole picture by unlocking historical illustration images that were designed high-quality within the scope of the project and contextualization skills in mind, piece by piece by giving correct answers to the questions. To achieve this, students unlock a part of the picture after each correct answer they give to questions that are asked randomly from a pre-prepared pool. This teaching tool allows for the addition of various types of questions and images, and allows for the teacher to choose how many parts the image will be divided into. If students answer any question incorrectly, feedback is given and a link to the visual history dictionary or another destination can be provided.

Concept Map

The "Concept Map" alternative teaching tool gives teachers and students the opportunity to create their own concept maps through an interactive activity. A concept map is a representation of interconnected concepts by specifying their relationship on a template or figure. Using this tool, students place sub-concepts appropriately around a main concept selected within the scope of the history course. They write the names of sub-concepts, determine their form and indicate their relationship with other concepts on the figure. Thus, an interactive concept map is designed. The student can update this interactive concept map at any time, and can make changes and additions to it. The concept map designed by the student can also be viewed by the teacher and other students. Thus, feedback and evaluation are that much easier to provide. In addition, a teacher can share a full, partially filled out, incorrect or empty concept map they have prepared with students. On this shared concept map, students can work on completing the map, find errors, and make updates.

Lens-Image Cropping

The alternative teaching tool, "Lens-Image Cropping", provides a high-resolution image regarding the subject at hand that contain multiple parts. Each part can be focused on separately. The difference between Seeing the Big Picture and this alternative teaching tool is that it proceeds from the whole to the parts instead of the opposite. It allows teachers to add various types of questions, select an image, and then also choose which parts of the image to focus on. If students answer any question incorrectly, feedback is given and a link to the visual history dictionary or another destination can be provided. The teacher selects an image to be seen by the students and uploads it to the system. For example, a visual representation of Central Asian Turks putting together a celebration event can be selected. This image is first presented as a whole. A question-answering activity can be done for the whole picture. Then, the various fragments of the visual can be focused on. Through this process, important parts of the entire image can be zoomed in on and viewed as a separate image altogether. Then, the student may be asked the following questions about the focused sections: "How can you date this part of the image? What is your evidence related to the dating of this image?". The student proceeds by answering questions about each part, thereby completing the activity.

SOLUTIONS AND RECOMMENDATIONS

The first of the main problems faced by history teaching is that it exposes the student to the danger of memorization directly. The reason for this is that instead of rebuilding the past, it only brings the remnants of the past side by side (Tekeli, 1998; 58) and it is shown that such an understanding of history, which does this in order not to damage the "objective" texture of history, is reflected in education (Yazıcı, 2008). It can be said that it is not correct to expect the student to sympathize with an area where he or she has to passively learn or memorize and cannot interact.

In this sense, it is possible to say that the works carried out within the scope of the project will break the ground in history education. Activities prepared with alternative teaching tools using digital historical materials prepared within the scope of the project involve students' historical thinking skills in the process of producing knowledge instead of passively acquiring or memorizing information. Thus, students actively participate in the process in history lessons, not as passive recipients.

The second problem is non-innovative applications in history lessons; material and teacher relationship (şimşek, 2016). The relevant literature reveals that although there are many materials that can be used in history lessons other than maps in our country, they are not used in the classroom environment and it is not possible to benefit from those used efficiently (Ulusoy 2009; Turan, 2013). Although historical thinking skills are included in detail in the history curriculum, which was put into practice in our country in 2018, it is seen that teaching methods could not be placed in professional historiography in practice. The reason for this is that many history teachers do not have enough information about the basic concepts that form the theoretical infrastructure of new curricula; On the other hand, it can be shown that those who have theoretical knowledge have difficulties in how to transfer the theory to practice (Aktekin&Öztürk;2009). In addition to the prevalence of the subject-centered teaching approach in history education in Turkey, it can be said that history textbooks are at the center of education as an important material for history teachers (Yazıcı& Şimşek, 2011) who have the habit of teaching lessons based on this. It can be said that the studies carried out within the scope of the project for this problem offer effective solutions.

The first of these solutions is to include historical illustrations, 3D models, videos prepared for learning outcomes in the visual history dictionary on the project page, and different materials that can be used in history lessons apart from the textbook. Another solution is to offer an innovative application to history teachers with alternative teaching tools. Therefore, it contributes to the professional development and transformation of history teachers. In particular, it helps history teachers, who are distant from the use of digital tools, to establish a bond between their students who are closer to these tools. In particular, it helps history teachers, who are distant from the use of digital tools, to establish a bond between their students who are closer to these tools. In addition, history teachers have the opportunity to produce activities in the E-Activity Design tab on the project's web page. Therefore, history teachers can design their own original activities apart from the ready-made activities they can implement, or they can use the activities produced by other colleagues by arranging them for their own classes. In this sense, the project carries the practices of history teachers beyond the traditional and unorthodox, and also offers them the opportunity to be professionally active and productive.

Today's students are located in a world where new technologies are constantly updated and these technologies shape 21st century literacy, skills and affect the way information is transmitted (Okeke, Van Wyk & Phasha; 2014). Growing up in the digital age means learners have endless knowledge over the internet, but also learn to behave sensibly and safely. Therefore, students need important skills such as critical thinking and responsibility. Therefore, history education should include the critical use of evidence, considering the values, knowledge and world of thought of the period studied, and a discussion about the relevance of this event to the present day. The activities produced with an alternative teaching tool within the scope of the project focus on these needs and suggestions. For this purpose, the visual history dictionary prepared within the scope of the project; both alternative teaching tools and professional development of history teachers, change and continuity; similarity and difference; cause and effect; It is based on historical thinking skills such as perceiving time/chronology, contextualization, and concepts such as fact and thought.

FUTURE RESEARCH DIRECTIONS

The purpose of education, which is one of the main articles of the United Nations 2030 Sustainable Development Agenda, is to provide inclusive, egalitarian, effective, sustainable and high-quality schooling and to promote lifelong learning opportunities for everyone. In this sense, education all over the world focuses on 21st century skills (Care, 2020). Although the need for skills such as reading and writing that are considered necessary to gain knowledge (Nokes, 2017) continue to exist, critical thinking, creativity, communication and collaborative learning are the main focus in today's world. In order to best prepare students for the changing world of academics, elements such as critical thinking skills, complex problem solving, collaboration, and multimedia communication has to be integrated into traditional teaching (Alpay & Özdemir, 2021).

In a current OECD study dated September 2020 (2020; 7) titled "Return to the Future of Education" four alternative pathways to education in 2040 are proposed. These are "increased schooling, outsourced education, learning-centered schools, learning by living and doing". In particular, the last three alternative ways directly affect learning environments. When a society is interested in educating its citizens, it is envisaged that there will also be a differentiation in traditional education systems. This means that history teachers may need to change their understanding of why and for what purpose they teach history (Seixas & Morton, 2013). This perspective is an approach that supports citizenship education through historical reasoning and reflection (Reisman, 2012). In this sense, digital technology is an important factor in learning environments, as education takes place with various, customized and flexible arrangements (OECD, 2020). Therefore, it is necessary to demolish the walls around schools and to integrate constantly changing forms of learning, civic participation and social innovation. Since education can take place anywhere and at any time by including technology in the process, boundaries and distinctions between formal and informal learning may not be clear. For this reason, digital competency for both history teachers and students is emerging as a rising trend of the future.

Digital technology allows for history teachers to use digital artifacts as an integral part of their pedagogical sense of teaching historical knowledge. From this point of view, history teachers should also be aware of the effects of digital technology on teaching and learning strategies and the structural elements in the presentation of their courses. Nowadays, history teachers may think that they don't need to change because they are successful without digital tools. This situation can cause a digital gap between history teachers and students, who are more acquainted with digital tools (Jansen & Van Der Merwe, 2015). As a matter of fact, the history teachers we worked with indicated that they did not want to use web-based teaching tools in their focus group interviews because they did not know which tool they would use and most of these tools were provided in English. In fact, many explained that they do not use these tools because they expected to lose their authority in the classroom if they made an attempt. Nevertheless, in order not to deepen the aforementioned gap in technological competency, it is important that history teachers feel more comfortable and start using web-based learning tools to support their professional development.

Work done within the scope of this project, historical materials and alternative teaching tools produced in accordance to needs of history teachers offers them the opportunity to use digital technology in an effective way and prepare functional activities that can be integrated into courses or even used outside the classroom. Also, these resources respond to the need for a methodological change that integrates active learning methods, digital resources and emerging technologies so that students can participate in asynchronous courses.

The fact that today's students do not even remember a time when they were not surrounded by technology requires history teachers to include technology and technological resources in their classrooms. As digital developments continue to affect our daily lives, most teachers are able to use technological resources such as digital storytelling, online simulations, and virtual history museums and web-based methodologies to build relationships with students and provide an effective history course. With the inclusion of these technological resources in the learning environment, students can begin to love history, or at least have increased motivation. This will undoubtedly contribute to students becoming knowledgeable citizens who have a positive impact on society (Fork, 2016).

The purpose of Cases on Historical Thinking and Gamification in Social Studies Education is stated as responding to the needs of social sciences and humanities studies teachers that have changed sharply during COVID-19. In this context, dissemination of research and innovation proposals about using digital resources regarding the use of gamification in the process of teaching social sciences and humanities lessons, using active learning methods in this course and about the change in the epistemological model of social sciences and humanities regarding history (historical thinking and historical consciousness) is stated as special purposes of Cases on Historical Thinking and Gamification in Social Studies Education. It can be said that the project examined and introduced within the scope of this section responds directly to the first two of these specific goals and indirectly to the other. Through the project, a needs analyses of history teachers was conducted and problems they faced in the learning-teaching process, topics they had difficulty teaching about and reasons for these difficulties were examined. Activities and lesson plans prepared using digital historical materials created in accordance with the needs of history teachers provide examples of the use of digital resources in these courses. In addition, alternative teaching tools designed at this scope provide opportunities to create active learning environments. Activities/lesson plans designed with the provided digital historical resources and alternative teaching tools can change students' contextualization skills and historical reasoning processes for the better by letting them access context appropriate information and be involved in the creation process. The opportunities provided through this project (the opportunity to use, change and create activities), also creates necessary space for history teachers to break the monotony and the stereotypic areas and let them be productive and create awareness about occupational development.

CONCLUSION

It is possible to say that the project also contributed to the professional development of history teachers, since history teachers actively participated in all of the studies carried out within the scope of the project. In this sense, the project focuses on the digital literacy skills of history teachers; it provides an opportunity for them to adapt to the process in today's education system, not only as the implementer but also as the designer in the teaching process. In addition, it can be said that the awareness of history teachers, who design the teaching process not only with a focus on knowledge, but also by incorporating the skills of their students into the process, is formed. This change and transformation can be observed in the activities designed by the teachers.

TEBİT (https://tebit.gazi.edu.tr/; http://tebit.cu.edu.tr/Authentication/Login?redirectAction=Index), which is a first in the field of history education in Turkey; It has a unique structure in terms of offering solutions to the problems in history education and presented under the above-mentioned titles. Of course, although this project does not completely solve the problems in question, it is seen as an important step taken in this sense. It offers history teachers digital historical resources and alternative teaching tools that they can use in history education so that students can gain high-level thinking skills as well as knowledge in history lessons. In this context, since the visual history dictionary on the web page of the project has a dynamic structure, the process of developing digital historical content to be used in history lessons continues.

Another important result is the alternative teaching tools designed in line with the needs of history teachers. In this sense, these tools, which also consider the working principles of the science of history, offer the opportunity to apply evidence-based history teaching in a digital sense. The implementation process of the tools has just started and the process has not been completed. In this process, since it has a dynamic structure like the visual history dictionary, the editing and development processes continue according to the feedback of the practitioner history teachers and their students. However, in the first application, history teachers stated that these tools created an effective area of use both inside and outside the classroom, and their students willingly participated in these practices. It is possible to say that the objectives of the project have been achieved.

ACKNOWLEDGMENT

This research was supported by the TÜBİTAK (The Scientific and Technological Research Council of Turkey), The Project "TEBAG"; Development of Alternative Teaching Tools to Improve the Contextualization Skill in History Education [Project No: 218K399].

REFERENCES

Aktekin, S. (2009). Türkiye'de tarih eğitimi. In Çok Kültürlü Bir Avrupa İçin Tarih ve Sosyal Bilgiler Eğitimi. Ankara: Harf Eğitim.

Alam, A. (2020). *Challenges and Possibilities of Online Education during Covid-19*. https://www.preprints.org/manuscript/202006.0013/v1

Alpay, A., & Özdemir, M. (2021). Güncel eğilimlerden hareketle gelecek eğitim politikalarına yönelik çıkarımlar. *İnsan ve İnsan*, *8*(27), 27-49.

Andrews, T., & Burke, F. (2007). What does it mean to think historically. *Perspectives on History*, *45*(1), 32–35.

Ata, B. (2013). *Tarih Öğretmenlerine Aktif Tarih Ortamı için 100 Etkinlik (edt)*. PegemA Yayıncılık.

Baron, C. (2016). Using embedded visual coding to support contextualization of historical texts. *American Educational Research Journal*, *53*(3), 516–540. doi:10.3102/0002831216637347

Bogdandy, B., Tamas, J., & Toth, Z. (2020). Digital Transformation in Education During Covid-19: A Case Study. In *2020 11th IEEE International Conference on Cognitive Infocommunications* (pp. 173-178). IEEE. 10.1109/CogInfoCom50765.2020.9237840

Bozkurt, A. (2020). Koronavirüs (Covid-19) pandemi süreci ve pandemi sonrası dünyada eğitime yönelik değerlendirmeler: yeni normal ve yeni eğitim paradigması. *Açık Öğretim Uygulamaları ve Araştırmaları Dergisi (AUAD)*, *6*(3), 112-142. https://dergipark.org.tr/en/download/article-file/1215818

Care, E. (2020). *Global Initiative around Assessment of 21st Century Skills*. https://bangkok.unesco.org/content/global-initiative-aroundassessment-21st-century-skills

Chapman, A. (2003). Conceptual awareness through categorising: Using ICT to get Year 13 reading. *Teaching History*, *111*, 38.

Davey, L. (2009). The application of case study evaluations. *Elementary Education Online*, *8*(2), 1–3.

Fork, R. (2016). Technological resources in the history classroom. *Learning and Teaching*, *5*(1). https://openjournals.utoledo.edu/index.php/learningtoteach/article/view/219/101

Gómez-Carrasco, C. J., Rodríguez-Medina, J., Chaparro-Sainz, Á., & Monteagudo-Fernández, J. (2021). Teaching Approaches and Profile Analysis: An Exploratory Study With Trainee History Teachers. *SAGE Open*, *12*(1).

Gültekin, F., & Akça Berk, N. 2018. İnsan, zaman ve mekân: sosyal bilgiler öğretmen adaylarının bağlamsallaştırma becerileri. In Uluslararası Tarih Eğitimi Sempozyumu Bildiri Kitabı (pp. 775-791). Academic Press.

Havekes, H., Coppen, P. A., Luttenberg, J., & van Boxtel, C. (2012). Knowing and doing history: A conceptual framework and pedagogy for teaching historical contextualisation. *International Journal of Historical Learning, Teaching and Research*, 11.

Jansen, C., & Van Der Merwe, P. (2015). Teaching Practice in the 21st Century: Emerging Trends, Challenges and Opportunities. *Universal Journal of Educational Research*, *3*(3), 190–199. doi:10.13189/ujer.2015.030304

Köksal, H. (2012). *Yenilikçi tarih öğretimi etkinlik örnekleri (Edt)*. Harf Eğitim Yayıncılığı.

Nokes, J. D. (2017). Historical reading and writing in secondary school classrooms. In *Palgrave handbook of research in historical culture and education* (pp. 553–571). Palgrave Macmillan. doi:10.1057/978-1-137-52908-4_29

Nokes, J. D., Dole, J. A., & Hacker, D. J. (2007). Teaching high school students to use heuristics while reading historical texts. *Journal of Educational Psychology*, *99*(3), 492–504. doi:10.1037/0022-0663.99.3.492

OECD. (2020). *Back to the Future of Education Four OECD Scenarios for Schooling*. OECD Publishing.

OECD. (n.d.). *Teachers as Designers of Learning Environments*. https://www.oecd-ilibrary.org/education/teachers-as-designers-oflearning-environments_9789264085374-en

Okeke, C., Van Wyk, M., & Phasha, N. (2014). The meaning and practice of educational theory. In Schooling, society and Inclusive Education: An Afrocentric perspective. Oxford University Press.

Öztürk, İ. H. (2011). Tarih öğretiminde anakronizm sorunu: Sosyal bilgiler ve tarih ders kitaplarındaki kurgusal metinler üzerine bir inceleme. *Sosyal Bilgiler Eğitimi Araştırmaları Dergisi*, *2*(1), 37–58.

Paricio, J., García-Ceballos, S., & Rubio-Navarro, A. (2022). Epistemic beliefs and pre-service teachers' conceptions of history ınstruction. In Frontiers in Education (Vol. 7, p. 865222). Frontiers Media SA.

Reisman, A. (2012). Reading like a historian: A document-based history curriculum intervention in urban high schools. *Cognition and Instruction*, *30*(1), 86–112. doi:10.1080/07370008.2011.634081

Safran, M., & Şimşek, A. (2009). Çocuklarda zaman algısının gelişimi. *Uluslararası Sosyal Araştırmalar Dergisi*, *2*(6), 542–548.

Safran, M. (2006). *Tarih Eğitimi Makale ve Bildiriler*. Gazi Kitabevi.

Sarı, T. & Nayır, F. (2020). Pandemi Dönemi Eğitim: Sorunlar ve Fırsatlar. *Electronic Turkish Studies, 15*(4).

Seixas, P., & Morton, T. (2012). *The Big Six Historical Thinking Concepts*. Nelson Education.

Şimşek, A. (2016). Yayın Kritiği: Taslak Tarih Öğretim Programı (Eleştiriler-Öneriler). *Turkish History Education Journal, 5*(1), 316–331.

Tekeli, İ. (1998). *Tarih Yazımı Üzerine Düşünmek*. Dost Kitabevi.

Ulusoy, K. (2009). Lise Öğrencilerinin Tarih Dersinin İşlenişi ile İlgili Düşünceleri (Ankara Örneği). *Çukurova Üniversitesi Sosyal Bilimler Enstitüsü Dergisi, 18*(1), 417-434.

Van Drie, J., & Van Boxtel, C. (2008). Historical reasoning: Towards a framework for analyzing students' reasoning about the past. *Educational Psychology Review, 20*(2), 87–110. doi:10.100710648-007-9056-1

VanSledright, B., & Reddy, K. (2014). Changing epistemic beliefs? An exploratory study of cognition among prospective history teacher. *Revista Tempo e Argumento, 6*(11), 28–68. doi:10.5965/2175180306112014028

Wansink, B. G. J. (2017). *Between fact and interpretation: Teachers' beliefs and practices in intepretational history teaching* (Doctoral dissertation). Utrecht University.

Wineburg, S. S. (1991). Historical problem solving: A study of the cognitive processes used in the evaluation of documentary and pictorial evidence. *Journal of Educational Psychology, 83*(1), 73–87. doi:10.1037/0022-0663.83.1.73

Wooden, J. A. (2008). "I had always heard Lincoln was a good person, but…": A study of sixth graders' reading of lincoln's views on black—white relations. *Social Studies, 99*(1), 23–32. doi:10.3200/TSSS.99.1.23-32

Yazıcı, F., & Şimşek, A. (2011). Tarih Öğretiminde Nesnellik Sorunu. *Tarih Okulu Dergisi, 2011*(XI), 13–32.

Yazıcı, F. (2008). Tarih Öğretmenlerinin Tarihsel Kanıt Algıları. In Uluslararası Sosyal Bilimler Eğitimi Sempozyumu Bildiri Kitabı (pp. 366-370). Çanakkale.

Yılmaz, K., & Koca, F. (2012). Tarihsel empati üzerine nitel bir araştırma: Tarih öğretmenlerinin algı, görüş ve deneyimlerinin incelenmesi. *Gaziantep Üniversitesi Sosyal Bilgimler Dergisi, 11*(3), 855–879.

APPENDIX 1

SECTION 1: ACTIVITY INSTRUCTION FOR TEACHERS
ACTIVITY NAME: Zero Point of History[1]
KEY QUESTION OF THE ACTIVITY:
What do we learn about human history from Göbeklitepe?
EARNINGS:
Program achievement:
9.2.1 Based on the evidence, students make inferences about the life of people who lived in the times before the invention of writing.
By examining the material cultural finds that have survived from the oldest known settlements of settled life and civilization such as Göbeklitepe, Çatalhöyük and Çayönü, the lifestyle of human beings, their relationship with nature and their struggle for survival (eating, drinking, dressing, and sheltering) are discussed until the invention of writing.
Activity gain:
By examining the effects of material culture finds from Göbeklitepe on the history of humanity, the life style of human beings, their relationship with nature and their struggle for survival (eating, drinking, dressing, and sheltering) are discussed until the invention of writing.
LEARNING OUTCOMES:
All students: Recognize the material culture finds from Göbeklitepe that have survived to the present day.
Many Students: Relates the material culture finds from Göbeklitepe to the people's lifestyles.
Some students: Examine the material culture finds from Göbeklitepe in terms of the variability of historical information.
CLASS LEVEL: 9th Grade
SCHEDULED TIME: 40 + 40 minutes
HISTORICAL THINKING SKILLS:
Historical Empathy
VALUES:
Respect
CONCEPTS:
Hunting-Gathering, Settlement Life, Religious Belief, Architectural Structure.
PROCESS:
One week before the activity, students are asked to position themselves in Göbeklitepe from the shared Padlet link. (When positioning, when Göbeklitepe is mentioned, students are asked to write the first three words that come to mind.) Considering the students who will use the pad for the first time, teachers should show the students how to position and add words.
Padlet link: https://padlet.com/volkancivelekkk/rqkpbzb5ghz32xqj
One week before the activity, students are asked to visit Göbeklitepe with a 3D virtual tour.
Suggested links for virtual tour:
https://www.360tr.com/gobekli-tepe-5-sanal-tur_2ab7166d45_tr.html
https://mekan360.com/sanaltur_gobekli-tepe-sanliurfa_2160.html
Students are also asked to find Göbeklitepe and see it from a bird's eye view on Google Earth.
https://bit.ly/3FI98T2

Before the activity, the teacher can design the classroom order to be the letter, T.
Stage 1:
With the teacher's choice, one of the students reads Text 1. After reading the text, the questions below are answered.
Stage 2:
First of all, the questions under Video 1 are asked to the students.
Then, Video-1 is watched and the answers given are discussed.
(If there is a question or topic that attracts the attention of the students anywhere in the video, the video can be stopped.)
Stage 3:
Göbeklitepe Virtual Exhibition is visited and students are provided to answer questions in the exhibition area.
(Since there is no clear/precise information about Göbeklitepe, it is very important that the teacher who manages the process guides the process through possible answers and assumptions).
At the end of the activity, the Padlet is opened and the 3 words written by the students before the activity are read.
At the end of the activity, it is asked whether these three words have changed. (Evaluation)

APPENDIX 2

ACTIVITY INSTRUCTION FOR STUDENT
INTRODUCTION:
What do we learn about human history from Göbeklitepe? Answer the question.
PROCESS:
Stage 1:
Read Text 1, which describes the first moments of Klaus Schmidt's journey.
Answer the questions under Text 1.
Look carefully at Figure 1. Answer the questions under Figure 1.
Stage 2:
Answer the questions below before watching Video 1.
Watch the video.
Stage 3:
Visit the Göbeklitepe virtual exhibition. Answer the questions in the virtual exhibition area.
Text- I
It was October 1994, and the atmosphere was covered with the intense colors of the autumn evening sun. Our path was passing through a field of slightly rising basalt blocks, which could not be understood at a glance. There were no traces of prehistoric humans, no walls, no potsherds, no stone tools. Reminiscent of many similar previous marches to spot prehistoric remains, the inevitably skepticism of the meaning of the march was growing. (Schmidt, 2018)

1. What are the first impressions of Klaus Schmidt's journey?
2. What could be the emotional state of Klaus Schmidt in the first moments of his journey?

Figure 5.
https://bit.ly/3jR5vRv (You can also access the image from the link)

1. Do you see archaeological remains in this image from 1995?
2. If you were in the excavation team, could you show where you would start the excavation on the image? Explain why?
3. Can you see the tree on the mound in the image? Could this tree have a special name?

Video-I

Before watching the video, the following questions are asked to our students.

1. How long did it take to build the entire area under the mound?
2. Where did the people who built and visited this structure come from?
3. Why did the people who lived in Göbeklitepe at that time buried these artifacts?

At the 1st Göbeklitepe Symposium, the answers of Mr.Klaus Schmidt to these questions are discussed at https://youtu.be/tx8EWfjjNuk.

Virtual Exhibition

https://www.emaze.com/@AOQLLIIIR/gbeklitepe You can access the virtual exhibition from this link.

[1] V.C., History Teacher, Rize, Turkey.

Chapter 11
What Do Secondary Students Know About Video Games?
Previous Ideas and Predisposition to Learning Social Sciences With Video Games

Rocío Jiménez-Palacios
https://orcid.org/0000-0003-0746-9170
COIDESO, University of Huelva, Spain

José María Cuenca-López
COIDESO, University of Huelva, Spain

Inmaculada López-Cruz
University of Huelva, Spain

EXECUTIVE SUMMARY

This chapter presents the results of a questionnaire given to secondary school students (12-13 years) about the use of video games for the teaching and learning of Social Sciences, and more specifically for History, as well as their opinions on the introduction of this resource in the classroom. This highlights the possibility of including new methods and methodological approaches in the formal context, taking into account the curriculum of the subject of Social Sciences in secondary education. The outcomes endorse the role of emotions and motivation through gamification in teaching and learning processes.

INTRODUCTION

Provide background on the history of the organization, type of business, products/services provided, management structure, financial status (including annual sales), strategic planning, organizational culture, economic climate and any other issues that you feel are necessary to provide the reader with a comprehensive understanding of the background of the case.

DOI: 10.4018/978-1-6684-5240-0.ch011

Currently there is a real concern in the field of research, innovation and teaching motivated by the use of new resources in the Social Science teaching and learning process. The application of teaching methods, methodologies and techniques is developing very slowly in this area, causing stagnation in the students' education, which continues along traditional lines typical of subjects framed within Social Sciences (Gómez & Miralles, 2015; Ibagón-Martín & Miralles-Martínez, 2021; Martín-Cáceres, Estepa-Giménez & Cuenca-López, 2021; Moreno-Vera, 2018). This statement stems from observation of the work of teachers in schools and research conducted on the use of technological resources in the classroom where, despite having the necessary tools, their use falls into minimal experiences or simply as a tool facilitating more immediate access to information (Martínez, Souto & Beltrán, 2005; Prats, 2002; Sancho & Alonso, 2011). It is logical to think that the use of different, more up-to-date resources involves a change in the methodology, assessment and practice of teaching per se, as well as a change in the roles of teachers and pupils (Muñoz, 2008). Increasing numbers of teachers are training and becoming involved in educational innovation, achieving very positive results in their students.

Although technological instruments are commonly used outside the classroom among young people in the education stage, their inclusion has not reached desirable levels in practice in the formal context, as they have often merely been used as consultation tools or, as a further step, to search for information. This does not mean that more innovative experiences have not been carried out, such as working with blogs, webquests and wikis, etc., as proposed by Barba (2005), Sobrino (2013) or Rivero & Mur (2015).

In this case, it goes one step further and the research examines a medium with which young people are well familiarised in their leisure time, namely video games. The aim pursued in this work is the proposal to introduce video gaming in the classroom as a teaching and learning tool, based on the knowledge that learners have about them, as well as their predisposition to use them to learn Social Sciences. To this end, it is intended to distance itself from games designed purely for learning, which are generally not very motivating, and instead use others designed for entertainment and fun, while always carefully monitoring the content provided. Specifically, the intention is to work on Social Sciences through an appropriate methodology, always keeping in mind that the video game acts as a medium of the teaching-learning process and not as the only source with which to work (González-González & Blanco-Izquierdo, 2012).

In this work, an initial approach was made to the students with whom we intended to implement a sequence of activities using a video game as a resource complemented with other activities, in order to improve the students' attitudes towards the learning process (Seixas, Gomes & Filho, 2016). This resource provides the development of skills similar to what the cinema did before, only that, in this case, you can also interact with it and make the player participate in their own learning (Vicent & Platas, 2018). The objectives set for this end are: to find out their personal experience with video games in general; to examine the use they make of them; to assess their predisposition to using video games to learn; and to analyse their position on the teaching-learning of Social Sciences through video games.

SOCIAL SCIENCE TEACHING THROUGH VIDEO GAMES

One of the first ideas that must be clear is that the study of Social Sciences allows us to analyse, interpret and know the context (both near and far) and participate in it in a coherent, committed and critical way. If we add to this that video games (mostly those in historical genres, graphic adventures, role-playing and similar) increasingly aim to resemble reality, one can even think that the historical and cultural aspects of society are virtually present in the design of many of the video games young people use today. The need to recreate a contextualised scenario and an appropriate environment in a given era means that creators and designers need to study, research and be aware of the appropriate elements, tools, characters, clothing, buildings, landscapes, etc., to achieve a reproduction as plausible as possible, although certain licence is taken when making the virtual story that is narrated in the game more attractive.

In these cases, it is most likely that the spatiotemporal elements will be part of historical genre games such as Imperivm, Age of Empire, Rome, Civilization, Europa Universalis, etc., where development of the video game is focused on a historical content and, therefore, the need to provide information for its development is essential for its users. However, they are not the only ones in which temporal contents are present. In many cases, video games that are not classified within the historical genre precisely resort to history or to the historical as something anecdotal inside the game itself, providing a part of reality close to the player, where use is made of vestiges to set and contextualise the different scenes in space and time. This can be seen in the latest games such as Assassin's Creed or Call of Duty, where History remains in the background but is important in the development of the game.

This leads us to raise the possibility of making use of these recreations for students to use the game as a virtual laboratory where they can experiment with the vestiges within a context, using an alternative teaching and learning methodology to the traditional one, such as problem solving, and which shall be examine more carefully in the following section (Cuenca & Martín, 2010).

When a child begins regulated education at the infant level, their learning is based on play, a fact that is practically abandoned in primary education and hardly appears in later levels. Gamification contains in itself a strong emotional component linked to motivation, since, by using the game or game mechanics in non-playful environments, it makes it present in the students and they are more receptive to learning. For this reason, it is increasingly used in classrooms where students learn as if they were playing, that is, using gamification (Parra-González & Segura-Robles, 2019).

As this is an emerging issue in recent years, there are not many experiences carried out even in the formal context, we do find a greater number of didactic proposals regarding their use in studies such as Gálvez de la Cuesta (2006), Cuenca, Martín & Estepa (2011), Jiménez-Palacios & Cuenca (2016), Egea, Arias & García-López (2017), Iturriaga & Medel (2017), Soler-Domínguez, Contero & Alcañiz (2017), Arias, Egea & García-López (2018), Vicent & Platas (2018).

HOW TO USE VIDEO GAMES FOR SOCIAL SCIENCE TEACHING AND LEARNING

Introducing a video game as a classroom resource entails several factors to be taken into account for the process to be fruitful. The crucial aspect before developing an experience with an innovative resource, in this case virtual games, is that the teacher must have perfect knowledge of the video game they are going to use and analyse its potential and deficiencies when it comes to designing the activity or activities to be carried out with the pupils. This is also linked with the objectives to be achieved, which must be clear to avoid ramblings that entail an unnecessary waste of time. Ouariachi, Olvera-Lobo & Gutiérrez-Pérez (2017) have designed a table depicting the different dimensions and criteria to assess the usefulness of online games in the classroom, which can be taken as reference to analyse the video game as a resource through a checklist, as well as the observation grid included in other works by Jiménez-Palacios & Cuenca (2015), where the variables are scored on a grading scale from 1 to 5, both useful as a step prior to choosing the resource.

It is important to emphasise the importance of the teacher being highly familiar with the video game, so that they have the capacity to resolve any doubts or issues that may arise in its use and development. In addition, it is necessary to be clear about the content that is intended to be addressed in order to meet the objectives set by the teacher (Egea-Vivancos & Arias-Ferrer, 2021).

Moreover, it must be kept in mind at all times that the video game should not be used as the only source of knowledge. In other words, just as when showing a documentary or a film, reading a text or going on a research visit, these activities are complemented with other tasks that involve reflection, critical thinking, the structuring of the knowledge obtained or the search for complementary information, among others (Cuenca-López & Jiménez-Palacios, 2018; Jiménez-Palacios, 2021).

Once these basic premises are met, the teacher can begin to design the activity, using appropriate methodologies for proper development of the teaching-learning process. There is no single way of using video games in the classroom, and this will depend on the objectives set by the teacher, the point of the of the didactic unit at which they are going to implement it and, more generally, on the time and resources available. Different ways to implement video games in the classroom could be:

- The video game as research resource
- The video game as a resource for development of a virtual narrative
- The video game as a knowledge assimilation resource (role plays)
- The video game as a problem-solving resource
- The video game as a learning strategy resource
- Other knowledge associated with use of video games

METHODOLOGICAL POSITIONING

Given the objectives stated, the methodology focuses on an interpretive paradigm with a qualitative approach through which the data collected is analyzed (Rodríguez & Valldeoriola, 2012). This research is based on the responses given by the informants through a questionnaire from which, a priori, quantifiable data were obtained, especially in the closed-ended questions. However, the data extracted are processed from a qualitative perspective, as the approach of this research requires it and the final results are considered more promise for future studies.

Due to the configuration of the main instrument of this work, the questionnaire, the researcher is obliged to engage in a reflexive analysis under a critical paradigm (Bisquerra, 2009), taking into account the questions that were designed, both open and closed. Although this may fall into the great error of subjectivism, the researcher's abstraction towards the answers given and the processing of the data that emerge from them should constitute the objective and thus reliable view of the results.

Informants

The informants in this research were 1st year students in Compulsory Secondary Education (ESO) from the El Galeón de Isla Cristina secondary school (Huelva), specifically in the Social Sciences subject. This is a case study involving a total of 30 students (11 male and 19 female) (Figure 1). The choice of the school and sample were not random. In the first place, it was vital to connect with a teacher whose teaching methodology moves away from the traditional, in favour of an innovative teaching approach suitable

Table 1. Survey questions

INFORMANTS' DATA		
Q.0 Sex		
Part I. What do you know about video games?		
Q.1 Do you know what a video game is?	Q.2 What kind of video games do you know?	Q.3 Do you play video games?
Q.4 When do you play video games?	Q.5 What do you like most about playing video games?	Q.6 Where do you play video games?
Q.7 How do you play?	Q.8 Which video games do you play?	
Part II Video games in the classroom		
Q.9 Do you think you can learn through video games?	Q.10 Would you like video games to be used in classes to learn?	Q.11 Do you know any video games you have learnt something from?
Q.12 Would you study more if video games were used in class?	Q.13 Which subjects do you think video games could be used in?	Q.14 What do you think you can learn playing video games?

Source: own creation

to the present day and, above all, to the interests of the pupils. This need is justified because this way, the pupils become acquainted with methodologies other than the traditional and teacher-centred, in such a way that the ideas and thinking are more open and have more potential when it comes to implementing an alternative didactic unit or a sequence of activities in which the work is done in an innovative way. Moreover, the informants are students from the same class group who, after this first contact with their opinions on the use of a video game for learning purposes, will take part in its future implementation to discover the real results of the practice of methodological innovation.

Research Instruments

A questionnaire was designed for data gathering purposes (Table 1). When preparing this instrument, two factors were taken into account. First, at whom it was aimed, and second, the objectives pursued to this end. Thus, as explained earlier, the questionnaire was filled in by pupils from the first year of the first cycle of Compulsory Secondary Education, so it was necessary to use language appropriate for their degree of reading and comprehension maturity. Likewise, and in line with the objectives set in this work, the questions were grouped into two parts, one of a more general nature about the knowledge and day-to-day use of video games: "What do you know about video games?" (8 questions) and a second focused on the teaching-learning process with video games, without having had a previous experience in the classroom: "Video games in the classroom" (6 questions). Based on these two major sections, a series of closed, semi-open and open questions were articulated in which the participants, totally anonymously, had the option to express their opinion and the knowledge already acquired based on previous experience regarding the question, as well as answering closed questions with a certain number of possibilities, making it possible to obtain quantitative results from the case, but always treating the data from a qualitative perspective.

To approach this instrument with the greatest possible reliability, a validation was carried out by a group of experts through which objections were raised and a final design of the questionnaire was finally agreed upon. The group of experts was formed with the teacher of the group to which the questionnaire

Table 2. Questionnaire analysis categories table

Categories	Subcategories	Indicators	Descriptors
1 What do you know about video games?	1 What is a video game?	Erroneous or confusing conceptualisation	The pupil is unaware of the concept being asked about, or confuses it.
		Simple conceptualisation	The pupil defines the concept from a simplistic viewpoint.
		Complex conceptualisation	The pupil defines and explains the concept.
	2 What use do pupils make of video games?	Entertainment/fun	The pupil conceives video gaming as an entertainment resource with which to experience adventures and pass the time.
		Fun and competitive	The pupil conceives video gaming as an entertainment resource in which they can compete against themselves and other players.
		Fun and learning resource	The pupil conceives video gaming as an entertainment resource from which they can also learn and develop abilities and skills.
2 Video games in the classroom	3 What are the pupils' attitudes towards learning with video games? (Without previous experience)	Contrary	The pupil does not think that video games serve as a learning resource.
		Agree	The pupil is receptive towards learning through video games, but does not know how.
		Enthusiastic	The pupil displays great interest in the use of video games for learning.
	4 What do they think they can learn using video games?	Conceptual contents	The pupil links the resource with the learning of concepts.
		Procedural contents	The pupil links the resource with the learning of procedures.
		Attitudinal contents	The pupil links the resource with the learning of attitudes.

Source: own creation from table of categories of the EPITEC project (Cuenca & Estepa, 2017).

was addressed, who is also a doctor in Social Science teaching, a doctor in the same area and a professor of Experimental Science Teaching. This way, through the judgment of these experts, the opinions and suggestions on the instrument and its suitability for the group of informants were taken into account.

For analysis of the questionnaire data, a table of categories was created (Table 2) which included the two categories of the questionnaire and with subcategories that included the answers provided in said instrument. The indicators are presented following a progression hypothesis, except in the fourth subcategory, where the three types of content that encompass the teaching-learning process appear.

A video game leaderboard was also applied (Table 3) in question 8, where the pupils named the video games they regularly play, to find out what types of games they use and in order to carry out a more in-depth analysis of the data collected.

Table 3. Video games classification, own creation

Video games				
General video games classification			**Classification of education-specific video games**	
Playing modes	**Game mechanics**	**Types of game**	**Socio-historical and problem-solving components**	**Aim**
• Action • Strategy • Adventure • Simulator • Simulation	• Recollection • Hunt/capture •Configuration/ construction • Skill/ • Race • Search	• Arcade • Simulation • Strategy • Board games • Escape games	• War and conflicts • Urbanism and territorial management • Environment • Economy/ • Business • Social relations • Citizens' social issues	Educational: • Serious Games Formative: • Epistemic games

Source: own creation

ANALYSIS AND RESULTS

Before begin this part, all the graphics are in the appendix but there are some ones that not are mentioned in the text but take part of this research, so are included in the appendix too.

Once the students completed the questionnaire, the researchers proceeded to scrutinise, analyse and reflect on their answers, bearing in mind the table of categories (Table 2) drawn up for this purpose.

An initial general overview found no special difference between male and female pupils regarding their experiences with video games and the opinions that they expressed about them in some of the questions.

The results were extracted from the most relevant questions. Thus, the informants of this research provided a simple definition of what a video game is, but through questions 2 and 5, the authors found that their knowledge is broader and more complex because, although it is not reflected in an initial conceptual definition, it is evident in the evaluation of the answers given about it explicitly. The pupils are quite clear about what the videogame concept refers to (Figure 2), as the majority defined it as a virtual game which can be played on different devices (mobile, computer, video game console ...). In addition, on this issue, 80% of the students stated that they use their smartphones to play, the computer being the least used. However, among the male students, videogame consoles are the platform most used, with 81.1% compared to 47.4% of female students who say they use video game consoles to play (Figure 7).

Moreover, the videogame themes most widely known, in both cases, are sports and fight/shooting games, compared to the traditional platforms/phases that are the least known among the informants. This is linked to the objectives and goals that they pursue when they play (Figure 6), of which none of the options proposed in the questionnaire stands out. Thus, 46,7% say that they play to beat their own record, showing in this case an important incentive to better themselves and therefore advocate the need to improve their game to achieve this. Analysing this observation in depth through Table 1, for the students, video games have a fun and competitive purpose that encourages the spirit of self-improvement and enhancement of their player skills. However, there is a greater gender difference in terms of the aim being to finish the game, where 52.6% of the female students stated this option as one of their goals, compared to 27.3% the male students. In this way, this use of video games in the female students is interpreted as entertainment, but without referring to competitiveness, in overcoming the different levels or development of the virtual story. It is notable that despite this competitiveness with other users that can be generated by video games, it is not precisely a reason for playing for the students who filled in this questionnaire, in which this choice and the option of living adventures were the least indicated.

The third question asked in the survey (Figure 4) gives us positive information on what can be derived from this work, i.e. the fact that 87% of the students are familiar with the use of video games points to a development of skills in them that is more natural when it comes to introducing the video game as a resource in the classroom, even though they have had no experience with the game with which they will soon be working. Alfageme and Sánchez (2002) summarised the skills that can be enhanced in users by video games according to Gros (1998), where the acquisition of psychomotor skills, the improvement and education of attention, the assimilation and retention of information, searching for information, decision making, etc., are part of a set of procedural and attitudinal contents that are developed through the use of video games.

From the response given by the students to question 8 on which video games they play, they obtained two graphs separated by gender, in order to better evaluate the question, although it is not included in the questionnaire, of whether girls and boys share games. In this first assessment, the video games the students claim to play in both cases are: FIFA, Call of Duty, Mario Bros, GTA, Just Dance, Minecraft and Block Hexa Puzzle. Video games that combine the traditional side of their invention with current events in their different versions. The second question arising from the outcomes of this question concerns which type of video games they use in their spare time. To answer this question, they used a classification table (Table 3) drawn up and published in previous works, which now includes the "Search" item as a new feature in the "Game mechanics" column, as a feature of video games where you have to search for information and not only collect objects.

Applying table 3 to the games the students have stated that they use, the researchers obtained significant results insofar as among the 43 games that were named in Q.8 (Figures 9 and 10), there were many video games whose player mode focuses mainly on action, with 28% compared to 12% of simulator games, which sometimes come together in the same game, especially when they are first person. In the Game mechanics column, 44% of the games are developed around skill/racing, probably fuelled by the competitiveness involved, either with oneself or with other players. Games that use the search and construction/configuration mode are also located in this column to a lesser extent, with 9.3% and 14% respectively. As for the types of game, simulation, arcade and strategy are very evenly matched, and in some cases they coincide in the same game. Arcade and strategy games make up 35% of the video games that the informants claimed to know and play.

The last two columns correspond to a more general category, the classification of specific video games for education, where you can see that there are a high number of video games with no possible classification. In the first of these columns there are 25 games and in the second column 32. This is an indicator that the video games used by young people at the age when they start Compulsory Secondary Education do not pay specific attention to contexts or settings that can help them in their learning, but are merely concerned with entertainment in their leisure time, although this does not mean that the respondents do not see the game as a resource with which to learn. This further reinforces what was previously noted about the subcategory in Table 1: What use do pupils make of video games?", which merely considers entertainment. Finally, regarding this question, the authors observe the confusion of some informants, who cite some social network applications as video games (Snapchat or Instagram). Although they are also focused on their entertainment, they are not considered video games per se, as their real purpose is to connect people.

Whereas the first part of the questionnaire proposed basic aspects of the students' experience with video games in their leisure time and situated the context of this work, the second part delves into the initial question that was raised: What is the students' predisposition when introducing the video game as a classroom resource? Some 90% of the students say they think they can learn with video games in the formal context (Q.9), so the intentionality pursued in future experimentation and research is enhanced by the positive expectations presented by the students. Similarly, the previous percentage increases to 97% in the next question (Q.10) showing a very good predisposition to the introduction of this resource for learning purposes. Only one female student took up a negative position towards this question. Both questions are linked to the hypothetical situation put forward in Q.12, where 73% answered affirmatively, which means these answers may be taken as a motivating incentive when introducing an innovative element in their study routine. In relation to these questions, in subcategory 3 of Table 1 an enthusiastic attitude of the students is appreciated when introducing the video game in the classroom as a new resource that they have not used before.

In the results shown in Figure 17 (Q.13), the students mostly state that video games are a resource applicable to all subjects making up the curriculum; only two female students indicated that they could not be used in any subjects, and 30% said that they could be used in some. However, when they were asked to say in which ones, although they pointed them out individually, they finally included all of them, which evidences the transversality and interdisciplinary nature of video games as a resource in the formal educational context from the point of view of the learners.

In the final question asked (Figure 18), they can appreciate the students' opinions regarding their positioning when it comes to learning from video games. A clear difference was noted in all the responses among 3 items: conceptual content, attitudinal content and they don't know what, but something is learnt. The female students were more convinced that they can learn and it is surprising that they referred not only to conceptual knowledge (31%), but also expanded their field of vision, adding the development of skills and abilities such as motivation, group work or fun through the gamification of learning, although to a lesser extent, with 5% of responses about it. On the other hand, the male students were more doubtful that learning can be achieved through the use of video games, unless the games are specifically educational or refer to a historic setting. They are more likely to say that they would achieve attitudinal (18%) learning rather than conceptual (9%). In both cases, there is a high percentage that do not know what they would learn (18% of male students and 26% of females), but they do value the resource as useful for teaching and learning

From the last two questions in the questionnaire, it is clear that the students are confident in application of the resource in their subjects, and that they can learn contents of a conceptual and attitudinal nature from them, but they do not contemplate the learning of procedures, as pointed out previously and thus categorised according to Table 1 of this paper.

DISCUSSION OF RESULTS

The results obtained in this work augur a positive future for an upcoming proposal of work with students in the classroom using video games. The informants of this research provide a complex conceptualisation of what a video game is. The work by Sánchez, Alfageme & Serrano (2011), examines the students' knowledge of video games in greater depth, determining not only the concept but also the classification they make about the types of games they know or use from a simple viewpoint.

On the other hand, the students were surveyed about the use that they will make of video games, which is generally quite different from what teachers do or intend to do when introducing this resource in the classroom. In this case, being something designed for the leisure of the users, it is evident that its use is of a playful nature as well as competitive, either with oneself or with other players. However, as their main aim is entertainment, no learning-related purposes are associated with video games in any case, unless imposed by the game itself (educational video games or serious games). For this reason, from the teachers' point of view, it is not only that the students are motivated but that they learn significantly, develop skills and abilities, etc. (Sánchez, Alfageme & Serrano, 2011; Delgado-Algarra, 2018).

Previous works carried out research in this same direction, but aimed at teachers in initial training, (Jiménez-Palacios & Cuenca, 2015), to determine whether, from the standpoint of teaching, future teachers would be prepared to apply innovative methodologies using video games as a resource. The outcomes were highly positive, as in our case, in which the majority of students were satisfied and some showed special enthusiasm. There is thus a clear predisposition from the teaching and learning perspective for the use of video games in the formal context, greatly enhancing motivation (Molins-Ruano, Sevilla, Santini, Haya & Sacha, 2014). The teachers' own knowledge and their attitudes towards the resource influences not only the classroom dynamic when it comes to implementation, but also the results that may be achieved afterwards (All, Núñez & Van Looy, 2016).

In relation to the latter and coinciding with this research, the study by Gómez-García, Planells & Chicharoo-Merayo (2017) reveals the belief of the informants in the potential that video games may have in educational activity, precisely citing History as a thematic area in which to apply this resource. The position found in this work is addressed not only to the teaching and learning of History, but to elevating that learning to the Social Sciences in general. In this way, historical education, which has not been as present as would be desired in teaching methodologies, would take on a relevant role in the formal context.

Although the perspective of this study moves away from the use of educational video games in favour of video games of a cultural nature and/or, as far as possible, commercial, research recently carried out has reported positive results in terms of the acquisition of significant knowledge through games whose main objective is for users to learn, using variations within the game itself that make it more interesting and, therefore, attractive in its use (Nebel, Schneider, Beege & Rey, 2017; Martínez, Egea & Arias, 2018). Along these lines, it is necessary to emphasise that in this work the students made no reference to the learning of procedures, although they did cite the acquisition and development of attitudinal as well as conceptual knowledge, the two types most mentioned when asked about what they think they can learn with video games.

It should be noted that there are increasing numbers of research works in which technology in general plays an important role as a nucleus in teaching-learning processes, whether in the classroom, in museums, interpretation centres, etc., and although it seems normal in the current technological era, the truth is that there is still much to work to be done to make the most of these resources.

CONCLUSIONS

In the light of the different questions posed in the questionnaire and their subsequent analysis, the authors observed that the resource in question is habitually used among the majority of the students surveyed and that this thus constitutes a certain advantage when it comes to using it, even though the video game that is going to be used is not known to the learners. The experience and knowledge that they have with video games, as well as the purpose for which they use them in some cases, point to the development of skills and abilities that would otherwise not be present.

On the other hand, a specific objective was pursued with this research, to determine the opinion and the predisposition that students might show towards the use of video games for the teaching and learning of Social Sciences, specifically focused on History education in the classroom. These outcomes obtained from a small sample represent an advance in the thinking of researchers and teachers who pursue the change towards alternative methodologies of an investigative nature, whereby the learners acquire more meaningful learning through virtual interaction with socio-historical elements, as well as the mere fact of gamifying the teaching-learning process.

The lack of reference by the students to the use of video games designed for educational purposes leads us to think that they are not exactly the most attractive kind in terms of their use for entertainment. This leads to the reflection that, although they fulfil an educational function, from the emotional point of view, their use does not favour an improvement in learning but a change of support to carry out activities or to study the teaching units in greater depth, from the textbook or blackboard to the screen.

From here and as future lines of action, the realization of experiences with different videogames that serve as an example of good practices in the teaching and learning of Social Sciences is proposed, because it is necessary a evolution in the didactic and using resources adapted to nowadays.

ACKNOWLEDGEMENT

This research is part of the Project I+D+i "Heritage Education for the territorial and emotional intelligence of citizens (EPITEC)" Project (EDU2015-67953-P) and *PID2020-116662GB-I00* funded by MCIN/AEI/ 10.13039/501100011033 and is part of the Center for Research in Contemporary Thought and Innovation for Social Development (COIDESO) Universidad de Huelva and in RED-14: Social Science Teaching Research Network, RED2018/102336/T, funded by MCIN/AEI/10.13039/501100011033.

REFERENCES

Alfageme González, B., & Sánchez, P. (2002). Aprendiendo habilidades con videojuegos. *Comunicar, 19*, 114–119.

All, A., Núñez, E. P., & Van Looy, J. (2016). Assessing the effectiveness of digital game-based learning: Best practices. *Computers & Education, 92*, 90–103. doi:10.1016/j.compedu.2015.10.007

Arias, L., Egea, A., & García-López, A. J. (2018). Aprender historia a través del juego de realidad virtual inmersiva "Carthago Nova". Propuesta 26 de integración de un serious game en el proceso de enseñanza-aprendizaje. *Clío: History and History Teaching, 44.*

Barba, C. (2005). La webquest y la didáctica de la historia. Monográfico dedicado a la Didáctica de las ciencias Sociales. *Quaderns Digitals, 37*, 1–9.

Bisquerra Alzina, R. (2009). *Metodología de la investigación educativa.* La Muralla S.A.

Cuenca, J. M., & Estepa, J. (2017). Educación patrimonial para la inteligencia territorial y emocional de la ciudadanía. *MIDAS. Museus e estudos interdisciplinares, 8*, 1-10.

Cuenca, J. M., Martín, M., & Estepa, J. (2011). Historia y videojuegos. Una propuesta de trabajo para el aula de 1o de ESO. *Íber: Didáctica de las Ciencias Sociales. Geografía e Historia, 69*, 64–73.

Cuenca-López, J. M., & Jiménez-Palacios, R. (2018). Enseñando historia y patrimonio a través de los videojuegos: investigación e innovación. *RiMe. Rivista dell'Istituto di Storia dell'Europa Mediterranea,* 43-64.

Cuenca-López, J. M., & Martín-Cáceres, M. J. (2010). Virtual games in social science education. *Computers & Education, 55*(3), 1336–1345. doi:10.1016/j.compedu.2010.05.028

Da Rocha Seixas, L., Gomes, A. S., & de Melo Filho, I. J. (2016). Effectiveness of gamification in the engagement of students. *Computers in Human Behavior, 58*, 48–63. doi:10.1016/j.chb.2015.11.021

Delgado-Algarra, E. J. (2018). Enseñanza de la Historia y compromiso ciudadano a través de los videojuegos Civilization VI y Stardew Valley: cómo seleccionar e integrar los videojuegos en el aula. *Clío. History & History Teaching, 44.*

Egea, A., Arias, L., & García-López, A. J. (2017). Videojuegos, historia y patrimonio: primeros resultados de una investigación educativa evaluativa en educación secundaria. *Revista interuniversitaria de investigación en Tecnología Educativa.*

Egea-Vivancos, A., & Arias-Ferrer, L. (2021). Principles for the design of a history and heritage game based on the evaluation of immersive virtual reality video games. *E-Learning and Digital Media, 18*(4), 383–402. doi:10.1177/2042753020980103

Gálvez de la Cuesta, M. C. (2006). Aplicaciones de los videojuegos de contenido histórico en el aula. *Icono, 14*(7), 1–13.

Gómez Carrasco, C. J., & Miralles Martínez, P. (2015). Pensar historicamente ou memorizar o passado? A avaliação dos conteúdos históricos na educação obrigatória na Espanha. *Revista de Estudios Sociales,* (52), 52–68.

Gómez-García, S., Planells, A. J., & Chicharro-Merayo, M. (2017). ¿Los alumnos quieren aprender con videojuegos? Lo que opinan sus usuarios del potencial educativo de este medio. *Educar, 53*(1), 49–66. doi:10.5565/rev/educar.848

González-González, C., & Blanco-Izquierdo, F. (2012). Designing social videogames for educational uses. *Computers & Education, 58*(1), 250–262. doi:10.1016/j.compedu.2011.08.014

Gros, B. (Coord.). (1998). *Jugando con videojuegos: educación y entretenimiento.* Bilbao, Desclée de Brouwer.

Ibagón-Martín, N. J., & Miralles-Martínez, P. (2021). Temas controversiales y educación histórica. In C. J. Gómez, X. M. Souto, & P. Miralles (Eds.), *Enseñanza de las ciencias sociales para una ciudadanía democrática: Estudios en homenaje al profesor Ramón López Facal* (pp. 123–137). Ediciones Octaedro.

Iturriaga, D., & Medel, I. (2017). La historia a través de los videojuegos. Evaluación mediante Civilization y Assassin's Creed. *Íber. Didáctica de las Ciencias Sociales. Geografía e Historia*, *86*, 30–36.

Jiménez-Palacios, R. (2021). El videojuego como recurso emocionante para educar en patrimonio. In J. M. Cuenca, J. Estepa, & M. Martín (Eds.), *Investigación y buenas prácticas en educación patrimonial entre la escuela y el museo: territorio, emociones y ciudadanía* (pp. 73–85). Trea.

Jiménez-Palacios, R., & Cuenca, J. M. (2016). Construyendo el conocimiento a través de videojuegos. El caso del 'El Códex del Peregrino. In L. Arias, A. I. Ponce, & D. Verdú (Eds.), *Estrategias y recursos para la integración del patrimonio y los museos en la educación formal* (pp. 237–247). Editum.

Jiménez-Palacios, R., & Cuenca-López, J.M. (2015). El uso didáctico de los videojuegos: concepciones e ideas de futuros docentes de Ciencias Sociales. *Clío. History and History teaching, 41*, 14-85.

Martín-Cáceres, M., Estepa-Giménez, J., & Cuenca-López, J. M. (2021). Los patrimonios controversiales en la educación patrimonial para la formación de la ciudadanía. In C. J. Gómez, X. M. Souto, & P. Miralles (Eds.), *Enseñanza de las ciencias sociales para una ciudadanía democrática: Estudios en homenaje al profesor Ramón López Facal* (pp. 109–122). Ediciones Octaedro.

Martínez, J. M., Egea, A., & Arias, L. (2018). Evaluación de un videojuego educativo de contenido histórico. La opinión de los estudiantes. *Revista Latinoamericana de Tecnología Educativa, 17*(1).

Martínez Valcárcel, N., Souto González, X. M., & Beltrán Llavador, J. (2005). Los problemas docentes en historia de bachillerato: La gran diversidad bajo la aparente uniformidad. *Didáctica de las Ciencias Experimentales y Sociales*, *19*, 33–55.

Molins-Ruano, P., Sevilla, C., Santini, S., Haya, P. A., Rodríguez, P., & Sacha, G. M. (2014). Designing videogames to improve students' motivation. *Computers in Human Behavior*, *31*, 571–579. doi:10.1016/j.chb.2013.06.013

Moreno-Vera, J. R. (2018). El pensamiento crítico en la enseñanza de la historia a través de temas controvertidos. *Actualidades Pedagógicas*, *1*(72), 15–28. doi:10.19052/ap.5215

Muñoz, J. M. (2008). NNTT, TIC, NTIC, TAC… en educación ¿pero esto qué es? *Quaderns digitals. Revista de Nuevas Tecnologías y Sociedad*, *51*, 1–9.

Nebel, S., Schneider, S., Beege, M., & Rey, G. D. (2017). Leaderboards within educational videogames: The impact of difficulty, effort and gameplay. *Computers & Education*, *113*, 28–41. doi:10.1016/j.compedu.2017.05.011

Ouariachi, T., Olvera-Lobo, M. D., & Gutiérrez-Pérez, J. (2017). Evaluación de juegos online para la enseñanza y aprendizaje del cambio climático. *Enseñanza de las ciencias, 35*(1), 193-214.

Parra-González, M. E., & Segura-Robles, A. (2019). Producción científica sobre gamificación en educación: un análisis cienciométrico. Scientific production about gamification in education: A Scientometric analysis. *Review of Education*, *386*, 113–135.

Prats, J. (2002). Internet en las aulas de educación secundaria. *Iber: Didáctica de las Ciencias Sociales, geografía e historia, 29*, 1-8.

Rivero, P., & Mur, L. (2015). Aprender Ciencias Sociales en la web 2.0. *Iber: Didáctica de las Ciencias Sociales, geografía e historia, 80*, 30-37.

Rodríguez, D., & Valldeoriola, J. (2012). *Metodología de la investigación*. Red Tercer Milenio.

Sánchez, P. A., Alfageme, B., & Serrano, F. J. (2011). Opiniones sobre los videojuegos del alumnado de Educación Secundaria Obligatoria. *Edutec. Revista Electrónica de Tecnología Educativa*, (38), 185. doi:10.21556/edutec.2011.38.386

Sancho, J. M., & Alonso Cano, C. (2011). *Cuatro casos, cuatro historias de uso educativo de las TIC*. Universitat de Barcelona, Esbrina-Recerca.

Sobrino, D. (2013). El trabajo con blogs en Ciencias Sociales, Geografía e Historia. *Clío. History and History teaching, 39*, 1-49.

Soler-Domínguez, J. L., Contero González, M., & Alcañiz, M. (2017). Press start!: Cinco estrategias para el despliegue efectivo del Aprendizaje Basado en Videojuegos. *Actas del V Congreso Internacional de Videojuegos y Educación (CIVE'17).*

Vicent, N., & Platas, M. (2018). ¡Juguemos en el Antiguo Egipto! Flipped classroom a través del videojuego Assassin's Creed: 41 Origins. *Clío: History and History Teaching, 44.*

APPENDIX 1

Figure 1. Q.0 Sex
Source: own creation

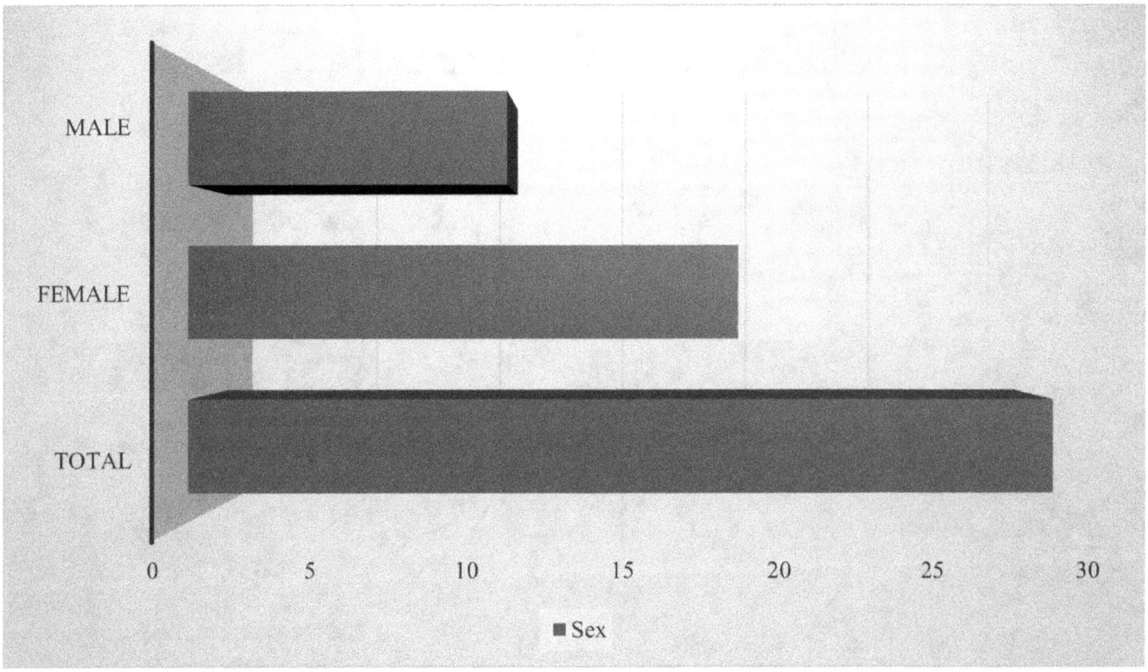

Figure 2. Q.1 Do you know what a video game is?
Source: own creation

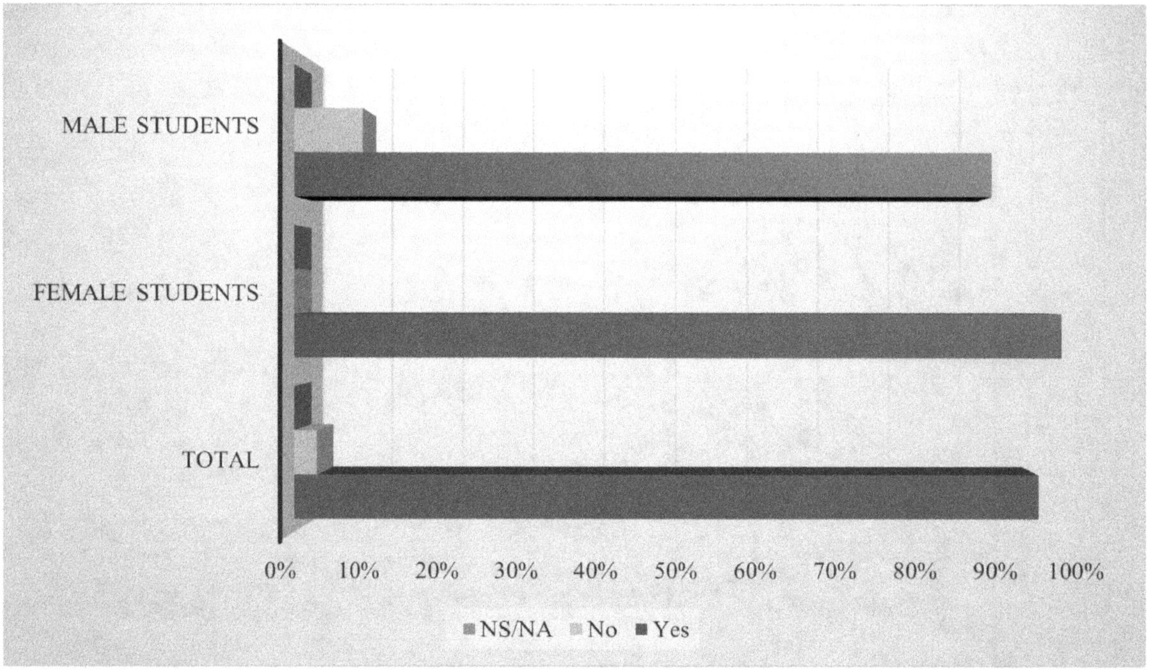

Figure 3. Q.2 What kind of video games do you know?
Source: own creation

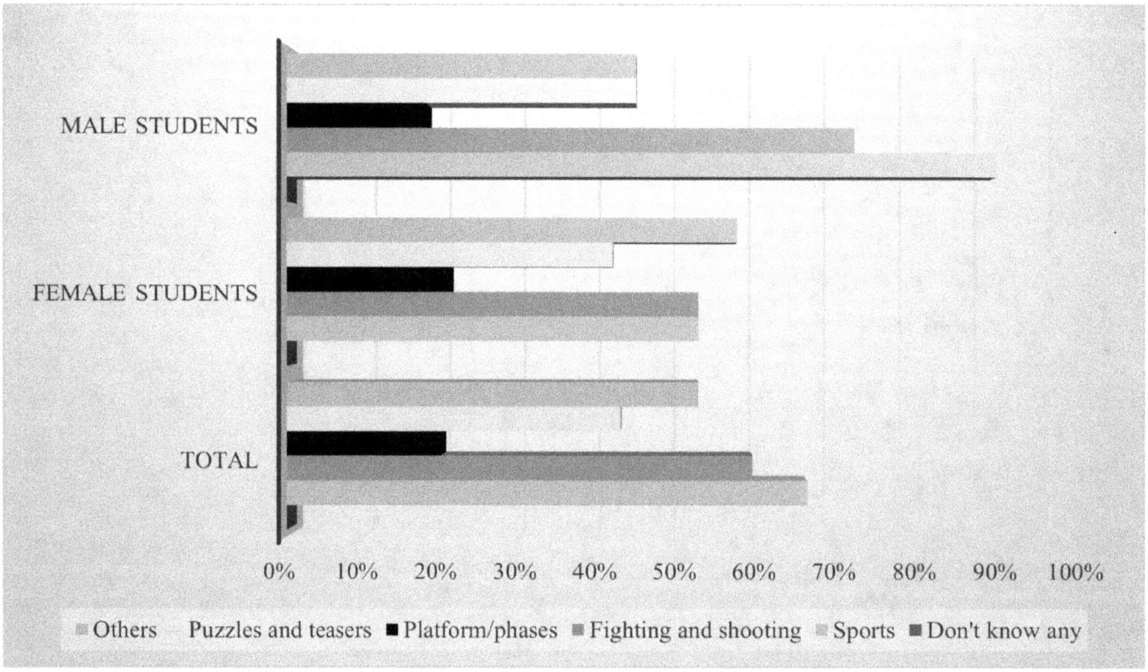

Figure 4. Q.3 Do you play video games?
Source: own creation

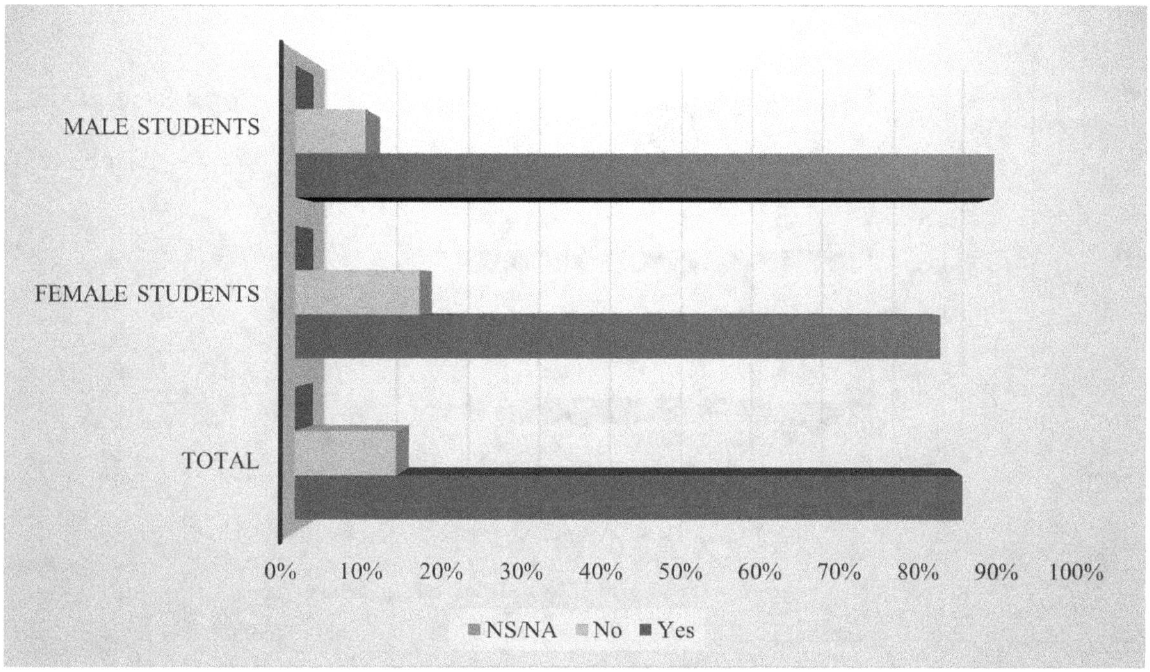

Figure 5. Q.4 When do you play video games?
Source: own creation

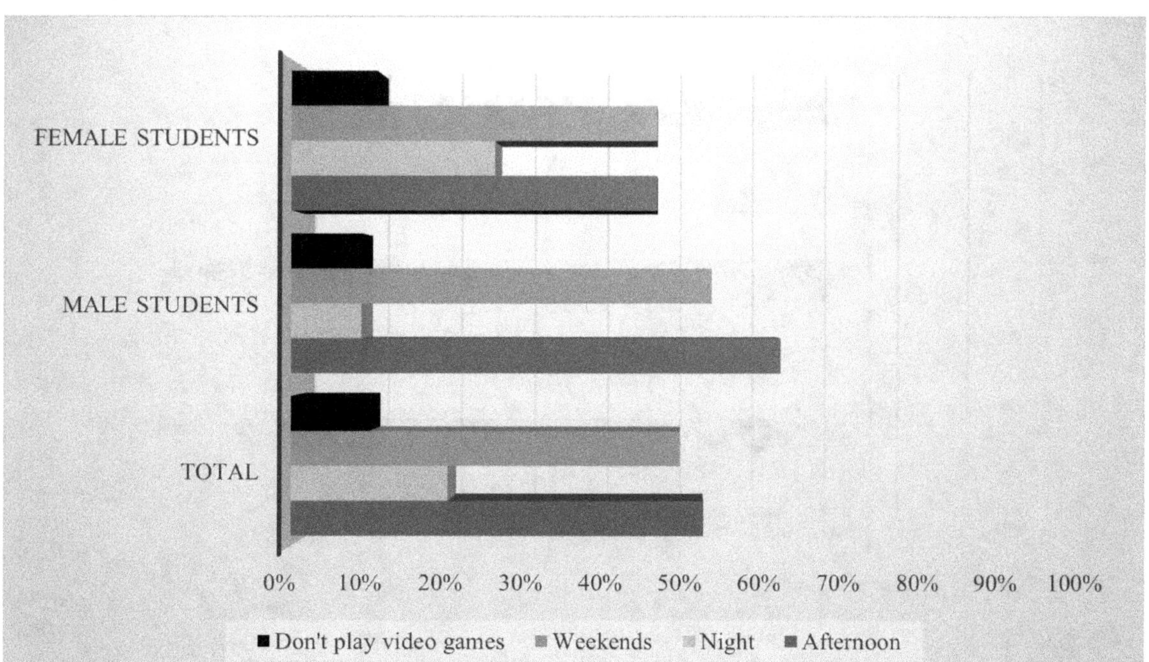

Figure 6. Q.5 What do you like most about playing video games?
Source: own creation

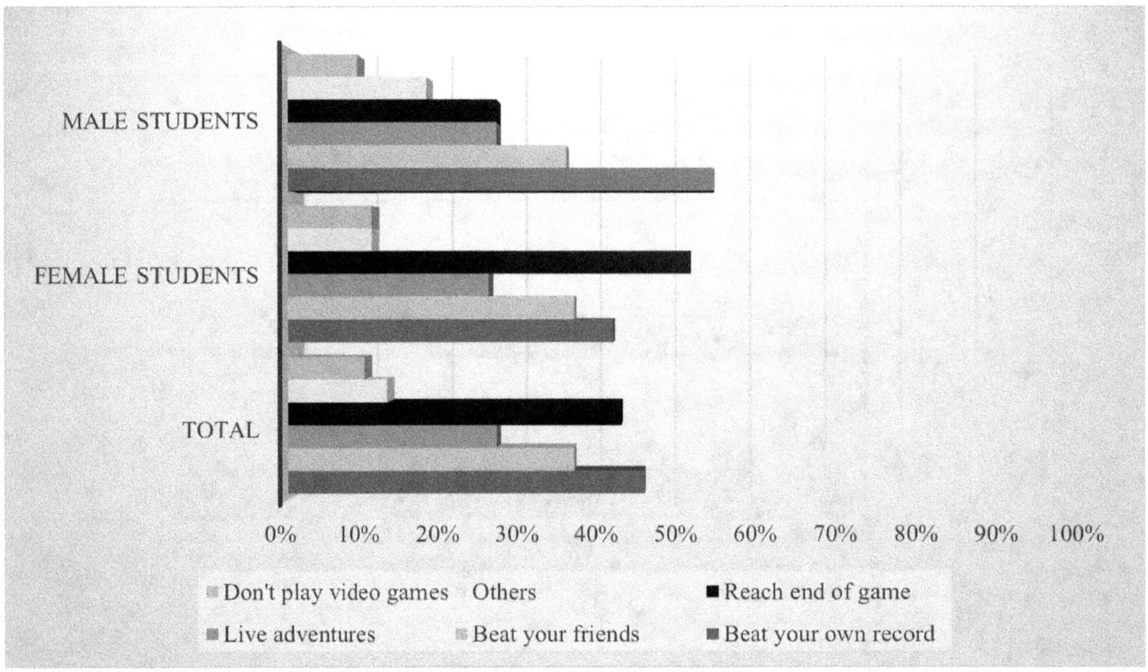

Figure 7. Q.6 Where do you play video games?
Source: own creation

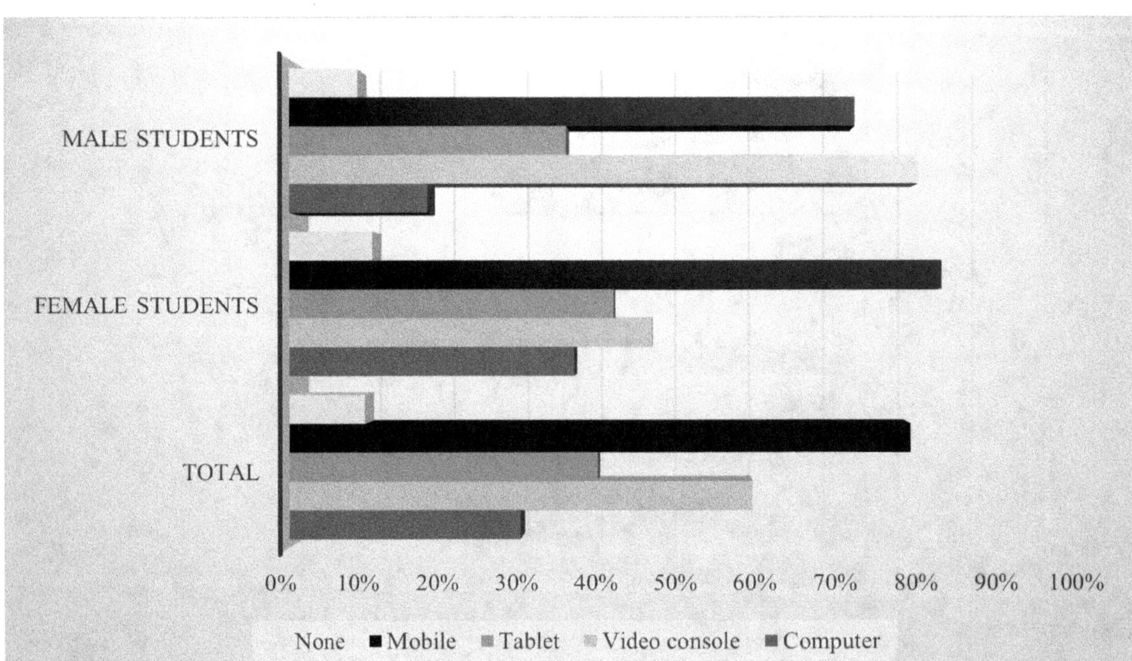

Figure 8. Q.7 How do you play?
Source: own creation

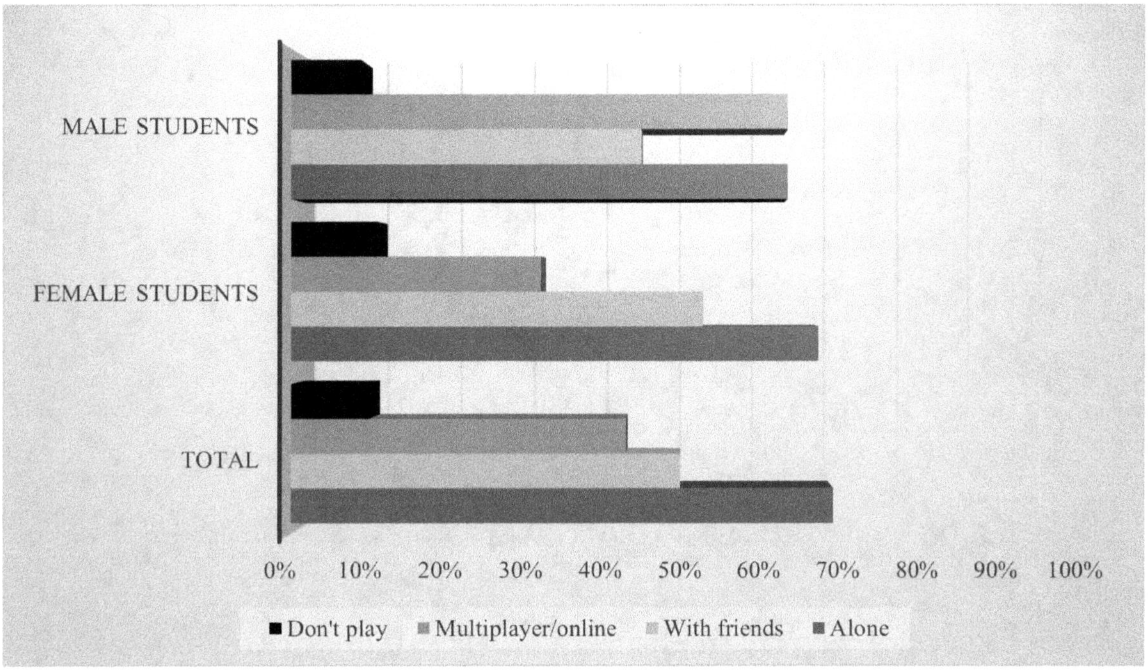

Figure 9. Q.8 Which video games do you play? (Female students)
Source: own creation

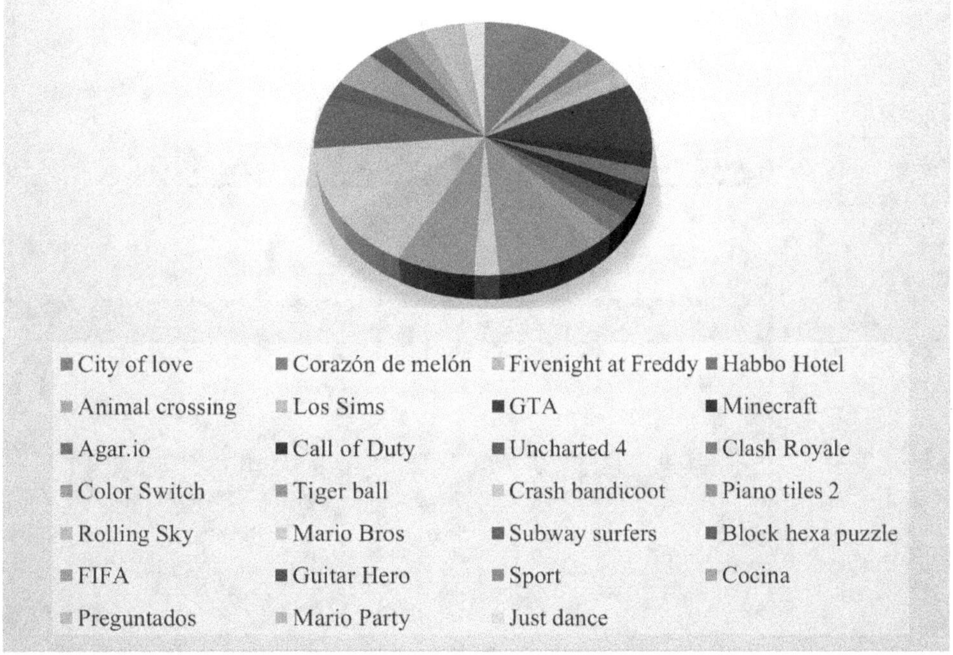

Figure 10. Q.8 Which video games do you play? (Male students)
Source: own creation

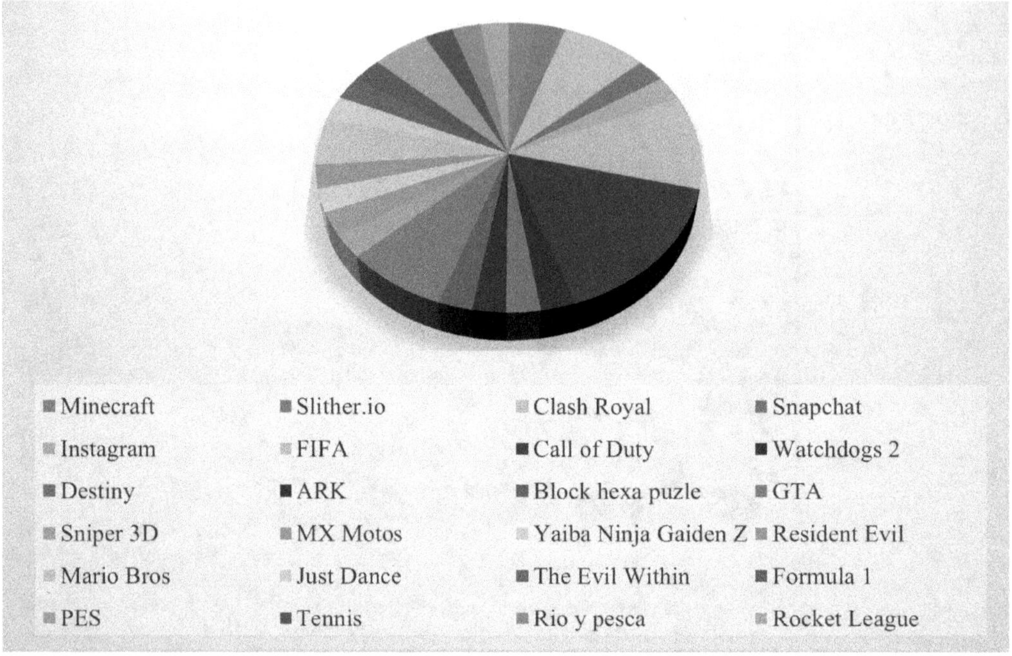

Figure 11. Q.9 Do you think you can learn through video games?
Source: own creation

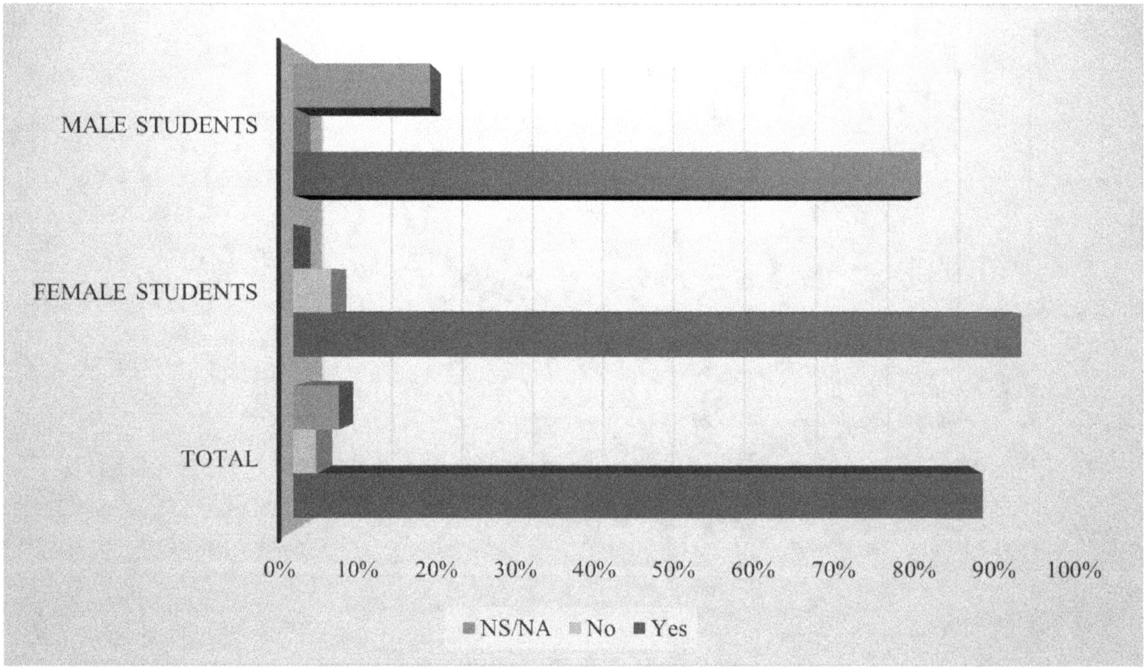

Figure 12. Q.10 Would you like video games to be used in classes to learn?
Source: own creation

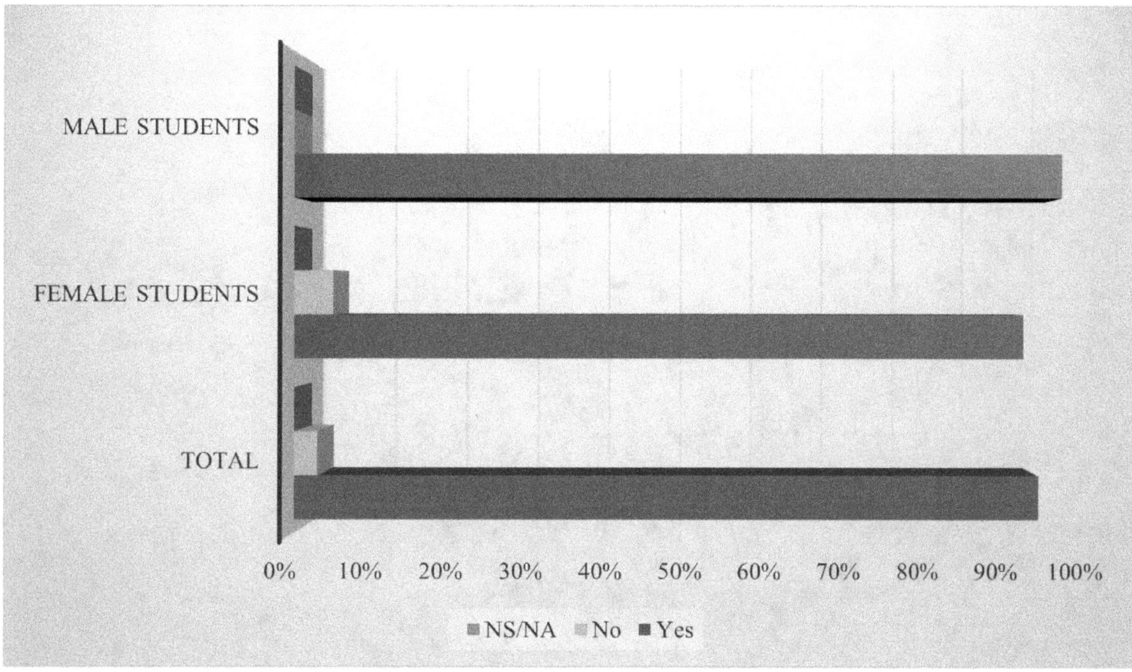

Figure 13. Q.11 Do you know any video games you have learnt something from?
Source: own creation

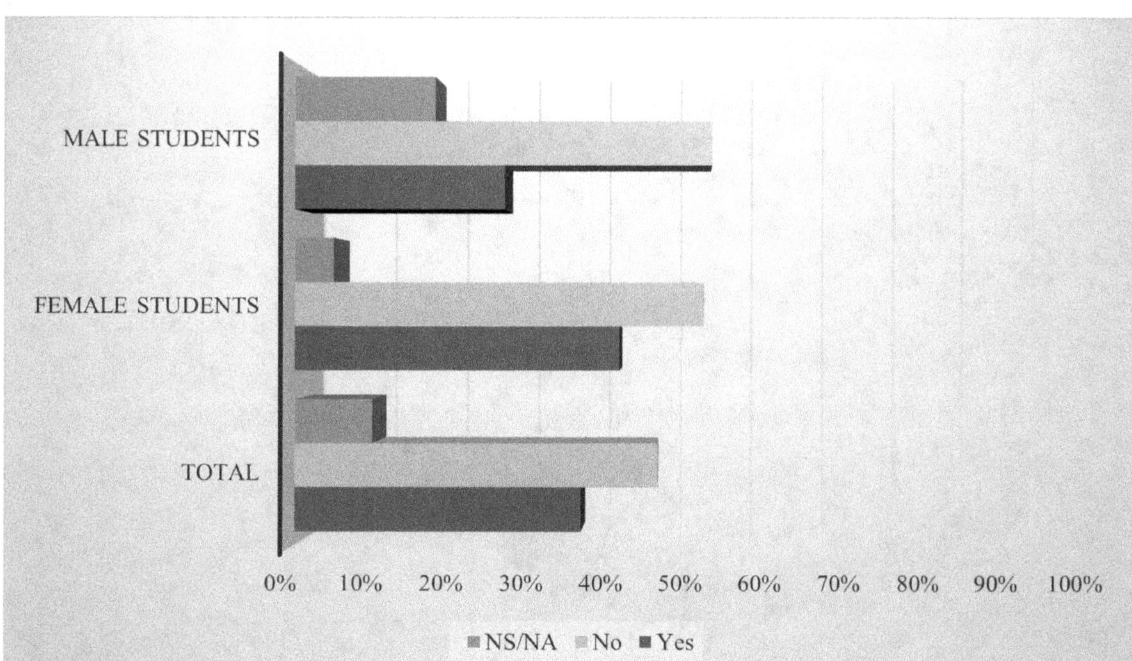

Figure 14. Q.11 Do you know any video games you have learnt something from? Which? (Female students)
Source: own creation

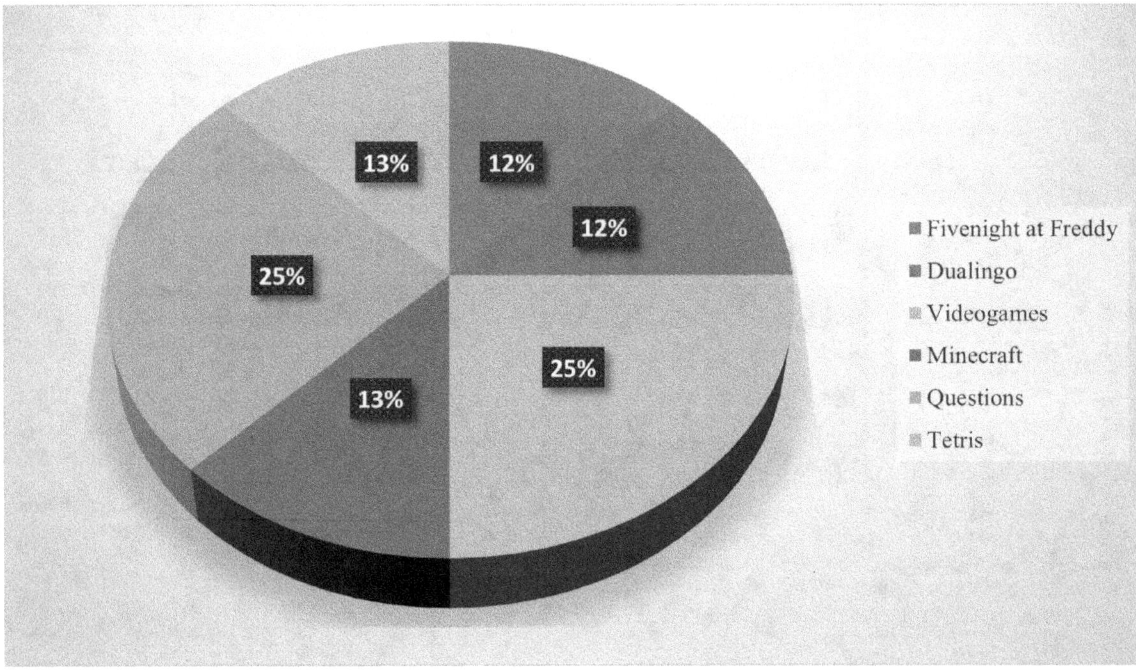

Figure 15. Q.11 Do you know any video games you have learnt something from? Which? (Male students)
Source: own creation

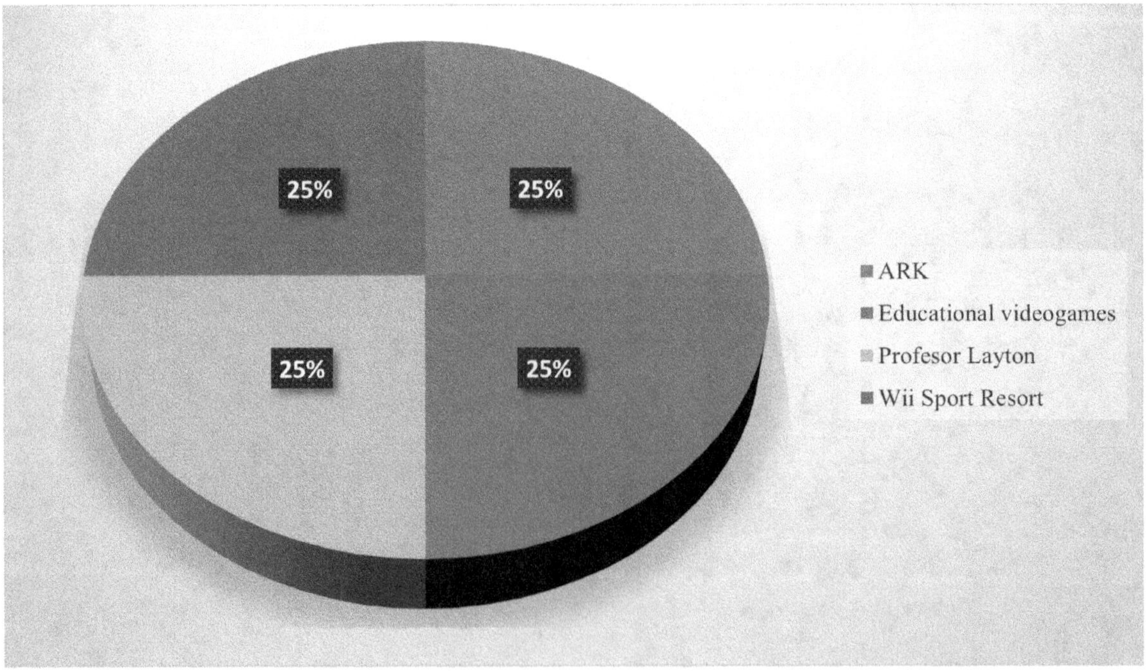

Figure 16. Q.12 Would you study more if video games were used in class?
Source: own creation

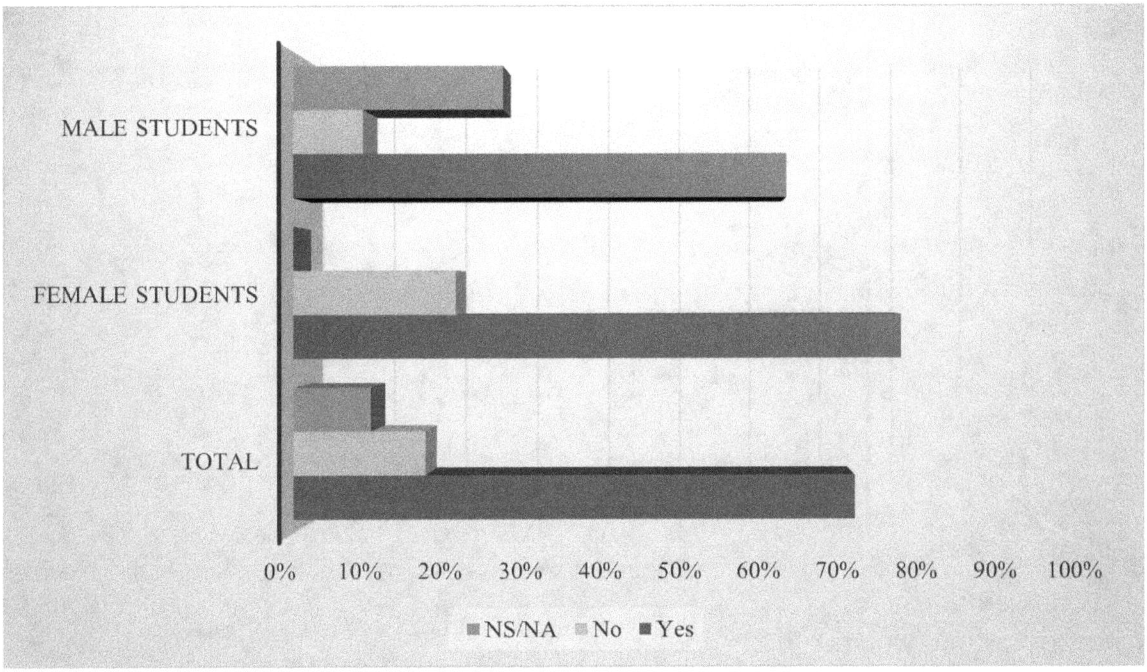

Figure 17. Q.13 Which subjects do you think video games could be used in?
Source: own creation

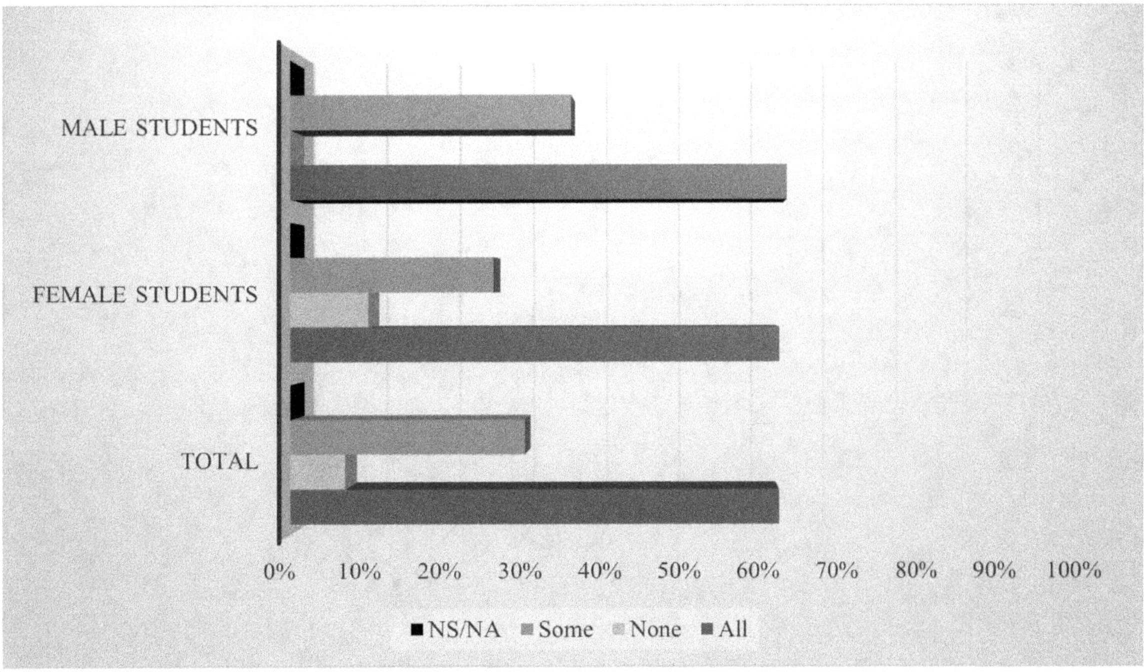

Figure 18. Q.14 What do you think you can learn playing video games?
Source: own creation

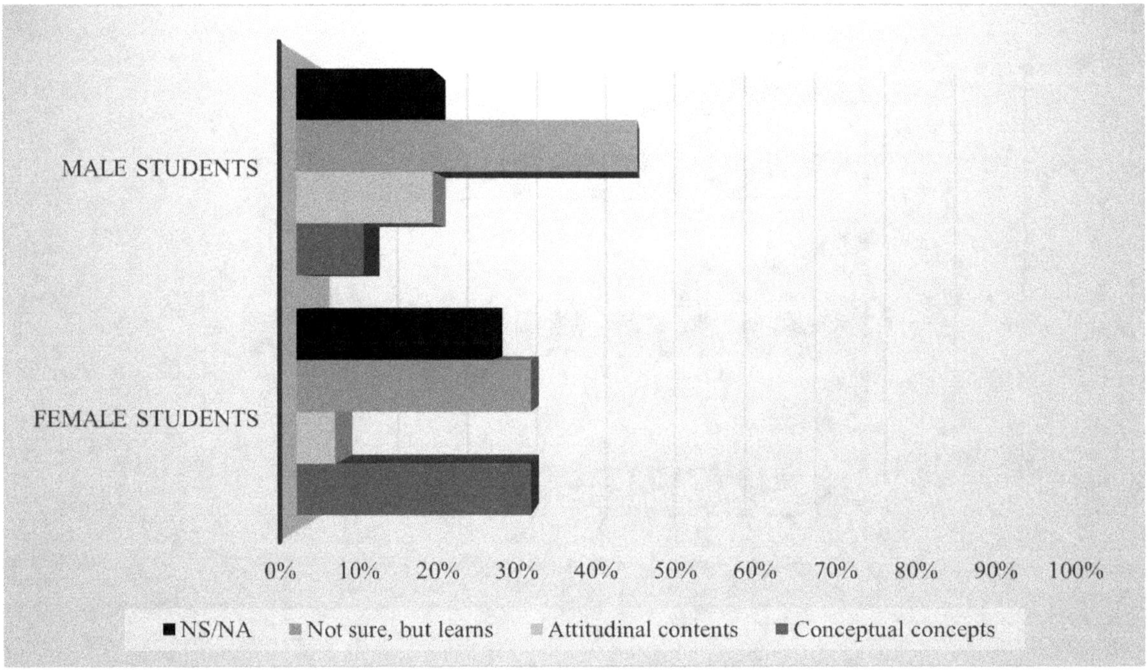

Chapter 12
Learning to Understand Historical Context:
Role-Playing Game "The Nuremberg Prosecutors"

Pilar Rivero
https://orcid.org/0000-0002-6757-7598
Research Group ARGOS, Faculty of Education, University of Zaragoza, Spain

Sergio Sánchez-Martínez
https://orcid.org/0000-0002-6382-8142
Research Group ARGOS, Faculty of Education, University of Zaragoza, Spain

Iñaki Navarro-Neri
https://orcid.org/0000-0001-8589-6659
Research Group ARGOS, Faculty of Education, University of Zaragoza, Spain

Miguel Ángel Pallarés
https://orcid.org/0000-0003-3459-5965
Research Group ARGOS, Faculty of Education, University of Zaragoza, Spain

EXECUTIVE SUMMARY

The development of historical thinking in students using active methodologies is an unavoidable opportunity to approach key events in the history of humanity, such as the Nuremberg trials. This chapter presents a proposal for gamification in the classroom through role-playing using a card game designed ad hoc in order to develop historical empathy in students. The objectives of this proposal are to determine the responsibilities of individuals and organisations for the execution of the German extermination programme, decide the seriousness of the facts proven through documentation and sources provided, value respect for life and tolerance as the foundations of democracy and human rights, investigate and become aware of the crimes committed by those involved, and value respect for life and tolerance as the foundations of democracy and human rights. This activity introduces students to a controversial topic such as the Nuremberg trials through activities such as the creation of a preliminary commission, the performance of the trial, and a debate.

DOI: 10.4018/978-1-6684-5240-0.ch012

HISTORICAL THINKING AND HISTORICAL EMPATHY IN THE CLASSROOM

Encouraging students' historical empathy has been a point of convergence for recent research into the development of historical thinking in the classroom (Brooks, 2008; Seixas and Morton, 2012; VanSledright, 2014; Wineburg, 2001). The work by Foster and Yeager (1998) stands out in theoretical reflection on historical empathy. These authors define historical empathy as the "ability to infer from given knowledge an explanation of certain actions" (p. 2) since "historical empathy combines the adductive and logical thinking associated with the use of evidence" with "the inferential and appropriately creative skills that seek to bridge the gap between what is known and what may be inferred from history" (p. 3). Other authors, such as Riley (1998), argue that empathy is nothing more than "a reconstruction of others' beliefs, values, and goals, any or all of which are not necessarily those of the historical investigator" (p. 33). Finally, Foster (1999) had already highlighted years earlier that the concept of empathy can be addressed by pointing out what it is not. For example, empathy does not require a student to identify with a historical figure since any attempt to do so "ignores the perspective of hindsight and is alien to the principle that historians are contemporary interpreters of past events" (p. 19). Empathy requires "cautious inquiry and close examination of available evidence" (p. 19). It concerns understanding the context and managing to reconstruct the perspective an individual or a group based their decision on at a precise historical moment (Paricio, 2019). Rather than a sentimental issue, it is a question of understanding the historical context to appreciate the actions of those who came before us and not to judge historical facts based on presentism.

Concerning empirical research, authors such as Ashby and Lee (1987) found in their early curricular experiences with historical empathy that students tended from the outset to assume people in the past held the same beliefs, ideas, and values they had in their own time. Other studies documented how students justified past actions that now are found unacceptable by claiming the perpetrators were, in some way, inferior (Lee et al., 1997; Lee and Ashby, 2001). Other research on historical empathy in the classroom has studied it using primary sources, for example (Carril-Merino et al., 2020; Dickinson and Lee, 1978; Shemilt 1987). This is particularly interesting due to the use of resources that are contemporary to the historical moment to understand.

In Spain, several research projects have conducted historical empathy exercises in the classroom using both a cognitive and an affective dimension (Domínguez, 1986, 2015; González et al., 2008; Guillén, 2016; Sáiz, 2013). Multiple educational proposals have also recently been documented to study historical empathy with preservice teachers (Carril-Merino et al., 2018, 2020, 2020b; San Pedro-Veledo and López-Manrique, 2017), thus indicating that this is an emerging line of educational innovation in Spain that will become consolidated.

WORKING ON THE HISTORICAL CONTEXT: AWAKENING HISTORICAL CONSCIOUSNESS IN STUDENTS

One of the major problems that has arisen since starting to develop historical empathy in the classroom is, undoubtedly, the confusion between empathy and sympathy (Paricio, 2019). The first documented experiences in which, for example, students were asked to write a letter as if they were World War I combatants, showed that the line between imagination and a true exercise of empathy is too thin (Coltham and Fines, 1971). However, this educational approach has become consolidated in current classroom practice with varying levels of complexity.

In recent years, several authors (Brooks, 2011; Endacott, 2010; Endacott and Brooks, 2013) have accepted the emotional and affective bond that can arise from these exercises, since historical empathy is "the process of students' cognitive and affective engagement with historical figures to better understand and contextualize their lived experiences, decisions, or actions. Historical empathy involves understanding how people from the past thought, felt, made decisions, acted, and faced consequences within a specific historical and social context" (Endacott and Brooks, 2013, p. 41). Endacott and Brooks (2013) understand that historical empathy includes three distinct processes: historical contextualization, perspective taking, and affective connection. As Davison (2012) put forward, rather than imagining "what an historical character might have felt" (pp. 12–13), the aim is to reconstruct the situation they were in with the utmost thoroughness so their experiences or possible interpretations of the situation can be analyzed in this character's general and specific context (Paricio, 2019).

Other authors such as Barton and Levstik (2004), Lévesque (2008, 2011) and Huijgen, van Boxtel, van de Grift and Holthuis (2016) also propose three pivotal aspects for conceiving and designing historical empathy activities: contextualization, a sense of otherness versus presentism, and understanding the perspective behind a way of acting. Contextualization is, therefore, always the starting point for any historical empathy exercise as locating any action in its complex world of facts, circumstances, and characteristics is vital, since they ultimately give meaning to any human action (Paricio, 2019).

THE COMPLEX HISTORICAL CONTEXT OF THE HOLOCAUST

Understanding people's actions during the Holocaust, one of the major genocides in the history of humankind, is extremely complex, as is the historical context surrounding it. However, teaching it through history instruction is vital. Aiming at making students understand the Holocaust and its historical context, this chapter presents a work proposal to address this based on a specific moment, the Nuremberg trials.

At the end of 1945, just after the end of World War II, the United Nations General Assembly (UNGA) created a specialized agency for education, the United Nations Educational, Scientific and Cultural Organization (UNESCO), in response to the horrors of the war and, particularly, to react to the crimes committed by Nazi Germany and its collaborators. Shortly afterwards, on December 9, 1948, this Assembly approved resolution 260 A (III) on the prevention and punishment of the crime of genocide, understood as the destruction or attempted destruction of a national, ethnical, racial, or religious group, with the intent to destroy human diversity (Valencia, 2000, pp. 87–88); the following day, resolution 217 A (III) was approved, known as the Universal Declaration of Human Rights, which recognizes every individual's dignity and equal rights, without distinction of any kind due to race, color, sex, language, religion, political opinion or other status (United Nations Organization, 1948).

It was during those three years that the Nuremberg trials were held, as the victorious powers decided to bring justice to bear on the main German leaders and organizations that had been responsible for the greatest atrocities during World War II (Overy, 2003). The process began with the London Agreement of August 8, 1945, which established the International Military Tribunal of Nuremberg. Subsequently, its article 6 inspired the norms dealing with genocide, crimes against humanity and war crimes, contained in the current Rome Statute of July 17, 1998, which created the permanent International Criminal Court (Pallarés and Sánchez, 2020, p. 123).

The Nuremberg trials represent more than just a trial of those responsible for the Holocaust. They marked a before and after in international law, which is still contravened to this day as accusations of genocide have not stopped. The examples of Rwanda, the war that broke up Yugoslavia, Yemen, and a long and unfortunate etcetera mean that explaining who is responsible for certain crimes needs to remain a subject taught in schools. As a consequence of various current political scenarios, it is no surprise that Holocaust denialism is still present in some circles, despite being a minority belief. Furthermore, the trials led to an in-depth debate on their legitimacy and on the concepts of justice and vengeance.

THE HOLOCAUST AS A CONTROVERSIAL TOPIC IN THE HISTORY CLASSROOM

The European Parliament issued a Recommendation in 2018 (to update the 2006 one) on key competences for lifelong learning. This defined social and civic competences to encourage active citizenship in a knowledge society and exerted a huge influence on European school curricula concerning tolerance, democratic coexistence, citizen participation, and respect for cultural diversity. Both recommendations emphasized the need for knowledge and critical understanding of past events and fostered the promotion of a culture of peace and non-violence (De Miguel and Sebastián López, 2020).

The United Nations resolution on Holocaust Remembrance (2005) urged member states to develop educational programs to prevent future acts of genocide, considering as such those committed with the intention of destroying a human group and based on a supremacist ideology. Another resolution two years later urged rejection of denialism and, in 2015, a new commitment was made, in which education was to play a crucial role, encouraging governments to usher in educational programs and projects that would contribute to preventing mass atrocities. UNESCO also supported this remembrance by creating an educational program in 2011 on the history of the Holocaust and, more generally, of genocides and mass atrocities, so that young people would become more aware of these historical events and understand the dynamics and processes that can lead to committing violence against certain groups (Hyang and Leicht, 2017).

Although the abundance of controversial topics stirs up intense emotions, raises difficult pedagogical questions and divides public opinion, the interest in working this topics in the classroom lies in their usefulness to help students develop their critical and analytical thinking, which is vital in the teaching of democracy and human rights as it contributes to form independent opinions, fosters intercultural dialogue, tolerance, and respect for others, aims to resolve conflicts peacefully and helps to acquire the tools needed to monitor the media in order to avoid manipulations (Kerr and Huddleston, 2015). However, studying controversial issues leads to intense emotions, difficult pedagogical questions, and divided public opinion. The priorities in Europe are to bolster the role of education in promoting European own values (democracy, human rights, and the rule of law) and to use it to defend against current social ills (radicalization, supremacism, xenophobia, anti-Semitism, violence and incitement to hatred, and loss of confidence in politics), which is why a democratic, inclusive education for the common good is needed (Díez, 2022). Teaching the Holocaust in class—while ensuring appropriate historical attention to detail and facing up to the past—contributes to achieving global political priorities through education, whose aims are to foster world citizenship, promote human rights, and engender a culture of peace and reconciliation. Studying the Holocaust shows how fragile all societies and institutions are, highlights aspects of human behavior that should be monitored, demonstrates the dangers of prejudice and discrimination, and explores issues such as the power of extremist ideologies and human possibilities in extreme situations. The aim is for students to become critically literate, socially connected and respectful of diversity, and to behave in a responsible, committed manner. Education should also promote values essential for coexisting—such as empathy, tolerance and a resolute attitude against racism and discrimination—which are so necessary in today's world. In short, students should be educated for global citizenship (Hyang and Leicht, 2017, pp. 18–25). By promoting critical thinking, history is understood as a debate whereby inaccuracies and distortions can be identified when the study of the past serves certain political or moral agendas.

CHALLENGES OF TEACHING ABOUT THE HOLOCAUST

Holocaust studies have gradually shaped one of the pioneering ways of recovering memory as a means of rethinking the past, which was soon transferred to the educational field (Davies, 2000; and Levy and Szneider, 2002). Although some voices underscore an excessive moral emphasis on this subject (Finkelstein, 2014), encompassing an emotional charge coupled with personal experiences that lend more authority to witnesses than to historical evidence, an empathetic attitude can be encouraged using heritage elements as a didactic resource (oral and material sources, images, testimonies, and narratives) concerning Nazi concentration and extermination camps. Consequently, several initiatives focused on recovering memory have been implemented in other countries. These include the International Holocaust Remembrance Alliance (IHRA) in 1998, the Stockholm International Forum on the Holocaust in 2000, the Education Working Group (EWG)—responsible for advising the signatory states on teaching the Holocaust in their curricula—the Salzburg Global Seminar, the U.S. Holocaust Memorial Museum, (Sánchez Macías, 2020, pp. 102–104), and, of course, Yad Vashem in Israel for decades.

These spaces should help people ask questions and reflect on the actions committed against humanity (Estepa and Delgado-Algarra, 2020). The fact memories clash should not impede a democratic society from assuming its responsibility to remember, nor, based on that act of remembering, from advocating and promoting opposing values to the ones leading to these events (for example, wars, dictatorships, and repressions). Education undoubtedly plays a crucial role in this regard and not only are there curricular examples in neighboring countries, but the European Union itself has also championed specific educational programs, primarily to address Holocaust remembrance (Prutsch, 2015), even though, as Joaquín Prats says, vindicating historical memory is the result of the supremacy of the present and some forgetting of history (Prats, 2020, p. 11).

Problems have been detected in the teaching and learning of the Holocaust, specifically when visiting concentration camps. These problems concern the type of museographic discourse in these spaces (mainly focused on what befell the Jewish people and on anti-Semitism), the kind of knowledge the students have before they visit, and interpreting the information and finding connections with current social problems, such as other genocides, xenophobia, and the treatment of immigrants. The classroom experience is similar, as the students' collective imagination primarily links the Holocaust to the genocide of Jews by the Nazis for racist reasons. Therefore, the Holocaust needs to be more present in school textbooks and approached in a more holistic manner without undervaluing any affected collective to make students reflect on xenophobic, discriminatory, and antidemocratic practices, and hate policies. Special attention should be paid to the importance of society's responsibility toward conflicts arising in its midst to help educate citizens that are critical, respectful, and mutually supportive (López Mateu, 2020). A report by UNESCO and the Georg Eckert Institute for International Textbook Research was published in 2015 on the international situation of Holocaust teaching in high-school education, focusing more on the concepts and specific narratives in textbooks and syllabuses rather than on the content, support, and time allocated. The report's conclusions are that the Holocaust is represented by common patterns using selective information and conveying recurrent geographical spatial and temporal scales, as well as protagonists, patterns, and interpretations (based on definitions, causes, relativization, or trivialization). The Holocaust is taught in history lessons on World War II in half the countries; in some it is studied with human rights; in others the words Holocaust or Shoah are avoided; and in just a few multicausality is addressed (in Germany and France), Hitler-centrism is overemphasized, and radical ideologies are cited (Fracapane, 2015). The Holocaust is not excessively mentioned in the textbooks in Spain (González and Núñez, 2020) and, therefore, their content can be improved.

Another difficulty when introducing the topic stems from the teachers' approach, since Nazism cannot be taught from a moral bias, with presentist prejudices; to think historically, students must explore Nazi rationality to understand why they acted as they did, meaning a multiperspective approach is required (Santos, 2020, pp. 66–67). Another failing found in some teachers is that they lack suitable preparation and time during the course needed to tackle the global regulatory framework that emerged after the Holocaust, since the Nuremberg trials involved a major legal problem: they were judging crimes not classified as such when they were committed (Valencia, 2000). The fact that teachers also lack preparation and time to work topics related to the subject ethical values, such as the Universal Declaration of Human Rights, is also a problem that need to be tackled. Furthermore, educators need to consider some specific challenges that must be faced in every educational context. First, informal factors outside the classroom (movies, video games, museums, cultural events, family stories, and national narratives), referred to as the "cultural curriculum," can wield a huge influence on how students learn about the Holocaust and can convey biases. Second, the subject raises complex ethical and emotional issues for both teachers and learners, which can result in historical narratives or personal ideologies being called into question (Hyang and Leicht, 2017, pp. 50–51).

At certain ages, students' cognitive capacity and previous knowledge about the Holocaust is scarce. However, even in more advanced grades, they may not show enough empathy with the victims because the experience is distant, the evidence is not appropriate, and young people's reactions may be more emotional than rational. For that reason, after providing the students with selected resources documenting classwork, teachers, who must remain neutral, should ask challenging questions about these topics; they must present problem situations that make controversial topics accessible so that students can try to understand other people's actions, whereby the experience of otherness inspires them to take a step back to understand that historical event (Núñez and González, 2021).

Learning about history, using interdisciplinary approaches and problem-based learning, teaching the subject over several years, having enough time to present the topic, with a scale of knowledge based on the students' age, and applying a gender focus should all be part of the curriculum. The recommendations for classroom practices are an open learning environment, applying participatory methods, differentiating between historical and moral lessons, addressing the complexity of the Holocaust, striving for precision in language and balancing perspectives, making distinctions between affected groups, examining acts of heroism, providing appropriate historical context, personalizing victims, adopting responsible methodological choices, and emphasizing that the Holocaust was not inevitable. The recommendations for non-formal education focus on cooperating with memorial centers, museums, and civil society (Hyang and Leicht, 2017, pp. 51–57, 62–69).

Fortunately, high-school teachers are now supported by specialized educational texts—such as those published by the University College of London (Pearce, 2020)—and by the guidelines established by UNESCO (Hyang and Leicht, 2017). In addition, Holocaust education is consolidated as a research and innovation line by its specificities, complexity and internationality (Foster et al., 2020). Although there is actually scant teaching material available on the Nuremberg trials, considered an epilogue of Nazism (Gray, 2015; Pearce, 2020, pp. 92–93), the Holocaust and Human Behavior monograph (Sigward, 2017, pp. 552–594) focuses on the process at length, and in its various sections it reflects on: revenge, legal settlements, and the establishment of the tribunal; the protagonists of the trials (defendants, judges, prosecutors, and witnesses); the losers' radical ideology and legal apparatus; the government of a state at the service of the perpetrators of genocide; the business of slave labor; parallel trials in Japan; the scope of justice; morality and legal dilemmas; and the limits of forgiveness. Each part is accompanied by a questionnaire to further explore and debate the subject, every chapter ends with a final analysis and reflection; therefore, it is a highly interesting tool for preparing educational activities.

ROLE-PLAYING: AN OPPORTUNITY FOR STUDENTS TO DEVELOP HISTORICAL THINKING

The Holocaust is one of what social science education refers to as controversial or conflicting topics. In Spain, for example, there are numerous studies on the implementation of controversial topics in the classroom such as the Spanish Civil War (Sospedra-Roca et al., 2022), migration and refugees (Santisteban-Fernández, A. 2019), terrorism (Aranguren-Juaristi et al., 2020; Vicent et al., 2021) or controversial heritage (Castro-Fernández et al., 2022) among others.

All the research cited in the previous paragraph, despite the fact that they do not share a common methodology, have a common objective: to know the students' perceptions of the topic in question. Therefore, working on controversial topics, in this case a topic of global relevance such as the Holocaust, through role-playing is an opportunity to achieve objectives such as finding out students' perceptions of the topic but, above all, developing their historical thinking and historical empathy.

Role-playing is an entertaining activity in which participants interpret behavioral models that are not their own (Brell, 2006). Students take on an active role by playing a specific character, placing themselves at the heart of learning, and, therefore, gaining first-hand experience of the situations and lessons to be acquired (Fernández Gavira et al., 2018).

This gamification of teaching primarily consists of choosing features from games and applying them in education, not only to improve the learning experience but also to motivate students (Özdener, 2018; Robson et al., 2015). However, as Martínez-Hita and Miralles (2020) point out, classes must obviously never turn into a game, since the aim is to learn, but from a motivational stance (Kapp, 2012).

Role-playing encompasses a series of benefits as an educational tool. First, it facilitates and gives meaning to the interdisciplinary teaching–learning process by analyzing and representing real situations and/or problems. This allows students to improve the quality of their learning, since they obtain a more holistic and in-depth knowledge. Furthermore, students' implicit commitment and participation result in more long-lasting learning (Fernández, 2006). Second, students develop more independence in a safe setting where there are no real risks or consequences (Marrón, 1996). Third, it arouses their curiosity and fosters critical thinking and other skills such as sociability, the spirit of cooperation, interculturality, and oral and written communication (Andreu, 2008). Fourth, it helps students take on a leading role in active learning and in a dynamic participatory classroom context (Quinquer, 2004). Fifth, it favors meaningful learning and discovery learning, since it builds on the skills students already have (Marrón, 1996). Sixth, it encourages students to develop empathy, since they not only learn to put content into practice, but also to be an individual by adopting behaviors, attitudes, and values such as empathy, tolerance, and respect (Biosca, 1997).

However, besides the aforementioned benefits, the use of role-playing in social science teaching involves a series of opportunities that clearly apply to historical role-playing (Hammer and Turkington, 2021); not only does it enable students to walk in the shoes of historical figures and make decisions, thereby helping them understand why they were made, it also forces them to adopt a historian's role and practices, either by explicitly taking on the role of historical researchers (Robbins, 2011) or by supporting the research the player undertakes as a key component of the role-play (Hammer and Heller, 2012). For example, role-playing games addressing complex issues such as slavery (Ellingboe, 2008), or colonialism (Burke, 2013) allow players to take on a role that probably lies far outside their own personal experience (Sampat, 2017).

In short, gamification fosters student involvement and participation because they feel encouraged by completing the proposed tasks (Rivero, 2017). Consequently, students are aided in developing historical thinking and also in combating their demotivation and perception of history as a boring discipline (Llopis and Balaguer, 2016).

THE "NUREMBERG PROSECUTORS" EXPERIENCE

High-school students' imagination contains notions about Nazism and the extermination of human beings during World War II. These notions usually stem from a variety of content consumed through the Internet, video games, documentaries on platforms, or conveyed directly by families engaged with history. They are abstract and undoubtedly unimaginable concepts, given the scope of the atrocity committed.

While understanding the past is a challenge for students, teaching it in a way that makes it understandable is equally complex. Sometimes high-school teachers use a textbook as an essential tool for unraveling the facts. However, they are more likely to use materials they create themselves, illustrated sources, testimonies, maps, and films; everything available is tested in the classroom to improve understanding of the past.

In this case, the aim is to present material prepared by the authors with several objectives. Fundamentally, the purpose is to involve the students in some research by carrying out the task the allied prosecutors performed in the main Nuremberg trail. They also play the role of judges and prosecutors, and finish with a simulation of the trial. Finally, they view previously selected film materials to consolidate their learning and stimulate discussions around the issues arising from the activity.

Design of the Materials

The activity was based on preparing illustrated material, whose structure and presentation is not dissimilar to the games students play in their leisure time. A compact, visual, and direct format was considered adequate to facilitate handling during the activity. For that reason, the selected format was a simple but direct card containing a summary of the information. This material was created using a selection of

Figure 1. Front and back of defendant Hans Frank's information card
Source: own creation

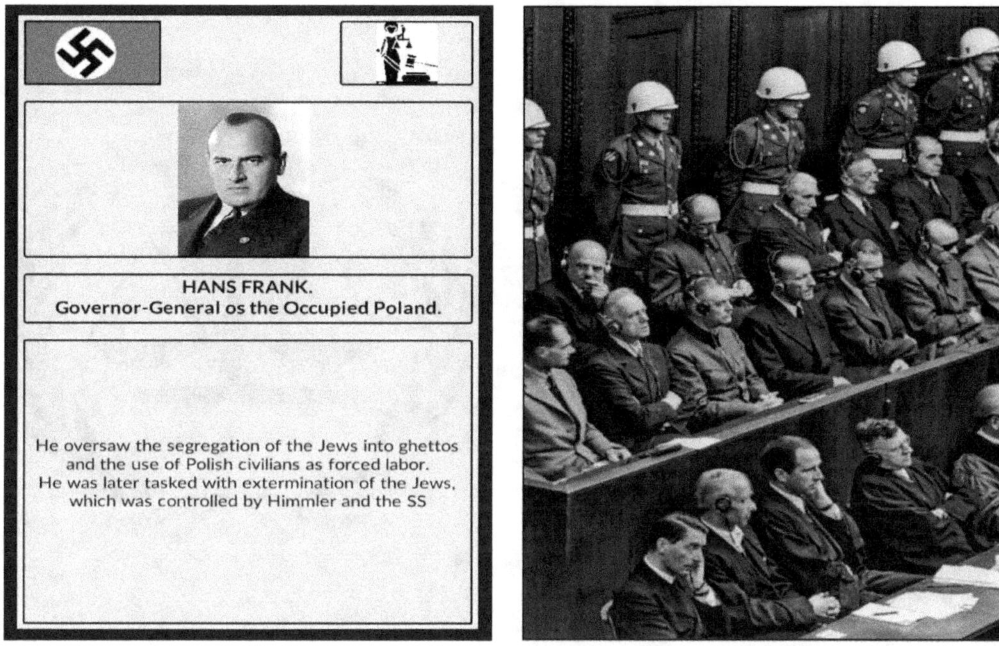

free-format images, texts prepared by the teachers, and illustrations identifying the role of each card in the activity through simple symbols.

The Cards

The materials used are based on the design of several groups of cards. These cards were created with the computer design program Card Creator (Pixelatto, 2017), as its interface and final design are easy to use. Several groups (five in total) of cards were created to set up the activity. The groups are divided based on a logical sequence in a judicial process: judges and chief prosecutor, defendants (figure 1), accusations, evidence, and convictions.

The first of the groups (five cards in total) comprises the four judges and the chief prosecutor who led the indictments. They are: General Nikitchenko, representing the Soviet Union; Francis Biddle, the United States; Geoffrey Lawrence (figure 2), the president ofthe tribunal and representing the United Kingdom; Henri Donnedieu de Vabres representing the Republic of France; and, finally, the American Robert H. Jackson, the chief prosecutor of the trial.

The cards representing the defendants total 38. While it is true that there were 24 defendants in the main Nuremberg trial, the possibility of including more defendants in the activity was considered. The criteria for selecting these 38 elements were first to represent the main trial with historical accuracy with the 24 historical defendants, but also to add organizations that had participated in the Holocaust in some way, or people who had died before the trial.

The aim of these criteria is to help the students learn and reflect. The defendants include organizations such as the Gestapo, the SD, the SS, and the Land, Sea, and Air forces of the Third Reich. The

Figure 2. Front and back of judge Geoffrey Lawrence's information card
Source: own creation

different organizations outlined above were selected because they are famous and historically relevant. In the context of the Third Reich, they all played a necessary role in promoting the war, occupying and controlling invaded countries, and implementing the machinery of the Holocaust in Europe. This helps students question the extent to which an organization can be held responsible for and accused of certain crimes, and the convictions or decisions that can be established as a result of its actions. Besides these organizations, figures that were not present at the trial for various reasons were also included. As with the organizations, these figures stand out due to their historical relevance in the events.

Therefore, cards representing people that had already died or whose whereabouts were unknown were introduced. The first corresponds to Adolf Hitler, due to his considerable relevance as leader of a totalitarian state and, ultimately, the instigator and person most responsible for anti-Semitism and the war. There is no text on this card since the students know this figure extremely well. The others are Goebbels, for his role in building the Nazi propaganda apparatus and spreading anti-Jewish ideas; Adolf Eichmann, for his direct responsibility in planning and executing the Holocaust; Himmler, for his role as head of the SS, the direct perpetrators of the mass murders and for managing the extermination camps; Mengele, for the atrocities committed during his experiments on human beings; and Rudolf Höss, commandant of Auschwitz. In short, these figures were selected for their historical relevance to the Holocaust. The purpose of these cards is to encourage discussion on determining responsibilities, even if the person is deceased. In most European legislations, the case ends if the accused has died. In this case, these defendants can be charged, proved guilty, and, if applicable, convicted. Finally, the cards of two figures that did not participate in the main trial, Wisliceny and Höss, were introduced because of the historical fame they gained in the Holocaust trial.

Figure 3. Back of the card of crimes against peace
Source: own creation

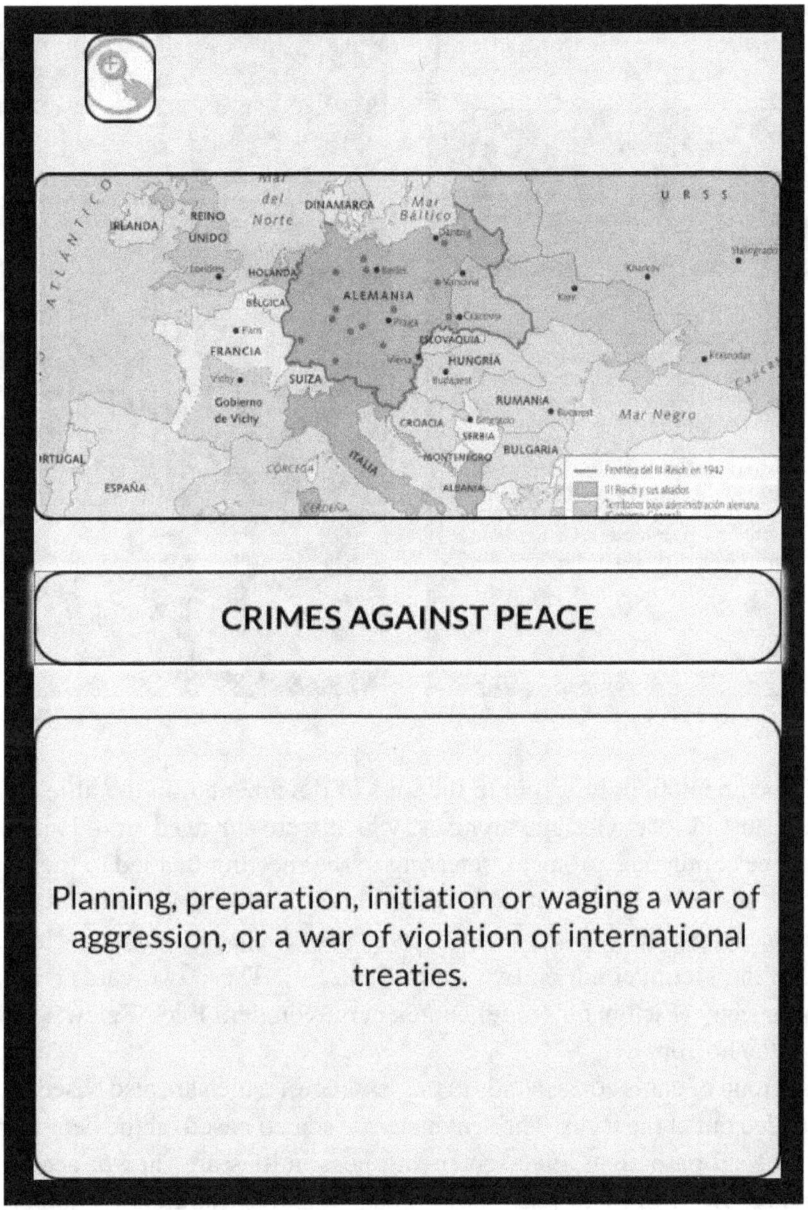

The types of crimes in the main trial were established and the legislation applied was simplified. These crimes are represented on seven cards corresponding to war crimes, crimes against peace (figure 3), murder, slavery, forced deportation, crimes against humanity, and genocide.

The next group of materials is the evidence that should be brought against the defendants and charges. This is a series of cards containing substantial and summarized information on the numerous pieces of evidence presented at the main trial. Given the extent of the evidence, the information was summarized and the most decisive in the trial was highlighted. This selection of evidence consists of the following

Figure 4. Front and back of "victim count" evidence card
Source: own creation

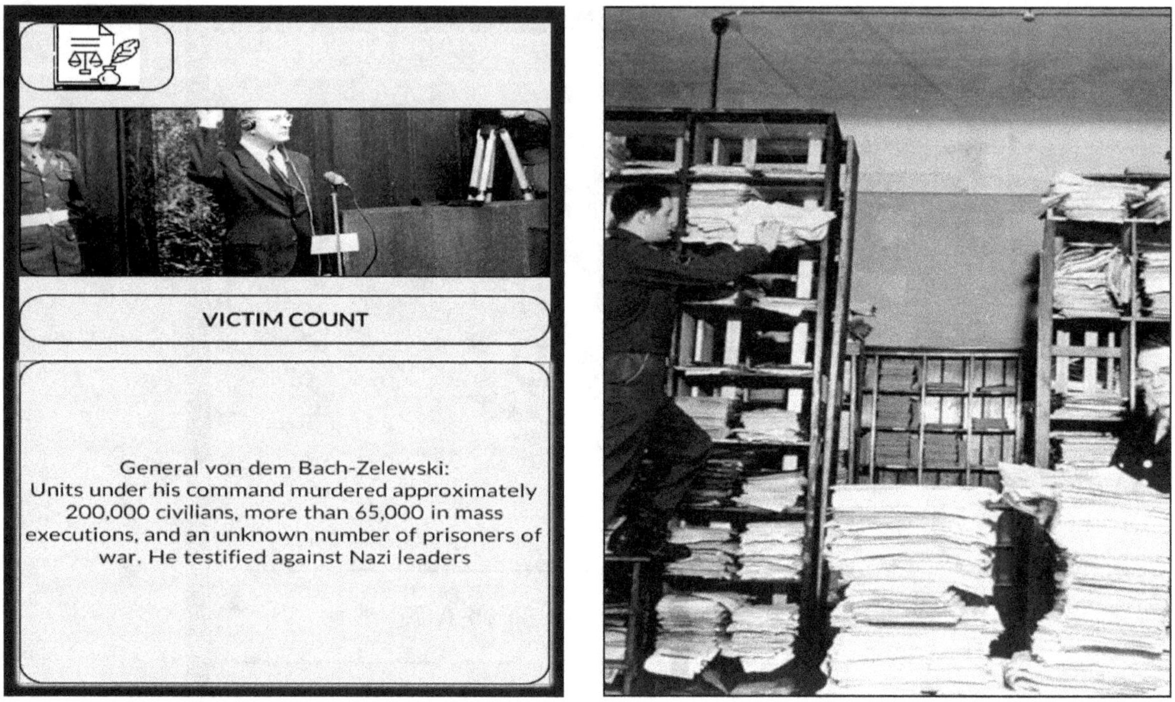

summary: seized documentation, referring to the tons of documentation the allies managed to obtain; copies on the Holocaust in local Gestapo archives, which were salvaged from local Third Reich headquarters; the Wannsee conference protocol, referring to the meeting that led to the "final solution"; the Stroop report, which served to document the destruction of the Warsaw ghetto, as well as other places; photographs taken in camps; first-person testimonies of people who suffered the Holocaust; testimonies of perpetrators; and the victim count on two cards (figure 4). These two cards represent the numbers given by Dieter Wisliceny (Eichmann's aide) and General von dem Bach-Zelewski, whose testimonies gave an account of the horror.

Finally, the last group of cards corresponds to the sentences, which are also based on a summary of the ones originally handed out at the trials. The sentences are scaled based on the defendant's responsibility and involvement in Nazi barbarism. Five sentencing possibilities are shown: acquittal, life imprisonment, prison sentences from 10 to 20 years, death penalty, and extradition to another country for trial.

Performing the Activity

The proposed activity is structured into three sessions and it can be extended if necessary. Like the activity, the material is presented as a flexible model that teachers can adapt to their classroom and syllabus contexts. From a curricular viewpoint, it should come after the contents of World War II and the Holocaust, since students should have some previous knowledge about the activity. However, given the magnitude of the topic, students have previous knowledge gleaned from non-formal education through information in books, novels, or documentaries. Consequently, the activity does not need too much presentation, since it is the culmination of previous knowledge and involves immersion in the historical event through simulation and historical empathy as fundamental factors. The activity is, therefore, useful in the fourth and last year of compulsory high-school education (ESO) in Spain in the subjects of geography and history, as well as in the baccalaureate subject of contemporary world history. However, the activity could also be implemented when teaching social psychology in the subject of psychology in the second year of the baccalaureate.

Regarding the activity's distribution, the first session is planned to be performed in small groups. Depending on classroom size, teams can comprise several members, although the ideal number is five. Each group should appoint a secretary whose role is to take notes of all the groups' deliberations, discussions, and decisions. Several handouts are provided for that purpose. The following should be written on them: the name of the defendant or organization, the crimes for which they will be tried, list of evidence for each crime, and a proposed sentence.

Based on the material—the cards—the teams must discuss whether the defendants are guilty or innocent, as well as the degree of involvement in the proposed crimes. Depending on the total number of groups in the class, between seven and eight accusation cards are distributed to each team. The teacher can choose which cards are handed out to adapt the materials to the number of students, although including at least the original 24 defendants is essential.

A complete set of crimes, evidence and convictions is distributed together with the cards of the defendants. By using the material in this way, the groups are immersed in simulating the work of the prosecutors' investigation teams at the Nuremberg trials. This session can be extended whenever possible. After completing the work of simulating the prosecutors' investigation, the groups can pool the difficulties they encountered in establishing crimes, evidence, and convictions.

The second session is simulating the trial. Four judges must be appointed as representatives of each of the teams and they will have a crucial role. Two prosecutors are also appointed to make the accusations. For the simulation, the cards of the judges are distributed among the students, and the card of the chief prosecutor, General Jackson, is given to the prosecutors. The classroom has to be transformed into a court of justice with four preferential places for the judges and a chair for the defendants.

Regarding the role of the defendants, this should ideally be played by the teacher to give it more drama, emphasis, and theatricality. Teachers should properly document themselves on the defendants' reactions during the trial. When the trial begins, the defendants are called to testify in the order the judges establish. The defendant must respond to the accusations and evidence presented by the prosecutors. The various ways the teachers choose to defend themselves must include phrases that cast doubt on the legality of the court, the idea of revenge on the defeated side, or following orders given by superiors. In the case of Göring, responsibility must be acknowledged, just as it was in the original trial.

After completing the representation of the trial, the judges must meet and pass sentence. The sentences are given defendant by defendant in a solemn tone, given the historical importance of the moment.

The third session is established in two parts. On the one hand, viewing scenes the teacher selects from the two-part series *Nuremberg* (Simoneau, 2001) and from the film *Judgment at Nuremberg* (Kramer, 1961), paying close attention to the closing argument of the German judge Ernst Janning portrayed by Burt Lancaster. A broad range of scenes has been selected so that teachers can choose the ones that accurately illustrate history and help students to better understand the importance of the trials and how chilling some of the testimonies were. These are short clips due to time constraints. For that reason, we have chosen the following scenes (with our own short titles) from the miniseries *Nuremberg* (Simoneau, 2001):

A) ***Trial objective***: DVD 1 (min. 13.10–14.25). This scene shows the debate on the end goals of the trial and underscores the importance of the idea of justice prevailing over that of vengeance in typical trials.
B) ***Start of the trial***: First part (min. 57.36–1h.03). This illustrates the solemnity and historical background of the activity. The scene shows how the judges, prosecutors, and defendants were arranged in the courtroom and the protocol for starting the trial.
C) ***Witness statements***: First part (min. 1h.13.10–1h.18.25). This provides students with some direct examples of people who survived the camps, especially as the statements made in the scene mirror original statements made during the trial.
D) ***Göring's speech***: Second part (min. 5.39–7.15). Göring's evidence was decisive during the trial since he recognized and revealed that both he and the other defendants were guilty. The scene provides students with a personal vision based on the testimony of one of the Third Reich's main perpetrators.
E) ***Statements by Streicher, Frank, Kaltenbrunner, Höss, Saukel, and Speer***: Second part (min. 40.00–50.04). Selection of statements made by several figures representative of their arguments. Students can see how the defendants reacted differently to the issue of the Nazi extermination actions.
F) ***The origin of evil***: Second part (min. 58.05–59.52). Fictitious scene showing the allies' main interrogator's thoughts on the origin of evil and malice when speaking with the chief prosecutor. This conversation demonstrates how incredulous the interrogators and prosecutors were when they learned about the historical events involving the mass murder of human beings and the defendants' absence of remorse due to an extreme lack of empathy.
G) ***Theclosing argument*** from the film *Judgment at Nuremberg* (min. 2h.15.30–2h.23.45). The final clip is the scene in which Judge Janning reflects on individual responsibility for events, and on the possibility of choosing when evil compels you to act.

At the end of the clips, a discussion takes place among the students and between them and the teacher on the activity itself and on the historical relevance and significance of the Nuremberg trials.

Pilot Experiences: Results

The experience of Hammer and Turkington (2021) was considered in both the design of materials and the implementation of the activity, in response to the challenges of Holocaust-related role-playing games these authors defined.

The education activity has been performed in two different groups: in the prison classroom of Zuera Correctional Center, in the context of high-school education for adults in the fourth year (corresponding to the fourth year of the Spanish ESO), and at an ESO and baccalaureate school in Aragon in the fourth year of ESO.

Although both contexts are the same academic year, they present a completely different and diverse range of students in terms of cognitive development, age stage, and learning objectives; however, their reflections and discussions were very similar. In both cases, the activity was concluded with a discussion group from whose most significant testimonies have been extracted in order to qualitatively exemplify the success of the didactic proposal presented in this chapter.

In the experience at Zuera Correctional Center, most students were surprised by how some defendants approached their defense: "I understand they may justify what they did because they had been ordered to do it, but that was barbaric." This was also seen in the response to the statement: "If you had been where they (the defendants) were, you would have done the same thing." These issues were repeated in the high school, where they added: "Well, I wouldn't have done it and I would have left the country." On the same issue we read: "Why couldn't they refuse to do it? Did they like hurting people or killing them?" On the Holocaust, in both cases they thought about the way people were exterminated with expressions such as: "it's inhuman"; "they were animals, they did not see them as people"; and "You must be crazy to do that because you want to."

In one of the groups at the Zuera Correctional Center there was considerable discussion on the legality of bringing a deceased person to trial. In this case, it concerned Goebbels's trial in the first session, and the following is worth quoting: "These people also have to be brought to trial, even though they are dead, because they were responsible for the genocide. And they must also be judged by history; the victims must be compensated with justice." There was also some debate as to how an entire organization can be judged: "You cannot judge the entire German army"; "You have to judge the officers, because they're the ones in charge." In contrast, at the high school, the students had no qualms about judging organizations: "If they're all responsible, they're all guilty." These were the aspects provoking most discussion. There were no discussions on political ideologies or ethnic issues; therefore, in the context of history instruction in Spain in the twenty-first century, it may not be appropriate to define the Holocaust as a controversial topic. It is hard to understand, especially in context, but it is not a matter of conflict that engages students in discussions forcing them to take very differentiated and opposing positions.

The participation and involvement of the students in the activity was outstanding at Zuera Correctional Center. The highly diverse students remarked on the clarity of the materials and how easy they were to use. Order, respect for others' opinions, and the contents made for a highly satisfactory educational experience. The knowledge was acquired by an experience in which students were the protagonists of history in both the defendant research and trial representation phases. Highlighted in relation to viewing the chosen scenes is the personal relationship they established between the events shown and the work they performed in the activity. The final discussion was extremely participatory and underlined how everyone takes responsibility for their life choices. These students had been tried and convicted for various crimes and all of them empathized with the Holocaust victims and not with the defendants. The sentences they gave stand out, since most were life imprisonment. There was only one death sentence for Höss for his brutality at Auschwitz. The main reason for giving various Nazi leaders life sentences lies in these students' personal experiences as they thought this was the worst possible sentence, even above the death penalty.

In an educational context of adolescents in the fourth year of ESO, the dynamics and the material were surprising as tools to facilitate learning. The students' immersion in history pinpointed a remarkable understanding of contents unlike a traditional explanation. The group work representing the committee of prosecutors was remarkable, with small discussions on whether it was possible to judge organizations or people who had died. The determination to judge everyone was unexpected, even if the case expired on the accused's death, since they had to be answerable to the victims and to history. As in the experience at Zuera, viewing the selected scenes was very illustrative, and the students' comments underscored their disbelief at the unrepentant statements. The structured discussion highlighted evil as the main driving force behind the atrocities. Unsurprisingly, they discussed whether something similar could happen again.

The students commented on the events of the Yugoslav Wars and the Rwandan Civil War, emphasizing the importance of knowing history as a reminder to prevent future atrocities.

CONCLUSIONS

Role-playing has been confirmed as a highly interesting method for developing students' historical thinking, since, to a certain extent, it enables them to reproduce a historical episode in the classroom. This game helps students improve their comprehension of its context, which is crucial for understanding the position adopted by every historical figure represented in it and for its dynamics to work in the classroom. Along these lines, authors such as Riley (1998) and Stern (1998) argue that, when studying events such as the Holocaust, the voices of men, women, and children can play a more important role in empathic reconstruction than the decisions made by the key figures involved (Brooks, 2008). Therefore, the testimonies provided in the role-play are vital to implement the experience properly. Particular thought must be given to designing the materials, selecting historical figures, information, and sources for the educational activity to be effective. Using cards is appropriate due to their visual and handling aspects.

Besides working on the context—the game's main objective—it was observed that the discussions led to a series of interesting reflections on the principle of agency, the person or persons behind historical changes and phenomena, which entails thinking about people's responsibility for actions and decisions made now and throughout history. This confirms interest in the subject, approached on the basis of civic education and values, and the relevance it acquires in the classroom for educating students (Chapman, 2020), since, irrespective of whether it can be considered a controversial topic in the Spanish context—as no divergent opinions were voiced—the students' reflections on this activity serve, in turn, to reflect on current conflicts (López Mateu, 2020) and to address in the classroom most of the problems arising from controversial topics: extremism, radicalization, xenophobia, anti-Semitism, incitement to hatred, loss of confidence in politics, and the negative effects of austerity measures (Kerr and Huddleston, 2015). Therefore, working controversial topics such as the Nuremberg trials through active and reflective educational activities conforms to the purpose of education in today's democratic societies and is very positive. The Holocaust may not be a controversial topic in Spain, but teaching and learning about it is an essential tool in the classroom for addressing a number of controversial aspects in most contemporary conflicts. As Chapman (2020) points out, this is a case of not only learning about the Holocaust, but, above all, learning from it.

ACKNOWLEDGMENT

This research wants to express its gratitude to the following people for their collaboration: the Subdirectorate of Treatment and J.M. Allue, educator at the Penitentiary Centre of Zuera and Enrique Vallespín Domínguez, teacher of Compulsory Secondary Education and High School.

This research was supported by the project: Competencias digitales, procesos de aprendizaje y toma de conciencia sobre el patrimonio cultural: Educación de calidad para ciudades y comunidades sostenibles MINECO/AEI[PID2020-115288RB-I00] and the research group ARGOS [S50_20R] Government of Aragón.

REFERENCES

Andreu, M. A. (2008). Simulación. In M. J. Labrador & M. A. Andreu (Eds.), *Metodologías activas. Grupo de Innovación en Metodologías Activas (GIMA)* (pp. 93–105). Universidad Politécnica de Valencia.

Aranguren-Juaristi, O., Apalaoza-Llorente, D., Echeberria Arquero, B., & Vicent, N. (2020). Testimonios de víctimas en el módulo educativo Adi-adian. Una mirada desde la didáctica de las ciencias sociales y la educación patrimonial. *Investigaciones En La Escuela, 101*(101), 15–24. doi:10.12795/IE.2020.i101.02

Ashby, R., & Lee, P. J. (1987). Children's concepts of empathy and understanding in history. In C. Portal (Ed.), *The history curriculum for teachers* (pp. 62–88). The Falmer Press.

Barton, K. C., & Levstik, L. (2004). *Teaching History for the Common Good.* Erlbau. doi:10.4324/9781410610508

Biosca, T. (1997). La història i els jocs didàctics de simulació. *L'Avenç. Revista de història i cultura, 217*, 52-53.

Brell, M. (2006). Juegos de rol. *Educación social: revista de intervención socioeducativa, 33*, 104-113.

Brooks, S. (2008). Displaying historical empathy: What impact can a writing assignment have? *Social Studies Research & Practice*, *3*(2), 130–146. doi:10.1108/SSRP-02-2008-B0008

Brooks, S. (2011). Historical Empathy as Perspective Recognition and Care in One Secondary Social Studies Classroom. *Theory and Research in Social Education*, *39*(2), 166–202. doi:10.1080/00933104.2011.10473452

Burke, L. L. (2013). *DogEatDog* [Game]. Liwanang Press.

Carril-Merino, Mª. T., Andreu-Mediero, B., De la Calle-Carracedo, M., & López-Torres, E. (2020). Fuentes orales para el desarrollo de la empatía histórica: un estudio en la formación del profesorado de Educación Infantil. *Panta Rei: revista digital de Historia y didáctica de la Historia, 14*(1),155-184. doi:10.6018/pantarei.444771

Carril-Merino, M. T., Sánchez-Agustí, M., & Miguel-Revilla, D. (2018). Perspectiva histórica y empatía: Su interrelación en futuros profesores de Educación Primaria. *Aula Abierta*, *47*(2), 221–228. doi:10.17811/rifie.47.2.2018.221-228

Carril-Merino, Mª. T., Sánchez-Agustí, M., & Muñoz-Labraña, C. (2020b). Empatía histórica en futuros profesores de primaria: El trabajo infantil en el siglo XIX. *Educação e Pesquisa*, *46*, 1–18. doi:10.1590/S1678-4634202046215492

Castro-Fernández, B., Jiménez-Esquinas, G., & López-Facal, R. (2022). Teacher Training Via Debate on the Way of St. James as Controversial Heritage. *Frontiers in Education*, *6*, 823122. doi:10.3389/feduc.2021.823122

Chapman, A. (2020). Learning the lessons of the Holocaust: A critical exploration. In S. Foster, A. Pearce, & A. Pettigrew (Eds.), Holocaust Education. Contemporary challenges and controversies (pp. 50-73). UCL Press. doi:10.2307/j.ctv15d7zpf.9

Coltham, J., & Fines, J. (1971). *Educational Objectives for the Study of History*. The Historical Association.

Davies, I. (Ed.). (2000). Teaching the Holocaust: Educational Dimensions, Principles and Practice. Continuum.

Davison, M. (2012). Teaching historial empathy and the 1915 Gallipoli campaign. In M. Harcourt & M. Sheehan (Eds.), *Historymatters: teaching and learninghistory in New Zealandsecondaryschools in the 21st century* (pp. 11–31). NZCER Press.

De Miguel, R. & Sebastián, M. (2020). Democracia, participación y ciudadanía europea: recursos didácticos cartográficos para la enseñanza de la convivencia y la integración europea. *Clio. History and History Teaching*, *46*, 14-29. doi:10.26754/ojs_clio/clio.2020465256

Dickinson, A. K., & Lee, P. (1978). Understanding and Research. In A. Dickinson & P. Lee (Eds.), *History Teaching and Historical Understanding* (pp. 95–120). Heinemann Educational Books.

Díez Gutiérrez, E. J. (2022). *Pedagogía antifascista. Construir una pedagogía inclusiva, democrática y del bien común frente al auge del fascismo y la xenofobia*. Octaedro.

Domínguez, J. (1986). Enseñar a comprender el pasado histórico: Conceptos y empatía. *Infancia y Aprendizaje*, *34*(34), 1–21. doi:10.1080/02103702.1986.10822113

Domínguez, J. (2015). *Pensamiento histórico y evaluación de competencias*. Graó.

Ellingboe, J. (2008). *Steal Away Jordan* [Game]. Stone Baby Games.

Endacott, J. L. (2010). Reconsidering Affective Engagement in Historical Empathy. *Theory & Research in Social Education, 38*(1), 6-47. doi:10.1080/00933104.2010.10473415

Endacott, J. L., & Brooks, S. (2013). An Updated Theoretical and Practical Model for Promoting Historical Empathy. *Social Studies Research & Practice*, *8*(1), 41–58. doi:10.1108/SSRP-01-2013-B0003

Estepa, J., & Delgado-Algarra, E. J. (2020). Construyendo un compromiso democrático: memoria histórica, patrimonio y educación ciudadana. In I. Sáez-Rosenkranz & J. Prats Cuevas (Eds.), *Memoria histórica y enseñanza de la Historia* (pp. 45–64). Ediciones Trea.

Fernández Gavira, J., Prieto Gallego, E., Alcaraz-Rodríguez, V., Sánchez-Oliver, A. J., & Grimaldi-Puyanal, M. (2018). Aprendizajes significativos mediante la Gamificación a partir del Juego de Rol: "Las Aldeas de la Historia". Espiral. *Cuadernos del Profesorado*, *11*(22), 69–78. doi:10.25115/ecp.v11i21.1919

Fernández, A. (2006). Metodologías activas para la formación de competencias. *Educatio siglo XXI, 24*, 35-56.

Finkelstein, N. G. (2014). *La industria del Holocausto. Reflexiones sobre la explotación del sufrimiento judío*. Akal.

Foster, S. J., & Yeager, E. A. (1998). The role of empathy in the development of historical understanding. *The International Journal of Social Education*, *13*(1), 1–7.

Foster, S. J. (1999). Using historical empathy to excite students about the study of history: Can you empathize with Neville Chamberlain? *Social Studies*, *90*(1), 18–24. doi:10.1080/00377999909602386

Foster, S., Pearce, A., & Pettigrew, A. (Eds.). (2020). Holocaust Education. Contemporary Challenges and Controversies.

Fracapane, K. (2015). *The international status of Education about the Holocaust. A global mapping of textbooks and curricula. Summary*. UNESCO.

González, N., Henríquez, H., Pagès, J., & Santisteban, A. (2008). Empathie historique pour un présent en mutation. L'enseignement et l'apprentissage de la compréhension historique à travers une expérience didactique. In *Colloque Didactiques de l'Histoire, de la Géographie et de l'Éducation à la Citoyenneté. Enjeux du Monde, enjeux d'apprentissage en histoire, géographie, éducation à la citoyenneté Quels apports des didactiques?* (pp. 1-10). Université de Nantes.

Gray, M. (2015). *Teaching the Holocaust. Practical approaches for ages 11-18*. Routledge. doi:10.4324/9781315763286

Guillén, M. (2016). Un viaje al siglo XVI a partir de los casos de un corsario y un bandolero. Una experiencia de empatía histórica en secundaria. *Clío. History and HistoryTeaching, 42.*

Hammer, J., & Heller, K. (2012). *Playing history: How Ars Magica players develop historical literacy. Proceedings of Meaningful Play*. Available in: https://meaningfulplay.msu.edu/proceedings2012/mp2012_submission_7.pdf

Hammer, J., & Turkington, M. (2021). Designing Role-Playing Games that Address the Holocaust. *International Journal of Designs for Learning*, *12*(1), 42–53. doi:10.14434/ijdl.v12i1.31265

Hayes, P., & Roth, J. K. (2010). *The Oxford Handbook of Holocaust Studies*. Oxford University Press. doi:10.1093/oxfordhb/9780199211869.001.0001

Huijgen, T., van Boxtel, C., van de Grift, W., & Holthuis, P. (2016). Toward Historical Perspective Taking: Students' Reasoning When Contextualizing the Actions of People in the Past. *Theory and Research in Social Education*, *45*(1), 110–144. doi:10.1080/00933104.2016.1208597

Hyang Choi, S., & Leicht, A. (Eds.). (2017). *Education about the Holocaust and preventing genocide: a policy guide*. UNESCO.

Kapp, K. M. (2012). *The Gamification of Learning and Instruction. Game-Based Methods and Strategies for Training and Education*. John Wiley &Sons.

Kerr, D., & Huddleston, T. (Eds.). (2015). *Teaching Controversial Issues. Through Education for Democratic Citizenship and Human Rights (EDC/HRE)*. Council of Europe.

Kramer, S. (Director and Producer). (1961). *Judgment at Nuremberg* [Film]. Roxlom Films.

Lee, P. J., & Ashby, R. (2001). Empathy, perspective taking, and rational understanding. In O. L. Davis Jr, E. A. Yaeger, & S. J. Foster (Eds.), *Historical empathy and perspective taking in the social studies* (pp. 21–50). Rowman & Littlefield Publishers, Inc.

Lee, P. J., Dickinson, A. & Ashby, R. (1997). "Just ano theremperor". Understanding action in the past. *International Journal of Educational Research. Explanation and understanding in learning History, 27*(3), 233-244. doi:10.1016/S0883-0355(97)89731-5

Lee, P., Dickinson, A., & Ashby, R. (2004). Las ideas de los niños sobre la historia. In M. Carretero & J.F. Voss (Coords.), Aprender y pensar la historia (pp. 217-248). Amorrortu.

Lévesque, S. (2008). *Thinking Historically: Educating Students for the 21st Century*. University of Toronto Press.

Lévesque, S. (2011). What It Means to Think Historically. In P. Clark (Ed.), *New possibilitie sfor the past: shaping history education in Canada* (pp. 115–138). UBC Press.

Levy, D., & Szneider, N. (2002). Memory Unbound: The Holocaust and the Formation of Cosmopolitan Memory. *European Journal of Social Theory*, *5*(1), 87–106. doi:10.1177/1368431002005001002

Llopis, M. A., & Balaguer, P. (2016). El uso del juego en educación. Gamificación. In O. Chiva & M. Martí (Coords.), Métodos pedagógicos activos y globalizadores (pp. 85-101). Graó.

López Mateu, G. (2020). La enseñanza del Holocausto: una oportunidad pedagógica para reflexionar sobre los conflictos sociales actuales. *Clio. History and History teaching*, *46*, 30-40. doi:10.26754/ojs_clio/clio.2020465300

Marrón, M. J. (1996). Los juegos de simulación como recurso didáctico para la enseñanza de la geografía. *Didáctica geográfica, 1*, 45-56.

Martínez-Hita, M., & Miralles-Martínez, P. (2020). Evaluación del diseño de un programa de intervención gamificado para el desarrollo del pensamiento histórico en el alumnado de Educación Primaria. *Revista Interuniversitaria De Formación Del Profesorado. Continuación De La Antigua Revista De Escuelas Normales*, *34*(2), 187–204. doi:10.47553/rifop.v34i2.78420

Núñez, M., & González, B. (2021). Didáctica de la pregunta, didáctica de la Shoah: Comprendiendo la Historia desde el cuestionamiento a las subjetividades. *Clio. History and History Teaching*, *47*(47), 267–275. doi:10.26754/ojs_clio/clio.2021475603

Overy, R. (2003). *Interrogatorios. El Tercer Reich en el banquillo*. Tusquets.

Özdener, N. (2018). Gamification for enhancing Web 2.0 based educational activities: The case of pre-service grade school teachers using educational Wiki pages. *Telematics and Informatics*, *35*(3), 564–578. doi:10.1016/j.tele.2017.04.003

Pallarés Jiménez, M. Á., & Sánchez Martínez, S. (2020). Enseñar los juicios de Núremberg en un centro penitenciario. Una propuesta educativa. *Clio. History and History Teaching*, *46*(46), 122–135. doi:10.26754/ojs_clio/clio.2020465293

Paricio, J. (2019). El valor de la historia. Estudio de alternativas curriculares en Secundaria (2). *Clio. History and History teaching, 45,* 330-356.

Pearce, A. (2020). Challenges, issues and controversies: The shapes of 'Holocaust education' in the early twenty-first century. In S. Foster, A. Pearce, & A. Pettigrew (Eds.), *Holocaust Education. Contemporany challenges and controversies*. UCL Press. doi:10.2307/j.ctv15d7zpf.7

Pixelatto creative games and tools (Developer and Editor) (2017). *Card Creator* [Videogame]. Author.

Prats, J. (2020). Memoria histórica y enseñanza de la Historia. In I. Sáez-Rosenkranz & J. Prats Cuevas (Eds.), *Memoria histórica y enseñanza de la Historia* (pp. 11–28). Ediciones Trea.

Prutsch, M. J. (2015). *European Historical Memory: Policies, Challenges and Perspectives. European Union*. Available in: https://www.europarl.europa.eu/studies

Quinquer, D. (2004). Estrategias metodológicas para enseñar y aprender ciencias sociales: Interacción, cooperación y participación. *Íber. Didáctica de las Ciencias Sociales. Geografía e Historia*, *40*, 7–22.

Riley, K. L. (1998). Historical empathy and the Holocaust: Theory into practice. *The International Journal of Social Education*, *13*(1), 32–42.

Rivero, P. (2017). Proceso de gamificación en el aula de ciencias sociales. *Íber. Didáctica de las Ciencias Sociales. Geografía e Historia*, *86*, 4–6.

Robbins, B. (2011). *Microscope* [Game]. Lame Mage Productions.

Robson, K., Plangger, K., Kietzmann, J. H., Mccarthy, I., & Pitt, L. (2015). Is it all a game? Understanding the principles of gamification. *Business Horizons*, *58*(4), 411–420. doi:10.1016/j.bushor.2015.03.006

Sáiz, J. (2013). Empatía histórica, historia social e identidades: Pensar históricamente la conquista cristiana de la Valencia musulmana con estudiantes de 2º ESO. *Clío. History and History Teaching*, *39*, 1–20.

Sampat, E. (2017). *Empathy Engines: Design GamesThat Are Personal, Political and Profound*. Create Space Independent Publishing Platform.

San Pedro-Veledo, M. B., & López-Manrique, I. (2017). Empatía histórica y aumento de la tolerancia hacia las figuras de los refugiados. *Revista de psicología y educación, 12*(2), 116-128. doi:10.23923/rpye2017.12.150

Sánchez Macías, I. (2020). Proyecto fotográfico Auschwitz: El escenario del horror. *Clio. History and History teaching*, *46*, 102-104. doi:10.26754/ojs_clio/clio.2020465299

Santisteban Fernández, A. (2019). La enseñanza de las Ciencias Sociales a partir de problemas sociales o temas controvertidos: Estado de la cuestión y resultados de una investigación. *El Futuro del Pasado*, *10*, 57–79. doi:10.14516/fdp.2019.010.001.002

Santos, A. (2020). Multiperspectiva frente al Nazismo en un contexto excepcional. *Clio. History and History teaching*, *46*, 65-77. doi:10.26754/ojs_clio/clio.2020465264

Seixas, P., & Morton, T. (2013). *The Big Six Historical Thinking Concepts*. Nelson College Indigenous.

Shemilt, D. (1984). Beauty and the Philosopher: Empathy in History and Classroom. In A. Dickinson, P. Lee, & P. Rogers (Eds.), *Learning History*. Heinemann Educational Books.

Sigward, D. (Ed.). (2017). *Holocaust and Human Behavior*. Facing History and Ourselves.

Sospedra-Roca, R., Hernàndez-Cardona, F. X., & Hernández-Pongiluppi, M. (2022). Digital iconography, conflict heritage, and the teaching of history: The case of the Spanish Civil War. *Cogent Education*, *9*(1), 2082087. doi:10.1080/2331186X.2022.2082087

Stern, B. S. (1998). Addressing the concept of historical empathy: Withfrauen: German women recall the third Reich. *The International Journal of Social Education, 13*(1), 43–48.

United Nations Organization. (1948). *Universal Declaration of Human Rights.* Available in: https://www.un.org/es/about-us/universal-declaration-of-human-rights

VanSledright, B. A. (2014). *Assessing historical thinking and understanding. Innovate designs for new standards.* Routledge.

Vicent, N., Albas, L., Gillate, I., & Ibáñez-Etxeberría, Á. (2021). What do our future teachers think about terrorism and politically motivated violence in the Basque Country? *Humanities and Social Sciences Communication, 8*(43), 43. Advance online publication. doi:10.105741599-021-00721-0

Wineburg, S. (2001). *Historical Thinking and other Unnatural Acts. Charting the Future of Teaching the Past.* Temple University Press.

ADDITIONAL READING

Barton, K. C. (2012). Agency, choice and historical action: How history teaching can help students think about democratic decision making. *Citizenship Teaching & Learning, 7*(2), 131–142. doi:10.1386/ctl.7.2.131_1

Bekerman, Z., & Zembylas, M. (2012). *Teaching contested narratives: Identity, memory and reconciliation in peace education and beyond.* Cambridge University Press.

Boltz, L. O. (2017). "Like Hearing From Them in the Past": The Cognitive-Affective Model of Historical Empathy in Videogame Play. *International Journal of Gaming and Computer-Mediated Simulations, 9*(4), 1–18. doi:10.4018/IJGCMS.2017100101

Chapman, A. (2009). Taking The Perspective of The Other Seriously? The Importance of HIstorical Argument. *Euroclio Bulletin, 28*, 13–18.

Lee, P. J., & Shemilt, D. (2011). The concept that dares not speak its name: Should empathy come out of the closet? *Teaching History, 143*, 39–49.

Mills, G. (2005). *Teaching sensitive and controversial issues in history.* History Teacher Education Network.

Psaltis, C., Carretero, M., & Čehajić-Clancy, S. (Eds.). (2017). *History Education and Conflict Transformation. Social Psychological Theories, History Teaching and Reconciliation.* Palgrave McMillan.

Van Boxtel, C., & Van Drie, J. (2012). "That's in the time of the Romans!" Knowledge and strategies students use to contextualize historical images and documents. *Cognition and Instruction, 30*(2), 113–145. doi:10.1080/07370008.2012.661813

Van Drie, J., & Van Boxtel, C. (2008). Historical reasoning: Towards a framework for analyzing students' reasoning about the past. *Educational Psychology Review, 20*(2), 87–110. doi:10.100710648-007-9056-1

KEY TERMS AND DEFINITIONS

Controversial Topics: Topics that have served as foundation for irreconcilable arguments. These events or historical figures are very interesting to work on in the classroom as they arouse the interest and participation of students, which, in turn, offers an opportunity for developing participatory and constructive learning proposals in the classroom.

Genocide: A crime that includes any act consisting of serious injury to the physical and/or mental integrity or death of the members of a group as well as intentionally subjecting them to living conditions resulting in their physical, partial, or total destruction. The term was coined by the Polish-Jewish jurist Raphael Lemkin in 1944 after he managed to escape and go into exile in the United States.

Historical Context: Material, social, political, ideological, and cultural circumstances that condition any historical event or character to be worked on in the classroom. A true understanding of historical events and characters can only be obtained by understanding the specific context of the historical event or character to be studied, such as the socio-economic circumstances of the time or the specific beliefs of certain historical figures.

Historical Empathy: Rational understanding, without neglecting emotional aspects, of the beliefs and values of past characters by making appropriate use of the available sources. This skill fosters understanding of actions and social practices that have already taken place, which, as Lee and Ashby point out, favours the understanding of history.

Holocaust: Systematic persecution and annihilation by the German state between 1933 and 1945 of Jews, Romanies, the disabled, homosexuals, Serbs, Poles, Soviet prisoners of war and political dissidents. The estimation is that this systematic repression took the lives of around five and six million Jews, 250,000 Romanies, 250,000 people with disabilities and three million Poles, etc.

Multiperspective: It consists in using as an excellent educational opportunity the existence of multiple stories of the past and the fact that all of them are true and, at the same time, none of them is. It means accepting the subjectivity of historians based on their beliefs, knowledge, interests, values, etc. as a guarantee for a multifaceted and polysemic learning of history in which the multiple versions of a historical event provide a better understanding of it.

Nuremberg Trials: A series of trials held between 20 November 1945 and 1 October 1946 in which the victorious Allies of World War II determined and punished the responsibilities of leaders, officials, organisations and collaborators of the German Third Reich between 1939 and 1945. These trials laid the foundations for a specific international jurisprudence on genocide, war crimes and crimes against humanity.

Role-Playing Game: An entertaining dynamic in which participants play the role of real or fictitious characters. They interpret models of behaviour that are not their own and acquire first-hand experience of different situations and lessons.

Chapter 13
The Use of WebQuests to Promote Democratic Education in a Higher Education Context

José María Campillo-Ferrer
https://orcid.org/0000-0001-8570-3749
University of Murcia, Spain

EXECUTIVE SUMMARY

During the last decades, literature has demonstrated the benefits of WebQuests as a potential resource for promoting critical thinking skills and knowledge. However, in higher education contexts, research on the use of WebQuests as a tool to promote democratic education is extremely scarce. Although there are some studies involving student teachers on the appropriateness and effectiveness of the WebQuest approach to learning, few studies have focused on the development of democratic education by students with the support of other ICT resources. The present study investigated the impact of WebQuests in higher education classrooms and on democratic education in the Region of Murcia, Spain. The design and planning of WebQuests was encouraged along with other electronic resources to help foster learning and networking among future teachers.

INTRODUCTION

Information and communication technologies (ICT) have become widespread in recent decades, influencing the evolution of social interactions in the 21st century (Levin-Goldberg, 2014). Their lasting impact on many fields, including health, business and education, has led to a great deal of research into new approaches that seek to engage individuals and groups in new forms of communication, collaboration and networking (Levitt & Piro, 2014).

The development of ICT in education has shown enormous potential to contribute effectively to achieving efficiency, improving quality and fostering innovative methods in this field (Kelly, 2000; Russell et al., 2008). In this respect, there has been a growing interest in addressing the impact of e-learning as

DOI: 10.4018/978-1-6684-5240-0.ch013

an innovative process that enables the acquisition of knowledge through electronic resources and frees learners from having to attend classes at a specific location and at the same time.

The intensive use of the Internet across the world as a versatile tool for interactive and cooperative study has paved the way for enhancing new learning processes and guiding students to structure their own knowledge. In fact, students' progressive access to the Internet increases their participation in activities both inside and outside the classroom, providing opportunities for cooperative work, research and information acquisition as well as for knowledge exchange with peers and teachers.

As a result, web-based learning approaches have emerged and have left behind traditional approaches, such as oral communication through memorisation and highly repetitive tasks that were once globally accepted. One of these novel approaches is based on the use of the WebQuest, which was first implemented by Bernie Dodge, a professor at San Diego State University, in 1995. He defined it as "an inquiry-oriented activity in which some or all of the information with which students interact comes from resources on the Internet, optionally supplemented by video conferencing" (Dodge, 1995b). The main aim of this study is to examine the impact WebQuests had on students' views on learning about democratic education issues. To achieve this aim, the following research objectives were set out:

RO1: To examine their views on the learning achieved in the core unit at the beginning and at the end of the term, according to participants' sex, experience and level of motivation.

RO2: To analyse their perspectives on the learning developed through the set of techniques and strategies used in the core unit, according to their sex, experience and level of motivation within this ICT-oriented approach.

BACKGROUND

WebQuests aim to foster meaningful learning by combining innovation and technology under a constructivist approach. Kujawa (2006) described it as an alternative solution to explicit teaching instruction that encourages students to uncover meaning and construct new knowledge for themselves. In this line, Churchill (2006) argues, WebQuests promote the active role of learners by shifting the focus of instruction from the teacher to the learners, who are responsible for setting the pace of their learning, improving their skills and developing their autonomy and independence in this virtual learning environment. March (2003) highlighted scaffolding as one of the main processes fostered by these ICT tools thanks to their multifaceted nature that helps learners to progress through various online tasks and, therefore, go beyond their current levels of skill and knowledge in order to lay the foundations for their own learning.

According to such a constructivist perspective, this online pedagogical tool can promote the efficient participation of students in the learning process, using the Internet as a rich source of information that is at their disposal to access, analyse and transform content related to the area they are studying into meaningful learning (Wu, 2021).

Given the wealth of information available on the Internet, WebQuests are very useful in helping students focus their attention on reliable content, preventing them from searching for information in unrelated areas. To ensure that students are on the right websites, WebQuests include tasks for them to complete, designed to make the most of their time and guide them meaningfully in developing their analytical and critical skills (Bansal & Dutt, 2020). In fact, these task-oriented practices are often broken down into clearer, smaller and more manageable steps so that learners know how to proceed in every moment. This "guidance on how to organise the information acquired may take the form of guiding questions, or prompts to complete organisational frameworks such as timelines, concept maps or cause-and-effect diagrams" (Dodge, 1995a). Thus, this scaffolded learning structure encourages students to explore the intellectually disciplined process of actively applying, analyzing, synthesizing and/or evaluating information to accomplish their assigned goals.

According to Dodge (1995a), there are at least two types of WebQuests as per the types of thinking or dimensions of learning previously described by Marzano et al. (1992): short-term and long-term. A short-term WebQuest is related to Dimension 2, whose main objective is to acquire and integrate knowledge. This type of WebQuest aims to encourage learners to work with new and meaningful information and grasp its meaning and make sense of it. Students usually have one to three lessons to complete it. The long-term WebQuest is related to Dimension 3, whose main objective is to extend and refine knowledge. Here, students are not only required to analyse a significant amount of information, but also to transform it and construct new meaning in order to use it in different ways and for different purposes. It usually takes learners about a week to a month to complete such lessons.

Dodge (1995a) also described the building blocks that make up a WebQuest, as follows:

1. An introduction that provides background information and describes what the WebQuest is about.
2. A task, which consists of inspirational assignments to engage learners' attention.
3. A set of information resources, which are essential for learners to complete the assignments. They can be integrated into the WebQuest through Internet links to data or through document attachments.
4. An explanation of the process that learners must follow to complete the task.
5. Some guidance on how to organise the information provided. These can be guiding questions or indications for completing the tasks, such as concept maps, diagrams or timelines.
6. A conclusion that brings the WebQuest to an end. This helps learners remember what they have learnt and paves the way for further practice in other areas.

A relevant advantage related to the use of WebQuests is the flexibility it provides to address important topics by drawing on different perspectives and information from many sources (Kaur & Kauts, 2018). In this sense, some relevant research has been conducted on the application of this tool in the development of teaching and learning processes in the Social Sciences. In particular, Vera & Pérez (2004) examined student teachers' perceptions of the use of WebQuests, and found that participants appreciated the benefits of their use for pedagogical purposes.

More specifically, given the importance of democratic education and human rights in social science education, it is essential to reflect on these issues and address possible challenges for educational purposes (Alshurman, 2015; Campillo & Miralles, 2022).

Therefore, promoting programmes, modules and units that address these key issues through the use of WebQuests can educate students to broaden their vision of the democratic challenges of the 21st century from a digital, innovative and motivating perspective (Miralles et al., 2013). Although there are not many studies that have addressed these questions, there is some relevant research such as that of Piedmont (2020) who analysed how pre-service teachers constructed civic knowledge and skills that promoted active democratic citizenship. She found that WebQuests benefited participants as responsible and democratic citizens and as future social studies teachers. Two years earlier, Byker and Thomas (2018) examined WebQuests as technological tools that fostered inquiry-based learning in social studies teaching and learning. They concluded that these online resources were highly motivating and helped students to engage in their own learning process, hone their inquiry-related skills and acquire cultural competencies in a participatory and democratic atmosphere.

MAIN FOCUS OF THE CHAPTER

Procedure and data analysis. The data collected during the the research question around which this study revolves is as follows: What effects did the use of WebQuests have on students' self-perception of learning and democratic education issues according to their sex, experience and level of motivation? To answer this question, a quasi-experimental design was applied through pre-test and post-test questionnaires, which were planned ad hoc to measure the impact of this ICT-based approach.

The questionnaire was composed of three main sections: general instructions, personal information and a section dedicated to learning and democratic education. The third section contained fifteen items divided into two main sub-sections: the impact of the use of WebQuests on students' learning and democratic education and their opinions on the effectiveness of the main strategies and techniques used within this approach. The items were rated on a five-point Likert scale, where one was "Very poor" and five was "Excellent", to measure the degree to which students agreed or disagreed with the statements presented.

A quantitative methodology was adopted to analyse the extent to which the objectives set out in this research were achieved. In accordance with this methodology, identical pre-and post-tests were given to students at the beginning and end of the term to examine comparative data, paying particular attention to significant differences in learning and democratic education.

The WebQuest approach was adopted in two groups of the core unit of Didactics of Social Sciences, which is a compulsory course in the second year of the Primary Education degree at the University of Murcia, Spain. The sample consisted of 80 student teachers aged between 19 and 46 years (M = 20.4, SD = 4.88). The majority of the participants were female (61 = 76.25%, and 19 males = 23.75%), and only two of students had repeated a year (2.5%). Three out of four participants (75%) had never used WebQuests. Informed consent was required and obtained from all student teachers before carrying out this study.

The main objective of the core unit was for students to acquire the relevant knowledge and mastery of communication, collaboration and adaptability skills needed to become social science teachers, with an emphasis on the cultivation of democratic citizenship and human rights education to foster reflection and exchange of good practices on these issues. In addition, students had to design, carry out and evaluate lesson plans for social sciences and justify the selected approach in primary education. The strategies used through the WebQuests were organised within an ICT-oriented framework as an effective context that can support learning and make it motivating and productive.

The core unit was designed to be taught in the first term of the 2021/2022 academic year (September–December) for thirteen weeks using a blended teaching model in which the students combined face-to-face instruction and online course delivery. Students were encouraged to use the resources available on the student portal, which were uploaded regularly every week. Throughout the term, they also had to create a WebQuest with the aim of raising democratic education issues such as human rights, equity, structural inequality and political engagement, among others, that could be used in real-life application and would inspire them to really delve into the subject. Before designing their own WebQuests in the first two weeks of the terms, students were provided with several ready-made examples to familiarise themselves with the format of these online resources and what they entail. Then, from the third to the last week, they were given tasks that helped them to design their WebQuests in a progressive and collaborative way, such as choosing a relevant topic, including effective resources, designing a meaningful task, providing steps to organise the work, among others.

METHODS

1. Data collection tools

Participants' views on the adoption of this ICT-oriented approach were collected through an ad hoc questionnaire, the main purpose of which is to report on the implementation of a flipped approach by collecting data at two points in time from a sample of university students. Several advantages have been identified in the use of this technique in terms of reliability, objectivity and representativeness (Cohen et al., 2017). Questionnaires are particularly valuable for data collection, as their quantifying nature and easy administration allow researchers to collect information from a large number of respondents. They are also considered quite reliable, as researchers do not need to be present when respondents fill them out, which means that they should provide similar results if administered by different researchers. However, some limitations have been observed due to their impersonal nature, given the researcher's detachment, or differences in interpretation that may distort respondents' answers and undermine the validity of the information provided (Beiske, 2002; Waidi, 2016).

The questionnaire was composed of thirty-six items divided into four main sections: self-perceived motivation, self-perceived acquisition of digital competencies, the effectiveness of this approach on students' learning processes, and reported views on students' learning of democratic education. The items were rated on a Likert scale of one to five points, where one was "Very poor" and five was "Excellent", to score the degree to which the respondents agreed with the statements presented.

2. Procedure and data analysis

The data collected during the research were analyzed in XLSTAT, which is the main data analysis and statistical solution for Microsoft Excel. The degree of reliability and validity of the questionnaire was measured prior to data analysis. The construct reliability was determined by means of Cronbach's alpha to determine whether the questionnaire consisting of a multiple-question Likert scale was reliable. In this regard, positive results were obtained ($\alpha = 0.87$). The validity of the instrument was also estimated using Bartlett's test of sphericity, and a significance level of 0.000 was obtained.

3. Results

The results shown in Table 1 are descriptive statistics and the results of Mann-Whitney tests based on our analysis of the first objective with a focus on the sex of the participants.

According to the results shown in Table 1, male students consider collaborative learning, active citizenship and cooperative work to be quite relevant, while female students focus more on the development of problem-solving skills, critical thinking and education for tolerance. No significant differences were found between students based on sex.

Table 1. Results of the Mann Whitney test in relation to undergraduate students' views on learning about democratic education issues and their gender

Democratic education issues	Men (n=19)		Women (n=61)		Mann-Whitney U	p	alpha
	Pre-test M (SD)	Post-test M (SD)	Pre-test M (SD)	Post-test M (SD)			
Collaborative learning	4.11 (0.65)	4.42 (0.61)	4.27 (0.71)	4.32 (0.78)	565.00	.933	.05
Active citizenship	3.94 (0.71)	4.31 (0.58)	4.13 (0.79)	4.14 (0.79)	633.00	.974	.05
Respect for human rights	3.94 (0.77)	4.21 (0.71)	4.19 (0.72)	4.31 (0,67)	622.50	.967	.05
Problem-solving skills	4.01 (0.74)	4.11 (0,73)	4.14 (0.65)	4.22 (0.76)	556.50	.517	.05
Collective responsibility	3.73 (0.73)	4.11 (0,73)	4.01 (0.77)	4.22 (0.76)	591.50	.759	.05
Critical thinking	3.84 (0.89)	4.11 (0.65)	4.03 (0.77)	4.16 (0.73)	604.50	.856	.05
Cooperative work with members of the educational community	3.78 (1.03)	4.21 (0.78)	4.11 (0.75)	4.14 (0.70)	639.00	.821	.05
Adoption of more tolerant attitudes	3.68 (0.88)	3.86 (0.83)	4.36 (0.68)	4.19 (0.85)	627.00	.929	.05
Identification of social movements	3.94 (0.71)	3.62 (1.09)	4.05 (0.84)	4.08 (0.78)	601.50	.325	.05
Overall/Total democratic education issues	3.88 (0.79)	4.21 (0.71)	4.11 (0.75)	4.21 (0.75)			

Similarly, students with experience in using WebQuests for educational purposes rated all democratic education issues higher than inexperienced participants, with medians above 4. In addition, significant differences were found between the two groups with respect to critical thinking, with the former rating this item significantly higher than the latter (see Table 2).

According to the students' level of motivation, highly motivated students rated all democratic education issues the highest, indicating a correlation between the students' level of motivation and their positive opinion on learning about democratic education issues (see Table 3). Moreover, significant differences were found in all items analysed, with the first subgroup, consisting of highly motivated students, rating significantly higher than the other two subgroups.

As we can see in table 4, in terms of the adoption of effective strategies and techniques in this learning context, no significant differences were identified between experienced and inexperienced learners, although the former had a more positive perception of them than the latter.

According to the level of motivation of the respondents (see Table 5), significant differences were found in their ratings, with highly motivated students rating the use of effective strategies higher than the other two less motivated subgroups.

Table 2. Results of the Mann Whitney test in relation to undergraduate students' views on learning about democratic education issues and their experience within the webquest-based approach

Democratic education issues	Experienced students (n=22)		Inexperienced students (n=58)		Mann-Whitney U	p	alpha
	Pre-test M (SD)	Post-test M (SD)	Pre-test M (SD)	Post-test M (SD)			
Collaborative learning	4.5 (0.59)	4.54 (0.74)	4.13 (0.68)	4.27 (0.73)	491.00	.088	.05
Active citizenship	4.27 (0.71)	4.36 (0.79)	4.11 (0.74)	4.12 (0.76)	516.00	.238	.05
Respect for human rights	4.31 (0.71)	4.51 (0.59)	4.05 (0.71)	4.21 (0,69)	494.50	.090	.05
Problem-solving skills	4.18 (0.79)	4.31 (0,78)	4.03 (0.62)	4.15 (0.74)	550.00	.307	.05
Collective responsibility	4.18 (0.79)	4.31 (0,71)	3.89 (0.67)	4.15 (0.69)	556.50	.521	.05
Critical thinking	4.13 (0.77)	4.36 (0.84)	3.94 (0.75)	4.06 (0.64)	465.00	.048*	.05
Cooperative work with members of the educational community	4.13 (0.77)	4.36 (0.65)	4.01 (0.78)	4.08 (0.73)	508.00	.150	.05
Adoption of more tolerant attitudes	4.18 (0.73)	4.27 (1.03)	3.96 (0.79)	4.22 (0.72)	560.50	.369	.05
Identification of social movements	4.04 (0.78)	4.31 (0.89)	3.93 (0.72)	3.98 (0.73)	467.00	.063	.05
Overall/Total democratic education issues	4.22 (0.72)	4.37 (0.78)	4.01 (0.72)	4.13 (0.71)			

ISSUES, CONTROVERSIES, PROBLEMS

In particular, when creating and using these web-based resources from a democratic perspective, the challenges involved in this inquiry-based teaching and learning process are sometimes related to the level of digital literacy of learners. This gap often makes all the difference between a learner gaining the training and experience they need or missing out on the opportunity to hone effective digital competence. In our study, 75% of respondents have not ever learnt through the use of WebQuests before, which obliged them to take supplementary online classes and access to virtual tutoring to cope with this challenging environment. And so, the need or the provision of training, monitoring and assessment of digital literacy among students seems essential to develop adapted structures and lay down coordinated guidelines for future programmes, plans and projects.

It goes without saying that the specific digital skills and competence levels of learners depend not only on the country or region in which they live, but also on the learners' particular situations (economic and social conditions). Seitkazy et al. (2016) examined teacher and student perceptions and attitudes towards the use of WebQuests when performing collaborative tasks in a democratic atmosphere. Their findings

Table 3. Results of the Kruskal Wallis test in relation to undergraduate students' views on learning about democratic education issues and their levels of motivation

Democratic education issues	High level of motivation (n=42)		Medium level of motivation (n= 34)		Low level of motivation (n=4)		Kruskal Wallis K	*p*
	Pre-test M (SD)	Post-test M (SD)	Pre-test M (SD)	Post-test M (SD)	Pre-test M (SD)	Post-test M (SD)		
Collaborative learning	4.23	4.54	4.21	4.17	4	3.75	6.759	.034*
	(0.75)	(0.59)	(0.64)	(0.83)	(1.14)	(0.95)		
Active citizenship	4.12	4.41	3.94	3.97	4.25	3.75	7.121	.028*
	(0.67)	(0.62)	(0.85)	(0.79)	(1.15)	(0.95)		
Respect for human rights	4.14	4.54	4.08	4.02	4.5	3.75	13.620	.001*
	(0.71)	(0.59)	(0.75)	(0.62)	(1.01)	(0.95)		
Problem-solving skills	4.16	4.57	4.01	3.79	4	3.75	22.230	.001*
	(0.62)	(0.54)	(0.73)	(0.72)	(1.14)	(0.95)		
Collective responsibility	4.09	4.41	3.76	4.01	4	3.75	7.305	.026*
	(0.71)	(0.58)	(0.81)	(0.73)	(0.81)	(0.95)		
Critical thinking	4.01	4.38	3.91	3.91	3.5	3.75	9.196	.010*
	(0.82)	(0.71)	(0.79)	(0.62)	(1.29)	(0.95)		
Cooperative work with members of the educational community	4.16	4.42	3.82	3.88	4	3.75	12.045	.002*
	(0.72)	(0.63)	(0.96)	(0.68)	(1.14)	(0.95)		
Adoption of more tolerant attitudes	4.09	4.51	3.73	3.97	4.25	3.75	9.565	.008*
	(0.69)	(0.67)	(0.86)	(0.87)	(1.15)	(0.95)		
Identification of social movements	3.97	4.35	3.76	3.76	4	3.75	10.436	.005*
	(0.78)	(0.61)	(0.74)	(0.85)	(1.14)	(0.95)		
Overall/Total democratic education issues	4,11	4.45	3.91	3.94	4.05	3.75		
	(0.71)	(0,61)	(0.79)	(0.74)	(1.11)	(0.95)		

revealed that lack of ICT resources and a slow Internet connection may hinder the quick and efficient implementation of Internet-based tasks and assignments. Similarly, Yenmez et al. (2017) conducted a study that aimed to analyse whether the implementation of WebQuests had a positive or negative impact on student's academic achievement. They found that the technical and network infrastructure plays an important role in implementing this ICT-oriented approach. As such, it can be concluded that the inability to gain quick access to Internet resources can affect students' progress, motivation and, hence, the development of their digital competence.

In a similar vein, Ritzhaupt et al. (2013) analysed students' digital skills and its relationship to their socioeconomic status, gender and ethnicity in Florida. They proved that there was a digital divide between different groups of students, in favour of learners of high socio-economic status and whites. So, in order to advance the use of digital technology and to promote not only social and economic growth and development, but also greater and more democratic equality of opportunity in the development of digital literacy, it is necessary for all learners to reach a satisfactory level of digital competence, in ad-

Table 4. Results of the Mann Whitney test in relation to the views of undergraduate students on the strategies used and their gender and experience

Strategies used within this approach	Sex	N	Mann Whitney U	p- value	Experience	N	Mann Whitney U	p- value
Points obtained in Webquest assignments	Male	19	690.00	.639	Experienced	22	609.00	.435
	Female	61			Inexperienced	58		
Kahoot!, Socrative quizzes	Male	19	510.50	.321	Experienced	22	454.00	.052
	Female	61			Inexperienced	58		
Blogs and learning gamification platforms	Male	19	651.50	.697	Experienced	22	545.00	.690
	Female	61			Inexperienced	58		
Instructional videos	Male	19	547.00	.537	Experienced	22	511.00	.157
	Female	61			Inexperienced	58		
Small group activities	Male	19	664.50	.923	Experienced	22	552.00	.530
	Female	61			Inexperienced	58		
Practical classroom activities	Male	19	515.50	.239	Experienced	22	602.00	.916
	Female	61			Inexperienced	58		

Table 5. Results of the Kruskal-Wallis test in relation to the views of undergraduate students on the learning strategies used and their levels of motivation

Strategies used within this approach	Levels of motivation	N	Kruskal Wallis K	p- value
Points obtained in Webquest assignments	High	42	15.704	.000*
	Medium	34		
	Low	4		
Kahoot!, Socrative quizzes	High	42	5.923	.052
	Medium	34		
	Low	4		
Blogs and learning gamification platforms	High	42	14.762	.0001*
	Medium	34		
	Low	4		
Instructional videos	High	42	12.068	.002*
	Medium	34		
	Low	4		
Small group activities	High	42	9.814	.007*
	Medium	34		
	Low	4		
Practical classroom activities	High	42	11.906	.003*
	Medium	34		
	Low	4		

dition to improving infrastructure and access. In this sense, slow web connectivity and limited access to the Internet are two of the main challenges for many students in different learning contexts.

In this context, some learners may feel lost on the Internet when searching for what they are asked for due to different causes, e.g., JavaScript pop-ups that spawn faster than learners can close them, links that do not head to expected sites, passwords required on some websites or other filters and unsolicited browsing. In this line, Unal (2008) addressed issues and problems when teaching through the use of WebQuests and found that establishing access permission can be quite difficult and challenging.

Focusing on links, March (2003) stresses their importance within this inquiry-based learning approach for students to follow a scaffolded learning pathway that enables them to access effective resources on the Internet. Therefore, it seems reasonable when creating WebQuests to promote democratic education issues, students should look for appropriate links that give access to interactive and contextualised resources and to check regularly for broken or blind links. Indeed, such links limit the flow of data in these virtual tools, which can have a negative impact on learning experiences. An improper URL inserted by the WebQuest designer or a lost link that no longer refers to the site because the webmaster removed it are some setbacks that can be avoided by regular checking.

Similarly, to maximise learning from democratic education through the use of this web-based resource, it is of utmost importance that links direct students not only to valid websites, but also to media-rich sites that foster motivation. In this study, motivation is a crucial factor for students to be more actively involved and encouraged to achieve specific democratic education goals. Consequently, web links should be sufficiently inspiring for learners to discover stimulating data that will encourage their personal curiosity and allow them to delve deeper into democratic education. Otherwise, with too many options to manage and understand, the risk of learners wandering the World Wide Web completely adrift is very high.

As Summerville (2000) states, "with the plethora of information, students quickly become frustrated with following links that lead them to useless information" (p.1). For this reason, the appropriate selection of links stands out as a crucial factor, as it can affect learners' democratic participation and thus their possible outcomes within this interactive framework. However, the vast amount of information available on the Internet can also slow down the identification of essential resources and thus minimise their potential for interactivity and coordination among learners. As March (2004) argues, encyclopaedic briefs, word searches and other resources that can be found both within and without the Internet are not sufficiently suitable for inclusion in WebQuests.

In addition, despite the WebQuests motivational power, some problems may arise within this inquiry-oriented approach with respect to the inflexible nature of curriculum, which sometimes limits educators' access to these resources due to constraints related to style and tempo. Considering the relevance of motivation as highlighted in this study, Prapinwong (2008) examined teacher and student perceptions and observations on the use of WebQuests in a higher education context in Thailand. Among the challenges, the author highlighted teachers' concerns about the limitations of curriculum and assessment when making use of WebQuests, which can lead to lower student motivation.

As a result, some of these ICT tools may not be helpful to meet curriculum standards, which may place learners at a disadvantage (Amini et al., 2020). In this regard, it is essential to overcome the barriers imposed by highly structured courses and programmes in the form of unified curricula, pre-selected material and standardised learning outcomes by exploring possible measures leading to significant changes to evolve this rigid structure into a more flexible, open and democratic framework. In this way, the application of pedagogical strategies that are not geared towards adjusting teaching practices to the needs and interests of learners, but rather to restrictive curricular guidelines, may not be effective enough to understand the substantial learning challenges that are continuously faced in real educational settings. Therefore, educators must have sufficient opportunities to incorporate Internet-based resources that cover democratic issues into the curriculum in order to focus on student progress and achievement, rather than addressing possible curricular constraints, such as time limitations and course content.

With this in mind, in this study we aimed to provide students with sufficient learning opportunities to create a WebQuest with ease. In fact, sufficient time was given throughout the term, and useful resources for creating a WebQuest were uploaded weekly to the student portal. Instructions were clear from the first to the thirteenth week, and queries were answered almost immediately. These facts may demonstrate that more flexible approaches could, in turn, favour the creation of freer and more interactive environments between students and teachers, which could enhance certain crucial skills related to problem solving and other reasoning abilities, among other benefits.

Another point to bear in mind is the crucial development of thinking processes among students for democratic educational purposes. At the core of these open Internet-based approaches is the transformation of newly obtained information into deeper understanding. In this context, learners are asked to identify key points and prioritise meaningful relationships by using up-to-date, interactive resources, which ultimately helps them construe a meaningful interpretation of the facts and ideas under consideration. Moreover, the validity of traditional assignments based on relocating existing information from web sources into pre-designed templates without modifying the original content is challenged within this inquiry-oriented framework. Thus, one of the main aims when using this online platform is to convey not only existing ideas but also new thoughts and perspectives from a critical point of view. Therefore, beyond the use of practical resources of powerful websites and relevant internet-based social media platforms, educators should seek to engage learners actively to respond to open-ended and probing questions. As such, it seems reasonable for educators to encourage students to witness and analyse the complexity of the democratic issues being debated, with particular emphasis on developing their higher-order thinking skills as an effective strategy for addressing these issues in a meaningful way.

However, some research has suggested that, despite the potential ability of students to develop some abstract thinking in multifaceted WebQuest tasks, in many cases, these ICT tools focus primarily on the development of lower order thinking skills (LOTS), which implies the development of less demanding cognitive processes. In this regard, Polly and Ausband (2009) examined the extent to which higher order thinking skills (HOTS) and levels of technology implementation (LoTI) were developed in the WebQuests under study. They concluded that a large number of tasks designed to be performed in these WebQuests promoted HOTS and low LoTI. And so, it is essential that learners play an active role in the use of WebQuests, connecting ideas and trying out solutions in real-life situations.

To achieve this, a proper orchestration of web-based information sources must be promoted and applied by educators in order to nourish students' innovative abstract thinking and thus enhance their learning experiences from a democratic perspective. However, some studies reveal that students may find the structure of the WebQuest rather rigid, which has several consequences. For instance, Gürgil et al. (2019) analysed the views of Turkish pre-service teachers on WebQuests in terms of the design process and the final outcomes. They found that the participants considered the main components of WebQuest design to be rather inflexible, as they limited their imagination and creativity.

Having described some of the main challenges educators face when designing WebQuests for educational purposes, solutions and proposals for improvement are suggested in the section below to enhance the dissemination of high-quality practices.

SOLUTIONS AND RECOMMENDATIONS

WebQuests aim to foster meaningful learning through the use of technology in inquiry-based, learner-centred approaches (Bayram et al., 2019; Ebadi & Rahimi, 2018; March, 2004). Some studies highlight the importance of evaluating these web-based tools in order to harmonise and coordinate all educational professionals and learners, and ultimately, maximise their potential benefits when promoting democratic education. To do so, researchers and educators should select the best criteria for evaluating the impact of these e-tools and, if possible, offer possible solutions to overcome possible constraints or limitations.

For instance, Gülbahar et al. (2010) analysed these ICT resources in detail and paid special attention to some key points, such as general design, grammar, navigation and technical issues. With a similar aim, Green (2001) stresses the importance of teaching students to evaluate the quality of websites. In particular, the author presents key proposals for improving the quality of websites by focusing on three main areas: purpose, content and functionality. Primarily, most focus is on the purpose of the website; more specifically, what it has been designed for, the quality of the information provided and the ease with which students can navigate through it and obtain the information they are looking for. Given the flexibility of e-platforms that allow their use and implementation in different learning environments, education professionals must adapt these assessment criteria and achievement levels according to the specific learners they are targeting. This move is crucial to meeting the learners' specific needs and, at the same time, align the democratic principles with the design of their course, module or unit.

It can be reasonably agreed that learner support resources that facilitate access to and understanding of democratic content improve students' autonomous learning skills, ultimately increasing their motivation and facilitating more effective task completion. It is, therefore, strongly recommended that such resources are designed appropriately to ensure good readability, accurate comprehension and user-friendliness.

In terms of readability, Schutten and McFarland (2009) suggest that WebQuest developers should ask themselves whether learners completing a task on this Internet-based resource have acquired sufficient knowledge to read and understand a text, which is to understand not only the instructions, but also the main ideas and supporting details that emerge from the text, in order to extract its precise meaning and do what is asked of them effectively. For example, when presenting a potential democratic political conflict in this digital approach, students must first know and understand the rules and procedures governing the application of democratic principles in the particular context in which these principles apply, in order to be able to discuss and reach a satisfactory solution. Similarly, other studies focus on other possible difficulties that impede a correct understanding of web content such as those linked to the proper formatting style of WebQuests, e.g., misplaced or missing images, incorrectly sized tables and other incorrect formatting (Fleissner et al., 2006; Pérez, 2016).

Educators should also be particularly concerned about the reliability of democratic resources in online environments, something learners may be unfamiliar with. Further, advice and guidance from educators is crucial to ensure that students are aware of security measures and give due consideration to reliability and privacy. WebQuest designers should also consider some effective ways to determine whether the web content they share is sufficiently trustworthy and secure, such as carefully reading websites' privacy policies, looking out for security seals or avoiding spammy websites. In particular, the use of modern anti-spam technology could be a good solution for educators and students to control IP addresses, block advertisements and prevent malware from running in their browser.

So what are the necessary features of Internet resources in order to engage students in the learning of democratic education under this ICT-oriented approach? According to March (2004), the key general attributes of effective websites should be interactivity, multi-perspectivity, contextualisation and contemporaneity, among others. The need to understand and explore different perspectives must be satiated so that learners feel they are able to gain a holistic view of a given situation or issue, enabling them to identify the cause of the problem and discover a solution that takes into consideration the feelings and interests of all those involved. For instance, from a democratic perspective, the use of media-rich resources such as primary source media or innovative timelines can encourage students to grasp the meaning of historic events and link them to larger themes. These resources can essentially help learners develop critical thinking skills and meaningful strategies for becoming active citizens within this enriched learning framework.

It is possible that irrespective of students' knowledge of democratic education issues, the more they are pushed to complete a reading task, the worse their comprehension of the text will be. For this reason, the integration of pedagogical support into the pre-selected readings in WebQuests can be effective in encouraging students to carry out the assignment with their own strategies. The use of simple instructions and practical examples can help learners to articulate the implications of a text more meaningfully, developing a range of skills such as summarising, prediction and attention to detail. Therefore, how educators design WebQuest activities within a democracy-oriented approach is one of the main criteria that can determine how learners make new connections, deductions and inferences, which can facilitate the development of their reading comprehension and ultimately enhance their learning of democratic education issues.

In consequence, learners should be provided with a scaffolded learning structure that indicates what the specific and measurable outcomes of the learners' work are, taking into account their goals and needs and mapping out the necessary steps to achieve them, for example, by allocating sufficient time to complete the task. Therefore, tasks on democratic education must be sufficiently motivating and authentic for them to adequately develop their decision-making mechanisms, considering that the activities they are carrying out are useful for dealing with real and contemporary issues. In relation to these issues, Vera & Pérez (2008) examined several social science webquests aimed at pupils in the last years of primary education in Spain and concluded that most of the webquests analysed effectively addressed the concept of citizenship, as well as the right to life, liberty and equality, through collaborative and motivating tasks. Similarly, Sánchez & Trigueros (2017) analysed the opinions of Spanish student teachers on the development of social and citizenship competences through the integration of ICT in primary education, and obtained positive results on the perceptions of the participants in relation to the use of WebQuests for this educational purpose.

In addition, ensuring an acceptable level of cognitive development in students is essential for them to feel that they are able to apply HOTS in real and intellectually demanding situations, for example, analysing some democratic issues related to active citizenship, respect for human rights or gender equity. In this sense, Delgado et al. (2020) analysed university students' perceptions of the creation of WebQuests to promote critical thinking, concluding that most participants agreed that the use of these tools clearly facilitated cognitive development. These results coincide with those obtained in this study, as critical thinking was one of the most positively valued items, especially by more experienced students. Another clear example of increasing learners' concentration, which can lead to greater effort and interest in completing the task, can be the use of open-ended questions (March, 2004). These questions can also be very useful in encouraging learners to discuss and find the best solution in a given challenging task (Koutsogianni, 2014).

Obviously, at the heart of these stimulating tasks is the critical thinking that is developed and enhanced for instructional purposes within this inquiry-oriented approach. Consequently, a focus on questions, ideas and reflections that trigger their curiosity about democratic issues is paramount for students to critically share their thoughts, while challenging and reconsidering ideological preconceptions for democratic educational purposes.

FUTURE RESEARCH DIRECTIONS

This study has just focused on student teachers' views on the use of WebQuests for democratic purposes. However, further research with a wider range of populations, including university professors, social science teachers and primary school pupils, would provide more accurate data that would improve our understanding of how to assess the effects of the application of these ICT tools in social studies teaching and learning from a pedagogical and democratic perspective.

In this study, student teachers attended a training programme on the use of these online resources, however, more training should be provided in the different core units of the primary education degree so that student teachers are well trained and prepared in this field. Consequently, the potential of WebQuests as effective cross-curricular resources has not been fully exploited or explored in some particular contexts of higher education, which is particularly evident in the field of democratic education. As stated by Sánchez & Trigueros (2017), there is a need for teacher education students to be better trained in the use and implementation of these ICT resources, given the positive assessment stated by students regarding the potential of these resources in the teaching of social sciences.

In summary, the implementation of media rich learning environments, and in particular, WebQuest-based ones is a major challenge that requires further research and more scrutiny for any potential bias. As a consequence, further research will be needed on how this web-based tool can facilitate effective multimodal teaching and learning for different audiences in order to improve our understanding of how to promote democratic education with precision, fluency and imagination (Barrett, 2020; Jónsson & Garces Rodriguez, 2021).

CONCLUSION

Educators, policy makers, administrations, stakeholders and other interested parties must explore the different possible approaches to introducing digital technology and democratic education in higher education contexts (Perkins & McKnight, 2005). It is of great important that the use of WebQuests is developed under a learner-centric approach and, therefore, within a constructivist framework (Drozd & O'Donoghue, 2007; Hassanien, 2006). In these scenarios, educators should mediate between knowledge and learners, encouraging the development of practical strategies that best suit learners' interests and preferences, in order for learners to progressively improve their digital competence and their social and democratic skills. Accordingly, the development of critical thinking skills such as classifying, comparing, analysing arguments, deducing, hypothesising, examining perspectives and problem solving should also be encouraged, as they are very effective in promoting communication, teamwork and knowledge sharing throughout the learning process.

Furthermore, the choice of essential Internet resources is a relevant principle of this scaffolded learning approach as well as an appropriate didactic strategy to engage learners in interactive participation and collaboration (Aydin, 2016). The use of effective digital resources with appropriate online tools supports their complex cognitive development in stimulating and motivating tasks from a democratic perspective. Thus, finding similarities and differences between different temporal dimensions of democracy, analysing citizens' capacity to participate in specific deliberations or examining the demands of democratic authorities are just a few examples of the analytical skills and effective resources needed to motivate students and address relevant democratic issues from a problem-solving perspective and within an ICT-oriented approach.

REFERENCES

Alshurman, M. (2015). Democratic education and administration. *Procedia: Social and Behavioral Sciences*, *176*, 861–869. doi:10.1016/j.sbspro.2015.01.551

Amini, M., Asgari, M., & Asgari, Z. (2020). Advantages and disadvantages of using Webquests in junior high school English classes in Iran. *Journal of Critical Studies in Language and Literature*, *1*(1), 35–43. doi:10.46809/jcsll.v1i1.43

Aydin, S. (2016). WebQuests as language-learning tools. *Computer Assisted Language Learning*, *29*(4), 765–778. doi:10.1080/09588221.2015.1061019

Bansal, R., & Dutt, S. (2020). Using WebQuest Based Instruction to Enhance Students' Critical Thinking. *Issues and Ideas in Education*, *8*(1), 1–8. doi:10.15415/iie.2020.81001

Barrett, M. (2020). The Council of Europe's Reference Framework of Competences for Democratic Culture: Policy context, content and impact. *London Review of Education*, *18*(1), 1–17. doi:10.18546/LRE.18.1.01

Bayram, D., Gökçe, K., & Derin, A. (2019). The Implementation of WebQuest-supported Critical Thinking Instruction in Pre-service English Teacher Education: The Turkish Context. *Participatory Educational Research*, *6*(2), 144–157. doi:10.17275/per.19.18.6.2

Byker, E. J., & Thomas, A. (2018). Culturally responsive WebQuests: Connecting technology with inquiry-based learning. *Teaching Social Studies*, *18*(2), 19–25.

Campillo, J. M., & Miralles, P. (2022, April). Impact of the flipped classroom model on democratic education of student teachers in Spain. *Education, Citizenship and Social Justice*. Advance online publication. doi:10.1177/17461979221084111

Churchill, D. (2006). Student-centred learning design: Key components, technology role and frameworks for integration. *Synergy*, *4*(1), 18–28.

Delgado, J., García, C., Guaicha, K., & Prado, M. (2020). La Webquest como herramienta didáctica para potenciar el pensamiento crítico en la formación de estudiantes universitarios. *Revista Tecnológica-Educativa Docentes 2.0*, *9*(1), 49-55.

Dodge, B. (1995a). WebQuests: A technique for internet-based learning. *Distance Education*, *1*(2), 10–13.

Dodge, B. (1995b). *Some Thoughts About WebQuests*. https://webquest.org/sdsu/about_webquests.html

Drozd, M., & O'Donoghue, J. (2007). The use of a WebQuest to support undergraduate nurses. *Teaching and Learning in Nursing*, *2*(3), 63–67. doi:10.1016/j.teln.2007.03.001

Ebadi, S., & Rahimi, M. (2018). An exploration into the impact of WebQuest-based classroom on EFL learners' critical thinking and academic writing skills: A mixed-methods study. *Computer Assisted Language Learning*, *31*(5-6), 617–651. doi:10.1080/09588221.2018.1449757

Fleissner, S., Chan, Y. Y., Yuen, T. H., & Ng, V. (2006, May). WebQuest markup language (WQML) for sharable inquiry-based learning. In *International Conference on Computational Science and Its Applications* (pp. 383-392). Springer. 10.1007/11751540_41

Green, T. (2001). Teaching students to critically evaluate web pages. *The Clearing House: A Journal of Educational Strategies, Issues and Ideas*, *75*(1), 32–34. doi:10.1080/00098650109599231

Gülbahar, Y., Madran, R. O., & Kalelioglu, F. (2010). Development and evaluation of an interactive WebQuest environment:"Web Macerasi. *Journal of Educational Technology & Society*, *13*(3), 139–150. https://www.jstor.org/stable/10.2307/jeductechsoci.13.3.139

Gürgil, F., Ünal, M., & Aksoy, B. (2019). Social Studies Preservice Teachers' Views on and Experiences with WebQuest. *Journal of Education and Training Studies*, *7*(4), 131–141. doi:10.11114/jets.v7i4.4061

Hassanien, A. (2006). An evaluation of the webquest as a computer-based learning tool. *Research in Post-Compulsory Education*, *11*(2), 235–250. doi:10.1080/13596740600769230

Jónsson, Ó. P., & Garces Rodriguez, A. (2021). Educating democracy: Competences for a democratic culture. *Education, Citizenship and Social Justice*, *16*(1), 62–77. doi:10.1177/1746197919886873

Kaur, S., & Kauts, A. (2018). Impact of webquest on student engagement. *Indian Journal of Public Health*, *9*(12), 1665–1669.

Kelly, R. (2000). Working with WebQuests: Making the web accessible to students with disabilities. *Teaching Exceptional Children*, *32*(6), 4–13. doi:10.1177/004005990003200601

Koutsogianni, E. (2014). Promoting motivation and autonomy through Webquest implementation in Junior High school EFL context. *Research Papers in Language Teaching & Learning*, *5*(1), 307–323.

Kujawa, J. (2006). WebQuests Travel to Higher Education. *Journal of Hospitality & Tourism Education*, *18*(3), 45–55. doi:10.1080/10963758.2006.10696863

Levin-Goldberg, J. (2014). Webquest 2.0: Best Practices for the 21st Century. *Journal of Institutional Research*, *3*, 73–82.

Levitt, R., & Piro, J. (2014). Game-changer: Operationalizing the common core using WebQuests and 'gamification'in teacher education. *International Journal of Web-Based Learning and Teaching Technologies*, *9*(3), 53–71. doi:10.4018/ijwltt.2014070104

March, T. (2003). *What WebQuests are (really)*. http://bestwebquests. com/what_webquests_are. asp

March, T. (2004). The learning power of WebQuests. *Educational Leadership*, *61*(4), 42–47.

Marzano, R. J., Pickering, D., Arredondo, D. E., Blackburn, G. J., Brandt, R. S., & Moffett, C. A. (1992). *Dimensions of learning*. Association for Supervision and Curriculum Development.

Miralles, P., Gómez, C. J., & Arias, L. (2013). Social sciences teaching and information processing. An experience using WebQuests in primary education teacher training. *International Journal of Educational Technology in Higher Education, 10*(2), 344–357.

Molebash, P., & Dodge, B. (2003). Kickstarting inquiry with WebQuests and Web inquiry projects. (Advancing Technology). *Social Education, 67*(3), 158–162.

Pérez, R. G. (2016). Teaching the use of WebQuests to master students in Pablo de Olavide University. In New perspectives on teaching and working with languages in the digital era. Research-publishing. net. doi:10.14705/rpnet.2016.tislid2014.425

Perkins, R., & McKnight, M. L. (2005). Teachers' attitudes toward WebQuests as a method of teaching. *Computers in the Schools, 22*(1-2), 123–133. doi:10.1300/J025v22n01_11

Piedmont, E. V. (2020). Exploring COVID-19 in a Social Studies Methods Course: Pre-Service Teachers Harness the Current Pandemic to Design Inquiry-Based Webquests for Elementary Learners. *Journal of International Social Studies, 10*(2), 113–126.

Polly, D., & Ausband, L. (2009). Developing higher-order thinking skills through WebQuests. *Journal of Computing in Teacher Education, 26*(1), 29–34.

Prapinwong, M. (2008). *Constructivist language learning through WebQuests in EFL context: an exploratory study* [Doctoral dissertation]. Indiana University.

Ritzhaupt, A. D., Liu, F., Dawson, K., & Barron, A. E. (2013). Differences in student information and communication technology literacy based on socio-economic status, ethnicity, and gender: Evidence of a digital divide in Florida schools. *Journal of Research on Technology in Education, 45*(4), 291–307. doi:10.1080/15391523.2013.10782607

Russell, C. K., Burchum, J. R., Likes, W. M., Jacob, S., Graff, J. C., Driscoll, C., Britt, T., Adymy, C., & Cowan, P. (2008). WebQuests: creating engaging, student-centered, constructivist learning activities. *CIN: Computers, Informatics, Nursing, 26*(2), 78–87. doi:10.1097/01.NCN.0000304774.63402.b8 PMID:18317258

Sánchez, D. O., & Trigueros, I. M. G. (2017). Las WebQuests y los MOOCs en la enseñanza de las Ciencias Sociales y la formación del profesorado de Educación Primaria. *Revista electrónica interuniversitaria de formación del profesorado, 20*(2), 205-220.

Schutten, M., & McFarland, A. (2009). Readability levels of health-based websites: From content to comprehension. *International Electronic Journal of Health Education, 12*, 99–107.

Seitkazy, P. B., Toleubekova, R. K., Amanova, A. K., Tashetov, A. A., Iskakova, G., & Demissenova, S. S. (2016). A Web-Quest as a teaching and learning tool. *International Electronic Journal of Mathematics Education, 11*(10), 3537–3549.

Summerville, J. (2000). WebQuests: An Aspect of Technology Integration for Training Preservice Teachers. *TechTrends, 44*(2), 31–35. doi:10.1007/BF02822950

Unal, Z. (2008, March). Addressing Issues and Problems to Increase Users' Motivation and Completion Rate of Student WebQuests with InstantWebQuest. In *Society for Information Technology & Teacher Education International Conference* (pp. 3188-3194). Association for the Advancement of Computing in Education (AACE).

Vera, M. I., & Pérez, D. (2004). El profesorado en formación de Ciencias Sociales y las TICs: situación y perspectivas. In M. I. Vera & D. Pérez (Eds.), *Formación de la ciudadanía: las TICs y los nuevos problemas* (pp. 1–20). https://dialnet.unirioja.es/descarga/articulo/1448326.pdf

Vera, M. I., & Pérez, T. D. (2008). Las WebQuests de Ciencias Sociales: un instrumento para formar ciudadanos en primaria. In R. M. Ávila, A. Cruz, & C. Díez (Eds.), *Didáctica de las Ciencias Sociales, Currículo Escolar y Formación del Profesorado* (pp. 631–641). Universidad de Jaén.

Wu, C. P. (2021). An Experiential Study on WebQuest and Higher Order Thinking Skills in an EFL Writing Class. In *Advancing Online Course Design and Pedagogy for the 21st Century Learning Environment* (pp. 191–205). IGI Global. doi:10.4018/978-1-7998-5598-9.ch011

Yenmez, A. A., Özpinar, İ., & Gökçe, S. (2017). Use of WebQuests in Mathematics Instruction: Academic Achievement, Teacher and Student Opinions. *Universal Journal of Educational Research*, *5*(9), 1554–1570. doi:10.13189/ujer.2017.050913

Chapter 14
The Perceptions of Pre-Service Teachers Regarding the Teaching Methodology of Primary Education Social Science Teachers

Catalina Guerrero-Romera
https://orcid.org/0000-0001-6080-1676
University of Murcia, Spain

EXECUTIVE SUMMARY

This chapter has been proposed with the aim of discovering and analysing how Social Sciences teachers represent and develop knowledge in their teaching practice through the perspective of pre-service teachers. To achieve this, the methodological model of primary education teachers will be analysed via observations carried out by students of an undergraduate degree in Primary Education during their period of teaching practice, paying particular attention to the development of the historical thinking skills and the use of ICT resources and of learning strategies, resources, and assessment. These observations by trainees reflect how pre-service teachers are more aware of the importance of encouraging a wider variety of learning and assessment strategies and activities for the achievement of historical thinking competences and more complex thinking skills.

INTRODUCTION

The change in approach to the teaching of History which has taken place over recent years emphasises the need to promote new learning strategies and models and a method of assessment for History which are more linked with the development of skills, particularly those of historical thinking (Carretero, 2019; Sáiz & Domínguez, 2017; Sáiz & Gómez, 2016; Metzger y Harris, 2018; Thorp y Persson, 2020). In this context, it is essential to analyse the conceptions held and the teaching approaches employed by

DOI: 10.4018/978-1-6684-5240-0.ch014

Social Science teachers, how they represent the knowledge they teach and what consequences this has on the strategies and resources which they consider most relevant for teaching (Guerrero, Sánchez & Miralles, 2022).

Nowadays, a less descriptive and conceptual approach to the teaching of History is advocated, one which is more geared towards developing the capacity to think historically and to foster competences such as the critical analysis of information, the use and interpretation of sources, seeing things from different perspectives and other skills related with the trade of the historian and the construction of historical knowledge (Thorp & Persson, 2020; Sáiz & Gómez, 2016; Prieto, Gómez & Miralles, 2013; Santisteban, González & Pages, 2010; Lévesque, 2008; VanSledright, 2011). This construction is obtained through teaching and learning processes of second-order contents related with this way of understanding history education based on the historical thinking skills: historical relevance, causes and consequences, change and continuity, the analysis of sources, empathy and historical consciousness (Seixas & Morton, 2013; VanSledright, 2014).

This implies encouraging more complex cognitive strategies, the development of a historical consciousness and a responsibility for a democratic and critical citizenship (Lucas & Delgado, 2018; Rüsen, 2015; Sáiz, 2013; Marín, 2017) which extends beyond a form of learning based essentially on the textbook and on taking standardised examinations (Prats, 2011; Herrera & Gil, 2015, Hernández, 2019; Gómez, Rodríguez & Miralles, 2014; Gómez, Rodríguez & Mirete, 2018).

This model advocates a form of history learning which combines the following two dimensions: knowledge of history and the use of historical skills and competences related with basic educational competences (Lee 2005 and 2011; Sáiz 2013). In this context, teaching staff are a fundamental element in the development and improvement of learning processes and are also a key aspect in the transformation of education and a change in learning models (Pagès, 2011). This change involves reviewing the models and practices carried out if teachers wish to be agents of the change towards sustainability and in the training of future citizens (Calero et al., 2019).

Santisteban (2019) has spoken of the need to shape a transformative citizenship, among whom the learning of social and citizenship competences is fostered. It is necessary to encourage a curriculum with a social vocation which develops competences and contents in accordance with the Sustainable Development Goals and the application of learning models based on higher-order thinking skills (Avendaño-Castro & Parada, 2013; López Facal et al., 2017; Lévesque & Clark, 2018) from a socio-cultural and humanistic perspective of history teaching connected with citizenship education and social problems (Barton & Levstik, 2004; Rüsen, 2015). This form of education is extremely committed to democracy and justice within the framework of the 2030 Agenda and the Sustainable Development Goals (Medir & Serra, 2021).

Within the teaching of historical contents, it is necessary, therefore, to promote new learning strategies and models and forms of History assessment linked to the development of these historical thinking skills, making it possible for them to be developed in the classroom from a critical perspective (Pagès, 1994; Miralles et al., 2014; Estepa, 2017). At the same time, it is also important to work on second-order contents and to promote a form of historical comprehension which involves the development of these skills via active student-based methods and resources (Guerrero et al., 2021; Miralles, Gómez & Rodríguez, 2017; Thorp & Persson, 2020; VanSledright, 2011).

The improvement of these approaches and models regarding the teaching of the social sciences should be based on the identification of the learning practices and processes being carried out in compulsory education as these can constitute an indicator of the educational change being brought about. Even at the present time, it is common to encounter educational practices in which perspectives based on memorisation are predominant in the teaching of History, along with the use of strategies and methods which do not favour critical and reflexive thinking on the part of the student or his/her involvement in the learning process (Andelique, 2011; Gómez, Ortuño & Molina, 2014; Sáiz & Gómez, 2016; Miguel-Revilla et al. 2020). Methodological practices should, therefore, encourage student participation from perspectives more based on experience and from constructivist approaches (Gómez, Miralles, López & Prats, 2017; Prats, 2011; Herrera &Gil, 2015; Hernández, 2019; Soler et al., 2018; Dejene, Bishaw & Dagnew, 2018).

In this context, teachers (as essential agents for the success of any teaching and learning process) are responsible for putting these approaches into practice, particularly the innovations developed in schools, especially if the use of a specific teaching model or approach could be related with the use of a specific method, strategy or resources in the classroom (Guerrero et al., 2021, 2022). The present study has been proposed with the aim of discovering and analysing how Social Sciences teachers represent and develop knowledge in their teaching practice through the perspective of pre-service teachers. To achieve this, the methodological model of primary education teachers will be analysed via observations carried out by students of an undergraduate degree in Primary Education during their period of teaching practice, paying particular attention to the development of the historical thinking skills and the use of ICT resources and of learning strategies, resources and assessment.

METHODOLOGY

As far as the methodology of this study is concerned, it is non-experimental with a quantitative approach based on an observation protocol which was specifically designed and validated. A Likert-scale was employed with the following five response options: never, rarely, sometimes, almost always and always. It contained 25 items for the analysis carried out by students performing teaching practice regarding the reality of the teaching observed during their period of training in the classroom, specifically relating to the methods, strategies and resources employed by teachers in their Social Sciences classes, along with other aspects relating to the development of the historical thinking skills. The informed consent of the participants was obtained for this purpose. As far as the participants are concerned, the protocol was administered to 53 students of an undergraduate degree in Primary Education in the 3rd-year subject of Teaching Practice II, tutored by teachers from the field of Social Sciences Teaching in the 2019-2020 academic year. The sample consisted of 82.5% women and 15.9% men, with 1.6% not specifying their gender (Table 1). The data handling and analysis was carried out using the SPSS v.19.0 statistical software. In order to analyse the data and interpret the results, basic descriptive statistics have been performed with the aim of being able to respond to the objectives proposed in the research.

RESULTS

The results of the analysis carried out of the teaching practice as far as the stated objectives are concerned are presented below. First of all, with regard to the method employed by the teachers observed when explaining the contents, 66% of the students undergoing training perceived that it was always based on the master class, with only 9.5% stating that this method was never or rarely used (Table 2). On the other hand, 45% stated that the teachers always or almost always connected their explanations with current

Table 1. Distribution of the participants according to sex

Sex	N	Valid percentage
Women	45	82.5
Men	8	15.9
No answer	1	1.6
Total	53	100

Source: Own.

events, with 38% considering that this was never or only rarely done (22.6% and 15.1%, respectively). As far as the use of different methodologies are concerned, only 39.6% believed that the teachers always employ different methods when providing their explanations, with 36% stating that this was never or almost never the case. Regarding the use of the analysis of sources such as documents, photographs, graphs or maps in the explanation of contents, 66% of the participants stated that the teachers always or almost always (27% and 28.6%, respectively) made use of such resources.

Table 2. Method employed by teachers for the explanation of contents based on the master class

		Frequency	Valid %
Method employed based on the master class	Never	2	3.8
	Rarely	3	5.7
	Sometimes	12	22.6
	Almost always	1	1.9
	Always	35	66
	Total	53	100.0

Source: Own

Furthermore, as far as the use of strategies focused on the student (gamification, flipped classroom, role plays, etc.) is concerned, 62.3% believed that this was always or almost always (25.4% and 27%, respectively) carried out. More specifically, in relation to whether these strategies were used to encourage students to think critically about the contents (project-based learning, problem-based learning, etc.) 54.7% perceived that the teachers always or almost always employed such strategies, while 36% stated that this was only done rarely or sometimes (Table 3).

With regard to the use of the textbook for the explanation of contents and activities, almost 50% of the participants stated that this resource is always or almost always still used for explanations. However, only 28.3% of teachers use it for doing activities, with 34% sometimes doing so. Furthermore, 65% were of the opinion that teachers combine several resources (textbook, presentations, documentaries, films and photographs) when explaining contents and 54.7% stated that the teacher always or almost always creates their own contents for their explanations (32.1% and 22.6%, respectively). As far as the use of ICT resources by teachers when explaining contents is concerned, 49% of the participants perceived that these were always or almost always used (28.3% and 20.8%, respectively).

Table 3. Use of student-focused strategies to encourage students to reflect critically on the contents

		Frequency	Valid %
Student-focused strategies	Never	17	32.1
	Rarely	2	3.8
	Sometimes	5	9.4
	Almost always	6	11.3
	Always	23	43.4
	Total	53	100.0

Source: Own

On the other hand, 49% of the participants believed that teachers design activities which encourage the analysis of sources and critical thinking among students and only 40% stated that debates are employed (Table 4). Likewise, 66% believed that educational field trips are carried out within the subject connected with the contents of Social Sciences.

Table 4. Use of debates by teachers

		Frequency	Valid %
Use of debates	Never	15	28.3
	Rarely	17	32.1
	Sometimes	0	0
	Almost always	11	20.8
	Always	10	18.9
	Total	53	100.0

Source: Own

With regard to groupings in the classroom, the pre-service teachers stated that 49% of the teachers always or almost always employ individual work in the classroom, 41.5% always or almost always in small groups and 38.1% always or almost always in pairs. As far as the use of different strategies or tools for assessment are concerned (notebooks, written work, rubrics, portfolios, etc.), 68% stated that the teachers always or almost always employ different tools (30.2% and 37.7%, respectively) and 50% considered that the mark of the examination is more than 50% of the total mark for the subject.

Secondly, with regard to working on the historical thinking skills in the classroom, the results described below stand out. Regarding "the identification of causes and consequences of historical events", 55% believed that this is rarely or only sometimes carried out. 64% stated that "the identification of historical aspects which have changed or persisted in spite of the passing of time" was also only rarely or sometimes taken into consideration. 41% stated that the "critical evaluation of historical events or processes" was always or almost always carried out, while the fact of "putting oneself in the shoes of a historical character (drama or simulation) in order to understand his/her actions was always or almost always employed by only 17% of teachers (3.8 and 13.2%, respectively) (Table 5). With regard to the issue of whether students

Table 5. Putting oneself in the shoes of a historical character (drama or simulation) in order to understand his/her actions

		Frequency	Valid %
Putting oneself in the shoes of a historical character	Never	10	18.9
	Rarely	16	30.2
	Sometimes	18	34.0
	Almost always	7	13.2
	Always	2	3.8
	Total	53	100.0

Source: Own

are taught in Social Sciences classes to understand the modification of the environment by humans via the interpretation and elaboration of maps, graphs, news related with the environment, the analysis of photographs and the use of ICT resources applied to geography (Wikiloc, Google Earth, etc.), 56.6% stated that this was only rarely or sometimes the case (18.9 and 37.7%, respectively).

Last of all, regarding the perception of pre-service teachers of whether Social Sciences classes prove motivating for students, only 45.3% of the respondents perceived that this was always or almost always the case (11.3% and 34%, respectively).

DISCUSSION

The results obtained via the perception of undergraduate students with a training in history indicate that teaching practices based on memorisation and the transmission of knowledge still persist, particularly in relation to the learning of the historical thinking skills (Gómez, Rodríguez & Mirete, 2018; Souto, Fuster & Sáiz, 2014; Guerrero et al., 2021), although a change can be noted in the way History is taught and in how positivist epistemological trends have been overcome (Sáiz & López-Facal, 2015; VanSledright, 2011 and 2014). However, the reality is that more than half of the Social Sciences teachers observed continue to use the textbook and make limited use of active methods and resources and different assessment strategies or make little use of ICT resources in teaching historical thinking skills in compulsory education. This would show that practices which do not foster reflexive thinking among students or an understanding of these concepts still persist in the classroom (Andelique, 2011; López & Valls, 2012; Dejene et al., 2018; VanSledright & Maggioni, 2016).

Furthermore, as far as the participants' perception regarding the issue of whether History classes prove motivating for students is concerned, the results do not present very high percentages. In this regard, several studies have shown the low degree of value which students attribute to History, associating it with a form of teaching which is based on memorisation, is not easily understood and is even boring (Prats, 2017; Ibagón, 2016; Gómez, Miralles & Molina, 2015; Barca, 2011). This lack of interest on the part of students is also demonstrated in other research and studies, such as those by VanSledright & Maggioni (2016), Sanz, Molero & Rodríguez (2017), Ortega (2015), Prats (2017) and Lévesque & Clark (2018).

Even so, it can be observed that teachers also propose pedagogical alternatives for the study of contents and the learning of cognitive historical skills which overcome these routines based on memorisation or encyclopaedic knowledge in the teaching of History (Seixas & Morton, 2013; Souto, Fuster & Sáiz, 2014; Montilla, Maraver, Romero & Martín, 2018; Lévesque & Clark, 2018; Thorp & Persson, 2020; Guerrero et al., 2021). In this regard, it is necessary to highlight the importance of the design and implementation of teaching and learning activities and the assessment of the historical thinking skills due to the fact that, as stated by García-Morís (2016), there is a lack of specific materials and teaching proposals which help teachers to pave the way for such active practices and a more motivating model of history teaching.

However, from the perspective of pre-service teachers, primary education teachers value and develop the historical thinking skills in their students, following a more competence-based approach to the social sciences and a more cognitive learning of history (Akhan, 2021; Sánchez, Guerrero & Miralles, 2021; Gómez, Chaparro, Felices & Cózar, 2020; Gómez & Sobrino, 2018; VanSledright, 2011). Furthermore, these observations by trainee teachers reflect how future teachers are more aware of the importance of fostering a wider variety of learning and assessment strategies and activities in order to achieve the historical thinking skills and more complex thinking skills oriented towards education for a democratic and critical citizenship (Domínguez, 2015; Ercikan & Seixas (2015); Prats 2020; Gómez, López-Facal & Rodríguez 2019; Gómez, Miralles, Rodríguez & Maquilón 2020).

As proposed by Sáiz & López-Facal (2015), teacher training should be analysed from this perspective, along with the knowledge held by teachers of new models of history education, the teaching models which they carry out and, especially, the decisions they take with regard to these models. In any case, the data obtained make it possible to observe how teachers undergoing their initial training are able to detect activities and strategies which can achieve a cognitive learning model of history (Miralles, Gómez & Rodríguez, 2017; VanSledright & Maggioni, 2016).

To conclude, it can be stated that it is still necessary to progress towards teaching approaches and practices which are more focused on the student and which favour not only the teaching of the historical thinking skills, but also the use of active methodologies which bring about the participation and involvement of students and interdisciplinarity, as well as the use of other innovative resources extending beyond the textbook, such as educational field trips, holding debates, drama and ICT resources (Gómez, Miralles, López & Prats, 2017; Roblizo, Sánchez & Cózar, 2016; Gómez, Miralles &Chapman, 2017; Gómez, Ortuño & Miralles, 2018; Thorp & Persson, 2020).

In this context, strategies and resources for learning and assessment which encourage the acquisition of second-order concepts and the assumption of current models for the teaching of history are of great importance via an effective and practical model of teacher training based on the identification of needs and a continual inter-relationship of theory and practice through on-going psychopedagogical training (de Groot-Reuvekamp, Ros and van Boxtel, 2018; Pagés, 2018; Imbernón, 2019).

Teacher training is, therefore, of vital importance when modifying this teaching approach in favour of another which is more student-focused and which encourages the teaching of historical contents oriented towards the education of a critical citizenship, making it possible for students to develop social and civic skills with a view to actively participating in society (Floden, 2015; Marín, 2017; Prats, 2020).

Last of all, as far as the limitations of this research are concerned, it could be pointed out that the size of the sample and the fact that it is limited to Spain, should be taken into account. In addition, it should be complemented with a mixed method in which teachers are asked about their approach in the classroom in order to reveal whether their perception of their teaching practice corresponds with the perspective held or manifested by the pre-service teachers. Future research it is recommended that the number of participants be increased and that it can be carried out in other contexts. On the other hand, it could include an analysis of the profile and training in the subject of History of pre-service and in-service teachers or an analysis of whether teachers perceive practice as an improvement of teaching as proposed by Seixas (2001) and Santisteban, González & Pagès (2015). This will allow more solid conclusions and recommendations to be drawn for the improvement of social science teaching. It should not be forgotten that the conceptual model of history education should contribute towards establishing teaching proposals which lead to quality learning, connected to the challenges of the current world and the development of critical and reflexive thinking.

NOTE

This research was supported by the Fundación Séneca-Agencia de Ciencia y Tecnología de la Región de Murcia (Spain): "The geographical and historical thinking of primary education students in the Region of Murcia: an innovative methodological proposal for quality education (20874/PI/18).

REFERENCES

Akhan, O. (2021). History teaching approaches preferred by Turkish and Russian history teachers. *World Journal of Education*, *11*(1), 62–74. doi:10.5430/wje.v11n1p62

Andelique, C. M. (2011). La didáctica de la historia y la formación docente: ¿qué profesor de historia necesitan las escuelas? *Clío & Asociados*, *15*(15), 256–269. doi:10.14409/cya.v1i15.1704

Avendaño-Castro, W., & Parada Trujillo, A. (2013). El currículo en la sociedad del conocimiento. *Educación y Educadores*, *16*(1), 159–174.

Barca, I. (2011). Narrativas e consciência histórica dos jovens. *Enseñanza de las Ciencias Sociales*, (10), 22–28.

Barton, K., & Levstik, L. (2004). *Teaching History for the Common Good*. Lawrence Erlbaum. doi:10.4324/9781410610508

Barton, K. C. (2010). Investigación sobre las ideas de los estudiantes acerca de la historia. *Enseñanza de las Ciencias Sociales*, (9), 97–114.

Calero Llinares, M., Mayoral García-Berlanga, O., Ull Solís, A., & Vilches Peña, A. (2019). La educación para la sostenibilidad en la formación del profesorado de ciencias experimentales en Secundaria. *Enseñanza de las Ciencias*, *37*(1), 157–175. doi:10.5565/rev/ensciencias.2605

Carretero, M. (2019). Pensamiento histórico e historia global como nuevos desafíos para la enseñanza. *Cuadernos de Pedagogía*, *495*, 59–63.

de Groot-Reuvekamp, M., Ros, A., & van Boxtel, C. (2018a). Improving elementary school students' understanding of historical time: Effects of teaching with "Timewise". *Theory and Research in Social Education*, *46*(1), 35–67. doi:10.1080/00933104.2017.1357058

Dejene, W., Bishaw, A., & Dagnew, A. (2018). Preservice Teachers' Approaches to Learning and Their Teaching Approach Preferences: Secondary Teacher Education Program in Focus. *Cogent Edu.*, *5*(1), 1502396. doi:10.1080/2331186X.2018.1502396

Domínguez, J. (2015). *Pensamiento histórico y evaluación de competencias.* Graó.

Ercikan, K., & Seixas, P. (2015). *New directions in assessing historical thinking.* Routledge. doi:10.4324/9781315779539

Estepa, J. (2017). *Otra didáctica de la Historia para otra escuela.* Universidad de Huelva.

Floden, R. (2015). Learning what research says about teacher preparation. In M. J. Feuer, A. I. Berman, & R. C. Atkinson (Eds.), *Past as prologue: The national academy of education at 50. Members reflect* (pp. 279–284). National Academy of Education.

García-Morís, R. (2016). Propuesta metodológica para el uso de las fuentes históricas demográficas de la Edad Moderna como recurso didáctico. *Revista de Didácticas Específ icas, 14*, 71-85.

Gómez, C., Miralles, P., & Molina, S. (2015). Presentación Evaluación, competencias históricas y educación ciudadana. *Revista de Estudios Sociales*, (52), 9–14.

Gómez, C., & Sobrino, D. (2018). Métodos activos de aprendizaje y adquisición de competencias en la clase de Historia. In P. Miralles & C. Gómez (Eds.), *La educación histórica ante el reto de las competencias Métodos, recursos y enfoques de enseñanza* (pp. 111–126). Octaedro.

Gómez, C. J., Chaparro, A., Felices, M. M., & Cózar, R. (2020). Estrategias metodológicas y uso de recursos digitales para la enseñanza de la historia. Análisis de recuerdos y opiniones del profesorado en formación inicial. *Aula Abierta*, *49*(1), 65–74. doi:10.17811/rifie.49.1.2020.65-74

Gómez, C. J., López-Facal, R., & Rodríguez-Medina, J. (2019). La investigación en Didáctica de las Ciencias Sociales en revistas españolas de Ciencias de la Educación. Un análisis bibliométrico (2007-2017). *Revista de Didáctica de las Ciencias Experimentales y Sociales*, *37*(37), 67–88. doi:10.7203/dces.37.14440

Gómez, C. J., Miralles, P., & Chapman, A. (2017). Los procedimientos de evaluación en la clase de Historia. Un análisis comparativo a través de las opiniones de los docentes en formación en España e Inglaterra. *Revista Electrónica Interuniversitaria de Formación del Profesorado*, *20*(2), 45–61. doi:10.6018/reifop/20.2.284631

Gómez, C. J., Miralles, P., López, R., & Prats, J. (2017). Las competencias históricas en el horizonte. Propuestas presentes y perspectivas de futuro. In R. López, P. Miralles, & J. Prats (Eds.), *Enseñanza de la historia y competencias educativas* (pp. 215–234). Graó.

Gómez, C. J., Miralles, P., Rodríguez-Medina, J., & Maquilón, J. (2020). Perceptions on the procedures and techniques for assessing history and defining teaching profiles. Teacher training in Spain and the United Kingdom. *Educational Studies*, *43*, 1–19. doi:10.1080/03055698.2019.1707069

Gómez, C. J., Ortuño, J., & Miralles, P. (2018). *Enseñar ciencias sociales con métodos activos de aprendizaje. Reflexiones y propuestas a través de la indagación.* Octaedro.

Gómez, C. J., Rodríguez, R. A., & Miralles, P. (2014). La enseñanza de la Historia en educación primaria y la construcción de una narrativa nacional. *Perfiles Educativos*, *37*(150), 20–38.

Gómez, C. J., Rodríguez-Pérez, R. A., & Mirete, A. B. (2018). Metodología didáctica y concepciones epistemológicas sobre la enseñanza de la historia. Una investigación con futuros maestros. *Revista Complutense de Educación*, *24*(1), 237–250.

Guerrero-Romera, C., Sánchez-Ibáñez, R., Escribano, V., & Vivas, V. (2021). The perceptions of active teachers regarding the most suitable resources for teaching history. *Humanities & Social Sciences Communications*, *8*, 61. doi:10.105741599-021-00736-7

Guerrero-Romera, C., Sánchez-Ibáñez, R., & Miralles-Martínez, P. (2022). Approaches to History Teaching According to a Structural Equation Model. *Frontiers in Education.*, *7*, 842977. doi:10.3389/feduc.2022.842977

Hernández, A. M. (2019). *Estrategias y recursos didácticos para la enseñanza de las Ciencias Sociales*. Ediciones Pirámide.

Herrera, Z., & Gil, M. D. C. (2015). Literatura, tecnologías de información y comunicación en clases de historia. *Revista de Ciencias Sociales*, *XXI*(2), 327–336.

Ibagón, N. J. (2016). Enseñar y aprender historia a partir del análisis de fuentes históricas. Una experiencia formativa en Educación Superior. Voces y silencios. *Revista Latinoamericana de educación, 7*(1), 121-133.

Imbernón Muñoz, F. (2019). La formación del profesorado de Secundaria: La eterna pesadilla. *Profesorado, Revista De Currículum Y Formación Del Profesorado, 23*(3), 151-163. doi:10.30827/profesorado.v23i3.9302

König, J., Ligtvoeta, R., Klemenza, S., & Rothlandb, M. (2017). Effects of opportunities to learn in teacher preparation on future teachers' general pedagogical knowledge: Analyzing program characteristics and outcomes. *Studies in Educational Evaluation*, *53*, 122–133. doi:10.1016/j.stueduc.2017.03.001

Lee, P. (2005). Putting principles intro practice: understanding history. In M. Donovan & J. Bransford (Eds.), *How students learn: History in the classroom* (pp. 31–77). National Academies Press.

Lee, P. (2011). History education and historical literacy. In I. Davies (Ed.), *Debates in History Teaching* (pp. 63–72). Routledge.

Lévesque, S., & Clark, P. (2018). Historical Thinking: Definitions and Educational Applications. In S. Metzger & L. M. Harris (Eds.), *The Wiley International Handbook of History Teaching and Learning* (pp. 119–148). John Wiley & Sons, Inc. doi:10.1002/9781119100812.ch5

López, R & Valls, R. (2012). La necesidad cívica de saber historia y geografía. *Educar para la participación ciudadana En la Enseñanza de las ciencias sociales. Volumen I. Asociación Universitaria de Profesorado de Didáctica de las Ciencias Sociales,* 185-192

López Facal, R., Gómez, C. J., Miralles, P., & Prats, J. (2017). Pensamiento histórico, enseñanza de la historia y competencias educativas. In R. López Facal, P. Miralles, J. Prats, & C. J. Gómez (Eds.), *Enseñanza de la historia y competencias educativas*. Graó.

Lucas, L., & Delgado, E. J. (2018). Educación para una ciudadanía comprometida en la enseñanza de las Ciencias Sociales: ¿Qué piensa el alumnado de un profesor innovador sobre su aprendizaje? *Didáctica de las Ciencias Experimentales y Sociales*, *35*(35), 3–16. doi:10.7203/dces.35.12572

Marín, V. (2017). La enseñanza de la historia y la construcción y la construcción de una ciudadanía crítica. In La enseñanza de la historia en el siglo XXI. Desarrollo y evaluación de competencias históricas para una ciudadanía democrática (pp. 95-112). Murcia: Editum.

Medir, R., & Serra, A. (2021). Una alianza entre los objetivos del desarrollo sostenible y la formación de maestras en ciudadanía sostenible. *Didacticae*, *9*, 79–83.

Metzger, S. A., & Harris, L. M. (Eds.). (2018). *The Wiley International Handbook of history teaching and learning*. Wiley. doi:10.1002/9781119100812

Miralles, P., Gómez, C., & Rodríguez, R. (2017). Patrimonio, competencias históricas y metodologías activas de aprendizaje. Un análisis de las opiniones de los docentes en formación en España e Inglaterra. *Estudios Pedagógicos (Valdivia)*, *43*(4), 161–184. doi:10.4067/S0718-07052017000400009

Miralles, P., Gómez, C., & Sánchez, R. (2014). Dime qué preguntas y te diré qué evalúas y enseñas. Análisis de los exámenes de ciencias sociales en tercer ciclo de Educación Primaria. *Aula Abierta*, *42*(2), 83–89. doi:10.1016/j.aula.2014.05.002

Montilla, M. V., Maraver, P., Romero, C., & Martín, A. (2018). Análisis de las expectativas del profesorado novel sobre su futura labor docente. *Aula Abierta*, *47*(2), 185–192. doi:10.17811/rifie.47.2.2018.185-192

Ortega, D. (2015). La enseñanza de las Ciencias Sociales, las TIC y el tratamiento de la información y competencia digital (TICD) en el grado de Maestro/a de Educación Primaria de las universidades de Castilla y León. *Enseñanza de las Ciencias Sociales*, (14), 121–134.

Pagés, A. (2011). ¿Qué se necesita saber y saber hacer para enseñar ciencias sociales? *Edetania*, (40), 67–81.

Pagés, A. (2018). Aprender a enseñar historia. Las relaciones entre la historia y la historia escolar. *Trayectorias Universitarias*, *4*(7), 53–59.

Pagés, J. (1994). La didáctica de las ciencias sociales, el currículum y la formación del profesorado. *Signos Teoria y Practica de la Educación, 5*(13), 38-51.

Prats, J. (Coord.). (2011). Didáctica de la Geografía y la Historia. Barcelona, España: Graó. Ministerio de Educación Cultura y Deporte, Secretaría General Técnica.

Prats, J. (2017). Retos y dificultades para la enseñanza de la historia. In La historia en el aula. Innovación docente y enseñanza de la historia en la educación secundaria (pp. 15-32). Milenio.

Prats, J. (Coord.). (2020). Ciencias sociales, ciudadanía y sociedad digital. In *Re-flexiones desde la educación*. Editorial Trea.

Prats, J. (2020). Didáctica de la historia en secundaria y en la universidad. Dos mundos que viven de espaldas. *Íber. Didáctica de las Ciencias Sociales. Geografía e Historia*, *100*, 10–14.

Prieto, J. A, Gómez, C. J. & Miralles, P. (2013). El uso de fuentes primarias en el aula y el desarrollo del pensamiento histórico y social. Una experiencia en Bachillerato. *Clío. History and Teaching, 39.*

Roblizo, M., Sánchez, M. C., & Cózar, R. (2016). El reto de la competencia digital en los futuros docentes de Infantil, Primaria y Secundaria: Los estudiantes de Grado y Máster de Educación ante las TIC. *Revista de Investigación Social, 15*, 254–295.

Rüsen, J. (2015). *Teoria da História. Uma teoria da história como ciencia*. Universidade Federal do Paraná.

Sáiz, J. (2013). Empatía histórica, historia social e identidades: Pensar históricamente la conquista cristiana de la Valencia musulmana con estudiantes de 2o ESO. *Clio*, 39.

Sáiz, J., & Domínguez, J. (2017). Aprender sobre la historia: Competencias metodológicas en educación secundaria. In Enseñanza de la historia y competencias educativas (pp. 23-47). Graó.

Sáiz, J., & Fuster, C. (2014). Memorizar historia sin aprender pensamiento histórico: Las PAU de Historia de España. *Investigación en la Escuela, 84*, 47–57.

Sáiz, J. & Gómez, C. J. (2016). Investigar el pensamiento histórico y narrativo en la formación del profesorado: fundamentos teóricos y metodológicos. *Revista electrónica interuniversitaria de formación de profesorado, 19*(1), 175-190.

Sáiz, J., & López-Facal, R. (2015). Competencias y narrativas históricas: El pensamiento histórico de estudiantes y futuros profesores españoles de educación secundaria. *Revista de Estudios Sociales*, *52*, 87–101.

Sánchez-Ibáñez, R., Guerrero-Romera, C., & Miralles-Martínez, P. (2021). The disciplinary training needs of teachers of the social sciences, *Humanities & Social Science Communication*, *8*, 26. doi:10.105741599-021-00705-0

Santisteban, A. (2019). La enseñanza de las Ciencias Sociales a partir de problemas sociales o temas controvertidos. Estado de la cuestión y resultados de una investigación. *El futuro del Pasado: revista electrónica de historia, 10*, 57-79.

Santisteban, A., González, N., & Pagès, J. (2010). Una investigación sobre la formación del pensamiento histórico. In *Metodología de investigación en Didáctica de las Ciencias Sociales* (pp. 115–128). I. Fernando el Católico-Diputación de Zaragoza-AUPDCS.

Sanz, P., Molero, J. M., & Rodríguez, D. (2017). La historia en el aula. Innovación docente y enseñanza de la historia en la educación secundaria. *Historia y Memoria de la Educación*, (6), 553–555.

Seixas, P. (2001). Review of Research on Social Studies. In Handbook Of Research On Teaching (4th ed.). American Educational Research Association.

Seixas, P., & Morton, T. (2013). *The Big Six Historical Thinking Concepts*. Nelson.

Soler, M. G., Cárdenas, F. A., & Hernández-Pina, F. (2018). Enfoques de enseñanza y enfoques de aprendizaje: Perspectivas teóricas promisorias para el desarrollo de investigaciones en educación en ciencias. *Ciência & Educação (Bauru)*, *24*(4), 993–1012. doi:10.1590/1516-731320180040012

Souto, X. M., Fuster, C., & Sáiz, J. (2014). Un camino de ida y vuelta. Reválidas y selectividad en las rutinas escolares de la enseñanza de la Geografía e Historia. In J. Pagés & A. Santisteban (Eds.), *Una mirada al pasado y una proyección de futuro. Investigación e innovación en didáctica de las ciencias sociales* (pp. 157–165). AUPDCS.

Thorp, R., & Persson, A. (2020). On historical thinking and the history educational challenge. *Educational Philosophy and Theory*, *52*(8), 891–901. doi:10.1080/00131857.2020.1712550

VanSledright, B. (2011). *The Challenge of Rethinking History Education. On practice, theories, and policy.* Routledge.

VanSledright, B. (2014). *Assessing historical thinking and understanding. Innovation design for new standards*. Routledge. doi:10.4324/9780203464632

VanSledright, B. A. (2004). What Does It Mean to Think Historically... and How Do You Teach It? *Social Education*, *68*(3), 230–233.

VanSledright, B. A., & Maggioni, L. (2016). Epistemic cognition in history. In J. A. Greene, W. A. Sandoval, & I. Bråten (Eds.), *Handbook of epistemic cognition* (pp. 128–146). Routledge.

Wineburg, S. (2018). *Why Learn History (When Itís Already on Your Phone)*. Chicago Univ. doi:10.7208/chicago/9780226357355.001.0001

Chapter 15
Evaluation of a Training Program for Trainee Teachers in Active Methodologies for Teaching Social Sciences

Ramón Méndez
https://orcid.org/0000-0002-6002-0017
University of Almería, Spain

Álvaro Chaparro-Sainz
University of Almería, Spain

Rubén Martínez Sánchez
Lideria International School, Spain

María del Mar Felices-De la Fuente
University of Almería, Spain

EXECUTIVE SUMMARY

The primary purposes of this study are to investigate the opinions and conceptions of primary education teachers undergoing initial training on active methodologies and to evaluate a training program that uses these methodologies with a particular focus on the teaching of Social Sciences. To this end, a mixed methodology has been employed, using an initial questionnaire and a focus group as research instruments. Following the data analysis, the results show a favorable assessment of these active methodologies. There were some gender differences, as women assigned greater value than men to the active strategies, resources, and evaluation approaches and were more focused on competency-based learning. Another result highlighted the suitability of using service-learning or inquiry methodology to teach Social Sciences. The authors conclude that improving the training program developed is necessary, offering more connections with practice and expanding initial teacher training in active methods.

DOI: 10.4018/978-1-6684-5240-0.ch015

INTRODUCTION

The introduction of competency-based teaching in school curricula has significantly affected how Social Sciences are taught in the classroom. In light of this new reality, in recent years, various studies have insisted on the need to renew training programs to ensure that teacher training programs enable an improvement of the teaching-learning processes according to the new demands (González & Skultety, 2018; Oliveira et al., 2019; Maloy et al., 2019; Moreno-Vera & Alvén, 2020; Raya & Navaridas, 2021).

In the field of Social Sciences teaching, research shows the need to shift toward a teaching model that encourages students to think critically through active methodologies, thus abandoning passive and rote learning practices (Moreno et al., 2021; Gómez et al., 2022). Thus, as opposed to traditional teaching, active learning methodologies have been postulated as the guarantors of the balance between knowledge, skills and abilities (Souto & García-Monteagudo, 2019; Ordoñez et al., 2021; Moreno-Vera et al., 2021; Gómez et al., 2020a).

The studies that analyze the inclusion of active learning methodologies in educational contexts focused on gamification (Hanus & Fox, 2015; Attali & Arieli-Attali, 2015; De Marcos et al., 2016; Han-Huey et al., 2018; Hakak et al., 2019; Durrani et al., 2022) and the Flipped Classroom (Gilboy et al., 2015; Hao & Lee, 2016; Yilmaz, 2017; Steen-Utheim & Foldnes, 2018; Shibukawa & Taguchi, 2019; Maloy et al., 2019; Ruiz et al., 2022) are particularly noteworthy. Moreover, these strategies receive the most attention from primary education trainee teachers (Blasco-Serrano et al., 2018; Gómez et al., 2019).

The results of some studies show how learning opportunities in training programs have a remarkable correlation with teachers' knowledge and competencies at the end of their training (Blömeke et al., 2014). Thus, the paper by Coll et al. (2018) has shown the close correlation between the methodology used in university classrooms with the professional development of graduates. In fact, among the most influential factors are problem-based learning, curricular practices and practical knowledge, results that, on the other hand, coincide with those shown by Hortigüela et al. (2018).

More specifically, in teaching social knowledge, the improvement of teaching processes must involve learning alternative methodologies to traditional teaching (Gómez et al., 2021). Furthermore, this situation requires a methodological change that favors the student's active participation in constructing social knowledge (Miralles et al., 2017). Thus, intervention in teacher training is essential as long as the development of knowledge, skills and teaching competencies in two areas are established: methodology and epistemology.

Authors such as Estepa (2017) justify the need for quality training based on the idea that a teacher usually bases their teaching methods on models already lived or experienced and their experiences as a student when faced with teaching for the first time. This may imply reproducing previously perceived models that generally tend to be attached to traditional models (Sánchez-Fuster, 2017). Currently, there are several studies within the area of Didactics of Social Sciences that have proved that teaching and learning social knowledge should be done from active methodological approaches (Gómez et al., 2018), involving the students in building their own knowledge and making possible for them to interpret their reality from a critical perspective so that they can participate in it and transform it. This diagnosis, in the framework of Higher Education, has, in recent years, entailed the design and implementation of training to supplement the current syllabus in the degrees that, precisely, are more oriented to the learning of methodological nature aspects (León & Crisol, 2011; Monteagudo et al., 2017).

Within the Spanish school system, the teaching of Social Sciences remains mainly traditional, based on replicating and rote learning (Souto & García-Monteagudo, 2019). Indeed, first-order concepts continue to play a more significant role in classrooms than second-order concepts, which are more procedural and attitudinal (VanSledright, 2014). The result is that students struggle to find the concepts being taught either meaningful, useful, or practical. Being aware of this reality, it is crucial that, from the teachers' initial training, future teachers are prepared to incorporate new strategies in the teaching of Social Sciences, transforming the inherited routines (Parra & Fuertes, 2019).

Concerning the teaching of history content, Lévesque and Zanazanian (2015) emphasize that in transforming educational practices, the fundamental role falls on the initial training of future teachers since only through it can we train our students in methodologies that could improve historical education. This teaching requirement is also crucial in university contexts in which future teachers demand to be trained in new and alternative teaching strategies to be fully prepared for the current educational reality, connecting the theory and the practice (Felices & Chaparro, 2021; Darouech & Felices, 2021).

Following the model adopted by many countries, such as the United Kingdom, Canada and the United States, Spain needs to redefine the social knowledge education model. This redefinition is based on introducing teaching methods that allow progressive knowledge acquisition following the guidelines of educational curricula that advocate the use of active learning methods (Gómez et al., 2021).

Thus, some previous studies have highlighted the importance of analyzing the teaching methods and strategies used in the teaching process in order to understand the level of student satisfaction with the training they receive (Chaparro & Ruiz, 2022). In this sense, recent studies have focused on knowing the ultimate value of indicators such as motivation, satisfaction and perceived learning in the opinion of the participating students to evaluate the suitability of a training plan, as well as the advisability of incorporating changes or possible improvements (Alqurashi, 2019).

Similarly, other works show the potential of implementing gamified training programs for the learning of historical contents in Primary Education. Thus, the results provided by Martínez-Hita (2022) show significantly higher learning compared to the academic results obtained by the students in the control group. Likewise, several studies confirm the teacher's need to adapt the gamified practice to the students' characteristics and subject contents (Sailer et al., 2017; Chapman & Rich, 2018). Also noteworthy are the studies that have revealed pedagogical benefits for teachers in initial training at the university stage (Urh et al., 2015; Da Rocha et al., 2016), which justifies its implementation in higher education processes.

Regarding the implementation of the Flipped-Classroom methodology, it is worth noting how this pedagogical approach has become a viable alternative in training processes (Vaughan, 2014) since it allows greater student activity by transmitting conceptual knowledge through the viewing of videos at home and, particularly, through practical work in the classroom (Abeysekera & Dawson, 2015). Research into their educational effectiveness is rarer (O'Flaherty & Phillips, 2015), although a sufficient number of them have demonstrated the benefits of implementing this methodology (Gilboy et al., 2015; Steen-Utheim & Foldnes, 2018). We should not ignore the studies that point to certain disadvantages in using this methodology, mainly subordinated to the students' daily classroom activities (Akçayir & Akçayir, 2018). However, Cai et al. (2019) noted that its success lies in proper teacher planning in terms of content, ease of use, and access to materials that can be meaningful for learning.

In this theoretical context and, specifically, being teachers of teachers ourselves, we begin with the motivation of preparing our students for their future profession as teachers, implementing a training program that incorporates active teaching methodologies to teach Social Sciences in Primary Education. The training program developed over three months was structured in the two principal methodologies used in educational contexts: Gamification and Flipped Classroom. This study notes the scientific results about the students' perceptions after finishing the program.

RESEARCH DESIGN

Research Objectives

The main objective of this research is to evaluate the impact of a training program on active methodologies for teaching Social Sciences in Primary Education. This main objective is further specified in other specific objectives such as:

- SO1. To know the opinions and conceptions of teachers in initial training on the use of active methodologies for teaching Social Sciences.
- SO2. To detect possible differences, according to gender, between the opinions of future teachers.
- SO3. To identify changes in the conceptions and opinions of teachers in training on the use of active methodologies after completing the training program.

Approach and Methodology

The present study responds to an evaluative investigation of a training program on active methodologies based on two fundamental pillars: gamification and flipped classroom. By connecting to a digital platform (Google classroom), the participants had individual access to the different materials, resources and activities proposed in the training program. The course was based on watching videos, reading texts and completing challenges at the end of each topic. The training was developed over a period of three months, dedicating approximately ten hours of training and having as final delivery the development of an intervention proposal that included contents, materials and resources seen during the training plan.

The data collection and analysis process sought a greater understanding of the teaching and learning process and has been carried out with a mixed approach, which includes the application of quantitative (questionnaires) and qualitative (focus groups) research instruments (Rodríguez-Medina and Rubia Avi, 2021). Initially, the training participants answered an initial questionnaire testing their knowledge of active learning methodologies for teaching Social Sciences (pretest). Students' participation and interests in the program's contents have been monitored during the process. Lastly, a group discussion was held with the participating students to gather qualitative information on the training process implemented.

Participants

The participants comprised the third-year students of the Primary Education Degree of the University of Almeria, enrolled in the subject Didactics of Social Sciences II (n=148). In terms of gender distribution, 63.5% of the participants are women, and 36.5% are men. Most students are under 23 years of age (77.7%) but with some previous teaching experience. Indeed, only 25% stated that they had no previous experience, while 47.1% stated that they had experience in formal education, and 28% reported experience in non-formal education or support roles in formal education.

Information Collection Instrument

Quantitative data were collected utilizing a questionnaire (Appendix 1) divided into four blocks and created from questionnaires validated in previous research on the use of active methodologies and their use in the teaching of Social Sciences.

The first block focused on the conceptions of active methodologies. To this end, the validated questionnaire Opiniones y Concepciones Docentes hacia la Utilización de Metodologías Docentes Activas (OCDUMA) (Opinions and Teaching Conceptions towards the Use of Active Teaching Methodologies, hereinafter, OCDUMA) was replicated. This instrument, designed to analyze the conceptions, opinions and perceptions of teachers of active methodologies (Arias & Rodríguez, 2020), is divided into five factors:

- Improvement of teaching (Items 1 to 8).
- Reluctance to use (Items 9 to 11).
- Spaces and resources (Items 12 to 13).
- Limiting factors (Items 14 to 16).
- Training in active methods (Items 17 to 18).

The other three blocks specifically focused on Social Science Teaching: Methodologies and Strategies; Materials and Resources; and Evaluation. The items of both blocks have been elaborated ad hoc from the instruments used in previous research in the field of knowledge (Gómez et al., 2020b).

The reliability of each of the blocks of the questionnaire was calculated using Cronbach's alpha test (Table 1). In three of the blocks, the test result was higher than 0.7, considered an acceptable value; in the Materials and resources block, the result was higher than 8, considered good (Frías-Navarro, 2020).

Table 1. Reliability of the questionnaire

Block	Items	Cronbach's alpha
Opinions and conceptions of teachers towards the use of active methodologies.	18	0.726
Methodologies and strategies for teaching social sciences.	8	0.728
Materials and resources for teaching the social sciences	16	0.860
Social Science Education and Assessment	8	0.734

The quantitative data collection was completed with a focus group in which nine students who had completed the training program participated. These students were selected by deliberate sampling based on their active participation during the classes and their commitment to the training developed (Barbour, 2007). Using five open questions (Table 2), the group was encouraged to engage in debate and discussion, thus contributing their opinions and enriching the discussion with their peers.

Similarly, discussion elements such as vignettes or examples were incorporated into the group to force the students to position themselves on the usefulness of ICT and the concept of innovation in relation to active methodologies. Data was collected from the focus group employing a recording, and a note-taking process was carried out in which the most salient features of the group dynamics and our impressions of the participants' comments were collected.

Table 2. List of open-ended questions from the focus group

Question	Statement
1	What do you consider to be active learning methodologies?
2	Has your opinion about these methodologies changed, and how useful has the training plan been in your learning?
3	Could you tell us the strengths and weaknesses of Flipped Classroom and Gamification?
4	What are the possibilities of these active methodologies for teaching Social Sciences?
5	Do you think you will use these methodologies in the future?

Procedure and Data Analysis

The quantitative analysis of the data was carried out with the statistical program SPSS v27.0 which, in this research, has allowed us to develop an analytical process at a descriptive level in order to know the conceptions and interests of future teachers regarding the use of active methodologies. An inferential study was also conducted to identify significant differences in students' responses grouped by gender and age.

The interventions of the focus group were coded following the codes established in the previous analysis to analyze the information extracted (Sáiz et al., 2019). The research team members then discussed the key ideas, linking them to students' opinions. From this work, the main contributions of the students are presented, enriching the quantitative work and providing the quality details that allow improving the program, as well as the training of future teachers.

RESULTS

Concerning the first subjective aspect of the research, aimed at finding out the conceptions and opinions of future teachers on the use of active methodologies, the results show that these methodologies are valued very positively. Within block 1 of the questionnaire used, related to the 18 items that make up the OCDUMA instrument, the results of factor 1, focused on measuring improvements in the teaching and learning processes, show that 90% of future teachers indicate that they "agree" or "strongly agree" with the improvement proposal linked to active methodologies, as can be seen in the first seven items (Figure 1).

In terms of reluctance, future teachers consider that fear of change is shown to be the most significant cause of not using active methodologies (91.2% of those surveyed "agree" or "totally agree"), followed by lack of motivation (89.2%) and the aging of the teaching staff (64.8%).

However, these are not the only difficulties pointed out by future teachers. The results of Factor 3, which focused on resources, and Factor 5, which is dedicated to training, show the lowest values given by future teachers, all below 2.5 mean and mode, with a median equal to 2. These results indicate that future teachers believe there is a critical lack of resources to develop educational proposals with active methodologies and that the training received is very low for the implementation of these proposals. Furthermore, future teachers point to the curriculum, bureaucracy, and increased workload as the most limiting factors for developing active methodologies (Appendix 2).

Figure 1. Block 1. OCDUMA Questionnaire. Concepts and opinions

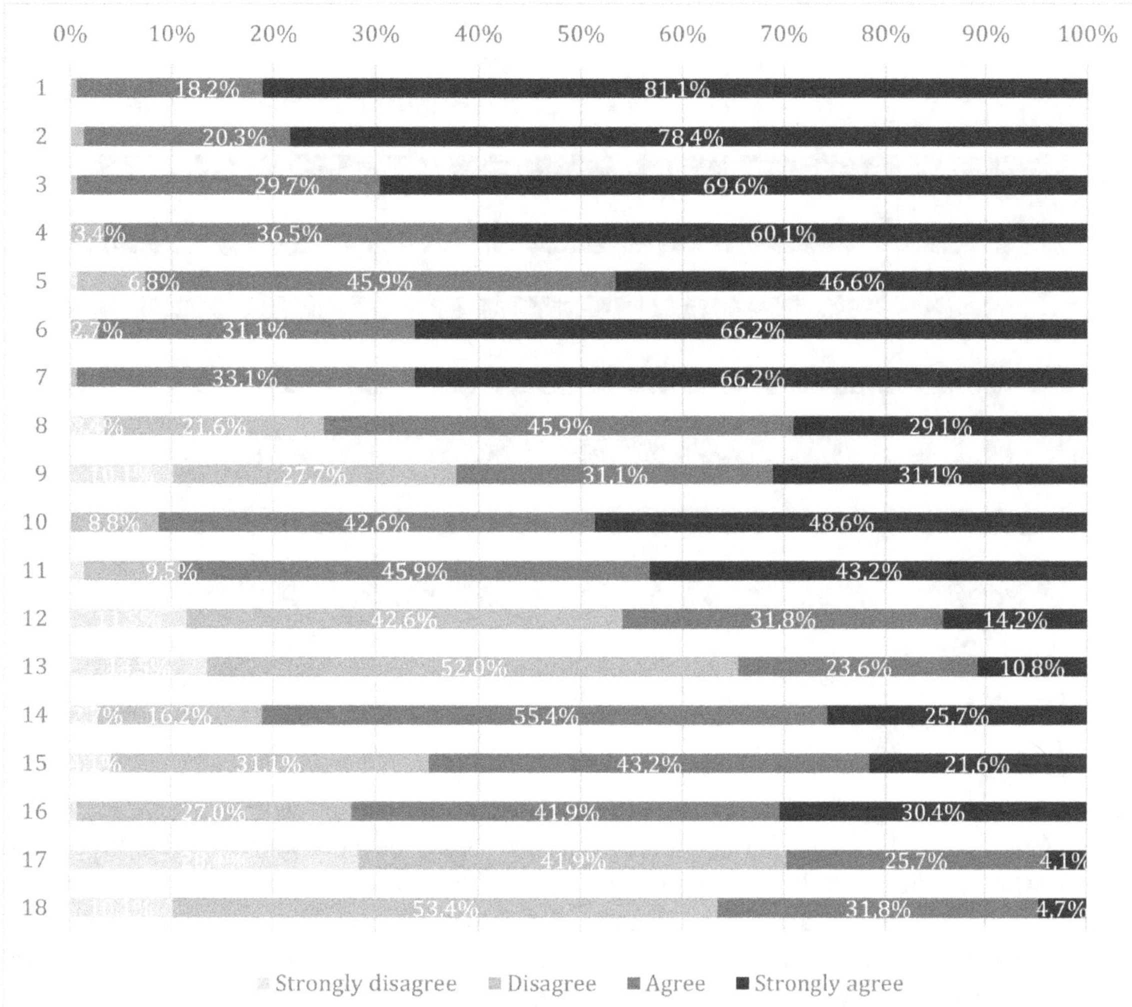

In response to the second specific objective of the research, using the comparison of means for independent samples (t), significant differences were found according to the gender of the participants. In the first seven items, women show higher average scores. However, these differences are statistically significant ($p<0.05$) in the first two items as it pertains to Item 1 (*the use of active methodologies enhances students' knowledge, processes and attitudes*), Item 2 (*active methodologies enhance students' competencies*), and Items 6 and 7, (*Training in active methodologies is necessary to generate methodological change,* and *The development of active methodologies requires teacher coordination)* (Appendix 2).

Regarding the descriptive items in block 2 of the questionnaire, the didactic strategies most highly valued by future teachers involve using the reality close to the students, leaving the classroom (Item 23) and using key current topics (Item 21). On the other hand, it is worth noting the low value given by students to the textbook and the teacher's explanation (Item 19). Indeed, 68.9% of the participants revealed that this didactic strategy is "not adequate" or "not at all adequate" (Figure 2).

Figure 2. Block 2. OCDUMA Questionnaire. Didactic strategies

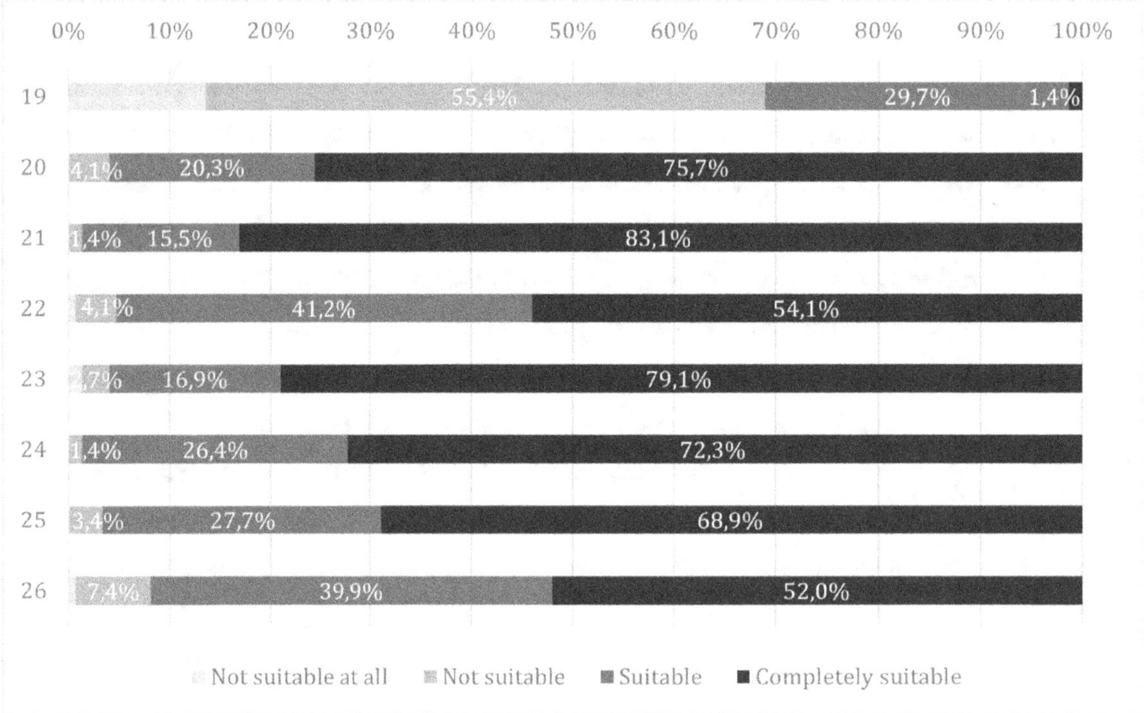

However, there are significant differences ($p<0.05$) between men and women (Table 3), with men considering the teacher's explanation supported by the textbook to be more valuable (Item 19) compared to women, who rate the use of key current topics (Item 21) higher, Service-Learning (Item 25), going out of the classroom (Item 23) and researching social problems (Item 22).

As for resources and materials, as shown in Figure 3, the most valued, considered as "adequate" or "totally adequate" by more than 90% of the participants, were the local and regional heritage sites (Item 39), museums (Item 33) and oral sources (Item 30). At the opposite extreme, we find the textbook (Item 27), valued by 74.3% of the participants as "not at all adequate" or "not adequate," followed by the teacher's notes (Item 32).

In relation to teaching resources and materials, prospective teachers also show divergences of opinion according to gender. We observed, for example, that the evaluation of the textbook (Item 27) as a resource is significantly different between men and women ($t=2.108$; $p<0.05$), the former evaluating it better as didactic material. Divergent responses according to gender are also observed in the use of the written and digital press (Item 31), a resource that women consider more appropriate for Primary Education classrooms ($t=2.408$; $p<0.05$) than men.

The evaluation approaches best valued by future teachers are historical empathy (Item 47), linked to the competence of historical perspective, and research on local environments (Item 48), linked to the ethical dimension of social sciences. The worst rated resources are the essays and questions on historical processes (Item 45) and the objective tests (Item 50). Thus, the graph (Figure 4) shows that assessments focused on active processes are considered much more adequate than tests focused on diagnosing memorized knowledge in the Social Sciences.

Table 3. Block 2. OCDUMA Questionnaire. Didactic strategies (gender differences)

Item	Gender	X	t	Sig** p≤0.05
Item 19	Women	2,04	-3,636	0,000**
	Men	2,44		
	Total	2,19		
Item 20	Women	3,74	0,853	0,395
	Men	3,67		
	Total	3,72		
Item 21	Women	3,88	2,320	0,023**
	Men	3,70		
	Total	3,82		
Item 22	Women	3,61	3,248	0,001**
	Men	3,28		
	Total	3,49		
Item 23	Women	3,83	2,412	0,018**
	Men	3,57		
	Total	3,74		
Item 24	Women	3,76	1,470	0,145
	Men	3,63		
	Total	3,71		
Item 25	Women	3,76	2,847	0,005**
	Men	3,48		
	Total	3,66		
Item 26	Women	3,48	1,124	0,263
	Men	3,35		
	Total	3,42		

Significant differences were found between men and women linked to the evaluation approach, consistent with the results obtained on strategies and resources. Males consider it significantly more adequate to evaluate knowledge about facts (t=-1.990) and historical processes (t=-2.738), while females consider it significantly more adequate to evaluate social explanation and causal reasoning (t=2.429).

The students' interventions enrich these quantitative data in the discussion group, which allowed us to verify the third sub-objective of the research, whether there have been changes in the conceptions of the students participating in this training program. It should be noted that, initially, the students, when questioned about the definition of active learning methodologies, did not articulate any answer that could be considered concise or clear. The students pointed out characteristics with which they identified active methodologies, listing examples of what, in their opinion, could be considered an active methodology. However, none of the participants presented a clear definition of active methodology that would allow establishing a framework or reference to which to link the term.

Figure 3. Block 2. OCDUMA Questionnaire. Resources and materials

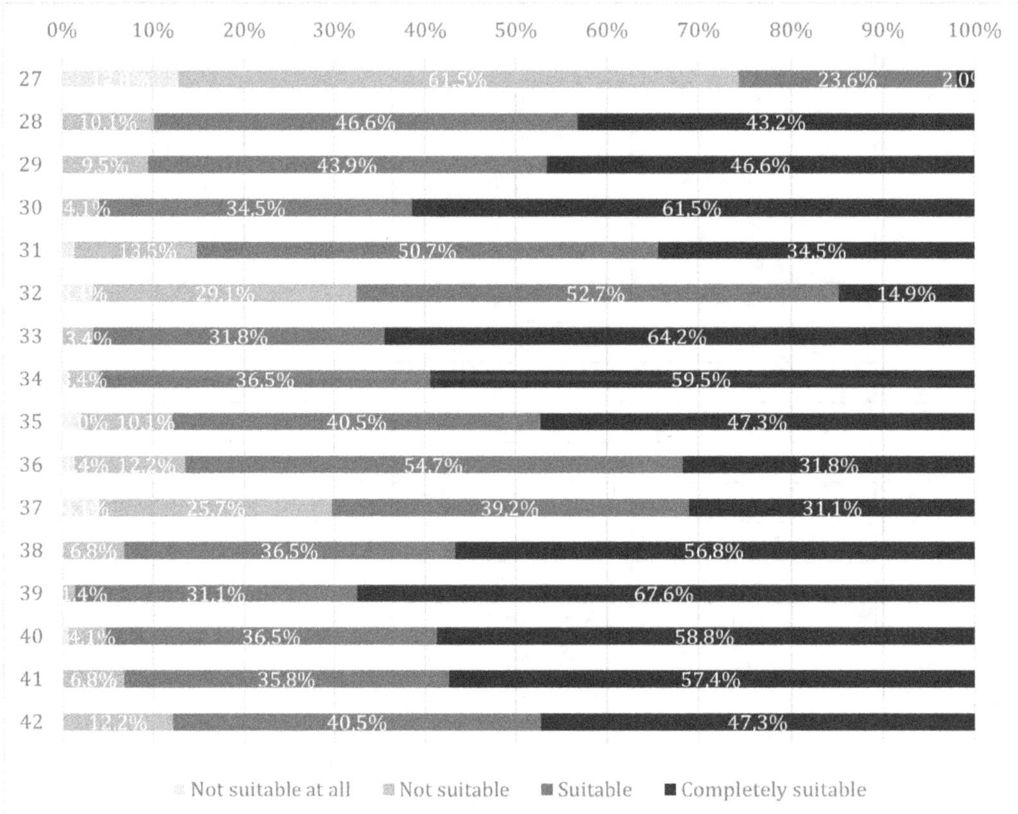

Figure 4. Block 4. OCDUMA Questionnaire. Evaluation approaches

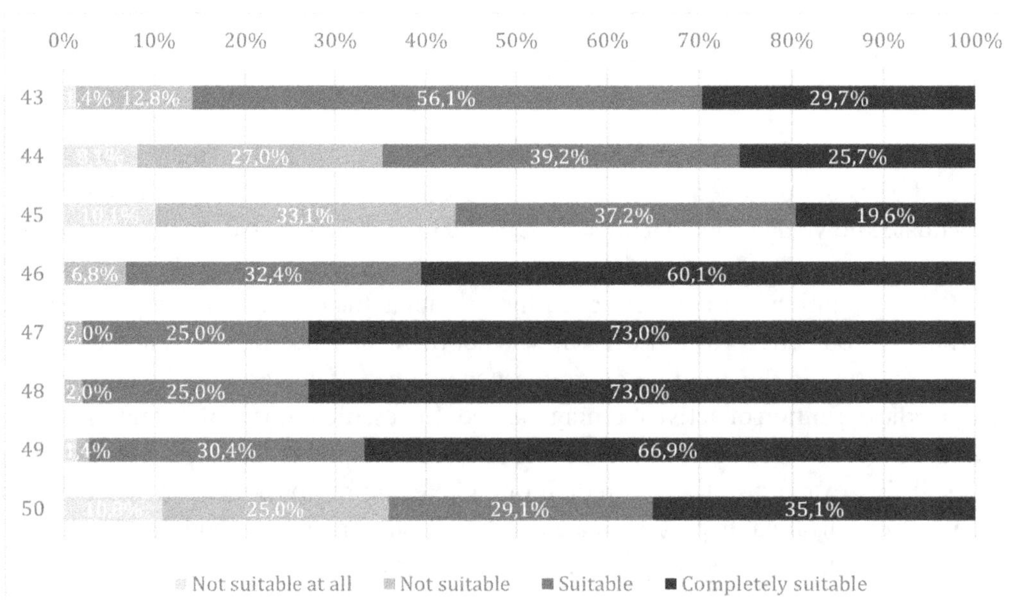

The students considered that the most crucial thing should be the implementation of the different teaching and learning strategies, with several of the participants emphasizing the importance of "knowing how to develop an active methodology in the classroom." In fact, the participants pointed out that they wanted to have direct, hands-on experience implementing these strategies or, in its absence, replace it by visualizing "an experience in primary education where these strategies are used." Students wanted to observe how a teacher would "implement that methodology" rather than hear or read about how it should be put into practice.

This situation may explain why the students have carried out, within the framework of the training plan developed, some "very idyllic case studies." This statement reveals the students' lack of experience with these methodologies, as it confirms the absence of references and guidelines that bring them closer to viable, implementable and realistic designs.

In this analytical framework, we consider it relevant to highlight that the principal affirmation of the group resided in the unanimous response regarding the future use of active methodologies in the classroom. The nine participants of the group affirmed that implementing these methodologies is fundamental for the teaching of Social Sciences, mainly because these methodologies allow students to act, participate and intervene in the teaching-learning processes, a recurrent demand in current educational precepts.

Regarding Social Sciences, the students linked the use of active methodologies with the possibility of "opening the point of view, opening the mind" in Primary Education and making it possible for students to "question things." In this sense, the discussion group affirmed that "Social Sciences can only be taught through an active learning methodology." However, the students participating in the focus group shared that "not everything is valid; there are limits" to implementing didactic strategies in the classroom.

Furthermore, participants in the discussion group pointed out the existence of teachers in initial training who, despite showing interest in the use of active methodologies in university classrooms, privately stated their intention to reject the use of such methodologies in the classroom because they do not find the necessary motivation to implement them or, simply because they preferred to opt for "the easy thing to do."

Paying particular attention to the strategies presented in the training plan, the students participating in the group agreed with the importance of linking the Didactics of Social Sciences with the Service-Learning method and inquiry projects. In fact, they affirmed that "the ones we have not seen [methodologies] are even more important than the ones we have worked on." In this regard, it should be noted that the participants identified the enormous potential of the methods worked in the classroom with an interdisciplinary teaching approach. Nonetheless, despite their correct assessment, the students demanded training in other methodologies since they consider them more appropriate for teaching the social and cultural environment.

Similarly, the focus group continued with the qualitative analysis and identified specific characteristics and situations in a SWOT matrix (Table 4).

As seen in the SWOT matrix, the students claimed the need for more training while also recognizing the need to invest their time when designing a didactic action with these methodologies as a weakness. In addition, students underlined as a threat the problems observed, especially during their school internships, related to teacher coordination when carrying out these strategies in the classroom. As a strength, in addition to those traditionally linked to the implementation of active methodologies with students, the participants highlighted the possibilities they offer for improving and facilitating attention to diversity. Finally, as an opportunity, the students highlighted the potential they offer for interdisciplinary work with students in different subjects.

Table 4. SWOT matrix resulting from the focus group

WEAKNESSES	THREATS
1. Requires more preparation time. 2. Lack of training. 3. They cannot always be adapted to meet diversity. 4. Parents are not adequately informed.	1. The assessment system. 2. Coordination of the teaching team. 3. Teachers using the textbook as the primary resource. 4. Reluctance of families to accept these methodologies.
1. Supports student diversity outreach. 2. The fear of rote learning is lost. 3. It is a methodology that connects students with their immediate reality.	1. The number of resources and applications is increasing every day. 2. Teaching interdisciplinary content.
STRENGTHS	**OPPORTUNITIES**

DISCUSSION

The results achieved in this research are similar to those obtained from the OCDUMA questionnaire on more than twelve thousand active teachers (Arias & Rodriguez, 2020); that is, teachers in training consider active learning methodologies to be highly positive (Arias & Rodríguez, 2020; Campillo & Miralles, 2022). Thus, the teaching and learning of social knowledge should be done from active methodological approaches, involving students in the construction of their own knowledge and the interpretation of their reality from a critical perspective (Gómez et al., 2018).

Undoubtedly, the ultimate goal must be one in which students are aware that they can participate in society and transform it. The need to change the teaching-learning processes from within is reflected in the students' opinions, aware that the experiences lived also determine their future actions (Estepa, 2017). Given this situation, students demand more and better training in these methodologies, as seen in recent studies (Chaparro-Sainz et al., 2022; Darouech& Felices, 2021).

Despite the interest shown in these strategies, in line with what has been observed in other studies (Blasco-Serrano et al., 2018), the discussion group students insisted on the suitability of using other active methodologies such as Service-Learning or inquiry to teach Social Science content in compulsory stages. Thus, despite the motivational nature linked to methodologies such as gamification or flipped-classroom (Da Rocha et al., 2016; Gómez et al., 2021), with respect to teaching social content, students showed greater interest in other methodological alternatives. A process already pointed out by Hanus and Fox (2015) when they pointed out the importance of thinking about the educational objective above the enthusiasm produced by the game and the competition.

It is worth noting how the student body perceived the possibility of these methodologies being adapted to the student body's characteristics are in accord with the scientific results of several studies (Sailer et al., 2017; Chapman & Rich, 2018). This fundamental adaptability becomes even more critical when referring to students with specific educational needs. In this line, the possibility offered by active methodologies in different educational contexts and situations justifies their implementation in Higher Education formative processes, as already pointed out by some research (Urh et al., 2015; Da Rocha et al., 2016).

Finally, as observed in other studies (Gómez et al., 2020b; Chaparro-Sainz et al., 2022), there are significant differences associated with the gender of the participants detected in this study. Thus, the differences between women and men always point in the same direction. Women place a higher value on active strategies, resources and approaches to assessment focused on competency-based learning, while men place a higher value on closed discourse and learning with more traditional methodologies.

CONCLUSION

The main conclusion of this study is that, despite the high value given to active methodologies in the initial questionnaire by trainee teachers, the implementation of these methodologies in the classroom does not represent an added value to the teaching and learning process. Implementing these methodologies in the classroom does not add value to the teaching and learning process but rather must be appropriate to the context, the characteristics of the students, and the subject being taught.

Thus, with specific regard to the teaching of Social Sciences, certain doubts about gamification as an adequate strategy for the competent learning of Social Sciences have been raised by the trainee teachers, both in the classroom and in the discussion group. Concurrently, the same students pointed out the use of Service-Learning or inquiry as a more appropriate methodology for teaching and learning social knowledge, given that, in their opinion, it favors reflection processes to a greater extent, as well as the application of knowledge to the reality being studied for its understanding, intervention and improvement.

The above notwithstanding, it cannot be ignored that future teachers link the term active methodologies with a change and an opportunity, although they demand more and better training in their application. In this sense, the students have valued the initiative very positively, as it is innovative and adapts to their interests. However, they state that this experience could be improved by working on real cases that show the reality of implementing these strategies in primary education contexts. Likewise, the participants have considered that the aspects that make it difficult to put these methodologies into practice can be overcome if some initial orientation experiences are included in their university training. These results undoubtedly invite reflection and the reinforcement of training actions in this line in the context of Higher Education.

However, as university teachers and trainers of future teachers, we also point out that these actions should not only focus on practice. It is also necessary to improve theoretical training, focusing on the meaning and definition of active methodologies so that they do not become a mere claim for their innovative or playful component. Likewise, we have found that students identify this concept or term (active methodologies) with very diverse processes, actions and strategies without having a precise definition of everything encapsulated when speaking of active learning methods. In their opinion, all definitions are valid unless referring to the direct transmission of knowledge by teachers or using a textbook as a sole resource. Thus, the term active methodologies can be used to identify strategies that, although innovative, such as the use of ICT, do not necessarily involve student participation in the construction of learning.

Regarding the improvement of teacher training, it has been considered that significant differences based on gender should also promote specific actions in university teaching-learning processes. In this sense, for example, when configuring work groups in particular subjects, teachers should be cautious when validating the configuration of groups formed exclusively of men since this can lead us away from the coeducation needed in educational contexts.

Finally, it is essential to highlight the learning that the program's hetero-evaluation process has had on two levels. On the one hand, the students' evaluation of the program has been recorded, allowing us to initiate a process of improvement for future courses. In addition, future teachers have participated in the process of metacognition on their learning and reflection on their teaching practice, which has an impact on the acquisition of competence that we consider key for their professional future, such as reflection on teaching action, due to the possibilities of improvement and adaptation that it offers to education professionals.

In short, as indicated at the beginning of this paper, the experience encourages further progress in training in teaching competencies that will bring about a fundamental transformation in teaching processes and contribute, in turn, to the development of competencies in Primary Education. If future teachers do not receive adequate training, it will be difficult to integrate methodologies in the classroom that contribute to the necessary preparation of children and the construction of critical and committed citizenship. Therefore, from Higher Education and as trainers of trainers, we have the challenge of making change possible and improving our university students' preparation.

ACKNOWLEDGMENT

This research was supported by the Spanish Ministry for Science and Innovation [grant number PID2020-113453RB-I00] funded by MCIN/AEI/10.13039/501100011033.

REFERENCES

Abeysekera, L., & Dawson, P. (2015). Motivation and cognitive load in the flipped classroom: Definition, rationale and a call for research. *Higher Education Research & Development, 34*(1), 1–14. doi:10.1080/07294360.2014.934336

Akçayir, G., & Akçayir, M. (2018). The flipped classroom: A review of its advantages and challenges. *Computers & Education, 126*, 334–345. doi:10.1016/j.compedu.2018.07.021

Alqurashi, E. (2019). Predicting student satisfaction and perceived learning within online learning environments. *Distance Education, 40*(1), 133–148. doi:10.1080/01587919.2018.1553562

Arias, A. R., & Rodríguez, A. (2020). Validación de la escala OCDUMA para analizar las concepciones, opiniones y percepciones del profesorado hacia las metodologías activas. *Aula abierta, 49*(4), 403-412. doi:10.17811/rifie.49.4.2020.403-412

Attali, Y., & Arieli-Attali, M. (2015). Gamification in assessment: Do points affect test performance? *Computers & Education, 83*, 57–63. doi:10.1016/j.compedu.2014.12.012

Barbour, R. (2007). *Los grupos de discusión en Investigación Cualitativa*. Morata.

Blasco-Serrano, A. C., Lorenzo, J., & Sarsa, J. (2018). Percepción de los estudiantes al invertir la clase mediante el uso de redes sociales y sistemas de respuesta inmediata. *RED. Revista de Educación a Distancia, 57*(6), 1-19. https://revistas.um.es/red/article/view/327391

Blömeke, S., Hsieh, F., Kaiser, G., & Schmidt, W. (2014). *International Perspectives on Teacher Knowledge, Beliefs and Opportunities to Learn*. Springer. doi:10.1007/978-94-007-6437-8

Cai, J., Yang, H. H., Gong, D., MacLeod, J., & Zhu, S. (2019). Understanding the continued use of flipped classroom instruction: A personal beliefs model in Chinese higher education. *Journal of Computing in Higher Education, 31*(1), 137–155. doi:10.100712528-018-9196-y

Campillo, J. M., & Miralles, P. (2022). Impact of the flipped classroom model on democratic education of student teachers in Spain. *Education, Citizenship and Social Justice*, 1–17. doi:10.1177/17461979221084111

Chaparro, A., & García, C. R. (Coords.). (2022). *Prácticas docentes universitarias en Didáctica de las Ciencias Sociales: investigaciones y experiencias*. Dykinson.

Chaparro-Sainz, Á., Méndez, R., & Felices-De la Fuente, M. M. (2022). El patrimonio en las aulas. Un estudio en prospectiva con estudiantes del Grado en Educación Primaria. *Contextos educativos. Review of Education*, *29*(29), 137–154. doi:10.18172/con.4950

Chapman, J. R., & Rich, P. J. (2018). Does educational gamification improve students' motivation? If so, which game elements work best? *Journal of Education for Business*, *93*(7), 315–322. doi:10.1080/08832323.2018.1490687

Coll, V., Pardo, C., & Pérez, P. J. (2018). Métodos de enseñanza-aprendizaje y su efecto en el desarrollo profesional y competencial de los egresados. *Cultura y Educación*, *30*(3), 556–583. doi:10.1080/11356405.2018.1494773

Da Rocha, L., Sandro, A., & De Melho, I. (2016). Effectiveness of gamification in the engagement of students. *Journal of Computer in Human Behavior*, *58*, 48–63. doi:10.1016/j.chb.2015.11.021

Darouech, S., & Felices, M. M. (2021). La formación inicial en Didáctica de las Ciencias Sociales según el alumnado egresado. *Didáctica de las Ciencias Experimentales y Sociales*, *41*, 57–72. doi:10.7203/dces.41.21294

De Marcos, L., García-López, E., & García-Cabot, A. (2016). On the effectiveness of game-like and social approaches in learning: Comparing educational gaming, gamification & social networking. *Computer Education*, *95*, 99–113. doi:10.1016/j.compedu.2015.12.008

Durrani, U. K., Al Naymat, G., Ayoubi, R. A., Kamal, M. M., & Hussain, H. (2022). Gamified flipped classroom versus traditional classroom learning: Which approach is more efficient in business education? *International Journal of Management Education*, *20*(1), 1–10. doi:10.1016/j.ijme.2021.100595

Estepa, J. (2017). *Otra didáctica de la historia para otra escuela. Lección inaugural del curso 2017-2018*. Universidad de Huelva. http://www.ub.edu/histodidactica/images/documentos/pdf/estepa%20libro.pdf

Felices-De la Fuente, M. M., & Chaparro-Sainz, Á. (2021). Opinions of Future Teachers on Training in Social Sciences Didactics. *Frontiers in Education*, *6*, 1–13. https://www.frontiersin.org/articles/10.3389/feduc.2021.803289/full. doi:10.3389/feduc.2021.803289

Gilboy, M. B., Heinerichs, S., & Pazzaglia, G. (2015). Enhancing student engagement using the flipped classroom. *Journal of Nutrition Education and Behavior*, *47*(1), 109–114. doi:10.1016/j.jneb.2014.08.008 PMID:25262529

Gómez, C. J., Chaparro, Á., Felices, M. M., & Cózar, R. (2020b). Estrategias metodológicas y uso de recursos digitales para la enseñanza de la historia: análisis de recuerdos y opiniones del profesorado en formación inicial. *Aula abierta*, *49*(1), 65-74. doi:10.17811/rifie.49.1.2020.65-74

Gómez, C. J., Ortuño, J., & Miralles, P. (2018). *Enseñar ciencias sociales con métodos activos de aprendizaje: reflexiones y propuestas a través de la indagación*. Octaedro.

Gómez, C. J., Rodríguez, J., Miralles, P., & Arias, V. (2021). Effects of a teacher training program on the motivation and satisfaction of history secondary students. *Revista de Psicodidáctica*, *26*(1), 45–52. doi:10.1016/j.psicoe.2020.08.001

Gómez, C. J., Rodríguez-Medina, J., Chaparro, Á., & Felices, M. M. (2022). Enseñar la historia de Europa desde métodos activos y compromiso cívico. Diseño y validación de una propuesta. In S. Alonso-García, G. Gómez, C. Rodríguez & M. Ramos (Coords.), La educación globalizada: experiencias e investigaciones (pp. 200-210). Dykinson.

Gómez-Carrasco, C. J., Monteagudo-Fernández, J., Moreno-Vera, J. R., & Sainz, M. (2019). Effects of a Gamification and Flipped-Classroom Program for Teachers in Training on Motivation and Learning Perception. *Education Sciences*, *9*(4), 1–15. doi:10.3390/educsci9040299

Gómez-Carrasco, C. J., Monteagudo-Fernández, J., Moreno-Vera, J. R., & Sainz, M. (2020a). Evaluation of a gamification and flipped-classroom program used in teacher training: Perception of learning and outcome. *PLoS One*, *15*(10), 1–15. doi:10.1371/journal.pone.0241892 PMID:33119687

González, G., & Skultety, L. (2018). Teacher learning in a combined professional development intervention. *Teaching and Teacher Education*, *71*, 341–354. doi:10.1016/j.tate.2018.02.003

Hakak, S., Fazmidar, N., Noor, M., Nizam, M., Affal, H., Hussin, M., Ahmed, M., & Imran, M. (2019). Cloud-assisted gamification for education and learning – Recent advances and challenge. *Computers & Electrical Engineering*, *74*, 22–34. doi:10.1016/j.compeleceng.2019.01.002

Han-Huey, C., Kofinas, A., & Luo, J. (2018). Enhancing student learning experience with technology-mediated gamification: An empirical study. *Computer Education*, *121*, 1–17. doi:10.1016/j.compedu.2018.01.009

Hanus, M. D., & Fox, J. (2015). Assessing the effects of gamification in the classroom: A longitudinal study on intrinsic motivation, social comparison, satisfaction, effort and academic performance. *Computers & Education*, *80*, 152–161. doi:10.1016/j.compedu.2014.08.019

Hao, Y., & Lee, K. S. (2016). Teaching in flipped classrooms: Exploring pre-service teachers' concerns. *Journal of Computer in Human Behavior*, *57*, 250–260. doi:10.1016/j.chb.2015.12.022

Hortigüela, D., Abella, V., Delgado, V., & Ausin, V. (2018). Valoración del aprendizaje obtenido en la formación inicial del profesorado en función del enfoque metodológico. *Profesorado. Revista de Currículum y Formación del Profesorado, 22*(2), 227-246. https://recyt.fecyt.es/index.php/profesorado/article/view/66372/0

León, M. J., & Crisol, E. (2011). Diseño de cuestionarios (oppumaugr y opeumaugr): la opinión y la percepción del profesorado y los estudiantes sobre el uso de las metodologías activas en la universidad. *Profesorado. Revista de currículum y formación del profesorado, 15*(2), 271-298. https://recyt.fecyt.es/index.php/profesorado/article/view/43508

Lévesque, S. G., & Zanazanian, P. (2015). Developing Historical Consciousness and a Community of History Practitioners: A Survey of Prospective History Teachers Across Canada. *McGill Journal of Education*, *50*(2-3), 389–412. doi:10.7202/1036438ar

Maloy, J., Fries, L., Laski, L., & Ramírez, G. (2019). Seductive details in the flipped classroom: The impact of interesting but educationally irrelevant information on student learning and motivation. *CBE Life Sciences Education*, *18*(3), 1–10. doi:10.1187/cbe.19-01-0004 PMID:31469621

Martínez-Hita, M. (2022). *El pensamiento histórico en Educación Primaria: diseño y evaluación de un programa de intervención gamificado*. PhD. Universidad de Murcia. https://digitum.um.es/digitum/handle/10201/116267

Miralles, P., Gómez, C. J., & Rodríguez, R. (2017). Patrimonio, competencias históricas y metodologías activas de aprendizaje. Un análisis de las opiniones de los docentes en formación en España e Inglaterra. *Estudios Pedagógicos (Valdivia)*, *43*(4), 161–184. doi:10.4067/S0718-07052017000400009

Monteagudo, J., Gómez, C. J., & Miralles, P. (2017). Evaluación del diseño e implementación de la metodología flipped-classroom en la formación del profesorado de ciencias sociales. *RED: Revista de Educación a Distancia*, *55*, 1–26. doi:10.6018/red/55/7

Moreno, A. J., Trujillo, J. M., & Aznar, I. (Coords.). (2021). *Metodologías activas para la enseñanza universitaria.* Graó.

Moreno-Vera, J. R., & Alvén, F. (2020). Concepts for historical and geographical thinking in Sweden's and Spain's Primary Education curricula. *Humanities & Social Sciences Communications*, *7*(1), 1–10. doi:10.105741599-020-00601-z

Moreno-Vera, J. R., Gómez-Carrasco, C. J., Monteagudo-Fernández, J., & Sainz-Gómez, M. (2021). Gamificación y flipped-classroom en la formación de Ciencias Sociales. Estudio exploratorio y validación de una escala. In M. C. Sánchez-Fuster, J. M. Campillo, & V. Navas (Eds.), *La formación del profesorado en didáctica de las ciencias sociales en el ámbito iberoamericano* (pp. 79–98). Editum.

O'Flaherty, J., & Phillips, C. (2015). The use of Flipped Classrooms in Higher Education: A Scoping Review. *The Internet and Higher Education*, *25*, 85–95. doi:10.1016/j.iheduc.2015.02.002

Oliveira, C., Lopes, J., & Spear-Swerling, L. (2019). Teachers' academic training for literacy instruction. *European Journal of Teacher Education*, *42*(3), 315–334. doi:10.1080/02619768.2019.1576627

Ordoñez, B. P., Ochoa, M. E., Erráez, J. L., León, J. L., & Espinoza, E. E. (2021). Consideraciones sobre aula invertida y gamificación en el área de ciencias sociales. *Revista Universidad y Sociedad, 13*(3), 497-504. https://rus.ucf.edu.cu/index.php/rus/index

Parra, D., & Fuertes, C. (Coords.). (2019). *Reinterpretar la tradición, transformar las prácticas: Ciencias Sociales para una educación crítica*. Tirant Lo Blanch.

Raya, E., & Navaridas, F. (2021). Formación para la competencia docente en la educación del siglo XXI. In E. Raya & F. Navaridas (Coords.), *Formación docente y desarrollo de competencias en el profesorado. Hacia un modelo para la calidad educativa* (pp. 23-26). Wolters Kluwer.

Rodríguez-Medina, J., & Rubia, B. (2021). Mixed methods in education research. In C. Gómez, P. Miralles, & R. López (Coords.), *Handbook of research on education in History and Geography* (pp. 35-52). Peter Lang.

Ruiz, M. C., Martínez-Jiménez, R., Licerán-Gutiérrez, A., & García-Martía, E. (2022). Students' attitude: Key to understanding the improvement of their academic RESULTS in a flipped classroom environment. *International Journal of Management Education*, *20*(2), 1–11. doi:10.1016/j.ijme.2022.100635

Sailer, M., Hense, J. U., Mayr, S. K., & Mandl, H. (2017). How gamification motivates: An experimental study of the effects of specific game design elements on psychological need satisfaction. *Journal of Computer in Human Behavior*, *69*, 371–380. doi:10.1016/j.chb.2016.12.033

Sáiz, M. C., Escolar, M. C., & Rodríguez-Medina, J. (2019). *Investigación cualitativa: aplicación de métodos mixtos y de técnicas de minería de datos*. Universidad de Burgos.

Sánchez-Fuster, M. C. (2017). *Evaluación de los recursos utilizados en Ciencias Sociales, Geografía e Historia*. PhD, Universidad de Murcia. https://digitum.um.es/digitum/handle/10201/54567

Shibukawa, S., & Taguchi, M. (2019). Exploring the difficulty on students' preparation and the effective instruction in the flipped classroom. A case study in a physiology class. *Journal of Computing in Higher Education*, *31*(2), 311–339. doi:10.100712528-019-09220-3

Souto, X. M., & García-Monteagudo, D. (2019). Conocer las rutinas para innovar en la geografía escolar. *Revista de Geografía Norte Grande*, *74*(74), 207–228. doi:10.4067/S0718-34022019000300207

Steen-Utheim, A. T., & Foldnes, N. (2018). A qualitative investigation of student engagement in a flipped classroom. *Teaching in Higher Education*, *23*(3), 307–324. doi:10.1080/13562517.2017.1379481

Urh, M., Vukovic, G., Jereb, E., & Pintar, R. (2015). The model for introduction of gamification into e-learning in higher education. *Procedia: Social and Behavioral Sciences*, *197*, 388–397. doi:10.1016/j.sbspro.2015.07.154

VanSledright, B. A. (2014). *Assessing Historical Thinking and Understanding. Innovation Design for New Standards*. Routledge.

Vaughan, M. (2014). Flipping the learning: An investigation into the use of the flipped classroom model in an introductory teaching course. *Education Research and Perspectives*, *41*(1), 25–41. https://www.erpjournal.net/

Yilmaz, R. (2017). Exploring the role of e-learning readiness on student satisfaction and motivation in flipped classroom. *Journal of Computer in Human Behavior*, *70*, 251–260. doi:10.1016/j.chb.2016.12.085

KEY TERMS AND DEFINITIONS

Active Learning Methods: Methods in which the teacher encourages students to take a leading role in their learning, through responsible participation, reflection in problem solving, creative activity and group work.

Flipped Classroom: Pedagogical model that changes the traditional learning system, since students study and prepare lessons outside of class and, later, in the classroom they do homework, interact and carry out more participatory activities.

Focus Groups: Qualitative research technique used to collect data through the interaction of a group made up of a small number of carefully selected people who discuss a given topic.

Gamification: Learning technique that transfers the mechanics of games to the educational field in order to achieve better results in terms of acquiring knowledge, improving some skill, or rewarding specific actions.

Inquiry Learning: Teaching methodology through which students must find solutions to a problem situation from a research process. This methodology focuses on tackling problems and cooperative work.

Metacognition: People's ability to reflect on their thought processes and the way they learn, becoming aware of their own cognition and acquired learning.

Service-Learning: Methodology that combines the academic curriculum with community service to enrich the educational experience, train citizenship, encourage social and civic participation throughout life, and strengthen the common good of communities.

APPENDIX 1

Table 5. OCDUMA questionnaire

Block 1. OCDUMA	
1	The use of active methodologies enhances students' knowledge, processes and attitudes.
2	Active methodologies enhance students' skills (autonomy, use of ICT, metacognition, entrepreneurship, social skills, etc.).
3	Active methodologies enhance and increase teacher-student interaction
4	The use of active methodologies promotes interdisciplinary content.
5	Active methodologies imply comprehensive evaluation models with the students.
6	Training in active methodologies is necessary to generate methodological change.
7	The development of active methodologies requires the coordination of the teaching staff.
8	Active methodologies focus on student learning rather than on the teaching process of the teacher.
9	Teacher aging hinders the implementation of active methodologies.
10	Fear of change explains the low use of active methodologies
11	Lack of motivation due to the absence of incentives slows down the use of active methodologies.
12	Teaching spaces in the centers facilitate the use of active methodologies.
13	The centers have the necessary resources to implement active methodologies.
14	The curriculum and study plans hinder the implementation of active methodologies.
15	External testing hinders the implementation of active methodologies.
16	The use of active methodologies implies more bureaucratic and organizational work on the part of teachers.
17	The initial training in active methodologies provided by the university is adequate.
18	The training provided by teacher training centers is extensive and adequate.
Block 2. Didactic strategies.	
19	The teacher explains with textbook support.
20	Empathy strategies, simulation or role-playing, or historical perspective.
21	Use key current issues to connect past and present.
22	Investigation of specific social problems through primary sources and presentation of the results.
23	Leave the classroom to go to museums, urban spaces, natural environment, places of economic activities, or places of historical interest.
24	Directed classroom discussions on social issues
25	Interdisciplinary or Service-Learning projects that interdisciplinarily connect the social and cultural environment with citizen participation locally and globally.
26	Work and elaboration of maps, sketches and analysis tools for the knowledge of the environment.
Block 3. Resources and materials.	
27	Textbook
28	Websites with historical, social and geographical content.
29	Primary documentary sources
30	Oral sources (interviews with grandparents, relatives, neighbors...)
31	Print or digital press
32	Teacher's notes
33	Museums and other heritage interpretation sites
34	Films and documentaries on social, historical and anthropological themes...
35	Historical novels, comics and children's literature

continued on following page

Table 5. Continued

36	Articles in popular magazines
37	Video games
38	Local festivals and traditions
39	Nearby local and regional heritage
40	Virtual recreations of museums and other centers of heritage interest.
41	Applications for cell phones and tablets with historical, geographical and heritage content
42	Maps, sketches and other spatial representations
Block 4. Evaluation approaches.	
43	Exercises requiring interpretation of texts and images.
44	Short questions about historical events or characters
45	Essays and developmental questions on historical processes
46	Fieldwork (collecting information, carrying out exercises) during a visit to a museum or other place of interest.
47	Empathy, simulation or historical perspective exercises.
48	Research in local or nearby environments
49	Questions that seek social, historical explanation and causal reasoning.
50	Objective tests (silent maps, multiple-choice tests, linking dates with events...)

(Data Source: Arias & Rodríguez, 2020).

APPENDIX 2

Table 6. Block 1. OCDUMA Questionnaire. Gender analysis

Item	$\bar{x}$	Mode	Median	Min	Max	Standard deviation	Gender	$\bar{x}$	t	sig
1	3,80	4	4	2	4	0,42	Women	3,86	2,14	0,03
							Men	3,70		
2	3,77	4	4	2	4	0,45	Women	3,85	2,71	0,01
							Men	3,63		
3	3,69	4	4	2	4	0,48	Women	3,70	0,43	0,67
							Men	3,67		
4	3,57	4	4	2	4	0,56	Women	3,63	1,73	0,09
							Men	3,46		
5	3,39	4	3	1	4	0,64	Women	3,45	1,54	0,12
							Men	3,28		
6	3,64	4	4	2	4	0,54	Women	3,73	2,77	0,01
							Men	3,46		
7	3,66	4	4	2	4	0,49	Women	3,73	2,49	0,01
							Men	3,52		
8	3,01	3	3	1	4	0,80	Women	3,00	-0,13	0,89
							Men	3,02		
9	2,83	3	3	1	4	0,99	Women	2,74	-1,41	0,16
							Men	2,98		
10	3,40	4	3	2	4	0,65	Women	3,44	0,93	0,35
							Men	3,33		
11	3,31	3	3	1	4	0,70	Women	3,34	0,68	0,50
							Men	3,26		
12	2,49	2	2	1	4	0,88	Women	2,49	0,05	0,96
							Men	2,48		
13	2,32	2	2	1	4	0,84	Women	2,23	-1,60	0,11
							Men	2,46		
14	3,04	3	3	1	4	0,73	Women	3,05	0,28	0,78
							Men	3,02		
15	2,82	3	3	1	4	0,81	Women	2,85	0,53	0,60
							Men	2,78		
16	3,02	3	3	1	4	0,78	Women	3,07	1,12	0,26
							Men	2,93		
17	2,05	2	2	1	4	0,84	Women	2,07	0,42	0,68
							Men	2,02		
18	2,31	2	2	1	4	0,72	Women	2,27	-1,00	0,32
							Men	2,39		

Compilation of References

Abeysekera, L., & Dawson, P. (2015). Motivation and cognitive load in the flipped classroom: Definition, rationale and a call for research. *Higher Education Research & Development*, *34*(1), 1–14. doi:10.1080/07294360.2014.934336

Acosta Barros, L. (2010). La enseñanza-aprendizaje de la historia en bachillerato y las TIC: La introducción de la estrategia Webquest. *Clío: History and History Teaching, 36*(8), 1–10. http://clio.rediris.es/n36/didactica/lmacosta_iehcan.pdf

Acosta, L.M. (2010). La enseñanza-aprendizaje de la historia en bachillerato y las TIC: la introducción de la estrategia Webquest. *Clío. History and History Teaching, 36*.

Adams, N. E. (2015). Bloom's taxonomy of cognitive learning objectives. *Journal of the Medical Library Association: JMLA*, *103*(3), 152–153. doi:10.3163/1536-5050.103.3.010 PMID:26213509

Ahmed, A., & Sutton, M. J. (2017). Gamification, serious games, simulations, and immersive learning environments in knowledge management initiatives. *World Journal of Science, Technology and Sustainable Development*, *14*(2/3), 78–83. doi:10.1108/WJSTSD-02-2017-0005

Akçayır, G., & Akçayır, M. (2018). The flipped classroom: A review of its advantages and challenges. *Computers & Education*, *126*, 334–345. doi:10.1016/j.compedu.2018.07.021

Akhan, O. (2021). History teaching approaches preferred by Turkish and Russian history teachers. *World Journal of Education*, *11*(1), 62–74. doi:10.5430/wje.v11n1p62

Aktekin, S. (2009). Türkiye'de tarih eğitimi. In Çok Kültürlü Bir Avrupa İçin Tarih ve Sosyal Bilgiler Eğitimi. Ankara: Harf Eğitim.

Alajaji, D., & Alshwiah, A. (2021). Effect of Combining Gamification and a Scavenger Hunt on Pre-Service Teachers' Perceptions and Achievement. *Journal of Information Technology Education*, *20*, 283–308. doi:10.28945/4809

Alam, A. (2020). *Challenges and Possibilities of Online Education during Covid-19*. https://www.preprints.org/manuscript/202006.0013/v1

Alarcón-San Lucas, M., & Millán-Ibarra, A. (2021). La relación entre el uso responsable de la tecnología y el aprendizaje en los estudiantes del Subnivel Básica Media de la Escuela Leónidas Plaza. *593 Digital Publisher CEIT, 6*(1), 120-138. doi:10.33386/593dp.2021.2-1.528

Alawadhi, A., & Abu-Ayyash, E. A. S. (2021). Students' perceptions of Kahoot!: An exploratory mixed-method study in EFL undergraduate classrooms in the UAE. *Education and Information Technologies*, *26*(4), 3629–3658. doi:10.100710639-020-10425-8

Alfageme González, B., & Sánchez, P. (2002). Aprendiendo habilidades con videojuegos. *Comunicar*, *19*, 114–119.

All, A., Núñez, E. P., & Van Looy, J. (2016). Assessing the effectiveness of digital game-based learning: Best practices. *Computers & Education*, *92*, 90–103. doi:10.1016/j.compedu.2015.10.007

Alonso-García, S., Martínez-Domingo, J. A., Berral-Ortiz, B., & De la Cruz-Campos, J. C. (2021a). Gamificación en Educación Superior. Revisión de experiencias realizadas en España en los últimos años. *Hachetetepé. Revista científica de Educación y Comunicación, 23*, 1-21. . doi:10.25267/Hachetetepe.2021.i23.2205

Alonso-García, S., Rodríguez-Jiménez, C., De la Cruz-Campos, J. C., & Santos-Villalba, M. J. (2021b). Applications of Gamification in the Context of Higher Education. A Theoretical Approach. In *International Conference in Methodologies and intelligent Systems for Techhnology Enhanced Learning* (pp. 147-155). Springer. 10.1007/978-3-030-86618-1_15

Alpay, A., & Özdemir, M. (2021). Güncel eğilimlerden hareketle gelecek eğitim politikalarına yönelik çıkarımlar. *İnsan ve İnsan*, *8*(27), 27-49.

Alqurashi, E. (2019). Predicting student satisfaction and perceived learning within online learning environments. *Distance Education*, *40*(1), 133–148. doi:10.1080/01587919.2018.1553562

Alshikhabobakr, H., Khan, S., Gedawy, H., Hussein, N., & Razak, S. (2020). Gamified Stories in History Classrooms. In *ICETC'20: 2020 12th International Conference on Education Technology and Computers* (pp. 76-81). Association for Computing Machinery. 10.1145/3436756.3437024

Alshurman, M. (2015). Democratic education and administration. *Procedia: Social and Behavioral Sciences*, *176*, 861–869. doi:10.1016/j.sbspro.2015.01.551

Altakhayneh, B. (2022). Impact of Using Flipped Classroom Strategy in Developing the Mathematical Thinking of Pre-Service Teachers in Open Education Systems in Jordan. *International Journal of Emerging Technologies in Learning*, *17*(3), 228–244. doi:10.3991/ijet.v17i03.24973

Álvarez, J. M., Díaz, Y., & Molina, J. (2021). *El Código Cuomo. Las fábulas de María: una niña a la que no le gustaba la escuela* [The Cuomo Code. Mary's fables: a girl who didn't like school]. Dykinson.

Álvarez, J. M., Miralles, P., Molina, J., & Trigueros, F. J. (2021). Secondary School Students' Perception of the Acquisition of Social Science Skill. *Social Sciences*, *10*(4), 126. Advance online publication. doi:10.3390ocsci10040126

Álvarez, J. M., Molina, J., Miralles, P., & Trigueros, F. J. (2021). Key Competences and the Transfer of Social Knowledge: Perceptions of Secondary School Pupils. *Sustainability*, *13*(4).

Álvarez, J. M., Molina, J., Trigueros, F. J., & Miralles, P. (2021). The Development of Historical Competencies in Secondary Education: A Study Based on the Analysis of Sources in Spanish and Italian History Textbooks. *International Journal of Learning, Teaching and Educational Research*, *20*(4), 137–151. doi:10.26803/ijlter.20.4.8

Álvarez, J. M., Trigueros, F. J., Miralles, P., & Molina, J. (2020). Assessment by Competences in Social Sciences: Secondary Students Perception Based on the EPECOCISO Scale. *Sustainability*, *12*(23), 1–15. doi:10.3390u122310056

Álvaro-Tordesillas, A., Alonso-Rodríguez, M., Poza-Casado, I., & Galván-Desvaux, N. (2020). Gamification experience in the subject of Descriptive Geometry for Architecture. *Educación XX1, 23*(1), 373-408. doi:10.5944/educxx1.23591

Alvén, F. (2017). *Tänka rätt och tycka lämplig: historieämnet I skärningspunkten mellan att fostra kulturbärare och förbereda kulturbyggare*. Malmö Högskola.

Amini, M., Asgari, M., & Asgari, Z. (2020). Advantages and disadvantages of using Webquests in junior high school English classes in Iran. *Journal of Critical Studies in Language and Literature*, *1*(1), 35–43. doi:10.46809/jcsll.v1i1.43

Andelique, C. M. (2011). La didáctica de la historia y la formación docente: ¿qué profesor de historia necesitan las escuelas? *Clío & Asociados*, *15*(15), 256–269. doi:10.14409/cya.v1i15.1704

Anderson, L. W., Krathwohl, D. R., Airasian, P., Cruikshank, K., Mayer, R., Pintrich, P., Raths, J., & Wittrock, M. (2001). *Taxonomy for Learning, Teaching, and Assessing, A: A Revision of Bloo''s Taxonomy of Educational Objectives*. Longman.

Andreu, M. A. (2008). Simulación. In M. J. Labrador & M. A. Andreu (Eds.), *Metodologías activas. Grupo de Innovación en Metodologías Activas (GIMA)* (pp. 93–105). Universidad Politécnica de Valencia.

Andrews, T., & Burke, F. (2007). What does it mean to think historically. *Perspectives on History*, *45*(1), 32–35.

Ansari, D., Coch, D., & De Smedt, B. (2011). Connecting education and cognitive neuroscience: Where will the journey take us? *Educational Philosophy and Theory*, *43*(1), 37–42. doi:10.1111/j.1469-5812.2010.00705.x

Arancibia, M., & Badia, A. (2013). Caracterización y valoración de los usos educativos de las TIC en 10 secuencias didácticas de historia en enseñanza secundaria. *Estudios Pedagógicos (Valdivia)*, *39*(Especial), 7–24. doi:10.4067/S0718-07052013000300002

Aranguren-Juaristi, O., Apalaoza-Llorente, D., Echeberria Arquero, B., & Vicent, N. (2020). Testimonios de víctimas en el módulo educativo Adi-adian. Una mirada desde la didáctica de las ciencias sociales y la educación patrimonial. *Investigaciones En La Escuela*, *101*(101), 15–24. doi:10.12795/IE.2020.i101.02

Area, M., & González, C. S. (2015). De la enseñanza con libros de texto al aprendizaje en espacios online gamificados. *Educatio Siglo XXI*, *33*(3), 15–38. doi:10.6018/j/240791

Arias, A. R., & Rodríguez, A. (2020). Validación de la escala OCDUMA para analizar las concepciones, opiniones y percepciones del profesorado hacia las metodologías activas. *Aula abierta*, *49*(4), 403-412. doi:10.17811/rifie.49.4.2020.403-412

Arias, L., Egea, A., & García-López, A. J. (2018). Aprender historia a través del juego de realidad virtual inmersiva "Carthago Nova". Propuesta 26 de integración de un serious game en el proceso de enseñanza-aprendizaje. *Clío: History and History Teaching*, *44*.

Artal, J. S., Casanova, O., Serrano, R. M., & Romero, E. (2017). Mobile devices and flipped classroom. A multidisciplinary experience of university teachers. *Edutec. Revista Electrónica de Tecnología Educativa*, *59*, 1–13. doi:10.21556/edutec.2017.59.817

Ashby, R., & Lee, P. J. (1987). Children's concepts of empathy and understanding in history. In C. Portal (Ed.), *The history curriculum for teachers* (pp. 62–88). The Falmer Press.

Assaly, I., & Smadi, O. M. (2015). Using Bloom's Taxonomy to evaluate the cognitive levels of Master class textebook's questions. *English Language Teaching*, *8*(5), 100–110. doi:10.5539/elt.v8n5p100

Ata, B. (2013). *Tarih Öğretmenlerine Aktif Tarih Ortamı için 100 Etkinlik (edt)*. PegemA Yayıncılık.

Athanassiou, N., McNett, J., & Harvey, C. (2003). Critical thinking in the management classroom: Bloom's taxonomy as a learning tool. *Journal of Management Education*, *27*(5), 533–555. doi:10.1177/1052562903252515

Attali, Y., & Arieli-Attali, M. (2015). Gamification in assessment: Do points affect test performance? *Computers & Education*, *83*, 57–63. doi:10.1016/j.compedu.2014.12.012

Avendaño-Castro, W., & Parada Trujillo, A. (2013). El currículo en la sociedad del conocimiento. *Educación y Educadores*, *16*(1), 159–174.

Aydin, S. (2016). WebQuests as language-learning tools. *Computer Assisted Language Learning*, *29*(4), 765–778. doi:10.1080/09588221.2015.1061019

Ayén, F. (2017). ¿Qué es la gamificación y el ABJ? *Íber. Didáctica de las Ciencias Sociales. Geografía e Historia*, *86*, 7–15.

Aznar-Díaz, I., Raso-Sánchez, F., Hinojo-Lucena, M. A., & Romero-Díaz de la Guardia, J. J. (2017). Percepciones de los futuros docentes respecto al potencial de la ludificación y la inclusión de los videojuegos en los procesos de enseñanza-aprendizaje. *Educar*, *53*(1), 11–28. doi:10.5565/rev/educar.840

Bai, S., Hew, K. F., & Huang, B. (2020). Does gamification improve student learning outcome? Evidence from a meta-analysis and synthesis of qualitative data in educational contexts. *Educational Research Review*, *30*, 100322. doi:10.1016/j.edurev.2020.100322

Bansal, R., & Dutt, S. (2020). Using WebQuest Based Instruction to Enhance Students' Critical Thinking. *Issues and Ideas in Education*, *8*(1), 1–8. doi:10.15415/iie.2020.81001

Barba, C. (2005). La webquest y la didáctica de la historia. Monográfico dedicado a la Didáctica de las ciencias Sociales. *Quaderns Digitals*, *37*, 1–9.

Barbour, R. (2007). *Los grupos de discusión en Investigación Cualitativa*. Morata.

Barca, I. (2011). Narrativas e consciência histórica dos jovens. *Enseñanza de las Ciencias Sociales*, (10), 22–28.

Baron, C. (2016). Using embedded visual coding to support contextualization of historical texts. *American Educational Research Journal*, *53*(3), 516–540. doi:10.3102/0002831216637347

Barrett, M. (2020). The Council of Europe's Reference Framework of Competences for Democratic Culture: Policy context, content and impact. *London Review of Education*, *18*(1), 1–17. doi:10.18546/LRE.18.1.01

Bartel, A., Figas, P., & Hagel, G. (2015). Towards a competency-based education with gamification design elements. In *Proceedings of the 2015 Annual Symposium on Computer-Human Interaction in Play* (pp. 457-462). 10.1145/2793107.2810325

Barton, K. C. (2005). "Best Not to Forget Them": Adolescents' Judgments of Historical Significance in Northern Ireland. *Theory and Research in Social Education*, *33*(1), 9–44. doi:10.1080/00933104.2005.10473270

Barton, K. C. (2010). Investigación sobre las ideas de los estudiantes acerca de la historia. *Enseñanza de las Ciencias Sociales*, (9), 97–114.

Barton, K., & Levstik, L. (2004). *Teaching History for the Common Good*. Lawrence Erlbau. doi:10.4324/9781410610508

Bayram, D., Gökçe, K., & Derin, A. (2019). The Implementation of WebQuest-supported Critical Thinking Instruction in Pre-service English Teacher Education: The Turkish Context. *Participatory Educational Research*, *6*(2), 144–157. doi:10.17275/per.19.18.6.2

Bécares, L., Busto, M., & de Hoyos, C. (2016). Sentarse, escuchar y repetir. ¿Existe otra forma de enseñar historia? *Ikastorratza.e-Revista de Didáctica*, (16), 15-38.

Becker, K. (2021). What's the difference between gamification, serious games, educational games, and game-based learning? *Academia Letters*. Advance online publication. doi:10.20935/AL209

Behl, A., Jayawardena, N., Pereira, V., Islam, N., Del Giudice, M., & Choudrie, J. (2022). Gamification and e-learning for young learners: A systematic literature review, bibliometric analysis, and future research agenda. *Technological Forecasting and Social Change*, *176*, 121–145. doi:10.1016/j.techfore.2021.121445

Bel, J. C. (2021). *La imaginación histórica en la didáctica de la historia: génesis del concepto, percepciones del profesorado y estudio de caso en Educación Primaria*. Universitat de València.

Belova, N., & Zowada, C. (2020). Innovating Higher Education via Game-Based Learning on Misconceptions. *Education Sciences*, *10*(9), 221. doi:10.3390/educsci10090221

Benito, A., & Cruz, A. (2007). *Nuevas claves para la Docencia Universitaria*. Narcea.

Bergmann, J., & Sams, A. (2012). *Flip your classroom: Reach every student in every class every day*. International Society for Technology in Education.

Berkling, K., & Thomas, C. (2013). Gamification of a software engineering course and a detailed analysis of the factors that lead to it's failure. *2013 International Conference on Interactive Collaborative Learning (ICL)*, 525–530. 10.1109/ICL.2013.6644642

Bernate, J. A., & Vargas, J. A. (2020). Desafíos y tendencias del siglo XXI en la educación superior. *Revista de Ciencias Sociales*, *26*(2), 141–154.

Bertram, C. (2016). Recontextualising principles for the selection, sequencing and progression of history knowledge in four school curricula. *Journal of Education*, *64*(64), 27–54. doi:10.17159/i64a02

Binkley, M., Erstad, O., Herman, J., Raizen, S., Ripley, M., Miller-Ricci, M., & Rumble, M. (2012). Defining twenty-first century skills. In *Assessment and teaching of 21st century skills* (pp. 17–66). Springer. doi:10.1007/978-94-007-2324-5_2

Biosca, T. (1997). La història i els jocs didàctics de simulació. *L'Avenç. Revista de història i cultura, 217*, 52-53.

Bisquerra Alzina, R. (2009). *Metodología de la investigación educativa*. La Muralla S.A.

Bisquerra, R. (Coord.). (2014). Metodología de la investigación educativa (4ª ed.). La Muralla.

Bisquerra, R. (1992). *Introducción a la estadística aplicada a la investigación educativa*. PPU.

Blasco-Serrano, A. C., Lorenzo, J., & Sarsa, J. (2018). Percepción de los estudiantes al invertir la clase mediante el uso de redes sociales y sistemas de respuesta inmediata. *RED. Revista de Educación a Distancia, 57*(6), 1-19. https://revistas.um.es/red/article/view/327391

Blömeke, S., Hsieh, F., Kaiser, G., & Schmidt, W. (2014). *International Perspectives on Teacher Knowledge, Beliefs and Opportunities to Learn*. Springer. doi:10.1007/978-94-007-6437-8

Bloom, B., Englehart, M. D., Furst, E. J., Hill, W. H., & Krathwohl, D. (1956). *Taxonomy of educational objectives: The classification of educational goals. In Handbook 1: Cognitive domain*. Longsman.

Bogdandy, B., Tamas, J., & Toth, Z. (2020). Digital Transformation in Education During Covid-19: A Case Study. In *2020 11th IEEE International Conference on Cognitive Infocommunications* (pp. 173-178). IEEE. 10.1109/CogInfoCom50765.2020.9237840

Bohan, C. H., & Davis, O. L. Jr. (1998). Historical Constructions: How Social Studies Student Teachers' Historical Thinking is Reflected in Their Writing of History. *Theory and Research in Social Education*, *26*(2), 173–197. doi:10.1080/00933104.1998.10505843

Bonwell, C., & Eison, J. (1991). *Active learning:creating excitement in the classroom*. The George Washington University.

Booth, M. B. (1983). Skills, concepts and attitudes: The development of adolescent children's historical thinking. *History and Theory*, *22*(4), 101–107. doi:10.2307/2505218

Booth, M. B. (1987). Ages and concepts: a critique of the Piagetian approach to history teaching. In C. Portal (Ed.), *The history curriculum for teachers* (pp. 22–38). The Falmer Press.

Boyle, E., Connolly, T., & Hainey, T. (2011). The role of psychology in understanding the impact of computer games. *Entertainment Computing*, *2*(2), 69–74. doi:10.1016/j.entcom.2010.12.002

Bozkurt, A. (2020). Koronavirüs (Covid-19) pandemi süreci ve pandemi sonrası dünyada eğitime yönelik değerlendirmeler: yeni normal ve yeni eğitim paradigması. *Açık Öğretim Uygulamaları ve Araştırmaları Dergisi (AUAD), 6*(3), 112-142. https://dergipark.org.tr/en/download/article-file/1215818

Brant, J., Chapman, A., & Isaacs, T. (2016). International instructional systems: Social studies. *Curriculum Journal*, *27*(1), 62–79. doi:10.1080/09585176.2015.1134340

Brell, M. (2006). Juegos de rol. *Educación social: revista de intervención socioeducativa, 33*, 104-113.

Brooks, S. (2008). Displaying historical empathy: What impact can a writing assignment have? *Social Studies Research & Practice*, *3*(2), 130–146. doi:10.1108/SSRP-02-2008-B0008

Brooks, S. (2011). Historical Empathy as Perspective Recognition and Care in One Secondary Social Studies Classroom. *Theory and Research in Social Education*, *39*(2), 166–202. doi:10.1080/00933104.2011.10473452

Brophy, J., & VanSledright, B. (1992). Storytelling, imagination and fanciful elaboration in children's historical reconstructions. *American Educational Research Journal*, *20*(4), 837–859.

Brophy, J., VanSledright, B., & Brendin, S. (1992). Fifth graders' ideas about history expressed before and after their introduction to the subject. *Theory and Research in Social Education*, *XX*(4), 440–489. doi:10.1080/00933104.1992.10505682

Buckley, P., & Doyle, E. (2016). Gamification and student motivation. *Interactive Learning Environments*, *24*(6), 1162–1175. doi:10.1080/10494820.2014.964263

Buisman, A. L. D., & van Eekelen, M. C. J. D. (2014) Gamification in educational software development. *Proceedings of the Computer Science Education Research Conference*, 55, 9–20. 10.1145/2691352.2691353

Burenheide, B. (2007). I Can Do This: Revelations on Teaching with Historical Thinking. *The History Teacher*, *41*(1), 55–61.

Burke, L. L. (2013). *DogEatDog* [Game]. Liwanang Press.

Byker, E. J., & Thomas, A. (2018). Culturally responsive WebQuests: Connecting technology with inquiry-based learning. *Teaching Social Studies*, *18*(2), 19–25.

Cabero-Almenara, J., Guillen-Gámez, F. D., Ruiz-Palmero, J., & Palacios-Rodríguez, A. (2022). Teachers' digital competence to assist students with functional diversity: Identification of factors through logistic regression methods. *British Journal of Educational Technology*, *53*(1), 41–57. doi:10.1111/bjet.13151

Cabero, J. (2021). And COVID-19 transformed the educational system: Reflections and experiences to learn. *International Journal of Educational Research and Innovation*, (15), 218–228. doi:10.46661/ijeri.5246

Cabero, J., Fernández, B., & Marín, V. (2017). Dispositivos móviles y realidad aumentada en el aprendizaje del alumnado universitario. *RIED-Revista Iberoamericana De Educación a Distancia*, *20*(2), 167–185. doi:10.5944/ried.20.2.17245

Cabero, J., & Llorente, M. C. (2013). The application of expert judgement as a technique for evaluating information technology (ICT). *Eduweb. Revista de Tecnología de Información y Comunicación en Educación*, *7*(2), 11–22.

Cai, J., Yang, H. H., Gong, D., MacLeod, J., & Zhu, S. (2019). Understanding the continued use of flipped classroom instruction: A personal beliefs model in Chinese higher education. *Journal of Computing in Higher Education*, *31*(1), 137–155. doi:10.100712528-018-9196-y

Cajani, L. (2006). Italian history textbooks on the brink of the twenty-first century. In J. Nicholls (Ed.), *School history textbooks across cultures: International debates and perspectives* (pp. 27-41). Symposium Books.

Calatayud, M. A. (2000). La supremacía del examen, la evaluación como examen: Su uso y abuso, aún, en la educación primaria [The supremacy of the test, assessment as test: its use and abuse, even in primary education]. *Bordón, 52*(2), 165–178.

Calero Llinares, M., Mayoral García-Berlanga, O., Ull Solís, A., & Vilches Peña, A. (2019). La educación para la sostenibilidad en la formación del profesorado de ciencias experimentales en Secundaria. *Enseñanza de las Ciencias, 37*(1), 157–175. doi:10.5565/rev/ensciencias.2605

Campillo, J. M., & Miralles, P. (2022, April). Impact of the flipped classroom model on democratic education of student teachers in Spain. *Education, Citizenship and Social Justice*. Advance online publication. doi:10.1177/17461979221084111

Campos, A., Batista, E., Signoretti, A., Gardiman, R., & Madeira, C. (2015). Gamifying activities in a higher education course. In*: Proceedings of the European Conference on Games-Based Learning* (pp. 117–124). Academic Conferences International Limited. Retrieved from https://www.proquest.com/conference-papers-proceedings/gamifying-activities-higher-education-course/docview/1728409632/se-2?accountid=14542

Campos, M. (2008). La evaluación por competencias, mitos, peligros, desafíos [Competency-based assessment, myths, dangers, challenges]. *Educere. Foro Universitario, 43*, 805–814.

Canales-Ronda, P., & Hernández-Fernández, A. (2019). Flipped classroom methodology in university teaching. *Revista Iberoamericana de Educación Superior, 10*(28), 116–130. doi:10.22201/iisue.20072872e.2019.28.432

Carbonell, J. (2015). *Pedagogías del siglo XXI: Alternativas para la innovación educativa*. Octaedro.

Carceller, C. J. (2016). Gamification in green mobile applications: Analysis of game components and game elements. *Sphera Publica, 1*(16), 95–113.

Care, E. (2020). *Global Initiative around Assessment of 21st Century Skills*. https://bangkok.unesco.org/content/global-initiative-aroundassessment-21st-century-skills

CARM (Comunidad Autónoma de la Región de Murcia) (2014). Decreto 198/2014, de 5 de septiembre, por el que se establece el currículo de la Educación Primaria en la Comunidad Autónoma de la Región de Murcia. *BORM (Boletín Oficial de la Región de Murcia), 206*, 6 de septiembre de 2014.

Carretero, M. (2019). Pensamiento histórico e historia global como nuevos desafíos para la enseñanza [Historical thinking and global history as new teaching challenges]. *Cuadernos de Pedagogía, 495*, 59–63.

Carretero, M. (2019). Pensamiento histórico e historia global como nuevos desafíos para la enseñanza. *Cuadernos de Pedagogía, 495*, 59–63.

Carretero, M., Berger, S., & Grever, M. (Eds.). (2017). *Palgrave Handbook of Research in Historical Culture and Education*. Palgrave Macmillan. doi:10.1057/978-1-137-52908-4

Carretero, M., & López, C. (2009). Estudios cognitivos sobre el conocimiento histórico: Aportaciones para la enseñanza y alfabetización histórica [Cognitive Studies on Historical Knowledge: Contributions to Historical Literacy and Education]. *Enseñanza de las Ciencias Sociales, 8*, 79–93.

Carretero, M., Pozo, J. I., & Asensio, M. (Eds.). (1989). *La enseñanza de las Ciencias Sociales*. Visor.

Carril-Merino, Mª. T., Andreu-Mediero, B., De la Calle-Carracedo, M., & López-Torres, E. (2020). Fuentes orales para el desarrollo de la empatía histórica: un estudio en la formación del profesorado de Educación Infantil. *Panta Rei: revista digital de Historia y didáctica de la Historia, 14*(1),155-184. doi:10.6018/pantarei.444771

Carril-Merino, M. T., Sánchez-Agustí, M., & Miguel-Revilla, D. (2018). Perspectiva histórica y empatía: Su interrelación en futuros profesores de Educación Primaria. *Aula Abierta, 47*(2), 221–228. doi:10.17811/rifie.47.2.2018.221-228

Carril-Merino, Mª. T., Sánchez-Agustí, M., & Muñoz-Labraña, C. (2020b). Empatía histórica en futuros profesores de primaria: El trabajo infantil en el siglo XIX. *Educação e Pesquisa, 46*, 1–18. doi:10.1590/S1678-4634202046215492

Casali Fuentes, A. (2007). Una adaptación del estructuralismo a la historia. La larga duración histórica: clave metodológica de las diferentes temporalidades. *Analecta: revista de humanidades, 2,* 1-17.

Castañeda, L., Esteve, F., & Adell, J. (2018). ¿Por qué es necesario repensar la competencia docente para el mundo digital? *Revista de Educación a Distancia, 56*(56), 1–20. doi:10.6018/red/56/6

Castro-Fernández, B., Jiménez-Esquinas, G., & López-Facal, R. (2022). Teacher Training Via Debate on the Way of St. James as Controversial Heritage. *Frontiers in Education, 6*, 823122. doi:10.3389/feduc.2021.823122

Chamoso, J. M., Durán, J., García, F., Martín, J., & Rodríguez, M. (2004). Análisis y experimentación de juegos como instrumentos para enseñar matemáticas. *Suma*, (47), 47–58.

Chaparro, A., & Ruiz, C. R. (Coords.). (2022). Prácticas docentes universitarias en Didáctica de las Ciencias Sociales: investigaciones y experiencias. Dykinson.

Chaparro-Sainz, Á., Méndez, R., & Felices-De la Fuente, M. M. (2022). El patrimonio en las aulas. Un estudio en prospectiva con estudiantes del Grado en Educación Primaria. *Contextos educativos. Review of Education, 29*(29), 137–154. doi:10.18172/con.4950

Chapman, A. (2020). Learning the lessons of the Holocaust: A critical exploration. In S. Foster, A. Pearce, & A. Pettigrew (Eds.), Holocaust Education. Contemporary challenges and controversies (pp. 50-73). UCL Press. doi:10.2307/j.ctv15d7zpf.9

Chapman, A. (2003). Conceptual awareness through categorising: Using ICT to get Year 13 reading. *Teaching History, 111*, 38.

Chapman, J. R., & Rich, P. J. (2018). Does educational gamification improve students' motivation? If so, which game elements work best? *Journal of Education for Business, 93*(7), 315–322. doi:10.1080/08832323.2018.1490687

Chick, R. C., Clifton, G. T., Peace, K. M., Propper, B. W., Hale, D. F., Alseidi, A. A., & Vreeland, T. J. (2020). Using Technology to Maintain the Education of Residents During the COVID-19 Pandemic. *Journal of Surgical Education, 77*(4), 729–732. doi:10.1016/j.jsurg.2020.03.018 PMID:32253133

Chuang, H. H., Weng, C. Y., & Chen, C. H. (2018). Which students benefit most from a flipped classroom approach to language learning? *British Journal of Educational Technology, 49*(1), 56–68. doi:10.1111/bjet.12530

Churchill, D. (2006). Student-centred learning design: Key components, technology role and frameworks for integration. *Synergy, 4*(1), 18–28.

Clark, P. (2018). History Education Debates: Canadian Identity, Historical Thinking and Historical Consciousness. *Arbor. Ciencia. Pensamiento y Cultura, 194*(788), 1–13. doi:10.3989/arbor.2018.788n2001

Codish, D., & Ravid, G. (2012) Personality based gamification: how differente personalities perceive gamification. *Proceedings of the 22nd European Conference on Information Systems*, 11. https://cutt.ly/gGnfmdE

Cohen, J. (1988). *Statistical Power Analysis for the Behavioral Sciences* (2nd ed.). Lawrence Erlbaum Associates.

Cohen, J. (1988). *Statistical power analysis for the behavioral sciences*. Erlbaum.

Coll, C. (2018). La personalización del aprendizaje escolar, una exigencia de la nueva ecología del aprendizaje. *Personalización del aprendizaje*, 5-11.

Coll, V., Pardo, C., & Pérez, P. J. (2018). Métodos de enseñanza-aprendizaje y su efecto en el desarrollo profesional y competencial de los egresados. *Cultura y Educación*, *30*(3), 556–583. doi:10.1080/11356405.2018.1494773

Colomer, J. C., Sáiz, J., & Morales, A. (2021). History and geographical thinking skills: between disciplinary knowledge and knowledge for teaching in Teacher Education. In Handbook of Research on Teacher Education in History and Geography (pp. 159-176). Peter Lang Publishing Group.

Colomer, J. C., Fuertes, C., & Parra, D. (2022). Tecnología educativa y enfoque sociocrítico en enseñanza de la Historia. ¿ Dónde estamos?¿ Hacia dónde vamos? *Con-ciencia social. Segunda Época*, (5), 143–160.

Colomer, J., Serra, T., Cañabate, D., & Bubnys, R. (2020). Reflective Learning in Higher Education: Active Methodologies for Transformative Practices. *Sustainability*, *12*(9), 3827. doi:10.3390u12093827

Colomo-Magaña, E., Sánchez-Rivas, E., Ruiz-Palmero, J., & Sánchez-Rodríguez, J. (2020). Percepción docente sobre la gamificación de la evaluación en la asignatura de Historia en educación secundaria [Teaching perception about gamification of the evaluation in the subject of History in secondary education]. *Información Tecnológica*, *31*(4), 233–242. doi:10.4067/S0718-07642020000400233

Coltham, J., & Fines, J. (1971). *Educational Objectives for the Study of History*. The Historical Association.

Concha-Maquisaca, J. A., & Álvarez-Lozano, M. I. (2021). Aplicación del sistema del conocimiento a través de herramientas tecnopedagógicas en Cañar durante el COVID-19. *Espisteme Koinonia*, *4*(8), 204–288. doi:10.35381/e.k.v4i8.1353

Connolly, T. M., Boyle, E. A., MacArthur, E., Hainey, T., & Boyle, J. M. (2012). A systematic literature review of empirical evidence on computer games and serious games. *Computers & Education*, *59*(2), 661–686. doi:10.1016/j.compedu.2012.03.004

Contreras, R. S. (2016). Digital games and gamification applied in the field of education. *RIED. Revista Iberoamericana de Educación a Distancia*, *19*(2), 27–33. doi:10.5944/ried.19.2.16143

Cooper, H. (2014). Why Are There No History Text Books in English Primary Schools? *Ensayos. Revista de la Facultad de Educación de Albacete*, *29*(1), 27–42.

Cornella, P., Estebanell, M., & Brusi, D. (2020). Gamificación y aprendizaje basado en juegos: Consideraciones generales y algunos ejemplos para la Enseñanza de la Geología. *Enseñanza de las ciencias de la tierra. Revista de la Asociación Española para la Enseñanza de las Ciencias de la Tierra*, *28*(1), 5–19.

Counsell, C., Burn, K., & Chapman, A. (2016). *MasterClass in history education. Transforming teaching and learning*. Bloomsbury. doi:10.5040/9781474285476

Cózar-Gutiérrez, R., & Sáez-López, J. M. (2016). Game-based learning and gamification in initial teacher training in the social sciences: An experiment with MinecraftEdu. *International Journal of Educational Technology in Higher Education*, *13*(2), 2. Advance online publication. doi:10.118641239-016-0003-4

Crawford, J., Butler-Henderson, K., Rudolph, J., Malkawi, B., Glowatz, M., Burton, R., & Lam, S. (2020). COVID-19: 20 countries' higher education intra-period digital pedagogy responses. *Journal of Applied Learning & Teaching*, *3*(1), 1–20. doi:10.37074/jalt.2020.3.1.7

Csikszentmihalyi, M. (1990). *Flow. The Psychology of Optimal Experience*. Harper & Row.

Cuenca, J. M., & Estepa, J. (2017). Educación patrimonial para la inteligencia territorial y emocional de la ciudadanía. *MIDAS. Museus e estudos interdisciplinares, 8*, 1-10.

Cuenca, J. M., Martín, M., & Estepa, J. (2011). Historia y videojuegos. Una propuesta de trabajo para el aula de 1o de ESO. *Íber: Didáctica de las Ciencias Sociales. Geografía e Historia, 69*, 64–73.

Cuenca-López, J. M., & Jiménez-Palacios, R. (2018). Enseñando historia y patrimonio a través de los videojuegos: investigación e innovación. *RiMe. Rivista dell'Istituto di Storia dell'Europa Mediterranea,* 43-64.

Cuenca-López, J. M., & Martín-Cáceres, M. J. (2010). Virtual games in social science education. *Computers & Education, 55*(3), 1336–1345. doi:10.1016/j.compedu.2010.05.028

Cuenca-López, J.-M., & Martín, M. (2010). La resolución de problemas en la enseñanza de las ciencias sociales a través de videojuegos. *Íber. Didáctica de las Ciencias Sociales. Geografía e Historia*, (63), 32–42.

Cuesta, R. (1998). *Clío en las aulas. La enseñanza de la Historia en España entre reformas, ilusiones y rutinas* [Clio in the classroom. History teaching in Spain between reforms, illusions and routines]. Akal.

Da Rocha-Seixas, L., Gomes, A. S., & De Melo-Filho, I. J. (2016). Effectiveness of gamification in the engagement of students. *Computers in Human Behavior, 58*, 48–63. doi:10.1016/j.chb.2015.11.021

Darouech, S., & Felices, M. M. (2021). La formación inicial en Didáctica de las Ciencias Sociales según el alumnado egresado. *Didáctica de las Ciencias Experimentales y Sociales, 41*(41), 57–72. doi:10.7203/dces.41.21294

Davey, L. (2009). The application of case study evaluations. *Elementary Education Online, 8*(2), 1–3.

Davies, I. (Ed.). (2000). Teaching the Holocaust: Educational Dimensions, Principles and Practice. Continuum.

Davison, M. (2012). Teaching historial empathy and the 1915 Gallipoli campaign. In M. Harcourt & M. Sheehan (Eds.), *Historymatters: teaching and learninghistory in New Zealandsecondaryschools in the 21st century* (pp. 11–31). NZCER Press.

De Groot-Reuvekamp, M., Ros, A., & Van Boxtel, C. (2018). A successful professional development program in history: What matters? *Teaching and Teacher Education, 75*, 290–301. doi:10.1016/j.tate.2018.07.005

de Groot-Reuvekamp, M., Ros, A., & van Boxtel, C. (2018a). Improving elementary school students' understanding of historical time: Effects of teaching with "Timewise". *Theory and Research in Social Education, 46*(1), 35–67. doi:10.1080/00933104.2017.1357058

De Marcos, L., García-López, E., & García-Cabot, A. (2016). On the effectiveness of game-like and social approaches in learning: Comparing educational gaming, gamification & social networking. *Computer Education, 95*, 99–113. doi:10.1016/j.compedu.2015.12.008

De Miguel, R. & Sebastián, M. (2020). Democracia, participación y ciudadanía europea: recursos didácticos cartográficos para la enseñanza de la convivencia y la integración europea. *Clio. History and History Teaching, 46*, 14-29. doi:10.26754/ojs_clio/clio.2020465256

De Sousa Borges, S., Durelli, V. H., Reis, H. M., & Isotani, S. (2014). A systematic mapping on gamification applied to education. In *Proceedings of the 29th annual ACM symposium on applied computing* (pp. 216-222). 10.1145/2554850.2554956

Dejene, W., Bishaw, A., & Dagnew, A. (2018). Preservice Teachers' Approaches to Learning and Their Teaching Approach Preferences: Secondary Teacher Education Program in Focus. *Cogent Edu., 5*(1), 1502396. doi:10.1080/2331186X.2018.1502396 del Pozo, M. M. (2015). Videojuegos y aprendizaje colaborativo. Experiencias en torno a la etapa de Educación Primaria. *Teoría de la Educación*, *16*(2), 69–89.

Delgado, J., García, C., Guaicha, K., & Prado, M. (2020). La Webquest como herramienta didáctica para potenciar el pensamiento crítico en la formación de estudiantes universitarios. *Revista Tecnológica-Educativa Docentes 2.0*, *9*(1), 49-55.

Delgado-Algarra, E. J. (2018). Enseñanza de la Historia y compromiso ciudadano a través de los videojuegos Civilization VI y Stardew Valley: cómo seleccionar e integrar los videojuegos en el aula. *Clío. History & History Teaching, 44.*

Delgado-Algarra, E. J. (2022). Gamification and Game-Based Learning: Motivating Social Sciences Education. In Information Resources Management Association (Ed.), Research Anthology on Developments in Gamification and Game-Based Learning (pp. 932-956). IGI Global.

De-Marcos, L., Domínguez, A., Saenz-de-Navarrete, J., & Pagés, C. (2014). An empirical study comparing gamification and social networking on e-learning. *Computers & Education*, *75*, 82–91. doi:10.1016/j.compedu.2014.01.012

Deterding, S., Dixon, D., Khaled, R., & Nacke, L. (2011). From game design elements to gamefulness: Defining "gamification". In A. Lugmayr (Ed.), *Proceedings of the 15th international academic MindTrek Conference: Envisioning future media environments* (pp. 9-15). ACM. 10.1145/2181037.2181040

Dewey, J. (1900). The aim of history in elementary education. *Elementary School Record*, *1*(4), 203.

Dicheva, D., Dichev, C., Agre, G., & Angelova, G. (2015). Gamification in education: A systematic mapping study. *Journal of Educational Technology & Society*, *18*(3), 75–88.

Dickinson, A. K., & Lee, P. (1978). Understanding and Research. In A. Dickinson & P. Lee (Eds.), *History Teaching and Historical Understanding* (pp. 95–120). Heinemann Educational Books.

Díez Gutiérrez, E. J. (2022). *Pedagogía antifascista. Construir una pedagogía inclusiva, democrática y del bien común frente al auge del fascismo y la xenofobia*. Octaedro.

Dodge, B. (1995b). *Some Thoughts About WebQuests*. https://webquest.org/sdsu/about_webquests.html

Dodge, B. (1995a). WebQuests: A technique for internet-based learning. *Distance Education*, *1*(2), 10–13.

Domínguez, J. (2016). Enseñar y evaluar el pensamiento histórico. Competencias, conceptos y destrezas cognitivas [Teaching and assessing historical thinking. Cognitive skills, concepts and competences]. *Íber: Didáctica de las ciencias sociales, geografía e historia, 82*, 43-49.

Domínguez, J. (2016). Enseñar y evaluar el pensamiento histórico: competencias, conceptos y destrezas cognitivas. *Íber, didáctica de las ciencias sociales, geografía e historia, 82,* 43-49.

Domínguez, A., Saenz-de-Navarrete, J., de-Marcos, L., Fernández-Sanz, L., Pagés, C., & Martínez, J. J. (2013). Gamifying learning experiences: Practical implications and outcomes. *Computers & Education*, *63*, 380–392. doi:10.1016/j.compedu.2012.12.020

Domínguez-Almansa, A., & López Facal, R. (2017). Patrimonios en conflictos. Competencias cívicas y formación profesional en educación primaria. *Review of Education*, *375*, 86–109. doi:10.4438/1988-592X-RE-2016-375-336

Domínguez, J. (1986). Enseñar a comprender el pasado histórico: Conceptos y empatía. *Infancia y Aprendizaje*, *34*(34), 1–21. doi:10.1080/02103702.1986.10822113

Domínguez, J. (2015). *Pensamiento histórico y evaluación de competencias*. Graó.

Drozd, M., & O'Donoghue, J. (2007). The use of a WebQuest to support undergraduate nurses. *Teaching and Learning in Nursing*, *2*(3), 63–67. doi:10.1016/j.teln.2007.03.001

Durrani, U. K., Al Naymat, G., Ayoubi, R. A., Kamal, M. M., & Hussain, H. (2022). Gamified flipped classroom versus traditional classroom learning: Which approach is more efficient in business education? *International Journal of Management Education*, *20*(1), 1–10. doi:10.1016/j.ijme.2021.100595

Ebadi, S., & Rahimi, M. (2018). An exploration into the impact of WebQuest-based classroom on EFL learners' critical thinking and academic writing skills: A mixed-methods study. *Computer Assisted Language Learning*, *31*(5-6), 617–651. doi:10.1080/09588221.2018.1449757

Egea, A., Arias, L., & García-López, A. J. (2017). Videojuegos, historia y patrimonio: primeros resultados de una investigación educativa evaluativa en educación secundaria. *Revista interuniversitaria de investigación en Tecnología Educativa*.

Egea-Vivancos, A., & Arias-Ferrer, L. (2018). El desafío de enseñar a pensar históricamente a través de la arqueología [The challenge of teaching historical thinking through archaeology]. In A. Egea-Vivancos, L. Arias-Ferrer, & J. Santacana-i-Mestre (Coords.), Y la arqueología llegó al aula: La cultura material y el método arqueológico para la enseñanza de la historia y el patrimonio (pp.329-343). Ediciones Trea.

Egea-Vivancos, A., & Arias-Ferrer, L. (2021). Principles for the design of a history and heritage game based on the evaluation of immersive virtual reality video games. *E-Learning and Digital Media*, *18*(4), 383–402. doi:10.1177/2042753020980103

Eisenberg, M., & Berkowitz, R. E. (1990). *Information Problem Solving: The Big Six Skills*. Linworth.

Elche, M., & Yubero, S. (2019). The influence of reading habits on the use of internet: A study with university students. *Investigación Bibliotecológica*, *33*(79), 51–66. doi:10.22201/iibi.24488321xe.2019.79.57985

Eliasson, P., Alvén, F., Yngveus, C. A., & Rosenlund, D. (2015). Historical consciousness and historical thinking reflected in large-scale assessment in Sweden. In K. Ercikan & P. Seixas (Eds.), *New directions in assessing historical thinking* (pp. 171–182). Routledge.

Ellingboe, J. (2008). *Steal Away Jordan* [Game]. Stone Baby Games.

Endacott, J. L. (2010). Reconsidering Affective Engagement in Historical Empathy. *Theory & Research in Social Education, 38*(1), 6-47. doi:10.1080/00933104.2010.10473415

Endacott, J. L., & Brooks, S. (2013). An Updated Theoretical and Practical Model for Promoting Historical Empathy. *Social Studies Research & Practice*, *8*(1), 41–58. doi:10.1108/SSRP-01-2013-B0003

Epstein, T., & Salinas, C. S. (2018). Research methodologies in history education. In S. A. Metzger & L. M. Harris (Eds.), *The Wiley International Handbook of history teaching and learning* (pp. 61–92). Wiley. doi:10.1002/9781119100812.ch3

Ercikan, K., & Seixas, P. (2015). Issues in designing assessment of historical thinking. *Theory into Practice*, *54*(3), 255–262. doi:10.1080/00405841.2015.1044375

Ercikan, K., & Seixas, P. (2015). *New directions in assessing historical thinking*. Routledge. doi:10.4324/9781315779539

Escobar-Pérez, J., & Cuervo-Martínez, Á. (2008). Validez de contenido y juicio de expertos: Una aproximación a su utilización. *Avances en Medición*, *6*, 27–36.

Espada, M., Rocu, P., Navia, J. A., & Gómez-López, M. (2020). Academic performance and university student satisfaction with the flipped classroom method. *Profesorado*, *24*(1), 116–135. doi:10.30827/profesorado.v24i1.8710

Estepa, J. (2017). *Otra didáctica de la historia para otra escuela. Lección inaugural del curso 2017-2018*. Universidad de Huelva. http://www.ub.edu/histodidactica/images/documentos/pdf/estepa%20libro.pdf

Estepa, J. (2017). *Otra didáctica de la Historia para otra escuela*. Universidad de Huelva.

Estepa, J., & Delgado-Algarra, E. J. (2020). Construyendo un compromiso democrático: memoria histórica, patrimonio y educación ciudadana. In I. Sáez-Rosenkranz & J. Prats Cuevas (Eds.), *Memoria histórica y enseñanza de la Historia* (pp. 45–64). Ediciones Trea.

Éthier, M. A., Demers, S. & Lefrançois, D. (2010). Las investigaciones en didáctica sobre el desarrollo del pensamiento histórico en la enseñanza primaria. Una panorámica de la literatura publicada en francés e inglés desde el año 1990. *Enseñanza de las ciencias sociales, 9*, 61-74.

Éthier, M. A., Demers, S., & Lefrançois, D. (2010). El desarrollo del pensamiento histórico de la literatura publicada en francés e inglés. *Enseñanza de las ciencias sociales: revista de investigación*, (9), 61-74.

Eukel, H., & Morrell, B. (2021). Ensuring Educational Escape-Room Success: The Process of Designing, Piloting, Evaluating, Redesigning, and Re-Evaluating Educational Escape Rooms. *Simulation & Gaming*, *52*(1), 18–23. doi:10.1177/1046878120953453

Fallace, T., & Fantozzi, V. (2017). The Dewey School as Triumph, Tragedy, and Misunderstood: Exploring the Myths and Historiography of the University of Chicago Laboratory School. *Teachers College Record: The Voice of Scholarship in Education, 119*(2). doi:10.1177/016146811711900205

Farías-Gaytán, S., Aguaded, I., & Ramírez-Montoya, M. S. (2022). Transformation and digital literacy: Systematic literature mapping. *Education and Information Technologies*, *27*(4), 1417–1437. doi:10.100710639-021-10624-x

Felices-De la Fuente, M. M., & Chaparro-Sainz, Á. (2021). Opinions of Future Teachers on Training in Social Sciences Didactics. *Frontiers in Education*, *6*, 1–13. https://www.frontiersin.org/articles/10.3389/feduc.2021.803289/full. doi:10.3389/feduc.2021.803289

Fernández Gavira, J., Prieto Gallego, E., Alcaraz-Rodríguez, V., Sánchez-Oliver, A. J., & Grimaldi-Puyanal, M. (2018). Aprendizajes significativos mediante la Gamificación a partir del Juego de Rol: "Las Aldeas de la Historia". Espiral. *Cuadernos del Profesorado*, *11*(22), 69–78. doi:10.25115/ecp.v11i21.1919

Fernández, A. (2006). Metodologías activas para la formación de competencias. *Educatio siglo XXI, 24*, 35-56.

Fernández, F. J., Fernández, M. J., & Rodríguez, J. M. (2018). El proceso de integración y uso pedagógico de las TIC en los centros educativos madrileños. *Educación XX1, 21*(2), 395-416. doi:10.5944/educxx1.17907

Fernández-Batanero, J. M., Cabero-Almenara, J., Román-Graván, P., & Palacios-Rodríguez, A. (2022). Knowledge of university teachers on the use of digital resources to assist people with disabilities. The case of Spain. *Education and Information Technologies*, 1–15. doi:10.100710639-022-10965-1 PMID:35340536

Fernández-Enguita, M. (2016). *La educación en la encrucijada*. Santillana.

Fernandez, S. (2021). Making space in higher education: Disability, digital technology, and the inclusive prospect of digital collaborative making. *International Journal of Inclusive Education*, *25*(12), 1375–1390. doi:10.1080/13603116.2019.1610806

Figg, C., & Jaipal-Jamani, K. (2018). Developing Teacher Knowledge About Gamification as an Instructional Strategy. In M. Niess & H. Gillow-Wiles (Eds.), *Handbook of Research on Teacher Education in the Digital Age* (pp. 663–690). IGI Global.

Finkelstein, N. G. (2014). *La industria del Holocausto. Reflexiones sobre la explotación del sufrimiento judío*. Akal.

Fleissner, S., Chan, Y. Y., Yuen, T. H., & Ng, V. (2006, May). WebQuest markup language (WQML) for sharable inquiry-based learning. In *International Conference on Computational Science and Its Applications* (pp. 383-392). Springer. 10.1007/11751540_41

Floden, R. (2015). Learning what research says about teacher preparation. In M. J. Feuer, A. I. Berman, & R. C. Atkinson (Eds.), *Past as prologue: The national academy of education at 50. Members reflect* (pp. 279–284). National Academy of Education.

Fontana, J. (2006). ¿Qué Historia para el siglo XXI? *Analecta: Revista de Humanidades, 1*, 1-12.

Fork, R. (2016). Technological resources in the history classroom. *Learning and Teaching*, *5*(1). https://openjournals.utoledo.edu/index.php/learningtoteach/article/view/219/101

Förster, M., Maur, A., Weiser, C., & Winkel, K. (2022). Pre-class video watching fosters achievement and knowledge retention in a flipped classroom. *Computers & Education*, *179*, 104399. doi:10.1016/j.compedu.2021.104399

Foster, S., Pearce, A., & Pettigrew, A. (Eds.). (2020). Holocaust Education. Contemporary Challenges and Controversies.

Foster, S. J. (1999). Using historical empathy to excite students about the study of history: Can you empathize with Neville Chamberlain? *Social Studies*, *90*(1), 18–24. doi:10.1080/00377999909602386

Foster, S. J., & Yeager, E. A. (1998). The role of empathy in the development of historical understanding. *The International Journal of Social Education*, *13*(1), 1–7.

Fracapane, K. (2015). *The international status of Education about the Holocaust. A global mapping of textbooks and curricula. Summary*. UNESCO.

Fraile-Delgado, F. J. (2020). Pensar en Clío: la evolución de las concepciones historiográficas del alumnado de 1° de Educación Secundaria Obligatoria. *Didáctica de las ciencias experimentales y sociales*, *39*, 3-16. doi:10.7203/dces.39.15512

Friesen, N. (2013). Learning analytics: Readiness and rewards. *Canadian Journal of Learning and Technology*, *39*(4), 1–12. doi:10.21432/T2J01B

Fuentes, C. (2002). La visión de la historia por los adolescentes: revisión del estado de la cuestión en Estados Unidos y el Reino Unido. *Enseñanza de las ciencias sociales, 1*, 55-68.

Fuentes, A., López, J., & Pozo, S. (2019). Análisis de la competencia digital docente: Factor clave en el desempeño de pedagogías activas con Realidad Aumentada. *Revista Electrónica Iberoamericana sobre Calidad, Eficacia y Cambio en Educación*, *17*(2), 27–42. doi:10.15366/reice2019.17.2.002

Fuentes, C. (2006). Concepciones de los alumnos sobre la Historia. *Educar em Revista*, *22*(spe), 219–239. doi:10.1590/0104-4060.407

Funkenstein, A. (1989). Collective memory and historical consciousness. *History & Memory*, *1*(1), 5–26. https://www.jstor.org/stable/25618571

Gadamer, H. G., & Fantel, H. (1975). The problema of historical consciousness. *Graduate Faculty Philosophy Journal*, *5*(1), 8–52. doi:10.5840/gfpj1975512

Gago, M. (2018). *Consciência histórica e narrativa na aula de História- concepções de professores*. Edições Afrontamento.

Gaitán, V. (2013). *Gamificación: el aprendizaje divertido*. Accessed on May 25, 2022, at https://www.educativa.com/blog-articulos/gamificacion-el-aprendizaje-divertido/

Gajardo, M. (1993). Ivan Illich. *Prospects*, *23*(3-4), 711–720. doi:10.1007/BF02195145

Gálvez de la Cuesta, M. C. (2006). Aplicaciones de los videojuegos de contenido histórico en el aula. *Icono*, *14*(7), 1–13.

García Fernández, G. A. (2021). Enseñar historia en las escuelas públicas del siglo XXI. ¿Qué historia enseñar y para qué? *Revista Didáctica de las Ciencias Experimentales y Sociales*, *40*(40), 35–50. doi:10.7203/dces.40.16835

García-Morís, R. (2016). Propuesta metodológica para el uso de las fuentes históricas demográficas de la Edad Moderna como recurso didáctico. *Revista de Didácticas Específicas, 14*, 71-85.

Gerge, K. J. (2005). Narrative, moral identity and historical consciousness. In J. Straub (Ed.), *Narration, identity and historical consciousness* (pp. 99–119). Berghahn Books.

Gilboy, M. B., Heinerichs, S., & Pazzaglia, G. (2015). Enhancing student engagement using the flipped classroom. *Journal of Nutrition Education and Behavior*, *47*(1), 109–114. doi:10.1016/j.jneb.2014.08.008 PMID:25262529

Giménez, J. E. (2019). Investigar para innovar: El caso del Ámbito de Investigación de las sociedades actuales e históricas. *Revista de Investigación en Didáctica de las Ciencias Sociales*, *1*, 4. doi:10.17398/2531-0968.04.4

Goldman, S. R. (2004). Cognitive aspects of constructing meaning through and across multiple texts. In N. Shuart Faris, & D. Bloome (Eds.), Uses of intertextuality in classroom and educational research (pp. 317-351). Information Age Publishing.

Gómez Carrasco, C. J., Molina, S., & Ortuño, J (2014). Aprender a pensar históricamente. Retos para la historia en el siglo XXI. *Tempo e argumento, 6*(11), 5-27. doi:10.5965/2175180306112014005

Gómez Carrasco, C. J., & Miralles Martínez, P. (2015). Pensar historicamente ou memorizar o passado? A avaliação dos conteúdos históricos na educação obrigatória na Espanha. *Revista de Estudios Sociales*, (52), 52–68.

Gómez Carrasco, C. J., Monteagudo, J., Moreno-Vera, J. R., & Sáinz, M. (2019). Effects of a gamification and flipped-classroom program for teachers in training on motivation and learning perception. *Education Sciences*, *9*(4), 299. doi:10.3390/educsci9040299

Gómez Carrasco, C. J., Monteagudo, J., Moreno-Vera, J. R., & Sáinz, M. (2020). Evaluation of a gamification and flipped-classroom program used in teacher training: Perception of learning and outcome. *PLoS One*, *15*(10), e0241892. doi:10.1371/journal.pone.0241892 PMID:33119687

Gómez Carrasco, C. J., Solé, G., Miralles, P., & Sánchez-Ibáñez, R. (2020). Analysis of cognitive skills in history textbook (Spain-England-Portugal). *Frontiers in Psychology*, *11*, 521115. doi:10.3389/fpsyg.2020.521115 PMID:33329167

Gómez, C. J. & Miralles, P. (2016). Las competencias históricas en educación obligatoria: evaluación, estrategias basadas en la indagación, y argumentación de los estudiantes [Historical competencies in compulsory education: assessment, inquiry-based strategies, and student argumentation]. *New approaches in educational research, 5*(2), 139-146. doi:10.7821/naer.2016.7.172

Gómez, C. J., Rodríguez-Medina, J., Chaparro, Á., & Felices, M. M. (2022). Enseñar la historia de Europa desde métodos activos y compromiso cívico. Diseño y validación de una propuesta. In S. Alonso-García, G. Gómez, C. Rodríguez & M. Ramos (Coords.), La educación globalizada: experiencias e investigaciones (pp. 200-210). Dykinson.

Gómez, C., Rodríguez, R., & Monteagudo, J. (2017). Las competencias históricas en los procesos de evaluación: libros de texto y exámenes [Historical competences in assessment processes: textbooks and exams]. In Enseñanza de la historia y competencias educativas [History teaching and educational competences] (pp. 141-165). Graó.

Gómez, C. J. (2014). Pensamiento histórico y contenidos disciplinares en los libros de texto. Un análisis exploratorio de la Edad Moderna en 2.° de la ESO. *Ensayos. Revista de la Facultad de Educación de Albacete*, *29*(1), 131–158.

Gómez, C. J., López-Facal, R., & Rodríguez-Medina, J. (2019). La investigación en Didáctica de las Ciencias Sociales en revistas españolas de Ciencias de la Educación. Un análisis bibliométrico (2007-2017). *Revista de Didáctica de las Ciencias Experimentales y Sociales*, *37*(37), 67–88. doi:10.7203/dces.37.14440

Gómez, C. J., & Miralles, P. (2015). ¿Pensar históricamente o memorizar el pasado? La evaluación de los contenidos históricos en la educación obligatoria en España [Thinking historically or memorising the past? The evaluation of historical content in compulsory education in Spain]. *Revista de Estudios Sociales*, *52*(52), 52–68. doi:10.7440/res52.2015.04

Gómez, C. J., Miralles, P., & Chapman, A. (2017). Los procedimientos de evaluación en la clase de Historia. Un análisis comparativo a través de las opiniones de los docentes en formación en España e Inglaterra. *Revista Electrónica Interuniversitaria de Formación del Profesorado*, *20*(2), 45–61. doi:10.6018/reifop/20.2.284631

Gómez, C. J., Miralles, P., López, R., & Prats, J. (2017). Las competencias históricas en el horizonte. Propuestas presentes y perspectivas de futuro. In R. López, P. Miralles, & J. Prats (Eds.), *Enseñanza de la historia y competencias educativas* (pp. 215–234). Graó.

Gómez, C. J., Miralles, P., Rodríguez-Medina, J., & Maquilón, J. (2020). Perceptions on the procedures and techniques for assessing history and defining teaching profiles. Teacher training in Spain and the United Kingdom. *Educational Studies*, *43*, 1–19. doi:10.1080/03055698.2019.1707069

Gómez, C. J., Ortuño, J., & Miralles, P. (2018). *Enseñar ciencias sociales con métodos activos de aprendizaje. Reflexiones y propuestas a través de la indagación*. Octaedro.

Gómez, C. J., Ortuño, J., & Miralles, P. (2018). *Enseñar ciencias sociales con métodos activos de aprendizaje: reflexiones y propuestas a través de la indagación*. Octaedro.

Gómez, C. J., Rodríguez, J., Miralles, P., & Arias, V. (2021). Effects of a teacher training program on the motivation and satisfaction of history secondary students. *Revista de Psicodidáctica*, *26*(1), 45–52. doi:10.1016/j.psicoe.2020.08.001

Gómez, C. J., Rodríguez-Medina, J., Miralles, P., & Arias, V. B. (2021). Efectos de un programa de formación del profesorado en la motivación y satisfacción de los estudiantes de historia en enseñanza secundaria. *Revista de Psicodidáctica*, *26*(1), 45–52. doi:10.1016/j.psicod.2020.07.002

Gómez, C. J., Rodríguez-Pérez, R. A., & Mirete, A. B. (2018). Metodología didáctica y concepciones epistemológicas sobre la enseñanza de la historia. Una investigación con futuros maestros. *Revista Complutense de Educación*, *24*(1), 237–250.

Gómez, C. J., Rodríguez, R. A., & Miralles, P. (2014). La enseñanza de la Historia en educación primaria y la construcción de una narrativa nacional. *Perfiles Educativos*, *37*(150), 20–38.

Gómez, C. J., Rodríguez, R. A., & Mirete, A. B. (2018). Percepción de la enseñanza de la historia y concepciones epistemológicas. Una investigación para futuros maestros [Perceptions of history teaching and epistemological conceptions. An investigation for future teachers]. *Revista Complutense de Educación*, *29*(1), 237–250. doi:10.5209/RCED.52233

Gómez, C., Miralles, P., & Molina, S. (2015). Presentación Evaluación, competencias históricas y educación ciudadana. *Revista de Estudios Sociales*, (52), 9–14.

Gómez, C., & Sobrino, D. (2018). Métodos activos de aprendizaje y adquisición de competencias en la clase de Historia. In P. Miralles & C. Gómez (Eds.), *La educación histórica ante el reto de las competencias Métodos, recursos y enfoques de enseñanza* (pp. 111–126). Octaedro.

Gómez-Carrasco, C. J., Chaparro Sainz, Á., Felices de la Fuente, M., & Cózar Gutiérrez, R. (2020). Estrategias metodológicas y uso de recursos digitales para la enseñanza de la historia. Análisis de recuerdos y opiniones del profesorado en formación inicial. *Aula Abierta*, *49*(1), 65–74. doi:10.17811/rifie.49.1.2020.65-74

Gómez-Carrasco, C. J., & Chapman, A. (2016). Pensamiento histórico y evaluación de competencias en el currículo de Inglaterra y España. Un estudio comparativo. In R. López-Facal (Ed.), *Ciencias Sociales, educación y futuro. Investigaciones en didáctica de las ciencias sociales* (pp. 432–445). Universidad de Santiago de Compostela.

Gómez-Carrasco, C. J., Martínez-Miralles, P., & López-Facal, R. (2021). *Handbook of Research on Teacher Education in History and Geography*. Peter Lang Publishing. doi:10.3726/b18091

Gómez-Carrasco, C. J., & Miralles Martínez, P. (2017). *Los espejos de Clío. Usos y abusos de la Historia en el ámbito escolar*. Sílex.

Gómez-Carrasco, C. J., & Miralles Martínez, P. (2018). Las competencias históricas en perspectiva comparada. Enfoques internacionales sobre su desarrollo y evaluación. *Educatio Siglo XXI*, *36*(1), 11–20.

Gómez-Carrasco, C. J., Rodríguez-Medina, J., Chaparro-Sainz, Á., & Monteagudo-Fernández, J. (2021). Teaching Approaches and Profile Analysis: An Exploratory Study With Trainee History Teachers. *SAGE Open*, *12*(1).

Gómez-García, S., Planells, A. J., & Chicharro-Merayo, M. (2017). ¿Los alumnos quieren aprender con videojuegos? Lo que opinan sus usuarios del potencial educativo de este medio. *Educar*, *53*(1), 49–66. doi:10.5565/rev/educar.848

González, N., Henríquez, H., Pagès, J., & Santisteban, A. (2008). Empathie historique pour un présent en mutation. L'enseignement et l'apprentissage de la compréhension historique à travers une expérience didactique. In *Colloque Didactiques de l'Histoire, de la Géographie et de l'Éducation à la Citoyenneté. Enjeux du Monde, enjeux d'apprentissage en histoire, géographie, éducation à la citoyenneté Quels apports des didactiques?* (pp. 1-10). Université de Nantes.

González-Acosta, E., Almeida-González, M., Torres-Chils, A., & Traba-Montejo, Y. M. (2020). La gamificación como herramienta educativa: El estudiante de contabilidad en el rol del gerente, del contador y del auditor. *Formación Universitaria*, *13*(5), 155–164. doi:10.4067/S0718-50062020000500155

González, D., Jeong, J. S., Cañada, F., & Gallego, A. (2017). The teaching of science content through a "Flipped" model: An instructional proposal for students in Primary Education. *Enseñanza de las Ciencias*, *35*(2), 71–87. doi:10.5565/rev/ensciencias.2233

González, G., & Skultety, L. (2018). Teacher learning in a combined professional development intervention. *Teaching and Teacher Education*, *71*, 341–354. doi:10.1016/j.tate.2018.02.003

González-González, C., & Blanco-Izquierdo, F. (2012). Designing social videogames for educational uses. *Computers & Education*, *58*(1), 250–262. doi:10.1016/j.compedu.2011.08.014

Grant, S. G. (2001). It's Just the Facts, or Is It? The Relationship between Teachers' Practices and Students' Understandings of History. *Theory and Research in Social Education*, *29*(1), 65–108. doi:10.1080/00933104.2001.10505930

Gray, M. (2015). *Teaching the Holocaust. Practical approaches for ages 11-18*. Routledge. doi:10.4324/9781315763286

Greenhow, C., Lewin, C., & Staudt Willet, K. B. (2021). The educational response to Covid-19 across two countries: A critical examination of initial digital pedagogy adoption. *Technology, Pedagogy and Education*, *30*(1), 7–25. doi:10.1080/1475939X.2020.1866654

Green, T. (2001). Teaching students to critically evaluate web pages. *The Clearing House: A Journal of Educational Strategies, Issues and Ideas*, *75*(1), 32–34. doi:10.1080/00098650109599231

Gros, B. (Coord.). (1998). *Jugando con videojuegos: educación y entretenimiento*. Bilbao, Desclée de Brouwer.

Gros, B. (Coord.). (2008). Videojuegos y aprendizaje. Barcelona, Spain: Graó.

Gros, B., & Garrido-Miranda, J. M. (2008). "Con el dedo en la pantalla": El uso de un videojuego de estrategia en la mediación de aprendizajes curriculares. *Teoría de la Educación. Educación y Cultura en la Sociedad de la Información*, *9*(3), 108–129.

Guerrero-Romera, C., López-García, A., & Monteagudo-Fernández, J. (2019). Development of historical thinking in the classroom through a training programme for Secondary Education. *Revista Electrónica Interuniversitaria de Formación del Profesorado*, *22*(2). Advance online publication. doi:10.6018/reifop.22.2.363911

Guerrero-Romera, C., Sánchez-Ibáñez, R., Escribano, V., & Vivas, V. (2021). The perceptions of active teachers regarding the most suitable resources for teaching history. *Humanities & Social Sciences Communications*, *8*, 61. doi:10.105741599-021-00736-7

Guerrero-Romera, C., Sánchez-Ibáñez, R., & Miralles-Martínez, P. (2022). Approaches to History Teaching According to a Structural Equation Model. *Frontiers in Education.*, *7*, 842977. doi:10.3389/feduc.2022.842977

Guevara, J. M., & Colomer, J. C. (2017). Minecraft y Eduloc en historia y geografía. *Íber. Didáctica de las Ciencias Sociales. Geografía e Historia*, *86*, 16–23.

Guevara, J. M., & Colomer, J. C. (2017). Minecraft y Eduloc, en historia y geografía. *Íber. Didáctica de las Ciencias Sociales. Geografía e Historia*, (86), 16–23.

Guillén, M. (2016). Un viaje al siglo XVI a partir de los casos de un corsario y un bandolero. Una experiencia de empatía histórica en secundaria. *Clío. History and HistoryTeaching, 42.*

Gülbahar, Y., Madran, R. O., & Kalelioglu, F. (2010). Development and evaluation of an interactive WebQuest environment:"Web Macerasi. *Journal of Educational Technology & Society*, *13*(3), 139–150. https://www.jstor.org/stable/10.2307/jeductechsoci.13.3.139

Gültekin, F., & Akça Berk, N. 2018. İnsan, zaman ve mekân: sosyal bilgiler öğretmen adaylarının bağlamsallaştırma becerileri. In Uluslararası Tarih Eğitimi Sempozyumu Bildiri Kitabı (pp. 775-791). Academic Press.

Gürgil, F., Ünal, M., & Aksoy, B. (2019). Social Studies Preservice Teachers' Views on and Experiences with WebQuest. *Journal of Education and Training Studies*, *7*(4), 131–141. doi:10.11114/jets.v7i4.4061

Haaranen, L., Ihantola, P., Hakulinen, L., & Korhonen, A. (2014) How (not) to introduce badges to online exercises. *Proceedings of the 45th ACM Technical Symposium on Computer Science Education*, 33–38. 10.1145/2538862.2538921

Hakak, S., Fazmidar, N., Noor, M., Nizam, M., Affal, H., Hussin, M., Ahmed, M., & Imran, M. (2019). Cloud-assisted gamification for education and learning – Recent advances and challenge. *Computers & Electrical Engineering*, *74*, 22–34. doi:10.1016/j.compeleceng.2019.01.002

Halawi, L., McCarthy, R., & Pires, S. (2009). An evaluation of E-Learning on the basis of Bloom's taxonomy: An exploration study. *Journal of Education for Business*, *84*(6), 374–380. doi:10.3200/JOEB.84.6.374-380

Hamari, J., Koivisto, J., & Sarsa, H. (2014). Does Gamification Work?– A Literature Review of Empirical Studies on Gamification. In R. H. Sprague (Ed.), *47th Hawaii International Conference on System Science (HICSS)* (pp. 3025-3034). IEEE Computer Society. /HICSS.2014.37710.1109/HICSS.2014.377

Hammer, J., & Heller, K. (2012). *Playing history: How Ars Magica players develop historical literacy. Proceedings of Meaningful Play.* Available in: https://meaningfulplay.msu.edu/proceedings2012/mp2012_submission_7.pdf

Hammer, J., & Turkington, M. (2021). Designing Role-Playing Games that Address the Holocaust. *International Journal of Designs for Learning*, *12*(1), 42–53. doi:10.14434/ijdl.v12i1.31265

Han-Huey, C., Kofinas, A., & Luo, J. (2018). Enhancing student learning experience with technology-mediated gamification: An empirical study. *Computer Education*, *121*, 1–17. doi:10.1016/j.compedu.2018.01.009

Hanus, M. D., & Fox, J. (2015). Assessing the effects of gamification in the classroom: A longitudinal study on intrinsic motivation, social comparison, satisfaction, effort, and academic performance. *Computers & Education*, *80*, 152–161. doi:10.1016/j.compedu.2014.08.019

Hao, Y., & Lee, K. S. (2016). Teaching in flipped classrooms: Exploring pre-service teachers' concerns. *Journal of Computer in Human Behavior*, *57*, 250–260. doi:10.1016/j.chb.2015.12.022

Hassanien, A. (2006). An evaluation of the webquest as a computer-based learning tool. *Research in Post-Compulsory Education*, *11*(2), 235–250. doi:10.1080/13596740600769230

Havekes, H., Coppen, P. A., Luttenberg, J., & van Boxtel, C. (2012). Knowing and doing history: A conceptual framework and pedagogy for teaching historical contextualisation. *International Journal of Historical Learning, Teaching and Research*, 11.

Hayes, P., & Roth, J. K. (2010). *The Oxford Handbook of Holocaust Studies*. Oxford University Press. doi:10.1093/oxfordhb/9780199211869.001.0001

Heller, A. (1990). *Can modernity survive?* University of California Press.

Hernández, A. M. (2019). *Estrategias y recursos didácticos para la enseñanza de las Ciencias Sociales*. Ediciones Pirámide.

Hernández-Fernández, A., Olmedo-Torre, N., & Peña, M. (2020). Is Classroom Gamification Opposed to Performance? *Sustainability*, *12*(23), 9958. doi:10.3390u12239958

Herrera, Z., & Gil, M. D. C. (2015). Literatura, tecnologías de información y comunicación en clases de historia. *Revista de Ciencias Sociales*, *XXI*(2), 327–336.

Hinojo-Lucena, F. J., Aznar-Díaz, I., Cáceres-Reche, M. P., & Romero-Rodríguez, J. M. (2019). Flipped Classroom Method for the Teacher Training for Secondary Education: A Case Study in the University of Granada, Spain. *International Journal of Emerging Technologies in Learning*, *14*(11), 202–208. doi:10.3991/ijet.v14i11.9853

Hoofman, J., & Secord, E. (2021). The Effect of COVID-19 on Education. *Pediatric Clinics of North America*, *68*(5), 1071–1079. doi:10.1016/j.pcl.2021.05.009 PMID:34538299

Hortigüela, D., Abella, V., Delgado, V., & Ausin, V. (2018). Valoración del aprendizaje obtenido en la formación inicial del profesorado en función del enfoque metodológico. *Profesorado. Revista de Currículum y Formación del Profesorado*, *22*(2), 227-246. https://recyt.fecyt.es/index.php/profesorado/article/view/66372/0

Howell, R. A. (2021). Engaging students in education for sustainable development: The benefits of active learning, reflective practices and flipped classroom pedagogies. *Journal of Cleaner Production*, *325*, 129–168. doi:10.1016/j.jclepro.2021.129318

Huang, W. H., & Soman, D. (2013). *Gamification Of Education*. Accessed on May 25, 2022, at https://mybrainware.com/wp-content/uploads/2017/11/Gamification-in-Education-Huang.pdf

Huang, B., Hew, K. F., & Lo, C. K. (2019). Investigating the effects of gamification-enhanced flipped learning on undergraduate students' behavioral and cognitive engagement. *Interactive Learning Environments*, *27*(8), 1106–1126. doi:10.1080/10494820.2018.1495653

Huang, R., Ritzhaupt, A. D., Sommer, M., Zhu, J., Stephen, A., Valle, N., Hampton, J., & Li, J. (2020). The impact of gamification in educational settings on student learning outcomes: A meta-analysis. *Educational Technology Research and Development, 68*(4), 1875–1901. doi:10.100711423-020-09807-z

Huda, M., Maseleno, A., Shahrill, M., Jasmi, K. A., Mustari, I., & Basiron, B. (2017). Exploring adaptive teaching competencies in big data era. *International Journal of Emerging Technologies in Learning, 12*(3), 68–83. doi:10.3991/ijet.v12i03.6434

Huijgen, T., van Boxtel, C., van de Grift, W., & Holthuis, P. (2016). Toward Historical Perspective Taking: Students' Reasoning When Contextualizing the Actions of People in the Past. *Theory and Research in Social Education, 45*(1), 110–144. doi:10.1080/00933104.2016.1208597

Hunicke, R., Leblanc, M., & Zubek, R. (2004). MDA: A formal approach to game design and game research. In D. Fu, S. Henke, & J. Orkin (Eds.), *Proceedings of the AAAI-04 Workshop on Challenges in Game AI* (pp. 1-5). AAAI Press.

Hunicke, R., Leblanc, M., & Zubek, R. (2004). MDA: A Formal Approach to Game Design and Game Research. In *Proceedings of the AAAI Workshop on Challenges in Game AI.* AAAI Press.

Hussein, M. T., & Fast, O. (2020). Gut feeling: A grounded theory study to identify clinical educators' reasoning processes in putting students on a learning contract. *Journal of Clinical Nursing, 29*(1-2), 75–84. doi:10.1111/jocn.15058 PMID:31512306

Hyang Choi, S., & Leicht, A. (Eds.). (2017). *Education about the Holocaust and preventing genocide: a policy guide.* UNESCO.

Ibagón, N. J. (2016). Enseñar y aprender historia a partir del análisis de fuentes históricas. Una experiencia formativa en Educación Superior. Voces y silencios. *Revista Latinoamericana de educación, 7*(1), 121-133.

Ibagón, N. J. (2021). El uso de fuentes históricas en la escuela y el desarrollo del pensamiento histórico del estudiantado [The use of historical sources in schools and the development of students' historical thinking]. In Educación histórica para el siglo XXI, principios epistemológicos y metodológicos [History Education for the 21st century, epistemological and methodological principles] (pp. 155-183). Universidad Icesi y Universidad del Valle.

Ibagón-Martín, N. J., & Miralles-Martínez, P. (2021). Temas controversiales y educación histórica. In C. J. Gómez, X. M. Souto, & P. Miralles (Eds.), *Enseñanza de las ciencias sociales para una ciudadanía democrática: Estudios en homenaje al profesor Ramón López Facal* (pp. 123–137). Ediciones Octaedro.

Ibagón, N. J., & Miralles, P. (2019). Historia a enseñar, historia enseñada e historia aprendida. Posibilidades investigativas en el campo de la educación Histórica en Iberoamérica [History to be taught, taught history and learned history. Research possibilities in the field of history education in Ibero-America]. *Historia y Espacio, 15*(53), 9–18.

Imbernón Muñoz, F. (2019). La formación del profesorado de Secundaria: La eterna pesadilla. *Profesorado, Revista De Currículum Y Formación Del Profesorado, 23*(3), 151-163. doi:10.30827/profesorado.v23i3.9302

Iturriaga, D., & Medel, I. (2017). La historia a través de los videojuegos. Evaluación mediante Civilization y Assassin's Creed. *Íber. Didáctica de las Ciencias Sociales. Geografía e Historia, 86*, 30–36.

Jagušt, T., Botički, I., & So, H. J. (2018). Examining competitive, collaborative and adaptive gamification in young learners' math learning. *Computers & Education, 125*, 444–457. doi:10.1016/j.compedu.2018.06.022

Jansen, C., & Van Der Merwe, P. (2015). Teaching Practice in the 21st Century: Emerging Trends, Challenges and Opportunities. *Universal Journal of Educational Research, 3*(3), 190–199. doi:10.13189/ujer.2015.030304

Jiménez-Palacios, R., & Cuenca-López, J. M. (2021). La enseñanza y aprendizaje de las Ciencias Sociales a través del patrimonio, videojuegos y emociones. Estudio de caso en un IES de Huelva (España). *Panta Rei. Revista digital de Historia y Didáctica de la Historia*, (15), 103-133.

Jiménez-Palacios, R., & Cuenca-López, J.M. (2015). El uso didáctico de los videojuegos: concepciones e ideas de futuros docentes de Ciencias Sociales. *Clío. History and History teaching, 41*, 14-85.

Jiménez-Palacios, R. (2021). El videojuego como recurso emocionante para educar en patrimonio. In J. M. Cuenca, J. Estepa, & M. Martín (Eds.), *Investigación y buenas prácticas en educación patrimonial entre la escuela y el museo: territorio, emociones y ciudadanía* (pp. 73–85). Trea.

Jiménez-Palacios, R., & Cuenca, J. M. (2016). Construyendo el conocimiento a través de videojuegos. El caso del 'El Códex del Peregrino. In L. Arias, A. I. Ponce, & D. Verdú (Eds.), *Estrategias y recursos para la integración del patrimonio y los museos en la educación formal* (pp. 237–247). Editum.

Johnson, R. T., Johnson, D. W., & Holubec, E. J. (1999). *El aprendizaje cooperativo en el aula*. Paidós.

Jónsson, Ó. P., & Garces Rodriguez, A. (2021). Educating democracy: Competences for a democratic culture. *Education, Citizenship and Social Justice*, *16*(1), 62–77. doi:10.1177/1746197919886873

Kapell, M. W., & Elliott, A. B. R. (2013). *Playing with the Past: Digital Games and the Simulation of History*. Bloomsbury.

Kapp, K. (2012). *The gamification of learning and instruction: Game-based methods and strategies for training and education*. John Wiley & Sons.

Kapp, K. (2012). *The Gamification of Learning and Instruction: Game-Based Methods and Strategies for Training and Education*. John Wiley & Sons.

Kapp, K. M. (2012). *The Gamification of Learning and Instruction. Game-Based Methods and Strategies for Training and Education*. John Wiley & Sons.

Kapp, K. M. (2012). *The Gamification of Learning and Instruction: Game-based Methods and Strategies for Training and Education*. John Wiley & Sons.

Karatas, I., Tunc, M., Yilmaz, N., & Karaci, G. (2017). An Investigation of Technological Pedagogical Content Knowledge, Self-Confidence, and Perception of Pre-Service Middle School Mathematics Teachers towards Instructional *Technologies. Journal of Educational Technology & Society*, *20*(3), 122–132. https://jstor.org/stable/26196124

Karsenti, T., Bugmann, J., & Gros, P. P. (2017). *Transforming Education with Minecraft? Results of an exploratory study conducted with 118 elementary-school students*. CRIFPE.

Kaur, S., & Kauts, A. (2018). Impact of webquest on student engagement. *Indian Journal of Public Health*, *9*(12), 1665–1669.

Keller, J. M. (1987). Development and use of the ARCS model of instructional design. *Journal of Instructional Development*, *10*(3), 2–10. doi:10.1007/BF02905780

Keller, J. M. (2010). *Motivational design for learning and performance: The ARCS model approach*. Springer US. doi:10.1007/978-1-4419-1250-3

Kelly, R. (2000). Working with WebQuests: Making the web accessible to students with disabilities. *Teaching Exceptional Children*, *32*(6), 4–13. doi:10.1177/004005990003200601

Kerr, D., & Huddleston, T. (Eds.). (2015). *Teaching Controversial Issues. Through Education for Democratic Citizenship and Human Rights (EDC/HRE)*. Council of Europe.

Kim, S., Song, K., Lockee, B., & Burton, J. (2018). What is Gamification in Learning and Education? In S. Kim, K. Song, B. Lockee, & J. Burton (Eds.), *Gamification in Learning and Education* (pp. 25–38). Springer International Publishing. doi:10.1007/978-3-319-47283-6_4

Kocakoyun, S., & Ozdamli, F. (2018). A Review of Research on Gamification Approach in Education. In R. Morese, S. Palermo & J. Nervo (Eds.), Socialization - A Multidimensional Perspective (pp. 51-72). IntechOpen. doi:10.5772/intechopen.74131

Köksal, H. (2012). *Yenilikçi tarih öğretimi etkinlik örnekleri (Edt).* Harf Eğitim Yayıncılığı.

König, J., Ligtvoeta, R., Klemenza, S., & Rothlandb, M. (2017). Effects of opportunities to learn in teacher preparation on future teachers' general pedagogical knowledge: Analyzing program characteristics and outcomes. *Studies in Educational Evaluation, 53*, 122–133. doi:10.1016/j.stueduc.2017.03.001

Körber, A. (2005). German history didactics: from historical consciousness to historical competencies and beyond? In H. Bjerg, C. Lenz, & E. Thorstensen (Eds.), *Historicizing the uses of the past. Scandinavian perspective on history culture, historical consciousness and didactics of history related to World War II* (pp. 145–164). Transcript Verlag.

Kori, K., Mäeots, M., & Pedaste, M. (2014). Guided reflection to support quality of reflection and inquiry in web-based learning. *Procedia: Social and Behavioral Sciences, 112*, 242–251. doi:10.1016/j.sbspro.2014.01.1161

Koutsogianni, E. (2014). Promoting motivation and autonomy through Webquest implementation in Junior High school EFL context. *Research Papers in Language Teaching & Learning, 5*(1), 307–323.

Kramer, S. (Director and Producer). (1961). *Judgment at Nuremberg* [Film]. Roxlom Films.

Krathwohl, D. R. (2010). A revision of Bloom's taxonomy: An overview. *Theory into Practice, 41*(4), 212–218. doi:10.120715430421tip4104_2

Kujawa, J. (2006). WebQuests Travel to Higher Education. *Journal of Hospitality & Tourism Education, 18*(3), 45–55. doi:10.1080/10963758.2006.10696863

Landers, R. N. (2014). Developing a Theory of Gamified Learning: Linking Serious Games and Gamification of Learning. *Simulation & Gaming, 45*(6), 752–768. doi:10.1177/1046878114563660

Lee, P. J., Dickinson, A. & Ashby, R. (1997). "Just ano theremperor". Understanding action in the past. *International Journal of Educational Research. Explanation and understanding in learning History, 27*(3), 233-244. doi:10.1016/S0883-0355(97)89731-5

Lee, P., & Ashby, R. (2000). Progression in Historical Understanding among Students Ages 7-14. In Knowing, Teaching, and Leaming History: National and Intemational Perspectives (pp. 199-222). University Press.

Lee, P., Dickinson, A., & Ashby, R. (2004). Las ideas de los niños sobre la historia. In M. Carretero & J.F. Voss (Coords.), Aprender y pensar la historia (pp. 217-248). Amorrortu.

Lee, J. J., & Hammer, J. (2011). Gamification in Education: What, How, Why Bother? *Academic Exchange Quarterly, 15*(2), 1–5.

Lee, P. (2005). Putting Principles into Practice: Understanding History. In M. S. Donovan & J. D. Bransford (Eds.), *How students learn: History in the classroom* (pp. 29–78). National Academies Press.

Lee, P. (2005). Putting principles intro practice: understanding history. In M. Donovan & J. Bransford (Eds.), *How students learn: History in the classroom* (pp. 31–77). National Academies Press.

Lee, P. (2011). History education and historical literacy. In I. Davies (Ed.), *Debates in History Teaching* (pp. 63–72). Routledge.

Lee, P. J. (1983). History Teaching and Philosophy of History. *History and Theory*, *22*(4), 19–49. doi:10.2307/2505214

Lee, P. J., & Ashby, R. (2001). Empathy, perspective taking, and rational understanding. In O. L. Davis Jr, E. A. Yaeger, & S. J. Foster (Eds.), *Historical empathy and perspective taking in the social studies* (pp. 21–50). Rowman & Littlefield Publishers, Inc.

Lee, P., & Ashby, R. (2000). Progression in Historical Understanding among Students Ages 7-14. In P. N. Stearns, P. Seixas, & S. Wineburg (Eds.), *Knowing, Teaching, and Learning History: National and International Perspectives* (pp. 199–222). New York University Press.

Lee, P., & Ashby, R. (2000). Progression in Historical Understanding among Students Ages 7-14. In P. N. Stearns, P. Seixas, & S. Wineburg (Eds.), *Knowing, Teaching, and Learning History: National and International Perspectives* (pp. 199–222). New York University Press.

León, M. J., & Crisol, E. (2011). Diseño de cuestionarios (oppumaugr y opeumaugr): la opinión y la percepción del profesorado y los estudiantes sobre el uso de las metodologías activas en la universidad. *Profesorado. Revista de currículum y formación del profesorado, 15*(2), 271-298. https://recyt.fecyt.es/index.php/profesorado/article/view/43508

Lévesque, S. (2008). Thinking historically: Educating students for the twenty-first century. Toronto University Press.

Lévesque, S. (2008). *Thinking Historically. Educating Students for the 21th Century*. University of Toronto Press.

Lévesque, S. (2008). *Thinking historically. Educating students for the twenty-first century*. University of Toronto Press.

Lévesque, S. (2008). *Thinking Historically: Educating Students for the 21st Century*. University of Toronto Press.

Lévesque, S. (2011). What It Means to Think Historically. In P. Clark (Ed.), *New possibilitie sfor the past: shaping history education in Canada* (pp. 115–138). UBC Press.

Lévesque, S. G., & Zanazanian, P. (2015). Developing Historical Consciousness and a Community of History Practitioners: A Survey of Prospective History Teachers Across Canada. *McGill Journal of Education*, *50*(2-3), 389–412. doi:10.7202/1036438ar

Lévesque, S., & Clark, P. (2018). Historical Thinking: Definitions and Educational Applications. In S. Metzger & L. M. Harris (Eds.), *The Wiley International Handbook of History Teaching and Learning* (pp. 119–148). John Wiley & Sons, Inc. doi:10.1002/9781119100812.ch5

Levin-Goldberg, J. (2014). Webquest 2.0: Best Practices for the 21st Century. *Journal of Institutional Research*, *3*, 73–82.

Levitt, R., & Piro, J. (2014). Game-changer: Operationalizing the common core using WebQuests and 'gamification' in teacher education. *International Journal of Web-Based Learning and Teaching Technologies*, *9*(3), 53–71. doi:10.4018/ijwltt.2014070104

Levy, D., & Szneider, N. (2002). Memory Unbound: The Holocaust and the Formation of Cosmopolitan Memory. *European Journal of Social Theory*, *5*(1), 87–106. doi:10.1177/1368431002005001002

Li, C., Lee, M., Lien, Y., Huang, Y., Wang, C., & Hou, H. (2019). A Real Escape Gamification Teaching Activity Integrated with Situated Learning and Multi-dimensional Scaffolding for Elementary School Social Studies Course. In *2019 8th International Congress on Advanced Applied Informatics (IIAI-AAI)* (pp. 1051-1052). IEEE. 10.1109/IIAI-AAI.2019.00222

Liceras, A. (2016). Las dificultades en la enseñanza y el aprendizaje de las ciencias sociales. In A. Liceras & G. Romero (Coords.), Didáctica de las Ciencias Sociales. Fundamentos, contextos y propuestas (pp. 95-118). Pirámide.

Liceras, A. (2016). Las dificultades en la enseñanza y el aprendizaje de las ciencias sociales. In Didáctica de las Ciencias Sociales. Fundamentos, contextos y propuestas (pp. 95-118). Pirámide.

Llopis, M. A., & Balaguer, P. (2016). El uso del juego en educación. Gamificación. In O. Chiva & M. Martí (Coords.), Métodos pedagógicos activos y globalizadores (pp. 85-101). Graó.

Loorbach, N., Peters, O., Karreman, J., & Steehouder, M. (2015). Validation of the Instructional Materials Motivation Survey (IMMS) in a self-directed instructional setting aimed at working with technology. *British Journal of Educational Technology*, *46*(1), 204–218. doi:10.1111/bjet.12138

López Facal, R., Velasco, L., Santidrián, V. M., & Armas Castro, X. A. (Coords.). (2011). *Pensar históricamente en tiempos de globalización: actas del I Congreso Internacional sobre enseñanza de la historia* [Thinking Historically in Times of Globalisation: Proceedings of the 1st International Conference on History Education]. Universidade de Santiago de Compostela.

López Facal, R., Gómez, C. J., Miralles, P., & Prats, J. (2017). Pensamiento histórico, enseñanza de la historia y competencias educativas. In R. López Facal, P. Miralles, J. Prats, & C. J. Gómez (Eds.), *Enseñanza de la historia y competencias educativas*. Graó.

López Facal, R., & Valls, R. (2012). La necesidad cívica de saber historia y geografía [The civic need to know history and geography]. In N. de Alba, F. F. García, & A. S. Fernández (Eds.), *Educar para la participación ciudadana en la enseñanza de las Ciencias Sociales* [Educating for civic participation in social science education] (pp. 185–192). Díada Editora. https://cutt.ly/2u5HA2R

López Mateu, G. (2020). La enseñanza del Holocausto: una oportunidad pedagógica para reflexionar sobre los conflictos sociales actuales. *Clio. History and History teaching*, *46*, 30-40. doi:10.26754/ojs_clio/clio.2020465300

López, R & Valls, R. (2012). La necesidad cívica de saber historia y geografía. *Educar para la participación ciudadana En la Enseñanza de las ciencias sociales. Volumen I. Asociación Universitaria de Profesorado de Didáctica de las Ciencias Sociales,* 185-192

López-Facal, R. (2014). La LOMCE y la competencia histórica. *Ayer*, *94*, 273–285.

Lucas, L., & Delgado, E. J. (2018). Educación para una ciudadanía comprometida en la enseñanza de las Ciencias Sociales: ¿Qué piensa el alumnado de un profesor innovador sobre su aprendizaje? *Didáctica de las Ciencias Experimentales y Sociales*, *35*(35), 3–16. doi:10.7203/dces.35.12572

Luelmo, M. J. (2018). Origen y desarrollo de las Metodologías Activas dentro del sistema educativo español. *Encuentro Journal*, (27), 4-21. http://www3.uah.es/encuentrojournal/index.php/encuentro/article/view/2

Lukacs, J. (1968). *Historical consciousness: the remembered past*. Transaction publishers.

Magalhães, O. (2013). Em torno da escolha do manual escolar: opções de professors. In T. García, M. A. Schmidt, & R. Valls (Eds.), Didática, História e manuais escolares: contextos ibero-americanos (pp. 231-246). Ijuí: Editora Unijuí.

Majuri, J., Koivisto, J., & Hamari, J. (2018). Gamification of education and learning: A review of empirical literature. In J. Koivisto & J. Hamari (Eds.), *Proceedings of the 2nd International GamiFIN Conference* (pp. 11–19). CEUR Workshop Proceedings.

Maloy, J., Fries, L., Laski, L., & Ramírez, G. (2019). Seductive details in the flipped classroom: The impact of interesting but educationally irrelevant information on student learning and motivation. *CBE Life Sciences Education*, *18*(3), 1–10. doi:10.1187/cbe.19-01-0004 PMID:31469621

Manzano-León, A., Camacho-Lazarraga, P., Guerrero, M. A., Guerrero-Puerta, L., Aguilar-Parra, J. M., Trigueros, R., & Alias, A. (2021). Between Level Up and Game Over: A Systematic Literature Review of Gamification in Education. *Sustainability*, *13*(4), 2247. doi:10.3390u13042247

March, T. (2003). *What WebQuests are (really)*. http://bestwebquests. com/what_webquests_are. asp

March, T. (2004). The learning power of WebQuests. *Educational Leadership*, *61*(4), 42–47.

Marczewski, A. (2014). *Thin Layer vs Deep Level Gamification*. Gamasutra. The Art and Business of Making Games. https://www.gamasutra.com/blogs/AndrzejMarczewski/ 20140120/208924/ Thin_Layer_vs_Deep_Level_Gamification. php

Marczewski, A. (2015). *Even Ninja Monkeys Like to Play: Gamification, Game Thinking and Motivational Design*. Independently Published.

Marczewski, A. (2015). *Even Ninja Monkeys Like to Play: Gamification, Game Thinking and Motivational Design*. CreateSpace Independent Publishing Platform.

Marín, V. (2017). La enseñanza de la historia y la construcción y la construcción de una ciudadanía crítica. In La enseñanza de la historia en el siglo XXI. Desarrollo y evaluación de competencias históricas para una ciudadanía democrática (pp. 95-112). Murcia: Editum.

Marrón, M. J. (1996). Los juegos de simulación como recurso didáctico para la enseñanza de la geografía. *Didáctica geográfica, 1*, 45-56.

Martens, A., & Mueller, W. (2016). Gamification - A Structured Analysis. *2016 IEEE 16th International Conference on Advanced Learning Technologies (ICALT),* 138-142. 10.1109/ICALT.2016.72

Martín-Cáceres, M., Estepa-Giménez, J., & Cuenca-López, J. M. (2021). Los patrimonios controversiales en la educación patrimonial para la formación de la ciudadanía. In C. J. Gómez, X. M. Souto, & P. Miralles (Eds.), *Enseñanza de las ciencias sociales para una ciudadanía democrática: Estudios en homenaje al profesor Ramón López Facal* (pp. 109–122). Ediciones Octaedro.

Martín, E., Pozo, J. I., Mateos, M., Martín, A., & Del Puy, M. (2014). Infant, primary and secondary teacher's conceptions of learning and teaching and their relation to educational variables. *Revista Latinoamericana de Psicología*, *46*(3), 211–221. doi:10.1016/S0120-0534(14)70024-X

Martínez Hita, M. (2022). *El pensamiento histórico en Educación Primaria. Diseño y evaluación de un programa de intervención gamificado* [Tesis de Doctorado, Universidad de Murcia]. Repositorio Institucional de la Universidad de Murcia.

Martínez Navarro, G. (2017). Tecnologías y nuevas tendencias en educación: aprender jugando. El caso de Kahoot. *Opción: Revista de Ciencias Humanas y Sociales, 33*(83), 252–277. https://produccioncientificaluz.org/index.php/opcion/article/view/23116

Martínez Valcárcel, N. (2014). *La historia de España en los recuerdos escolares*. Nau Llibres.

Martínez Valcárcel, N., Souto González, X. M., & Beltrán Llavador, J. (2005). Los problemas docentes en historia de bachillerato: La gran diversidad bajo la aparente uniformidad. *Didáctica de las Ciencias Experimentales y Sociales*, *19*, 33–55.

Martínez, J. M., Egea, A., & Arias, L. (2018). Evaluación de un videojuego educativo de contenido histórico. La opinión de los estudiantes. *Revista Latinoamericana de Tecnología Educativa, 17*(1).

Martínez-Hita, M. (2022). *El pensamiento histórico en Educación Primaria. Diseño y evaluación de un programa de intervención gamificado* [Historical thinking in Primary Education. Design and evaluation of a gamified intervention programme] [Doctoral thesis, University of Murcia]. Digitum: Repositorio Institucional de la Universidad de Murcia. http://hdl.handle.net/10201/116267

Martínez-Hita, M. (2022). *El pensamiento histórico en Educación Primaria: diseño y evaluación de un programa de intervención gamificado*. PhD. Universidad de Murcia. https://digitum.um.es/digitum/handle/10201/116267

Martínez-Hita, M., & Gómez, C. J. (2016). Diferentes enfoques sobre la enseñanza de la historia y del pensamiento histórico en el currículo español y canadiense. In J. Maquilón, C. J. Gómez, & M. B. Alfageme (Eds.), De la investigación a la mejora educativa en las aulas (pp. 19–32). Academic Press.

Martínez-Hita, M. (2019). Análisis comparativo del modelo cognitivo y conceptos históricos en el currículum español e inglés. In *IV Jornadas Doctorales Escuela Internacional de Doctorado de la Universidad de Murcia (EIDUM)* (pp. 560–563). Editum.

Martínez-Hita, M., & Gómez, C. J. (2018). Cognitive level and thinking historically competencies in history textbooks from Spain and England: A comparative study. *Review of Education, 379*, 136–159.

Martínez-Hita, M., & Gómez, C. J. (2018). Nivel cognitivo y competencias de pensamiento histórico en los libros de texto de Historia de España e Inglaterra. Un estudio comparativo. *Review of Education, 379*, 145–169. doi:10.4438/1988-592X-RE-2017-379-364

Martínez-Hita, M., Gómez-Carrasco, C. J., & Miralles-Martínez, P. (2021). The effects of a gamified project based on historical thinking on the academic performance of primary school children. *Humanit Soc Sci Commun, 8*(1), 122. doi:10.105741599-021-00796-9

Martínez-Hita, M., & Miralles, P. (2020). Evaluación del diseño de un programa de intervención gamificado para el desarrollo del pensamiento histórico en Educación Primaria. *RIFOP, 34*(2), 187–204. doi:10.47553/rifop.v34i2.78420

Martínez-Jiménez, R., Pedrosa-Ortega, C., Licerán-Gutiérrez, A., Ruiz-Jiménez, M. C., & García-Martí, E. (2021). Kahoot! as a tool to improve student academic performance in business management subjects. *Sustainability, 13*(5), 2969. doi:10.3390u13052969

Martins, E. (2019). História, historiografia e pesquisa em educação histórica [History, historiography and research in history education]. *Educar em Revista, 35*(74), 17–33. doi:10.1590/0104-4060.63035

Marzano, R. J., Pickering, D., Arredondo, D. E., Blackburn, G. J., Brandt, R. S., & Moffett, C. A. (1992). *Dimensions of learning*. Association for Supervision and Curriculum Development.

Maté, I. (2017). Juegos de rol. Pautas para su uso en clase. *Íber. Didáctica de las Ciencias Sociales. Geografía e Historia, 86*, 24–29.

McCall, J. (2012). Gaming the past: Using video games to teach secondary history. In *Gaming the Past: Using Video Games to Teach Secondary History*. Routledge.

McDaniel, R., Lindgren, R., & Friskics, J. (2012) Using badges for shaping interactions in online learning environments. *IEEE International Professional Communication Conference*, 12–15. 10.1109/IPCC.2012.6408619

McGonigal, J. (2013). *Por qué los videojuegos pueden mejorar tu vida y cambiar el mundo?: un encuentro entre el mundo virtual y el real en el que las personas salen favorecidas*. Siglo XXI.

Medir, R., & Serra, A. (2021). Una alianza entre los objetivos del desarrollo sostenible y la formación de maestras en ciudadanía sostenible. *Didacticae*, *9*, 79–83.

Mee, R. W., Shahdan, T. S., Ismail, R., Ghani, K. A., Pek, L. S., Von, W. Y., Woo, A., & Rao, Y. S. (2020). Role of gamification in classroom teaching: Pre-service teachers' view. *International Journal of Evaluation and Research in Education*, *9*(3), 684–690. doi:10.11591/ijere.v9i3.20622

Mekler, E. D., Brühlmann, F., Tuch, A. N., & Opwis, K. (2017). Towards understanding the effects of individual gamification elements on intrinsic motivation and performance. *Computers in Human Behavior, 71*, 525-534. https://doi.org/10.1016/j.chb.2015.08.048

Méndez, P., Lage, F., & Cataldi, Z. (2013). M-learning in higher education: Application for mobile devices focusing on self-assessment. In 1er Congreso Nacional de Ingeniería Informática/Sistemas de Información. Proceedings (pp. 1–10). National Technological University.

Mendioroz-Lacambra, A., & Erce-Domínguez, A. (2020). El método arqueológico simulado para desarrollar competencias históricas en educación infantil [Working with archeology in early childhood education to develop historical skills]. *Arte. Individuo y Sociedad*, *32*(3), 767–781. doi:10.5209/aris.65825

Metzger, S. A., & Harris, L. M. (Eds.). (2018). *The Wiley International Handbook of history teaching and learning*. Wiley. doi:10.1002/9781119100812

Meyer, C., & Jones, T. (1993). *Promoting active learning: Strategies for the college classroom*. Jossey-Bass.

Mhlanga, D., & Moloi, T. (2020). COVID-19 and the Digital Transformation of Education: What Are We Learning on 4IR in South Africa? *Education Sciences*, *10*(7), 1–11. doi:10.3390/educsci10070180

Michael, D. R., & Chen, S. L. (2005). Serious Games: Games That Educate, Train, and Inform. *Education*, 1–95. https://dl.acm.org/doi/abs/10.5555/1051239

Miguel-Revilla, D., Carril-Merino, T., & Sánchez-Agustí, M. (2020). An examination of epistemic beliefs about history in initial teacher training: A comparative analysis between primary and secondary education prospective teachers. *Journal of Experimental Education*, *89*(1), 54–73. doi:10.1080/00220973.2020.1718059

Mingorance, A. C., Trujillo, J. M., Cáceres, P., & Torres, C. (2017). Improving academic performance through the inverted classroom methodology focused on active learning for university students of educational sciences. *Journal of Sport and Health Research*, *9*(1), 129–136. doi:10.36097/rsan.v0i31.601.s244

Minte, A., & Ibagón, N. (2017). Pensamiento crítico ¿competencia olvidada en la enseñanza de la historia? [Critical thinking, a neglected skill in history teaching?]. *Revista Entramado*, *13*(2), 186–198. doi:10.18041/entramado.2017v13n2.26228

Miragall, M., & García-Soriano, G. (2016). Transforming an undergraduate psychology class into a flipped classroom. *@tic. Revista d'innovació educativa, 17,* 21–29. doi:10.7203/attic.17.9097

Miralles Martínez, P., Gómez Carrasco, C. J., & Monteagudo Fernández, J. (2019). Percepciones sobre el uso de recursos TIC y «MASS-MEDIA» Para la enseñanza de la historia. Un estudio comparativo en futuros docentes de España-Inglaterra. *Educación XX1, 22*(2). doi:10.5944/educxx1.21377

Miralles, P., & Gómez, C. J. (2021). El pensamiento histórico del alumnado y su relación con las competencias [Students' historical thinking and its relationship to competences]. In Educación histórica para el siglo XXI, principios epistemológicos y metodológicos [History Education for the 21st century, epistemological and methodological principles] (pp. 83-114). Universidad Icesi y Universidad del Valle.

Miralles, P., Molina, S., & Ortuño, J. (2011). La Investigación en Didáctica de las Ciencias Sociales [Research in Social Sciences Didactics]. *Educatio Siglo XXI, 29*(1), 149-174. https://revistas.um.es/educatio/article/view/119921/112891

Miralles, P., & Gómez, C. J. (2021). El pensamiento histórico del alumnado y su relación con las competencias. In *Educación histórica para el siglo XXI. Principios epistemológicos y metodológico.* (pp. 83-114). Universidad del Valle y Universidad Icesi.

Miralles, P., Gómez, C. J., & Arias, L. (2013). Social sciences teaching and information processing. An experience using WebQuests in primary education teacher training. *International Journal of Educational Technology in Higher Education, 10*(2), 344–357.

Miralles, P., Gómez, C. J., & Sánchez, R. (2014). Dime qué preguntas y te diré qué evalúas y enseñas. Análisis de los exámenes de Ciencias Sociales en tercer ciclo de Educación Primaria [Tell me what questions you ask and I will tell you what you assess and teach. Analysis of the Social Sciences examinations in the third cycle of Primary Education]. *Aula Abierta, 42*(2), 83–89. doi:10.1016/j.aula.2014.05.002

Miralles, P., Gómez, C., & Rodríguez, R. (2017). Patrimonio, competencias históricas y metodologías activas de aprendizaje. Un análisis de las opiniones de los docentes en formación en España e Inglaterra. *Estudios Pedagógicos (Valdivia), 43*(4), 161–184. doi:10.4067/S0718-07052017000400009

Molebash, P., & Dodge, B. (2003). Kickstarting inquiry with WebQuests and Web inquiry projects.(Advancing Technology). *Social Education, 67*(3), 158–162.

Molina, S., Ortuño, J., & Miralles, P. (2011). El comentario de fuentes primarias como herramienta para la evaluación de competencias básicas en Historia [The commentary of primary sources as a tool for the assessment of basic skills in History]. In P. Miralles, S. Molina, & A. Santisteban (Eds.), *La evaluación en el proceso de enseñanza y aprendizaje de las ciencias sociales* [Assessment in the teaching and learning process in the social sciences] (Vol. 1, pp. 295–306). AUPDCS.

Molina, S., Rodríguez, R., & Sánchez, R. (2013). Investigar, enseñar y divulgar la historia social: La experiencia del Seminario y grupo de investigación Familia y Élite de Poder de la Universidad de Murcia [Researching, teaching and disseminating social history: the experience of the Seminar and research group Family and Power Elite at the University of Murcia]. *Clio*, 39.

Moliner, L., & Alegre, F. (2021). COVID-19 Restrictions and Its Influence on Students' Mathematics Achievement in Spain. *Education Sciences, 12*(2), 105. doi:10.3390/educsci12020105

Molins-Ruano, P., Sevilla, C., Santini, S., Haya, P. A., Rodríguez, P., & Sacha, G. M. (2014). Designing videogames to improve students' motivation. *Computers in Human Behavior, 31*, 571–579. doi:10.1016/j.chb.2013.06.013

Monteagudo-Fernández, J., Rodríguez Pérez, R. A., Escribano-Miralles, A., & Rodríguez García, A. M. (2020). Percepciones de los estudiantes de Educación Secundaria sobre la enseñanza de la historia, a través del uso de las TIC y recursos digitales. *Revista Electrónica Interuniversitaria de Formación del Profesorado, 23*(2). Advance online publication. doi:10.6018/reifop.417611

Monteagudo, J., Gómez, C. J., & Miralles, P. (2017). Evaluación del diseño e implementación de la metodología flipped-classroom en la formación del profesorado de ciencias sociales. *RED: Revista de Educación a Distancia, 55*(55), 1–26. doi:10.6018/red/55/7

Montilla, M. V., Maraver, P., Romero, C., & Martín, A. (2018). Análisis de las expectativas del profesorado novel sobre su futura labor docente. *Aula Abierta, 47*(2), 185–192. doi:10.17811/rifie.47.2.2018.185-192

Morais, L., Goncalves, V., & De Assis, L. B. (2021). A Case Study on the use of Gamification in the Flipped Classroom. *16th Iberian Conference on Information Systems and Technologies, CISTI. Code 170402*. 10.23919/CISTI52073.2021.9476257

Morales, P., & Landa, V. (2004). Aprendizaje Basado en Problemas. *Theoria*, 145–157. https://cmapspublic.ihmc.us/rid=1152868048651_1396346847_11204/pbl1.pdf

Moreno, A. J., Trujillo, J. M., & Aznar, I. (Coords.). (2021). *Metodologías activas para la enseñanza universitaria*. Graó.

Moreno, E. (2019). El "Breakout EDU" como herramienta clave para la gamificación en la formación inicial de maestros/as. EDUTEC. Revista electrónica de tecnología educativa, (67), 66-79. doi:10.21556/edutec.2019.67.1247

Moreno, N., López, E., & Leiva, J. (2018). El uso de tecnologías emergentes como recursos didácticos en ámbitos educativos. *International Studies on Law and Education*, *29*(30), 131–146. http://www.hottopos.com/isle29_30/131-146Moreno.pdf

Moreno-Vera, J. R. (2018). El pensamiento crítico en la enseñanza de la historia a través de temas controvertidos. *Actualidades Pedagógicas*, *1*(72), 15–28. doi:10.19052/ap.5215

Moreno-Vera, J. R., & Alvén, F. (2020). Concepts for historical and geographical thinking in Sweden's and Spain's Primary Education curricula. *Humanities & Social Sciences Communications*, *7*(1), 107. doi:10.105741599-020-00601-z

Moreno-Vera, J. R., Gómez-Carrasco, C. J., Monteagudo-Fernández, J., & Sainz-Gómez, M. (2021). Gamificación y flipped-classroom en la formación de Ciencias Sociales. Estudio exploratorio y validación de una escala. In M. C. Sánchez-Fuster, J. M. Campillo, & V. Navas (Eds.), *La formación del profesorado en didáctica de las ciencias sociales en el ámbito iberoamericano* (pp. 79–98). Editum.

Moreno-Vera, J. R., Ponsoda-López de Atalaya, S., & Blanes-Mora, R. (2021). By Toutatis! Trainee Teachers' Motivation When Using Comics to Learn History. *Frontiers in Psychology*, *27*, 778792. Advance online publication. doi:10.3389/fpsyg.2021.778792 PMID:34777186

Moreno-Vera, J. R., Ponsoda-López de Atalaya, S., López-Fernández, J. A., & Blanes-Mora, R. (2020). Holistic or Traditional Conceptions of Heritage among Early-Childhood and Primary Trainee Teachers. *Sustainability*, *12*(21), 8921. doi:10.3390u12218921

Moseikina, M., Toktamysov, S., & Danshina, S. (2022). Modern Technologies and Gamification in Historical Education. *Simulation & Gaming*, *53*(2), 135–156. doi:10.1177/10468781221075965

Mugueta, Í. (2019). El campus escolar «Historia y videojuegos»: Diseño, resultados y conclusiones. *Clío: History and History Teaching*, (44), 9–25.

Mullins, J. K., & Sabherwal, R. (2020). Gamification: A cognitive-emotional view. *Journal of Business Research*, *106*, 304–314. doi:10.1016/j.jbusres.2018.09.023

Muñoz, J. M. (2008). NNTT, TIC, NTIC, TAC… en educación ¿pero esto qué es? *Quaderns digitals. Revista de Nuevas Tecnologías y Sociedad*, *51*, 1–9.

Nacke, L. E., & Deterding, S. (2017). The maturing of gamification research. *Computers in Human Behavior*, *71*, 450–454. doi:10.1016/j.chb.2016.11.062

National Institute of Educational Technologies and Teacher Training. (2017). *Marco de Competencia Digital*. Ministerio de Educación, Ciencia y Deportes.

Nebel, S., Schneider, S., Beege, M., & Rey, G. D. (2017). Leaderboards within educational videogames: The impact of difficulty, effort and gameplay. *Computers & Education*, *113*, 28–41. doi:10.1016/j.compedu.2017.05.011

Nicholson, S. (2015). A recipe for meaningful gamification. In *Gamification in education and business* (pp. 1–20). Springer. https://scottnicholson.com/pubs/recipepreprint.pdf

Nokes, J. D. (2017). Historical reading and writing in secondary school classrooms. In *Palgrave handbook of research in historical culture and education* (pp. 553–571). Palgrave Macmillan. doi:10.1057/978-1-137-52908-4_29

Nokes, J. D., Dole, J. A., & Hacker, D. J. (2007). Teaching high school students to use heuristics while reading historical texts. *Journal of Educational Psychology, 99*(3), 492–504. doi:10.1037/0022-0663.99.3.492

Nousiainen, T., Kangas, M., Rikala, J., & Vesisenaho, M. (2018). Teacher competencies in game-based pedagogy. *Teaching and Teacher Education, 74*, 85–97. doi:10.1016/j.tate.2018.04.012

Núñez, M., & González, B. (2021). Didáctica de la pregunta, didáctica de la Shoah: Comprendiendo la Historia desde el cuestionamiento a las subjetividades. *Clio. History and History Teaching, 47*(47), 267–275. doi:10.26754/ojs_clio/clio.2021475603

O'Flaherty, J., & Phillips, C. (2015). The use of flipped classrooms in higher education: A scoping review. *Internet and Higher Education, 25*, 85–95. doi:10.1016/j.iheduc.2015.02.002

OECD. (2020). *Back to the Future of Education Four OECD Scenarios for Schooling*. OECD Publishing.

OECD. (n.d.). *Teachers as Designers of Learning Environments.* https://www.oecd-ilibrary.org/education/teachers-as-designers-oflearning-environments_9789264085374-en

Okeke, C., Van Wyk, M., & Phasha, N. (2014). The meaning and practice of educational theory. In Schooling, society and Inclusive Education: An Afrocentric perspective. Oxford University Press.

Oliveira, C., Lopes, J., & Spear-Swerling, L. (2019). Teachers' academic training for literacy instruction. *European Journal of Teacher Education, 42*(3), 315–334. doi:10.1080/02619768.2019.1576627

Olmos, R. (2017). Kahoot: ¡Un, dos, tres! Análisis de una aplicación de cuestionarios. *Íber. Didáctica de las Ciencias Sociales, Geografía e Historia, 86*, 51-56. Available at: https://dialnet.unirioja.es/ejemplar/456181

Olmos, R. (2018). Kahoot! Una aplicación para la gamificación en el aula [Kahoot! An application for classroom gamification]. In *EDUNOVATIC 2017. Conference Proceedings. 2nd Virtual International Conference on Education, Innovation and ICT* (pp. 862-869). Adaya Press.

Order ECD/65/2015, of 21 January, which describes the relationships between the competences, contents and assessment criteria of primary education, compulsory secondary education and baccalaureate. (2015, January). *Boletín Oficial del Estado, 25*(29), 6986–7003.

Ordoñez, B. P., Ochoa, M. E., Erráez, J. L., León, J. L., & Espinoza, E. E. (2021). Consideraciones sobre aula invertida y gamificación en el área de ciencias sociales. *Revista Universidad y Sociedad, 13*(3), 497-504. https://rus.ucf.edu.cu/index.php/rus/index

Organic Law 3/2020 of 29 December 2020, which amends Organic Law 2/2006 of 3 May on Education. (2020, December). *Boletín Oficial del Estado, 340*(30), 122868–122953.

Ortega Sánchez, D. (2018). Las mujeres en la historia enseñada: Resultados de un programa docente en formación inicial del profesorado. *Enseñanza de las Ciencias Sociales, 17*(2018.17), 13–21. doi:10.1344/ECCSS2018.17.2

Ortega, D. (2015). La enseñanza de las Ciencias Sociales, las TIC y el tratamiento de la información y competencia digital (TICD) en el grado de Maestro/a de Educación Primaria de las universidades de Castilla y León. *Enseñanza de las Ciencias Sociales*, (14), 121–134.

Ortiz-Colón, A. M., Jordán, J., & Agredal, M. (2018). Gamificación en educación: Una panorámica sobre el estado de la cuestión. *Educação e Pesquisa*, *44*(0), 1–17. doi:10.15901678-4634201844173773

Ortiz-Martínez, E., Santos-Jaén, J. M., & Palacios-Manzano, M. (2022). Games in the classroom? Analysis of their effects on financial accounting marks in higher education. *International Journal of Management Education*, *20*(1), 100584. doi:10.1016/j.ijme.2021.100584

Orts, M. (2019). El uso de móviles en el instituto. Reflexiones en el instituto Jaume Vicens Vives (Girona). *Aula de Secundaria, 32*, 35-39.

Ouariachi, T., Olvera-Lobo, M. D., & Gutiérrez-Pérez, J. (2017). Evaluación de juegos online para la enseñanza y aprendizaje del cambio climático. *Enseñanza de las ciencias, 35*(1), 193-214.

Overy, R. (2003). *Interrogatorios. El Tercer Reich en el banquillo*. Tusquets.

Özdener, N. (2018). Gamification for enhancing Web 2.0 based educational activities: The case of pre-service grade school teachers using educational Wiki pages. *Telematics and Informatics*, *35*(3), 564–578. doi:10.1016/j.tele.2017.04.003

Öztürk, İ. H. (2011). Tarih öğretiminde anakronizm sorunu: Sosyal bilgiler ve tarih ders kitaplarındaki kurgusal metinler üzerine bir inceleme. *Sosyal Bilgiler Eğitimi Araştırmaları Dergisi*, *2*(1), 37–58.

Pagés, J. (1994). La didáctica de las ciencias sociales, el currículum y la formación del profesorado. *Signos Teoria y Practica de la Educación, 5*(13), 38-51.

Pagés, A. (2011). ¿Qué se necesita saber y saber hacer para enseñar ciencias sociales? *Edetania*, (40), 67–81.

Pagés, A. (2018). Aprender a enseñar historia. Las relaciones entre la historia y la historia escolar. *Trayectorias Universitarias*, *4*(7), 53–59.

Pagès, J. (2002). Aprender a enseñar historia y ciencias sociales: El currículo y la didáctica de las ciencias sociales [Learning to teach history and social sciences: the curriculum and the didactic of social sciences]. *Pensamiento Educativo: Revista de Investigacion Educacional Latinoamericana*, *30*(1), 255–269.

Pagès, J., & Santisteban, A. (2010). La enseñanza y el aprendizaje del tiempo histórico en Educación Primaria. *Cad. Cedes, Campinas*, *30*(82), 281–309. doi:10.1590/S0101-32622010000300002

Palacios, R. J. (2020). *Experimentación y análisis del uso de los videojuegos para la Educación Patrimonial. Estudio de caso en 1.º de ESO*. Universidad de Huelva.

Pallarés Jiménez, M. Á., & Sánchez Martínez, S. (2020). Enseñar los juicios de Núremberg en un centro penitenciario. Una propuesta educativa. *Clio. History and History Teaching*, *46*(46), 122–135. doi:10.26754/ojs_clio/clio.2020465293

Papadopoulos, P. M., Lagkas, T., & Demetriadis, S. N. (2016). How revealing rankings affects student attitude and performance in a peer review learning environment. In S. Zvacek, M. T. Restivo, J. Uhomoibhi, & M. Helfert (Eds.), *CSEDU 2015. CCIS* (Vol. 583, pp. 225–240). Springer. doi:10.1007/978-3-319-29585-5_13

Paricio, J. (2019). El valor de la historia. Estudio de alternativas curriculares en Secundaria (2). *Clio. History and History teaching, 45,* 330-356.

Paricio, J., García-Ceballos, S., & Rubio-Navarro, A. (2022). Epistemic beliefs and pre-service teachers' conceptions of history ınstruction. In Frontiers in Education (Vol. 7, p. 865222). Frontiers Media SA.

Parkes, R. J., & Donnelly, D. (2014). Changing conceptions of historical thinking in History education: An Australian case study. *Revista Tempo e Argumento*, *6*(11), 113–136. doi:10.5965/2175180306112014113

Parra, D., & Fuertes, C. (Coords.). (2019). *Reinterpretar la tradición, transformar las prácticas. Ciencias Sociales para una educación crítica*. Tirant humanidades.

Parra, D., & Fuertes, C. (Coords.). (2019). *Reinterpretar la tradición, transformar las prácticas: Ciencias Sociales para una educación crítica*. Tirant Lo Blanch.

Parra-González, M. E., López-Belmonte, J., Segura-Robles, A., & Moreno-Guerrero, A. J. (2021). Gamification and flipped learning and their influence on aspects related to the teaching-learning process. *Heliyon, 7*(2), e06254. doi:10.1016/j.heliyon.2021.e06254 PMID:33659757

Parra-González, M. E., & Segura-Robles, A. (2019). Producción científica sobre gamificación en educación: un análisis cienciométrico. Scientific production about gamification in education: A Scientometric analysis. *Review of Education, 386*, 113–135.

Pearce, A. (2020). Challenges, issues and controversies: The shapes of 'Holocaust education' in the early twenty-first century. In S. Foster, A. Pearce, & A. Pettigrew (Eds.), *Holocaust Education. Contemporany challenges and controversies*. UCL Press. doi:10.2307/j.ctv15d7zpf.7

Peck, C., & Seixas, P. (2008). Benchmarks of Historical Thinking: First Steps. *Canadian Journal of Education, 31*(4), 1015–1038.

Pelletier, K., Brown, M., Brooks, D. C., McCormack, M., Reeves, J., Arbino, N., Bozkurt, A., Crawford, S., Czerniewicz, L., Gibson, R., Linder, K., Mason, J., & Mondelli, V. (2021). *2021 EDUCAUSE Horizon Report Teaching and Learning Edition*. EDU. https://www.learntechlib.org/p/219489/

Pérez, R. G. (2016). Teaching the use of WebQuests to master students in Pablo de Olavide University. In New perspectives on teaching and working with languages in the digital era. Research-publishing.net. doi:10.14705/rpnet.2016.tislid2014.425

Pérez-López, I., & Rivera, E. (2017). Training teachers, training people: Analysis of the learning achieved by university students from a gamification experience. *Signo y Pensamiento, 36*(70), 112–129. doi:10.11144/Javeriana.syp36-70.fdfp

Perkins, R., & McKnight, M. L. (2005). Teachers' attitudes toward WebQuests as a method of teaching. *Computers in the Schools, 22*(1-2), 123–133. doi:10.1300/J025v22n01_11

Piedmont, E. V. (2020). Exploring COVID-19 in a Social Studies Methods Course: Pre-Service Teachers Harness the Current Pandemic to Design Inquiry-Based Webquests for Elementary Learners. *Journal of International Social Studies, 10*(2), 113–126.

Pixelatto creative games and tools (Developer and Editor) (2017). *Card Creator* [Videogame]. Author.

Polly, D., & Ausband, L. (2009). Developing higher-order thinking skills through WebQuests. *Journal of Computing in Teacher Education, 26*(1), 29–34.

Polo, I. (2010). La evaluación de las competencias básicas [The assessment of basic skills]. *Avances en supervisión educativa, 12*.

Powell, Ch. (2003). Challenging the pluralism of our past: Presentism and the selective tradition in historical fiction written for young people. *Research in the Teaching of English, 37*, 425–466.

Prados Sánchez, G., Cózar-Gutiérrez, R., del Olmo-Muñoz, J., & González-Calero, J. A. (2021). Impact of a gamified platform in the promotion of reading comprehension and attitudes towards reading in primary education. *Computer Assisted Language Learning*, 1–25. Advance online publication. doi:10.1080/09588221.2021.1939388

Prapinwong, M. (2008). *Constructivist language learning through WebQuests in EFL context: an exploratory study* [Doctoral dissertation]. Indiana University.

Prats, J. (2002). Internet en las aulas de educación secundaria. *Iber: Didáctica de las Ciencias Sociales, geografía e historia, 29*, 1-8.

Prats, J. (2017). Retos y dificultades para la enseñanza de la historia. In La historia en el aula. Innovación docente y enseñanza de la historia en la educación secundaria (pp. 15-32). Milenio.

Prats, J. (Coord.). (2011). Didáctica de la Geografía y la Historia. Barcelona, España: Graó. Ministerio de Educación Cultura y Deporte, Secretaría General Técnica.

Prats, J. (Coord.). (2020). Ciencias sociales, ciudadanía y sociedad digital. In *Re-flexiones desde la educación*. Editorial Trea.

Prats, J. (2020). Didáctica de la historia en secundaria y en la universidad. Dos mundos que viven de espaldas. *Íber. Didáctica de las Ciencias Sociales. Geografía e Historia*, *100*, 10–14.

Prats, J. (2020). Memoria histórica y enseñanza de la Historia. In I. Sáez-Rosenkranz & J. Prats Cuevas (Eds.), *Memoria histórica y enseñanza de la Historia* (pp. 11–28). Ediciones Trea.

Prats, J., & Santacana, J. (2001). *Enseñar historia: notas para una didáctica renovadora*. Junta de Extremadura.

Prieto, J. A, Gómez, C. J. & Miralles, P. (2013). El uso de fuentes primarias en el aula y el desarrollo del pensamiento histórico y social. Una experiencia en Bachillerato. *Clío. History and Teaching, 39.*

Prieto, J. M. (2020). Una revisión sistemática sobre gamificación, motivación y aprendizaje en universitarios. *Teoría de la Educación. Revista Interuniversitaria*, *32*(1), 73–99. doi:10.14201/teri.20625

Prutsch, M. J. (2015). *European Historical Memory: Policies, Challenges and Perspectives. European Union*. Available in: https://www.europarl.europa.eu/studies

Pujolà, J. T., & Herrera, F. J. (2019). Gamificación. In J. M. Basols, E. Gironzetti, & M. Lacorte (Eds.), *The Routledge Handbook of Spanish Language Teaching. Metodologías, contextos y recursos para la enseñanza del español L2* (pp. 583–595). Routledge.

Putz, L. M., Hofbauer, F., & Treiblmaier, H. (2020). Can gamification help to improve education? Findings from a longitudinal study. *Computers in Human Behavior*, *110*, 106392. doi:10.1016/j.chb.2020.106392

Quinquer, D. (2004). Estrategias metodológicas para enseñar y aprender ciencias sociales: Interacción, cooperación y participación. *Íber. Didáctica de las Ciencias Sociales. Geografía e Historia*, *40*, 7–22.

Quintero, D. (2018). Didáctica de las Ciencias Sociales a través de los videojuegos: Investigación y experimentación del juego Assassin's Creed Origins, para posible propuesta didáctica sobre la enseñanza del patrimonio y la cultura del Antiguo Egipto. *Clío: History and History Teaching*, (44), 1–28.

Ramlo, S. E. (2021). Universities and the COVID-19 Pandemic: Comparing Views about How to Address the Financial Impact. *Innovative Higher Education*, *46*(6), 777–793. doi:10.100710755-021-09561-x PMID:34177079

Rapp, A. (2017). From games to gamification: A classification of rewards in World of Warcraft for the design of gamified systems. *Simulation & Gaming*, *48*(3), 381–401. doi:10.1177/1046878117697147

Raya, E., & Navaridas, F. (2021). Formación para la competencia docente en la educación del siglo XXI. In E. Raya & F. Navaridas (Coords.), Formación docente y desarrollo de competencias en el profesorado. Hacia un modelo para la calidad educativa (pp. 23-26). Wolters Kluwer.

Reisman, A. (2012). Reading like a historian: A document-based history curriculum intervention in urban high schools. *Cognition and Instruction, 30*(1), 86–112. doi:10.1080/07370008.2011.634081

Riazi, A. M., & Mosalanejad, N. (2010). Evaluation of Learning Objectives in Iranian High-School and Pre-University English Textbooks Using Bloom's Taxonomy. *The Electronic Journal for English as a Second Language, 13*(4), 1-16.

Riley, K. L. (1998). Historical empathy and the Holocaust: Theory into practice. *The International Journal of Social Education, 13*(1), 32–42.

Ritzhaupt, A. D., Liu, F., Dawson, K., & Barron, A. E. (2013). Differences in student information and communication technology literacy based on socio-economic status, ethnicity, and gender: Evidence of a digital divide in Florida schools. *Journal of Research on Technology in Education, 45*(4), 291–307. doi:10.1080/15391523.2013.10782607

Rivero, P. (Coord.). (2017). Gamificación para aprender ciencias sociales. *Íber: Didáctica de las ciencias sociales, geografía e historia*, 86.

Rivero, P., & Mur, L. (2015). Aprender Ciencias Sociales en la web 2.0. *Iber: Didáctica de las Ciencias Sociales, geografía e historia, 80*, 30-37.

Rivero-Guerra, A. O. (2019). Impact of three teaching models in university general botany courses on the academic results of students. *Formación Universitaria, 12*(3), 67–80. doi:10.4067/S0718-50062019000300067

Rivero, P. (2017). Proceso de gamificación en el aula de ciencias sociales [Gamification process in the social sciences classroom]. *Íber. Didáctica de las Ciencias Sociales. Geografía e Historia, 86*, 4–6.

Rivero, P. (2017). Proceso de gamificación en el aula de ciencias sociales. *Íber. Didáctica de las Ciencias Sociales. Geografía e Historia, 86*, 4–6.

Rivero, P. (2017). Procesos de gamificación en el aula de Ciencias Sociales. *Íber. Didáctica de las Ciencias Sociales. Geografía e Historia, 86*, 5–6.

Robbins, B. (2011). *Microscope* [Game]. Lame Mage Productions.

Roblizo, M., Sánchez, M. C., & Cózar, R. (2016). El reto de la competencia digital en los futuros docentes de Infantil, Primaria y Secundaria: Los estudiantes de Grado y Máster de Educación ante las TIC. *Revista de Investigación Social, 15*, 254–295.

Robson, K., Plangger, K., Kietzmann, J. H., McCarthy, I., & Pitt, L. (2015). Is it all a game? Understanding the principles of gamification. *Business Horizons, 58*(4), 411–420. doi:10.1016/j.bushor.2015.03.006

Rodríguez, D., & Valldeoriola, J. (2012). *Metodología de la investigación*. Red Tercer Milenio.

Rodríguez, F., & Santiago, R. (2015). *Gamificación: Cómo motivar a tu alumnado y mejorar el clima en el aula*. Digital Text.

Rodríguez-Fernández, L. (2017). Smartphones and learning: The use of Kahoot in the university classroom. *Revista Mediterránea de Comunicación, 8*(1), 181–190. doi:10.14198/MEDCOM2017.8.1.13

Rodríguez, M. A., & Gutiérrez, D. (2016). Innovación en el aula de ciencias sociales a través de los videojuegos. *Revista Iberoamericana de Educación, 72*(2), 181–200.

Rodríguez-Medina, J., & Rubia, B. (2021). Mixed methods in education research. In C. Gómez, P. Miralles, & R. López (Coords.), Handbook of research on education in History and Geography (pp. 35-52). Peter Lang.

Rojas-Viteri, J., Álvarez-Zurita, A., & Bracero-Huertas, D. (2021). Uso de Kahoot como elemento motivador en el proceso enseñanza-aprendizaje. *Revista Cátedra*, *4*(1), 98–114. doi:10.29166/catedra.v4i1.2815

Romero-Rodríguez, J. M., Aznar-Díaz, I., Hinojo-Lucena, F. J., & Gómez-García, G. (2020). Mobile Learning in Higher Education: Structural Equation Model for Good Teaching Practices. *IEEE Access: Practical Innovations, Open Solutions*, *8*(1), 91761–91769. doi:10.1109/ACCESS.2020.2994967 PMID:34192098

Rosenthal, R. (1991). *Meta-analytic procedures for social research* (2nd ed.). Sage. doi:10.4135/9781412984997

Ros, G., & Rodríguez, M. T. (2021). Influence of the flipped classroom in the scientific training of pre-service teachers: Benefits in the teaching-learning process, attitudes and expectations towards science. *Revista de Investigación Educacional*, *39*(2), 463–482. doi:10.6018/rie.434131

Ross, D. (1984). Historical consciousness in nineteenth-century America. *The American Historical Review*, *89*(4), 909–928. doi:10.2307/1866398

Royal Decree 126/2014, of 28 February, establishing the basic curriculum for Primary Education. (2014, March). *Boletín Oficial del Estado*, *1*(52).

Royal Decree 157/2022, of 1 March, which establishes the orientation and minimum teachings of Primary Education. (2022, March). *Boletín Oficial del Estado*, *2*(52).

Royal Decree 984/2021, of 16 November, which regulates assessment and promotion in Primary Education, as well as assessment, promotion and qualifications in Compulsory Secondary Education, Baccalaureate and Vocational Training. (2021, November). *Official State Gazette*, *17*(275), 141583–141595.

Ruiz, M. C., Martínez-Jiménez, R., Licerán-Gutiérrez, A., & García-Martía, E. (2022). Students' attitude: Key to understanding the improvement of their academic RESULTS in a flipped classroom environment. *International Journal of Management Education*, *20*(2), 1–11. doi:10.1016/j.ijme.2022.100635

Rüsen, J. (2012). Tradition: A principle of historical sense-generation and its logic and effect in historical culture. *History and Theory*, *51*(4), 45–59. doi:10.1111/j.1468-2303.2012.00646.x

Rüsen, J. (2015). *Teoria da História. Uma teoria da história como ciencia.* Universidade Federal do Paraná.

Russell, C. K., Burchum, J. R., Likes, W. M., Jacob, S., Graff, J. C., Driscoll, C., Britt, T., Adymy, C., & Cowan, P. (2008). WebQuests: creating engaging, student-centered, constructivist learning activities. *CIN: Computers, Informatics, Nursing*, *26*(2), 78–87. doi:10.1097/01.NCN.0000304774.63402.b8 PMID:18317258

Sáez, J. M., Cózar, R., & Domínguez, J. (2016). Realidad aumentada en Educación Primaria: Comprensión de elementos artísticos y aplicación didáctica en ciencias sociales. *Digital Education Review*, *34*, 59–75.

Sáez-Pérez, M. P. (2011). *Metodologías Activas y Aprendizaje. Propuesta de innovación en el grado de ingeniería de edificación*. Universidad de Granada.

Safran, M. (2006). *Tarih Eğitimi Makale ve Bildiriler*. Gazi Kitabevi.

Safran, M., & Şimşek, A. (2009). Çocuklarda zaman algısının gelişimi. *Uluslararası Sosyal Araştırmalar Dergisi*, *2*(6), 542–548.

Sailer, M., Hense, J. U., Mayr, S. K., & Mandl, H. (2017). How gamification motivates: An experimental study of the effects of specific game design elements on psychological need satisfaction. *Journal of Computer in Human Behavior*, *69*, 371–380. doi:10.1016/j.chb.2016.12.033

Sailer, M., & Homner, L. (2020). The Gamification of Learning: A Meta-analysis. *Educational Psychology Review, 32*(1), 77–112. doi:10.100710648-019-09498-w

Sáiz, J. & Colomer, J. C. (2014). ¿Se enseña pensamiento histórico en libros de texto de Educación Primaria? Análisis de actividades de historia para alumnos de 10-12 años de edad. *CLIO. History and History teaching, 40.*

Sáiz, J. & Gómez, C. J. (2016). Investigar el pensamiento histórico y narrativo en la formación del profesorado: fundamentos teóricos y metodológicos. *Revista electrónica interuniversitaria de formación de profesorado, 19*(1), 175-190.

Sáiz, J. (2011). Actividades de libros de texto de Historia, competencias básicas y destrezas cognitivas, una difícil relación: análisis de manuales de 1° y 2° de ESO. *Didáctica de las ciencias experimentales y sociales, 25*, 37-64.

Sáiz, J. (2013). Alfabetización histórica y competencias básicas en libros de texto de historia y en aprendizajes de estudiantes. *Didáctica de las ciencias experimentales y sociales*, (27), 43-66.

Sáiz, J. (2013). Alfabetización histórica y competencias básicas en libros de texto de historia y en aprendizajes de estudiantes. *Didáctica de las ciencias experimentales y sociales, 27*, 43-66. doi:10.7203/dces.27.2648

Sáiz, J., & Domínguez, J. (2017). Aprender sobre la historia: Competencias metodológicas en educación secundaria. In Enseñanza de la historia y competencias educativas (pp. 23-47). Graó.

Sáiz, J. (2013). Alfabetización histórica y competencias básicas en libros de texto de historia y en aprendizaje de los estudiantes. *Didáctica de las Ciencias Experimentales y Sociales, 27*, 43–66.

Sáiz, J. (2013). Empatía histórica, historia social e identidades: Pensar históricamente la conquista cristiana de la Valencia musulmana con estudiantes de 2o ESO. *Clio*, 39.

Sáiz, J. (2013). Empatía histórica, historia social e identidades: Pensar históricamente la conquista cristiana de la Valencia musulmana con estudiantes de 2° ESO. *Clío. History and History Teaching, 39*, 1–20.

Sáiz, J., & Colomer, J. C. (2014). ¿Se enseña pensamiento histórico en libros de texto de Educación Primaria? Análisis de actividades de historia para alumnos de 10-12 años de edad. *Clío: History and History Teaching*, (40), 1–19.

Sáiz, J., & Fuster, C. (2014). Memorizar historia sin aprender pensamiento histórico: Las PAU de Historia de España. *Investigación en la Escuela, 84*, 47–57.

Sáiz, J., & López-Facal, R. (2015). Competencias y narrativas históricas: El pensamiento histórico de estudiantes y futuros profesores españoles de educación secundaria. *Revista de Estudios Sociales, 52*, 87–101.

Sáiz, J., & López, R. (2015). Competencias y narrativas históricas: El pensamiento histórico de estudiantes y futuros profesores de educación secundaria [Historical skills and narratives: the historical thinking of students and prospective secondary school teachers]. *Revista de Estudios Sociales, 52*(52), 87–101. doi:10.7440/res52.2015.06

Sáiz, M. C., Escolar, M. C., & Rodríguez-Medina, J. (2019). *Investigación cualitativa: aplicación de métodos mixtos y de técnicas de minería de datos*. Universidad de Burgos.

Sáiz-Serrano, J., Gómez-Carrasco, C. J., & López-Facal, R. (2018). Historical thinking, causal explanation and narrative discourse in trainee teachers in Spain. *Historical Encounters: A Journal of Historical Consciousness, Historical Cultures, and History Education, 5*(1), 16-30. http://hdl.handle.net/10347/17000

Sajinčič, N., Sandak, A., & Istenič, A. (2022). Pre-Service and In-Service Teachers' Views on Gamification. *International Journal of Emerging Technologies in Learning, 17*(3), 83–103. doi:10.3991/ijet.v17i03.26761

Sampat, E. (2017). *Empathy Engines: Design GamesThat Are Personal, Political and Profound.* Create Space Independent Publishing Platform.

San Pedro-Veledo, M. B., & López-Manrique, I. (2017). Empatía histórica y aumento de la tolerancia hacia las figuras de los refugiados. *Revista de psicología y educación, 12*(2), 116-128. doi:10.23923/rpye2017.12.150

Sánchez Macías, I. (2020). Proyecto fotográfico Auschwitz: El escenario del horror. *Clio. History and History teaching, 46*, 102-104. doi:10.26754/ojs_clio/clio.2020465299

Sánchez, D. O., & Trigueros, I. M. G. (2017). Las WebQuests y los MOOCs en la enseñanza de las Ciencias Sociales y la formación del profesorado de Educación Primaria. *Revista electrónica interuniversitaria de formación del profesorado, 20*(2), 205-220.

Sánchez, R., Campillo, J. M., & Guerrero, C. (2020). Percepciones del profesorado de primaria y secundaria sobre la enseñanza de la historia [Primary and secondary school teachers' perceptions of history teaching]. *Revista Interuniversitaria de Formación del Profesorado, 34*(3), 57-76. https://www.redalyc.org/journal/274/27468063003/html/

Sánchez, A., & Colomer, J. C. (2017). Gamificación y construcción del pensamiento histórico: Desarrollo de competencias en actividades gamificadas. *Clío: History and History Teaching*, (43), 1–12.

Sánchez-Cruzado, C., Sánchez-Compaña, M. T., & Ruiz-Palmero, J. (2019). Experiences of flipped classroom as a methodological strategy in university education. *Publicaciones, 49*(2), 39–58. doi:10.30827/publicaciones.v49i2.8270

Sanchez, D. R., Langer, M., & Kaur, R. (2020). Gamification in the classroom: Examining the impact of gamified quizzes on student learning. *Computers & Education, 144*, 103666. doi:10.1016/j.compedu.2019.103666

Sánchez-Fuster, M. C. (2017). *Evaluación de los recursos utilizados en Ciencias Sociales, Geografía e Historia.* PhD, Universidad de Murcia. https://digitum.um.es/digitum/handle/10201/54567

Sánchez-Ibáñez, R., Famà, K., & Escribano Miralles, A. (2020). I livelli cognitivi nei manuali di storia dell'Istruzione Secondaria Superiore in Italia. *Didattica Della Storia, Journal of Research and Didactics of History, 2*(1), 180-195. doi:10.6092/issn.2704-8217/11020

Sánchez-Ibáñez, R., Guerrero-Romera, C., & Miralles-Martínez, P. (2021). Primary and secondary school teachers' perceptions of their social science training needs. *Humanities and Social Sciences Communications, 8*(1), 26. doi:10.105741599-021-00705-0

Sánchez, M. M. (2012). Designing digital resources for e-learning environments in university education. *RIED. Revista Iberoamericana de Educación a Distancia, 15*(2), 53–74.

Sánchez-Mena, A., & Martí-Parreño, J. (2017). Drivers and Barriers to Adopting Gamification: Teachers' Perspectives. *The Electronic Journal of e-Learning, 15*(5), 434-443.

Sánchez, P. A., Alfageme, B., & Serrano, F. J. (2011). Opiniones sobre los videojuegos del alumnado de Educación Secundaria Obligatoria. *Edutec. Revista Electrónica de Tecnología Educativa*, (38), 185. doi:10.21556/edutec.2011.38.386

Sancho, J. M., & Alonso Cano, C. (2011). *Cuatro casos, cuatro historias de uso educativo de las TIC.* Universitat de Barcelona, Esbrina-Recerca.

Santacana, J. (2005). Reflexiones en torno al laboratorio escolar de ciencias sociales, *Íber: Didáctica de las Ciencias Sociales. Geografía e Historia, 43*, 7–14.

Santisteban Fernández, A. (2019). La enseñanza de las Ciencias Sociales a partir de problemas sociales o temas controvertidos: Estado de la cuestión y resultados de una investigación. *El Futuro del Pasado, 10*, 57–79. doi:10.14516/fdp.2019.010.001.002

Santisteban, A. (2010). La formación de competencias de pensamiento histórico. *Clío & Asociados, 14*, 34-56.

Santisteban, A. (2019). La enseñanza de las Ciencias Sociales a partir de problemas sociales o temas controvertidos. Estado de la cuestión y resultados de una investigación. *El futuro del Pasado: revista electrónica de historia, 10*, 57-79.

Santisteban, A. (2010). La formación de competencias de pensamiento histórico. *Clio y Asociados*, (14), 34–56. doi:10.14409/cya.v1i14.1674

Santisteban, A. (2017). Del tiempo histórico a la conciencia histórica: Cambios en la enseñanza y el aprendizaje de la historia en los últimos 25 años [From historical time to historical consciousness: changes in the teaching and learning of history in the last 25 years]. *Diálogo Andino, 53*, 87–99.

Santisteban, A., González, N., & Pagès, J. (2010). Una investigación sobre la formación del pensamiento histórico. In *Metodología de investigación en Didáctica de las Ciencias Sociales* (pp. 115–128). I. Fernando el Católico-Diputación de Zaragoza-AUPDCS.

Santos, A. (2020). Multiperspectiva frente al Nazismo en un contexto excepcional. *Clio. History and History teaching, 46*, 65-77. doi:10.26754/ojs_clio/clio.2020465264

Santos-Rego, M. (2017). La educación intercultural y el pluralismo religioso: Propuestas pedagógicas para el diálogo [Intercultural education and religious pluralism: pedagogical proposals for dialogue]. *Educación (Lima), 21*(1), 1–4. doi:10.5944/educxx1.17489

Sanz, P., Molero, J. M., & Rodríguez, D. (2017). La historia en el aula. Innovación docente y enseñanza de la historia en la educación secundaria. *Historia y Memoria de la Educación*, (6), 553–555.

Sanz, P., Molero, J. M., & Rodríguez, D. (Eds.). (2017). *La historia en el aula. Innovación docente y enseñanza de la historia en la educación secundaria*. Milenio.

Sarı, T. & Nayır, F. (2020). Pandemi Dönemi Eğitim: Sorunlar ve Fırsatlar. *Electronic Turkish Studies, 15*(4).

Schmidt, M. (2019). El turno de la didáctica de la historia: contribuciones para un debate [The turn of history didactics: contributions to a debate]. *Historia y espacio, 15*(53), 21-42.

Schmidt, M. A. & Fronza, M. (2018). Jovens, consciência histórica e avaliação da aprendizagem: o caso do Exame Nacional do Ensino Médio no Brasil entre 2009/2015. *Educatio Siglo XXI, 36*, 149-171. doi:10.6018/j/324211

Schutten, M., & McFarland, A. (2009). Readability levels of health-based websites: From content to comprehension. *International Electronic Journal of Health Education, 12*, 99–107.

Seaborn, K., & Fels, D. I. (2015). Gamification in theory and action: A survey. *International Journal of Human-Computer Studies, 74*, 14–31. doi:10.1016/j.ijhcs.2014.09.006

Seitkazy, P. B., Toleubekova, R. K., Amanova, A. K., Tashetov, A. A., Iskakova, G., & Demissenova, S. S. (2016). A Web-Quest as a teaching and learning tool. *International Electronic Journal of Mathematics Education, 11*(10), 3537–3549.

Seixas, P. (2001). Review of Research on Social Studies. In Handbook Of Research On Teaching (4th ed.). American Educational Research Association.

Seixas, P. (2006). *Benchmarks of historical thinking: a framework for assessment in Canada*. Centre for the Study of Historical Consciousness.

Seixas, P. (2006). *Teacher Notes: Benchmarks of Historical Thinking, a framework for Assessment in Canada.* UBC: Centre for the Study of Historical Consciousness. https://www.edu.gov.mb.ca/k12/cur/socstud/foundation_gr8/tns/tn1.pdf

Seixas, P., & Morton, T. (2013). The big six historical thinking concepts. Academic Press.

Seixas, P. (2004). *Theorizing historical consciousness*. University of Toronto Press. doi:10.3138/9781442682610

Seixas, P. (2017). Historical Counsciousness and Historical Thinking. In M. Carretero, M. Grever, & S. Berger (Eds.), *Palgrave Handbook of Research in Historical Culture and Education* (pp. 59–72). Palgrave McMillan. doi:10.1057/978-1-137-52908-4_3

Seixas, P., & Morton, T. (2013). *The Big Six Historical Thinking Concepts*. Nelson Education Ltd.

Seixas, P., & Morton, T. (2013). *The big six historical thinking concepts*. Nelson Education.

Seixas, P., & Morton, T. (2013). *The big six: historical thinking concepts*. Nelson College Indigenous.

Seixas, P., & Peck, C. (2004). Teaching historical thinking. In A. Sears & I. Wright (Eds.), *Challenges and Prospects for Canadian Social Studies* (pp. 109–117). Pacific Educational Press.

Seva, F., Vera, M. I., & Soriano, M. C. (2017). La percepción del alumnado de Ciencias Sociales ante la utilización de las tecnologías de la información y la comunicación en clase. Las TIC favorecen el aprendizaje de las Ciencias Sociales, según el alumnado [Social Studies pupils' perception of the use of information and communication technologies in class. According to pupils, ICT favour the learning of Social Sciences.]. In *Investigación en Didáctica de las Ciencias Sociales. Retos, preguntas y líneas de investigación* [Research in Didactics of Social Sciences. Challenges, questions and lines of research] (pp. 782-799). Asociación Universitaria de Profesorado de Didáctica de las Ciencias Sociales. http://rua.ua.es/dspace/handle/10045/71843

Shabatura, J. (2014). *Bloom's Taxonomy verb chart*. University of Arkansas. Retrieved May 10, 2022, from https://tips.uark.edu/blooms-taxonomy-verb-chart/

Shavab, O. A. K., Yulifar, L., Supriatna, N., & Mulyana, A. (2021). Gamification in History Learning: A Literature Review. In *6th International Conference on Education & Social Sciences (ICESS 2021)* (pp. 254-258). Atlantis Press. 10.2991/assehr.k.210918.047

Shemilt, D. (1984). Beauty and the Philosopher: Empathy in History and Classroom. In A. Dickinson, P. Lee, & P. Rogers (Eds.), *Learning History*. Heinemann Educational Books.

Shemilt, D. (1987a). Adolescent ideas about evidence and methodology in History. In C. Portal (Ed.), *The history curriculum for teachers* (pp. 39–61). The Falmer Press.

Shemilt, D. J. (1987b). El proyecto «Historia 13-16» del Schools Council: pasado, presente y futuro. In *La geografía y la Historia dentro de las Ciencias Sociales: hacia un currículum integrado* (pp. 173–208). Centro de Publicaciones del M.E.C.

Shibukawa, S., & Taguchi, M. (2019). Exploring the difficulty on students' preparation and the effective instruction in the flipped classroom. A case study in a physiology class. *Journal of Computing in Higher Education*, *31*(2), 311–339. doi:10.100712528-019-09220-3

Sierra, M. C., & Fernández-Sánchez, M. R. (2019). Gamificando el aula universitaria. Análisis de una experiencia de Escape Room en educación superior. *REXE-Revista de Estudios y Experiencias en Educación*, *18*(36), 105–115. doi:10.21703/rexe.20191836sierra15

Sigward, D. (Ed.). (2017). *Holocaust and Human Behavior*. Facing History and Ourselves.

Şimşek, A. (2016). Yayın Kritiği: Taslak Tarih Öğretim Programı (Eleştiriler-Öneriler). *Turkish History Education Journal*, *5*(1), 316–331.

Singer, L., & Schneider, K. (2012) It was a bit of a race: gamification of version control. *2012 2nd International Workshop on Games Software Engineering (GAS)*, 5–8. 10.1109/GAS.2012.6225927

Snow, E.L., Allen, L.K., Jackson, G.T., & McNamara, D.S. (2015) Spendency: students' propensity to use system currency. *Int. J. Artif. Intell. Educ., 25*(3), 407–427. doi:10.1007/s40593-015-0044-1

Sobrino, D. (2013). El trabajo con blogs en Ciencias Sociales, Geografía e Historia. *Clío. History and History teaching, 39*, 1-49.

Solbes, J. (2007). El desinterés del alumnado hacia el aprendizaje de la ciencia: implicaciones en su enseñanza. *Didáctica de las ciencias experimentales y sociales*, (21), 91-117.

Solé, G., & Barca, I. (2018). *O Manual Escolar no Ensino da História: Visões Historiográficas e Didática.* Associação de Professores de História. Available at: https://aph.pt/o-manual-escolar-no-ensino-da-historia-visoes-historiograficas-e-didaticas/

Soler-Domínguez, J. L., Contero González, M., & Alcañiz, M. (2017). Press start!: Cinco estrategias para el despliegue efectivo del Aprendizaje Basado en Videojuegos. *Actas del V Congreso Internacional de Videojuegos y Educación (CIVE'17).*

Soler, M. G., Cárdenas, F. A., & Hernández-Pina, F. (2018). Enfoques de enseñanza y enfoques de aprendizaje: Perspectivas teóricas promisorias para el desarrollo de investigaciones en educación en ciencias. *Ciência & Educação (Bauru), 24*(4), 993–1012. doi:10.1590/1516-731320180040012

Soria, G. M. (2014). El pensamiento histórico en la educación primaria: Estudio de casos a partir de narraciones históricas. *Enseñanza de las Ciencias Sociales*, (14), 83–95.

Sospedra-Roca, R., Hernàndez-Cardona, F. X., & Hernández-Pongiluppi, M. (2022). Digital iconography, conflict heritage, and the teaching of history: The case of the Spanish Civil War. *Cogent Education, 9*(1), 2082087. doi:10.1080/2331186X.2022.2082087

Souto, X. M., Fuster, C., & Sáiz, J. (2014). Un camino de ida y vuelta. Reválidas y selectividad en las rutinas escolares de la enseñanza de la Geografía e Historia. In J. Pagés & A. Santisteban (Eds.), *Una mirada al pasado y una proyección de futuro. Investigación e innovación en didáctica de las ciencias sociales* (pp. 157–165). AUPDCS.

Souto, X. M., & García-Monteagudo, D. (2019). Conocer las rutinas para innovar en la geografía escolar. *Revista de Geografía Norte Grande, 74*(74), 207–228. doi:10.4067/S0718-34022019000300207

Steen-Utheim, A. T., & Foldnes, N. (2018). A qualitative investigation of student engagement in a flipped classroom. *Teaching in Higher Education, 23*(3), 307–324. doi:10.1080/13562517.2017.1379481

Stern, B. S. (1998). Addressing the concept of historical empathy: Withfrauen: German women recall the third Reich. *The International Journal of Social Education, 13*(1), 43–48.

Stott, A., & Neustaedter, C. (2013). *Analysis of gamification in education.* http://clab.iat.sfu.ca/pubs/Stott-Gamification.pdf

Strayer, J. F. (2012). How learning in an inverted classroom influences cooperation, innovation and task orientation. *Learning Environments Research, 15*(2), 171–193. doi:10.100710984-012-9108-4

Summerville, J. (2000). WebQuests: An Aspect of Technology Integration for Training Preservice Teachers. *TechTrends, 44*(2), 31–35. doi:10.1007/BF02822950

Swacha, J. (2021). State of Research on Gamification in Education: A Bibliometric Survey. *Education in Science, 11*(2), 69. doi:10.3390/educsci11020069

Talan, T., Doğan, Y., & Batdı, V. (2020). Efficiency of digital and non-digital educational games: A comparative meta-analysis and a meta-thematic analysis. *Journal of Research on Technology in Education*, *52*(4), 474–514. doi:10.1080/15391523.2020.1743798

Tarman, B., & Kuran, B. (2015). Examination of the cognitive level of questions in social studies textbooks and the views of teachers based on Bloom Taxonomy. *Educational Sciences: Theory and Practice*, *15*(1), 213–222. doi:10.12738/estp.2015.1.2625

Teixes, F. (2014). *Gamificación: fundamentos y aplicaciones*. Editorial UOC.

Tekeli, İ. (1998). *Tarih Yazımı Üzerine Düşünmek*. Dost Kitabevi.

Thorp, R., & Persson, A. (2020). On historical thinking and the history educational challenge. *Educational Philosophy and Theory*, *52*(8), 891–901. doi:10.1080/00131857.2020.1712550

Tirado-Olivares, S., Cózar-Gutiérrez, R., García-Olivares, R., & González-Calero, J. A. (2021). Active learning in History teaching in higher education: The effect of inquiry-based learning and a student response system-based formative assessment in teacher training. *Australasian Journal of Educational Technology*, *37*(5), 61–76. doi:10.14742/ajet.7087

Toda, A. M., Valle, P. H., & Isotani, S. (2017). The dark side of gamification: An overview of negative effects of gamification in education. In *Researcher links workshop: higher education for all* (pp. 143–156). Springer. doi:10.1007/978-3-319-97934-2

Trejo, H. (2019). Recursos tecnológicos para la integración de la gamificación en el aula. *Tecnología. Ciência & Educação (Bauru)*, *13*, 75–117.

Ulusoy, K. (2009). Lise Öğrencilerinin Tarih Dersinin İşlenişi ile İlgili Düşünceleri (Ankara Örneği). *Çukurova Üniversitesi Sosyal Bilimler Enstitüsü Dergisi, 18*(1), 417-434.

Unal, Z. (2008, March). Addressing Issues and Problems to Increase Users' Motivation and Completion Rate of Student WebQuests with InstantWebQuest. In *Society for Information Technology & Teacher Education International Conference* (pp. 3188-3194). Association for the Advancement of Computing in Education (AACE).

UNESCO. (1980). *El niño y el juego Planteamientos teóricos y aplicaciones pedagógicas. Estudios y documentos de educación*. UNESCO.

United Nations Organization. (1948). *Universal Declaration of Human Rights*. Available in: https://www.un.org/es/about-us/universal-declaration-of-human-rights

Urh, M., Vukovic, G., Jereb, E., & Pintar, R. (2015). The model for introduction of gamification into e-learning in higher education. *Procedia: Social and Behavioral Sciences*, *197*, 388–397. doi:10.1016/j.sbspro.2015.07.154

Valls, R., & López-Facal, R. (2011). ¿Un nuevo paradigma para la enseñanza de la historia? Los problemas reales y las polémicas interesadas al respecto en España y en el contexto del mundo occidental. *Enseñanza de las ciencias sociales, 10*, 75-86.

Van der Schilden, R., & Heijltjes, B. (2017). Herald. How Wispfire used history to create fiction. In A. A. A. Mol, C. E. Ariese-Vandemeulebroucke, & K. H. J. Boom y Aris Politopoulos (Eds.), *The interactive past: Archaeology, heritage & video games* (pp. 73–82). Sidestone Press.

Van Drie, J., & van Boxtel, C. (2008). Historical reasoning: Towards a framework for analyzing students' reasoning about the past. *Educational Psychology Review*, *20*(2), 87–110. doi:10.100710648-007-9056-1

Van Straaten, D., Wilschut, A., & Oostdam, R. (2018). Measuring students' appraisals of the relevance of history: The construction and validation of the Relevance of History Measurement Scale (RHMS). *Studies in Educational Evaluation*, *56*, 102–111. doi:10.1016/j.stueduc.2017.12.002

VanSledright, B. (2011). *The Challenge of Rethinking History Education. On practice, theories, and policy.* Routledge.

VanSledright, B. (2011). *The challenge of rethinking history education: on practices, theories, and policy.* Routledge.

Vansledright, B. (2013). *Assessing historical thinking and understanding. Innovate designs for new standards*. Routledge. doi:10.4324/9780203464632

VanSledright, B. (2014). What Does It Mean To Think Historically… and How To Teach It? *Social Education*, *68*(3), 230–233.

VanSledright, B. A. (2004). What Does It Mean to Think Historically... and How Do You Teach It? *Social Education*, *68*(3), 230–233.

VanSledright, B. A. (2004). What Does lt Mean to Think Historically ... and How Do You Teach It? *Social Education*, *68*(3), 230–233.

VanSledright, B. A. (2011). *The Challenge of Rethinking History Education. On Practice, Theories, and Policy.* Routledge.

VanSledright, B. A. (2014). *Assessing Historical Thinking and Understanding. Innovation Design for New Standards.* Routledge.

VanSledright, B. A., & Maggioni, L. (2016). Epistemic cognition in history. In J. A. Greene, W. A. Sandoval, & I. Bråten (Eds.), *Handbook of epistemic cognition* (pp. 128–146). Routledge.

VanSledright, B., & Reddy, K. (2014). Changing epistemic beliefs? An exploratory study of cognition among prospective history teacher. *Revista Tempo e Argumento*, *6*(11), 28–68. doi:10.5965/2175180306112014028

Vaughan, M. (2014). Flipping the learning: An investigation into the use of the flipped classroom model in an introductory teaching course. *Education Research and Perspectives*, *41*(1), 25–41. https://www.erpjournal.net/

Vera, M. I., & Pérez, D. (2004). El profesorado en formación de Ciencias Sociales y las TICs: situación y perspectivas. In M. I. Vera & D. Pérez (Eds.), *Formación de la ciudadanía: las TICs y los nuevos problemas* (pp. 1–20). https://dialnet.unirioja.es/descarga/articulo/1448326.pdf

Vera, M. I., & Pérez, T. D. (2008). Las WebQuests de Ciencias Sociales: un instrumento para formar ciudadanos en primaria. In R. M. Ávila, A. Cruz, & C. Díez (Eds.), *Didáctica de las Ciencias Sociales, Currículo Escolar y Formación del Profesorado* (pp. 631–641). Universidad de Jaén.

Vicent, N., & Platas, M. (2018). ¡Juguemos en el Antiguo Egipto! Flipped classroom a través del videojuego Assassin's Creed: 41 Origins. *Clío: History and History Teaching, 44.*

Vicent, N., Albas, L., Gillate, I., & Ibáñez-Etxeberría, Á. (2021). What do our future teachers think about terrorism and politically motivated violence in the Basque Country? *Humanities and Social Sciences Communication*, *8*(43), 43. Advance online publication. doi:10.105741599-021-00721-0

Vygotsky, L. S. (1988). *El desarrollo de los procesos psicológicos superiores.* Editorial Crítica.

Wansink, B. G. J. (2017). *Between fact and interpretation: Teachers' beliefs and practices in intepretational history teaching* (Doctoral dissertation). Utrecht University.

Weintraub, K. J. (1975). Autobiography and historical consciousness. *Critical Inquiry*, *1*(4), 821–848. doi:10.1086/447818

Werbach, K., & Hunter, D. (2012). *For the Win: How Game Thinking Can Revolutionize Your Business*. Wharton Digital Press.

Werbach, K., & Hunter, D. (2015). *The Gamification Toolkit: Dynamics, Mechanics, and Components for the Win*. Wharton School Press.

Whitty, G. (1989). The new right and the national curriculum: State control or market forces? *Journal of Education Policy*, *4*(4), 329–341. doi:10.1080/0268093890040402

Wineburg, S. (1999). Historical Thinking and Other Unnatural Acts. *Phi Delta Kappan*, *80*(7), 488–499.

Wineburg, S. (2001). *Historical Thinking and other Unnatural Acts. Charting the Future of Teaching the Past*. Temple University Press.

Wineburg, S. (2001). *Historical thinking and other unnatural acts: charting the future of teaching the past*. Temple University Press.

Wineburg, S. (2002). *Historical thinking and Another unnatural acts. Charting the future of teaching the past*. Temple University Press.

Wineburg, S. (2018). *Why Learn History (When It's Already on Your Phone)*. Chicago University Press. doi:10.7208/chicago/9780226357355.001.0001

Wineburg, S. S. (1991). Historical problem solving: A study of the cognitive processes used in the evaluation of documentary and pictorial evidence. *Journal of Educational Psychology*, *83*(1), 73–87. doi:10.1037/0022-0663.83.1.73

Wooden, J. A. (2008). "I had always heard Lincoln was a good person, but…": A study of sixth graders' reading of lincoln's views on black—white relations. *Social Studies*, *99*(1), 23–32. doi:10.3200/TSSS.99.1.23-32

Wu, C. P. (2021). An Experiential Study on WebQuest and Higher Order Thinking Skills in an EFL Writing Class. In *Advancing Online Course Design and Pedagogy for the 21st Century Learning Environment* (pp. 191–205). IGI Global. doi:10.4018/978-1-7998-5598-9.ch011

Yazıcı, F. (2008). Tarih Öğretmenlerinin Tarihsel Kanıt Algıları. In Uluslararası Sosyal Bilimler Eğitimi Sempozyumu Bildiri Kitabı (pp. 366-370). Çanakkale.

Yazıcı, F., & Şimşek, A. (2011). Tarih Öğretiminde Nesnellik Sorunu. *Tarih Okulu Dergisi*, *2011*(XI), 13–32.

Yenmez, A. A., Özpinar, İ., & Gökçe, S. (2017). Use of WebQuests in Mathematics Instruction: Academic Achievement, Teacher and Student Opinions. *Universal Journal of Educational Research*, *5*(9), 1554–1570. doi:10.13189/ujer.2017.050913

Yildiz, İ., Topçu, E., & Kaymakci, S. (2021). The effect of gamification on motivation in the education of pre-service social studies teachers. *Thinking Skills and Creativity*, *42*, 100907. doi:10.1016/j.tsc.2021.100907

Yılmaz, K., & Koca, F. (2012). Tarihsel empati üzerine nitel bir araştırma: Tarih öğretmenlerinin algı, görüş ve deneyimlerinin incelenmesi. *Gaziantep Üniversitesi Sosyal Bilgimler Dergisi*, *11*(3), 855–879.

Yilmaz, R. (2017). Exploring the role of e-learning readiness on student satisfaction and motivation in flipped classroom. *Journal of Computer in Human Behavior*, *70*, 251–260. doi:10.1016/j.chb.2016.12.085

Zainuddin, Z., Chu, S. K. W., Shujahat, M., & Perera, C. J. (2020). The impact of gamification on learning and instruction: A systematic review of empirical evidence. *Educational Research Review*, *30*, 100326. doi:10.1016/j.edurev.2020.100326

Zambrano-Álava, A. P., Lucas-Zambrano, M. D. L. Á., Luque-Alcívar, K. E., & Lucas-Zambrano, A. T. (2020). La Gamificación: Herramientas innovadoras para promover el aprendizaje autorregulado. *Dominio de las Ciencias*, *6*(3), 349–369. doi:10.23857/dc.v6i3.1402

Zanazanian, P. (2015). Historical consciousness and metaphor: Charting new directions for grasping human historical sense-making patterns for knowing and acting in time. *Historical Encounters*, *2*, 16–33.

Zarmati, L. (2019). Future of Education and Skills 2030: Curriculum analysis. Learning progression in History. OECD.

Zou, D. (2020). Gamified flipped EFL classroom for primary education: Student and teacher perceptions. *Journal of Computers in Education,* 1-16. doi:10.1007/s40692-020-00153-w

Zuhir, A., Mohammed, E. Y., Al Arab, A. R., Alara, M., & Al-Rawashdeh, B. (2021). Advantages and Disadvantages of Using e-Learning in University Education: Analyzing Students' Perspectives. *Electronic Journal of e-Learning, 19*(3), 107-117. doi:10.34190/ejel.19.3.2168

About the Contributors

María Martínez-Hita has a PhD (2022) by University of Murcia (Spain). Master's degree in Research and Innovation in Preschool and Primary School Education (2016). Bachelor's degree in Primary Education with Mention in English as a foreign language (2015). Primary school teacher since 2016. Winner of the XXIV Congress of Young Researchers (2011) and representative of Spain in the XXIV European Union Contest for Young Scientists (EUCYS) (2012). Main research interests focus on teaching and learning of social sciences, gamification, history education, historical thinking, primary education, and teaching method innovations. Orcid ID: https://orcid.org/0000-0002-0341-6795

Cosme Jesús Gómez Carrasco is Senior Lecturer in Social Sciences Teaching at University of Murcia (Spain). He is PhD in History from the University of Castilla-La Mancha (Spain), and he has been postdoctoral researcher at the EHESS (Paris, France) and at the University Carlos III of Madrid (Spain). Also, he has been visiting professor at the Centre de Recherches Historiques (EHESS, France) and Honorary Researcher Associate at University College of London - Institute of Education (United Kingdom). He is the coordinator of the DICSO research group (University of Murcia). He has coordinated national R&D&i project and European project (ERASMUS + KA220). He has published more than 100 articles and book chapters in publishers and journals of high national and international impact. He has collaborated with evaluation agencies (State Research Agency, Andalusian Knowledge Agency), with the Ministry of Education and Vocational Training, and has been selected for the group of experts of Observatory of History Teaching in Europe (Council of Europe).

Pedro Miralles-Martínez has been a Teacher and Professor for 39 years in all levels of education: adult education; primary education; geography and history teacher and professor in secondary education; Senior Lecturer and Full Professor in the Teaching of the Social Sciences at University. He has worked in permanent teacher training in two Teacher and Resources Centers. He has directed or participated in thirty research and innovation projects on the teaching and learning of the social sciences, history education, historical thinking, assessment, competencies, teacher training, textbooks and citizenship education in pre-school, primary and secondary education. He is the author of more than two hundred publications and been an invited speaker at more than a hundred conferences and scientific meetings. As far as management is concerned, he has performed the following roles: head of studies and principal at a public school, principal at a secondary school, secretary and director of a University Department. He was the coordinator of the first PhD program in Social Sciences Teaching; he has coordinated the Pedagogical Aptitude Course in Geography and History, the master's and doctorate programs in Research and Innovation in Primary Education, as well as the master's degree 'Teaching Innovation in Infant and

Primary Education' and the Doctorate program 'Teaching and Educational Innovation'. He was also the Principal Investigator of the research group 'Teaching of Social Sciences' (2009-2022). In addition, he has been vice-rector of Training and Innovation of the University of Murcia (2014-2018).

* * *

Neval Akça Berk is an expert the application of historical reenactment in history education. Innovative applications and alternative teaching tools in history education, creative drama, the use of historical places in history education, and out-of-school history teaching are among the fields of study.

Santiago Alonso-García is currently Professor at the University of Granada. Diploma in Early Childhood Education, Degree in Psychopedagogy and PhD in Curriculum, Teaching and Educational Institutions from the University of Granada. My teaching experience since 2006 until now, includes working with MENAS (immigrant children), adult education, early childhood and primary education, secondary education in PCPI and higher education in Spanish universities (UCLM, UNIZAR, US, UGR) and abroad (UNACH, UNAE). I have participated in more than 50 national and international research and innovation projects, supported by more than 100 publications that can be consulted at https://scholar.google.es/citations?hl=es&user=KFLih3AAAAAJ, https://www.scopus.com/authid/detail.url?authorId=57198780913, https://orcid.org/0000-0002-9525-709X, https://dialnet.unirioja.es/servlet/autor?codigo=1111119.

Borja Aso holds a degree in History from the University of Zaragoza (2012), along with a master's degree in Teacher Training for Secondary Education (2013) and a master's degree in Lifelong Learning: Initiation to Research (2018), both from the University of Zaragoza. He has a PhD in Education from the University of Zaragoza (qualification of Outstanding "Cum Laude" with International Mention), with the Doctoral Thesis entitled "Educación Patrimonial en tiempos digitales. Study of the educommunication in social networks of the Diocesan Museum of Jaca". He currently works as an Associate Professor at the Faculty of Humanities and Education in Huesca (University of Zaragoza) and as a teacher of secondary education at the La Salle Santo Ángel school in Zaragoza. He has several publications with impact factor (indexed in JCR and SCOPUS) and has participated in various national and international congresses. His research interests focus on the analysis of the use of ICT and social networks for heritage educommunication, as well as the study of heritage education in the fields of knowledge related to History and Literature for secondary education. Orcid ID: https://orcid.org/0000-0002-3023-4516.

Inmaculada Aznar-Díaz is a Full Professor in the Department of Didactics and School Organisation at the University of Granada. PhD in Educational Sciences from the University of Granada. Degree in Psychopedagogy from the University of Granada. Director of the Research, Innovation & Technology in Education (RITE, SEJ-607) research group.

Fatih Berk is working his PhD thesis on digital history and its applications. He has studies on history textbooks, out-of-school history teaching, concept teaching, scale development in history and social studies.

Blanca Berral-Ortiz is currently Predoctoral Research Staff in Training. Graduated in Early Childhood Education from the University of Granada, obtaining an average grade of 9.161. Obtaining the prize paid to the "best records" for the course 2019-2020. Master's Degree in Research and Innovation in Curriculum and Training (University of Granada). I have received a Collaboration Grant from the Ministry of Education in the Department of Didactics and School Organization. Also, a grant for Research Initiation in the Master of the same department of the University of Granada. Linked to both grants I have made several publications such as articles, book chapters (Dykinson and Octaedro) focused mainly on active methodologies, ICT, social networks, appropriate or abusive use of technologies, among others. Likewise, I have participated in congresses as an assistant, collaborator and scientific committee as well as communication director. I have also collaborated in innovation projects at the University of Granada. ORCID ID: https://orcid.org/0000-0001-8139-8468.

Pilar Cáceres is a Full Professor in the Department of Teaching and School Organisation at the University of Granada. PhD in Educational Sciences from the University of Granada. Degree in Psychopedagogy from the University of Granada. Director of the Leadership, Development and Educational Research Group (LEADER Group, SEJ 604).

José María Campillo-Ferrer has a Diploma in Education from the University of Murcia since 2003 and a PhD in Didactics of Social Sciences from the same university since 2018. He has worked as a teacher for 20 years at various educational levels: professor for adult education, secondary school teacher, infant and primary school teacher and associate lecturer. He belongs to the Didactics of Social Sciences research group since 2017. He currently combines his job as an associate lecturer in the Faculty of Education of the University of Murcia since 2017 with his job as a primary school teacher in a state school, CEIP El Mirador, in San Javier, Murcia, Spain. He is the author of 11 publications (10 articles and 1 book chapter). His publications in WOS (JCR) and SCOPUS journals such as Sustainability or Palgrave Communications stand out. In management, he has held positions as a member of the management team of an adult education centre and a primary school (Secretary (2005-2006) and (2012-2015) and as a Coordinator in Primary Education (2016-2018).

Álvaro Chaparro-Sainz is Senior Lecturer at the Department of Education at the University of Almeria (Spain). He is Doctor in History with an extraordinary award from the University of the Basque Country (2010). Previously, he was Lecture professor at the University of Malaga (Spain) from 2018 to 2020, professor at the University of Murcia (ISEN) from 2015 to 2018. Also, he was postdoctoral researcher in differents universities in France: University of Lyon II (2010-2011), Casa de Velázquez (2011-2013); and research assistant at University of Nice (2013-2014) and University of Clermont-Ferrand (2014). He is researcher of Surclio research group (University of Almeria) colaborate researcher of DICSO research group (University of Murcia). Among other publications, he is the author of three monographs, three journals issues and more of fifty scientific articles in differents indexed journals (Palgrave communications, Encounters in Theory and History Education, Aula Abierta, etc.).

Juan Carlos Colomer Rubio holds a PhD in History from the Universitat de València, an Interuniversity Master's Degree in Contemporary History and a Master's Degree in Research in Specific Didactics from the same institution. He has been a FPU scholarship holder of the Ministry of Education in the Department of Contemporary History at the University of Valencia and has taught formal and non-formal education for more than a decade in several Valencian volunteer organizations. Specialized in recent history, his publications have dealt with the analysis of the teaching of history, its textbooks or the design of educational activities in new digital media (ICT). In addition, he has participated in several conferences and seminars related to his specialty, collaborating in several scientific research projects. He has made stays at the Harvard School of Education and has been a visiting professor at the University of Alagoas (Brazil). In addition, he has held the position of Vice-Dean of Professional Culture and Educational Technology at the Faculty of Education. Currently, he is a professor at the Department of Experimental and Social Sciences Teaching of the Facultat de Magisteri (València).

Ramón Cózar-Gutiérrez is an associate professor of the Department of History at the University of Castilla-La Mancha. He is co-leader of the research group LabinTic at the Faculty of Education of Albacete. His research interests in education include teaching and learning of History, teacher training, and educational technology.

José María Cuenca-López is Professor of Social Sciences Education at the University of Huelva, Doctor in heritage education. Researcher responsible for the R + D + i project "Heritage Education for the Territorial and Emotional Intelligence of Citizens" - EPITEC (EDU2015-67953-P) and "Controversial heritage for the ecosocial formation of citizenship. An investigation of heritage education in formal education (EPITEC2)", reference PID2020-116662GB-100, funded by MCIN/AEI/10.13039/501100011033, also in the research group "Initial Training and Professional Development of Teachers" - DESYM (HUM168 del Andalusian Research, Development and Innovation Plan), member of the Center for Research in Contemporary Thought and Innovation for Social Development (COIDESO) of the University of Huelva and coordinator in Huelva of the "Research Network in the Teaching of Social Sciences" - Red14 (RED2018-102336-T). It has 5 sections of teaching, 3 of research and 1 of research transfer by the CNEAI. Director of 8 PhD theses and 6 contracted researchers.

Juan Carlos de la Cruz Campos is a Lecturer in the Department of Didactics and School Organisation at the University of Granada. PhD in Cum Laude in Educational Sciences from the University of Granada, Degree in Physical Activity and Sport Sciences, Diploma in Teaching specialising in Physical Education from the University of Granada, Graduate in Primary Education from the Catholic University of Murcia, Master's Degree in Research in Physical Activity and Sport from the University of Malaga and Master's Degree in Educational Innovation and Knowledge Management from the University of Malaga. Expert in Personal Training from the University of Granada and Senior Sports Technician Level III in Football. He is a member of the AREA Research Group (HUM-672) since February 2020. He has experience as a teacher in Compulsory Secondary Education and as a member of the management team of an educational centre. He currently teaches full time in official degrees at the University of Granada, Double Degree in Primary Education and Physical Activity and Sport Sciences, Degree in Early Childhood Education, Degree in Social Education and Master's Degree in Teaching at the Melilla Campus. ORCID ID: https://orcid.org/0000-0002-9263-6799.

María del Mar Felices-De la Fuente is Lecturer in the Department of Education at the University of Almería (Almeria, Spain). She is Doctor in Arts and Humanities, with European Mention (University of Almería, 2011). She has also been Lecturer at the University of Malaga (2016-2017). Since 2014, she has been developing his teaching and research work in the area of Didactics of Social Sciences. She is researcher at the Surclio research group (University of Almería) and has almost eighty publications including books, book chapters and journal articles, some of them being published in the main quartiles of recognized databases. His research has focused on the development of historical thinking skills, the teaching practices of university teaching of Didactics of Social Sciences and the initial training of Social Sciences teachers.

Silvia García-Ceballos is a professor and researcher in the Specific Didactics Department (Social Sciences Didactics area) at the University of Zaragoza. PhD in Transdisciplinary Research in Education from the University of Valladolid, Bachelor of Fine Arts and Bachelor of Art History, both from the University of Salamanca. She has participated in numerous national and international research projects, as well as in several prestigious conferences. She has numerous publications of impact that reflect her main lines of research, among which are heritage education, program evaluation, educommunication and the development of teaching skills in heritage education, art education, didactics of history, art and social sciences in general. She is a member of the ARGOS research group, IUCA, RED14 and researcher of the Spanish Heritage Education Observatory. Orcid ID: https://orcid.org/0000-0002-7661-3001.

Catalina Guerrero-Romera is a PhD in Philosophy and Educational Sciences and lecturer in the Department of Theory and History of Education at the University of Murcia. She is a member of several networks, including the International Network for Scientific and Technical Cooperation at European and Latin American level in the field of Teacher Training and Innovation, the International Observatory of the Teaching Profession and the University Network of Virtual Campuses. His current lines of research are related to vocational training, employment and social inclusion, competence assessment and the teaching-learning of geography and history, education for citizenship and the development of more transformative and innovative values, models, and methodologies.

Erhan Güneş is a PhD graduate on Education Technology. He is the head of Computer Education and Instructional Technology Department at Kırşehir Ahi Evran University. He also gained experience in Distance Education (Director of Distance Education Research Center, 2016-2021). His areas of interest are distance education, teacher training, e-content and instructional material development, digital literacy and coding education. He has given courses about project management, distance education, programming and ICT in education. He has studied on e-learning, interaction, digital literacy and educational e-content development. He has many scientific publications in these subjects. He participated in various projects regarding technology and education. He has coordinated an Erasmus+ KA203 project. He is also a researcher in two ongoing TUBITAK (The Scientific and Technological Research Council of Turkey) projects. Moreover, he has consulted certain organisations' projects on teacher education and technology.

Şerifnaz Gülin Karabağ received her BA degree in history at Ankara University, Faculty of Languages, History and Geography. She finished her MA in Curriculum Studies at Goldsmiths College in London and holds a PhD degree in History in Education (focusing on Historical Empathy) from Gazi Institute of Educational Science. As for the professional career, she started as a research assistant at Gazi University between 1992-2007 and continued her career as an associated professor between 2016-2021 as a teacher trainer and a researcher. Currently, Karabag is a professor in the History Teaching Department at Faculty of Education. She is lecturing several courses (Materials Development and Adaptation, Teaching History to Young Learners, Methodology of History, Teaching Experience, History Teaching and ICT, History Teaching and History Textbooks, Teaching in History Lessons, History Teaching and Creative Drama) at both undergraduate and graduate levels. Her research interest is mainly on historical empathy, cultural heritage, history textbooks, special teaching methods and teaching materials. She has also published articles about creative drama and social studies education. Karabag is a member of the Turkish Association of History Educators. She participated in the EUROCLIO/Matra Project "A Key to Europe: Innovative Methodology for Turkish School History". She was also co-manager of the CHISE (The Cultural Heritage and Its Sustainability in Europe) project. She also worked in inclusive education project about Syrian students and teachers held by UNICEF and PIKTES after the outbreak of Syrian crisis in Turkey. In these projects, she was responsible for the developing and teaching modules. Karabag also worked for Turkey`s Ministry of National Education, to develop primary and secondary school social studies and history curricula and to edit both courses' textbooks for almost ten years. She studied "Leadership and Management in Higher Education" in Washington DC.

Selahattin Kaymakcı was born in Tosya/Kastamonu, located in the north of Turkey. In 2003, he graduated form Karadeniz Technical University, Fatih Faculty of Education, Social Studies Teacher Education Program. In 2006 he completed his MA on history education at the same university. He did his PhD on social studies education at Gazi University in 2010. He started to work as a research assistant at Karadeniz Techinical University, Fatih Faculty of Education in 2004. During the half of PhD process (2009-2010), he worked as a visiting scholar at University of Illinois at Urbana-Champaign. He became assistant professor in 2011, then he got his associate degree in 2014. He became full time professor in 2019. Now he is working at Kastamonu University, Faculty of Education, Social Studies Teacher Education Program. His research areas focus on social studies, history and life studies teaching.

Inmaculada López-Cruz is a Doctor in Didactics of Social Sciences. Teacher of Social Science in a Secondary School. Researcher in the Research Group "Initial Training and Professional Development of Teachers" - DESYM (HUM168 of the Andalusian Plan for Research, Development and Innovation), member of the EPITEC Project (EDU2015-67953-P) and PID2020-116662GB-I00 funded by MCIN/AEI/ 10.13039/501100011033 and "Controversial heritage for the ecosocial formation of citizenship. An investigation of heritage education in formal education (EPITEC2)", reference PID2020-116662GB-100, funded by MCIN/AEI/10.13039/501100011033. Coordinator of the project "Live and feel the heritage".

Carlota López-Fernández is a member of the research group Labintic (Lab of Technology Integration in Classrooms). Her lines of research focus on the teaching and learning of History, the application of active methodologies, and educational technology.

Ramón Méndez graduated in History from the Universidad Complutense de Madrid and holds postgraduate studies in both formal and informal education. In 2011 he started working at the Museo del Ferrocarril de Madrid and developed his doctoral thesis in Education at the Universidad Autónoma de Madrid. His research work is focused on Heritage Education and more specifically on the relationship between schools and museums. From 2020 up to date, he works as a teacher in the area of Didactics of Social Sciences of the Department of Education of the University of Almería.

Jesús Molina Saorín exercises his professional activity as University Professor and researcher in the Department of Didactics and School Organization of the Faculty of Education (University of Murcia and National University of Distance Education -UNED), and as Associate Professor at the Autonomous University of Ciudad Juarez (Mexico). Trained in Pedagogy (with extraordinary award of degree) and also in Physical Education, he finished his first European doctorate at the University of Murcia, with research stays at the Universidade do Porto (Portugal) and Universität zu Köln (Germany) thanks to which he achieved the mention of European Doctor in Pedagogy (with the highest qualification and published thesis). Graduated in Portuguese (Universidade de Lisboa), he completed a second doctorate in Sports Science, entirely taken at the Universidade do Porto (Portugal), achieving again the mention of European Doctor in Sports Science (with the highest qualification) by that university.

Iñaki Navarro is a Teacher and Researcher at the University of Zaragoza in the Department of Specific Didactics. PhD with International Mention at the University of Zaragoza in the PhD Programme in Education, with the qualification of "Cum Laude" with the Doctoral Thesis entitled "Educomunicación en Twitter de los museos arqueológicos españoles. Estudio de estrategias de educación patrimonial". Graduate in History from the University of Navarra and with specific studies in Education and Heritage: Master's Degree in History, Space and Heritage and Master's Degree in Teaching, specialising in Social Sciences, both from the Public University of Navarra. Member of the ARGOS research group and of the University Institute for Research in Environmental Sciences of Aragon (IUCA) in the area of Heritage and member of the RED 14 Group. Main lines of research: Educommunication of heritage on the web 2.0 and development of historical thinking in students and teachers in training. ORCID: 0000-0001-8589-6659.

Rocío Palacios is a Doctor in Didactics of Social Science. Professor at the University of Huelva in the area of Social Sciences Teaching. Degree in History with a postgraduate degree in Research in Teaching and Learning of Experimental, Social and Mathematical Sciences. Researcher in the Research Group "Initial Training and Professional Development of Teachers" - DESYM (HUM168 of the Andalusian Plan for Research, Development and Innovation), member of the "Heritage Education for the Territorial and Emotional Intelligence of Citizens" - EPITEC (EDU2015-67953-P) and PID2020-116662GB-I00 funded by MCIN/AEI/ 10.13039/501100011033 and in "Controversial heritage for the ecosocial formation of citizenship. An investigation of heritage education in formal education (EPITEC2)", reference PID2020-116662GB-100, funded by MCIN/AEI/10.13039/501100011033 and RED 14 (RED2018-102336-T) and "Research Network in the Teaching of Social Sciences". He is part of the training staff of COIDESO "Center for Research in Contemporary Thought and Innovation for Social Development" at the University of Huelva.

Miguel Ángel Pallarés Jiménez holds a degree and PhD in History from the University of Zaragoza (Spain). Nowadays he is a professor in its Faculty of Education, in the Department of Specific Didactics, and member of Argos Research Group and University Institute for Research in Environmental Sciences of Aragon (IUCA). He was the curator of the Sanz Briz Year in Zaragoza in 2020, and was in charge of the exhibition and catalogue on this diplomat, recognised by Yad Vashem as Righteous Among the Nations. In the same year he was coordinator of the International Symposium "Teaching the Holocaust", organised by Argos; and also editor, together with his colleague María Sebastián, of the monographic issue on the Holocaust. of the monographic issue on the Holocaust of the journal Clio: History and History Teaching.

Santiago Pozo-Sánchez is Doctor cum laude in Educational Sciences from the University of Granada. He holds a Master's degree from the University of Granada, as well as the Bachelor of Music History and Sciences from the University from La Rioja. He also has a Master's Degree in Teacher Training in Secondary Education by the Alfonso X el Sabio University, as well as the Degree in Spanish: Language and Literature and the Degree in History and Heritage from the University of Burgos. He teaches at the Faculty of Education and Technology of Ceuta, at the University of Granada, Spain. He is a member of the AREA Research Group (HUM-672) of the University of Granada. He has extensive scientific production in the form of publications included in prestigious international magazines and publishers. Likewise, he has obtained in multitude of research projects and teaching innovation, as well as in congresses of national and international scope. His lines of research focus mainly in educational innovation and the implementation of techno-pedagogical resources in the classroom, with special emphasis on the flipped learning pedagogical model. ORCID ID: https://orcid.org/0000-0001-8125-4990.

Pilar Rivero is a PhD in History from the University of Zaragoza (Spain) and PhD in Didactics of Social Sciences and Heritage from the University of Barcelona (Spain). She is professor in Didactics of Social Sciences at the University of Zaragoza, principal investigator of ARGOS group and of several research projects in the field of heritage and history education. Member of University Institute for Research in Environmental Sciences of Aragon (IUCA). Her mail lines of research are technologies for History and Heritage education and development of historical thinking in students and teachers in training. She has been coordinator of the teaching master's degree and the master's degree in "Lifelong learning: initiation to research", at the University of Zaragoza. She is currently the Director of the Department of Specific Didactics and a member of the management team of the Master in Museums: education and communication. She is a Member of the Advisory Council for the teaching of History of the Government of Aragon (Spain). Orcid code: 0000-0002-6757-7598.

José-María Romero-Rodríguez is a Professor at the Department of Didactics and School Organization of the University of Granada. PhD in Educational Sciences from the University of Granada. Master's Degree in Research and Innovation in Curriculum and Training from the University of Granada. Master's Degree in Innovation and Knowledge Management from the University of Malaga. Graduate in Pedagogy from the University of Granada. Member of the research group Laboratorio de Innovación en Educación (LabinED, SEJ-655).

Ana María Rubio Leiva works as a secondary school teacher and is also a member of the DIDE Research Group at the University of Murcia. She is an architect and is specialised in architectural heritage conservation at the Polytechnic University of Valencia in conjunction with the University of Rome, La Sapienza.

Alodia Rubio-Navarro is a PhD student of Education in the Specific Didactics Department (Social Sciences Didactics area) at the University of Zaragoza. Her thesis project, which has been awarded by a research grant from the Autonomous Community of Aragón (2021-2025), focuses on the use of digital technologies to communicate and promote local heritage as an educational tool. It is part of the state-funded project PID2020-115288RB-I00: "Digital competences, learning processes and cultural heritage awareness: quality education for sustainable cities and communities" driven by the University of Zaragoza. She has developed her work experience mainly in the field of museum education. Additionally, she has recently started her career in formal education, taking a master's degree in Teacher Training for Secondary Education (2021). Orcid ID: https://orcid.org/0000-0002-0908-9385.

Rubén Martínez Sánchez works as a teacher of Special Education at Lideria International School. He, in turn, is coordinator of graduate courses at the Domingo Savio Private University and Loyola University. Thanks to his work, it has led him to win the IMPORTANT 2020 award in the education category and recognition of the educational work of Latin America. He, in turn, has been named the second best teacher in Spain at the EducaAbanca 2021 awards and is currently nominated for these same awards in the 2022 edition.

Sergio Sánchez has a degree in History, a Diploma in Tourism, a Master's in Research and Advanced Studies in History and has the National Defense Course from CESEDEN and the Ministry of Defense. He is a professor of Compulsory Secondary Education and Baccalaureate of the Government of Aragon and an associate professor at the Department of Specific Didactics of the University of Zaragoza. Member of Environmental Sciences Institute (IUCA). As a secondary school teacher, he has launched several gamification, empathy and historical relevance projects in the classroom. As an associate professor of the Master's Degree in Teacher Training, his research lines are related to Video Games as a tool to learn History and another about War and Violence in History. He has been responsible for the implementation of the educational project on the Nuremberg trials at the Zuera Prison, in collaboration with Enrique Vallespín and Miguel Ángel Pallarés.

Raquel Sánchez Ibáñez is an Associate Professor and Researcher in Social Sciences Didactics (University of Murcia).

Maria Glória Parra Santos Solé is an Assistant Teacher at the University of Minho, Institute of Education (Portugal). Is a professor of the Department of Integrated Studies Literacy, Teaching and Supervision. PhD in Child Studies from the University of Minho with a thesis: Primary History: Time concepts and historical understanding in children and context for their development. Is member of the Research Center of Education (CIEd)- University of Minho. Member of the team that conducted the "Learning out comes" to History published online by the Ministry of Education (DGIC, 2010). Member of CiCe Association (Children's Identity & Citizenship in Europe- CICE). Member of History Educational International Research Network (HEIRNET) and IRAHSSE. Member of The Historical Association. Member of Associação de Professores de História (APH). Her research is related to Historical Education, on historical cognition, especially examines students' understanding such as historical evidence and historical time, and Heritage Education. She as published numerous articles, book chapters, and communications related to the teaching of History for children.

Mustafa Tanrıverdi completed his undergraduate degree in Gazi University Gazi Education Faculty Computer and Instructional Technologies, and his master's and doctorate degrees in Gazi University Informatics Institute Management Information Systems. He did his master's thesis on mobile learning environment development and his doctoral thesis on decision making systems for load distribution in mobile cloud environments. Between 2007-2021, he worked as a software developer at Gazi University Computer Center. He has been working as a Doctor Faculty Member in the Department of Management Information Systems of the Faculty of Applied Sciences since 2021, and as Assistant Director at Gazi University Distance Education Application and Research Center since 2022. He took part as a researcher in many national and international projects. He has many studies on software development, blockchain, mobile applications, cloud computing, database management and business intelligence.

Sergio Tirado-Olivares is a primary teacher and predoctoral fellow. His lines of research focus on the application of playful-active learning methodologies with primary education students and pre-service teachers in STEAM disciplines, the development of active methodologies in the school setting and the development of new formative assessment approaches.

Muhammet Ahmet Tokdemir had his graduation from Educational Faculty and worked as a teacher in difference governmental schools for nine years (2000-2009). He had his master and PhD degree in the field of teaching history. In 2009, he started to work as a research assistant in the academy and become assistant professor. Then he started to work for State Archives of Turkey (2015). He continues to work as an administrator under the State Archives. He has publications on the use of archival resources in history teaching, value teaching in history education, discussion and communication in history classes, history teaching and the history of education, and continues his research on these subjects.

Francisco Javier Trigueros Cano is a Doctor in Education. Collaborating Professor at the University of Murcia, he has a degree in Geography and History. He has been a Primary Education Teacher and advisor to the Centro de Profesores y Recursos. He has participated in several R+D+i projects in Social Sciences Didactics, and his lines of research revolve around the evaluation of geography and history in Primary and Secondary Education, and curricular analysis.

Juan Manuel Trujillo Torres is a Full Professor at the Department of Didactics and School Organisation of the University of Granada. PhD in Educational Sciences from the University of Granada. Degree in Pedagogy from the National University of Distance Education (UNED Spain). Director of the Department of Didactics and School Organization at the University of Granada. Director of the research group ÁREA (HUM-672).

Mutlu Tahsin Üstündağ is a PhD graduate on Education Technology. He is currently working in Gazi University Computer Education and Instructional Technologies Department. He also works as the director of Gazi University Distance Education, Application and Research Center since 2020. His areas of interest are distance education, teacher training, blockchain, web3 technologies, implementation of ICTs in education and instructional design. He gives lectures on algorithms, data structures, visual programming, rapid application development in education and business, internet programming, database management, project management and ICT utilization in education. He has many scientific publications in these subjects and has participated in various projects regarding technology and education. He has also worked in many national and international projects. He is a member of Turkish National Commission for UNESCO.

Mevlüt Uysal has a PhD in Management Information Systems. He works as a lecturer at Gazi University Distance Education Application and Research Center. His areas of interest are software development, web technologies, algorithms, decision support systems, optimization, data analysis and educational technology. The software he developed as a result of his master's thesis titled "Creating an Expandable Decision Tree for Data Analysis, Developing of Web and Mobile Applications" guides researchers in choosing the most appropriate statistical data analysis method. He developed an optimization-based decision support system as a result of his doctoral thesis titled "A Decision Support System for Part Logistics in the Automotive Sector". He has taken part in national and international projects in the fields of decision support systems, decision trees, blockchain, web technologies and educational technology and has academic studies in these fields. He teaches Management Information Systems, Blockchain and Web Technologies at Gazi University.

Rafael Villena-Taranilla is currently working as a Primary Teacher in San Cristóbal school (Albacete), where he is the Coordinator of the Longlife Learning Programme. His research interests include virtual reality, augmented reality, gamification, and educational robotics.

Index

F

G

H

I

K

L

M

www.ingramcontent.com/pod-product-compliance
Lightning Source LLC
LaVergne TN
LVHW080019210926
848481LV00011B/3056
* 9 7 8 1 6 6 8 4 5 2 4 4 8 *